Assessing Students with Special Needs

Second Edition

John J. Venn
University of North Florida

Merrill,
an imprint of Prentice Hall
Upper Saddle River, New Jersey   Columbus, Ohio

Library of Congress Cataloging-in-Publication Data

Venn, John.
      Assessing students with special needs / by John Venn. — 2nd ed.
         p.   cm.
      Rev. ed. of: Assessment of students with special needs. c1994.
      Includes bibliographical references and indexes.
      ISBN 0-13-781204-3
      11. Handicapped children—Education—United States.   2. Educational
tests and measurements—United States.   3. Handicapped children-
-Psychological testing—United States.   4. Behavioral assessment of
children—United States.   I. Venn, John.   Assessment of students
with special needs.   II. Title.
LC4031.V46 2000
371.9—dc21   99-19137
                                                                                CIP

Cover Art: Angel Ratliff, West Central School, Columbus, Ohio, Franklin County Board of Mental
      Retardation and Development Disabilities
Editor: Ann Castel Davis
Developmental Editor: Gianna M. Marsella
Production Editor: Sheryl Glicker Langner
Production Coordination: JaNoel Lowe/Custom Editorial Productions, Inc.
Photo Coordinator: Anthony Magnacca
Design Coordinator: Diane C. Lorenzo
Cover Designer: Curt Besser
Production Manager: Laura Messerly
Editorial Assistant: Pat Grogg
Electronic Text Management: Karen L. Bretz
Director of Marketing: Kevin Flanagan
Marketing Manager: Meghan McCauley
Marketing Coordinator: Krista Groshong

This book was set in New Baskerville by Custom Editorial Productions, Inc., and was printed and
bound by R.R. Donnelley & Sons Company. The cover was printed by Phoenix Color Corp.

© 2000, 1994 by Prentice-Hall, Inc.
Pearson Education
Upper Saddle River, New Jersey 07458

Photo Credits: pp. 1, 52, 144, 242, 444, 590, Barbara Schwartz/Merrill; pp. 20, 192, 274,
Anne Vega/Merrill; pp. 82, 318, 564, Tom Watson/Merrill; pp. 106, 120, 378, 480, Scott Cunningham/
Merrill; pp. 356, 528, Anthony Magnacca/Merrill; pp. 412, 502, Todd Yarrington/Merrill

Printed in the United States of America

10 9 8 7 6 5 4 3 2 1

ISBN: 0-13-781204-3

Prentice-Hall International (UK) Limited, *London*
Prentice-Hall of Australia Pty. Limited, *Sydney*
Prentice-Hall of Canada, Inc., *Toronto*
Prentice-Hall Hispanoamericana, S. A., *Mexico*
Prentice-Hall of India Private Limited, *New Delhi*
Prentice-Hall of Japan, Inc., *Tokyo*
Prentice-Hall (Singapore) Pte. Ltd., *Singapore*
Editora Prentice-Hall do Brasil, Ltda., *Rio de Janeiro*

Preface

This book is for special and general education majors who want to learn how to assess students with special needs. The text provides instructors and students at undergraduate and graduate levels with comprehensive information about assessment principles and practices from an applied, practical perspective. In addition to serving as a college textbook, the book is also an excellent reference tool. As a result, the audience for the book includes special and general education teachers, school counselors, psychologists, educational diagnosticians, staffing specialists, speech pathologists, reading specialists, early intervention specialists, and professionals in the health-related professions.

This second edition of the book offers many additions and revisions. The additions include new chapters on portfolio assessment, assessment in inclusive settings, selecting and evaluating assessment instruments, and technology issues in assessing students with special needs. Revisions include expanded coverage of important topics such as curriculum-based assessment, cultural diversity, steps in the assessment process, Individual Education Plans (IEPs), and evaluation of academic achievement. The second edition also provides updated reviews of tests, and each chapter has been revised to provide comprehensive coverage of the most important assessment information. Readers will also find many new instructional features, including the following:

- Test summary tables at the end of a number of chapters that outline all of the tests reviewed in the chapter.
- A special section in each chapter that connects assessment with instruction.
- Additional vignettes that focus on assessment from a practical, applied perspective.
- Numerous examples, illustrations, checklists, charts, and graphs.
- Focus boxes that highlight special assessment considerations.
- Extensive chapter reviews and application activities.

The purpose of this book is to present comprehensive coverage of assessment in a single volume. To achieve this goal, the book covers assessment of students with special needs at all age levels, beginning with preschoolers and continuing through high school and into adulthood. Also included is material appropriate for assessing students across a broad range of performance levels including mild, moderate, and severe disabilities. College and university students, teachers, and others who read this text and learn the material will acquire essential knowledge and skills that will help them meet the often unique assessment needs of children and youth with disabilities.

The book is organized into five parts. The first part, Chapters 1–4, lays a foundation for assessing students with special needs. This part covers the steps in the assessment process and investigates test scores and their meaning. The second part, Chapters 5 and 6, introduces practical applications and considerations in the assessment process, including how to select and evaluate assessment instruments and procedures for giving, scoring, and interpreting tests. The third part, Chapters 7–13, covers general assessment considerations, including intelligence testing, evaluation of student behavior, developmental assessment, and career assessment. The fourth part, Chapters 14–17, focuses on assessing academic achievement and includes coverage of both formal, norm-referenced achievement tests and informal, curriculum-based procedures for evaluating academic progress. The fifth part, Chapters 18–20, investigates special assessment considerations, including portfolio assessment, assessment in inclusive settings, technology issues in assessment, and future perspectives.

Acknowledgments

Many caring and dedicated individuals deserve special recognition for their contributions to the development of this book. I extend sincere appreciation and thanks to the following reviewers: Andrew Cognard-Black, The Ohio State University; Libby G. Cohen, University of Southern Maine; Grace L. Denison, University of Maine, Farmington; Dan Fennerty, Central Washington University; Christine Givner, California State University, Los Angeles; Blanche Jackson Glimps, Kentucky Christian College; Judith J. Ivarie, Eastern Illinois University; Kenneth A. Kavale, University of Iowa; Nancy L. Mamlin, Appalachian State University; and Darcy Miller, Washington State University.

Special thanks are due to my students and colleagues who provided many valuable suggestions for improving this edition. Among the students who provided assistance and input were Peggy McBride, Linda Grenda, and Anna Mahan. I genuinely appreciate my colleagues who assisted me in various ways with this project, in particular Robert Drummond, for his encouragement; Kathe Kasten, Thomas Serwatka, and Lynne Raiser, for their continuing support; and Patricia Hollis, for all of her assistance.

The talented, patient, and committed personnel at Merrill/Prentice Hall Publishing deserve special thanks including Ann Davis, Administrative Editor, who provided continual support, encouragement, and guidance throughout the revision process; Gianna Marsella, Developmental Editor, whose exceptional skills, commitment, creativity, and dedication helped to make this second edition a reality; Pat Grogg, Editorial Assistant; and Sheryl Langner, Production Editor. Thanks also to JaNoel Lowe, Project Editor, at Custom Editorial Productions.

Finally, I wish to express sincere gratitude to my family. Thanks to Jeffrey, Sarah, and Jason for their kindness, patience, and understanding during this project. My wife, Janelle, deserves special acknowledgment for all of her efforts. She helped with many of the writing tasks, but I am most indebted for her loving reassurance and inspiration when I needed it most. I especially dedicate this book to her.

Discover Companion Websites: A Virtual Learning Environment

Technology is a constantly growing and changing aspect of our field that is creating a need for content and resources. To address this emerging need, we have developed an online learning environment for students and professors alike—Companion Websites—to support our textbooks.

In creating a Companion Website, our goal is to build on and enhance what the textbook already offers. For this reason, the content for each user-friendly website is organized by chapter and provides the professor and student with a variety of meaningful resources. Common features of a Companion Website include:

For the Professor

Every Companion Website integrates **Syllabus Manager™,** an online syllabus creation and management utility.

- **Syllabus Manager™** provides you, the instructor, with an easy, step-by-step process to create and revise syllabi, with direct links into Companion Website and other online content without having to learn HTML.
- Students may logon to your syllabus during any study session. All they need to know is the web address for the Companion Website, and the password you've assigned to your syllabus.
- After you have created a syllabus using **Syllabus Manager™,** students may enter the syllabus for their course section from any point in the Companion Website.
- Class dates are highlighted in white and assignment due dates appear in blue. Clicking on a date, the student is shown the list of activities for the assignment. The activities for each assignment are linked directly to actual content, saving time for students.
- Adding assignments consists of clicking on the desired due date, then filling in the details of the assignment—name of the assignment, instructions, and whether or not it is a one-time or repeating assignment.
- In addition, links to other activities can be created easily. If the activities are online, a URL can be entered in the space provided, and it will be linked automatically in the final syllabus.
- Your completed syllabus is hosted on our servers, allowing convenient updates from any computer on the Internet. Changes you make to your syllabus are immediately available to your students at their next login.

For the Student

- **Chapter Objectives**—outline key concepts from the text
- **Interactive self-quizzes**—complete with hints and automatic grading that provide immediate feedback for students

After students submit their answers for the interactive self-quizzes, the Companion Website **Results Reporter** computes a percentage grade, provides a graphic representation of how many questions were answered correctly and incorrectly, and gives a question by question analysis of the quiz. Students are given the option to send their quiz to up to four email addresses (professor, teaching assistant, study partner, etc.).

- **Message Board**—serves as a virtual bulletin board to post—or respond to—questions or comments to a national audience
- **Net Searches**—offer links by key terms from each chapter to related Internet content
- **Web Destinations**—links to www sites that relate to chapter content

To take advantage of these resources, please visit the *Assessing Students with Special Needs* Companion Website at www.prenhall.com/venn

Contents

Chapter 4

Test Scores and What They Mean   82

Chapter 5

Selecting and Evaluating Assessment Instruments   106

Chapter 6

Test Administration, Scoring, Interpretation, and Reporting 120

Chapter 10
Assessment of Language   274

Chapter 11
Assessment of Behavior   318

Chapter 12
Assessment of Adaptive
Behavior   356

Major Tests Discussed

For a complete listing of all tests that appear in the book, refer to the Test Index that begins on page 653. Also see the test review tables at the end of Chapters 7 through 17 for chapter-by-chapter summaries of tests.

Defining and Describing Assessment of Children With Special Needs

Overview

Perhaps one of the most valuable tools available to the special education teacher is assessment, the process of using tests and other formal and informal means of measurement to make educational decisions. Special education teachers need a working knowledge of assessment (its testing concepts and procedures) to effectively and efficiently address student needs and to provide a full range of appropriate educational services.

In this chapter we investigate assessment basics beginning with the key terms, concepts, and processes of assessment. We also review the evolution of testing as it applies to special education from the early 1900s through current federal legislation, and we consider the various legal and ethical concerns that influence present assessment measures.

From this point, we proceed in Chapter 2 to investigate the various stages of assessment, including screening students, classifying and placing students, educational intervention with students, and measuring student progress. We see how the initial stages of assessment differ from the subsequent stages and how all the stages are interconnected. In Chapters 3 and 4 we examine the basic measurement ideas involved in testing, including statistical and measurement concepts, test scoring, and interpretation. Chapters 5 and 6 focus on practical applications: procedures for selecting assessments, for giving tests, for interpreting results, and for reporting assessment findings. In Chapters 7 through 17 we learn how to test students specifically for intelligence, for developmental skills, for academic achievement, for perception and motor proficiency, for classroom behavior, for adaptive behavior, and for career and vocational skills. We also learn how to use the information gathered from these tests as groundwork for building individual education programs that will guide your students' learning. Finally, in Chapters 18, 19, and 20 we examine special assessment considerations related to portfolio assessment and assessment in inclusive settings, and we consider current issues and future trends.

As you can see from this overview of the chapters, a true understanding of assessment goes far beyond the understanding necessary to administer a test to a student. This book provides that understanding. First, however, we must cover the basics—what assessment is and why it is important.

Objectives

After reading this chapter, you will be prepared to do the following:

- Use the terms *test, measurement,* and *assessment* and discuss the similarities and differences among these terms.
- Understand the effect of historical events on current decision making.
- Investigate the major legal and ethical obligations controlling assessment in special education.

Definition of Assessment

All of us know about assessment from personal experiences as students. We have all taken a variety of tests, ranging from teacher-made tests in the classroom to standardized tests such as college entrance exams. Our skills and abilities have also been assessed with checklists, observations, and interviews. Although personal experiences help us understand the definition of assessment, personal experiences fail to convey fully the meaning of assessment in special education.

Broadly stated, **assessment** is the process of using tests and other measures of student performance and behavior to make educational decisions. Assessment consists of an assortment of techniques and procedures for evaluating, estimating, appraising, and drawing conclusions about students with special needs. Unlike the assessment process used in a typical educational setting, assessment in special education takes into account the unique needs of students; therefore, assessment becomes different for each student. One goal of assessment in special education is to adapt the process to fit individual student needs rather than to fit the student into a particular assessment procedure. For example, using an intelligence test that contains mostly language items with students who are hearing impaired or who have language problems fails to take into account the unique needs of these students. One of the appropriate modifications in this situation involves using a specially designed intelligence test that omits verbal language items.

Testing

Testing is a specific type of assessment procedure. A **test**, which is usually given once, contains a standard set of questions that produce a score, a set of scores, or some other numerical result. Most tests are given in a prescribed manner and in a structured setting. Special educators rely on many types of tests, including standardized commercial tests and classroom-based teacher-made tests.

Measurement

Measurement is the process of determining the ability or performance level of students. Testing is one type of measurement, but special educators use many other types as well, including observing behavior, conducting interviews, completing rating scales, filling out checklists, and performing clinical evaluations. Teachers usually give some measures of performance (such as tests) only once, but they conduct other measures (such as observations of student behavior) repeatedly. The purpose of measurement is to produce objective information such as numbers, scores, or other quantitative data. Like testing, measurement plays a key role in the assessment process in special education.

☑ Comprehension Checklist

Whereas the terms *assessment, testing,* and *measurement* are somewhat interchangeable, specific differences do exist among them. In fact, the differences actually involve the relationship of all three to one another. *Assessment,* the broadest term, subsumes testing and measurement because it involves the use of tests and other measures to make educational decisions about students with special needs.

Testing, the most specific term, refers to a set of questions given in a structured setting. *Measurement* is less specific and includes testing as well as many other procedures for quantifying behavior. The decision-making process is the key element that makes assessment the most general term.

Importance of Assessment

Perhaps one of the best ways to discover the importance of assessment is through the eyes of teachers, parents, and students with special needs. The following narrative sketches illustrate the importance of assessment in the lives of real people.

Shamikah's mother, Ms. Tisdale, was scared and worried because of her daughter's behavior problems in school. Shamikah often brought home notes describing behavior such as disturbing other students, refusing to complete work, and other disruptions. Shamikah also brought home incomplete and incorrect papers. Ms. Tisdale, although unsure about the source of the problem, wanted to do something about it.

Shamikah's teacher, Ms. Garcia, was also concerned about her behavior and grades, so she scheduled a conference with Ms. Tisdale to discuss the situation. At the conference, the teacher suggested referring Shamikah for assessment to help determine the nature and extent of her problem.

The assessment results revealed that Shamikah was significantly below average in academic achievement. More important, the results indicated that Shamikah had a visual learning deficit, which explained much of her difficulty with tasks such as copying from the board, completing worksheets, and reading. After reviewing the results, the mother and the teacher agreed that Shamikah's academic and behavior problems were due, in part, to her deficit in visual learning.

Based on the assessment, Ms. Garcia implemented instructional modifications to accommodate Shamikah's visual learning deficit. Shamikah also received assistance from a special education teacher, and Ms. Tisdale arranged for tutoring after school. As a result of these changes, the teachers and the parent noticed improvements in Shamikah's academic performance and behavior, although she still experienced problems from time to time.

This scenario illustrates the importance of assessment in identifying a student's learning problem and in selecting instructional intervention strategies that respond to specific problems. The following story illustrates the importance of assessment in meeting the needs of a student with a severe disability.

Juan was born with Down's syndrome, a condition that causes severe mental retardation. Knowing Juan's condition, the special education teacher used assessment to develop an individualized family service plan for Juan when he enrolled in a preschool program at age 3. Assessment assisted the teacher in identifying his current levels of performance, selecting priorities for educational programming, developing learning objectives, and measuring his progress.

In these sketches assessment plays a key role in identifying learning problems and in developing intervention strategies. In both cases, assessment was essential in developing appropriate, individualized education programs. Although not all situations are resolved so easily, the cases of Shamikah and Juan illustrate the importance of assessment in special education and demonstrate that understanding assessment is critical for the special education teacher.

Influences on Assessment

Assessment of students with special needs is a complex and far-reaching collection of procedures and practices that reflect the influence of a number of disciplines and points of view. Indeed, the variety of influences affecting assessment procedures accounts for the complexity and multiplicity of the process. For example, many of the tests available in the assessment pool originated from models designed in other disciplines; this accounts for the diversity of assessment instruments. In addition, federal laws that mandate assessment practices, along with the ethical obligations and professional standards that dictate professional concerns, complicate the assessment process significantly. Furthermore, assessment in special education includes implementation of a storehouse of tests appropriate to different levels of assessment. This requires that the assessor understand the multilayered structure of the assessment process, which belies the simplicity of a single test. A summary of the influences on assessment appears in Figure 1–1.

A Historical Perspective

One of the best ways to develop an understanding of the influences on assessment is to examine assessment from a historical perspective. The history of assessing students with special needs encompasses contributions from many disciplines, including psychology, medicine, and educational measurement. Assessment practices

Figure 1–1   Influences on Assessment of Students With Special Needs

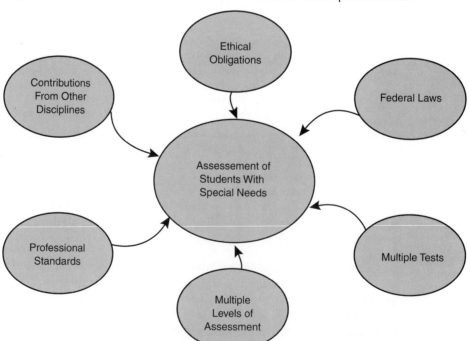

have also been shaped by federal laws and court decisions. Ethical obligations and professional standards are another important factor contributing to the development of assessment as we know it today. Contemporary assessment practices have emerged from these influences. A list of historical landmarks in assessment of students with special needs appears in Table 1–1. This is followed by a discussion of the historical significance of each landmark.

Intelligence Testing

One of the major historical contributions to assessment in special education was the development of the concept of intelligence. In 1905 A. Binet, a psychologist, and T. Simon, a physician, published the first effective intelligence test. Used in French schools to identify children who could not benefit from educational instruction, the test consisted mostly of verbal items, including (1) naming objects and pictures of objects, (2) supplying missing words at the end of simple sentences, and (3) answering questions such as "What is the thing to do when you are sleepy?" and "What do you do when you are cold?"

When Binet and Simon published an expanded and revised edition of this test in 1908, they introduced the concept of mental age as a way of reporting test results. Thorndike, Hagen, and Sattler published the most recent revision of this test, *The Stanford–Binet Intelligence Scale* (fourth edition), in 1986. Although the *Stanford–Binet* is still in widespread use, the *Wechsler Intelligence Scale for Children* (third edition) *(WISC-III)* (Wechsler, 1991) is currently the most frequently used test of this type. First published in 1949 as the *Wechsler Intelligence Scale for Children,* the WISC built on the Binet–Simon intelligence-measuring procedure by adding a wider variety of items and providing separate scores for individual parts of the test.

Assessing Large Groups

The U.S. Army first introduced the practice of assessing large groups during World War I when millions of recruits took the Army Alpha and Army Beta mental ability tests. Literate recruits took the Army Alpha test, and illiterate recruits took the Army Beta test. Army staffing specialists used the results to place the recruits in various roles. Those receiving high scores received training for technical jobs and served as officers, whereas those with low scores became foot soldiers.

Although the testing was an overall success, a major problem surfaced. The test authors failed to consider ethnic and cultural diversity in selecting items or interpreting results. Consequently, the tests were unfair to soldiers from minority groups and to those with limited English proficiency. This meant that some men received low scores due to test bias rather than low ability. Despite this significant problem, the army's use of the tests marked the first time in history that large groups of people were placed according to their test scores. Eventually psychologists refined and expanded these initial tests of mental ability for use during World War II. In addition, testing specialists developed other types of group tests after World War I, including the first of the group achievement tests.

Published in 1923, the *Stanford Achievement Test (SAT)* was the original large-group achievement test. Two similar tests, the *California Achievement Test* and the *Iowa Test of Basic Skills,* appeared in 1933 and 1936, respectively. These timed tests

Table 1–1   Historical Landmarks in Assessing Students With Special Needs

Intelligence Tests

1905   Binet and Simon published the first intelligence test, which later became the *Stanford–Binet Intelligence Scale.*

1908   The revised *Binet and Simon Intelligence Test* introduced the concept of mental age.

1949   Wechsler published the *Wechsler Intelligence Scale for Children* (*WISC*), which was the first edition of what has become the foremost intelligence test.

1974   Wechsler published the *Wechsler Intelligence Scale for Children* (Revised).

1986   Thorndike, Hagen, and Sattler published the *Stanford–Binet Intelligence Scale* (fourth edition).

1991   Wechsler published the *Wechsler Intelligence Scale for Children* (third edition).

Group Tests

1917   The U.S. Army used the Army Alpha and Army Beta tests in World War I, marking the first widespread use of a group intelligence test.

1923   The *Stanford Achievement Test* (*SAT*) was published. This was the first widely used group achievement test.

1933   The *California Achievement Test,* a group achievement test, was published.

1936   The *Iowa Test of Basic Skills,* a group achievement test, was published.

Adaptive Behavior Tests

1935   Doll published the *Genetic Scale of Social Maturity,* a measure of adaptive behavior.

1984   Sparrow, Balla, and Cicchetti published the most recent revision of the instrument, titled the *Vineland Adaptive Behavior Scales.*

Developmental Scales

1941   Gesell and Armatruda published *Developmental Diagnosis,* containing one of the original developmental scales.

Individual Diagnosis and Prescription

1876   Seguin, a medical doctor who developed many diagnostic procedures for assessing children with disabilities, established one of the first professional organizations in special education, now known as the American Association on Mental Retardation.

Individual Achievement Tests

1959   Dunn wrote the original *Peabody Picture Vocabulary Test* (*PPVT*), an individually administered test of receptive language vocabulary widely used in special education.

1965   Dunn updated the original version of the *PPVT.*

1970   Dunn and Markwardt created the original *Peabody Individual Achievement Test* (*PIAT*), a screening test of academic achievement.

1971   Connolly, Nachtman, and Pritchett published the first version of the *KeyMath Diagnostic Test of Arithmetic,* a comprehensive inventory of essential mathematics.

1981   Dunn and Dunn published the revised version of the *PPVT.*

1988   Connolly revised and expanded the *KeyMath Diagnostic Test of Arithmetic.* The new edition added a companion set of teaching and practice materials.

1989   Markwardt revised and expanded the *Peabody Individual Achievement Test* with new items, new norms, and an additional subtest.

1998   American Guidance Services publishes new editions of the *PPVT,* the *KeyMath Diagnostic Test of Arithmetic,* and the *Peabody Individual Achievement Test.*

Table 1-1 *(continued)*

Behavioral Assessment

1968   B. F. Skinner, the preeminent behavioral psychologist, published *The Technology of Teaching.* Skinner's behavior modification techniques led to the development of behavioral assessment procedures.

Nonbiased Assessment

1978   Jane Mercer introduced the *System of Multicultural Pluralistic Assessment* (*SOMPA*). Mercer's assessment approach includes consideration of sociocultural and health factors as an integral part of the assessment process.

Curriculum-Based Assessment

1982   Gronlund wrote about developing curriculum-based assessment procedures using teacher-made tests that offer high accuracy and validity. (See Focus 1–1.)

1985   Blankenship described the use of curriculum-based assessment data to make instructional decisions.

Assessment in Inclusive Settings

1975   The term *mainstreaming* emerged and gained general usage with the passage of Public Law 94-142 in 1975. Mainstreaming grew out of the **least restrictive environment** requirement in the law.

1985   The Regular Education Initiative (REI), a proposal advocating that general education accept primary responsibility for educating students with disabilities, was introduced. The REI called for significant changes in assessment practices for students with special needs.

1988   The concept of inclusion was introduced. Inclusion involved placing students with disabilities in general education classrooms in neighborhood schools and community settings.

use multiple-choice questions to measure attainment of academic skills such as reading, math, and language. Measuring the achievement of large groups of students with paper-and-pencil tests is standard procedure today. Similarly, business, industry, and government now routinely use large-group tests for a variety of purposes.

FOCUS 1–1

Assessment and Diversity

Since the introduction of these original group tests, the problem of bias in the use and interpretation of tests with minority and other groups whose experiences and culture differ from those of the general population has received a great deal of attention. This problem includes concerns about testing students with special needs. The major test publishers now invest significant effort in making their tests fair for females and for members of ethnic minority groups, linguistic minority groups, and disability groups. Significant progress has been made in finding solutions to the issues related to deciding what test modifications yield the most accurate and equitable decisions for all people. In later chapters our discussion will include more specific questions regarding assessment and diversity.

Assessing Adaptive Behavior

Adaptive behavior is the ability to adapt to the environment by developing independent personal and social behavior and by adjusting to changes in the environment. Unlike the concept of intelligence, which focuses on mental abilities, and the concept of achievement, which focuses on academic abilities, adaptive behavior concentrates on functional and practical abilities such as communication, activities of daily living, and social interaction. In 1935 Doll introduced the concept of assessing adaptive behavior with the *Genetic Scale of Social Maturity,* which Doll originally developed to assess children and adults with mental retardation. Over the years, this scale has remained one of the most widely used measures of adaptive functioning. Sparrow, Balla, and Cicchetti published the current revision of the instrument, the *Vineland Adaptive Behavior Scales,* in 1984. Many tests of this type are now available and are all built on Doll's initial idea of assessing functional and practical abilities.

Assessing Developmental Skills

Developmental psychologists introduced the notion of testing the developmental skills of young children from birth through 6 years of age. These psychologists included a group at Yale who studied the developmental patterns of young children and found a remarkably predictable sequence of skill development and learning. In 1941 Gesell and Armatruda, two psychologists in the Yale group, published *Developmental Diagnosis.* This test measured development in motor, language, personal–social, and adaptive skills. Gesell and Armatruda's work inspired others to design additional scales, and, as a result, a large number and variety of developmental tests are now available.

Individual Diagnosis and Prescription

Pioneers from many disciplines, especially medicine, developed the assessment concept of individual diagnosis and prescription. Early work by physicians established clinical procedures for diagnosing disabilities that cause mental retardation, physical handicaps, and health impairments. In 1876 Edouard O. Seguin, a medical doctor, played a major role in developing these diagnostic procedures and in that year established one of the first professional organizations in special education, the American Association for the Study of the Feebleminded. This organization, which later became the American Association on Mental Deficiency (AAMD), now is known as the American Association on Mental Retardation (AAMR). More recently, physical and occupational therapists have created new methods for improved diagnosis and treatment of neurological disorders.

Individual diagnosis and instruction have become a cornerstone of assessment in special education. This process resembles the procedure that physicians follow in diagnosing and treating medical conditions. A physician observes the symptoms of the patient, conducts medical tests to diagnose the cause, and then writes a prescription to treat the condition. In a similar way, a special education teacher uses individual diagnosis and prescription to develop for a student an instructional plan based on observation and testing. Both physician and teacher rely on direct observation as well as certain tests and other measures to assess the condition; in both cases the process is individualized to meet the needs of the particular patient or student.

Individual Achievement Testing

Special educators established widespread application of individual diagnosis and prescription using standardized, individually administered tests of academic achievement with the introduction of two tests: the *Peabody Individual Achievement Test (PIAT),* initially published in 1970 (Dunn & Markwardt), and the *KeyMath Diagnostic Test of Arithmetic,* first published in 1971 (Connolly, Nachtman, & Pritchett). These tests and other similar measures gave diagnosticians and special education teachers formal, standardized tools for assessing the learning needs of individual students and for developing specific teaching and intervention activities. Unlike group achievement tests, which report results as test scores and general levels of performance, these individually administered tests provide specific data and information for diagnosing remediation needs and for prescribing explicit intervention activities. Special educators currently rely on revised versions of the *PIAT* (Markwardt, 1998) and the *KeyMath Diagnostic Test of Arithmetic* (Connolly, 1998), which have become firmly established since their introduction in the early 1970s.

In 1959 Lloyd Dunn created the prototype for the *PIAT,* the *KeyMath Diagnostic Test of Arithmetic,* and many other individually administered tests by developing the *Peabody Picture Vocabulary Test.* Revised in 1965 and later in 1981, many special educators, psychologists, and speech pathologists use the current edition of the *Peabody Picture Vocabulary Test* (third edition) *(PPVT-III)* (Dunn & Dunn, 1997) to measure the receptive language vocabulary skills of students with special needs.

The tests are significant, in part, because they were among the first tests developed by special educators. These instruments incorporate the importance of individual rather than group testing for students with special learning needs.

Behavioral Assessment

Behavioral psychologists contributed the idea of assessing student performance over time using direct observation and continuous data collection. B. F. Skinner was the pioneer among these psychologists. The discipline was in its infancy in the late 1920s when Skinner shaped behavioral psychology as both a science and a philosophy. Skinner's voluminous research and writings included a book entitled *The Technology of Teaching* (1968), in which he described a behavioral approach to education emphasizing direct assessment of student behavior by charting rather than indirect assessment by pencil-on-paper testing. Skinner also recommended developing teaching machines that would provide information in small well-sequenced steps, give immediate feedback, and measure progress continuously. Computers now perform many of the functions of Skinner's teaching machines.

Evaluation techniques based on behavioral principles have become an integral part of current assessment in special education. The behavioral model emphasizes assessing students through direct observation rather than with tests. **Direct observation** involves listening to or watching a student for a period of time in a structured, systematic manner. Direct observation incorporates repeated measurement of student performance over time rather than single measurement using a standardized test. As a result of direct observation and repeated measurement, behavioral assessment provides a more realistic, practical measure of behavior than standardized tests yield. Examples of inexpensive and unobtrusive behavioral assessment techniques include keeping progress graphs on students, teaching students how to chart their own performance, counting incidents of misbehavior to establish a baseline for evaluating subsequent treatment, and using audio- or videotapes to measure change in behavior over time.

Nonbiased Testing

Nonbiased testing has been a critical concern in special education for some time. One of the most significant historical contributions to reducing bias in testing is an approach called the *System of Multicultural Pluralistic Assessment (SOMPA)* developed by Jane Mercer (Mercer & Lewis, 1978). *SOMPA* evaluates language and cultural differences as an integral part of the assessment process and attempts to minimize racial and cultural bias in measuring learning ability. *SOMPA* accomplishes this goal by enabling evaluators to consider sociocultural and health factors in estimating a child's learning potential.

SOMPA includes two major components and requires administration by a team of certified professionals. A social worker gives the parent interview components to the primary caregiver in the home. A psychologist or educational diagnostician gives assessment components to the student in a school setting. In addition to using the resulting test scores in a traditional manner, *SOMPA* also uses an innovative scoring system that accounts for social and cultural background. This creative system produces an estimated learning potential score. Unlike traditional test scores, the estimated learning potential score compares the child with other children who have similar backgrounds. According to Jane Mercer, use of estimated learning potential scores reduces the possibility of bias in testing.

Culturally sensitive assessment approaches such as *SOMPA* have been especially helpful in preventing students, especially minority students, from being diagnosed as retarded when they are not considered retarded in their home or community. When *SOMPA* was introduced in the late 1970s, it provided special educators, psychologists, and diagnosticians with a procedure for responding to a major bias-in-testing issue: the disproportionate number of students from minority groups who receive low scores on standardized tests of learning ability.

Curriculum-Based Assessment

Curriculum-based assessment is an evaluation approach that measures performance based on progress in the local school curriculum rather than in relation to scores on standardized, norm-referenced tests. Also referred to as *authentic assessment* and *performance assessment,* curriculum-based assessment relies on teacher-made tests, classwork, homework assignments, and teacher impressions to formulate assessment decisions. In 1982 Gronlund wrote about developing curriculum-based assessment procedures using teacher-made tests that offer high accuracy and validity.

In 1985 Blankenship described the use of curriculum-based assessment data to make instructional decisions. The primary advantage of curriculum-based assessment is its ability to evaluate student performance in direct relation to what has been taught in the curriculum. Special education teachers are especially interested in this type of assessment because it provides a direct link between evaluation and instruction.

Assessment in Inclusive Settings

Inclusion involves participation of children and youth with disabilities in the general education classroom and in the general curriculum, with appropriate aids and services. Inclusion is a controversial issue, with some advocating full inclusion of all students and others supporting inclusive placement as one alternative in a continuum of services (Council for Exceptional Children, 1996). The inclusion movement can be traced to mainstreaming, which emerged with the passage of Public Law 94-142 in 1975 and the **Regular Education Initiative (REI)** introduced in 1985. **Mainstreaming** refers to retaining students with disabilities in the "mainstream" of education rather than placing them in separate programs. The REI encouraged general education to accept primary responsibility for educating students with disabilities (Davis, 1989). Introduced in the 1980s, the REI recommended radical change in the treatment of students with special needs and contained two key elements: complete integration of students with disabilities into regular classes and removal of labels for students with disabilities (Kauffman, 1989).

Inclusive education has resulted in new opportunities for special educators to share and expand their expertise. As a result, skill in assessing students with special needs in inclusive settings is becoming an essential for all educators. For this reason, this book includes a complete chapter on assessment in inclusive settings designed to help you acquire a knowledge base in this increasingly important subject.

☑ Comprehension Checklist

Historically, significant contributions by professionals from many disciplines, including medicine, psychology, and educational measurement, have shaped current assessment practices in special education. For example, A. Binet and T. Simon developed the concept of intelligence and published the first effective intelligence test in 1905. Similarly, U.S. Army psychologists first introduced procedures for assessing large groups during World War I. This led to the development of the *Stanford Achievement Test* and other large-group tests. In the 1800s, pioneers such as E. Seguin introduced clinical procedures for individual diagnosis and prescriptive treatment that have become an integral part of current assessment in special education. Lloyd Dunn, a special educator, created the prototype for standardized, individually administered testing with the publication of the *Peabody Picture Vocabulary Test (PPVT)* in 1959. Finally, behavioral psychologists, including B. F. Skinner, created procedures for assessing students' performance by direct observation and continuous data collection techniques. These contributions provided the foundation for contemporary assessment practices and procedures for students with special needs. Improvements and innovations continue as a result of proposals such as inclusion and curriculum-based assessment.

Legal and Ethical Considerations in Assessment

Several federal laws have influenced assessment of students with special needs. One of the major legal and ethical considerations is protection of the right of the student and the family to privacy in connection with assessment in general and testing in particular. Both the Family and Educational Rights and Privacy Act and the Individuals with Disabilities Education Act (IDEA) affirm the right to privacy by carefully limiting legal access to a student's test scores and results. In addition, IDEA requires a school to obtain specific permission from the parents or legal guardian before testing to determine eligibility for special education. Finally, the requirements of the Infants and Toddlers Program, which is part of IDEA, mandate assessment of family needs and the development of an Individual Family Service Plan. A summary of the legal requirements mandated by these legislative acts appears in Table 1–2.

The IDEA Amendments of 1997

The Individuals with Disabilities Education Act Amendments of 1997 (IDEA 97) were signed into law on June 4, 1997. IDEA 97 substantially changes the law that was originally passed in 1975 as the Education of All Handicapped Children Act. Some of these are significant changes; others fine-tune the processes already in place for schools and parents to follow in planning and providing special education and related services for children with special needs.

What are the most significant changes in IDEA 97, and how do they affect assessment of children with special needs? Basically, the changes fall into several categories (*NICHCY News Digest*, 1997). These include the following:

* New requirements for participation of children and youth with disabilities in state and district assessment (testing) programs.
* Updated requirements for developing and reviewing Individualized Education Programs (IEPs), including increased emphasis on participation in general education with appropriate support services.
* More flexibility in conducting reevaluations.
* Changes in transition planning.

Participation of Children and Youth With Disabilities in Assessment Programs
Whether to include children and youth with disabilities in state and district assessments

Table 1–2   Summary of the Impact of Federal Laws on Assessment in Special Education

Law		Impact
Family & Educational Rights and Privacy Act	→	Guarantees privacy and access rights for student and parents
Individuals with Disabilities Education Act	→	Requires permission for testing, mandates an IEP, and calls for participation in general education
Infants and Toddlers Program	→	Requires assessment of family needs and mandates an Individual Family Service Plan

has been a continuing issue for many years. IDEA 97 resolves this issue by requiring states to include children with disabilities in state and district testing programs, with accommodations as necessary. For children who cannot participate in regular assessments, states must develop alternative assessments. However, questions about providing testing accommodations and modifications remain. The purpose of providing test accommodations is to ensure that students with disabilities have the opportunity to demonstrate what they know. For example, students who are deaf have the right to a sign language interpreter during testing. Students with other disabilities may benefit from other types of accommodations. A complete discussion of test accommodations with additional examples of typical modifications appears in Chapter 6, which, in addition to describing test accommodations, covers processes and procedures for administering, scoring, and interpreting tests.

IEP Requirements   Although the basic structure of the IEP remains intact, IDEA 97 calls for several key changes in IEP requirements. These changes have direct assessment implications. One of the most significant changes is more emphasis in the IEP on involving students with disabilities in the general curriculum and in the general education classroom. The law also reinforces the mandate that students who participate in regular education must receive appropriate support services. Chapter 2 details the basic IEP requirements and discusses recent changes in these requirements related to participation in regular education. In addition, Chapter 19 deals with the question of assessing children with special needs in inclusive settings, such as the general education classroom.

Conduct of Reevaluations   Under the previous version of IDEA, schools were required to reevaluate each student with disabilities every three years. The purpose of reevaluation is to determine continued eligibility and need for special education and related services. IDEA 97 has streamlined this process so that now the IEP team (which includes the parents) must, at least every three years, review existing assessment data to determine whether additional assessment is needed. If the team decides that more assessment data are needed, they may call for reevaluation. On the other hand, if the team decides that sufficient assessment data exist to address the needs of the child, then the school system is not required to reevaluate the child.

Changes in Transition Planning   IDEA 97 also modified the requirements for providing transition services to youth with disabilities. The most notable change is that when the students reach 14 years of age (instead of 16 as previously mandated), their IEPs must contain statements describing needed transition services such as vocational education, supported employment, and job placement. More detailed information regarding assessment and transition planning appears in Chapter 13, which covers processes and procedures for assessing career and vocational skills.

Ethical Considerations and Professional Standards

In addition to understanding the legal mandates for assessment, teachers must also be familiar with the ethical considerations and professional standards related to assessment in special education. The *Joint Technical Standards for Educational and Psychological Testing* (American Educational Research Association & National Council on Measurement in Education, 1984) provides one of the most comprehensive descriptions of ethics in testing. The *Code of Fair Testing Practices in Education* (Joint Committee on

Testing Practices, 1988) is another excellent source of information on the ethical responsibilities of professionals who develop and use tests. The standards from these professional organizations include guidelines that explain many of the basic principles of assessment, including obtaining permission for testing, ensuring the privacy of test results, and following standardized administration procedures.

Obtaining Permission Before Testing   Specific regulations for obtaining permission before testing students with disabilities appear in the federal regulations for implementing the Individuals with Disabilities Education Act (IDEA). This legislation refers to testing used selectively with an individual child to determine if the child has a disability and to identify the special education and related services the child needs. It excludes basic tests given to all children in a school, grade, or class. The legislation requires the school to fully inform parents of all information relevant to the testing. The information must be given to parents in their native language or in another appropriate mode of communication. The parents must give informed written consent for testing prior to the evaluation. Furthermore, parents must understand that granting of consent for testing is voluntary on their part and may be revoked at any time.

Specific regulations regarding permission for testing such as those in IDEA apply in many testing situations. In fact, obtaining permission for testing is one of the broad principles of assessment that is widely accepted and often mandated by law. Even when permission is not required, evaluators should make sure that test takers have relevant information regarding the testing. This means that the test giver is responsible for ensuring that test takers understand relevant information about the test, such as the purpose for testing, the type of testing, and the application of the test results. (American Educational Research Association & National Council on Measurement in Education, 1984).

Ensuring the Privacy of Test Results   Ensuring the privacy of test results is another of the basic assessment standards. This standard prohibits the release of test results identified by the names of individual test takers to any person or institution without the permission of the test taker, parent, or legal guardian. The need for privacy also includes test results on file that should be protected from inappropriate disclosure (American Educational Research Association & National Council on Measurement in Education, 1984).

Following Standardized Test Administration Procedures   Most formal tests include standardized administration procedures that specify how the test giver should administer and score the instrument. As a general rule, test givers should carefully follow these standardized procedures for giving the test and for obtaining scores from the test. This means that test givers should learn and strictly observe procedures for giving instructions to the test taker, setting time limits, presenting the test items, and using test materials. In general, deviations from standardized procedures should be made only on the basis of carefully considered professional judgment. When a test giver departs from standardized procedures, careful notes must be made, and the changes must be documented in the testing reports with appropriate cautions regarding the possible effects of such modifications on validity (American Educational Research Association & National Council on Measurement in Education, 1984).

New Professional Standards   In addition to these existing standards, the American Psychological Association (APA), in concert with other professional organizations, is finalizing new standards that reflect current assessment developments and issues. These soon-to-be-published assessment standards will likely contain many new guidelines, including an entire section on testing individuals with disabilities. The section on individuals with disabilities will focus on accommodations, modifications, and adaptations in testing. Specific accommodation strategies will most likely include standards for modifying and adapting test administration, media, timing, settings, and content.

Recent advances in scientific knowledge, medical practices, and social policies have resulted in more inclusive participation of individuals with disabilities in education and employment. These advances have raised new issues regarding assessment of students with disabilities that have created considerable debate. In particular, many questions are associated with modified administration of large-scale standardized tests for students with disabilities. The problem is that score reports from some large-scale standardized tests include an asterisk next to the score report or some other designation or flag that denotes modified test administration. The controversy centers around the efficacy of adding a flag on a test score to indicate an accommodation for a disability. Such flags may conflict with legal and social policy regarding fairness in testing individuals with disabilities. For this reason, the APA will most likely recommend that score reports from modified administrations avoid flags or other indicators in most situations. Flags are needed only when a score from a modified administration is not comparable to a score from a nonmodified administration.

☑ Comprehension Checklist

Federal legislation, along with various ethical concerns, makes assessment of students with special needs particularly complex and demanding. Because laws and ethics are vital to protect the rights of students, special education teachers must understand and apply them. By doing this, teachers are better able to safeguard their students from the potentially negative effects of testing.

Summary

Assessment, which is the use of tests and other measures to make educational decisions, is an elaborate process with a multifaceted structure. Contributions from testing specialists representing many disciplines account for much of the diversity in the process. Specific legal mandates and various ethical considerations further contribute to the complex nature of assessment. For this reason, a generic model fails to meet unique needs; therefore, assessment in special education consists of a combination of approaches to fit individual student needs and to provide accurate data for making educational decisions. Because it is so complicated, those who serve students with disabilities should be well versed in available assessment procedures and the appropriateness of those procedures in given situations. Assessment can have a significant positive or negative effect on the lives of students with disabilities. Therefore, it is imperative to understand assessment procedures, select appropriate measurement instruments, and conduct assessment skillfully. Assessment gives special educators an essential tool for providing the best possible services to those who require and are entitled to them.

Chapter Review and Application

Multiple Choice

Directions: Read each item carefully. In the blank beside each item, write the letter of the best response to the statement. Each item contains only one best answer. Check your answers with the answer key at the end of the book.

_____ **1.** The purpose of the first intelligence test was to
   a. identify students who could not benefit from educational instruction.
   b. identify gifted and talented students.
   c. identify adults with the highest intelligence.
   d. place army recruits in suitable roles.

_____ **2.** The practice of assessing large groups was first introduced
   a. in French schools at the turn of the century.
   b. by the U.S. army in World War II.
   c. by the U.S. army in World War I.
   d. by physicians who wished to diagnose children with special needs.

_____ **3.** The concept of adaptive behavior focuses on
   a. mental abilities.
   b. academic abilities.
   c. developmental skills.
   d. functional and practical abilities.

_____ **4.** Instruments that measure the development of motor, language, and personal–social skills in children from birth to about 6 years of age are usually referred to as _____ tests.
   a. achievement
   b. intelligence
   c. developmental
   d. behavioral

_____ **5.** Individual diagnosis and instruction has become a cornerstone of assessment in special education. Pioneers from many disciplines, especially _____, developed the assessment concept of individual diagnosis and prescription with students who have special needs.
   a. education
   b. medicine
   c. the army
   d. law

_____ **6.** Widespread application of the concept of individual diagnosis and prescription with students who have special needs using standardized, individually administered tests of academic achievement was established by
   a. army psychologists.
   b. French psychologists.
   c. behavioral psychologists.
   d. special educators.

_____ **7.** _____ contributed the idea of assessing student performance over time using direct observation and continuous data collection.
   a. Behavioral psychologists
   b. Special educators

      c. Medical and health-related professionals

      d. Regular educators

_____ **8.** Which evaluation approach relies on teacher-made tests, classwork, homework assignments, and teacher impressions to make assessment decisions?

      a. Intelligence testing

      b. Behavioral assessment

      c. Curriculum-based assessment

      d. Developmental assessment

_____ **9.** This law places more emphasis on participation of students with disabilities in general education.

      a. Family and Educational Rights and Privacy Act

      b. Individuals with Disabilities Education Act

      c. Infants and toddlers program

_____ **10.** This law requires assessment of family needs.

      a. Family and Educational Rights and Privacy Act

      b. Individuals with Disabilities Education Act

      c. Infants and toddlers program

_____ **11.** Which of the following ethical considerations prevents schools from giving test results to other agencies or institutions without written permission from the parents or legal guardians?

      a. Obtaining permission before testing

      b. Ensuring the privacy of test results

      c. Following standardized test administration procedures

_____ **12.** Which of the following ethical considerations requires schools to secure informed consent for testing from parents or legal guardians?

      a. Obtaining permission before testing

      b. Ensuring the privacy of test results

      c. Following standardized test administration procedures

_____ **13.** Which of the following ethical considerations requires test givers to learn and strictly observe procedures for giving instructions to the test taker, setting time limits, presenting test items, and using test materials?

      a. Obtaining permission before testing

      b. Ensuring the privacy of test results

      c. Following standardized test administration procedures

Match Terminology

Directions: Match the following terms with the appropriate description. Select from these terms: *assessment* (A), *test* (T), or *measurement* (M). In the blank beside each question, write the letter that is the best match for the description. You may use the terms more than once. Use the answer key at the end of the book to check your answers.

_____ **1.** The process of determining ability or performance.

_____ **2.** A process usually given once for the purpose of producing a score.

_____ **3.** A process used to make educational decisions.

_____ **4.** A process usually given in a prescribed manner and in a structured setting.

_____ **5.** An observation of student behavior.

_____ **6.** The broadest term.

_____ **7.** The most specific term.

Match Historical Figures

Directions: Match the following historical figures with their accomplishments: Skinner, Dunn, Gesell, Doll, Seguin, and Binet. In the blank beside each question, write the name of the historical figure that best matches the achievement. Use each name only once. Use the answer key at the end of the book to check your answers.

_____ 1. Played a major role in developing the assessment concept of individual diagnosis and prescription.
_____ 2. Introduced the concept of assessing adaptive behavior.
_____ 3. Introduced the notion of testing the developmental skills of young children.
_____ 4. Developed the first intelligence test.
_____ 5. Created the prototype for the *Peabody Individual Achievement Test,* the *Key-Math Diagnostic Test of Arithmetic,* and other individually administered achievement tests for assessing students with special needs.
_____ 6. Contributed the idea of assessing student performance over time using direct observation and continuous data collection.

List Assessment Influences

Directions: List the six influences on assessment of students with special needs that make the process so complex and multilayered. After listing the influences, check your list with the answer key at the end of the book.

8. _____
9. _____
10. _____
11. _____
12. _____
13. _____

Short Answers

Directions: Review your understanding of the material in this chapter by answering the following short answer items. After you have responded to each item, compare your responses to the sample answers. Your responses should contain information that is similar to but not exactly the same as the information in the sample answers at the end of the book.

1. Review the historical landmarks in assessment described in this chapter, and identify the three most significant landmarks that have influenced current assessment practices in special education. Explain the significance of each landmark you identify.
2. Describe three of the changes in assessment brought about by the IDEA amendments of 1997. In your opinion, which of these changes will have the most impact on assessment in special education? Why?
3. Why are ethics and professional standards important in assessing students with special needs? What is a practical, applied example that illustrates the importance of ethics and standards?

References

American Educational Research Association & National Council on Measurement in Education. (1984). *Joint Technical Standards for Educational and Psychological Testing.* Washington, D.C.: American Psychological Association.

Binet, A. & Simon, T. (1905). Méthodes nouvelles pur le diagnostic du niveau intéllectual des anormaux. *L'Annee Psychologique* 11, 191–244.

Blankenship, C. (1985). Using curriculum-based assessment data to make instructional decisions. *Exceptional Children* 52, 233–38.

Connolly, A., Natchman, W., & Pritchett, E. (1971). *KeyMath Diagnostic Arithmetic Test.* Circle Pines, MN: American Guidance Service.

Connolly, A. J. (1998). *KeyMath–Revised: A Diagnostic Inventory of Essential Mathematics.* Circle Pines, MN: American Guidance Service.

Council for Exceptional Children. (1996). Inclusion: Where are we today? *CEC Today* 3(3), 1, 5, 15.

Davis, W. E. (1989). The Regular Education Initiative debate: Its promises and problems. *Exceptional Children* 55, 440–46.

Doll, E. (1935). A genetic scale of social maturity. *The American Journal of Orthopsychiatry* 5, 180–188.

Dunn, L. M. (1959). *Peabody Picture Vocabulary Test.* Circle Pines, MN: American Guidance Service.

Dunn, L. M., & Dunn, L. M. (1997). *Peabody Picture Vocabulary Test* (3d ed.). Circle Pines, MN: American Guidance Service.

Dunn, L. M., & Markwardt, F. C. (1970). *Peabody Individual Achievement Test.* Circle Pines, MN: American Guidance Service.

Gesell, A., & Armatruda, C. S. (1941). *Developmental Diagnosis.* New York: Hoeber.

Gronlund, N. (1982). *Constructing Achievement Tests* (3d ed.). Englewood Cliffs, NJ: Prentice-Hall.

Individuals with Disabilities Education Act (October 30, 1990). *United States Statutes at Large* (vol. 104). Washington, D.C.: U.S. Government Printing Office, 1103–51.

Joint Committee on Testing Practices. (1988). *Code of Fair Testing Practices in Education.* Washington, D.C.: American Psychological Association.

Kauffman, J. M. (1989). The Regular Education Initiative as Reagan–Bush education policy: A trickle-down theory of education of the hard-to-teach. *Journal of Special Education* 23, 256–78.

Markwardt, F. C. (1998). *Peabody Individual Achievement Test* (rev. ed.) *(PIAT-R).* Circle Pines, MN: American Guidance Service.

Mercer, J. R., & Lewis, J. F. (1978). *System of Multicultural Pluralistic Assessment (SOMPA).* San Antonio, TX: Psychological Corporation.

NICHCY News Digest. (August, 1997). The IDEA amendments of 1997. Washington, D.C.: National Information Center for Children and Youth with Disabilities, 1–39.

Skinner, B. F. (1968). *The Technology of Teaching.* New York: Appleton-Century-Crofts.

Sparrow, S. S., Balla, D. A., & Cicchetti, D. V. (1984). *Vineland Adaptive Behavior Scales: Expanded Form Manual* (interview ed.). Circle Pines, MN: American Guidance Service.

Thorndike, R. L., Hagen, E., & Sattler, J. (1986). *The Stanford–Binet Intelligence Scale* (4th ed.). Chicago: Riverside Publishing.

Wechsler, D. (1991). *Manual for the Wechsler Intelligence Scale for Children* (3d ed.). San Antonio, TX: Psychological Corporation.

C H A P T E R   2

Steps in the
Assessment Process

Overview

The process of assessing students with special needs occurs in several stages and consists of multiple layers. In this chapter we investigate the different steps of the assessment process. Our study begins with an examination of assessment as it relates to screening students. Next we study the process of classifying and placing students into special education. We also focus in this chapter on the relationship between assessment and Individual Educational Plans (IEPs). This section includes the IEP requirements for assessing students, quality indicators for IEP assessment, and sample IEPs that show evaluation criteria and appraisal procedures. Later in the chapter we consider the kinds of assessment associated with instructional intervention and measuring student progress. Our examination of the goals and types of assessment associated with each step will help you understand the complex, multifaceted nature of the process. Our study also provides the basis for learning about specific tests and appraisal procedures in later chapters. The chapter also includes four case studies, one for each step in the assessment process. These biographical cases provide a link between assessment theory and instructional practice. Later chapters will refer to these cases; therefore, these early profiles serve as a foundation for more specific information in subsequent chapters.

Objectives

After reading this chapter, you will be prepared to do the following:

- Understand the role of assessment in screening students for special education.
- Explain the role of assessment in classifying and placing students in special education.
- Integrate assessment into the process of writing IEPs.
- Understand the purposes and uses of assessment in instructional intervention with students who have special needs.
- Use assessment to measure student progress.

Overview of the Assessment Process

Assessment in special education takes place in several different stages or steps. Each step has a different goal and produces assessment data or information of a specific type. By examining these steps, you will build an understanding of assessing students with special needs. However, because assessment is so complex, overlap between stages occurs with certain tests and procedures. Despite this overlap, grouping assessment into stages produces an orderly sequence that matches the steps taken to serve students with disabilities.

The first step in the process is screening students to determine if they have a potential problem that needs further assessment. When the screening process reveals a potential problem that requires additional evaluation, the student enters the second stage, called *classification and placement*. The purpose of classification and placement is to identify students who qualify for special education services. After students have been classified as having a disability and they begin to receive special education services, the next step is to obtain the assessment data needed to develop an instructional intervention program. The final phase in the process is measuring student progress, which includes assessing student performance and monitoring program effectiveness. A description of the purpose of each step appears in Table 2–1.

Use of Assessment in Screening Students

A variety of assessment activities occurs as part of the **screening process,** which refers to the assessment procedures that schools must follow to identify students who may have special needs. Screening begins when a professional or a parent observes a child

Table 2–1   Steps in the Assessment Process in Special Education

Step	Purpose	Assessment Questions
Screening students	To identify general levels of performance	Does a potential problem exist that requires further assessment?
Classifying and placing students	To determine who qualifies for special education services and to begin developing the students' individual education plans	Does the student have a specific disability? What area is the student struggling in?
Instructional intervention with students	To obtain data for making instructional decisions based on IEP goals	What instructional objectives are appropriate for the student? What are the priorities for intervention with the student?
Measuring student progress	To assess student performance, to see if the student is achieving IEP goals, to monitor program effectiveness and appropriateness of the IEP	Is the student making progress? Do the services meet the student's needs?

whose performance or behavior is so different that it causes significant concern. In many cases, regular class teachers make the initial referral. The purpose of screening is to determine if a child's general level of performance or behavior falls outside average or normal ranges. Screening helps alert parents and professionals to students who may have serious learning or behavior problems. Like all assessment processes, screening relies on specialized tests and evaluation procedures to identify students with potential problems that need further assessment. These assessments provide a sketch or an overall picture of child performance rather than a detailed analysis of specific strengths and weaknesses. Screening focuses on one question: Does a potential problem exist that requires further attention?

The screening process takes many forms, including use of the following:

- Standardized screening tests such as the *Comprehensive Scales of Student Abilities* (Hammill & Hresko, 1994), which is a 68-item, quick teacher rating scale of student ability.
- Screening checklists, scales, and inventories such as the *Early Screening Profiles* (Harrison & Knoff, 1990).
- Observations of behavior, speech, and language.
- Vision and hearing test results.
- Medical reports.
- Progress records.
- Intervention records.
- Educational history.
- Attendance history.
- Records of parent contacts and conferences.

Special Considerations and Precautions for Screening Students

Professionals must consider many factors and take special precautions during the screening process. Peterson (1987) identified the following considerations and precautions:

- The best screening programs check all aspects of child growth and development and include follow-up services. Without follow-up services, screening serves no practical purpose. Child Find is perhaps the best example of a screening program that meets these criteria. All states offer Child Find services, including screening programs designed to identify students with special needs and to arrange for follow-up services in response to identified needs.
- Screeners should plan specific procedures based on the number and the ages of the children (individual, small-group, or large-group screening).
- Screeners should design procedures in response to particular student characteristics, such as the nature of the potential problem, ethnic or racial background, native language, geographic region (urban, suburban, or rural), and family income level.
- Screeners should ensure that screening is a component in a continuum of services that includes diagnostic assessment and treatment or intervention.
- Parents or guardians must receive enough information to ensure their full participation in the screening process.

Professionals must avoid labeling as a result of the screening. This is important because screening can lead to early intervention that may prevent future learning and behavior problems or reduce their severity.

Child-Study Teams

Most schools rely on a core team of professionals, often called a **child-study team,** to coordinate screening and other activities associated with identifying students with special needs. These teams usually consist of a school administrator, a counselor, regular education teachers, and special education teachers. Referrals to the child-study team put into motion a series of screening activities, including the following:

- Observing student behavior.
- Meeting with parents.
- Documenting intervention efforts.
- Administering screening tests.
- Completing behavior rating scales, including teacher-designed instruments and published rating scales such as the *Behavior Rating Profile-2 (BRP-2)* (Brown & Hammill, 1990).

After these screening activities are completed, the child-study team reviews the data and decides whether to forward the case as a referral to a staffing team. If the child-study team sends a referral forward, the staffing team conducts comprehensive eligibility testing to determine if the student qualifies for special education services.

Screening Instruments

Screening instruments include a number of brief, easy-to-administer tests, rating scales, checklists, and direct observation techniques. Screening instruments include group and individual tests. Because they provide an overview or a sketch of behavior rather than a detailed analysis, test authors design screening instruments to measure performance with a limited number of items. Limiting the items enables evaluators to administer screening instruments in a short time. Evaluators usually need about 15 to 20 minutes to give and score a screening test, fill out a rating scale, complete a checklist, or record the results of a direct observation session. This means that an evaluator can screen one child during a brief time or a group of children in an entire day. Two of the best and most widely used screening instruments are the *Peabody Individual Achievement Test* (revised) *(PIAT-R)* (Markwardt, 1998) and the *Developmental Indicators for the Assessment of Learning* (third edition) *(DIAL-3)* (Mardell-Czudnowski & Goldenberg, 1998). The *PIAT-R* is designed for use with students from kindergarten through twelfth grade. The *DIAL-3* is for children from ages 2 through 6.

Limitations of Screening

Test developers create screening tests to measure overall performance rather than specific strengths and weaknesses. For this reason, professionals must avoid using screening tests in place of comprehensive assessment. Instead, they should rely on screening to help identify students who need more in-depth assessment and to obtain ideas about where to begin intervention while awaiting comprehensive diagnostic evaluation.

FOCUS 2–1

Why Do We Use Assessment To Screen Students?

- To confirm our observations and impressions
- To document potential problems
- To decide if further testing is needed

Why Do We Use Assessment to Screen Students?

Several reasons exist for assessing students as part of the referral process. First, when we suspect that a student may have special needs, we use assessment to confirm our observations and impressions. Second, we use assessment results to document that a student has a potential problem. For example, if a student receives a low score on a screening test, that low score can serve as evidence of a possible disability. Third, we use assessment as the basis for deciding whether to conduct more extensive evaluation to identify a student as having a particular disability. (See Focus 2–1.)

Practical Application of the Screening Process

We use many different types of screening activities with students who have special needs. These activities range from giving a quick screening test to more involved screening processes that lead to comprehensive testing to determine if a student qualifies for special education services. One of the most common and most important types of screening with students who have special needs involves prereferral activities. The purpose of prereferral is to screen students with potential problems to determine if they should be referred for comprehensive testing. The following narrative documents this process.

Jerrold Johnson, a bright, energetic child, has been a student at City Center Elementary School since kindergarten. Although Jerrold occasionally displays acting-out behavior, he has earned a reputation as a hard-working student who is well liked by his teachers and peers. Unfortunately, Jerrold has experienced academic difficulty in prereading and reading tasks since he began school. Although Jerrold's mother and his teachers noticed this problem, they attributed the difficulty to developmental delay and hoped he would catch up in reading without the need for special services. Unfortunately, Jerrold continued to have reading difficulty in the second grade. Mrs. Romero, Jerrold's second-grade teacher, described Jerrold as one of the poorest readers in her class based on his reading group performance. In particular, Mrs. Romero noticed that Jerrold had the most difficulty with word recognition, such as learning new words and remembering previously learned words.

Because of his continuing reading difficulties, Mrs. Romero decided to confirm her observations and impressions by asking the school's child-study team to screen Jerrold for a possible reading disability. Mrs. Romero was familiar with the child-study team screening process and knew that the team would require specific prereferral information if she brought his case to them. This information included observations of Jerrold's behavior, evidence of meetings with

Figure 2–1   Observation of Behavior

Name of Student _____ *Jerrold* _____

Name of Observer _____ *Ms. Breslav* _____

Length of Observations

_____ *55 minutes (11-2) & 40 minutes (11-4)* _____

Location of Observation

_____ *Jerrold's classroom* _____

Observation Notes

I observed Jerrold because of his difficulty in reading. For this reason, I planned my observations during the regular morning reading lesson. Jerrold exhibited some acting-out behavior during my observations. Specifically, Jerrold seemed to become restless and distracted when he had difficulty with the assigned reading tasks. However, he tried to complete all of his work, and his overall conduct was acceptable.

parents to discuss the problem, and documentation showing that the teacher had tried educational interventions in an attempt to solve the problem.

Mrs. Romero obtained one observation of Jerrold's behavior by having another second-grade teacher observe during a reading lesson. This teacher documented her observations by writing the brief narrative that appears in Figure 2–1. Mrs. Romero obtained a second observation by asking Jerrold's first-grade teacher to complete the rating scale that appears in Figure 2–2. The observations indicated that, although Jerrold displayed occasional behavior problems, his behavior was generally acceptable.

Mrs. Romero knew that her meetings with Jerrold's mother to discuss her son's reading problems were a critical step in the referral process. She knew that she must convince Jerrold's mother to consent to any testing that might be needed if the child-study team used the screening information to recommend testing for classification and placement. The conference notes from Mrs. Romero's two meetings with Jerrold's mom appear in Figure 2–3.

Mrs. Romero had attempted a number of different educational interventions in an effort to help Jerrold overcome his reading problems. As part of the child-study team screening and prereferral process, she documented these attempts in a written narrative description. Her description of educational interventions appears in Figure 2–4.

After these screening activities were completed, the child-study team met with Mrs. Romero to decide whether to forward the case to a staffing team for comprehensive testing. As a result of the thorough and precise screening information provided by Mrs. Romero, the team decided to recommend in-depth eligibility testing to determine if Jerrold qualified for classification as a student with a disability and placement in a special education class to help him with his reading difficulties.

This case study illustrates one role of assessment in the screening process. We will revisit Jerrold's case later in this chapter as we investigate IEPs, and we will see Jerrold later in Chapter 7 as we examine other types of tests.

Figure 2–2 Checklist of Classroom Conduct

Student ___Jerrold___

Rater ___Mrs. Kelly___

Date ___November 3___

How often did you observe these behaviors?	1=never 5=always				
	1	2	3	4	5
Often fidgets, squirms, or displays restlessness				✔	
Has difficulty remaining seated		✔			
Is easily distracted		✔			
Often blurts out during class		✔			
Has difficulty paying attention in class				✔	
Often talks excessively				✔	
Often interrupts others		✔			
Has difficulty listening		✔			
Often plays loudly		✔			
Other notable behavior (specify)					

Comments _Jerrold was a student in my first-grade class last year. I filled out this rating scale based on his behavior in my class._

Figure 2–3 Conference Notes

Conference One

Date ___November 4___

During the conference with Mrs. Johnson, we discussed Jerrold's difficulties in reading and the educational interventions (see Figure 2–4) that we have used to help Jerrold improve his reading skills. I mentioned to Ms. Johnson that the school might ask her for permission to test Jerrold for a possible reading disability if Jerrold continued to experience difficulties.

Conference Two

Date ___December 12___

During this conference, I told Mrs. Johnson that the school was going to ask for permission to test Jerrold, and I asked her if she would sign the permission forms. Mrs. Johnson said that she would go ahead and sign the forms.

Figure 2–4   Educational Interventions

Intervention One

One of the main interventions designed to help Jerrold improve his reading skills was placement in a special reading group. This group was specifically designed to have a smaller number of students so that Jerrold could receive additional help from the teacher.

Intervention Two

A second intervention was to provide Jerrold special help with new vocabulary words and words he was having difficulty with prior to introducing the words in Jerrold's reading group.

Intervention Three

Several other interventions have been provided, including special seating for Jerrold next to the teacher so he could receive extra help, assignment of a peer to help him with his reading, help from a teaching assistant two days a week, and special homework for Jerrold. The homework was arranged with Jerrold's mother, Mrs. Johnson. Mrs. Johnson asked for the special homework so that she could reinforce what he was learning at school.

☑ Comprehension Checklist

Screening, the first level in the assessment process, provides a sketch or overall picture of a child's performance that focuses on one question: Does a potential problem exist that requires further attention? Answering this question involves using rating scales, checklists, direct observation techniques, or brief, easy-to-administer tests. Because they measure overall performance rather than specific strengths and weaknesses, screening tests should not be used in place of comprehensive assessment. Instead, screening helps to identify students who need more in-depth assessment and to obtain ideas about where to begin intervention and what to do while awaiting comprehensive diagnostic evaluation. Comprehensive diagnostic evaluation occurs at the next level of the assessment process: classifying and placing students.

Use of Assessment in Classifying and Placing Students

The purposes of **classifying and placing students** are to determine the nature and severity of the problem, to decide eligibility for special education services, and to place students in appropriate programs. The general procedures for classifying and placing students are mandated by federal laws. In addition, each state has specific regulations. For example, some states rely on the traditional classification categories that include learning disabilities, emotional disturbance, and mental retardation. Other states use a generic classification system with categories such as educationally handicapped and severely handicapped.

Regardless of the classification system, federal law and state regulations include specific rules concerning assessment. For example, the law requires that certified specialists conduct the testing according to regulations that prescribe the tests that must be used. The law also mandates full parent participation and gives parents specific rights and responsibilities. These include parent permission for testing, parent participation in meetings, and informed consent regarding classification and placement decisions. For example, in the case study that we just reviewed involving Jerrold, the mother, Mrs. Johnson, had the right to refuse to sign the forms giving permission for testing. Without permission the school system could not have proceeded with the referral. This is the reason that the teacher in the case, Mrs. Romero, held special conferences with Mrs. Johnson to discuss Jerrold's reading difficulties and to describe the benefits of special services. The law also includes procedural safeguards to protect parents and their children. (See Focus 2–2.) These safeguards include the right to independent evaluations and due process procedures for resolving disagreements.

The process of classifying and placing students in special education requires the use of an interdisciplinary assessment team. Depending on the disability, specialists from various disciplines work together to obtain a complete diagnosis of the student's specific condition and needed services. A physical therapist working in concert with a physician, for example, may conduct specific tests and evaluation procedures to determine the nature and extent of a physical handicap. Based on the diagnosis, the IEP may include physical therapy services. Similarly, an audiologist may conduct specific tests to identify the type and degree of a hearing loss. In almost every case, a psychologist or an educational diagnostician administers a test to identify intellectual ability and developmental status or scholastic ability. The most commonly used test of intellectual ability is the *Wechsler Intelligence Scale for Children* (third edition) *(WISC-III)* (Wechsler, 1991). The *Battelle Developmental Inventory* (Newborg, Stock, Wnek, Guidubaldi, & Svinicki, 1984) is an example of a test for measuring developmental status. The *Kaufman Test of Educational Achievement (K-TEA)* (Kaufman & Kaufman, 1998) is an example of a widely used test of

FOCUS 2–2

Assessment and Diversity

For parents with limited English proficiency, the school system is responsible for providing the information the parents need in their native language. This means that permission for testing forms and other paperwork must be in the parent's native language. Likewise, the school should provide parents with an interpreter at meetings. This also applies to deaf parents who may need a sign language interpreter.

scholastic ability. Other specialists, including speech and language pathologists, occupational therapists, and medical specialists, may also participate as members of the assessment team, depending on the reason for testing and the nature of the problem.

Assessment Instruments for Classifying and Placing Students

Assessment at this level involves the use of comprehensive diagnostic tests and procedures administered by psychologists, educational diagnosticians, and other certified professionals. Unlike brief screening tests, these tests and procedures consist of in-depth, complex instruments and measurement systems that take several hours to administer, score, and interpret. In most cases, evaluators give a battery of standardized, individually administered diagnostic tests. Depending on the needs of the student and the reason for the evaluation, the battery may include instruments that assess intelligence, academic achievement, behavior, and perceptual skills. One of the most widely used tests for classifying and placing students with disabilities, especially students with learning disabilities, is the *Woodcock–Johnson Psycho-Educational Battery* (revised) *(WJ-R)* (Woodcock & Johnson, 1989). The test includes comprehensive tests of intellectual ability, academic achievement, and oral language skills. The academic achievement tests include measures of written expression, reading, math, science, social studies, and humanities. The *WJ-R,* which has an age range of preschool through retirement, takes several hours to administer.

Limitations of Classifying and Placing Students

The process of classifying students with a disability label and placing them in special education relies heavily on test scores. Although test scores are dependable, they sometimes fail to predict true behavior or ability accurately. Problems with test scores occur for various reasons. For example, some students fail to perform well on tests, especially pencil-on-paper tests given in testing situations. Other students, however, perform well in testing situations but display learning or behavior problems in the classroom and other natural settings. Furthermore, test scores indicate—but do not prove—a student's ability level. For this reason, we should use test scores with caution, keeping these limitations in mind at all times. Despite limitations, however, federal and state laws require the use of scores derived from standardized, norm-referenced assessment instruments. Scores from standardized, norm-referenced tests provide an objective measure that protects children from decisions based on the subjective impressions of professionals. Subjective impressions, such as opinions and judgments about student ability, performance, and behavior, are difficult to quantify and can result in biased and unfair decisions about students.

Why Do We Use Assessment to Classify and Place Students?

We assess students as part of the classification and placement process for several reasons. The primary reason is to obtain a comprehensive diagnosis of student strengths, weaknesses, and learning needs. We use this diagnosis as a basis for making classification and placement decisions that respond to the individual and unique needs of the student. Second, we use assessment in response to legal requirements and state and district regulations. Third, and perhaps the most important, we use assessment to

FOCUS 2–3

Why Do We Use Assessment to Classify and Place Students?

- To diagnose learning needs
- To meet legal requirements
- To protect the rights of children
- To determine eligibility for services

protect the rights of children and their families. The purpose of assessment for classification and placement is to determine if a child has a disability, and, if so, to decide the types of special education or related services needed to provide an appropriate education. These are legal decisions that label a student as eligible for special education services, and, because of the legalities involved, they rely heavily on results from norm-referenced, standardized tests. In the vast majority of cases, parents agree with the school systems regarding classification and placement recommendations, but parents can challenge a school's recommendation, and schools can also dispute parent requests. When such disputes cannot be resolved, they must be decided in a court of law. For this reason, the process includes a variety of procedural safeguards to protect the student, the parents, and the school system; however, these necessary and important safeguards sometimes make the process lengthy and cumbersome. (See Focus 2–3.)

Practical Application of Assessment in Classification and Placement

Let's take a look at the story of Mrs. Sharon Pinkney and her daughter Angel.

Mrs. Pinkney had long suspected that her daughter Angel had learning problems, and her suspicions were confirmed when she met with Angel's teacher. In the meeting, the teacher described Angel's learning problems and asked for permission to refer Angel to a school-based child-study team for advice on ways to help Angel. Mrs. Pinkney, who was both concerned about Angel's academic difficulties and relieved that the teacher had also identified them, agreed. The teacher indicated that the team might recommend testing to determine if Angel needed special help. About a month later, the teacher called Mrs. Pinkney to inform her that the school team had recommended further testing by a psychologist and that she would be receiving permission forms in the mail. When she received the forms, she signed them and returned them to the school.

About a month later, the school counselor called to ask Mrs. Pinkney to come in for a meeting to discuss the testing results. Mrs. Pinkney entered the conference room and was introduced to several specialists: a psychologist, a staffing specialist, a school counselor, an assistant principal, and the teacher who was the chair of the school's child-study team. The school counselor began the meeting with a brief introduction. Then the school counselor asked Mrs. Pinkney several questions about Angel's achievement and behavior. This gave Mrs. Pinkney the opportunity to describe her daughter to the professionals at the meeting and to talk about Angel's academic difficulties. Next, the school psychologist began her report. In her assessment of Angel, she identified a "significant discrepancy" between Angel's ability to learn, which was "normal" (as measured by an intelligence test), and her achievement, which was "below average" (as measured by an achievement test). The psychologist indicated that Angel had the most difficulty with reading, especially reading comprehension. During testing, Angel had difficulty answering specific questions about passages she had read, such as "What was the dog's name?" She was unable to tell the sequence of stories that were read, and she failed to recall the main idea in stories. After the psychologist's report, the school counselor asked Mrs. Pinkney if she had any questions about the report. As a result, the staffing team recommended that Angel be placed in a program that could provide her with special instruction in reading and that her IEP focus on objectives designed to help her improve reading comprehension skills such as remembering basic facts, recalling sequences, and recognizing main ideas in reading passages. Mrs. Pinkney had an opportunity to participate with the professionals on the team in developing the program placement recommendation and in designing the IEP goals and objectives.

When the staffing team recommended placement with a teacher who specialized in reading disabilities, Mrs. Pinkney was relieved. She learned that she could review the special education services each year and approve any changes. The conference with Angel's teacher and the education specialists made Mrs. Pinkney feel much better about Angel's learning problems and the possibility that she could overcome them. Several weeks later, Angel began attending her new class and, over time, the extra instruction helped Angel to improve her reading comprehension and build her self-confidence.

☑ Comprehension Checklist

This account shows many of the steps in the second level of assessment: the process of classifying and placing students into special education. Because of the number of steps involved, placing a student can take 6 months or longer in some situations. We have seen that assessment enables diagnosis of specific disabilities, which serves as the basis for making classification and placement decisions. After placement, the special education teacher uses the initial IEP to develop specific teaching and learning activities. Developing specific intervention activities falls into a third level of assessment: instructional intervention with students. However, before initiating an intervention program, students with special needs must have an IEP that responds to their unique learning needs.

Assessment and the Individual Education Plan (IEP)

After a student is identified as having a disability, the focus of assessment changes from screening and classification to instructional intervention and measuring progress. The **individual education plan (IEP)** is the document that guides the development and implementation of the instructional intervention program and the process of measuring student progress. The IEP, which is mandated by the Individuals with Disabilities Education Act, is a written document developed jointly by parents, professionals, and, if appropriate, the student. The initial IEP is developed by the staffing team as part of the placement process, but once a student begins to receive special education services, subsequent IEPs are developed by a school-based team. By law the IEP must include certain components that describe an appropriate

Table 2–2 The Components of Individualized Education Plans (IEPs)

1. A statement of the child's present levels of educational performance, including how the disability affects involvement and progress in the general curriculum

2. A statement of measurable annual goals, including benchmarks or short-term instructional objectives related to meeting the child's needs that result from the child's disability to enable the child to be involved in and progress in the general curriculum; and meeting each of the child's other educational needs that result from the child's disability

3. A statement of the specific special education and related services to be provided, and a statement of program modifications and supports provided for the child to attain the annual goals, to participate in the general curriculum, and to be educated and participate with other children with disabilities and nondisabled children in educational activities

4. An explanation of the extent, if any, to which the child will not participate with nondisabled children in the regular class and related activities

5. A statement of individual modifications in the administration of state- or districtwide assessments

6. The projected date for initiation of services and the anticipated duration of the services

7. Beginning at age 14, a statement of transition service needs

8. A statement of how the child's progress toward the annual goals will be measured and how the child's parents will be regularly informed of their child's progress, and the extent to which that progress is sufficient to enable the child to achieve the goals by the end of the year

education for a student who receives special education services. The law requires that special education teachers join with parents and other professionals as part of a team to develop the IEP. A list of the components of an IEP appears in Table 2–2.

IEPs and the Diagnostic–Prescriptive Model

The IEP components clearly set forth several legal mandates, including specific guidelines for assessing students who receive special education services. The basis of assessment in the IEP process is an appraisal method known as the **diagnostic–prescriptive model,** which is a system of assessment that involves the following:

- Conducting an initial evaluation to identify present levels of performance (diagnosis).
- Using the results to determine appropriate annual goals and benchmarks or short-term objectives (prescription).
- Measuring progress toward meeting the annual goals and determining the extent to which that progress is sufficient to achieve the goals by the end of the year.

Perhaps a better name for this model is the test-teach-test-teach method. When teachers use this method, they pretest students to determine learning needs and then teach using a curriculum based on those needs. After instruction, teachers posttest their students to measure progress and revise their teaching as appropriate. As specified in the IEP, implementing this model involves a series of steps. A diagram

Figure 2–5 Diagram of the Diagnostic–Prescriptive Model

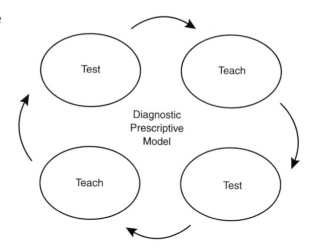

of the steps in the diagnostic–prescriptive model appears in Figure 2–5; Table 2–3 lists and describes each step in the process along with the IEP component that matches each step.

Individual Family Service Plans and Transition IEPs

The Infants and Toddlers Program, which is part of IDEA, mandates use of a similar planning process for very young children with disabilities. For children younger than age 3, the program calls for development of an Individual Family Service Plan that includes assessment of the needs of the child and the family. Similarly, IDEA calls for a specialized transition IEP for all students beginning at age 14. The purpose of the transition IEP is to facilitate movement from school to postschool activities. Specific information regarding these specialized IEPs appears in later chapters; specifically, Chapter 8 includes a discussion of Individual Family Service Plans, and Chapter 13 describes transition IEPs.

Table 2–3 IEPS and the Diagnostic–Prescriptive Model

	Assessment Step		IEP Component
Diagnose	Test	Test the student to identify present levels of educational performance	1 Present levels of educational performance
Prescribe	Teach	Teach the student based on annual goals and short-term objectives	2 State the annual goals, including short-term instructional objectives
Diagnose	Test	Test the student to determine progress in meeting goals	8 State how the child's progress toward meeting the annual goals will be measured
Prescribe	Teach	Teach the student based on new goals developed from the reevaluation	The law requires that the IEP be rewritten annually

The IEP, the Individual Family Service Plan, and the Transition IEP are written plans developed by a team that includes the parents. The plans must be based on assessment of the individual and unique needs of the child. The plans, developed at a team meeting, include annual goals and at least one short-term objective for each annual goal. The plans must also include evaluation criteria, procedures, and schedules.

Practical Application of Assessment and the IEP Process

Three sample IEPs that illustrate appropriate use of assessment in the IEP process appear in Figures 2–6, 2–7, and 2–8. The first IEP, in Figure 2–6, is an initial IEP

Figure 2–6 Individual Education Plan

Identifying Information

Name	Johnny Lees
School	Woodland Acres
Age	12
Grade	6
Parents	Ken & Melissa King
Address	377 5th Street
City	Johnson City
Phone	

Process Checklist

10/12	Referral date
10/17	Permission for testing
11/1	Testing completed
11/8	Meeting scheduled
11/15	Meeting held
11/15	IEP signed

Special Education Services

Service	Beginning Date	Anticipated Duration	Other Information
Instruction in self-management skills	12/4	One year	Daily resource room class
Individual Counseling	12/4	One year	Twice a week

Extent to Which the Student Will Not Participate in General Education

Service	Percent of Time	Purpose
Resource Room	30%	Academic instruction, socialization

Committee Members

Jeanne Prince	Joyce Glover Patricia Hollis
LEA Representative	Teachers
Melissa King	
Parents	Others
Student	Others

Figure 2–6   *(continued)*

Annual Goals and Short-Term Instructional Objectives
(Complete additional pages as needed)

Student's Name _____*Johnny Lees*_____   Domain ___*Personal/Social Skills*___

Present Level of Educational Performance

Teacher observations and data from behavior checklists indicate that Johnny becomes easily frustrated and may become aggressive when faced with difficult tasks or demanding situations in school. Johnny's priority for intervention is to develop self-control in school so that he can fully participate in general education.

Annual goal

1. Johnny will use a sequence of 4 self-management skills to maintain self-control in school. Attaining this goal will help Johnny fully participate in the general education classroom. Johnny's parents will receive a progress report each nine weeks.

Short-Term Instructional Objectives	Start Date	Assessment Procedures		
		Measurement	Process	Outcome
1.1 Johnny will identify the sequence of 4 skills (i.e., identify the problem, self-verbalize his feelings, use self-instruction to get back on task, & use self-reinforcement	Jan	Each step for 5 consecutive days	Teacher interview & self-evaluation	Achieved on 1/14
1.2 Johnny will use the skill in the resource room.	Feb	Each step 9 out of 10 times	Structured observation & self-evaluation	Achieved on 2/14
1.3 Johnny will use the self-control strategy in general classes.	Mar	Each step 9 out of 10 times	Structured observation & self-evaluation	

---

developed by a staffing team during the placement process. It includes a cover page and a short-term-objectives page. The cover page includes identifying information, a list of services to be provided, a description of the extent to which the student will not participate in general education, and the signatures of the committee members who developed the plan. The short-term-objectives page covers the social–emotional domain. This section includes a description of the present level of performance, the annual goal, and three short-term objectives, with assessment procedures for each objective. The second IEP, in Figure 2–7, shows a short-term-objectives page in the vocational/career domain. The third IEP, in Figure 2–8, shows a short-term-objectives page in the domain of curriculum and learning for Jerrold Johnson, the student whom we met in the section on screening at the beginning of this chapter. (Information about writing IEPs using computer software programs appears in Focus 2–4.)

Figure 2–7   Annual Goals and Short-Term Objectives

(Use additional pages as needed)

Student's Name _____Nancy McBride_____   Domain _____Vocational/Career_____

Annual Goal 1. Nancy will master the ten basic skills for her job as a nursing home cafeteria helper. Attaining this goal will enable Nancy to fully participate in the general work/study program. Nancy's parents will receive a progress report every nine weeks.

Short-Term Instructional Objectives	Date	Assessment Procedures		
		Measurement	Process	Outcome
1.1 Nancy will master the skills related to mopping the floor.	Nov	Meets nursing home standards	Observation form	Met on 11/12
1.2 Nancy will master the skills related to cleaning the tables and chairs.	Dec	Meets nursing home standards	Observation form	Met on 12/12
1.3 Nancy will master the operation of the dishwasher.	Jan	Meets nursing home standards	Observation form	
1.4 Nacny will master the skills related to setting the tables.	Feb	Meets nursing home standards	Observation form	

Quality Indicators for the Development of IEPs

The Florida Department of Education (Burke & Beech, 1997, p. 49) has developed a set of quality indicators for the development of IEPs that includes items for measuring the assessment elements of IEPS, including evaluation criteria, procedures, and schedules in the IEP. Teachers may use the checklist that appears in Figure 2–9 as a guide for checking the quality of the assessment data in IEPs that they help develop.

FOCUS 2–4

Technology Tip

Many school systems have purchased or developed special education management software for teachers and administrators to help them prepare IEPs, evaluations, and reports for state agencies. To find out more about this software, conduct an Internet search using *IEPs* as the key word. To see an example of a commercial IEP software management system, point your browser to the following Internet address: www.tera-sys-inc.com

Figure 2–8   Annual Goals and Short-Term Objectives

(Use additional pages as needed)

Student's Name _____ Jerrold Johnson _____   Domain _____ Curriculum & Learning _____

Present Level of Educational Performance

Jerrold reads at the first-grade level. Although he has good comprehension skills, he has difficulty with word recognition and decoding words using phonics. Jerrold practices his reading daily. He participates in his reading group and he completes his individual reading assignments. Jerrold's priority for educational intervention is to develop word recognition and decoding skills.

Annual Goals

1. Jerrold will develop word-recognition skills, especially in the areas of word recognition and decoding.
2. Jerrold will understand and apply 20 phonic rules.
Attaining these goals will enable Jerrold to participate in the general education reading program without daily special education support services.

Short-Term Instructional Objectives	Date	Assessment Procedures		
		Measurement	Process	Outcome
1.1 Jerrold will read beginning level 2nd grade passages 2.1 Jerrold will recognize and use 5 phonics rules	End of 1st term	90 correct wpm	Teacher observation Individually designed phonics worksheets	Achieved on 12/12
2.1 Jerrold will read upper level 2nd grade passages 2.2 Jerrold will recognize and use 10 phonics rules	End of 2nd term	90 correct wpm	Teacher observation Individually designed phonics worksheets	
3.1 Jerrold will read 3rd grade passages 3.2 Jerrold will recognize and use 15 phonics rules	End of 3rd term	90 correct wpm	Teacher observation Individually designed phonics worksheets	

IEPs and Participation in the Regular Classroom

New IEP requirements in IDEA 97 emphasize participation in the general education curriculum. These new requirements call attention to accommodations and adjustments necessary for children with disabilities to access the regular curriculum. The

Figure 2–9 Quality Indicators for Evaluation Criteria, Procedures, and Schedules

	Requirement		
Evaluation Criteria, Procedures, and Schedules	Appropriate objective criteria and evaluation procedures and schedules for determining, on at least an annual basis, whether the short-term instructional objectives are being achieved (Rule 6A-0.03028(I)(e),FAC)		
Quality Indicators		*Meets Criterion*	*Doesn't Meet Criterion*
Reflects evaluation schedules that include ongoing and frequent measurement of objectives.			
Specifies criteria that match the objective.			
Uses criteria that are attainable yet challenging in relation to the student's ability.			
Provides evaluation procedures that include home, work, community, and school settings for measuring objectives logically carried out in a specific setting.			
Reflects a variety of appropriate evaluation methods and procedures.			
Includes documentation of mastery of short-term instructional objectives.			
Comments:			

requirements also highlight the need for special services that facilitate appropriate participation in particular areas of the curriculum. By law each student's IEP must include a statement describing the extent, if any, to which the child will not participate with nondisabled children in the regular class and in extracurricular and other nonacademic activities. These new IEP requirements clearly strengthen the connection between special education and the general education curriculum. The requirements are also the legal basis for inclusion and mainstreaming programs and procedures. Because of the increasing focus on placing students with disabilities in regular education, Chapter 19 in this book is devoted to assessment in inclusive settings. Chapter 19 investigates processes and procedures for assessing students with special needs who receive all or part of their education in general education classrooms and other regular settings.

 Comprehension Checklist

For students with disabilities, the IEP guides the development and implementation of instructional intervention programs and the process of measuring progress. An IEP is a written plan developed jointly by parents, professionals, and, if appropriate, the student. The IEP is also the legal document that describes the elements of an appropriate education for students who receive special education services. The basis of assessment in the IEP process is an appraisal method known as the *diagnostic–prescriptive model,* which uses a test-teach-test-teach instructional approach. Recently revised IEP guidelines emphasize the need for students with disabilities to receive their education in the general education classroom and to participate in the general education curriculum with supplementary aids and services as appropriate.

Use of Assessment in Instructional Intervention

Teachers use assessment as part of **instructional intervention** to obtain the information necessary for making educational decisions related to developing instructional objectives, to establishing intervention priorities, and to evaluating the effectiveness of curricula and materials. Instructional intervention uses assessment in the classroom as a regular part of daily instruction so that the teaching process includes evaluation of student performance in relation to specific instructional objectives articulated in the IEP. For the special education teacher, assessment for instructional intervention is one of the most important of the assessment processes. Without it, teachers have difficulty developing and tailoring individual programs that respond to the performance levels and learning needs of their students.

Assessment Instruments for Instructional Intervention With Students

Although the process of instructional intervention with students uses standardized commercial tests such as the *Peabody Individual Achievement Test* (revised) (Markwardt, 1998) and the *KeyMath* (revised) (Connolly, 1998), it relies primarily on classroom-based, teacher-designed assessment instruments and procedures. These instruments and procedures include a variety of measures designed for practitioners, such as checklists of student performance, minimum competency tests, and teacher-made tests. Teacher observations and impressions are also an important component of assessment for instructional intervention. Salvia and Hughes (1990) defined observations as structured and unstructured ways of listening to and watching a student for the purpose of making programming decisions. An example of structured observation is the use of charts to illustrate student behavior. Impressions are unstructured and less systematic conclusions and judgments that teachers make after interacting with students for a period of time. For example, a teacher may decide to use a certain intervention approach based on an impression formed after working directly with a student and consulting with other teachers.

Limitations of Assessment in Instructional Intervention With Students

Assessment for instructional intervention with students relies, in part, on subjective evaluation based on impressions and opinions. Although subjective information is an important component in instructional intervention, it can be arbitrary and biased against a student. For this reason, assessment should include more than subjective appraisal as the basis for determining instructional objectives and priorities for intervention. Instead, it should reflect a variety of appropriate assessment methods and procedures. A teacher might, for example, combine clinical judgment with results from a checklist of skills and a score from a standardized test to try to ensure a fair, objective outcome and to develop the best possible IEP goals.

Why Do We Use Assessment in Instructional Intervention?

We use assessment as part of instructional intervention for many reasons. First, assessment helps us to identify student readiness for instruction and to determine strengths, weaknesses, interests, motivation, and learning style. In some situations, we use formal tests such as the *Test of Written Language-2* (Hammill & Larsen, 1986) or the *Gates–MacGinitie Reading Tests* (third edition) (MacGinitie & MacGinitie, 1989) to accomplish this, and in other situations we rely on less formal, teacher-made measurements such as classroom quizzes, direct observations, or checklists of skills. Second, as teachers we need to know what students have already learned. This knowledge then helps us determine what students need to learn next. The purpose of this type of diagnostic assessment is to obtain information for planning instructional interventions that respond to the needs of the students who will be receiving the instruction. In other words, appropriate assessment is necessary to make the best possible intervention decisions. These decisions include establishing intervention priorities, developing instructional objectives, and evaluating a curriculum and materials. (see Focus 2–5.)

Practical Application of Assessment in Instructional Intervention

Ms. Brenna Bateh is a very special teacher who has earned a reputation for innovative and student-based, individualized instruction. One of the ways she accomplishes this is by using instructional interventions to continually assess her students' academic performance and interests. She also seeks new ways to measure achievement and motivation; Ms. Bateh reads about new assessment procedures and relies on her own creativity and experience to devise a variety of ways to evaluate her students' performance.

Ms. Bateh learned, in her preservice classes, that assessment as part of instructional intervention could help her establish learning goals and plan ways to help students achieve the goals set in their IEPs. When Ms. Bateh began her teaching career, she practiced answering the following questions as part of her instructional planning: What do my students need to learn in my class, and how much of this material do they already know? How can I best determine if my students have accomplished these goals? What are the students' skills and knowledge as they enter the class? What level of motivation and interest do the students bring to the class?

FOCUS 2–5

Why Do We Use Assessment in Instructional Intervention?

- To identify instructional needs
- To establish intervention priorities
- To develop instructional objectives
- To evaluate curriculum and materials

To decide what students should know by the end of the class, Ms. Bateh relies on a variety of sources: her experience, other teachers' experiences, curriculum requirements, instructional and curriculum materials, and student interests. After deciding what students should learn in the class, Ms. Bateh pretests the students to identify how much of the material they know prior to entering the class or before beginning a new topic. She does this by preparing a simple teacher-made test that usually contains about ten multiple-choice and matching questions. Results from these pretests divulge what the students already know, and the pretests show the students what they will be responsible for learning. Ms. Bateh also uses posttest probes at the end of some lessons to decide if the students have learned the material and to summarize the material for the students. The information she receives from the probes provides essential information regarding student needs and their strengths and weaknesses—an important goal of instructional intervention. Pretest results from Ms. Bateh's classes revealed that her students had diverse needs that required many opportunities to practice skills, followed by extensive feedback. Ms. Bateh realized that she would need to individualize instruction in her classes as much as possible because all students have unique learning needs that cause them to work at different levels of performance and motivation. This is especially true with students who have disabilities.

Ms. Bateh was initially overwhelmed by the challenge of meeting the needs of all her students. She tried conventional methods for individualizing within the group and included peer teaching and cooperative learning in her teaching methods. When her assessments and instructional interventions showed that she needed to incorporate more reflective teaching and learning activities to motivate her students, she included more portfolio-based instruction and assessment activities such as portfolio conferences to help students learn reflection and self-evaluation.

As you can see, Ms. Bateh continually strives for improvement. Even after she finds solutions to instructional dilemmas, she searches for even better ways to help her students. Ms. Bateh is a good example of how to do instructional intervention successfully because she has learned how to use assessment as a regular part of instruction rather than as an extra element added on to meet state and district guidelines.

☑ Comprehension Checklist

The purpose of conducting assessment as part of instructional intervention is to obtain the information necessary for making educational decisions concerning instructional objectives, intervention priorities, and the effectiveness of curricula and materials. Teachers also conduct assessment during instructional intervention to obtain data for writing and revising IEPs. For the special education teacher, assessment for instructional intervention is one of the most important of the assessment processes. Without it, teachers have difficulty developing individual programs that respond to the performance levels and learning needs of their students. Assessment as part of instructional intervention relies primarily on classroom-based, teacher-designed assessment instruments and procedures such as checklists of student performance, minimum competency tests, and teacher-made tests. Teacher observations and impressions are also an important part of assessment for instructional intervention.

Use of Assessment in Measuring Student Progress

Assessment for **measuring student progress** involves ongoing evaluation as well as intermittent measurement of overall progress. According to Bricker and Gumerlock (1988), measuring and evaluating student progress entails assessment of progress on daily lessons, progress over time, and general progress. Teachers and administrators also rely on assessment of student progress to monitor program effectiveness, to ensure that special education services respond to the individual needs of students, and to determine how well the IEP is working.

Assessment Instruments for Measuring Student Progress

When practitioners measure the progress of students on daily lessons, they rely primarily on informal evaluation procedures, including teacher-made tests and other measures of student progress that are directly related to the curriculum. Examples of these tests and measures include the following:

- Scores from class tests, worksheets, and papers.
- Results of task analysis and error-pattern analysis.
- Teacher observations and impressions.
- Information from student portfolios.
- Behavior-management data.

Teachers use a variety of techniques to monitor daily progress, including recording performance in grade books, graphing data from behavior-management programs, and writing narrative reports from observations and impressions.

When teachers measure the progress of students over time, such as a term or a semester, they rely on curriculum-based assessment instruments. Examples of curriculum-based instruments include skills checklists from curriculum guides and competency tests, including minimum skills tests and objectives for which students must demonstrate mastery. These curriculum-based tests and checklists are best when they represent the instructional content of the daily lessons in the classroom or program.

Measuring the overall progress of students, usually on an annual basis, requires that teachers use commercial standardized tests rather than informal measures. Examples of formal standardized measures include commercial tests of individual academic achievement such as the *Peabody Individual Achievement Test* (revised) *(PIAT-R)* (Markwardt, 1998) and standardized behavior rating scales such as the *Comprehensive Behavior Rating Scale for Children (CBRS)* (Neeper & Lahey, 1988). Measuring global progress provides information for making decisions about the effectiveness of the program and supplies data for comparing the performance of one student to others.

Limitations of Measuring Student Progress

Measuring student progress can be a time-consuming process that takes away from instructional time. This occurs most often at the end of the school year when teachers are required to give group-administered, standardized achievement tests such as the *Stanford Achievement Test (SAT)* or the *Comprehensive Test of Basic Skills (CTBS)* and minimum competency tests (designed to measure global progress) in addition to keeping up with their routine assessment activities. One of the ways that teachers manage this problem is to use a type of classroom evaluation often referred to as *curriculum-based assessment (CBA)*, which is specifically designed for teachers to use in instructional situations. A key feature of CBA is that it enables teachers to measure progress as a regular part of instruction rather than as a separate activity. Because CBA is an ingredient of instruction, not a disconnected activity, teachers

and other measures, such as checklists and teacher judgment, that relate directly to the instructional curriculum. The reasons for measuring student progress are to obtain information for making instructional decisions, to monitor the appropriateness of the IEP, and to provide students with feedback. Measuring student progress also provides a way to monitor program effectiveness with the goal of ensuring that the services students receive are responsive to their individual needs.

Summary

The process of assessing students with special needs involves several steps, including the following:

- Screening students.
- Classifying and placing students.
- Establishing an IEP.
- Developing an instructional intervention program for students.
- Measuring student progress.

Although distinctions and differences exist among these steps in the assessment process, similarities exist among the stages as well. The differences involve the purpose of assessment at each level and the type of assessment procedures in each stage of the process. Screening students is usually the initial phase in the assessment process. Screening is usually a brief and relatively uncomplicated process. In contrast, classifying and placing a student usually involves lengthy, complicated, and formal diagnostic testing procedures. For students with disabilities, the IEP guides their instructional intervention programs and the process of measuring their progress. Both instructional intervention with students and measuring student progress rely on less formal assessment procedures that are directly tied to the instructional process. The similarities among the assessment categories involve the goal of all assessment in special education: to contribute information for designing an appropriate education for students with special needs.

Chapter Review and Application

Multiple Choice

Directions: Read each item carefully. In the blank beside each item, write the letter of the best answer for the statement. Each item contains only one best answer. Check your answers with the answer key at the end of the book.

_____ 1. When teachers decide what objectives to teach, they are making which of the following decisions?
   a. A screening
   b. A placement
   c. An instructional intervention
   d. A pupil progress

_____ 2. Which step in the assessment process involves evaluating student performance over time?
   a. A screening
   b. A placement

    c. An instructional intervention
    d. A pupil progress

____ **3.** Which assessment relies primarily on individually administered, standardized diagnostic tests?
    a. A screening
    b. A placement
    c. An instructional intervention
    d. A pupil progress

____ **4.** Which assessment decides who qualifies for special education?
    a. A screening
    b. A placement
    c. An instructional intervention
    d. A pupil progress

____ **5.** Which assessment involves monitoring program effectiveness?
    a. A screening
    b. A placement
    c. An instructional intervention
    d. A pupil progress

____ **6.** The referral process is part of which assessment?
    a. A screening
    b. A placement
    c. An instructional intervention
    d. A pupil progress

____ **7.** The IEP process is a part of which assessment?
    a. Screening
    b. Placement
    c. Instructional intervention

____ **8.** The staffing team arranges for Johnny to take an individually administered intelligence test. This occurs at which level of assessment?
    a. Screening
    b. Placement
    c. Instructional intervention
    d. Pupil progress

____ **9.** When Mrs. Wilson uses assessment information to decide if a student should be referred for further testing, she is operating at which level of assessment?
    a. Screening
    b. Placement
    c. Instructional intervention
    d. Pupil progress

____ **10.** After noticing that Jimmy has difficulty reading, Mrs. Robbins suspects that he may have a visual processing problem. What level of assessment does this concern?
    a. Screening
    b. Placement
    c. Instructional intervention
    d. Pupil progress

Match Levels of Assessment

Match the level of assessment with the description. Select from these choices:
screening, classification and placement, instructional intervention, and measuring
progress. Use each choice once.

_____ 1. Class grades and student self-assessment
_____ 2. Observations of behavior, parent conferences, and attempted educational interventions
_____ 3. What are the instructional priorities for my students?
_____ 4. A significant discrepancy between ability as measured by an intelligence test and achievement as measured by an achievement test

Short Answers

Directions: Review your understanding of the material in this chapter by answering
the following short answer tasks. Compare your responses to the sample answers.
Your responses should contain information that is similar to but not exactly the
same as the information in the sample answers at the end of the book.

1. Complete the evaluation plan section for the sample IEP (Figure 2–11) by developing criteria, procedures, and results for each of the three short-term objectives.

Figure 2–11 Annual Goals and Short-Term Instructional Objectives

(Complete additional pages as needed)

Student's Name _____Georgiana Forkner_____ Domain _____Behavioral_____

Present Level of Educational Performance
Teacher and staff observations indicate that Georgiana sometimes fails to follow the rules of student conduct for the classroom, the school, and the bus.

Annual Goal
Georgiana will follow the rules for the classroom, the school, and the bus.

Short-Term Instructional Objectives	Date	Assessment Procedures		
		Measurement	Process	Outcome
1.1 Georgiana will obey the rules established in the classroom.	Ongoing			
1.2 Georgiana will obey the Code of Student Conduct established in the school.	Ongoing			
1.3 Georgiana will obey the rules established for the school bus.	Ongoing			

2. Analyze the quality of the sample IEP that you completed in #1 by filling out the Checklist of Quality Indicators for Evaluation Criteria, Procedures, and Schedules (Figure 2–12) to determine if the IEP meets all of the criteria.

Figure 2–12   Quality Indicators for Evaluation Criteria, Procedures, and Schedules

	Requirement	
Evaluation Criteria, Procedures, and Schedules	Appropriate objective criteria and evaluation procedures and schedules for determining, on at least an annual basis, whether the short-term instructional objectives are being achieved (Rule 6A-0.03028(I)(e),FAC)	
Quality Indicators	*Meets Criterion*	*Doesn't Meet Criterion*
Reflects evaluation schedules that include ongoing and frequent measurement of objectives.		
Specifies criteria that match the objective.		
Uses criteria that are attainable yet challenging in relation to the student's ability.		
Provides evaluation procedures that include home, work, community, and school settings for measuring objectives logically carried out in a specific setting.		
Reflects a variety of appropriate evaluation methods and procedures.		
Includes documentation of mastery of short-term instructional objectives.		
Comments:		

References

Brown, L. L., & Hammill, D. D. (1990). *Behavior Rating Profile-2 (BRP-2)*. Austin, TX: Pro-Ed Corporation.

Burke, D. A., & Beech, M. (1997). *Developing Quality Individual Education Plans: A Guide for Instructional Personnel*. Tallahassee: Florida Department of Education.

Connolly, A. J. (1998). *KeyMath Revised: A Diagnostic Inventory of Essential Mathematics*. Circle Pines, MN: American Guidance Service.

Hammill, D. D., & Hresko, W. P. (1994). *Comprehensive Scales of Student Abilities*. Austin, TX: Pro-Ed.

Hammill, D. D., & Larsen, S. C. (1986). *Test of Written Language-2*. Austin, TX: Pro-Ed.

Harrison, P. L., & Knoff, H. M. (1990). *AGS Early Screening Profiles*. Circle Pines, MN: American Guidance Service.

Individuals with Disabilities Education Act (October 30, 1990). *United States Statutes at Large* (vol. 104). Washington, DC: U.S. Government Printing Office, 1103–51.

Kaufman, A. S., & Kaufman, N. L. (1998). *Kaufman Test of Educational Achievement (K-TEA)*. Circle Pines, MN: American Guidance Service.

MacGinitie, W. H., & MacGinitie, R. K. (1989). *Gates–MacGinitie Reading Tests* (3d. ed.). Chicago: Riverside.

Mardell-Czudnowski, C. D., & Goldenberg, D. S. (1998). *Developmental Indicators for the Assessment of Learning Revised (DIAL-3)*. Edison, NJ: Childcraft Education Corporation.

Markwardt, F. C. (1998). *Peabody Individual Achievement Test-Revised (PIAT-R)*. Circle Pines, MN: American Guidance Service.

Neeper, R., & Lahey, B. B. (1988). *Comprehensive Behavior Rating Scale for Children (CBRS)*. San Antonio, TX: The Psychological Corporation.

Newborg, J., Stock, J., Wnek, L., Guidubaldi, J., & Svinicki, J. (1984). *Battelle Developmental Inventory*. Allen, TX: DLM Teaching Resources.

Peterson, N. (1987). *Early Intervention for Handicapped and At-Risk Children*. Denver, CO: Love.

Salvia, J., & Hughes, C. (1990). *Curriculum-Based Assessment: Testing What is Taught*. New York: Macmillan.

Wechsler, D. (1991). *Wechsler Intelligence Scale for Children* (3d. ed.). Cleveland, OH: The Psychological Corporation.

Woodcock, R. W., & Johnson, M. B. (1989). *Woodcock–Johnson Psycho-Educational Battery* (rev. ed.). Allen, TX: DLM Teaching Resources.

C H A P T E R   3

Measurement Concepts

Overview

Knowledge of the basic concepts of measurement is essential to understanding assessment in special education. This chapter aids you in developing a knowledge base in this critical area. To achieve this goal, we examine the following key measurement concepts: basic statistics, accuracy in assessment, and effectiveness of tests and evaluation procedures. We also investigate the meaning of the terms *criterion-referenced* and *norm-referenced measurement,* and we consider the uses, advantages, and disadvantages of each. At the conclusion of this chapter, we review some practical measurement concepts and procedures for evaluating tests from an applied, functional perspective.

Objectives

After reading this chapter, you will be prepared to do the following:

- Understand the basic statistical concepts of distributions, central tendency, and variability.
- Understand test reliability and give examples of the four major types of reliability.
- Understand test validity and give examples of the three major types of validity.
- Describe norm-referenced and criterion-referenced testing and discuss their differences.
- Understand norms and describe the norm-development process.
- Understand the process of standardizing tests.
- Use practical measurement concepts to assist in selecting and evaluating tests for children with special needs.

Introduction

The basic concepts of measurement are a fundamental element of assessment in special education. These concepts provide the basis for accurately and effectively quantifying the abilities, skills, and behaviors of students with special needs. As a special educator, you will benefit from knowledge of these concepts in several ways. Understanding them enables you to use test manuals properly, especially the technical sections on scoring and interpreting results. Teachers and other professionals rely on the measurement concepts to communicate assessment information as part of the team process in special education. The concepts also assist special educators by helping to select assessment procedures to fit the individual needs of particular students. Finally, appropriate application of measurement procedures helps teachers to ensure the collection of accurate and meaningful instructional data in the classroom and in other settings.

This chapter emphasizes basic concepts rather than the more technical aspects of measurement, such as statistical techniques and test-development procedures. These concepts build on the overview of assessment presented in Chapters 1 and 2 and set the stage for examining test scores and their meaning in Chapter 4.

Basic Statistical Concepts

Statistics are special kinds of numbers that summarize and give meaning to large groups of data, including test scores, by putting them into manageable form. Examples of statistics that people rely on in daily living include interest rates, the inflation rate, and the unemployment rate. Teachers in special education routinely use other statistics, such as percent correct scores on classwork, percentile scores on standardized tests, and the number of items mastered on skills checklists. Teachers also rely on statistics to summarize scores from class tests. To illustrate this point, a large set of hypothetical test scores from several of Ms. Street's classes appears in Table 3–1. This random listing of scores has little meaning, demonstrating the difficulty of drawing conclusions from large groups of unorganized numbers. However, summarizing these scores with statistics converts the information into practical form. The three basic types of statistics are as follows:

1. Distributions, which are frequently graphed.
2. Measures of central tendency, often called *averages*.
3. Measures of variability, sometimes referred to as *dispersions*.

Distributions

Establishing a **distribution** is a procedure for classifying a large set of scores in a meaningful arrangement that visually summarizes and illustrates the relationship among the scores in the set. The process involves organizing scores in rank order from highest to lowest, grouping them in intervals, and graphing them. Placing scores in rank order and grouping them displays the pattern of the scores and arranges them for easy graphing. To illustrate this procedure, the random list of scores from Ms. Street's classes (Table 3–1) appears in Table 3–2 in rank order and

Table 3–1   Random Listing of Test Scores From Ms. Street's Classes

Student	*Number of Correct Answers*	*Student*	*Number of Correct Answers*
Robert	38	Vicki	29
Knute	24	Chiquita	29
Charmane	36	Lisa	25
Nadira	40	Grant	36
Todd	37	Nader	41
Julie	37	Clint	24
Blythe	29	Patrick	33
Debbie	44	Lynne	41
Jason	44	Lib	39
Jeffrey	35	Sharian	44
Lasonya	38	Latanya	32
Nathan	34	Kathe	43
Karly	27	Molly	29
Asher	46	Johnny	31
Katrina	35	Justin	34
Soo	46	Elliot	26
Bobby Joe	32	Lashanette	37
Donna	39	Charlene	35
Connie	32	Qadi	33
Elmo	33	Rossi	35
Chris	26	David	36
Ann Marie	40	Carver	35
Casey	29	Mary	40
Lacy	42	Sebastion	39
Peggy	35	Shawanda	37

in groups spanning three intervals. Graphing distributions with bar or line charts visually depicts the pattern of the scores. Graphs of the data from Ms. Street's classes appear in Figures 3–1 and 3–2. The vertical axis of each graph displays the frequency of occurrence of each group of scores, and the horizontal axis displays the individual scores.

The test scores from Ms. Street's classes shown in Figures 3–1 and 3–2 fall into a pattern called a **normal distribution.** In a normal distribution most of the scores cluster around the average score of the distribution, with fewer high and low scores. The scores also follow an even pattern, with an equal number of scores falling above and below the average score. Because the shape when graphed looks somewhat like a bell, another name for the normal distribution is the *bell-shaped curve* or *bell curve*. Use of normal distributions in assessment is based on the concept that cognitive, psychological, and emotional characteristics are evenly distributed in the population. This is an important theoretical assumption in test development. When developers create new tests, they expect the scores to fall into a normally distributed pattern. Similarly, when teachers give a test in class, they usually expect the resulting scores to be distributed in a normal curve with a few high scores and a few low scores but with the majority of scores in the midrange.

Table 3–2   Rank Order of Test Scores From Ms. Street's Classes

Student	No. of Correct Answers	No. of Scores in Group	Student	No. of Correct Answers	No. of Scores in Group
Asher	46		Jeffrey	35	
Soo	46		Katrina	35	
Debbie	44	5	Peggy	35	
Jason	44		Rossi	35	
Sharian	44				
			Justin	34	
Kathe	43		Nathan	34	
Lacy	42	4	Elmo	33	
Lynne	41		Patrick	33	
Nader	41		Qadi	33	8
			Bobby Joe	32	
Nadira	40		Latanya	32	
Ann Marie	40		Connie	32	
Mary	40				
Lib	39		Johnny	31	
Donna	39	8	Casey	29	
Sebastian	39		Chiquita	29	6
Lasonya	38		Molly	29	
Robert	38		Blythe	29	
			Vicki	29	
Shawanda	37				
Lashanette	37		Karly	27	
Julie	37		Chris	26	3
Todd	37		Elliot	26	
Charmane	36				
David	36		Lisa	25	
Grant	36	13	Knute	24	3
Carver	35		Clint	24	
Charlene	35				

An **abnormal** or **skewed distribution** occurs when scores cluster at either the high or the low end rather than at the middle or average of a distribution. This happens, for example, when teachers give easy or difficult tests, in which most students receive very high or very low scores, respectively. With a positive skew, scores cluster around the low end, and with a negative skew, scores bunch up at the high end. An illustration of positive skew appears in Figure 3–3. This type of distribution characterizes scores, such as those from a class test, in which almost all the marks range from 60 to 70 (when the highest possible score is 100). In contrast, a negative skew, as appears in Figure 3–4, occurs when most scores on a class test fall in the 90–100 range.

The most desirable characteristic for a set of test scores is a normal distribution. Skewed distributions are undesirable. Teachers avoid giving tests that produce skewed

Figure 3–1 Bar Chart of Test Scores From Ms. Street's Classes

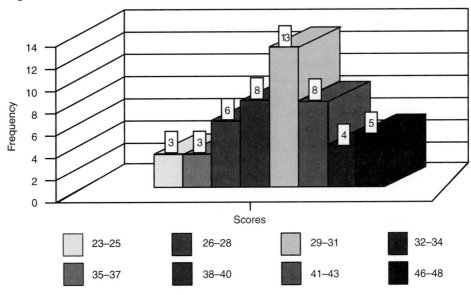

results, because if most students score 100% on a test, not only is the test probably too easy, but the results fail to discriminate among the students. Similarly, if most students receive low marks on a test, the skewed results fail to distinguish among the students.

Establishing distributions provides a method of describing groups of scores; graphing distributions produces a visual picture of the pattern of the scores. Another way to describe large groups of numbers with statistics is by measuring the central tendency.

Figure 3–2 Line Graph of Test Scores From Ms. Street's Classes

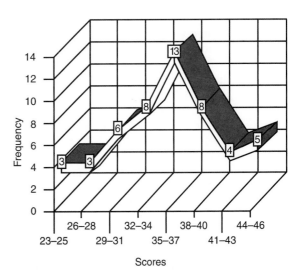

Figure 3–3   A Positively
Skewed Distribution

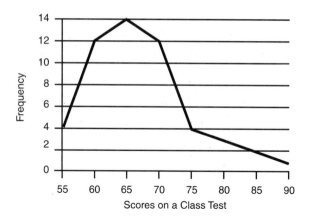

Figure 3–4   A Negatively
Skewed Distribution

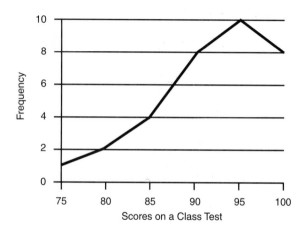

Measures of Central Tendency

The **measures of central tendency** are statistics that describe the typical, or representative, scores in a group of scores. They provide an indication of the trend or most numerous score in a distribution and include several types of averages, including the mean, the median, and the mode. The **mean** denotes the average number in a distribution and is the most commonly used measure of central tendency. In most instances, the term *average* refers to the mean rather than to the other specific measures of central tendency. The **mode** indicates the most frequently occurring score in a distribution. The **median** marks the midpoint, or middle figure, in a distribution.

When teachers give class tests, they usually describe the performance of the group by reporting the mean, or average, score. Teachers also rely on the mean to characterize the performance of individual students by averaging scores across several class tests. The formula for calculating the mean involves summing all of the scores and dividing by the number of scores as follows:

$$\text{Mean} = \frac{\text{Sum of all the scores}}{\text{Number of scores}}$$

Mathematical calculations rely on symbols as a form of notation for each of the operations in a formula. The formula for the mean uses the following mathematical symbols:

$\bar{X}$ or M = mean X = any score
Σ = sum N = number of scores

When the formula is depicted with these symbols, it appears as follows:

$$\bar{X} = \frac{\Sigma X}{N}$$

When the scores from Ms. Street's class tests are used, the calculation for the mean score is

ΣX = 1,761 (the sum of the test scores)
N = 50 (the total number of test scores)
$\bar{X}$ = 1,761/50 = 35 (the mean, or average, score on the test)

When a mean is calculated, the number of scores in the distribution is an important characteristic because, as the number of scores increases, the accuracy of the mean increases. Conversely, as the number of scores in a distribution decreases, the accuracy of the mean also decreases. This happens because with only a few scores in a group, an extreme score significantly changes the mean. However, with many scores in a distribution, an extreme score fails to significantly alter the mean.

The examples in Table 3–3 illustrate the effect of an extreme score on the mean. Distribution A contains only 5 scores, including 1 extreme score. In this small distribution, the extreme score significantly lowers the mean. Distribution B contains 15 scores, including the same extreme score. Because this is a larger distribution, the extreme score has little effect on the mean.

Because the number of scores in a distribution is such an important characteristic, experts recommend cautious use of the mean with small groups of scores, especially if one or more of the scores is an extreme score. According to most testing authorities, small distributions contain fewer than 15 scores. Although distributions with at least 15 scores are generally sufficient, distributions with 30 or more scores are ideal in size. The measures of central tendency, especially the mean, provide highly useful statistics for describing groups of scores. The measures of variability supply a complementary method for characterizing large sets of numbers.

Measures of Variability

Unlike the mean, which describes central tendency, the **measures of variability** summarize the spread, or dispersion, of distributions. The two most important measures of variability in assessment are the standard deviation and the standard error of measurement. The standard deviation summarizes the variability of groups of scores by measuring the average distance of individual scores from the mean of the distribution. In other words, the standard deviation describes the magnitude of the distance of individual scores from the average score. Distributions with higher variability yield larger standard deviations than distributions with lower variability. Educators rely on the standard deviation, by far the most common measure of variability, for functions such as interpreting the meaning of test scores, determining

Table 3–3   Effect of an Extreme Score on the Mean in a Small and a Large Distribution

Scores in Distribution A	Scores in Distribution B
90	90
95	95
90	90
95	85
15	90
$\Sigma X = 385$	95
	90
$N = 5$	85
	90
$\bar{x} = \Sigma\dfrac{X}{N} = \dfrac{385}{5} = 77$	85
	90
	95
	85
	95
	15
	$\Sigma X = 1{,}275$
	$N = 15$
	$\bar{x} = \Sigma\dfrac{X}{N} = \dfrac{1{,}275}{15} = 85$

the amount of error in test scores, and reporting scores derived from formal standardized tests.

The statistical notation for standard deviation is SD, S, s, or σ (the Greek letter *sigma*). To calculate the standard deviation, use the following formula:

$$SD = \sqrt{\frac{(X-\bar{x})^2}{N}}$$

where SD = standard deviation
  $\sqrt{}$ = square root
  Σ = sum
  X = raw score on the test
  $\bar{x}$ = mean of the test
  N = number of test scores

Calculating the standard deviation (using the scores from Ms. Street's classes) involves several steps (Table 3–4). The first step is to find the mean by adding all the scores and dividing the total by the number of scores. The mean test score from Ms. Street's classes was 35 (1,761/50 = 35). The next step involves subtracting the mean from each score. This procedure is shown in the third column. Next, the differences from the mean in the third column are squared, as shown in the fourth column. The subsequent step is to sum the squared differences from the mean,

Table 3–4 Calculating the Standard Deviation of the Scores
From Ms. Street's Classes

Student	*Test Score*	*X − x̄*	*(X − x̄)²*
Asher	46	46 − 35 = 11	11 × 11 = 121
Soo	46	46 − 35 = 11	11 × 11 = 121
Debbie	44	44 − 35 = 9	9 × 9 = 81
Jason	44	44 − 35 = 9	9 × 9 = 81
Sharian	44	44 − 35 = 9	9 × 9 = 81
Kathe	43	43 − 35 = 8	8 × 8 = 64
Lacy	42	42 − 35 = 7	7 × 7 = 49
Lynne	41	41 − 35 = 6	6 × 6 = 36
Nader	41	41 − 35 = 6	6 × 6 = 36
Nadira	40	40 − 35 = 5	5 × 5 = 25
Ann Marie	40	40 − 35 = 5	5 × 5 = 25
Mary	40	40 − 35 = 5	5 × 5 = 25
Lib	39	39 − 35 = 4	4 × 4 = 16
Donna	39	39 − 35 = 4	4 × 4 = 16
Sebastian	39	39 − 35 = 4	4 × 4 = 16
Lasonya	38	38 − 35 = 3	3 × 3 = 9
Robert	38	38 − 35 = 3	3 × 3 = 9
Shawanda	37	37 − 35 = 2	2 × 2 = 4
Lashanette	37	37 − 35 = 2	2 × 2 = 4
Julie	37	37 − 35 = 2	2 × 2 = 4
Todd	37	37 − 35 = 2	2 × 2 = 4
Charmane	36	36 − 35 = 1	1 × 1 = 1
David	36	36 − 35 = 1	1 × 1 = 1
Grant	36	36 − 35 = 1	1 × 1 = 1
Carver	35	35 − 35 = 0	0 × 0 = 0
Charlene	35	35 − 35 = 0	0 × 0 = 0
Jeffrey	35	35 − 35 = 0	0 × 0 = 0
Katrina	35	35 − 35 = 0	0 × 0 = 0
Peggy	35	35 − 35 = 0	0 × 0 = 0
Rossi	35	35 − 35 = 0	0 × 0 = 0
Justin	34	34 − 35 = −1	−1 × −1 = 1
Nathan	34	34 − 35 = −1	−1 × −1 = 1
Elmo	33	33 − 35 = −2	−2 × −2 = 4
Patrick	33	33 − 35 = −2	−2 × −2 = 4
Qadi	33	33 − 35 = −2	−2 × −2 = 4
Bobby Joe	32	32 − 35 = −3	−3 × −3 = 9
Latanya	32	32 − 35 = −3	−3 × −3 = 9
Connie	32	32 − 35 = −3	−3 × −3 = 9
Johnny	31	31 − 35 = −4	−4 × −4 = 16
Casey	29	29 − 35 = −6	−6 × −6 = 36
Chiquita	29	29 − 35 = −6	−6 × −6 = 36
Molly	29	29 − 35 = −6	−6 × −6 = 36
Blythe	29	29 − 35 = −6	−6 × −6 = 36
Vicki	29	29 − 35 = −6	−6 × −6 = 36
Karly	27	27 − 35 = −8	−8 × −8 = 64
Chris	26	26 − 35 = −9	−9 × −9 = 81
Elliot	26	26 − 35 = −9	−9 × −9 = 81
Lisa	25	25 − 35 = −10	−10 × −10 = 100
Knute	24	24 − 35 = −11	−11 × −11 = 121
Clint	24	24 − 35 = −11	−11 × −11 = 121
	Σ = 1,761		Σ(X − x̄)² = 1,635

which in this case is 1,635 (this number appears at the bottom of the fourth column), and divide by the number of scores (there are 50 scores). Thus 1,635 divided by 50 equals 32.7 (1,635/50 = 32.7). The resulting value of 32.7 is the variance, defined as the average squared deviation of scores from the mean. One more calculation is necessary to obtain the standard deviation. The variance is the average squared deviation from the mean. The standard deviation is the average deviation from the mean. To obtain the standard deviation, the square must be eliminated from the variance by determining the square root of the variance. In this case the square root of 32.7 is 5.72. The square root of a specific number is the number that, when multiplied by itself, produces that specific number. For example, the square root of 100 is 10, and the square root of 36 is 6. Most mathematics books contain a table of square roots for the numbers 1 through 100. Many calculators also have a square root function.

Standard Deviation and the Bell-Shaped Curve

The concept of the **standard deviation** can be explained by relating it to the normal distribution, or **bell-shaped curve.** In a normal distribution a precise relationship exists between the standard deviation and the number of scores. This relationship depends on the percentage distribution of cases in the normal curve, as illustrated in Figure 3–5. Here standard deviation units appear on the line under the curve marked to show one, two, and three standard deviations (SD) from the mean, which is marked with a 0. The percentage of scores falling within each standard deviation unit also appears in Figure 3–5. For example, the percentage of cases between the mean (0) and +1 SD is 34.13%. The same percentage of scores, 34.13%, occurs between the mean and –1 SD from the mean. A majority, or 68.26% (34.13 + 34.13 = 68.26), of the scores occurs between +1 and –1 SD from the mean. In other words, in a normal distribution most of the scores cluster around the mean, or average. Almost all, or 95.44%, of the scores occur between +2 and –2 standard deviations from the mean.

Understanding the percentage distribution of cases in a normal curve helps in interpreting standardized test scores. For example, characteristics such as achievement tend to be normally distributed among students in the school population. Most students have average achievement, and their scores on standardized tests

Figure 3–5   Percentage
Distribution of Cases in the
Normal Curve

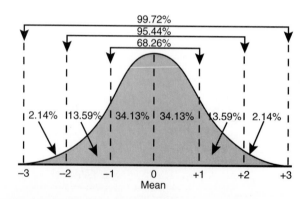

cluster around the middle of a bell-shaped curve. Relatively few students have significantly high or low achievement, and their scores fall near the ends of the bell-shaped curve.

In special education, however, the distribution of achievement takes on a positive skew. Standard test scores of students in special education usually fall at the low end of the bell-shaped curve. Students in special education sometimes score in the bottom 2% on standardized tests. This is more than 2 SD below the mean. In fact, in order to qualify for some special education programs, students must score at least 2 SD below the mean. Therefore, teachers in special education instruct a significant number of students whose scores on standardized tests are lower than 98% of all students in the school.

According to most specialists in statistics, the standard deviation along with the mean represent the two most important basic statistics. Testing experts often report these two statistics together because of the special relationship between them.

Relationship Between the Standard Deviation and the Mean

An illustration of the relationship between the standard deviation and the mean appears in Table 3–5. For demonstration purposes, the example relies on a small group of 10 scores rather than a larger set of scores. In this example, both sets of scores produce the same mean, $\bar{X} = 90$. In other words, the central tendency of the two sets of scores is identical. However, summarizing these distributions in terms of the mean leaves out vital information because of the large difference in the standard deviation, or variability, of the two groups of scores. The standard deviation of the scores in Group 1 is 2.2, and the standard deviation of the scores in Group 2 is 7.3. In other words, the variability of the scores in Group 2 is significantly greater than that of the scores in Group 1. The normal distribution provides the basis for interpreting the differences in the standard deviations of the two groups. In a normal

Table 3–5 Illustration of the Relationship Between the Standard Deviation and the Mean

Scores from Group 1	Scores from Group 2
90	98
88	82
90	98
94	82
86	85
92	95
90	82
88	97
90	83
92	98
Mean = 90	Mean = 90
SD = 2.2	SD = 7.3

distribution approximately 68% of the scores fall between 1 SD below the mean and 1 SD above the mean. In Group 1 the mean score is 90 and the standard deviation is 2.2. One standard deviation below the mean is 87.8 (90 − 2.2 = 87.8), and 1 SD above the mean is 92.2 (90 + 2.2 = 92.2). Therefore, 68% of the scores in Group 1 occur between 87.8 and 92.2. In Group 2 the mean is also 90, but the standard deviation is 7.3. For this group, 1 SD below the mean is 82.7 (90 − 7.3 = 82.7), and 1 SD above the mean is 97.3 (90 + 7.3 = 97.3). Therefore, 68% of the scores in this group occur between 82.7 and 97.3.

The mean and the standard deviation for the scores from Ms. Street's classes may be used to further illustrate the interpretation of standard deviation and the relationship between the standard deviation and the mean. The mean score from Ms. Street's classes was 35, and the standard deviation was 5.72. Therefore, 1 SD below the mean is 29.28 (35 − 5.72 = 29.28), and 1 SD above the mean is 40.72 (35 + 5.72 = 40.72). Therefore, 68%, or more than two thirds, of the scores from Ms. Street's classes were between 29.28 and 40.72. In other words, a majority of the scores fell within the range of 29 to 40 and clustered around 35. Relatively few students scored above 40 or below 29.

In many situations the best statistics for describing groups of numbers are the mean and the standard deviation. Statisticians suggest that if you can report only two statistics to describe a group of numbers, you should probably select the mean and the standard deviation. However, another statistic, the standard error of measurement, also has special meaning in assessment.

Standard Error of Measurement

The **standard error of measurement** is an estimate of the variability of individual test scores. Also called the *standard error of a score*, testing specialists use this statistic as a measure of the accuracy or reliability of tests. The essential notion of standard error of measurement originates from the idea that giving a test many times to the same student (assuming no learning occurs from the repeated testing) produces scores that vary somewhat each time. All test scores contain some of this measurement error or variability, but some test scores contain more variability or error than others. A test score with higher variability yields a larger standard error of measurement than a test score with lower variability.

The statistical symbols for expressing standard error of measurement include the notations SEM and SE_{meas}. The formula for the standard error of measurement is as follows:

$$SE_{meas} = S_X \sqrt{} - r_{XX}$$

where SE_{meas} = standard error of measurement
S_X = standard deviation of the test
$\sqrt{}$ = square root
r_{XX} = reliability coefficient of the test

The following example explains the concept of standard error of measurement from a more practical viewpoint. Assume that a test developer gave an intelligence test to a single student 100 times. If it were possible to give a test this many times, the developer could calculate the mean and standard deviation of the resulting 100 test scores to provide an index of the amount of error in the test scores. Because of measurement error, the 100 individual scores would vary each time in the pattern of a bell-shaped curve, or normal distribution. The mean of the distribution of these 100 scores represents the true score. In other words, the true score refers to the average of the 100 individual scores. The standard deviation represents the amount of variability in the scores around the true score. Unfortunately, it is not feasible to give the same test to a single student 100 times because of constraints such as student fatigue and the learning that takes place during repeated testing.

Because actually giving a test repeatedly is not possible, mathematicians developed the standard error of measurement statistic to estimate the amount of error in a test score. This statistic defines a confidence band, or confidence interval, that delineates a student's true score and accounts for any measurement error in testing. Teachers rely on the confidence band concept when they use test scores as estimates of student performance rather than as exact scores. The idea of a confidence band encourages reporting test performance as a range of scores rather than as a single score.

A practical example of the confidence band involves a situation in which a student receives an intelligence quotient (IQ) score of 70 on a test of mental ability. If the standard error of measurement for the test is 5 IQ points, then placing 5 points on either side of the score of 70 ($70 \pm 5 = 65$ to 75) defines the confidence interval. In this example, the confidence band ranges from 65 to 75. This means that the student's true score falls somewhere within the interval of 65 to 75 IQ points but may not be exactly 70. In other words, if a student took the same test over again, it is likely that the resulting score would be somewhere between the interval of 65 to 75, but probably not exactly 70, on the second administration. Likewise, if a student receives a score of 85 on an intelligence test and the standard error of measurement for the test is 4, then the confidence band extends to 4 points on either side of 85, or 81 to 89.

The standard error of measurement provides an indication of the technical quality of a test and helps in interpreting test results. Each test produces a different standard error of measurement, and most test authors report this statistic in the technical section of their manual. The concept suggests interpreting individual test scores within a band or range of possible scores rather than as one absolute number.

Teachers, psychologists, diagnosticians, and other professionals rely on the standard error of measurement statistic when they judge the accuracy of a student's score with respect to the test taken. For example, professionals must be cautious when they interpret the meaning of the student's performance on tests that exhibit high standard errors of measurement. In such cases, professionals often interpret the test score result as falling within a band of possible scores rather than as an absolute score. On the other hand, they can be more confident when interpreting scores from tests that display low standard errors of measurement. Furthermore, because the standard error of scores increases at the extremes of a test, professionals must be careful when interpreting student scores that fall into high and low ranges.

☑ Comprehension Checklist

Knowledge of the statistical concepts of distributions, central tendency, and variability sets the groundwork for considering additional measurement topics. Distributions visually summarize and illustrate the relationships among a set of scores. The measures of central tendency, consisting of the mean, the median, and the mode, describe the average score or most numerous score in a distribution. The measures of variability summarize the spread, or dispersion, of distributions. The next section uses these concepts in considering the process of measuring the reliability of assessment instruments.

Reliability

Reliability, an essential technical quality of assessment instruments, refers to the accuracy and consistency of test scores and other measures of the skills, abilities, and behaviors of students. A reliable test produces similar scores across various conditions and situations, including different evaluators and testing environments.

A helpful way to grasp the concept of reliability is to think of a test score as consisting of two parts: error and true score. Error is a random, unexplained variation in a test score that reduces reliability. True score is a nonrandom, or explainable, variation in a test score that increases reliability. Although error exists in all tests, reliable tests minimize the amount of error present in a score. One method for estimating the amount of error and the true score in a test is the standard error of measurement statistic. Test authors use the standard error of measurement and other measures of reliability as part of the process of developing new tests, and they report it in the technical section of the test manual.

The statistic for expressing reliability, the reliability coefficient, consists of values from 0 to 1.00. The mathematical notation for reliability is r, and a reliability coefficient of $r = 0$ indicates a total lack of reliability, whereas a coefficient of 1.00 represents perfect reliability. In general, acceptable reliability coefficients begin at r = .90 and rise to as much as $r = .98$. Coefficients below $r = .90$ usually indicate inadequate reliability, except in special circumstances involving assessment of difficult-to-measure behaviors such as social interaction, self-concept, and behavior problems. One way of describing reliability coefficients involves thinking of a coefficient such as $r = .90$ as an expression of the accuracy of a test in which 90% of the variability of a test score consists of true variability and 10% consists of error or unexplained variance. In most testing situations, an accuracy rating of 90% or more represents an acceptable level for making educational decisions; thus, coefficients of $r = .90$ and above indicate adequate test reliability. However, a test with a reliability coefficient of $r = .75$, for example, fails to provide acceptable reliability because approximately 25% of the score may be due to error or unexplained variance.

The different methods for estimating the reliability of assessment instruments include test-retest, alternate-form, split-half, and interrater reliability. A summary of these types of reliability appears in Table 3–6.

Test-Retest Reliability

Test-retest reliability is a process for estimating accuracy that involves giving a test twice to a carefully selected group and using the resulting scores to calculate a reliability

Table 3–6 Summary of Different Methods for Estimating the Reliability of
Assessment Instruments

Type of Reliability	Description
Test-retest	Compares scores obtained on two administrations of a test
Alternate form	Compares the scores from two forms of the same test
Split half	Correlates two halves of the same test
Interrater	Compares the direct observations of two observers

coefficient that describes the consistency among the two sets of scores. The reliability coefficient expresses the correlation between the scores obtained by the same
students on two administrations of a test. A critical factor with test-retest reliability is
the length of time between testing and retesting. Too little time between testing and
retesting inflates the reliability coefficient, whereas too much time deflates the reliability coefficient. In most situations, a 2-week interval allows enough time to adjust
for any learning that may take place from the first testing experience. Longer intervals may reduce the reliability estimate due to maturation of the students or the influence of outside events. However, the length of time between testing also depends
on the type and nature of the test. Because it requires two administrations of a test,
the procedure for estimating test-retest reliability is time consuming, expensive,
and error producing. For these reasons, test developers often prefer other methods
for measuring reliability, including alternate-form reliability.

Alternate-Form Reliability

Alternate-form reliability, also called equivalent-form reliability, is a process for estimating accuracy that compares the scores from two forms of the same test. Estimating this type of reliability involves writing two forms of the same test, giving both
forms to a carefully selected group, and comparing the scores from the two forms.
The reliability coefficient in this case describes the correlation between the scores
obtained by the same students on the two forms of the test. This type of reliability
avoids the problem of giving the same test twice, as in test-retest reliability. The use
of equivalent forms also provides the advantage of a second form for use when a student needs testing twice during a short time.

A disadvantage of this type of reliability estimation is the necessity for making
two equivalent forms of the same test. Developing two forms, such as Form A and
Form B, requires writing twice as many items and then arranging the items equally.
This process entails extra expense and difficulty in test development; thus, test developers often turn to a third type of reliability, split-half reliability, which avoids this
obstacle.

Split-Half Reliability

Split-half reliability is a procedure for determining accuracy that involves correlating
two halves of the same test. The steps in the process include giving a test once, splitting the test items in half, and comparing the results of the two halves to each other.
The reliability coefficient obtained is an estimate of the correlation between the

items in each half of the test. Test researchers split the test in half in several differ-ent ways. One technique involves comparing even-numbered and odd-numbered test items. Another procedure consists of comparing the first half of the test to the second half. Dividing the test items randomly into two halves also splits the test for comparison purposes. The method of dividing a test depends on the type of test; however, most developers use an odd-even split.

Because it relies on a single administration of one test, split-half reliability actu-ally involves measuring the internal consistency of an assessment tool. For this reason some experts refer to split-half reliability as a type of internal consistency re-liability. Testing specialists also use the standard error of measurement statistic de-scribed earlier to estimate the internal consistency of tests. The essential concept of both split-half reliability and standard error of measurement is that all tests have some measurement error within themselves, but tests with the best internal consis-tency minimize this type of variability.

Split-half reliability offers several advantages over the other types of reliability. Giving a test once is less expensive, faster, and easier. More important, because it uses only one administration and one form, split-half reliability produces more ac-curate results than other techniques by reducing the chances for error. With the other types of reliability estimation, test developers face many more uncontrollable events resulting from giving a test twice or from giving two forms of the same test. For these reasons, many test authors prefer split-half reliability.

Interrater Reliability

Interrater reliability, often referred to as *interobserver reliability,* is an estimate of the observations from two observers who directly watch or listen to a student. Many applications exist for interrater reliability in special education, including assess-ment related to behavior-management programs. The reliability coefficient ob-tained in this case correlates the observations of two independent observers. The procedure involves having two raters independently observe and record specified behaviors, such as out-of-seat or off-task behavior, during the same time periods. Comparing the ratings of the observers produces an estimate of the percentage of agreement between the two observations. The most common formula for calcu-lating interrater reliability is the percentage of agreement formula (Wolery et al., 1988):

$$\frac{\text{Number of agreements}}{\text{Number of agreements} + \text{Disagreements}} \times 100 = \text{Percentage of agreements}$$

However, estimating interrater reliability involves more than simply collecting and calculating the percentage of agreement between two raters. Barlow and Hersen (1984) point out that establishing interrater reliability involves a series of steps, in-cluding the following:

- Selecting the behaviors to be observed.
- Deciding the conditions under which the data will be gathered.
- Choosing a unit of analysis.
- Modifying the data collection plan if necessary.

Following these steps helps to ensure the collection of consistent, accurate data that professionals can rely on for making the best possible educational decisions.

☑ Comprehension Checklist

Reliability refers to the consistency or accuracy of test scores and other measures of behavior. A summary of the different types of reliability appears in Table 3–7. Although reliability plays an essential role in the basic measurement process, verifying the technical adequacy of a test also involves providing evidence of test validity.

Validity

Validity, which is the effectiveness of assessment instruments, is considered the most important technical characteristic of tests. The basic question of validity is, "How well does the test measure what it was designed to measure?" or "Does the test do what it is supposed to do?" Developers establish initial validity as part of the test-development process, but validity research often continues after publication of an assessment tool. The concept of validity includes the notion that the uses of a test should be validated, not just the test itself (Rubin, 1988). This view points out the importance of considering the consequences of tests as part of the process of determining the effectiveness of a test. The three major types of test validity are content, criterion related, and construct validity.

Content Validity

Content validity refers to how well a test covers the domain, or learning area, measured by the test. A test with good content validity includes a representative sample of the behavior in the domain, or learning area. A valid test of language, for example, includes items that measure performance in the relevant language skill areas. Likewise, a valid test of reading consists of items to assess the proficiency of relevant reading skills. The process of establishing content validity involves several steps, including the following:

- Developing test specifications based on a complete review of the content area.
- Writing test items to fit the test specifications.

Table 3–7 Summary of the Types of Reliability

Type of Reliability	Process	Source of Variability
Test-retest	Give the test twice	Time between tests
Alternate form	Give two forms of the test	Variation between tests
Split half	Divide the test in half	Variation between test halves
Standard error of measurement	Calculate a confidence interval	Reliability of individual scores
Interrater	Use two observers	Reliability across observers

- Conducting field tests by giving the test to carefully selected groups.
- Reviewing and revising the test after the initial field tests.
- Compiling the final test.

These steps rely heavily on the expert opinion of professionals in the field, who include teachers, curriculum experts, college professors, and test-development specialists. In most cases developers use a team of professionals. Several test-development teams may work together to develop a large commercial test; small teams consisting mainly of the test authors themselves write most of the noncommercial tests.

Teachers validate the content of a test when they evaluate the quality of the items on a test before giving it to their students. Test developers use a similar process. In fact, many test developers hire teachers to review tests before publication as part of the content validation process. Test users can evaluate content validity by reviewing the information provided by the test developer in the test manual. Test users can also evaluate content validity by reviewing the quality and relevance of the test items themselves.

Other measures of test effectiveness related to content validity include face validity and cash validity. Face validity, a superficial type of nontechnical validity, involves quickly reviewing a test to determine whether it appears valid on the surface. Although it is a desirable feature, face validity fails as a substitute for well-established content validity. Another type of nontechnical validity, cash validity, concerns the sales volume of a commercial test. However, high sales volume is not an appropriate criterion for evaluating test effectiveness, and test users should avoid selecting an instrument on this basis. Furthermore, just because a test sells well and is therefore readily available, it is not necessarily valid for use in a particular situation.

Criterion-Related Validity

Criterion-related validity involves analyzing the relationship between a test and other independent criteria of effectiveness. Criterion-related validity includes predictive validity, which entails measuring the effectiveness of a test in predicting future performance, and concurrent validity, which involves correlating a test with a comparable test or other measure of proven validity.

Establishing the predictive validity of a test entails evaluating the performance of students on the test against a direct but independent criterion. For example, the criterion for an achievement test might be the grade-point averages of the students during the following year. The criterion for a vocational aptitude test might be performance on the job. Predictive validity consists of correlating test performance with performance on the predictive measure. Highly positive correlations indicate good predictive validity. Inadequate predictive validity results from test scores that fail to correlate with scores on the predictive measure.

Educational decisions such as classifying students as disabled and placing them in programs require tests with good predictive validity. Educational decisions related to instruction and program planning rely on tests with good concurrent validity. Concurrent validity entails comparing scores from a new test with scores from a valid test that measures the same content. In this case, the developer gives both tests to a carefully selected group of students and compares the results. Results that produce highly positive correlations between performance on the new test and performance on the concurrent measure indicate good validity. Results that fail to show a correlation between the new test and the concurrent measure suggest poor concurrent validity. Another method for establishing concurrent validity involves comparing a test with some currently available criterion other than another test score. For example, correlating student performance on a test of social skills with a teacher's ratings of a student's social skills provides a means for establishing concurrent validity without the use of another test.

Construct Validity

More abstract than the other types of validity, **construct validity** refers to how well a test measures a theoretical construct, or attribute. Examples of constructs include traits such as intelligence, mathematical reasoning ability, receptive language vocabulary, and gross motor skills. The lengthy process of establishing construct validity entails synthesizing scientific research data about the relationship between test performance and the theoretical construct measured by the test. However, no specific step-by-step procedures exist for establishing this form of validity. In fact, Angoff (1988), who described construct validity as an evolving concept rather than a set of techniques, suggested that the essence of construct validity relates to the interpretation drawn from the test scores. According to Angoff, examining construct validity includes the following types of research: "correlational studies, factorial studies, studies of differences with respect to groups, situations, tasks, and times, observational studies of change, and studies of experimentally induced change" (p. 30). Construct validity is a characteristic that emerges from a systematic review of research and is based on an accumulation of evidence that supports the adequacy of a test.

Tests such as the *Wechsler Intelligence Scale for Children* (third edition) *(WISC-III)* (Wechsler, 1991) demonstrate construct validity based on hundreds of research studies covering a variety of topics. The accumulated knowledge from these studies provides clear evidence that the *WISC-III* measures the construct called intelligence. Other tests, however, lack evidence to support construct validity. For example, accumulated knowledge from research studies with the *Wide Range Achievement Test-3 (WRAT-III)* (Wilkinson, 1993) suggests that this particular instrument fails to measure the construct called wide range achievement.

Because establishing construct validity entails a long and involved process, most tests provide little information about this type of validity. Only the most well established tests in special education present solid evidence of construct validity. On the other hand, all but the most informal tests provide information about the other two types of validity: content and criterion related.

☑ Comprehension Checklist

Validity, the most important of the technical characteristics of tests, includes three major types: content, criterion related, and construct. A summary of the distinctive characteristics of each type appears in Table 3–8. The process of validating a test cannot be separated from the process of determining test reliability. In fact, an unusual and surprising relationship exists between the two concepts in that a test can be reliable without being valid but cannot be valid without being reliable. In

Table 3–8   Distinctive Characteristics of the Types of Validity

Type of Validity	Technical Question	Practical Question
Content	Do the test items represent the behavior in the domain or learning area?	Do the test scores predict Sarah's performance in the content area?
Criterion related (predictive)	Do the test scores predict future behavior?	Does the test score indicate how well Jason will perform in math during the next semester?
Criterion related (concurrent)	How well do the scores from the new test correlate with scores from a valid test in the same content area?	Do Jeffrey's scores on the test currently used in the program correspond to his scores on the new test that will be used next year?
Construct	How well does the test assess the theoretical trait it was designed to measure?	Is the test useful for measuring Emily's intelligence?

other words, reliability must be established before validity. One way of explaining this relationship is by analogy with a clock. For example, it is possible for a clock to be reliable without being valid, in that a clock can be consistently 43 minutes slow. In this case, the slow clock is reliable but not valid. This is analogous to a test that consistently underestimates student achievement by two grade levels. In this instance, the test is reliable but it is certainly not valid.

Norm-Referenced and Criterion-Referenced Testing

Norm-referenced and criterion-referenced testing represent two fundamentally different ways of interpreting performance. **Norm-referenced testing** involves interpreting student performance compared to the performance of others. **Criterion-referenced testing,** on the other hand, refers to interpreting student performance in relation to some functional level or criterion.

Norm-Referenced Testing

Norm-referenced testing relates an individual score or group of scores to the scores of those in a comparison group, called the *norm group* or *normative sample,* which consists of a carefully selected group of students who take the test in a precise manner. The norms constitute sets of scores for each age or grade level of the test based on the average scores of the subjects from the norm group. With norm-referenced testing the criterion of reference is the "place" or "rank" of a student compared to other students. A student with a 25th percentile score on a standardized test, for example, ranks in the lowest 25% compared to the norm group students. This ranking procedure illustrates how norm-referenced scores show relative standing. Although many uses exist for norm-referenced testing, it is most useful for making classification and placement decisions about students with special needs.

Criterion-Referenced Testing

Criterion-referenced testing, which involves interpreting student performance in relation to a specific functional level or criterion, is closely related to instruction and measures student knowledge on relatively small and discrete units. When the criterion relates to content, test performance is compared to a standard of mastery or proficiency for a skill or set of skills. For example, the *Brigance Diagnostic Inventory of Basic Skills* (Brigance, 1977), a criterion-referenced test of academic skills, measures competencies such as word-attack skills, phonetic skills, subtracting two-digit numbers, and solving mathematical word problems. Giving the *Brigance* entails evaluating performance in terms of student mastery of the specific skills on the test. Criterion-referenced assessment information is most helpful for making instructional decisions, such as determining what skills a student has mastered and which skills a student needs to learn next.

The criterion of reference can also be the individual student. When the criterion of reference is the individual, a student's performance is related to earlier performance on the same test. For example, giving the *Brigance* to a student at the beginning and again at the end of the school year enables measurement of progress over time. In this case the comparison involves the performance of a student on the first and second administrations of the test.

Use of Norm- and Criterion-Referenced Tests

Kubiszyn and Borich (1990) recommend that evaluators specify the reason for testing and the type of information needed before deciding whether to use norm-referenced, criterion-referenced, or both types of testing. Their recommendation highlights the importance of considering the information needed before testing to ensure that the resulting data will be helpful. An illustration of this decision-making process appears in Figure 3-6, which depicts the relationship between the purpose of testing and the type of test. As shown in Figure 3–6, evaluators should avoid using

Figure 3–6 Relationship Between the Purpose of Testing and the Type of Test Needed

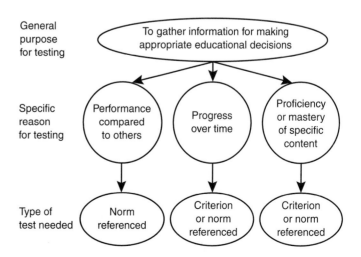

criterion-referenced testing to compare students with others because valid comparison among students depends on norms. However, in certain situations evaluators may use norm-referenced tests in a criterion-referenced manner. The procedure for accomplishing this involves interpreting results from norm-referenced testing without association to the norm group. Instead, the evaluator relates student performance on the norm-referenced test to the content of the test or to the student's earlier test scores. When using a norm-referenced test in a criterion-referenced manner, the evaluator must make sure that the test has enough items to adequately measure the specific content that serves as the criterion of reference.

Test Norms

Test norms are sets of scores developed from the scores of the subjects in the norm group, which is a carefully selected sample of students who take a test in a precise manner. Many types of norms exist, including national, state, and local norms.

National norms exist for virtually all norm-referenced tests. Good national norms, calculated from the results of testing a large sample group of students from all parts of the country, represent all students in the U.S. population. A well-selected national norm group includes students who represent a variety of socioeconomic circumstances, ethnic backgrounds, and geographic areas. National norms are useful for comparing the performance of individual children and groups of children to the performance of similar children from the norm sample group. For children with performance deficits, this information regarding relative standing helps determine the nature and severity of a child's deficits. For example, for a child with a reading problem, norm-referenced test results can reveal how far behind the child is in reading compared with other children of the same age and grade. Likewise, if a child is making excellent progress in reading achievement, norm-referenced test results can help a teacher determine how much progress the child has made in relation to similar children.

State and local norms exist for some, but not all, tests. However, state and local norms, which compare the performance of an individual with those of other students in the same state, school system, or class, may be more valuable than national norms, depending on the purpose of testing (Brown, 1980). Local norms developed from a representative sample of students in a specific school or district, for example, allow comparisons with other local students rather than comparisons at a national level. Information about classroom norms appear in Focus 3–1, and information about norms for students appears in Focus 3–2.

The soundness of a norm-referenced test score depends on the soundness of the norm group. Valid comparisons occur when the characteristics of the norm group represent the characteristics of the student. On the other hand, invalid comparisons happen when the characteristics of the norm group differ from those of the student. Sattler (1992) identified three important factors in evaluating the validity of a norm group: representativeness, size, and relevance. Representativeness refers to whether a norm group typifies the particular group of students for whom the test was designed, and includes characteristics such as age, grade level, gender, geographic region, ethnic group, and socioeconomic status. Size refers to the number of subjects in the norm group. According to Sattler, adequate norms include at least 100 subjects

FOCUS 3–1

Classroom Norms

Many teachers develop informal, but highly useful, classroom norms for frequently taught courses. The process for developing teacher-made norms involves collecting the results of class tests for a period of time and using this collection of data as the basis for comparisons. Although these norms cannot be used to place or label children, teachers find them helpful for evaluating the instructional program and the performance of individuals and groups of children.

for each age or grade level on the test. Relevance concerns the applicability of the norm group to the student taking the test. Some tests provide more than one norm group for comparison purposes. When this occurs, the evaluator should select the most relevant norm group.

Standardization

Standardization refers to structuring test materials, administration procedures, scoring methods, and techniques for interpreting results. Standardization makes it possible for evaluators to give, score, and interpret tests in a controlled manner that minimizes erratic, unpredictable results. This helps to ensure accuracy and consistency in measuring progress, determining levels of performance, and comparing performance to others.

All norm-referenced tests include standardized procedures that evaluators must follow if they plan on using the norms. Giving a normed test in a nonstandard manner invalidates the norms because the individual student receives a score based on modified testing conditions, whereas the norm group received their scores based on standard testing conditions. Although some criterion-referenced tests include standardized procedures just like norm-referenced tests, most criterion-referenced

FOCUS 3–2

Norms for Children With Disabilities

A few national norms exist for certain groups of students with disabilities, including students who are deaf and blind. For example, norms for children who are deaf are available for the performance subtest of the Wechsler Intelligence Scale for Children-Revised. These norms allow comparison of the performance of individual deaf children with the performance of deaf peers in the norm sample group. Likewise, the Vineland Adaptive Behavior Scales offer regular norms plus supplementary norms derived from samples of children with mental retardation, emotional disabilities, visual impairments, and hearing impairments.

tests include adaptable administration procedures that encourage flexibility in testing. This flexibility gives an evaluator opportunities to fit the test to the needs of the student.

Standardization helps to prevent bias in testing against certain students. However, standardizing a test fails to eliminate the possibility of bias completely, especially against students with disabilities. Standardized tests that require manipulation of materials such as blocks, for example, set up a barrier to students with physical impairments. In the same way, standardized tests that measure cognitive ability primarily through language and vocabulary skills introduce bias against students with hearing impairments. The critical issue of bias in testing will be examined in more detail in later chapters.

☑ Comprehension Checklist

Distinct differences exist between criterion-referenced and norm-referenced testing. The differences center around the purpose of testing. The purpose for norm-referenced testing involves comparison to others, whereas the goal of criterion-referenced testing involves measuring performance in relation to a functional criterion. Both types of testing serve necessary and important functions as part of assessment in special education. Although it is important to understand these technical measurement concepts, it is also important to consider certain practical measurement concepts.

Practical Measurement Concepts

Practical measurement concepts focus on the applied functional features of assessment instruments. Experts in testing (Cronbach, 1988; Messick, 1988) suggest that the validation process should include review of the practical aspects of tests. Teachers are especially sensitive to the practical perspective because they see firsthand the effects of testing. Practical considerations described by Drummond (1996) appear in checklist form in Table 3–9.

The items in the checklist in Table 3–9 focus on practical measurement concepts applicable to tests in general, not just to tests used with students who have special needs. Additional measurement considerations specifically for assessing students with special needs appear in Table 3–10.

☑ Comprehension Checklist

The pragmatic functional features of assessment instruments are an important aspect of the measurement process, especially for practitioners. In addition, the practical measurement concepts complement the more technical aspects of measurement by providing an applied viewpoint. Comprehensive analysis of the measurement features of assessment instruments and procedures involves both practical and technical considerations. Later chapters include additional information about the practical aspects of measuring the behavior and performance of students with disabilities. Chapter 5, for example, includes a checklist for conducting an overall evaluation of assessment instruments.

Table 3–9 Checklist of Practical Measurement Concepts

Item	Yes	No	Comments
1. Is the time involved in testing reasonable, given the purpose of the testing and the expected benefits?	___	___	
2. Is the cost of the test reasonable?	___	___	
3. Is the test well designed in an attractive and durable package with high-quality materials?	___	___	
4. Is the reading level of the test appropriate?	___	___	
5. Are the administration procedures clearly described and easy to follow?	___	___	
6. Are the response booklets and scoring sheets well designed?	___	___	
7. Are the scoring procedures clearly described and easy to follow?	___	___	
8. Are the interpretation procedures explained with examples and case studies?	___	___	
9. Are aids available for the evaluator (e.g., audio cassettes, computer software)?	___	___	
10. Is the manual clear and complete?	___	___	

Table 3–10 Checklist of Practical Measurement Concepts for Assessing Students With Special Needs

Item	Yes	No	Comments
1. Does the test provide modifications for use with students who have specific disabilities?	___	___	
2. Are norms for disability groups available?	___	___	
3. Was the test developed specifically for use with students who have disabilities?	___	___	
4. Are the response sheets on which students write their answers appropriately designed (e.g., sufficient space for answers, clear layout)?	___	___	
5. Are the test materials attractively designed and motivating to students?	___	___	

Summary

Knowledge of measurement concepts and techniques serves as a foundation for understanding assessment in special education. Measurement begins with basic statistics and extends to considering the practical value of tests. The basic statistical concepts furnish a way to describe numbers such as test scores. Other measurement procedures enable evaluation of the reliability and validity of assessment instruments. Furthermore, measurement concepts define the two distinct types of testing: criterion referenced and norm referenced. Virtually all aspects of testing and assessing students with special needs are based on measurement principles and practices.

Teaching in special education requires skillful measurement of student behavior and proper selection of accurate measurement tools in each situation. The way in which teachers and other professionals apply measurement procedures influences, either beneficially or harmfully, the lives of students with disabilities. By using measurement techniques carefully, cautiously, and correctly, teachers support the rights of students and their families to receive appropriate educational services.

Chapter 4 applies the basic concepts of measurement to the topic of test scores and their significance. Later chapters rely on the measurement concepts in examining the wide range and variety of tests and other evaluation procedures that make up assessment in special education.

Chapter Review and Application

Multiple Choice

Directions: Read each item carefully. In the blank beside each item, write the letter of the best response. Each item contains only one best answer. After completing all of the items, check your answers with the answer key at the end of the book.

_____ 1. Which statistical procedure estimates the variability of individual test scores?
   a. The mean
   b. The standard deviation
   c. The standard error of measurement

_____ 2. Experts recommend cautious use of the mean with _____ groups of scores.
   a. small
   b. large
   c. very large

_____ 3. If the standard deviation of scores for a sample group of children is 15 and the mean is 100, then approximately 68% of the scores occur between _____ and _____.
   a. 92.5 and 107.5
   b. 85 and 115
   c. 85 and 100
   d. 100 and 115

_____ 4. Ms. Bertowski gave a class test in which most of the scores ranged from 90 to 100 (the highest possible score was 100). Which of the following distribution patterns best describes these scores?
   a. Negative skew
   b. Positive skew
   c. Normal distribution

    5. La'Keisha received a score of 128 on a norm-referenced test with a standard error of measurement of 6. La'Keisha's true score is between _____ and _____.
    a. 122 and 128
    b. 128 and 134
    c. 125 and 132
    d. 122 and 134

    6. Mrs. Keoni notices that the mean is about the same for the test scores from her three math classes, yet one class has a much broader range of scores. Which statistic would Mrs. Keoni use to determine the magnitude of the range of scores?
    a. Median
    b. Standard error of measurement
    c. Mode
    d. Standard deviation

    7. A test must be _____ before it can be _____.
    a. valid, reliable
    b. reliable, valid
    c. norm referenced, valid
    d. norm referenced, reliable

    8. Which type of reliability applies to assessment related to behavior-management programs for students with behavior problems?
    a. Test-retest
    b. Alternate form
    c. Split-half
    d. Interrater

    9. Which type of validity involves analyzing the correlation between a test and some comparable measure of proven validity?
    a. Content
    b. Predictive
    c. Construct
    d. Concurrent

Short Answers

Directions: Review your understanding of the material in this chapter by answering the short answer questions below. After you have responded to each question, compare your responses with the sample answers. Your responses should contain information that is similar to but not exactly the same as that in the sample answers.

1. What is validity, why is it important in testing, and what is the basic question of validity?
2. If another teacher told you that a particular test had high validity, what questions would you ask to confirm this?
3. A special education teacher constructed a test for use in all the learning disabilities programs in the school without obtaining input from the other teachers of children with learning disabilities. What effect might this have on the validity of the test? Why? How could the teacher improve the validity of the test?

4. What is reliability, and why is it important in testing?
5. In reviewing reliability data in a test manual, a teacher noted the following reliability coefficients:

Test A

   Correlation of split-half (odd-even) reliability = .95
   Correlation of test-retest reliability = .90
   Correlation of alternate-form reliability = .95

Test B

   Correlation of split-half (odd-even) reliability = .80
   Correlation of test-retest reliability = .85
   Correlation of alternate-form reliability = .80

   What conclusion can you draw about the reliability of Test A compared with Test B? Why?

6. Which of the following represents a criterion-referenced interpretation and which a norm-referenced interpretation?
    a. Shameka mastered 85% of the competencies on the high school vocational skills checklist.
    b. Jung scored higher than 87% of the fourth graders on the reading comprehension test.
    c. When Martin took the reading test at the end of the semester, his score had improved significantly compared with his score at the beginning of the semester.
    d. Maria's math score placed her near the bottom of the class.

7. What is the value of using national norms? Under what conditions is it possible for a teacher to develop and use classroom norms?
8. Can a norm-referenced test be interpreted in both a criterion-referenced and a norm-referenced manner? If so, describe the conditions in which a teacher could use a norm-referenced test in a criterion-referenced manner.
9. A student has been given the *Wechsler Intelligence Scale for Children* four times during her school career, and her cumulative record includes the following fluctuations in intelligence quotient: 85 in 1989, 89 in 1992, 81 in 1995, and 87 in 1998. What significance should be attached to these fluctuations in scores? What term is used to describe these fluctuations?

References

Angoff, W. H. (1988). Validity: An evolving concept. In H. Wainer & H. I. Braun (Eds.), *Test Validity*. Hillsdale, NJ: Lawrence Erlbaum, 19–32.

Barlow, D. H., & Hersen, M. (1984). *Single Case Experimental Designs: Strategies for Studying Behavior Change* (2d ed.). New York: Pergamon.

Brigance, A. H. (1977). *Brigance Diagnostic Inventory of Basic Skills*. North Billerica, MA: Curriculum Associates.

Brown, F. G. (1980). *Guidelines for Test Use: A Commentary on the Standards for Educational and Psychological Tests*. Ames, IA: National Council on Measurement in Education.

Cronbach, L. J. (1988). Five perspectives on the validity argument. In H. Wainer & H. I. Braun (Eds.), *Test Validity*. Hillsdale, NJ: Lawrence Erlbaum, 3–18.

Drummond, R. J. (1996). *Appraisal Procedures for Counselors and Helping Professionals* (3d ed.). Englewood, NJ: Merrill/Prentice-Hall.

Kubiszyn, T., & Borich, G. (1990). *Educational Testing and Measurement: Classroom Application and Practice* (3d ed.). Glenview, IL: Scott, Foresman.

Messick, S. (1988). The once and future issues of validity: Assessing the meaning and consequences of measurement. In H. Wainer & H. I. Braun (Eds.), *Test Validity*. Hillsdale, NJ: Lawrence Erlbaum, 33–46.

Rubin, D. B. (1988). Discussion. In H. Wainer & H. I. Braun (Eds.), *Test Validity*. Hillsdale, NJ: Lawrence Erlbaum, 241–56.

Sattler, J. M. (1992). *Assessment of Children* (3d ed.). San Diego: Author.

Wechsler, D. (1991). *Manual for the Wechsler Intelligence Scale for Children* (3d ed.), San Antonio, TX: Psychological Corporation.

Wilkinson, G. S. (1993). *Wide Range Achievement Test-3*. Wilmington, DE: Wide Range, Inc.

Wolery, M., Bailey, D. B., & Sugai, G. M. (1988). *Effective Teaching: Principles and Procedures of Applied Behavior Analysis With Exceptional Students*. Boston: Allyn & Bacon.

CHAPTER 4

Test Scores and What They Mean

Overview

Assessing students with special needs requires the use of an assortment of test scores. In this chapter, you study the various test scores used in assessment, discover what they mean, and consider how to interpret them. You will also investigate the two fundamentally different categories of test scoring: criterion- referenced and norm-referenced scoring. The scoring associated with each category is the focus of the chapter, and for every score there is a definition, a practical example, a description of advantages, and a description of limitations. At the conclusion of the chapter, you consider practical principles for the use of scores in the classroom and in other settings.

Objectives

After reading this chapter, you will be prepared to do the following:

- Explain the standards for scoring, including procedures for accurately reporting results.
- Understand and use raw scores.
- Understand the purpose and use of norm-referenced and criterion-referenced test scores.
- Interpret and use criterion referenced scores, including simple numerical reports, percent correct scores, letter grades, and graphical reports.
- Interpret and use age- and grade-equivalent scores.
- Interpret and use percentile scores, including quartiles and deciles.
- Interpret and use the standard scores, including intelligence quotients, stanines, t-scores and z-scores, and normal curve equivalents.
- Apply the principles of using test scores.

Using Test Scores Properly

Mrs. Weinroth is a special education teacher who teaches students with mild and moderate disabilities. She has never interpreted test scores before, but because she has heard so much about test scores of late, she is wondering how she could use them in her class. But first, she asks herself, what test scores are available, and what kinds of test scores are best? How many different kinds are there? Next, she asks, why use test scores? Is the use of test scores valuable to teachers, and can they really make a difference in learning and teaching? What can they do for her that other assessment methods do not? What about her students—what can test scores do for them?

Mrs. Weinroth does some research, consults some educators, and decides she would like to learn more about test scores. She gets some helpful information from these resources on how to use test scores in a general education classroom. She does not know, however, how to tailor the test scores for her students with disabilities. None of the articles she has read mentioned this, and none of her colleagues have much experience with test scores for students with special needs. She wonders if her students' scores would be different from those of "typical" students? She decides to visit with the district's diagnostic teacher and consult a special education teacher in another school who uses test scores with success.

Definition of Test Scores

Simply defined, **test scores** are the numerical result of testing. Scores summarize test results through the use of numbers, and these results provide an effective and efficient way to describe student performance in an objective manner. Professionals rely on them for a variety of purposes in special education. Psychologists and diagnosticians rely on test scores to classify and place students in special education. Teachers depend on test scores to plan and evaluate instruction. Administrators use them to evaluate programs. Counselors and others relate test scores to student performance in communicating with parents about the progress or lack of progress of their children. In all of these situations, professionals use test scores to make educational decisions and to communicate information about those decisions.

Although test scores provide essential information, mistakes may occur unless other factors are considered. For this reason, experts caution against the use of scores in isolation as the sole criterion in decision making. Testing specialists recommend using scores together with qualitative information about a student and the setting in which the student is expected to perform. Qualitative information includes teacher judgment about what is best for the student and subjective impressions based on observing and interacting with students.

The goal is to strike a balance between quantitative and qualitative information. Striking this balance is not easy, but is necessary to make decisions in the best interests of the student, the parents, and the teacher. Fortunately, published standards for the use of test scores are available that serve as a guide for scoring and interpreting tests in an equitable and accurate manner. (See Focus 4–1.)

Problems With Test Scores

Mary Beth once had a teacher who told her parents that she was profoundly retarded with an IQ of 25 or lower. This test score meant, according to the teacher, that Mary Beth could not progress beyond a very low level of functioning. Furthermore, the teacher said that Mary Beth

FOCUS 4–1

Standards for Scoring

Revised **standards for scoring** will be published by the American Psychological Association in the near future. Revised standards are needed because the current *Standards for Scoring*, which were published in 1985, fail to reflect contemporary issues such as computer-based scoring. Although the exact language of the new standards has not been finalized, it is anticipated that the new standards will include the following guidelines:

- Accurate test scoring requires test administration and scoring according to the developer's instructions.
- Test scores should be interpreted with other information, including norms, measurement error, and descriptions of test content.
- Interpretations of test scores by computers require validation to ensure accuracy.
- Score reports should be provided in a form that is easily understandable to those receiving the report.
- The test giver is responsible for explaining the limitations of test scores and the relationship of test scores to other information.

The standards also require that the test giver ensure accuracy in scoring and interpreting results. This means that test givers should check all steps in the testing process, including spot checking computer- or machine-scored tests. Accuracy is essential because even a small scoring error can ultimately result in making the wrong educational decision. For example, if a test giver calculates the chronological age of a student incorrectly, the resulting test score will be inaccurate. Likewise, if a test giver enters a raw score into a computer-assisted scoring program incorrectly, the transformed score will be inaccurate. For this reason, test givers must make sure that the test administration and scoring process is error free.

was progressing so slowly that her developmental age as an adult would be no higher than that of a 5- or 6-year-old child. Last year Mary Beth enrolled in a supported employment program and, with the help of a job coach, began work at a print shop, running a copy machine. After extensive training, Mary Beth learned to operate the copy machine and is now successfully employed.

This true story and the one that follows illustrate some of the problems with test scores: Were the scores correct? Were they fair and unbiased? Were the test scores interpreted accurately? Do test designers fail to delineate limits of their tests to predict future performance? Do teachers sometimes use scores to forecast potential or lack of potential without carefully limiting the validity of their estimates?

One successful teacher of Mexican-American descent tells this story about himself: He received a low score on an intelligence test in elementary school, was labeled mentally retarded, and was placed in a special education class. His parents were told his intelligence was so low that he would never progress any higher than the fifth- or sixth-grade level in academic learning. Now he has earned a doctorate and is a professor at a junior college.

Unfortunately, teachers sometimes use test scores inappropriately, as illustrated in the following example.

Janet has a severe learning disability. In high school, her special education teacher told her that she could never succeed in college because test scores showed she could not score high enough on the entrance exam, and her learning disability was too severe. Today Janet is a school psychologist with a doctoral degree, and she often lectures in college classes on assessment in special education.

All of these cases involve real people, and each is based on an actual testing situation. The scenarios portray situations in which teachers and others in decision-making positions failed to interpret the meaning of test scores accurately. Although most professionals strive to avoid such mistakes, the cases illustrate how easy it is to misinterpret test scores. This occurs because of the misconceptions and myths that surround such results. Fortunately, college students preparing for careers in teaching learn about test scores in personnel preparation programs, and, after accepting teaching positions, most teachers continue to expand their knowledge of the subject. Learning as much as possible about test scores is necessary because of the complexity of the topic and the continuing changes in their use. Surprisingly, even the specialists in assessment have trouble keeping up to date with this complicated subject.

Fortunately, in most situations professionals interpret test scores accurately, and the cases just cited are exceptions rather than typical occurrences. The following account shows one of the many positive ways in which professionals use test scores.

Accurately Interpreting Test Scores

Joseph's difficulty with school work started in kindergarten, but his problems intensified in the first grade when the curriculum focus shifted from developmental to academic skills. Concerned about his severe lack of progress in academics, Joseph's teacher referred him to the child-study team. After completing the initial steps in the referral process, the team arranged for an assessment specialist to evaluate Joseph with a battery of diagnostic tests. In the diagnostic report, the specialist reported test scores in reading, math, and writing that fell into the significantly below-average range. Likewise, the specialist reported an intelligence quotient that fell below the cutoff level for mental retardation. In addition, the specialist described adaptive behavior scores that were also significantly below average.

The placement team relied on these test scores as critical information in identifying Joseph as mildly retarded and recommending placement in a special education program. In fact, the law required the team to obtain these test scores as part of the process of identifying Joseph as disabled and placing him in a special program. As is often the case, the special program was well suited to Joseph's individual learning needs, and, after a few weeks in the special class, he began to succeed in school work for the first time.

The cases cited emphasize the need to understand the diverse collection of available test scores, starting with the meaning of test scores in general. The ultimate intent of this chapter is to develop an understanding of the different test scores, what they mean, when to use them, and how to interpret them.

☑ Comprehension Checklist

As you can see, interpreting test scores involves many considerations. Special educators should follow the professional standards and legal responsibilities for scoring to ensure the highest possible accuracy with all types of test scores. Special education teachers are also responsible for following the standards and laws when they modify test administration procedures for students with special needs. The goal is to protect the rights of students and to maintain accuracy in all scoring activities.

Types of Test Scores

Teachers and others in special education rely on many types of test scores. However, the raw score is usually the first score obtained in testing.

Raw Scores

A **raw score** is the simple numerical result of testing, typically the number of items answered correctly. In most situations, evaluators avoid using raw scores to report test results. Instead, they convert raw scores into various types of transformed scores because most raw scores, such as 39 on a mathematics test, are meaningless in isolation. Likewise, a raw score of 128 on a motor performance test gives no information for making educational decisions. Furthermore, raw scores from different tests are not comparable. For example, if a student takes two tests, in which Test 1 consists of 50 items and Test 2 consists of 100 items, a raw score of 40 correct on the first test does not mean the same thing as a raw score of 40 correct on the second test. In this example, the two raw scores are not comparable because the tests are of different lengths, and they may differ in level of difficulty. For these reasons, most tests provide a procedure for converting raw scores into various other scores.

The two major categories of transformed scores, norm referenced and criterion referenced, represent fundamentally different ways of describing student performance. Whereas norm-referenced scores are formal and standardized, criterion-referenced scores are less formal and more flexible.

Norm-Referenced Scores

A **norm-referenced score** interprets student performance in relation to the performance of others by comparing an individual score with the average score of corresponding students in a norm sample group. The soundness of a single score depends on the soundness of the norm group scores. A score is sound when compared to scores from a representative norm group with similar characteristics; a score is unsound and of limited value when compared to scores from an unrepresentative norm group. For example, when evaluators test children with the *Wechsler Individual Achievement Test* (Wechsler, 1992), they compare an individual's score to scores from an equivalent sample group of children using the norms for the test. Fortunately, this edition of the test has excellent norms based on a representative sample group of children, which includes youngsters from a wide range of cultural, ethnic, geographic, and economic backgrounds.

Some widely used tests, however, have inadequate norms. For example, a test that was widely used throughout the United States and internationally for many years had a norm sample consisting almost entirely of students from an urban, middle-class background. Giving the test to a student from an urban, middle-class background produced a valid score because the student's performance was compared to that of others from a similar background. However, giving the test to students from rural, poor backgrounds or to students with disabilities produced invalid, biased scores because the norm group failed to include students from similar backgrounds. This shows that the usefulness of an individual score depends on the adequacy of the norms.

Teachers sometimes use norm-referenced scores in a criterion-referenced manner. A discussion of this use of norm-referenced scores appears in Focus 4–4.

Criterion-Referenced Scores

A **criterion-referenced score** interprets performance from a different viewpoint. It explains results in relation to a functional level of performance rather than in relation to the performance of others. When the criterion of reference is content related, the soundness of an individual score depends on the soundness of the content of the test. If the test items accurately reflect the instructional content, then the test score is sound; if the content of the test fails to represent the instructional content, then the value of the score is limited. For example, if, after teaching addition skills, the teacher gives a teacher-made test covering those addition skills, the resulting test scores will be sound. If, on the other hand, the content of the teacher-

FOCUS 4–2

Using Norm-Referenced Scores in a Criterion-Referenced Manner

Teachers sometimes use a score from a norm-referenced test in a criterion-referenced manner by giving a test at the beginning and again at the end of the year to measure individual student progress over time. In this situation, previous performance rather than the performance of students in the norm group serves as the criterion of reference. Although teachers use norm-referenced tests in this manner, and many test manuals suggest that teachers do so, such use may jeopardize reliability. The problem occurs because most norm-referenced tests measure only a few items corresponding to a given instructional objective, making it difficult to determine whether those items serve as a representative sample for any given objective. Therefore, deciding whether a student demonstrates competency by using a few items from a norm-referenced test is not the best way to determine skill level. In most situations, teachers should determine mastery of content with criterion-referenced assessment tools that assess students with many items across a skill.

made test includes addition and subtraction, the value of the resulting scores will be limited.

When the criterion relates to the student over time, the soundness of the score depends on administering and scoring the test in the same manner for each administration of the test. For example, if a teacher uses a test to measure proficiency in a certain skill area before and after instruction, the soundness of the score depends on administering and scoring the pretest and posttest in the same manner.

☑ Comprehension Checklist

Norm- and criterion-referenced scores define the two broad categories of test scores. The difference in the categories involves the purpose for testing and the methods of scoring and interpreting the results. A variety of specific scores appear within each category, and one type of score, the graphical score report, occurs in each of the categories.

Specific Criterion-Referenced Scores

Raw scores convert into a variety of specific criterion-referenced scores that include simple numerical reports, percent correct scores, letter grades, and graphical score reports.

Simple Numerical Reports

Transforming a raw score into a **simple numerical report** produces one of the most useful criterion-referenced scores. A simple numerical report is the number of right and wrong answers on a test. An example of this type of score is 45 of 50 correct responses, often expressed as 45/50. Teachers frequently report this type of score on class tests, papers, worksheets, and homework assignments. The score is also useful with skills checklists, task analysis, minimum competency tests, and other curriculum-based assessment procedures.

Percent Correct Scores

A **percent correct score** is a criterion-referenced score that describes performance as the percentage of correct answers on a test. Calculating a percent correct score involves dividing the number of correct answers by the total number of items on the test. For example, if a student answers 8 items correctly on a test with 10 items, then the percent correct score is 80%. This traditional score provides a convenient and straightforward way of converting raw scores into a more useful form. Like the simple numerical report score, the percent correct score is useful with class tests, checklists, minimum competency tests, and a variety of other curriculum-based assessment instruments.

Teachers should avoid using percent correct scores to compare performance across tests. This limitation is necessary because a percent correct score of 87% on an easy spelling test, for example, is not equivalent to a score of 87% on a difficult spelling test. Likewise, a score of 68% on a math test is not equivalent to a score of 68% on a reading test. This same limitation applies to numerical report scores.

Letter Grades

A **letter grade** is a classic means of describing student performance. Most teachers derive letter grades from percent correct scores and assign them according to a grading scale. An example of a letter-grade scale based on percent correct scores appears in Table 4–1. Sometimes subjective information, such as teacher opinion or impressions, serves as the basis for grade scores rather than objective test score data. Such arbitrary assignment limits the value of letter grades. Although not a score in a technical sense, a letter grade provides a way to describe student performance quickly and easily, in a manner familiar to most people. Within this context, letter grades serve as a practical tool for communicating student performance in the classroom.

Many teachers rely on alternative grading procedures to meet the unique needs of students with disabilities. Widely used alternative grading procedures include pass/fail grading, multiple grading, grading for effort, and portfolio-based grading. Detailed information on these and other alternative grading procedures appears in Chapter 19.

Graphical Reports

Converting raw scores into a **graphical report** produces profiles or visual representations of performance. Graphical reports illustrate progress over time and provide a way to analyze strengths and weaknesses across skills. Graphical reports include profiles on test scoring sheets and behavior charts. A completed age/grade profile for Maria from the *Woodcock Language Proficiency Battery* (revised) appears in Figure 4–1. This profile depicts the student's level of performance in several oral language skill areas and serves as an assessment tool for determining intervention priorities.

Data sources for graphical reports include test scores, scores from written work, homework grades, data on student behavior, and simple numerical reports from checklists. Plotting these types of data on profiles illustrates student performance graphically and simplifies the process of communicating assessment information to students, parents, and others. The use of profiles is not limited to criterion-referenced scores. Profiles serve an equally useful purpose with norm-referenced scores.

Table 4–1 Example of a Letter-Grade Scale

Percent Correct	Grade
93–100	A
85–92	B
75–84	C
65–74	D
Less than 65	F

Figure 4–1 Completed Age/Grade Profile for Maria From the *Woodcock Language Proficiency Battery-Revised*

Appendix A

Sample Completed Test Record: Sixth-grade Girl, Maria, Referred for Learning Problems

9-21650
Richard W. Woodcock

Woodcock Language Proficiency Battery–Revised

WLPB-R

TEST RECORD

Name *Maria Martin* ID _____ Sex. M ☐ F ☑ Examiner *F. Schrank*

Grade Placement *6.4* Years Retained *1* Years Skipped *0*

School/Agency *Schimelpfenig* Teacher/Department *D. Dailey* City/State *Plano, TX*

	Year	Month	Day
Testing Date:	91 90	12	37
Birth Date:	78	6	23
Difference:	12	6	14
Age:	12 – 6		

(Round to whole months)

LANGUAGE USE SURVEY: 1. What language was *first* learned by the subject? *Spanish*

HOW MUCH OF THE TIME (Check nearest percent) 0% 25% 50% 75% 100%

2. What language is primarily spoken by the subject at *home*? *English* ☐ ☐ ☐ ☑ ☐ Any other language/s? *Spanish* ☐ ☑ ☐ ☐ ☐

3. What language is primarily spoken by others in the subject's *home*? *Spanish* ☐ ☐ ☐ ☑ ☐ Any other language/s? *English* ☐ ☑ ☐ ☐ ☐

4. What language is primarily spoken by the subject in *informal social situations* (playground, cafeteria, or on the street)? *English* ☐ ☐ ☐ ☑ ☐ Any other language/s? *Spanish* ☐ ☑ ☐ ☐ ☐

5. What language is primarily spoken by the subject in the *classroom*? *English* ☐ ☐ ☐ ☐ ☑ Any other language/s? ☐ ☐ ☐ ☐ ☐

Adult Subjects: Education _____ Occupation _____

Other Information

Does the subject have glasses? ☑ Yes ☐ No Were they used during testing? ☑ Yes ☐ No
Does the subject have a hearing aid? ☐ Yes ☑ No Was it used during testing? ☐ Yes ☑ No

Age/Grade Profile: *Tests* RMIs and PRs based on: ☐ Age _____ ☑ Grade *6.4* EASY ← → DIFFICULT Instructional Range

Test		W	RMI	PR
1 Memory for Sentences		483	45/90	10
2 Picture Vocabulary		494	63/90	15
3 Oral Vocabulary		505	87/90	42
4 Listening Comprehension		500	82/90	34
5 Verbal Analogies		498	75/90	29

ORAL LANGUAGE

From Woodcock, R. W. (1991). *Woodcock Language Proficiency Battery-Revised.* Itasca, IL: Riverside Publishing. Reprinted with permission of the Riverside Publishing Company.

☑ Comprehension Checklist

Criterion-referenced scores range from simple numerical reports to more complex graphical reports. Teachers frequently rely on this type of scoring in the classroom and in other instructional environments. Criterion-referenced scores help to plan intervention programs, measure student progress, and report on student performance. The essential notion of criterion-referenced scoring is interpretation of performance in relation to some functional level. In contrast, the basic idea of norm-referenced scoring is interpretation of performance in relation to the performance of others.

Specific Norm-Referenced Scores

Norm-referenced scores include age scores, grade scores, percentiles, and standard scores. All norm-referenced scores, also referred to as *derived scores,* originate from the norms developed for a test. With most norm-referenced tests, the test giver chooses the score to report from a selection of several scores. Understanding all the available scores makes it possible to select the most appropriate score in a given situation. The appropriate score in one situation may not be appropriate in another: The goal is to select the score that fulfills the purpose of testing and fits the needs of the individual student.

Age Scores

An **age score** describes the typical or average performance of different age groups. For example, a 6-year-old who performs as a 5-year-old on a developmental test obtains an age score of 5. In this example, the age score of 5 symbolizes the highest average age level of performance on the test.

Test developers can formulate age scores for tests measuring any characteristic that changes with age. However, the most common use of age scores is with intelligence and achievement tests. Binet and Simon originally developed the ***mental age*** (MA) concept and score when they revised their intelligence test in 1908. An MA score represents mental ability in relation to the average performance of the individuals in the norm group at each successive chronological age. For example, a child's mental age might be described as follows:

Three months ago, Timmy, whose chronological age was 6 years, 2 months (expressed as 6.2), received an MA of 9 years, 9 months (expressed as 9.9) on the WISC-III intelligence test.

Developmental Age Scores   **Developmental age** is a type of age score designed to measure the performance of infants, toddlers, and preschoolers in a range from birth through 6 years of age. A few developmental scales measure skills after 6 years of age, but most end at age 6.

When tested with a developmental scale, Jason, who was 3 years old at the time, received the following developmental age scores: 1 year in language development, 4 years in gross motor development, 4 years in fine motor development, 3 years in social skills, and 3 years in self-help skills.

Quotient Scores A **quotient score** is an extension of an age score. The most common quotient score is a ratio intelligence quotient (**ratio IQ**). A ratio IQ is an age score derived from an intelligence test that expresses mental ability based on the ratio of a student's mental age to chronological age. The formula for calculating a ratio IQ is

$$\frac{\text{Mental age}}{\text{Chronological age}} \times 100 = \text{Ratio IQ}$$

When Warren was 11 years, 9 months old, he received an MA score of 9.9 on an intelligence test. A ratio IQ score was obtained by dividing the MA of 9.9 by Warren's chronological age of 11.9. The resulting number, 0.83, was multiplied by 100 to obtain a ratio IQ of 83.

$$\frac{9.9}{11.9} \times 100 = 83$$

Warren's score of 83 is interpreted in relation to the average IQ, which is 100. A score of 100 indicates a student with average intelligence. Warren's score of 83 is 17 points below the average and reflects below-average intellectual development. If Warren had obtained an MA of 9.9 on the test, his ratio IQ would have been normal, or average.

$$\frac{9.9}{9.9} \times 100 = 100$$

Although the logic of this type of test score is straightforward and seems reasonable, this score and all similar age-based scores are subject to misinterpretation for reasons explained later in this chapter in the section listing the disadvantages of such scores.

Other Quotient and Age Scores

Similar quotient scores exist for other tests, including **developmental quotients** (DQs), **social quotients** (SQs), **learning quotients** (LQs), and **achievement quotients** (AQs). Test developers give specific names to many other age scores. Examples of specific names include social age, fine motor age, and receptive language age.

Grade Scores

A **grade score** describes student performance according to scholastic grade levels. A grade score, however, is actually a specific type of age score rather than a separate score. A grade score expresses performance in association with a scholastic grade rather than a chronological age. Other terms for grade score include *grade-equivalent score, grade-referenced score,* and *grade-placement score.* For example, a seventh grader who achieves as a ninth grader on an academic test receives a grade score of ninth grade, which signifies the highest average grade level of attainment on a test.

Sarah received an overall grade-level score of third grade, fifth month (3.5) on an academic achievement test. She received scores of 4.4 on the reading recognition subtest, 4.1 on the reading comprehension subtest, 2.3 on the mathematics subtest, and 2.6 on the spelling subtest.

The overall score placed Sarah at the third grade, fifth month in academic achievement. More specifically, Sarah's academic strength was in reading, where she performed at a fourth-grade level. She was weaker in the academic areas of mathematics and spelling. In these areas she scored at about one grade level behind her overall average level of achievement.

Although generally correct, this interpretation is not necessarily accurate, depending on the age of the student. For a 21-year-old student, these scores would indicate a significantly low level of functioning; for a 4-year-old child, these scores would indicate a significantly advanced level of performance. In addition, the actual academic performance in a classroom situation of a 21-year-old and a 4-year-old with these scores would be much different, and the intervention approach would also vary considerably.

Advantages of Age and Grade Scores

Age and grade scores seem more practical and appealing than most other scores because it makes so much sense to think of scores in these terms. The concept of age and grade scoring appears easy to understand, making it possible to describe test performance in a more concrete way than with other scores. In addition, more people recognize age scores than the other norm-referenced scores. Although advantages exist in the use of age scores, especially with tests for very young children, many disadvantages also exist.

Disadvantages of Age and Grade Scores

Despite the many advantages and the widespread use of age and grade scores, specialists continue to document the disadvantages of age and grade scores with convincing evidence that condemns further use in most situations (Anastasi, 1988; Hoy & Gregg, 1994; McLoughlin & Lewis, 1994; Sattler, 1992). Furthermore, the Standards for Educational and Psychological Testing (American Psychological Association, 1985; Brown, 1980) advocate the elimination of age and grade scores altogether. Because of the many drawbacks associated with these scores, professionals should use them cautiously with a full understanding of the possible misinterpretations (Linn & Gronlund, 1995). A list of the disadvantages that lead to misinterpretations appears in Table 4–2, followed by a description of each drawback.

Table 4–2   Disadvantages of Age and Grade Scores

- Age and grade scores lead to inaccurate generalizations.
- Reliability decreases as student's age increases.
- Age and grade scores shrink independent of behavior change.
- Age and grade units are not equal.
- Age and grade scores from different tests are not comparable.
- Age and grade scores cannot be averaged.
- Some tests estimate certain age and grade scores.
- Age and grade scores may not indicate skill development.

Inaccurate Generalizations Experts in assessment maintain that age and grade scores lead to inaccurate generalizations about overall performance. This serious limitation exists in particular with students in special education, who often receive extremely low scores. For example, assuming that a 10-year-old who receives an age score of 3 on a developmental test behaves like a normal 3-year-old is probably an inaccurate generalization. Although a 10-year-old may receive an age score of 3 on a test, the pattern of development of a 10-year-old with this score may be completely different from the pattern of development of an average 3-year-old. A more accurate description of a 10-year-old who receives a developmental age score of 3 is that the student performs some skills typical of a child younger than age 3, some skills typical of a 3-year-old, and some skills above the 3-year-old age level. On the other hand, a typical 3-year-old performs most skills at the 3-year-old level and few skills above or below the 3-year-old age level. Another example of the problem is a 12th grader who receives a score of 3rd grade on a reading test. In this instance, the 12th grader probably does not read like a typical 3rd grader. This illustrates how age scores lead to inaccurate generalizations about performance.

Decreasing Reliability The reliability of age and grade scores tends to decrease with age because as children grow older, their pattern of skill development becomes unpredictable. Although the age scores of infants and preschoolers tend to be reliable and stable, the age scores of adolescents and adults tend to be unreliable and unstable. Children up to the age of about 6 years learn most skills in a remarkably similar sequence and pattern. This predictability in skill development fades with children above age 6.

Independent Decline Age scores and grade scores decline or shrink with increasing chronological age. This decrease in scores occurs independent of behavior change because as students age, it becomes easier for them to fall farther and farther behind. Although a 1-year-old cannot fall more than 1 year behind in development, a 12-year-old can easily fall more than a year behind in development. In fact, a 12-year-old can be as much as 12 years behind. Likewise, a 1st grader cannot fall more than one grade level behind, but a 12th grader can be as many 12 years below grade level. This shrinkage is more pronounced with scores at older age levels. It is less of a problem with young children because behavior change is relatively rapid in infants, toddlers, and preschoolers. For this reason, most experts believe it is appropriate to use developmental age scores in the birth-to-6-year-old range.

Unequal Units Another problem contributing to inaccuracy concerns the inequality of age- and grade-score units. This problem relates to the larger difference that exists among the reading behaviors of 1st and 2nd graders when compared to the reading behaviors of 11th and 12th graders. Likewise, larger differences exist in the language development of 1- and 2-year-old infants when compared with the language development of 9- and 10-year-old children. These examples illustrate the inequality of age-score units, which make the scores less effective measures of behavior than some of the other norm-referenced scores.

Scores From Different Tests Are Not Comparable Age and grade scores from different tests are not directly comparable because of differences in content and standardization procedures among the tests. This means that if a child has age scores from several different tests, comparisons across the tests may not be valid. Although all comparisons across tests should be done cautiously, comparisons using age scores tend to be especially inaccurate.

Averaging Distorts Performance   Age and grade scores show relative standing, not absolute differences; therefore, averaging the results of various scores to show overall achievement distorts performance. For example, averaging a reading score of second grade and a math score of eighth grade for an overall average level of achievement of fifth grade misrepresents achievement. Although the overall average is fifth grade, a student with these scores does not perform at all like a fifth grader in reading and mathematics.

Some Tests Estimate Certain Scores   Some tests estimate some scores such as grade scores sucha s 12th grade, 9th month, expressed as 12-9, or 7th grade, 2nd month, expressed as 7-2. Test developers estimate some grade scores because of the difficulty in including students from every specific grade level and month in the norm sample group. For example, if the third-grade students in the norm group were given the test at the beginning of the school year and the fourth-grade students were given the test in the middle of the school year, then the test developer must estimate grade scores for the months in between because no norm group scores exist. For this reason, grade scores from tests may not fit the teacher's informal observations about the skills of a student. Therefore teachers should use grade scores cautiously, especially when placing students in instructional groups.

Scores May Not Indicate Skill Development   Unfortunately, age scores may not indicate skill development because the obtained score does not always reflect the student's present level of performance. The following scenario illustrates this dilemma: If a second grader scores sixth grade on a math test, it does not necessarily mean that the student functions at the sixth-grade level in math. How can a second grader perform sixth-grade math when sixth-grade skills have not been taught yet? In reality, this test result means that the second grader obtained a grade-equivalent score of sixth grade on the second-grade test. It does not mean that the second grader performs math like a typical sixth grader. If the second grader took the sixth-grade test, the resulting score would be lower than if the second grader took the second-grade test.

Percentiles

In response to the many problems associated with grade and age scores, many experts recommend use of percentiles instead of grade and age scores. A **percentile score** shows relative standing by ranking a student in comparison to those in the corresponding norm group. A percentile is any 1 of 99 scores divided into a distribution of 100 equal ranks ranging from 1 to 99. The 50th percentile signifies the average ranking or average performance. A score below 50 connotes a below-average ranking; above 50 represents an above-average ranking.

Mary received a percentile score of 50 on a test of vocational skills. This score ranks in the middle range and indicates average performance.

Noah received a percentile score of 24 on a test of vocational skills. This score ranks in the bottom fourth or bottom 25% and signifies below-average performance.

Gail received a percentile score of 76 on a test of vocational skills. This score ranks in the top fourth or top 25% and denotes above-average performance.

Percentiles, also called *centiles,* divide scores into 100 equal units. **Quartiles,** another type of percentile, divide scores into 4 units or fourths: 1–25, 26–50, 51–75, and 76–99. The fourth, or upper, quartile (77–99) designates the top quarter or top fourth of all scores. The first, or lower, quartile (1–25) marks the bottom quarter or bottom fourth of all scores. **Deciles,** also a type of percentile, divide scores into tenths, or 10 equal units: 1–9, 10–19, 20–29, and so forth. A percentile of 92 signifies performance in the top 10%, whereas a percentile of 32 designates performance in the bottom 30%. A scale of 1 to 10 provides a convenient way to describe performance in deciles. For example, a decile of 9 is a 9 on a scale of 1 to 10; a decile of 3 is a 3 on a scale of 1 to 10.

Percentile scores should not be confused with percent correct scores, which are used in informal assessment and are criterion referenced. On the other hand, percentile scores are norm referenced for use in formal assessment. If a student receives a percent correct score of 90% by answering 90 of 100 questions correctly on a test, this does not mean that the score ranks in the 90th percentile. The percentile rank of a raw score of 90 depends on where this score stands in the distribution of all the scores.

Advantages of Percentiles   The advantages of percentiles include applicability to all age levels and suitability for scoring performance across domains, including intellectual, academic, social, and physical. Percentiles are reasonably easy to understand and are less susceptible to misinterpretation than age scores.

Disadvantages of Percentiles   The major drawback of percentiles involves the unequal length of percentile units, especially at the extremes. This characteristic results in a tendency to overemphasize differences near the middle and underemphasize differences near the ends. In other words, the difference between 50 and 55 may be less than the difference between 90 and 95. This inequality occurs because percentiles, which are calculated from ranked data, designate relative standing, not absolute differences.

Standard Scores

A **standard score** is a general term for a variety of scores that express performance by comparing the deviation of an individual score from the mean or average score for students in a norm group of the same chronological age or scholastic grade level. The standard deviation, or average variability, of the scores in the norm group provides the basis for calculating standard scores. Standard scores have the advantage of enabling comparison of performance across tests. This makes them especially useful in the process of classifying and placing students. Although test developers can set up standard scores with different means and standard deviations, the most widely used standard score has a mean ($\bar{x}$) of 100 and a standard deviation (SD) of 15. Originally designed for intelligence testing, this particular standard score is now available for use with a variety of tests.

When used with intelligence tests, a standard score with a mean of 100 and a standard deviation of 15 is called an intelligence quotient (IQ) or **deviation IQ.** A deviation IQ is a standard score that provides an index of general mental ability based on the deviation between a student's score and the average score for students in a norm group of the same age. Other tests use a similar quotient score. For example, some achievement tests use an achievement quotient (AQ), and certain developmental tests rely on a developmental quotient (DQ).

The basis for interpreting standard scores, including those with a mean of 100 and a standard deviation of 15, is the normal distribution or bell-shaped curve. This distribution is depicted in Figure 4–2 (p. 101). In a normal distribution, most scores fall into the average range, which is within 15 points of the mean, or between 85 and 115 (100 − 15 = 85 and 100 + 15 = 115). More specifically, about 68% of all scores in a normal distribution occur between 1 SD below the mean (85) and 1 SD above the mean (115). Relatively few scores (about 16%) rise above 1 SD (above 115) or below 1 SD (below 85). The following examples describe the process for interpreting standard scores with a mean of 100 and a standard deviation of 115, using this bell-shaped distribution pattern.

Jeffrey received a standard score (in this case a deviation IQ) of 95 on an intelligence test. This placed Jeffrey's score in the average range (about the middle of the bell-shaped curve) of intellectual ability compared to other students.

Angelo received a standard score of 105 on an intelligence test. This placed Angelo's score in the average range (about the middle of the bell-shaped curve) of intellectual ability compared to other students.

Tom received a standard score of 120 on an achievement test. This placed Tom's score in the above-average range of academic achievement.

Bob received a standard score of 80 on an achievement test. This positioned Bob's score in the below-average range of academic achievement.

Standard scores between 115 and 130 are above-average scores because they are 1 SD above the mean (100 + 15 = 115). Likewise, standard scores between 70 and 85 represent below-average scores because they are 1 SD below the mean (100 − 15 = 85).

Sharian received a standard score of 135 on a test of creativity. This indicates that Sharian scored in the significantly above-average range (at the positive end of the bell-shaped curve) in creative ability.

Nancy received a standard score of 65 on an intelligence test. This score indicated that she performed in the significantly below-average range (at the negative end of the bell-shaped curve) in intellectual ability.

Standard scores of 130 or higher are in the significantly above-average range because they are 2 SD above the mean (100 + 30 = 130). In contrast, standard scores of 70 or below fall into the significantly below average range because they are 2 SD below the mean (100 − 30 = 70).

Although the standard scores with a mean of 100 and a standard deviation of 15 are the most common standard scores, other valuable and widely used standard scores exist as well, such as z-scores, t-scores, stanines, and normal curve equivalents.

z-scores and t-scores

A **z-score** is a standard score with a mean of 0 and a standard deviation of 1. A z-score of 0 is average, whereas a z-score of +1 is 1 SD above the mean or above average. Likewise, a z-score of –1 is 1 SD below the mean or below average. Unfortunately, z-scores employ negative numbers, making them difficult to understand and communicate. Although researchers frequently use z-scores, they rarely appear in other situations.

Similar to a z-score without the negative numbers, a **t-score** is a standard score with a mean of 50 and a standard deviation of 10. A t-score of 50 is average, whereas a t-score of 40 is 1 SD below the mean or below average, and a t-score of 60 is 1 SD above the mean or above average. Because t-scores do not use negative numbers, interpreting them is not as difficult as interpreting z-scores. A t-score of 50 represents the performance of a typical or average child. A score of 40 indicates that the student performed at a level below approximately 84% of the students in the norm group based on interpreting the score in relation to the bell-shaped curve. A score of 60 suggests superior performance and indicates a score better than approximately 84% of the students in the corresponding norm group. Whereas z-scores rarely appear except in research, subtests on intelligence and achievement tests often use t-scores as the unit of measure.

Stanines

A **stanine** is a standard score with a mean of 5, a standard deviation of 2, and a range of 1 to 9. Psychologists originally developed stanines during World War II for use with mental ability tests. The psychologists needed a one-digit test score to fit a computer punch card with limited space. Therefore they set up a scale with a top score of 9. Because they use a scale of 1 to 9 and average scores occur around the mean of 5, stanines are convenient for communicating test results, especially with nonprofessionals. Stanines above 1 SD from the mean (5 + 2 = 7) fall in the above-average range, and stanines below 1 SD (5 – 2 = 3) fall in the below-average range.

Normal Curve Equivalents

A **normal curve equivalent** (NCE) is a statistically transformed standard score that fits a normal curve of equal units. Created by a research corporation for use in the U.S. Office of Education, the developers initially designed NCEs for researchers engaged in government-funded projects (Lyman, 1991). Since NCEs were originally developed, however, test authors have adopted them for use with numerous standardized tests, especially tests of academic achievement. Statistical experts recommend NCEs for use only with large and representative sample groups. In these situations, test developers transform raw scores into NCEs to correct for small measurement errors in a test. Like all standard scores, NCEs are expressed with a mean and a standard deviation. NCEs have a mean equal to 50 and a standard deviation equal to 21.06. Although a standard deviation of 21.06 appears unusual, it has the advantage of arranging the normal curve into 100 equal units beginning with 1 and ending with 99. Thus NCE values within 21.06 points of 50 (50 ± 21.06, or 71.06 to

28.94) represent average scores. Scores of 28.94 and lower fall more than 1 SD from the mean of 50 and indicate below-average test performance. Scores of 71.06 and higher are more than 1 SD from the mean and represent above-average values.

Advantages of Standard Scores

All of the aforementioned standard scores, except for the NCEs, maintain their original position of standing relative to the distribution of scores when transformed. This desirable statistical quality allows more accurate comparison of test scores across students on the same test and with students on different tests. This characteristic of accuracy allows the reporting of scores across various age and grade levels with less chance for misinterpretation than with other norm-referenced scores.

Disadvantages of Standard Scores

Standard scores are more difficult to interpret than some of the other available norm-referenced scores, especially percentiles. Difficulties with interpretation occur because grasping the precise meaning of standard scores requires application of some basic statistical concepts, such as the normal curve. This causes obstacles in the use of standard scores in communicating test results to others, especially with parents and students.

The use of standard scores from different tests with differing standard deviations can also cause interpretation problems. For example, a standard score of 70 on a test with a mean of 100 and a standard deviation of 15 is 2 SD below the mean $(100 - 30 = 70)$. This score is not directly comparable to a score of 70 on a test with a mean of 100 and a standard deviation of 16. The comparable score on the test with a standard deviation of 16 is 68 $(100 - 32 = 68)$. Care must be taken in the use of standard scores to avoid this type of misinterpretation, particularly when classifying students on the basis of test scores and communicating results with others.

Relationship Among Percentiles and Standard Scores

The normal curve provides the statistical basis for both percentiles and standard scores. An illustration of the relationship among these scores and the normal, bell-shaped curve appears in Figure 4–2.

☑ Comprehension Checklist

Age and grade scores are widely used because they are practical, easy to interpret, and suitable for communication with others, especially parents. Unfortunately, experts caution against their continued use because misinterpretation occurs so frequently. For this reason, test authors routinely omit such scores from new tests and from revisions of older tests. Test users should also begin to report other scores whenever possible. The exception to this rule remains in the use of developmental age scores for describing the performance of infants and young children. Fortunately, more acceptable norm-referenced scores exist as replacements for age scores.

Figure 4–2 Relationship Among Scores and the Normal Curve

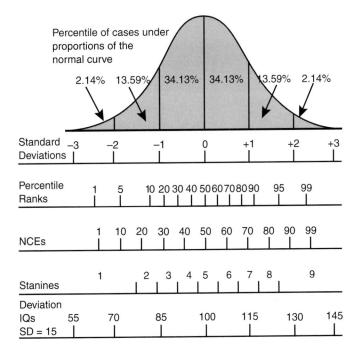

Percentile of cases under proportions of the normal curve

2.14% 13.59% 34.13% 34.13% 13.59% 2.14%

Standard Deviations   −3   −2   −1   0   +1   +2   +3

Percentile Ranks   1   5   10 20 30 40 50 60 70 80 90   95   99

NCEs   1   10   20   30   40   50   60   70   80   90   99

Stanines   1   2   3   4   5   6   7   8   9

Deviation IQs 55   70   85   100   115   130   145
SD = 15

Most experts agree that percentiles are probably the best all-around norm-referenced score for general use because of the many advantages and few limitations. Percentile scores indicate relative rank by comparing student performance to students in a corresponding norm group.

The most accurate of all the norm-referenced scores are the standard scores. Standard scores allow comparison of results across different tests, and this facilitates the process of assessment in special education, especially the difficult step of identifying and placing students with special needs. In fact, many aspects of assessment in special education, including the identification and placement process, prescribe the use of standard scores to provide objective information for making educational decisions.

Principles of Using Test Scores

Lyman (1991) described some of the most important **principles of using test scores.** These practical suggestions for using test scores accurately and effectively, with appropriate caution to avoid errors, appear in summary form in Table 4–3.

Know the Score

Always make sure that you know what kind of score you are using: a standard score, a raw score, a percentile, or something else. Misunderstanding results from confusing similar scores, such as percentile and percent correct. At times you have no choice in what score to use. In this case be aware of any limitations of the score. At other times

Table 4–3   Principle of Using Test Scores

- Know the score.
- Know the norms.
- Consider all available information.
- Use caution.
- Communicate effectively.
- Use a testing specialist.

---

choices among scores may be available. Knowing the score and what it means assists in making the best choice in each situation.

Know the Norms

Always make sure of the norms for the tests you are using. Some of the norms for tests in wide use in special education are inadequate. Other tests in wide use do not have norms at all. The norm sample must be sound and must represent the tested student; otherwise, the norms are not valid. If these conditions are not met, the resulting score is not appropriate.

Consider All Available Information

Consider all available information when interpreting test results, not just the test score. A test score reported in isolation has little meaning. Always report the name of the test and the date of testing along with the test score. Consider all available information related to the test score, even if it is not derived from a test. This may include, but is not limited to, the purpose of testing, the setting for the testing, and the response of the student to the test.

Use Caution

Test scores suggest the ability level of the student; they do not prove ability. Use test scores with caution, keeping their limitations in mind at all times. Careful, cautious use of test scores avoids problems and protects the sensitive egos of students who receive low scores.

Communicate Effectively

Give all necessary information and interpret the score in a practical, understandable manner. Because many, although not all, students with disabilities frequently score low on tests, use test scores carefully in positive ways rather than in ways that contribute to poor self-concept and feelings of failure.

Use a Testing Specialist

Interpreting complicated test scores requires specialized knowledge and skills. Most school systems have testing specialists who should be available to those who would like assistance. If you are not sure about the meaning of a particular score, ask for help from a testing specialist.

☑ Comprehension Checklist

The principles of using test scores serve as guidelines for their appropriate use. Adhering to the principles helps prevent mistakes in scoring and assists in the difficult task of staying up to date with the latest changes in test scores and test scoring procedures. Additional procedures for scoring tests appear in later chapters, including Chapter 6, which provides a checklist for evaluators to use in assessing their proficiency in conducting evaluations and scoring tests.

Summary

Test scores play a central role in assessment. Defined as the numerical result of testing, all tests provide scores. As a teacher in special education, you will encounter many different kinds of scores. Criterion-referenced scores function as a key ingredient of informal assessment in the special education classroom and in other instructional settings. Norm-referenced scores serve as a principal component of more formal assessment, especially testing for the purpose of classifying and placing students with special needs.

Although scores perform the essential function of describing the performance of students objectively, many pitfalls exist in scoring, and some aspects of the process confuse even the experts. The pitfalls include misuse of test scores, misinterpretation of test results, and misunderstanding of the meaning of scores. Fortunately, the standards for scoring and the principles of using test scores serve as a guide to avoid these hazards. By following these standards and principles, teachers ensure accuracy and fairness in the test scoring aspects of assessment in special education.

Chapter Review and Application

Multiple Choice

Directions: Read each item carefully. In the blank beside each item, write the letter of the best response. Each item contains only one best answer. After answering all of the items, check your answers with the answer key in the back of the book.

_____ 1. A percent correct score of 90% means which of the following?
  a. The student correctly answered 90% of the questions.
  b. The student correctly answered 10% of the questions.
  c. The score ranks in the top 10% in comparison with score in the norm group.
  d. The score ranks in the top 90% in comparison with scores in the norm group.

_____ 2. A percentile rank score of 90 means which of the following?
  a. The student correctly answered 90% of the questions.
  b. The student correctly answered 10% of the questions.
  c. The score ranks in the top 10% in comparison with scores in the norm group.
  d. The score ranks in the top 90% in comparison with scores in the norm group.

_____ **3.** Which score has a range of 1–99?
  a. Standard score
  b. Percentile
  c. Stanine
  d. Normal curve equivalent
_____ **4.** A score of 75 on a standardized test with a mean of 100 and a standard deviation of 15 falls into what range?
  a. Above-average
  b. Average
  c. Below-average
  d. Significantly below-average
_____ **5.** This score has a range of 1 to 9.
  a. Standard score
  b. Percentile
  c. Stanine
  d. Normal curve equivalent
_____ **6.** This standard score has a standard deviation of 21.06.
  a. Standard score
  b. Percentile
  c. Stanine
  d. Normal curve equivalent
_____ **7.** Norm-referenced scoring interprets student performance by comparing an individual score with what?
  a. The average score of corresponding students in a norm sample group.
  b. To a functional level of performance.
  c. The scores of the other students in the class.
_____ **8.** Criterion-referenced scoring interprets student performance by comparing an individual score with which of these?
  a. The average score of corresponding students in a norm sample group.
  b. To a functional level of performance.
  c. The scores of the other students in the class.

Short Answers

Directions: Review your understanding of the material in this chapter by answering the following short answer items. After you have responded to each item, compare your responses to the sample answers. Your responses should contain information that is similar to but not exactly the same as the information in the sample answers.

1. Describe the meaning of raw scores and transformed scores.
2. A ninth-grade student received a grade-equivalent score of second grade on a standardized reading test. What arguments might be made for and against using this score to interpret this student's performance?
3. Consider the following test score result: Shemika, a seventh grader, received a grade-level score of third grade on a standardized reading test. The most accurate interpretation of this score is that Shemika received a score of third grade on the seventh-grade reading test. Unfortunately, most professionals and parents inaccurately interpret this score to mean that Shemika is reading on the third-grade level. Why is the first interpretation accurate but the second is not?

4. Explain the following statements:
   a. Grade-equivalent scores provide unequal units that are unpredictable.
   b. Percentile scores provide systematically unequal units.
   c. Standard scores provide approximately equal units.
5. Assuming that all of the following scores were obtained from the same norm group, which score represents the highest performance? Which score represents the lowest performance?
   a. Percentile score = 35
   b. NCE score = 35
   c. Standard score = 65
   d. Stanine = 4
6. What is the main advantage of reporting test performance using norm-referenced scoring?
7. What is the main advantage of reporting test performance using criterion-referenced scoring?
8. Suppose you are the director of testing for a school district and you are planning a one-day workshop on test scores and their meaning for special education teachers. What topics would you include, and which would you emphasize?
9. The chapter discussed several types of test scores. Which criterion-referenced and norm-referenced scores do you prefer to use? Why?
10. A child in the sixth grade received a percentile score of 25 on a standardized reading test. How would you interpret this score?
11. Lake View School uses an average grade-equivalent score from a standardized achievement test to place transfer students in a grade. For example, students with grade equivalents of 5 are placed in the fifth grade, regardless of their age or previous school placement. List the advantages and limitations of this practice.

References

American Psychological Association. (1985). *Standards for Educational and Psychological Testing*. Washington, DC: Author.

Anastasi, A. (1988). *Psychological Testing* (6th ed.). New York: MacMillan.

Brown, F. G. (1980). *Guidelines for Test Use: A Commentary on the Standards for Educational and Psychological Tests*. Ames, IA: National Council on Measurement in Education.

Hoy, C., & Gregg, N. (1994). *Assessment: The Special Educator's Role*. Pacific Grove, CA: Brooks/Cole.

Kaufman, A. S., & Kaufman, N. L. (1993). *Kaufman Survey of Early Learning and Academic Skills*. Circle Pines, MN: American Guidance Service.

Linn, R. L., & Gronlund, N. E. (1995). *Measurement and Assessment in Teaching* (7th ed.). Upper Saddle River, NJ: Merrill/Prentice Hall.

Lyman, H. B. (1991). *Test Scores and What They Mean* (5th ed.). Englewood Cliffs, NJ: Prentice Hall.

McLoughlin, J. A., & Lewis, R. B. (1994). *Assessing Special Students* (4th ed.). New York: Merrill/Macmillan.

Sattler, J. M. (1992). *Assessment of Children* (3d ed.). San Diego: Author.

Wechsler, D. (1992). *Wechsler Individual Achievement Test*. San Antonio, TX: Psychological Corporation.

CHAPTER 5

Selecting and Evaluating
Assessment Instruments

Overview

One of the necessary competencies in the knowledge base of assessing children with special needs is the ability to locate, select, and evaluate assessment instruments. In this chapter you have the opportunity to develop your skills in this area. The chapter focuses on finding information about particular tests and selecting the right test from the range of available options.

As you investigate the process of selecting and evaluating assessments, you will discover that whether a particular test is appropriate depends on many factors, including technical adequacy—a major factor—and the need to fulfill the purpose for testing and to respond directly to meeting the individual and often unique needs of the student. Because high-quality tools with good technical characteristics produce the best possible assessment results, the quality of the chosen instruments often determines the value of the results. For this reason, you will investigate specific criteria for judging the quality of tests.

Objectives

After reading this chapter, you will be prepared to do the following:

- Explain the decision model for locating, selecting, and evaluating assessment instruments.
- Understand the wide range and variety of assessment decisions made by special educators.
- Determine the information needed to make the best possible assessment decision.
- Identify what information is already available.
- Identify what additional information is needed.
- Use the sources of test information to locate available assessment instruments.
- Use the assessment analysis checklist to evaluate available instruments.
- Use the assessment instrument review form to appraise various instruments.

The Decision Model

A decision model developed by Drummond (1996) illustrates the processes and procedures for locating, selecting, and evaluating assessment instruments. Focus 5–1 provides a summary of the questions in the decision model. The questions are arranged to show the sequential steps in the model, beginning with identification of the assessment decision. An explanation of each step in the model follows.

Assessment Decisions

Special education teachers make a wide range and variety of assessment decisions regarding the education of students with special needs, ranging from initial referral decisions to daily instructional decisions. For example, when special educators serve as members of child-study teams and student staffing committees, they help make placement decisions. In contrast, when special educators assess the strengths and weaknesses of students with reading disabilities, they use the evaluation results to help design reading remediation programs. Likewise, when teachers use spelling and math quizzes to help them prepare the lesson for the next day, they are making instructional decisions. Teachers are also called upon to make many educational progress decisions based on classroom assessment data.

Special education teachers also make important assessment decisions when they help develop Individual Education Plans (IEPs), Individual Transition Plans (ITPs), and Individual Family Service Plans. IEPs are planning documents that define the elements of an appropriate education for each individual student with a disability. ITPs are planning documents for students who will soon graduate from school and enter the world of work. Individual Family Service Plans are for infants and toddlers and their families. When teachers help develop IEPs, ITPs, and Individual Family Service Plans, they make vital educational planning decisions that affect the quality of the lives of children with special needs.

These are just a few examples of the many kinds of assessment decisions and judgments that teachers make. Good decisions emerge from information. The key

FOCUS 5–1

The Decision Model

1. What assessment decisions have to be made?
2. What information is needed to make the best decisions?
3. What information is already available?
4. What assessment methods and instruments will provide the needed information?
5. How should appropriate instruments be located?
6. What criteria should be used in selecting and evaluating assessment instruments?

is to determine as clearly as possible the kind of assessment decision that must be made before proceeding to the next step.

Required Assessment Information

The second step in the decision-making model involves specifying the required assessment information. This ensures that enough data are provided to make the best possible decision and to avoid unnecessary assessment. For example, most placement and staffing decisions require explicit assessment information. If a student is being tested for a learning disability, then school district procedures define the tests that must be given and the way in which those test results are used to make the eligibility decision. In other situations, the type of information needed is not mandated. For example, the assessment information needed to place a student in a work-study job in the community includes the student's work experience, job interests, and work aptitudes. Data and information about the student's educational achievement and interests, as well as job openings and appropriate job placement sites, are other dimensions that might be relevant to the placement decision.

Assessment Information Available

The third step is to identify what needed information is already available. In initial referral situations there are specific activities that must be completed and documented. These include observing the student, attempting educational interventions to help resolve the problem, and meeting with the parents. Some of these assessments may have already occurred prior to the referral. If so, this information should be used to avoid replicating assessments. In most school settings, each student has a cumulative folder that contains a social and an educational history, test results, attendance records, health information, and miscellaneous records, which can be very helpful in the decision-making process. However, when students are being placed, certain evaluations must be conducted regardless of the amount of prior information. Unfortunately, this sometimes leads to overtesting, especially with students who have special needs. For example, some students with disabilities have been tested so many times with individually administered, standardized achievement tests that, by the time they reach high school, they may resist or even refuse further testing.

Methods and Instruments to Obtain
Needed Assessment Information

After identifying the type of information that is needed and the information that is already available, the next step is to determine the methods and instruments for obtaining additional data. For example, if additional information is needed to make curricular and instructional decisions for students in a new class, then testing all of the new students with classroom-based instruments might be appropriate. If the goal is to staff a student into another program, then individual testing with formal standardized instruments may be necessary. If assessment information is needed to

design a behavior-management program for a child with aggressive, acting-out behavior, then the teacher may need to obtain a baseline of the inappropriate behavior. In other words, the particular assessment methods and instruments depend
on the purpose for conducting the assessment and the needs of the child.

Locating Appropriate Assessment Instruments

Thousands of tests are available for purchase from test publishers. Many more are
developed locally, statewide, or for specific projects. Although no single source exists
for all instruments, several popular and widely used sources for locating tests exist.

Tests in Print

One of the best sources for locating tests is *Tests in Print* (4th ed.) (Murphy, Conoley,
& Impara, 1994). This reference book, often referred to as *TIP-IV*, is available in
most colleges, universities, and large public libraries and lists more than 3,000 instruments available from commercial publishers. Commercial tests are those available for purchase through a test publisher. *TIP-IV* is revised periodically, and each
new edition replaces the earlier one by adding new tests and taking out tests that
are no longer in print.

Tests

The reference book titled *Tests: A Comprehensive Reference for Assessments in Psychology, Education, and Business* (Maddox, 1997) is similar to *TIP-IV* in that both are
encyclopedias with information about thousands of testing instruments used in
psychology, education, and business. *Tests* contains information on approximately
2,000 assessment instruments in 89 subcategories. Like *TIP-IV*, *Tests* does not review or evaluate tests; instead, each entry contains a statement of the instrument's
purpose, a brief description of the instrument, scoring procedures, cost, and publisher information.

Noncommercial Tests

Although *TIP-IV* and *Tests* are valuable reference tools, they fail to list the most recently published instruments, and they do not include noncommercial tests. Noncommercial tests are not available for purchase; instead they appear in books and
articles in professional journals. Other noncommercial tests are published locally
by schools, school districts, and state departments of education. Locating noncommercial and unpublished tests can be difficult; however, one of the best sources of
information about unpublished tests is *Tests in Microfiche*. Developed by the Educational Testing Service (ETS), the *Tests in Microfiche* collection includes an index of
unpublished tests and copies of the tests on microfiche. Many university libraries
subscribe to the ETS *Tests in Microfiche* collection. ETS has also begun listing and
describing the tests in this collection on the Internet. Another source of information about unpublished tests is the *Directory of Unpublished Experimental Measures*.
Volume five is the most recently published version of this directory (Goldman &
Mitchell, 1990).

Other Sources

Other major sources of information are the ERIC Clearinghouse on Assessment and Evaluation (ERIC/AE) and the Educational Testing Service (ETS). ERIC/AE is located at Catholic University of America (209 Boyle Hall, Washington, D.C., 20064, telephone (800) 464-3742 and it can also be accessed on the Internet at http:// www.ericae.net/. ERIC/AE provides comprehensive information concerning educational assessment and resources to encourage responsible test use. ETS is the world's largest private nonprofit educational assessment and measurement institution. Founded in 1947 by the American Council on Education, the Carnegie Foundation for the Advancement of Teaching, and the College Entrance Examination Board, ETS participates with many agencies and organizations in developing and implementing assessments for educational purposes. Both ERIC/AE and ETS publish newsletters and other valuable materials. ERIC/AE publications include *Measurement Update,* and the ETS newsletter is called *News on Tests.*

Once a particular test or group of tests has been located, more detailed information is available from several sources. Current textbooks on assessment, available in university libraries, are excellent sources for locating tests and obtaining detailed information about particular tests. Test publishers' catalogues are another good source of information. Lists of publishers appear in reference books such as *TIP-IV* and *Tests.* Most publishers provide 1-800 telephone information numbers. Obtaining a catalogue is usually as simple as calling the 1-800 number and making a request. Most publishers also maintain web sites on the Internet with catalogue information. For example, American Guidance Service, one of the largest and best publishers of tests for students with special needs, provides extensive on-line information at their web site www.ags net.com.

Testing centers in local school systems and measurement centers at many universities are another source of information. These centers usually maintain a collection of current catalogues, and they also have specimen sets for review and checkout. Hands-on examination of the tests themselves, along with a review of the test manuals, provides practical firsthand information about the suitability of particular tests. Test manuals contain descriptions of the purpose of the instrument, directions for administration and scoring, guidelines for interpretation, and information about reliability, validity, and other technical qualities.

Locating Tests on the World Wide Web

Web sites on the Internet are excellent sources for locating, selecting, and evaluating tests. Among the most useful sites are the ERIC Clearinghouse on Assessment and Evaluation (EIRC/AG) (http://www.ericae.net/), the National Center for Research on Evaluation, Standards, and Student Teaching (CRESST) (http://cresst96.cse.ucla.edu/index.htm), and the Buros Institute of Mental Measurements (http:///www.unl.edu. buros/index.html). A description of the information available from the ERIC/AE Test Locator appears in Focus 5–2. CRESST is another excellent source of information on how to locate and evaluate tests. The Buros Institue of Mental Measurements sites includes extensive information about tests and test reviews along with news, articles, and links.

FOCUS 5–2

Assessment Information Available From ERIC/AE

The ERIC/AE Internet site is sponsored by the ERIC Clearinghouse on Assessment and Evaluation. The site features assessment FAQs, a bookstore, a full-text library, and a test locator. The test locator includes the following components:

- The ETS/ERIC Test file (contains records on over 10,000 tests)
- The Test Review Locator
- The Buros/ERIC Test Publisher Locator
- The CEEE/ERIC Test Database (tests commonly used with LEP students)
- The Code of Fair Testing Practices
- Test Selection Tips

This excellent source of information for locating, selecting, and evaluating tests is available on the Internet (http://www.ericae.net/).

Evaluating Assessment Instruments

Catalogues and other materials from test publishers focus on selling tests rather than on critical evaluation by external reviewers. For this reason, it is useful to consider independent sources for external reviews, which may be found in the *Mental Measurements Yearbooks, Test Critiques,* professional journals, specimen sets, and newsletters. The Council for Exceptional Children has a division, the Council for Educational Diagnostic Services (CEDS), dedicated to testing and assessing children with special needs. CEDS serves professionals engaged in diagnosing and testing children. CEDS publishes *Diagnostique,* a professional journal on testing, and *Communiqué,* a quarterly newsletter, both of which provide helpful information on selecting and evaluating tests for children with special needs. Consulting with teachers and other professional colleagues can also yield valuable information. From among this wide range of resources, the first source to consider for in-depth reviews is the *Mental Measurements Yearbooks.*

Mental Measurements Yearbooks

The *Mental Measurement Yearbooks (MMY)* (Conoley & Impara, 1995), published by the Buros Institute for Mental Measurements, are large reference books that contain thousands of test reviews arranged alphabetically by title. The *MMY* includes timely, consumer-oriented reviews that promote and encourage informed test selection. Most *MMY* entries include descriptive information, two professional reviews of each instrument, and a list of references to relevant literature. The professional reviews contain detailed information about reliability, validity, norms, administration, scoring, and interpretation. Each *MMY* volume has six indexes for locating tests by title, acronym, subject, publisher, author, and score. These indexes help locate specific tests and groups of tests in a particular category. *MMY* is available in most university libraries and many large public libraries. In 1989, *MMY* began publishing the Supplement to the *Mental Measurements Yearbook* (*MMY-S*) (Impara & Conoley, 1997), which provide access to reviews prepared since the previous *MMY* edition.

Test Critiques

Test Critiques (Keyser & Sweetland, 1994) are similar in content and style to the *Mental Measurements Yearbooks*. Like *MMY, Test Critiques* provides in-depth reviews of the most frequently used psychological, educational, and business-related tests. Each volume contains a list of all reviewed tests and cumulative indexes organized by title, publisher, author, and subject.

Practical Criteria for Test Selection and Evaluation

Special educators should consider several criteria when selecting and evaluating assessment tools. Matching the assessment to student needs is a primary consideration, but evaluators should weigh other factors as well, including the age range of the instrument, test content, and assessment features. The ultimate goal is to choose an instrument or procedure that provides valid and practical assessment information. Two instruments designed to assist in test selection and evaluation appear in Figure 5–1. The Assessment Analysis Checklist is an informal checklist of key factors that special educators should consider in the selection process. The Assessment Instrument Review Form is a more formal, comprehensive guide for reviewers.

Assessment Analysis Checklist

The Assessment Analysis Checklist in Figure 5–1 is an informal guide for reviewing the adequacy of new or existing assessment instruments. Scoring the checklist involves assigning a *yes* or *no* mark to each item. The form contains space to include comments and remarks.

Assessment Instrument Review Form

The Assessment Instrument Review Form: A Guide for Reviewers that appears in Figure 5–2 was derived from an evaluation and assessment training manual developed by Graham (1992). The form lists the elements that should be considered in conducting formal, comprehensive reviews of tests. Prior to completing the form, reviewers should have a specimen set of the test to be reviewed that contains all the materials, including the manual. Completing the form usually takes about 30–45 minutes.

Figure 5–1   Assessment Analysis Checklist

Test Name: _____

	Yes	No
1. Does the instrument match student needs in design and implementation?	_____	_____
2. Is the age range appropriate?	_____	_____
3. Does the content match the student's curriculum?	_____	_____
4. Does the instrument provide clear administration instructions?	_____	_____
5. Does the instrument include precise scoring procedures?	_____	_____
6. Does the instrument include specific instructions for interpreting results?	_____	_____
7. Does the instrument include a curriculum or activity guide?	_____	_____
8. Does the instrument exhibit adequate technical qualities?	_____	_____

Additional observations regarding the suitability of the instrument:

_____

_____

_____

_____

Figure 5–2   Assessment Instrument Review Form: A Guide for Reviewers

Name of Instrument _____

Author(s) _____

Date of Publication _____   Publisher _____

1. List the subtests (e.g., learning areas) addressed.

   _____

   _____

2. Describe the age range. _____

3. State the purpose. _____

   _____

4. Describe the examiner qualifications. _____

   _____

   _____

Figure 5–2 *(continued)*

5. List the available scores. _____

   _____

   _____

6. Does the instrument display adequate technical qualities (i.e., validity, reliability, norms, and other research)?

   _____

   _____

7. Is this the instrument suitable (or can it be adapted) for students with limited English proficiency? yes _____ no _____

   Comments:_____

   _____

8. Are the administration procedures well designed and easy to follow?

   _____

   _____

9. What is the approximate administration and scoring time? _____

   _____

10. Is the instrument appropriate for use with children who have disabilities?

    _____

    _____

11. Can the instrument be adapted for use with children who have special needs?

    _____

    _____

12. Are the scoring procedures well designed and easy to follow?

    _____

    _____

13. What are the strengths of the instrument? _____

    _____

    _____

14. Does the instrument display any weaknesses? _____

    _____

    _____

15. Additional comments, information, and observations: _____

    _____

    _____

Summary

Teachers of students with special needs should know how to locate, select, and evaluate assessment instruments. Although no single source can list or describe all instruments that might be useful in specific situations, several databases and reference tools are readily available. Widely used sources for locating tests include *Tests in Print IV, Tests in Microfiche,* and the *Dictionary of Unpublished Experimental Mental Measures.* Sources for evaluating tests include the *Mental Measurements Yearbooks, Test Critiques,* and reviews in professional journals. Other useful sources of tes information include specimen sets, publishers' catalogues, newsletters, the ERIC Clearinghouse on Assessment and Evaluation, textbooks on assessment, and the World Wide Web.

Chapter Review and Application

Multiple Choice

Directions: Read each item carefully. In the blank beside each item, write the letter of the best response. Each item contains only one best answer. Check your answers with the answer key at the back of the book.

_____ 1. What is the first step in Drummond's Decision Model?
   a. What criteria should be used in selecting and evaluating assessment instruments?
   b. How should appropriate instruments be located?
   c. What information is needed to make the best decisions?
   d. What assessment decisions have to be made?

_____ 2. What is the last step in Drummond's Decision Model?
   a. What criteria should be used in selecting and evaluating assessment instruments?
   b. How should appropriate instruments be located?
   c. What information is needed to make the best decisions?
   d. What assessment decisions have to be made?

_____ 3. Which acronym describes a planning document for teenagers with special needs who are nearing graduation?
   a. MMY
   b. IEP
   c. ITP
   d. TIP-IV

_____ 4. Which publication includes two professional reviews of each test with timely, consumer-oriented information that promotes and encourages informed test selection?
   a. *Mental Measurements Yearbook*
   b. *Test Critiques*
   c. *Tests in Microfiche*
   d. ERIC Clearinghouse on Assessment and Evaluation

_____ **5.** Locating noncommercial and unpublished tests can be difficult; however, one of the best sources of information about unpublished tests is the following:
   a. *Mental Measurements Yearbook*
   b. *Test Critiques*
   c. *Tests in Microfiche*
   d. ERIC Clearinghouse on Assessment and Evaluation

_____ **6.** Which of the following descriptions best applies to *Tests in Print?*
   a. Includes copies of tests.
   b. Is an encyclopedia of more than 3,000 published tests.
   c. Lists and describes tests on the Internet.
   d. Provides critical reviews of major tests.

_____ **7.** Which of the following sources is available on the World Wide Web?
   a. Standardized tests for children with special needs.
   b. *Diagnostique.*
   c. ERIC/AE Test Locator.
   d. *Test Critiques.*

_____ **8.** The Council for Educational Diagnostic Services (CEDS), a division of the Council for Exceptional Children, publishes _____, a professional journal on testing and evaluation.
   a. *Measurement Update*
   b. *Diagnostique*
   c. *Mental Measurements Yearbook*
   d. *Test Critiques*

Short Answers and Practical Application Activities

Directions: Review your understanding of the material in this chapter by answering the short answer items and by completing the practical application activities that follow. After you have responded to the questions and activities, compare your responses to sample answers at the end of the book. Your responses should contain information that is similar to but not exactly the same as that in the sample answers.

1. How would you locate and select the most recent suitable test in one of your teaching areas?
2. What types of information would you expect to find in each of the following: *Mental Measurements Yearbook, Test Critiques,* a test manual?
3. Obtain the catalogues of two test publishers and read the descriptions of several tests of the same type. What type of information is provided? How adequate is the information? How objective is the presentation of the test?
4. Locate the latest *Mental Measurements Yearbook* and read the reviews of a test in one of your teaching areas. What strengths and weaknesses do the reviewers emphasize? Do the reviewers agree?
5. Use the Assessment Analysis Checklist to conduct an informal review of a test in one of your teaching areas.
6. Use the Assessment Instrument Review Form to conduct an in-depth review of a test in one of your teaching areas (Use a different test from the one you used in part 5).

References

Conoley, J. C., & Impara, J. C. (Eds.). (1995). *The Twelfth Mental Measurements Yearbook*. Lincoln, NE: Buros Institute of Mental Measurements.

Drummond, R. J. (1996). *Appraisal Procedures for Counselors and Helping Professionals* (3d ed). Columbus, OH: Merrill.

Goldman, B. A., & Mitchell, D. F. (1990). *Directory of Unpublished Experimental Measures* (vol. 5). Dubuque, IA: Wm. C. Brown.

Graham, M. A. (1992). *Evaluation and Assessment of Infants and Toddlers: Participant Guide*. Tallahassee, FL: Center for Prevention and Early Intervention Policy, FSU Institute of Science and Public Affairs.

Impara, J. C., & Conoley, J. C. (Eds.). (1997). *Supplement to the Twelfth Mental Measurements Yearbook*. Lincoln, NE: Buros Institute of Mental Measurements.

Keyser, D. J., & Sweetland, R. C. (1994). *Test Critiques*. Austin, TX: Pro-Ed.

Maddox, T. (Ed.). (1997). *Tests: A Comprehensive Reference for Assessments in Psychology, Education, and Business*. Austin, TX: Pro-Ed.

Murphy, L . L., Conoley, J. C., & Impara, J. C. (1994). *Tests in Print* (4th ed.). Lincoln, NE: Buros Institute of Mental Measurements.

CHAPTER 6

Test Administration, Scoring, Interpretation, and Reporting

Overview

All teachers administer and score tests and other evaluations as part of the instructional process. For this reason, teachers must understand the techniques and procedures for accurate test administration, scoring, interpretation, and report writing. This chapter builds on the knowledge and skills you have developed in your study of locating, selecting, and evaluating tests in the previous chapter. In this chapter you explore practical techniques for giving and scoring tests and reporting test results. At the end of the chapter you review several case-study examples of written reports.

Objectives

After reading this chapter, you will be prepared to do the following:

- Understand why we use assessment to document teaching and learning.
- Implement the key elements in preparing for assessment.
- Establish an appropriate assessment environment.
- Respond to students' needs during assessment.
- Provide reasonable accommodations during testing.
- Use appropriate prompts during assessment.
- Include anecdotal assessment information on scoresheets and in written reports.
- Select the best possible assessment tool.
- Prepare written reports.

frequently becomes more pronounced during assessment. To help overcome test anxiety, the evaluator should begin, whenever possible, with known tasks that are easy to complete successfully. This helps a student feel more confident and willing to proceed. Most standardized tests already include a set of relatively easy example items for this purpose. Special educators should also include warm-up tasks as part of curriculum-based assessment.

Session Length

In general, evaluators should avoid assessment sessions longer than 45 minutes to an hour. However, with some students, especially young children, individual sessions may need to be even shorter. To ensure physical comfort and prevent undue fatigue, the evaluator should schedule short breaks into sessions. Lengthy assessments should take place during more than one sitting. Ensuring physical comfort includes attention to factors such as room temperature. Rooms that are too hot or cold may reduce student concentration and motivation. If factors such as temperature affect a student's performance, the assessor should make a notation of the circumstances on the scoresheet and in the assessment report.

Test Accommodations

Students with special needs have the right to and can benefit from reasonable **accommodations in testing,** which are modifications and adjustments in test administration that give students with special needs a better opportunity to demonstrate their knowledge and skills. For children with disabilities, the Individuals with Disabilities Education Act (IDEA) guarantees the right to test accommodations. For children with special needs who elect not to receive or are ineligible for special education services, Section 504 of the Vocational Rehabilitation Act ensures their right to receive reasonable accommodations in testing (Educational Testing Service, 1998a).

Testing accommodations should reflect the particular needs of the individual student. A child with blindness, for example, may request a braille or a cassette version of a test. Other common test accommodations include a reader or a scribe, a sign language interpreter, extra testing time, or adjustable desks for children who use wheelchairs. Test accommodations allow children with disabilities a better opportunity to demonstrate their knowledge and skills, but not all modifications are reasonable or appropriate. The IEP is the document that educators should look to for guidance regarding appropriate modifications for each individual student. Additional information about this topic appears in Chapter 19.

Examples of accommodations that may be provided during standardized testing include those in the following list:

- Enlarged-print test book (14-point).
- Large-block answer sheet.
- Braille test book.
- Reader.
- Sign language or oral interpreter.
- Additional testing time.

- Rest breaks.
- More than one test day.
- Dictionary.
- Calculator.
- Spell-check for essay.
- Word processor for essay.
- Color overlay.
- Magnifier, slate, stylus, visual tec, or other tools used by examinees who are blind or visually impaired.
- Distraction-free testing room.
- Permission to record answers in the test book rather than on the answer sheet.
- Typewriter or computer for examinees who cannot handwrite their essays; examinees who are blind or visually impaired may use a braille typewriter, slate, or stylus to compose their essays.
- Kensington Track Ball.
- HeadMaster Mouse.
- ZOOMTEXT.

These particular accommodations are among those offered to people with disabilities by the Educational Testing Service (1998b). Some of these accommodations are available only for computer-based tests.

Practical Considerations in Providing Test Accommodations

When testing children with disabilities, keep the following considerations in mind (Educational Testing Service, 1998a); see Focus 6–2:

- Keep records documenting a child's history of accommodations. These records will help the child obtain such accommodations in higher education and outside of school.
- Because each child is unique, children with the same disability may need different accommodations. In other words, accommodations for one student may not work for another student with the same disability. The child's IEP or 504 plan should guide decisions regarding specific accommodations.
- Children should become informed consumers. This means that teachers, parents, and children should become familiar with accommodations, especially those that best help each child in the classroom and while taking various types of tests.
- Students should register early for special versions of standardized tests because it may take time to develop a special test format or modification.
- Students should receive special and individualized guidance prior to taking standardized tests. Guidance will help all children, especially those who tend to experience greater than average test anxiety. Students should understand how to take standardized tests, handle different types of test questions, and pace their efforts.
- Students should practice taking standardized tests well in advance. Experience with practice materials before taking the actual test boosts confidence and reduces anxiety. Students should take practice tests with the same accommodations that they would use during the actual testing.

FOCUS 6-2

Accommodations in Testing

- Document a child's history of accommodations.
- Children with the same disability may need different accommodations.
- Teachers, parents, and children should become familiar with appropriate accommodations
- Students should register early for special versions of standardized tests.
- Students should receive special and individualized guidance prior to taking standardized tests.
- Students should practice taking standardized tests.
- Students should be advised of their options concerning testing accommodations.
- Students should learn test score policies and what their test scores mean.

- Students should be advised of their options concerning testing accommodations. Options include more testing time, longer breaks between sections, and extra time for specific types of materials.
- Students should learn test score policies, what their test scores mean, and why their score reports may be marked "nonstandard administration." Nonstandard administration refers to test administrations that differ so significantly from the usual administration that the test results may not be comparable to those obtained from tests given under regular conditions. As a result, some score reports may contain the notation "nonstandard administration."

☑ Comprehension Checklist

Responding to student needs represents an important practical consideration in assessment. Assessment measures levels of performance and ability, and students, like all people, are affected by how they feel. For this reason, evaluators should respond to a student's personal needs when conducting an assessment and remain sensitive to physical comfort, communication preferences, and anxiety levels. Students with disabilities also need advice regarding testing accommodations that will give them a better opportunity to demonstrate their knowledge and skills. Attention to these practical elements helps to create a positive environment in which students feel as relaxed as possible. When this happens, assessment results accurately reflect actual performance levels and abilities.

Prompting During Assessment

Prompting during assessment refers to the appropriate use of verbal cues, modeling, and physical prompts while administering a test or conducting another type of assessment procedure. Because some tests specifically prohibit use of prompts, and others mandate particular methods of prompting, no absolute guidelines exist concerning prompting during assessment. To find out if a test calls for specific procedures, the evaluator should check the manual for instructions on prompting. If the administration procedures do not prohibit prompting, then evaluators may find the following procedures useful in many situations. However, when evaluators use special prompts, they should clearly note them on the scoresheet and in the assessment report to avoid misinterpretation of the results.

Most tests and assessment procedures specify whether a student can perform a skill independently. However, when a student fails to perform a task, the teacher needs to know the amount of assistance the student needs to accomplish the task. This is why special educators often use prompts to determine a student's need for assistance. Levels of assistance include verbal prompts, modeling, and physical prompts. Special educators often refer to these as the "tell, show, guide" prompting techniques.

Verbal Cues

In most assessment situations, an evaluator administers items by verbally requesting a student to do a task. For example, an evaluator may give a general instruction such as "Complete the math problems on this page in the test booklet." If a student fails to follow the instruction or begins to complete the math problems but stops before finishing, the evaluator usually provides a verbal cue or prompt. The evaluator may say, "Keep working until you have finished all of the problems," "Try to complete each problem," or "Do the best you can." If the student completes the task only after receiving multiple cues, then the evaluator indicates that the student failed to complete the tasks independently but successfully performed them when given verbal assistance in the form of prompting to finish the work.

Modeling

Unfortunately, some students fail to perform certain tasks even when given verbal prompts. When this happens, an evaluator may have to model appropriate task completion. When evaluators model a task, they demonstrate how to complete the task and then have the student imitate the performance.

Physical Prompts

In some assessment situations, especially with young students or students with severe disabilities, the evaluator may need to provide physical prompts to enable task completion. Evaluators should use physical prompts only after unsuccessful attempts with modeling and verbal prompting. Physical prompting usually involves actually guiding a student's hand through a task such as using a computer, completing a manipulative activity (e.g., putting together a puzzle), or performing some other task that requires movement.

☑ Comprehension Checklist

The "tell, show, guide" method gives a student the opportunity to perform a task with additional assistance: by hearing verbal prompts, by seeing an evaluator perform the task, and by feeling what is expected. It helps an evaluator to distinguish the difference between a student's lack of understanding and actual skill deficiency. It also provides important information about the focus of future intervention. For students who fail most tasks, this approach provides a way to identify what a student can do with assistance.

Assessment Proficiency Checklist

Teachers are often called upon to give and score tests and assessments. In order to ensure accurate assessment, teachers need to practice giving and scoring new tests. The **Assessment Proficiency Checklist (APC)** is a helpful tool for validating competence in tests administration and scoring. See Figure 6–1. The APC consists of two parts. Part I measures proficiency in administering tests and assessments. Part II measures proficiency in scoring tests and assessments. Teachers who wish to self-check their administration and scoring skills can use the APC as a self-evaluation tool by completing both parts of the checklist after giving a practice test or assessment to a student. Alternatively, an observer may watch a teacher giving and scoring a practice test. After the testing, the observer completes the APC form and reviews the results with the teacher. The APC is also an excellent tool for use in in-service and pre-service training activities that involve learning how to administer and score tests.

Scoring involves marking the checklist with a *yes*, a *no*, or *NA* (not applicable) as appropriate. Dividing the total number of items marked *yes* by the total number of items marked *yes* or *no* produces a percent correct score for each part of the checklist, which also includes space for adding relevant notes and comments.

Providing Anecdotal Assessment Information

Even the most thorough assessment tool does not always ask the "right" questions or provide space for additional comments. **Anecdotal assessment information** includes notes, comments, and other information about student needs, behaviors, and test performance that an evaluator adds to scoresheets or includes in written reports. Deciding to provide additional information involves identifying important facts that someone not familiar with a student should know, for example: a student who has a hearing aid but does not like to wear it even though it improves the ability to follow directions; a student who performs better for men than women; a student more willing to do a task when asked to do it, rather than when told to do it; a student who becomes red in the face prior to a seizure; a student who responds best when reinforced with extra time with the teacher or time with a radio.

Maladaptive Behavior

For some students the most important additional information concerns behavior such as noncompliance, aggression, withdrawal, or the need for special reinforcement during assessment. In cases involving severe behavior problems, the anecdotal information should concern the specific problem. Regardless of the severity of the behavior, however, most teachers find that additional information is almost always helpful. For example, with a student who has been on a behavior program for several months, an evaluator may decide to attach the resulting program data. This assists others who may work with this student in the future by providing information for developing the best possible intervention plan.

Figure 6–1   Assessment Proficiency Checklist

Student's Name _____   Date _____

Evaluator's Name _____   Location _____

Observer's Name _____

Part I: Administration Proficiency

Item	Score		
The evaluator:	Yes	No	NA
1. Reviewed prior assessment results and student needs prior to testing.			
2. Prepared a suitable location with necessary materials and equipment.			
3. Established rapport prior to assessment.			
4. Explained the purpose of assessment in an appropriate manner.			
5. Maintained student attention during the assessment.			
6. Used appropriate prompting procedures.			
7. Repeated or demonstrated items as appropriate.			
8. Administered items in correct order and gave all items.			
9. Provided appropriate feedback to student responses to the items.			
10. Properly managed inappropriate behavior.			
11. Ended the assessment positively with appropriate praise.			

Notes and Comments:

Part II: Scoring Proficiency

Item	Score		
The evaluator:	Yes	No	NA
1. Completed the cover sheet correctly (including the chronological age).			
2. Established accurate basal levels.			
3. Established accurate ceiling levels.			
4. Included appropriate notes about student responses to particular items.			
5. Calculated accurate raw scores.			
6. Calculated and recorded accurate transformed scores.			
7. Correctly completed the scoring profile.			

Notes and Comments:

Part 1: Administration Proficiency Score
Number of "Yes" Items _____   Number of "No" Items _____   Percent Correct Score _____

Part 2: Scoring Proficiency Score
Number of "Yes" Items _____   Number of "No" Items _____   Percent Correct Score _____

_____   _____
Signature of observer   Signature of evaluator

The Importance of Accuracy

When evaluators include additional information, they must avoid opinions or subjective impressions. For example, if a student refuses to follow instructions, an evaluator should ensure this behavior is typical in other settings before including statements about noncompliance as anecdotal information. If an evaluator includes incorrect information that becomes part of a permanent record, it may unfairly limit opportunities for that student in the future. Therefore, evaluators must exercise caution to ensure the accuracy of all assessment information.

☑ Comprehension Checklist

Providing anecdotal assessment information is an important practical aspect of assessment. Evaluators can include additional data in the form of written notes about particular student needs or, in cases involving maladaptive behavior, in the form of results from behavior-management programs.

Report Writing

Not only must special educators read, interpret, and apply reports by psychologists, diagnosticians, and other professionals, but they also are called on to write assessment reports themselves. The content and format of written reports depend on who will receive the report and the reasons for assessment. Most written reports, however, contain the following components:

- Identifying information.
  Student's name, address, date of birth, chronological age, and gender.
  Evaluator's name.
  Date or dates of evaluation.
  Location of evaluation.
- Background information.
  Reason for the assessment.
  Relevant educational, family, social, and medical histories.
  Observation of the student's behavior during the evaluation, including physical appearance, general behavior, responses to the testing session, specific behavior (e.g., activity level, communication style, unusual conduct).
- Summary of the test score results.
  Tests administered.
  Total and subtest scores.
  Standard error of measurement for the scores (if available).
  Purpose of the test.
  Means and standard deviations of the scores.
- Discussion and interpretation of results.
  Description of student performance in relevant areas and interpretation of student strengths, weaknesses, and gaps in performance overall and in each area assessed.

- Recommendations.

  Responses to referral questions, placement suggestions, and suggestions for intervention, including instructional, material, and equipment considerations.

  This content outline is a guide rather than a fixed, inflexible way of preparing a report. Report content depends on a variety of factors, including the student's needs, the writer's preferences, the intended uses of the report, and the nature of the assessment being reported.

Report-Writing Guidelines

In a comprehensive review of report-writing procedures, Sattler (1992) described the following principles. Special educators should use these principles as a guide to preparing written reports and as suggestions about what to look for when they are reading reports written by others.

- Organize assessment findings by detecting common themes through and across procedures, integrating the main findings, and using a theoretical focus.
- Include in the report relevant material and delete potentially damaging material.
- Use all relevant sources of information about the child—including reliable and valid tests results, behavioral observations, individual test responses, interview data, and the case history—in generating hypotheses, formulating interpretations, and arriving at recommendations. Avoid undue generalizations.
- Be definitive in your writing when the findings are clear; be cautious in your writing when the findings are problematic.
- Interpret the meaning and implications of a child's scores, rather than simply citing test names and scores.
- Use percentile ranks whenever possible to describe a child's scores because they will be easily understood by most readers.
- Interpret the implications of subtest or test variability with extreme caution, making use of all available sources of information.
- Refrain from making diagnoses about psychopathology or educational diagnoses solely on the basis of test scores; consider all sources of information.
- Communicate clearly and eliminate unnecessary technical material to enhance readability.
- Attend carefully to grammatical and stylistic points in your writing (Sattler, 1992, pp. 732–46).

Examples of Written Reports

Sample case-study reports of how to describe test performance in narrative form appear in Table 6–1 and Figure 6–2. The first report is from the *Peabody Individual Achievement Test-Revised, Normative Update (PIAT-R/NU)* (Markwardt, 1998). The *PIAT-R* report (Table 6–1) interprets the performance of a second grader with an IQ of 120. Because the *PIAT-R* is a screening test, the report is not as long or detailed as reports from more comprehensive instruments. The second report is a computer-generated case study from the *KeyMath-Revised, Normative Update: A Diagnostic Inventory of Essential Mathematics* (Connolly, 1998). This report (Figure 6–2), generated by the KeyMath-Revised Automated System for Scoring and Interpreting Standardized

Table 6–1   Sample Narrative Report from the *Peabody Individual Achievement Test–Revised*

This section presents a case study of Bill, whose test scores were presented in Figure 3.2 (see Figure 14–1, p. 422) and profiled in Figures 3.3–3.5; Figure 3.3 is reprinted as Figure 14–1(b), 3.4 as Figure 14–1(c), and 3.5 as Figure 14–1(d) on p. 423. Bill is a second-grader, aged 7-9, with an IQ of 120.

Accurate interpretation of *PIAT-R* results depends on many factors specific to the testing situation. Relevant factors include the reasons for testing, the decisions or plans that might be influenced by the results, the educational and psychometric background of the interpreter, and the audience to whom the results are to be communicated. Test results are commonly interpreted in terms of the following questions: How is the individual doing in relation to others at the same grade or age level? Is the individual doing as well as might be expected for his or her ability? What are the areas of strength and weakness?

The profile in Figure 3.3 indicates that Bill is doing better than the average of his age-mates in all areas except spelling—the confidence intervals for his scores other than Spelling are entirely above the reference line drawn at his chronological age level. Because the shaded interval for Spelling nearly overlaps the reference line, it appears that Bill is approximately average for his age in this area. In general, then, when Bill's scores are compared with those of other children his age, it appears that he is doing as well as or better than average.

A different picture emerges when the *PIAT-R* results are compared with Bill's ability as indicated by the reference line for his mental age (Figure 3.3; Figure 14–1(b), p. 423). From this perspective, Bill is doing as well as expected in encyclopedic knowledge—the confidence interval for General Information is above the mental age line. Bill appears to be achieving less than expected for his ability level on all the other areas tested.

The test results point to spelling as Bill's weakest area, since the confidence interval for Spelling is below the other intervals. Further evaluation of Bill's spelling skills is recommended. Evaluation can be performed by the use of diagnostic tests appropriate for Bill's spelling level or through informal analysis of his errors in the Spelling subtest, in the Written Expression story or in other writing compositions.

Bill's attitude toward spelling should be explored to determine whether it is a significant factor in his performance. Moreover, Bill may have a visual or perceptual problem. This possibility is strengthened by the fact that performance on Reading Recognition, which is his next lowest result, is also heavily dependent on visual or perceptual skills. Given Bill's low Reading Recognition score in relation to his ability, it might be appropriate to recommend diagnostic work on his word attack skills. Concern about Bill's word attack skills is further reinforced by his high General Information score. Considered together, the two scores suggest that although Bill probably has a large hearing and speaking vocabulary he may have difficulty identifying words in print.

In terms of strengths, Bill clearly excels at acquiring knowledge—his highest score is on General Information. The level of his general knowledge in comparison with his skills in the other areas suggests that Bill may be better at listening and observing than at reading. In any event, Bill's general knowledge provides a good basis for reinforcing his efforts in school and encouraging him to concentrate further on his studies. Bill's teacher might use his apparent interest in general knowledge when selecting instructional materials to develop his weaker achievement areas. Because his achievement in acquiring general knowledge from sources both inside and outside the school is greater than his achievement in developing curriculum-specific skills such as spelling, it might be appropriate to investigate his general attitude toward school and his study habits.

Bill's scores indicate that he is generally achieving at or above the level of his peers—as might be expected of someone with his better-than-average ability—but that in most areas

Table 6–1   *(continued)*

he is not achieving up to expectation for his ability level. When communicating these findings to Bill, his teachers, and his parents, the test interpreter should encourage further efforts on Bill's part while discouraging the complacency that might arise if Bill were compared only with the average of his age-mates.

Interpreting Written Expression. Interpretation of Bill's results on Written Expression is necessarily more speculative than for the other subtests. As discussed earlier, the psychometric qualities of Written Expression precluded the use of the derived scores and estimates of measurement error that are used with the other subtests. The derived scores available for Written Expression provide fewer levels of differentiation of achievement and, therefore, less precise descriptions of achievement levels. Interpretations of results on this subtest should be viewed as *hypotheses* about the subject rather than as highly accurate judgments or firm conclusions.

Bill's raw score of 28 on Level II, Prompt A (see Figure 3–2, p. 422) converts to a stanine score of 5 when compared with the scores of other second-graders. Thus, he is at the average for his grade level in written expression skills. Given his above-average IQ, Bill may be achieving below expectations in written expression, although it is not possible to determine the probability level for that conclusion.

In comparison with the performance of the Level II standardization sample, Bill's raw score corresponds to a developmental scaled score of 5. This scaled score places him approximately one standard deviation below the mean of the Level II standardization sample.

Any comparisons of Bill's Written Expression stanine with stanines on the other subtests must be made with caution—particularly because the written expression skills of a second-grader are at an early point in development. His average score for his grade on Written Expression and well-above-average score on General Information suggest a real difference in performance. Considering this difference and the earlier discussion of his reading scores, it would appear that Bill has a greater interest and ability in acquiring general knowledge than in the fundamental skills of reading, writing, spelling, and mathematics.

Similarly, Bill's score on Spelling suggests that he has stronger skills in written expression than in spelling. Although on the surface this difference is perplexing, as discussed in Part IV spelling is not considered in the scoring of Level II because the *PIAT-R* has a separate subtest devoted to spelling.

A comparison of Bill's Written Expression stanine score with the other *PIAT-R* stanine scores does not suggest other significant differences, but instead an essentially consistent level of achievement.

Interpreting the optional Written Language composite. Bill's Written Language composite standard score was obtained by following the procedures described in Appendix I. His age-based standard score of 95 indicates an approximately average level of achievement in Written Language. This finding is consistent with Bill's average performance on Spelling and Written Expression, the subtests that make up the Written Language composite.

Bill's standard score on Written Language may be compared directly with his IQ because both scales are age-based and have a mean of 100 and a standard deviation of 15. The discrepancy of 25 standard score points between his IQ of 120 and his Written Language composite score of 95 may be expressed as 1.7 (25/15) standard deviation units. This discrepancy exceeds the guideline of 1.5 standard deviation units established by some states to identify a possible learning disability. Although the discrepancy for Bill slightly exceeds that guideline, users should be cautious in drawing conclusions. Ability-achievement comparisons such as this ignore regression effects present when two measures are not perfectly correlated, and such comparisons introduce unknown effects that occur when scores on tests with different norming samples are compared. Therefore, further study of Bill's results is warranted.

Figure 6–2 Sample Computer-Generated Narrative Report from the *KeyMath Revised/NU: A Diagnostic Inventory of Essential Mathematics*

01/15/1998   *KeyMath Revised/NU*
Name: Bertelli, Brenda   Test Date: 01/05/1998
Age: 9-1   Grade: 4

SCORE NARRATIVE
Age Norms

The *KeyMath-R* is an individually administered test that provides a comprehensive assessment of important mathematics concepts and skills. The test identifies an individual's strengths and weaknesses in three broad areas—Basic Concepts, Operations, and Applications. These areas are composed of 13 subtests or "strands" (e.g., Numeration) which are composed of 43 substrands or domains (e.g., Multi-Digit Numbers).

This computer-generated report assesses Brenda's *KeyMath-R* performance and makes instructional recommendations. It is suggested that you prioritize and select those recommendations that best fit Brenda's needs. For a more comprehensive listing of instructional recommendations tailored for Brenda, see the report entitled "Item Objectives and TAP Resources." In planning her instruction, try to capitalize on Brenda's personal strengths to provide developmental support.

Total Test Performance

The total test mean is 100, and the standard deviation is 15. Brenda's total test standard score was 91. Her performance yielded a percentile rank of 27, meaning that Brenda outperformed 27 percent of her age-level peers on the total test. This level of performance is typically achieved by individuals at age 8-2 (i.e., equals an age equivalent of 8-2). Her achievement on *KeyMath-R* was at the 4th stanine. Collectively, these indicators describe Brenda's overall test performance as average. Brenda recently obtained a standard score of 93 on the DAS GCA Composite. Her actual achievement, based on the Total Test, is lower than the expected achievement score of 95. The percent of the population with the same size of discrepancy or greater is 34.

Area Performance

A mean of 100 and a standard deviation of 15 are also used to analyze an individual's performance in the three broad areas of Basic Concepts, Operations, and Applications. Brenda's performance in each area was compared with the performance achieved by individuals at her age level in the norm group. Her performance in these areas is as follows:

Basic Concepts: This area addresses the knowledge of quantity and space. Brenda achieved a standard score of 88, a percentile rank of 21, and an age equivalent of 7-9. This is below average and suggests a need for remedial instruction.

Operations: This area addresses both written and mental computation. Brenda achieved a standard score of 94, a percentile rank of 34, and an age equivalent of 8-5. This is within the average range, but may reflect some specific content on which remedial instruction will be helpful.

Figure 6–2   *(continued)*

Applications: This area requires the practical use of mathematical knowledge and operational skills. Brenda achieved a standard score of 89, a percentile rank of 23, and an age equivalent of 7-10. This is below average and suggests a need for remedial instruction.

A statistical analysis was completed on the variance present in Brenda's performance among the three areas. Basic Concepts and Operations have a standard score difference of 6 points, which is nonsignificant. Basic Concepts and Applications have a standard score difference of 1 point, which is nonsignificant. Operations and Applications have a standard score difference of 5, which is nonsignificant. The presence of no significant differences is a further indication that Brenda's test performance evidences no major patterns of strengths and weaknesses that should be considered when planning instruction. To be effective, prescriptive instruction will need to focus on strengths and weaknesses that may exist on specific concepts and skills. These become evident through a review of her performance on the different subtests and their respective content.

Subtest Performance

Brenda's performance on each subtest was compared with the performance achieved by individuals at her age level in the norm group. To make that comparison, her performance on each subtest was reported on a scale having a mean of 10 and a standard deviation of 3, and ranging from 1 to 19. Within that range, the scores from 9 to 11 and slightly beyond are considered average. Compared to her peers on subtests, Brenda displays no specific strengths. She displays the following weaknesses relative to the performance of her peers: Rational Numbers, Geometry, Measurement, Time and Money, and Estimation.

Below is a discussion of how Brenda performed on each of the 13 subtests. Instructional recommendations are included primarily for use with individuals who exhibit specific subtest weaknesses.

1. NUMERATION: Brenda's scaled score of 9 and percentile rank of 37 indicate that, in numeration and whole numbers, she is performing at an average level. The content on which Brenda needs to focus is three-digit numbers. Concepts developed with two-digit numbers, including place value, ordering, renaming, and rounding, need to be reinforced here. The place value and renaming concepts are essential to the effective handling of computation involving regrouping. Instruction should involve a variety of manipulative and pictorial models; activities may include base ten blocks, color-coded cubes, chip trading, hundreds charts, money (dollars, dimes, and pennies), and number lines.

2. RATIONAL NUMBERS: Fractions, decimals, and percents are difficult for many subjects. Brenda achieved a scaled score of 8 and a percentile rank of 25 in rational numbers. These scores indicate that her performance is slightly below average. Brenda's current level of functioning involves constructing and labeling fraction and decimal representations. The instructional emphasis for her work on fractions should be placed on part/whole models, with attention first directed to the denominator value and then to the numerator value. You might say, "A shape is folded into four parts of the same size. Three of the four parts are colored red, so three-fourths

Figure 6–2   *(continued)*

of the shape is red." When Brenda can effectively use part/whole models, instruction should progress to part/group models (e.g., two red marbles in a set of five marbles [2/5]; six red marbles in a set of eight marbles [3/4]).

3. GEOMETRY: Brenda's scaled score of 7 and percentile rank of 16 reveal that, in geometry, she is performing below average. Brenda has generally progressed beyond the recognition of common two-dimensional figures and is now into content involving coordinate planes. The use of grids, geoboards, and dot matrices can be particularly helpful in developing and applying concepts involving symmetry, parallel and intersecting line segments, and angles.

4. ADDITION: A scaled score of 9 and percentile rank of 37 indicate that, in addition, Brenda is functioning at an average level. Brenda has general mastery of addition facts and partial mastery of algorithms for whole numbers. Before she can effectively add two- and three-digit numbers with regrouping, she must have mastered the ability to rename numbers. Dimes and pennies are particularly useful in developing this skill (e.g., using different combinations of dimes and pennies to represent the value 42 cents). It is easy to build on such activities by having her record the value in each of two sets of dimes and pennies, and then represent and record their combined value using no more than nine pennies in the total. When Brenda can represent and record the addition algorithm with numbers at this level, it will be easy for her to transfer to the addition of multidigit numbers.

5. SUBTRACTION: Brenda's scaled score of 11 and percentile rank of 83 reveal that, in subtraction, she is functioning at an average level. Brenda has achieved general mastery of the subtraction facts and partial mastery of the subtraction algorithm with whole numbers. Before she can successfully subtract with regrouping, she must establish the ability to rename two- and three-digit numbers. This skill is most easily acquired through activities involving dimes and pennies, base ten blocks, chip trading, and the like. Many individuals find it helpful to begin subtraction by completely renaming the minuend where needed, rather than regrouping during the subtraction process. This allows them to concentrate on one task at a time.

6. MULTIPLICATION: The scaled score of 9 and percentile rank of 37 reveal that, in multiplication, Brenda is functioning at an average level. She needs to work on multiplication models and facts. It may be helpful to have her represent several like sets (e.g., 4 fives) and record them as repeated addition ($5 + 5 + 5 + 5 = 20$) and as multiplication ($4 \times 5 = 20$). Brenda should also learn to associate such facts with arrays (e.g., four rows with five in each). Multiplication facts with zero are difficult for many individuals. If she is having such difficulty, use slips of paper as place holders for sets. When empty, these slips effectively show that four sets of zero cubes equals zero. When Brenda can represent and record such facts, use frequent oral drills to maintain mastery.

7. DIVISION: Brenda's scaled score of 9 and percentile rank of 37 indicate that, in division, she is functioning at an average level. Brenda needs to work on division models and facts. Instruction should include separating amounts into equal-sized groups, evenly distributing amounts into a given number of sets, and recording

Figure 6–2 *(continued)*

these actions with division number sentences. All division facts should be associated with the inverse multiplication facts, because the latter are easier for individuals to recall and represent. When Brenda can represent and record division facts, provide frequent oral drills to maintain mastery.

8. MENTAL COMPUTATION: A scaled score of 10 and percentile rank of 50 reveal that, in mental computation, Brenda is functioning at an average level. Brenda's performance suggests that practice with orally presented mental computation chains would be useful in developing number and fact facility. Begin with relatively easy chains such as "four, plus six, minus eight, equals -?-" and progress to more difficult chains such as "nine, minus four, plus twenty, minus ten, equals -?-." (Pause at each comma for about one second.) Provide practice on such chains on a weekly basis for intense three- or four-minute sessions in a game-like atmosphere. Adjust the content, speed, and number of computations to conform to Brenda's progress.

9. MEASUREMENT: Brenda's scaled score of 7 and percentile rank of 16 indicate that, in measurement, she is performing below average. Brenda has generally moved beyond making simple comparisons and is now using nonstandard units to measure length, weight, area (space covered), and capacity (amount held). Instruction should include all these topics as well as the selection of appropriate units for given measurement tasks (e.g., paper clips rather than pencils as a unit for measuring the length of a comb). Related experiences with weights and a pan balance would be helpful.

10. TIME AND MONEY: In time and money, Brenda achieved a scaled score of 8 and percentile rank of 25, indicating that she is functioning slightly below average. Brenda should work on using the monthly calendar to determine days, dates, and time intervals (e.g., "What day is the 17th?" "What is the date of the fourth Monday?" "What is the date two weeks after the first Friday?"). She should also work on reading a clock and recording the times to the minute. In the area of money, Brenda should work at using different coin combinations to make values up to one dollar and to make change up to 25 cents.

11. ESTIMATION: A scaled score of 8 and percentile rank of 25 indicate that Brenda's ability to estimate is slightly below average. Brenda is still learning to estimate quantities and can benefit from practice using subsets and feedback on prior guesses to improve estimates. She is also beginning to estimate measurements using nonstandard and some standard units. A useful instructional technique is to have her estimate a measurement (e.g., the room is 24 shoe lengths wide) and, after part of the measurement is completed, allow her an opportunity to "refine" the estimate. Such "refinements" might be allowed two or three times per exercise. These efforts will enhance Brenda's ability to make estimates (judgments) and strengthen her measurement skills.

12. INTERPRETING DATA: In interpreting data, Brenda achieved a scaled score of 10 and percentile rank of 50, a performance that is at an average level. Brenda is now ready to make use of charts and tables in practical situations, such as interpreting transportation schedules and simple mileage charts. Instruction should

Figure 6–2   *(continued)*

include the construction and use of one- and two-attribute bar graphs, pictographs employing keys, and line and circle graphs.

13. PROBLEM SOLVING: Brenda's performance on the problem solving subtest yielded a scaled score of 9 and percentile rank of 37, indicating that she is functioning at an average level. Brenda is still working to relate computation with word problems. Practice in determining the "action" in problem situations would be particularly helpful. By identifying the action, she can reliably infer the operation that is required. For example, combining unlike amounts is always done with addition, combining a set of like amounts is most efficiently done with multiplication, separating and comparing amounts is done with subtraction, and separating a large amount into smaller, like amounts is most efficiently done with division.

Brenda can also benefit from practice analyzing word problems to determine key information, extraneous information, and information that is missing but necessary for a problem's solution. Her progress in the development of problem-solving skills will be greatly influenced by the amount of instructional time devoted to such efforts and the diversity of such experiences.

Tests (ASSIST) software program (Rodgers, 1998), shows the way in which a microcomputer software program describes the performance of a student. The *KeyMath-Revised,* a single-subject diagnostic test, also provides sufficient information for making detailed recommendations, including specific learning activities. However, because the sample report is computer generated, the report fails to include specific observations of the student's behavior during the testing session.

✓ Comprehension Checklist

Special educators are frequently called on to write assessment reports that describe the performance of their students. The particular content and format of written reports depend on who will receive the report and the reasons for writing the report. Most written reports contain the following common elements: identifying information, background information, summary of results, discussion and interpretation of results, and recommendations. The content and format of the report depend on a variety of factors, including the student's needs, the writer's preferences, the intended uses of the report, and the nature of the reported assessment.

Summary

The practical aspects of assessment refer to applied procedures for giving and scoring tests, for conducting other evaluation procedures, and for interpreting, reporting, and using assessment data. These practical considerations are important because accurate administration, scoring, and reporting produce useful assessment data. All special education teachers need to master the practical aspects of testing so that they can administer tests skillfully and interpret the results appropriately.

Because teaching students with disabilities includes measurement and evaluation as key components, the practical aspects of the process are an essential element in the knowledge base of assessment in special education. Not only do special education teachers need to understand the theoretical aspects of testing, but they should also be well trained in the practical elements.

Chapter Review and Application

Multiple Choice

Directions: Read each item carefully. In the blank beside each item, write the letter of the best response. Each item contains only one best answer. Check your answers with the answer key at the end of the book.

_____ 1. Evidence of learning for students with special needs is best documented with _____.
   a. personal teacher observations
   b. student self-evaluation
   c. objective assessment measures
   d. time spent on task

_____ 2. Appropriate preparation for a testing session should include _____.
   a. noting the time of day when the student appears most alert
   b. ensuring that the student has no prior knowledge of when testing will be conducted to avoid test anxiety
   c. remaining unbiased by avoiding information from other teachers about the student

_____ 3. Evaluators are advised to do which of the following prior to testing sessions?
   a. Remain flexible and spontaneous so the student will be unaware that testing is scheduled to occur.
   b. Carefully check and organize test materials.
   c. Allow the student to handle and inspect test materials.
   d. Inform the student of specific test questions.

_____ 4. What is the primary goal when selecting an assessment setting?
   a. Approximating classroom conditions present during group instruction
   b. Choosing an unfamiliar, formal environment to reflect the seriousness of the testing
   c. Providing built-in distractors to measure their influence on the student
   d. Maximizing student comfort

_____ 5. Which statement best describes appropriate consideration of student anxiety during assessment?
   a. Most standardized test instructions do not allow accommodations for student anxiety.
   b. Student anxiety is secondary to maintaining a formal assessment atmosphere.
   c. Most standardized tests include a set of relatively easy example items to help overcome test anxiety.
   d. Test anxiety is usually not a problem with students who have special needs.

_____ 6. Which statement provides the most accurate information about appropriate testing accommodations for students with disabilities?
  a. Children with the same disability all need the same accommodations.
  b. Avoid giving individualized guidance prior to standardized testing.
  c. Become familiar with appropriate accommodations for each student.

_____ 7. Which statement describes appropriate use of prompts during testing?
  a. Standardized testing protocols usually allow for wide-ranging examiner discretion in using prompts.
  b. Examiners need not note the use of special prompts on scoresheets.
  c. Testing manuals usually give specific instructions regarding prompting.

_____ 8. Which list illustrates the suggested order for giving prompts when protocol allows?
  a. Modeling, verbal cues, physical prompts.
  b. Physical prompts, modeling, verbal cues.
  c. Verbal cues, modeling, physical prompts.
  d. Verbal cues, physical prompts, modeling.

_____ 9. What is the most important reason for avoiding examiner opinions and subjective impressions when recording anecdotal information concerning issues of noncompliance during testing?
  a. Others may interpret it as a sign of inadequate examiner skills.
  b. It may unfairly limit future opportunities for the student.
  c. It is unimportant when making placement decisions.
  d. Testing results would seldom be affected by noncompliance.

Short Answers

Directions: Review your understanding of the material in this chapter by answering the following short answer items. After you have responded to each item, compare your responses with the sample answers. Your responses should contain information that is similar to but not exactly the same as the information in the sample answers at the end of the book.

1. Explain why assessment may appear to be just more paperwork, but, in reality, "appearances can be deceiving."
2. Which steps in the process of preparing for assessment seem most important? Why?
3. What test accommodations would you consider for a child with a learning disability? How would these accommodations differ from the accommodations you might provide for a child with another type of disability, such as deafness?
4. What is the value of anecdotal assessment information, especially in cases involving severe behavior problems?
5. What content would you include in a brief written report from a screening test? Why? What content would you include in a comprehensive diagnostic report? Why?
6. Use the guidelines for writing written reports to critique the sample case-study report on Bill that appears in Table 6–1.
7. Review the computer-generated report in Figure 6–2. Evaluate the usefulness of this report. What are its strengths and weaknesses?

CHAPTER 7

Assessing the Intelligence of Children With Special Needs

Overview

Intelligence testing, the complex and sometimes controversial process of measuring the learning ability of students, is an essential part of assessing students with special needs. Most intelligence testing occurs during the initial stage of identifying students with special needs. Assessment teams use intelligence test results, along with other assessment information, to classify and place those students who qualify for special education services.

This chapter helps you to develop knowledge of the content and the processes associated with intelligence testing in special education. We begin by investigating the basic concepts and the critical issues in testing the intelligence of students with special needs. Next we review individually administered intelligence tests, group intelligence tests, specialized tests, and intelligence tests for infants, toddlers, and preschoolers. As we explore each test, we will review the purpose of the instrument, the administration and scoring procedures, the technical characteristics, and the uses of the tool in special education. Finally, we will examine practical guidelines for teachers in the use of intelligence tests. The ultimate goal is to help you acquire an understanding of the various intelligence tests, their meaning, their interpretation, and their use with students who have special needs.

Objectives

After reading this chapter, you will be prepared to do the following:

- Explain the term *intelligence* and apply its various definitions.
- Consider the types of behaviors measured by intelligence tests.
- Explain the uses of intelligence testing in special education.
- Become aware of the current issues in intelligence testing.
- Name and describe the uses of individually administered intelligence tests.
- Name and describe the uses of group intelligence tests.
- Name and describe the uses of specialized intelligence tests.
- Name and describe the uses of intelligence tests for infants, toddlers, and preschoolers.
- Apply the guidelines for teachers in the use of intelligence test results.

Introduction to Intelligence Testing

The following narrative illustrates some of the most frequently asked questions that special education teachers have about intelligence tests.

The school psychologist was asked to describe to teachers the types of intelligence testing services she provided to the school. Because she was asked to focus on intelligence testing of students with special needs, she decided to talk about the intelligence tests used most frequently with exceptional children, including children who are gifted. Her presentation emphasized the questions most frequently asked by teachers. During the meeting, teachers raised many questions and concerns such as these: What are the group tests, and are they useful in special education? What individually administered tests are used most often with children who have special needs, and what purposes do they serve? Are there special tests for very young children and children with severe disabilities? Can teachers use intelligence test results to help plan curricula and to place their students in the most appropriate learning groups? During the presentation, one of the teachers asked the psychologist to tackle a key issue: "Since we know that many students with special needs have non-average intelligence (e.g., gifted, mentally retarded), how sensitive are the intelligence tests to extreme scores at both the high and low ends of the scale?" The psychologist explained that this central question illustrates the most critical aspect of intelligence tests and their interpretations. She indicated that because intelligence tests, like all tests, are less accurate at the extremes, teachers must exercise caution in interpreting scores in the abnormal range.

This chapter answers these important questions and provides other relevant information about intelligence testing with students who have special needs.

Purpose of Intelligence Testing

Most intelligence testing occurs during the classification and placement stage of assessment in special education. During this stage, assessment teams use intelligence test results, along with other measures of student ability and performance, to identify students who qualify for special education services. Despite the widespread use of intelligence tests in special education, the meaning of intelligence and the efficacy of using intelligence tests remains a topic of debate for several reasons. One reason involves the initial (and difficult) task of defining intelligence. Developing tests of intelligence based on a particular definition is an even greater challenge. Finally, the central focus of the debate concerns the role and use of intelligence tests to classify and place students in special education. Although some experts argue for the elimination of intelligence testing, most contend that no valid substitutes for intelligence testing exist at present. Most experts feel that as intelligence testing improves, we should continue to use intelligence test results, along with other valid measurements, to obtain a comprehensive picture of student learning ability and performance.

Defining Intelligence

What is intelligence? Is it the ability to change behavior based upon experience? Is it what intelligence tests measure? Is it a complex theoretical concept that explains certain types of behavior? Is it a score on an IQ test? Is it the measurement of one general trait or the separate measurement of different traits or characteristics? What makes a person intelligent? How should intelligence be measured?

These questions illustrate the difficulties in defining intelligence. Answers to these questions provide valuable insight into the challenge of defining the term and understanding the tests that measure it.

Most experts agree on the general definition of **intelligence** as a trait or construct associated with cognitive or intellectual capacity and directly related to the potential or ability to learn. Intelligence is an abstract quality associated with all types of intellectual processes including abstract thinking, mental reasoning, using sound judgment, and making rational decisions. Intelligence is distinct from other personality characteristics such as affective behavior. In defining intelligence, specialists note that the term represents a concept, not an object. A concept is an idea or theoretical construct developed, in the case of intelligence, to describe a behavior or a set of behaviors. A concept such as intelligence is not a thing or concrete object like a chair that can be seen, touched, or moved. A more sensible approach is to describe intelligence according to what a person does or fails to do rather than describing it according to what a person is (Murphy & Davidshofer, 1988). (See Focus 7–1 for a discussion of multiple inteligences.) From this perspective, a reasonable conclusion is that intelligence consists of a range of behaviors requiring mental ability rather than one single behavior. Furthermore, the purpose of intelligence testing is to measure various levels of intellectual ability within and across individuals. In special education many students manifest below average intelligence and, in some cases, students exhibit extremely low levels of intelligence. For this reason, special education teachers need to be aware of the levels of intelligence of their students and, more importantly, need to understand the instructional implications of intelligence.

Instructional Implications of Intelligence The concept of levels of intelligence suggests that the learning rates and patterns of students with abnormal intelligence are quantitatively and qualitatively different from the learning rates and patterns of students with normal intelligence. Further, students at the same levels of intelligence often display similar learning characteristics. Although intelligence is only one variable in the learning process, teachers use many specialized methods and materials with students who have significantly high or low levels of cognitive ability. For example, students with abnormally low intelligence learn at a slower rate. As a result, teachers use techniques such as overlearning (e.g., repeated practice) and creative repetition to help compensate for the cognitive deficits. Likewise, teachers carefully introduce new tasks only after students have mastered all of the prerequisite skills. Teachers also avoid tasks that are beyond a child's level of mental ability because such tasks quickly become frustrating and often lead to failure for the student and the teacher. In contrast, students with abnormally high levels of intelligence learn at a higher rates than average students. Highly intelligent students also benefit from unique teaching methods and materials. For example, teachers of gifted students use tasks that encourage divergent thinking and creativity. Knowledge of the instructional implications of intelligence helps in understanding the process of assessing the intellectual capacity of children with special needs.

Although psychologists agree about the general meaning of intelligence, a great deal of disagreement occurs concerning more specific definitions of the term. For example, Wechsler and Binet, the two foremost authors of intelligence tests, offer contrasting descriptions of intelligence. According to Wechsler, author of the *Wechsler Scales*

FOCUS 7–1

Assessing Multiple Intelligences

The concept of **multiple intelligences** (Gardner, 1994) refers to different dimensions of intelligence and recognizes that all children have unique cognitive behaviors and cognitive learning styles. Although demand exists for standardized pencil-on-paper tests of multiple intelligences, few, if any, such measures exist. Chen and Gardner (1997) suggest that appropriate assessment of multiple intelligences requires significant departures from traditional testing. For this reason, as experts develop measures of multiple intelligences, alternative forms of assessment will emerge, which will include new instruments, materials, and frameworks designed to tap the divergent behaviors associated with each intellectual capacity. For example, bodily intelligence can be assessed by recording how well a child learns and remembers a new dance or physical exercise. Likewise, assessing interpersonal intelligence requires accurate measurement of how a child interacts with and influences others in different social situations. At present, teachers rely on informal assessment of multiple intelligences using techniques such as observation of student behavior. One of the commercially available measures is the *Teele Inventory for Multiple Intelligences (TIMI)* (Teele, 1997). *TIMI* is one of the few commercially available assessment tools for making practical use of multiple intelligences. The *TIMI* includes an intelligence inventory, answer sheets, and a teacher's guide. Teachers can use the *TIMI* to put multiple intelligences theory into action in their classrooms, identify their students' strengths and talents, and gain valuable information about how to teach more effectively. In the future, many formal measures like the *TIMI* may become available for teachers to use in the classroom.

of Intelligence, intelligence is a global ability to act in a purposeful manner, to think reasonably, and to adjust appropriately to the environment (Wechsler, cited in Sattler, 1992). In contrast, Binet, the originator of intelligence tests, believed that intelligence consists of a group of abilities including judgment, good sense, initiative, and the ability to adjust to changes in the environment (Binet & Simon, cited in Sattler, 1992). These definitions also explain why different authors construct different types of intelligence tests, depending on their interpretation of the meaning of the term.

Behaviors Measured by Intelligence Tests

Intelligence tests measure learning ability by sampling various behaviors (Horn, 1985; Salvia & Ysseldyke, 1991). Although similarities exist in the behaviors measured by intelligence tests, different tests measure different behaviors. Because each test relies on a unique sample of behaviors, professionals should always reference a specific test when using intelligence test scores (often referred to as *IQ scores*). Naming a test is necessary because an IQ score from a group screening test of intelligence, such as the *Otis-Lennon School Ability Test (OLSAT)* (Otis & Lennon, 1982), for example, is derived from a different sample of behaviors than an IQ score from an individually administered, general test of intelligence, such as the *Wechsler Intelligence Scale for Children-Third Edition (WISC-III)* (Wechsler, 1991). When an IQ score appears in isolation, we must ask the question, "IQ as measured by which test?" The following overview of the behaviors sampled by different types of intelligence tests illustrates the significance of this question.

Intelligence tests can be grouped into four categories: individually administered tests of general intelligence, group intelligence tests, specialized intelligence tests, and intelligence tests for infants, toddlers, and preschoolers. An overview of each category follows.

Individually Administered Tests of General Intelligence

The individually administered tests of general intelligence widely used in special education include subtests that sample a variety of behaviors, including verbal language behaviors and performance behaviors. The **verbal language** items require responses to oral questions from an evaluator. For example, tasks such as answering factual and comprehension questions, defining vocabulary words, identifying similarities, and solving arithmetic problems all involve verbal language. Specific examples of such items include these questions:

> "Who invented the telephone?" "What is a paragraph?" "How are a window and a door similar?" (Wechsler, 1991).

Other verbal language items require definitions of increasingly difficult words, such as *string, spring, novel,* and *facetious.* Absurdities are another type of verbal language item on some tests. These require students to identify the nonsense in presented pictures (e.g., an elephant with wings).

In contrast to the verbal language items, the general intelligence tests also include items that measure performance such as fine motor proficiency and perceptual ability. **Performance behaviors** require that students respond to test items using motor and perceptual skills. Performance items rely on language only in the instructions. Many performance items assess ability based on speed of task completion (measured with a stopwatch) and the number of errors. Examples include putting together puzzle pieces to form complete objects, tracing a path through mazes of increasing complexity, and arranging blocks according to visually presented designs. Because performance items avoid use of language, they are useful for testing students with intact motor and perceptual processes but impaired verbal language.

The individually administered, general tests of intelligence contain subtests that sample a variety of behaviors. Other types of intelligence tests, including the group intelligence tests, rely on more restricted samples of behavior.

Group Intelligence Tests

Most group intelligence tests measure cognitive ability by having students pencil in responses to multiple-choice questions on machine-scored answer sheets. The *Otis–Lennon School Ability Test* (Otis & Lennon, 1982) is one of the widely used group intelligence tests that rely on this format. The multiple-choice format limits the variety of content that test developers can include on group intelligence tests. As a result, group tests tend to measure intelligence with a restricted sample of behaviors. In addition, the pencil-on-paper format requires that test takers have good reading skills and experience with "bubble-in" scoring sheets. Although this format is appropriate for most students, it causes difficulties for students with special needs, especially those who have visual perception problems. These children often have reading deficits and may have difficulty accurately transferring their answers to the scoring sheet.

Specialized Intelligence Tests

Like group tests, the specialized intelligence tests for students with severe and multiple disabilities (such as deafness, blindness, physical impairments, or severe mental retardation) also rely on restricted samples of behaviors. For example, the *Universal Nonverbal Intelligence Test (UNIT)* (Bracken & McCallum, 1997) is a test of visual memory and visual reasoning ability that requires no verbal and minimal motor responses. Developed for testing children with hearing impairments or receptive and expressive language disabilities and children who are non- or limited English proficient (LEP), the *UNIT* does not require reading, writing, or speaking skills. The *UNIT* consists of pictures and abstract drawings on cards that students respond to by pointing to the correct drawing or, if necessary, using an eye-blink communication system. Tests such as the *UNIT* sample **visual reasoning behaviors,** which require students to use visual-perception ability to make perceptual discriminations and to remember visual images. Perceptual discriminations involve simple perceptual classifications and abstract manipulation of symbolic concepts. Perceptual classification tasks usually consist of discrimination of colors, shapes, numbers, and objects. Abstract manipulation of symbolic concepts involves tasks such as visual discrimination (recognizing small differences in objects such as geometric drawings), visual sequencing (identifying the progressive relationship in a series of geometric figures), and recognition of details (identifying missing parts in pictures). Visual memory involves tasks such as remembering symbols, memory for designs, and object memory. Illustrations of some visual-reasoning tasks appear in Figure 7–1.

Figure 7–1   Sample Visual Reasoning Tasks

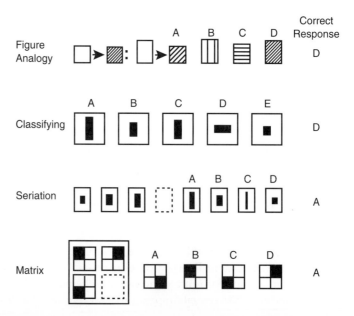

Intelligence Tests for Infants, Toddlers, and Preschoolers

Specialized tests for infants, toddlers, and preschoolers estimate learning potential based on samples of the behavior appropriate for very young children. The *Bayley Scales of Infant Development* (second edition) (Bayley, 1993), for example, consist of subscales of mental ability, motor skills, and behavior. The mental scale samples sensory and perceptual skills, vocalizations, and early verbal communication; the motor scale measures gross motor and fine motor skills; and the behavior scale is a rating scale completed by a primary care giver. The *Ordinal Scales of Psychological Development* (Uzgiris & Hunt, 1975) are another test that samples a specific set of behaviors representative of cognitive ability in young children. The *Ordinal Scales of Psychological Development*, which are based on the Piagetian stages of development, are especially useful for assessing the intellectual potential of children with severe and profound disabilities (Dunst, 1980). These scales measure a child's ability to visually follow objects, understand means-ends relationships, engage in gestural and vocal imitation, and play with objects.

Intelligence tests for children consist of samples of behavior. The individually administered, general tests sample the widest variety of behaviors. The specialized tests tend to rely on more restrictive samples of behavior. In addition to the group tests, specialized tests exist for special populations including infants, toddlers, preschoolers, and students with severe handicaps. However, evaluators rely on these tests only in situations that preclude use of more general measures.

Why Do We Use Intelligence Tests With Students Who Have Special Needs?

The primary use of intelligence testing in education is to identify and classify students (see Focus 7–2). As part of this process, students referred for special education services routinely receive an individually administered test of intelligence to estimate their learning ability. The way assessment teams interpret this estimate depends on the student's suspected disability. When assessment teams suspect learning disabilities, for example, they look for a significant difference between learning ability (as measured by an intelligence test) and achievement (as measured by an achievement test). The student with learning disabilities will also likely display normal intelligence and a learning profile that has significant strengths and weaknesses rather than a flat profile. When assessment teams suspect emotional disturbance, they look for normal intellectual abilities because eligibility requirements exclude students with mental retardation from such programs. When team members suspect mental retardation, they rely on intelligence testing to obtain evidence of significantly below-average learning ability that exists concurrently with deficits in adaptive behavior.

Although many states have replaced the traditional categories of learning disabilities, emotional disturbance, and mental retardation with more generic categories such as educational handicapped, learning handicapped, and severely handicapped, all states employ some form of intelligence testing in identifying, classifying, and placing students into special education programs. In addition, regulations require periodic reevaluation of intelligence to determine if a student should remain

FOCUS 7–2

Why Do We Use Intelligence Tests With Students Who Have Special Needs?

- To obtain an estimate of learning ability
- To identify students with disabilities
- To classify students according to their specific disability
- To periodically reevaluate the learning ability of students

in the current placement, transfer to another special education program, or transfer out of special education entirely.

You may recall the account of Jerrold Johnson that first appeared in Chapter 2, which illustrated critical steps in the screening and referral process. As a result of this process, Jerrold was recommended for comprehensive testing to determine if he qualified for special education services. The following account illustrates how intelligence testing helped to identify Jerrold's reading disability.

When the child-study team forwarded Jerrold's case to a staffing team for comprehensive testing, the psychologist assigned to the case decided to administer the Wechsler Intelligence Scale for Children-Third Edition (WISC-III). *The purpose was to determine Jerrold's aptitude. His* WISC-III *scores were in the normal range, and he received an overall standard score (IQ score) of 97. In addition to giving Jerrold an intelligence test, the psychologist administered a diagnostic achievement test, the* Wechsler Individual Achievement Test (WIAT). *The* WISC-III *and the* WIAT, *developed by the same author, have the advantage of being co-normed. This means that they were standardized using the same groups of children. As a result, scores from the two tests can be directly compared. In order to qualify as learning disabled, Jerrold's test scores would have to show significant discrepancy between aptitude as measured by the* WISC-III *and achievement as measured by the* WIAT. *His scores on the* WIAT *were much lower than his* WISC-III *scores, especially in reading recognition (a standard score of 81) and reading comprehension (a standard score of 77). Because of this significant difference between aptitude and achievement, Jerrold qualified for special education services. As a result, he enrolled in a program for students with learning disabilities designed to meet his individual learning needs.*

Jerrold's case illustrates the role of intelligence testing in identifying a student with a learning disability. In contrast, the next scenario illustrates the role of intelligence testing in identifying a student with mental retardation.

The psychologist evaluated Johnny, a student in Mrs. Johnson's second-grade class, for special education placement due to poor academic performance and inappropriate classroom behavior. In Johnny's case, the intelligence test results estimated his learning ability in the form of an intelligence quotient score of 64 on the Wechsler Intelligence Scale for Children-Third Edition (WISC-III). *This score fell well below the cutoff (80) for mental retardation used in this particular state. In addition to intelligence testing, the psychologist administered a test of academic achievement and an adaptive behavior scale before making an eligibility and placement decision. Johnny's achievement was consistently low in all academic areas, resulting in a flat profile. His adaptive behavior also fell into the significantly below-average range. In making their recommendation, the assessment team found that the test data clearly supported placing Johnny in a program for students with mild mental retardation.*

In Johnny's case the intelligence test results provided clear-cut data for a placement decision. In other situations, however, intelligence testing may not provide conclusive information. The next example illustrates this point.

The intelligence test score Walter received (an IQ of 80 on the Stanford–Binet Intelligence Scale: Fourth Edition [SB4]) *placed him directly on the eligibility borderline for the mental retardation program. Because the test score fell on the cutoff line, the assessment team turned to other assessment data to help make their decision. Unfortunately, Walter's levels of performance in achievement and adaptive behavior also fell near the borderline for eligibility. Because the assessment data failed to clearly indicate a disability, the team carefully considered Walter's social and family history before making a placement decision. Walter, a minority student, had grown up in a deprived and culturally different environment characterized by poverty and lack of experience. Therefore, the assessment team reasoned, environmental deprivation rather than mental retardation was a possible cause of his poor school performance. In deciding that the test data failed to support placement in special education, the assessment team strongly considered the economic and cultural factors. They recommended continued placement in the first grade and helped Walter's teacher to identify additional interventions to try in class. The assessment team also made arrangements for Walter to enroll in a remedial reading program where he received additional instructional assistance. Finally, the assessment team made arrangements for Walter to be retested in 1 year to obtain another estimate of his learning ability and achievement.*

In contrast to the first example, Walter's case illustrates a situation in which test data failed to provide conclusive evidence for making a placement decision.

Issues in Intelligence Testing

Although experts agree that it represents one of the most important contributions in the field of psychology, intelligence testing remains a controversial aspect of assessment in special education. Concerns center around several drawbacks of intelligence testing, including limited ability to predict nonacademic and vocational success, the inaccuracy of IQ scores at the extremes, and cultural bias against minority groups.

Effectiveness of Intelligence Testing in Predicting Nonschool Behavior

Many experts question the effectiveness of using intelligence test results to predict nonschool behaviors, such as potential for vocational success and preferred learning style. The question stems, in part, from misunderstanding the purpose of intelligence testing. Most people, including some psychologists, believe that intelligence testing measures natural ability or potential. However, little evidence exists to support this theory. From a historical perspective, it is clear that the originators of intelligence testing did not design them to predict nonschool behaviors. In 1905, Binet and Simon wrote the first intelligence test as a tool for identifying students with limited potential for success in school. As a result of testing, educators excluded students with low scores from the school system. Thus, the original purpose for testing intelligence was to predict school success. More recently, however, psychologists and others have come to rely on intelligence test results to predict learning style, vocational aptitude, and other abilities even though the validity of such practices is questionable.

Accuracy of Intelligence Tests

Another issue concerns the inaccuracy of intelligence tests at the extremes of high and low performance. Intelligence test scores, like all test scores, lose accuracy at extremely high and low levels of performance. This creates an acute problem in special education because many students receive scores that fall into the extreme ranges. Students with mild disabilities often receive IQ scores in the below-average range of 70 to 85 while students with severe and profound disabilities typically receive IQ scores of 55 and lower. On the other end of the IQ scale, students who are gifted typically score in the IQ range of 130 and above. The standard error of measurement (an estimate of the accuracy of a score) in these extreme ranges is much higher than for scores in the midrange of intelligence tests (around 100 IQ points). For this reason, assessment teams must treat extreme scores with caution to avoid misuse in identifying, classifying, and placing students.

Bias of Intelligence Tests Against Certain Groups of Students

A third issue, bias against certain groups of students, represents the greatest area of concern in intelligence testing. The long-running debate about bias pertains to the correct use of intelligence tests with students from deprived and culturally different backgrounds. This includes students with limited English language proficiency as well as students with disabilities. Many experts point out that intelligence tests are not culture fair. **Culture fair** refers to the fairness or equity of tests to all students regardless of cultural background. Culture-fair tests attempt to provide students of different cultures and life experiences equal opportunities for success. As a result, developers of culture-fair tests must limit test content to material that is common to all cultures or that is unfamiliar or new for students from various different cultural backgrounds. Although developing a completely culture-fair test may be impossible, most test writers today attempt to reduce, as much as possible, the influence of cultural factors in testing. Test writers accomplish this goal by eliminating "culturally loaded" items from tests, such as pictures or vocabulary that may be biased against certain groups. The classic example of such an item is a question from an early edition of the *Wechsler Intelligence Scale for Children*. The question involved asking children what they should do if a much smaller child hit them. "Correct" answers included telling an adult or ignoring the smaller child. "Incorrect" answers included hitting the child back. The question is culturally loaded because children in some cultures learn that hitting a much younger child back is appropriate, whereas children in other cultures learn the opposite. Dr. Wechsler removed this item from later editions of the test.

Despite these efforts, evidence suggests that intelligence tests favor students from middle-class, urban backgrounds and discriminate against students from low socioeconomic backgrounds, rural areas, and minority groups (Miller-Jones 1989). For this reason, test developers continue their efforts to eliminate bias in intelligence testing. In response to the problem of partiality, Mercer and Lewis (1978) developed the *System of Multicultural Pluralistic Assessment,* or *SOMPA,* which attempts to prevent bias against minority groups in testing for placement in special education. The system (explained in greater detail later in this chapter in the section on specialized intelligence tests) consists of a complete program including assessment of language and cultural factors through the use of sociocultural scales, health history inventories, and norms for black, Hispanic, and white children. *SOMPA* and other similar systems illustrate one response to solving this persistent problem.

Those who question efforts to create culture-fair tests argue that an intelligence test is unfair only if it fails to predict academic success. They contend intelligence tests effectively predict students who perform well in school by identifying those with good verbal skills and high abstract reasoning ability (Robinson & Robinson, 1965). However, the issue of bias in testing is more than pedagogical because millions of students receive intelligence tests each year, and educational placement depends, in large part, on their performance on these tests.

☑ Comprehension Checklist

Intelligence testing represents a complicated and controversial area of assessment in special education. Although intelligence generally refers to the ability to learn based on experience, many complex definitions exist for the term. Likewise, psychologists have created many types of intelligence tests, most of which measure intelligence by using a combination of verbal language, motor performance, and visual reasoning items, although verbal items predominate. Controversies surrounding intelligence testing further contribute to its complicated nature. These controversies include questions about the role of intelligence testing in special education and concerns about the predictive validity of such tests. However, the greatest controversy centers around the extent to which bias affects the intelligence test scores of students from minority groups. Psychologists and special educators continue to develop procedures that reduce bias in intelligence testing and in assessment in general. The four categories of intelligence tests are individually administered tests of general intelligence, group intelligence tests, specialized intelligence tests, and intelligence tests for infants, toddlers, and preschoolers.

Individually Administered Intelligence Tests

The measurement of learning ability with individually administered intelligence tests represents one of the primary applications of psychology in special education. Psychologists have developed a large number of such tests, including instruments for measuring general ability as well as highly specialized measures for special populations. An evaluator administers **individually administered intelligence tests** to only one student at a time. Individual tests exist for all age groups of students, including infants, preschoolers, and adults. Whereas the group tests measure only one type of ability, most individual tests contain subtests that measure different abilities, such as verbal skills, motor performance, and visual reasoning skills. This format enables the assessment team to gauge intellectual abilities and overall intelligence. Because examiners present test items orally or with pictures, students need not read, and most individually administered tests require limited written responses. Examiners administer the tests in a one-on-one setting and usually prepare a formal written report of results. The foremost individually administered intelligence test in special education is the *Wechsler Intelligence Scale for Children-Third Edition.* Comprehensive reviews of this test and other widely used intelligence tests follow.

Wechsler Intelligence Scale for Children-Third Edition (WISC-III)

The most widely used test of general intellectual ability in special education today is the *Wechsler Intelligence Scale for Children-Third Edition (WISC-III)* (Wechsler, 1991). Designed for students from age 6 to 16, the *WISC-III* contains excellent technical qualities, well-designed administration and scoring procedures, and many additional features. The *WISC-III* is one of a group of three tests spanning all ages. The other two tests are the *Wechsler Preschool and Primary Scale of Intelligence-Revised (WPPSI-R)* (Wechsler, 1989), which measures the intellectual ability of preschoolers from age 4 through 6 years and 6 months of age, and the *Wechsler Adult Intelligence Scale-Revised (WAIS-R)* (Wechsler, 1981), which assesses the general learning ability of adults from 16 years through retirement. Table 7–1 summarizes the *WISC-III.*

General Description and Purpose of the *WISC-III*   The *WISC-III*, which consists of a verbal scale and a performance scale, assesses global intellectual ability by measuring student behavior on a variety of tasks. The test estimates overall learning potential as well as relative strengths and weaknesses in verbal and performance skills. The *WISC-III* consists of 13 subtests: 10 required and 3 supplementary. Evaluators use the supplements as alternates or extra subtests if time permits. The **verbal scale** subtests contain items that require students to listen to questions and answer verbally.

Table 7–1   *Wechsler Intelligence Scale for Children-Third Edition (WISC-III)*

Type of Test:	Norm referenced
Purpose:	A general measure of intellectual ability
Content Areas:	Verbal ability and performance ability
Administration Time:	Approximately 1 hour
Age Levels:	6–16 years
Suitable for:	Students with mild, moderate, and severe disabilities, including learning disabilities, behavior disorders, mental retardation, visual impairments (verbal scale), hearing impairments (performance scale), and physical handicaps (verbal scale)
Scores:	Verbal, performance, and full-scale IQ scores; four factor-based index scores (verbal comprehension, perceptual organization, freedom from distractibility, and processing speed); & scaled scores for each subtest
In Short:	The *WISC-III* is a well-designed intelligence test with superior technical characteristics. The improvements in this edition make it an outstanding assessment instrument.

Verbal Scale

Subtest	Description
General Information	Answering specific factual questions
General Comprehension	Understanding questions about vocabulary
Arithmetic	Solving arithmetic problems
Similarities	Identifying similarities or commonalities
Vocabulary	Defining words
Digit Span (supplementary)	Immediately recalling orally presented digits

The **performance scale** subtests consist of items requiring visual reasoning ability and fine motor responses.

Performance Scale

Subtest	Description
Picture Completion	Identifying missing parts in pictures
Picture Arrangement	Comprehending and sequencing relationships
Block Design	Copying visually presented stimulus designs
Object Assembly	Putting together puzzle pieces to form complete objects
Coding	Associating and copying specified symbols
Mazes (supplementary)	Tracing a path through mazes
Symbol Search (supplementary)	Identifying if a target symbol is in a search group

Materials for the *WISC-III* Materials supplied with the *WISC-III* include a test manual; a set of scoring forms; booklets for the mazes, coding subtests, and symbol search; and a booklet for arithmetic problems, picture completion, and block design subtests. Manipulative materials for the performance subtests include cards for the picture arrangement subtest, block design cubes, and parts for the object assembly subtest. The materials fit in a briefcase for ease of storage and transport. Supporting materials include WISC-III Writer: The Interpretive Software System and Scoring Assistant for the Wechsler Scales (SAWS), which is an interactive software program that enables one to write individualized, comprehensive reports on a personal computer. The program automatically converts raw scores into scaled scores, percentiles, factor scores, composites, and confidence intervals. The program also provides three report formats: an extensive interpretive report, a parent report, and a tables-and-graphs report. The SAWS automates the process of generating profile reports including score difference analysis, norm table conversions, scaled scores, standard scores, confidence intervals, and ability/achievement discrepancies.

Administration of the *WISC-III* The *WISC-III* takes 50 to 75 minutes to give, depending on the response speed of the student. Specially trained evaluators administer the test following standardized procedures. Administration involves alternating the presentation of performance and verbal subtests in a specified order. This alternating procedure makes taking the test more interesting for the student. Specific training and certification are required for evaluators, and test use is limited to psychologists and diagnosticians who have met these conditions.

Scoring of the *WISC-III*   Evaluators can obtain deviation IQs for the verbal scale, the performance scale, and the full scale. These IQ scores have a mean of 100 and a standard deviation of 15. The standard error of measurement ranges from 3 at the mean to as much as 5.61 for extremely high and low scores. In addition, evaluators can also calculate four factor-based index scores. The subtests for each index score consist of the following:

Verbal Comprehension	*Perceptual Organization*
Information	Picture Completion
Similarities	Picture Arrangement
Vocabulary	Block Design
Comprehension	Object Assembly
Freedom From Distractibility	*Processing Speed*
Arithmetic	Coding
Digit Span	Symbol Search

Like the IQ scores, the index scores have a mean of 100 and a standard deviation of 15. However, because the *WISC-III* developers did not include normative data for the index scores in the manual, evaluators should use the scores only for explaining a student's performance. Evaluators should avoid including index scores in written reports. An expanded scoring form, available as a supplement, provides more room to record student responses, examiner notes, and behavioral observations. Scoring may also include use of a supplementary computer software report program that analyzes results and generates a four-page interpretive report. The evaluator summarizes the testing results on a form that includes identifying information, subtest and overall IQs, and graphs that profile the results. A sample summary form appears in Figure 7–2.

Interpretation of the *WISC-III*   The full-scale IQ obtained from the *WISC-III* indicates a student's general intellectual ability, whereas IQ scores from the verbal and performance scales provide a profile of intelligence. Performance on the verbal scale depends on a student's ability to orally answer questions presented verbally. In contrast, the performance scale depends on a student's ability to quickly perform nonverbal problem-solving tasks, using visual and fine motor skills. Discrepancies of more than 12 IQ points between the verbal and performance scales may have diagnostic implications. For example, a student with a full-scale IQ score of 85, a performance-scale IQ score of 90, and a verbal-scale IQ score of 72 exhibits a difference of 18 points between the verbal and performance scales ($90 - 72 = 18$). A difference of this magnitude represents a significant discrepancy between performance and verbal ability.

Identifying discrepancies helps the evaluator interpret student performance when notable differences exist between functioning levels in performance and verbal ability. Sattler (1992) identified several possible reasons for discrepancies, including interest or learning styles (e.g., a student with strong verbal skills but weak performance skills), cognitive styles, the presence of disabilities, sensory deficits, and information processing deficits (e.g., strengths or weaknesses in auditory or visual processing skills). Sattler cautioned against drawing conclusions based solely on significant discrepancies. Rather, the evaluator should base interpretations on all relevant information, including the student's overall performance, educational history and family background, and present learning difficulties.

Figure 7–2   Sample Summary Form From the *WISC-III*

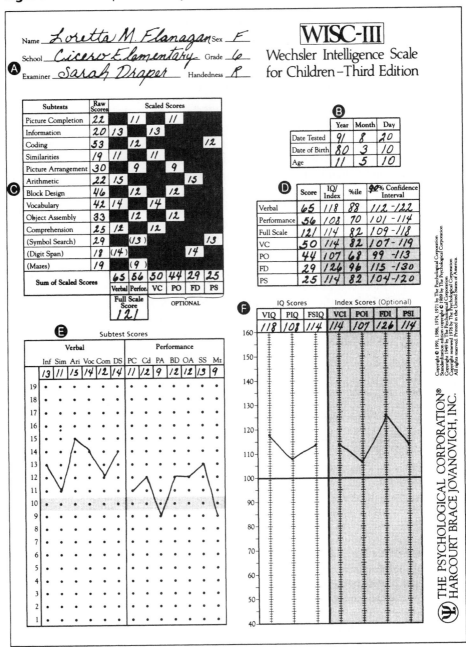

Source: Weshler, D. (1991). *Wechsler Intelligence Scale for Children* (3d ed.). San Antonio, TX: Psychological Coproration. Reprinted with permission of the Psychological Corporation.

WISC-III scores can also be interpreted in conjunction with scores from the *Wechsler Individual Achievement Test (WIAT)* (Wechsler, 1992). The *WIAT* was standardized on a sample matched to the *WISC-III* in demographic variables and ability. Because these tests were matched, a more accurate interpretation of the discrepancy between ability and achievement is possible than with unmatched tests. Interpreting this discrepancy is a necessary step in identifying students with learning disabilities. A comprehensive review of the *WIAT* appears in Chapter 14.

Technical Characteristics of the *WISC-III*   As might be expected from the premier test of its kind, the *WISC-III* exhibits outstanding technical characteristics in all areas. The norms are excellent, the validity is well established, and the reliability is superior (Sandoval, 1995). Split-half reliability coefficients range from .77 to .87 for the individual verbal subscales and from .69 to .87 for the individual performance subscales. Average reliability coefficients for the verbal, performance, and full-scale IQs are much higher at .95, .91, and .96, respectively. Because the reliability coefficients of the subscale scores fall below those of the full-scale IQ scores, the accuracy of interpretations based on subscale scores is limited. The *WISC-III* exhibits excellent concurrent validity based on numerous research studies, including investigations of the relationship between performance on the *WISC-III* and the *Wechsler Preschool and Primary Scale of Intelligence (WPPSI)*, the *Wechsler Adult Intelligence Scale (WAIS)*, and the *Stanford–Binet Intelligence Scale*. Other studies provide strong evidence of excellent content and construct validity.

The test developers obtained normative data by using a stratified sampling plan to ensure the selection of a representative sample group. Sampling variables included age, sex, race, geographic region, occupation of the head of the household, and urban-rural residence. The developers did not include children with disabilities in the standardization sample. Some bilingual children were tested if they demonstrated proficiency in speaking and understanding English.

Critical Reviews of the *WISC-III*   In a review of the standardization of the *WISC-III*, Roid (1990) indicated that this revision gives the test a needed update while maintaining the major features of its predecessor. Improvements include expanding the object assembly subtest, modernizing the artwork, updating the coding subtest, extending the norms of the subtests, modifying items to minimize bias, and developing supplementary materials, including a co-normed achievement test and computer-interpretative software. According to reviews by Bortner (1985) and Detterman (1985) of the earlier version of the *WISC* (Wechsler, 1974), several reasons account for the popularity of the test among examiners, including high-quality administration and scoring procedures, excellent standardization, and clarity of the test manual. The newest edition maintains these benefits. On the other hand, the latest version of the test retains earlier weaknesses as well, including limited validity with students who receive very low or very high scores (e.g., IQs less than 70 and greater than 130). This limitation results from the unreliability of extreme scores and occurs when evaluators fail to consider the standard error of measurement in judging the meaning of low and high IQ scores. Another problem concerns incorrect interpretation of index and subscale scores by evaluators who may overgeneralize differences in such scores. According to Witt & Gresham (1985), the problem with overgeneralizing subscale scores concerns their low reliability. For this reason, evaluators should avoid

References

Connolly, A. J. (1998). *KeyMath Revised: A Diagnostic Inventory of Essential Mathematics*. Circle Pines, MN: American Guidance Service.

Educational Testing Service. (1998a). Available gopher://etsis4.ets.org:70/11/president

———. (1998b). What Every School Should Know About Testing Students With Disabilities. Online, Internet. Available http://www.ets.org/praxis/prxdisab.html

Markwardt, F. C. (1998). *Peabody Individual Achievement Test-Revised*. Circle Pines, MN: American Guidance Service.

Newborg, J., Stock, J., Wnek, L., Guidubaldi, J., & Svinicki, J. (1984). *Battelle Developmental Inventory*. Allen, TX: DLM Teaching Resources.

Rodgers, D. (1998). *KeyMath-Revised ASSIST*. Circle Pines, MN: American Guidance Service.

Sattler, J. M. (1992). *Assessment of Children* (3d ed.). San Diego, CA: Author.

concluding that students manifest a particular type of learning deficit just because they receive a low score on a specific factor or subscale. For example, a student who receives a low score on the digit span subscale does not necessarily have a deficit in auditory memory. Despite these criticisms, Braden (1995) suggested that the *WISC-III* is likely to remain the favorite test among practitioners and clinical researchers because of the many positive characteristics and features.

Summary of the *WISC-III*   The *WISC-III*, which conceptualizes intelligence as a global ability, assesses student ability through a series of verbal and manipulative tasks. With a research base of more than 5,000 studies, the *WISC-III* represents an important diagnostic tool for assessing educational potential and evaluating disabilities. Examiners rely on the test extensively in the process of identifying students who qualify for special education services.

Stanford–Binet Intelligence Scale: Fourth Edition

The *Stanford–Binet Intelligence Scale,* first published by Binet and Simon in 1905, is the oldest of the intelligence tests in current use. Originally designed to identify students in French schools who could not benefit from instruction, psychologists brought it to the United States soon after initial publication. In the United States, the scales were revised and published again in 1916 (Terman & Merrill) as the *Stanford– Binet Intelligence Scale.* Later revisions were published in 1937 (Terman & Merrill) and in 1960. The 1960 (Terman & Merrill) edition introduced use of the deviation IQ rather than a ratio IQ, and this significant improvement increased the accuracy and precision of the test scores. The norms for the 1960 scale were revised and published as the *Stanford–Binet: Fourth Edition (SB4)* (Thorndike et al., 1986a–c), although the test items, administration, and scoring procedures remained similar to the 1960 edition (see Table 7–2). Although not as widely used as the *WISC-III*, the *SB4* continues to serve as a useful instrument for measuring general intellectual ability.

Table 7–2   *Stanford–Binet Intelligence Scale: Fourth Edition*

Type of Test:	Norm referenced
Purpose:	A general measure of intellectual ability
Content Areas:	Verbal reasoning, quantitative reasoning, abstract/visual reasoning, and short-term memory
Administration Time:	Approximately 1 hour
Age Levels:	2–16 years
Suitable for:	Students with mild, moderate, and severe disabilities, including learning disabilities, behavior disorders, and mental retardation
Scores:	Deviation IQ scores for the total test and each of the four test areas; normalized standard scores for each of the 15 subtests
In Short:	Because it was the original intelligence test, first introduced in 1905, the *Stanford–Binet* is historically significant. The well-designed and widely used *SB4* is the most recent edition of this classic instrument.

General Description and Purpose of the *SB4* The *SB4* measures the general intellectual ability of children between the ages of 2 and 16 years. For the early ages the test requires fine motor skills such as using building blocks, matching shapes, and stringing beads, but the vast majority of the test consists of verbal language items, such as answering questions, defining words, and remembering sentences. Because of this emphasis, most specialists recommend against use of the *SB4* with children who have auditory processing deficits or other language-based problems. For these children, a low score on the test may reflect a language or processing deficit rather than low intelligence. The four areas and 15 subtests of the *SB4* include the following:

Verbal Reasoning	*Abstract/Visual Reasoning*
Vocabulary	Pattern analysis
Comprehension	Copying
Absurdities	Matrices
Verbal relations	Paper folding and cutting

Quantitative Reasoning	*Short-Term Memory*
Quantitative	Bead memory
Number Series	Memory for sentences
Equation Building	Memory for digits
	Memory for objects

Materials for the *SB4* Contained in a briefcase-type kit, the test materials include the manipulative items, the scoring sheets, and the test manual.

Administration of the *SB4* The test takes about 45 minutes to administer to a young child and as long as 2 hours to an adolescent. An evaluator gives the *SB4* in a clinical interview format that requires the child to answer many verbal language questions. The test items are grouped by age in the 15 subtests; the evaluator begins giving them at the approximate age of the child (the basal level) and stops giving items when the child misses a certain number (the ceiling level). Because evaluators must obtain specific training and certification, use of the *SB4* is limited to psychologists, diagnosticians, and other professionals who have received this training.

Scoring of the *SB4* Deviation IQs, called *standard age scores (SASs)* (M = 100, SD = 16) by the *SB4*, are available for the four areas of the test and for the total score. The *SB4* also provides normalized standard scores with a mean of 50 and a standard deviation of 8 for the 15 subtests. However, evaluators should interpret subtest scores cautiously because of the inherent limitations of subscale scoring. The evaluator records the child's response to each item in a 40-page record booklet. The overall results of the testing are recorded on the front page of the booklet.

Interpretation of the *SB4* The total IQ score from the *SB4* indicates overall intellectual performance, whereas the four area scores provide a profile of intellectual development across the domains of verbal reasoning, quantitative reasoning, abstract/visual reasoning, and short-term memory. Because the standard deviation of the IQ scores is 16 rather than the more common standard deviation of 15, interpreting scores from the *SB4* must account for this one-point difference. For example, a score of 68 from the *SB4* (2 SDs below the mean of 100, or $100 - 32 = 68$) equals a score of 70 from most tests ($100 - 30 = 70$).

Technical Characteristics of the *SB4*   The *SB4* provides very good overall technical qualities. Reliability estimates for the test include measures of the internal consistency for the composite IQ, the area IQs, and the subtest scores. Highly reliable test-retest estimates for preschool and elementary children exist, but no estimates of test-retest reliability with junior high and high school students are available. Evidence of test validity includes many concurrent validity studies comparing the scale to other IQ tests, as well as several studies using factor analysis to examine the validity of the area scores. Glutting (1989), who reviewed the factor analysis research on the test, concluded that many of the area scores failed to measure separate factors. For this reason, interpretation of differences in student performance based on such scores should be done cautiously. Normative data were obtained on the basis of a sample group of more than 5,000 individuals from 2 through 23 years of age, and this large group yielded satisfactory norms.

Critical Reviews of the *SB4*   Critical reviews of the *SB4* by Cronbach (1989) and Anastasi (1988) praised the efficient administration and scoring of the test but criticized some of the technical characteristics. The reviewers noted that the norms overrepresent children from affluent backgrounds and criticized the lack of available data to support the validity of the area scores. This suggests a need for more information on interpreting *SB4* test scores. For these reasons, the reviewers concluded that the *SB4* failed to demonstrate clear advantages over similar tests such as the *WISC-III*.

Summary of the *SB4*   As the original intelligence test, it is difficult to overstate the historical effect of the *Stanford–Binet Intelligence Scale* on the major institutions in Western society. One outgrowth of this pioneering assessment tool has been the reliance on such tests by all of the major institutions in society, including business, industry, the military, and education. The initial *Binet Intelligence Scale* demonstrated, for the first time, a procedure for accurately and effectively measuring intellectual ability. Acceptance of the *Stanford–Binet* and other intelligence tests led to widespread use of other types of tests, such as achievement and aptitude tests.

Woodcock–Johnson Psycho-Educational Battery-Revised

The *Woodcock–Johnson Psycho-Educational Battery-Revised (WJ-R)* (Woodcock & Johnson, 1989) assesses multiple skills and consists of two parts. Part 1, the tests of cognitive ability, measures general intellectual ability. Part 2, the tests of achievement, measures academic achievement. Together the two parts make up a complete test collection that the authors designed for use with children and adults between the ages of 2 through retirement. A parallel Spanish version of the *WJ-R* is also available. The *Batería Woodcock–Muñoz-Revisada (Batería-R)* (Woodcock & Muñoz-Sandoval, 1996) assesses the cognitive abilities and achievement levels in Spanish-speaking children. All tests in the *Batería-R* have been carefully adapted from the *WJ-R*, and information can be directly compared. Although the *WJ-R* has many excellent features, it is not as widely used as the *WISC-III* in identifying students with disabilities.

General Description and Purpose of the *WJ-R* Part 1 of the *WJ-R*, the tests of cognitive ability, consists of 7 standard subtests and 14 supplemental subtests. The *WJ-R* recommends use of the 7 standard subtests for obtaining a cognitive score in the shortest possible time and also with preschool students or students with severe disabilities. The supplemental subtests complement the standard subtests and provide additional scores in the areas of cognitive factors, scholastic aptitudes, and oral language skills. The test manual provides specific guidelines for when to use the supplemental tests.

The standard subtests consist of the following:

Subtest	Description
Memory for names	Long-term memory
Memory for sentences	Short-term memory
Visual matching	Visual processing
Incomplete words	Auditory processing
Visual closure	Visual processing
Picture vocabulary	Receptive language
Analysis-synthesis	Reasoning ability

The 14 supplemental subtests include the following:

Subtest	Description
Visual-auditory learning	Delayed recall: Memory for names
Memory for words	Delayed recall: Visual-auditory learning
Cross out	Numbers reversed
Sound blending	Sound patterns
Picture recognition	Spatial relations
Oral vocabulary	Listening comprehension
Concept formation	Verbal analogies

The tests of achievement are co-normed with the tests of cognitive ability and, like the cognitive tests, consist of a standard battery and a supplemental battery of tests. The nine tests in the standard battery provide achievement scores in reading, math, written language, and knowledge and consist of the following:

Letter-word identification	Humanities
Passage comprehension	Social studies
Calculation	Science
Applied problems	Writing samples
Dictation	

The authors designed the tests in the supplemental battery for selective use with the standard battery to obtain additional information in basic reading, reading comprehension, basic math, math reasoning, basic writing, and written expression. The supplemental battery subtests include the following:

Word attack	Handwriting
Reading vocabulary	Usage
Quantitative concepts	Spelling
Proofing	Punctuation
Writing fluency	

Materials for the *WJ-R* Contained in a briefcase-type kit, the test materials for the *WJ-R* include two easel-type booklets containing test items, scoring sheets, and two spiral-bound test manuals. *WJ-R* software includes a computer scoring program and a computer reporting program (Schrank & Woodcock, 1995). Other resources include a clinical interpretation book (McGrew, 1994), an instructional guide (Mather, 1991), a recommendations and reports resource manual (Mather & Jaffe, 1992), and a guide for using and interpreting the *WJ-R* (Hessler, 1993).

Administration of the *WJ-R* Both the cognitive tests and the achievement tests are organized into a standard battery and a supplemental battery. This enables evaluators to utilize the supplemental tests in a flexible manner, depending on the needs of the student and time constraints. Giving the standard cognitive battery usually takes less than 1 hour, but giving all 21 cognitive tests may take several hours and require more than one sitting. Likewise, giving the standard achievement battery takes about an hour, but additional time is needed for the supplemental tests.

Scoring and Interpretation of the *WJ-R* No other test provides as many scores and profiles as the *WJ-R*. These include cluster scores for seven cognitive factors, cluster scores for four scholastic aptitudes, an extended broad cognitive ability score, individual test scores, intracognitive discrepancy scores, an oral language cluster score, and an oral language aptitude score. Examiners may obtain age and grade scores as well as percentile ranks and standard scores for each content area and cluster. Because the two parts of the *WJ-R* are co-normed, the *WJ-R* is ideally suited for identifying students with significant discrepancies between learning ability and academic achievement. Such comparisons are a necessary step in the process of making classification and placement decisions for students with specific learning disabilities.

Technical Characteristics of the *WJ-R* The *WJ-R*, standardized on a sample of more than 6,300 individuals, included more than 100 different localities in the norming process. Reliability coefficients average in the .90s for the cluster scores, and concurrent validity coefficients range from .60 to .70. Overall, the *WJ-R* displays more than adequate technical qualities.

Critical Reviews of the *WJ-R* In a comprehensive review of the *WJ-R*, Lee (1995) concluded that the battery is one of the most advanced tests for measuring the cognitive and achievement skills of children. Likewise, Cummings (1995), in another comprehensive review, indicated that the battery is one of the most outstanding norm-referenced psychoeducational tests because of its theoretically sound cognitive section and the achievement section that measures multiple dimensions of important academic skills.

Summary of the *WJ-R* Because the *WJ-R* provides a variety of scores and options for in-depth diagnosis, it is a valuable tool for making placement decisions and planning individual programs. Although scoring of the subtests is difficult and time consuming because of the complexity of the scoring procedure, the *WJ-R* rates consideration in settings that require a complete testing program. A summary of the *WJ-R* appears in Table 7–3.

Table 7–3   *Woodcock–Johnson Psycho-Educational Battery-Revised*

Type of Test:	Norm referenced
Purpose:	A general measure of intellectual ability and academic achievement
Content Areas:	Broad cognitive ability, academic achievement, and a variety of subtest and individual test scores
Administration Time:	1 hour to several hours
Age Levels:	2 years–retirement
Suitable for:	Students with mild and moderate disabilities, including learning disabilities, behavior disorders, and mental retardation
Scores:	Provides a large variety of standard scores, percentiles, and age and grade scores for the overall test and each subtest
In Short:	The *WJ-R* has unique features not available in other intelligence and achievement tests.

Kaufman Assessment Battery for Children

The *Kaufman Assessment Battery for Children (K-ABC)* (Kaufman & Kaufman, 1983) represents another well-designed intelligence test battery that, like the *WISC-III* and the *WJ-R*, includes assessment of intellectual ability and achievement. The *K-ABC* reflects contemporary concerns such as nondiscriminatory assessment, specific procedures for use with students with disabilities, and procedures for identifying a student's preferred learning style. Although it includes many useful features, the *K-ABC* is not as widely used as some of the other individually administered tests of general intellectual ability such as the *WISC-III*. Encompassing an age range of 2 years and 5 months to 12 years and 5 months, the *K-ABC* consists of 16 subtests, of which only 13 are administered to any one child based on age. A summary of the *K-ABC* appears in Table 7–4. The subtests are grouped into three scales as follows:

Scale	*Subtest*
Sequential processing	Hand movements
	Number recall
	Word order
Simultaneous processing	Magic window
	Face recognition
	Gestalt closure
	Triangles
	Spatial memory
	Photo series
Achievement	Vocabulary
	Faces & places
	Arithmetic
	Riddles
	Reading/decoding
	Reading/understanding

Table 7–4   *Kaufman Assessment Battery for Children (K-ABC)*

Type of Test:	Norm referenced
Purpose:	A general measure of intellectual ability and academic achievement
Content Areas:	Sequential processing, simultaneous processing, achievement, and nonverbal (optional)
Administration Time:	30 to 90 minutes
Age Levels:	2.5–12.5 years
Suitable for:	Students with mild, moderate, and severe disabilities, including learning disabilities, emotional disturbance, and mental retardation
Scores:	Standard scores (M = 100, SD = 15), percentiles, age equivalents, and grade equivalents for the achievement subtests
In Short:	Special features of the *K-ABC* include test items that appeal to children and specific procedures for testing students from minority groups and students with disabilities.

Materials for the *K-ABC*   The complete *K-ABC* kit includes all test materials, an administration and scoring manual, an interpretive manual, and 25 individual test records.

Administration and Scoring of the *K-ABC*   Designed for school and clinical psychologists and other qualified professionals, the *K-ABC* limits use to those with specific training and certification. Administration and scoring follow consistent rules, with minimal verbal directions. An optional videotape demonstration of an evaluator giving the test helps new users learn the administration procedures. Administration time varies from about 45 minutes for young children to an hour and a half for older children.

Available scores include standard scores (M = 100, SD = 15), percentiles, sociocultural percentiles, and age equivalents for the following scales: sequential processing, achievement, simultaneous processing, nonverbal, and mental processing. Sociocultural percentiles, normed on a special sample of minority and nonminority students, provide an additional score that evaluators can use along with standard scores in making assessment decisions with minority students. This avoids the problem of labeling based on use of a single mental ability score. The scales for mental processing and achievement were normed on the same sample to facilitate comparison of ability and achievement. This feature helps in diagnosing learning disabilities. An optional workshop for teachers shows how to identify a student's preferred learning style and how to interpret *K-ABC* mental processing scores in instructional situations. Subtest scores for mental processing and achievement are also available.

Technical Characteristics of the *K-ABC*   Standardized on a national sample of over 2,000 children stratified for gender, geographic location, parental education, ethnic group, and community size, the *K-ABC* sample included representative proportions of white, black, Hispanic, Asian, and Native American children. About 7% of the children in the sample were in special education programs. Special sociocultural norms, based on an additional sample of 469 black children and 119 white children, may be used with the general norms or to provide additional interpretive information. Coefficients for both split-half and test-retest reliability estimates average in the .70 to .80 range for subtests and in the .80 to .90 range for the global scores. A large number and variety of research studies support the construct, concurrent, and predictive validity of the test.

Summary of the *K-ABC*   The *K-ABC*, attractively packaged with test items that appeal to and interest children, takes an innovative approach by defining intelligence as the ability to solve problems through the use of simultaneous and sequential cognitive processing skills. The *K-ABC* was based on current research and theory in cognitive development; particularly noteworthy features of the *K-ABC* include special attention to nondiscriminatory assessment and specific procedures for use with students who have disabilities.

☑ Comprehension Checklist

Assessment with individually administered tests of general intelligence is an integral step in identifying, classifying, and placing students in special education. Although professionals may choose from a number of instruments, the *WISC-III* remains the most widely used test. The *WISC-III* estimates global learning potential along with separate measures of verbal and performance ability. The *SB4* estimates global potential by a similar process for assessing intelligence and includes four separate measures of specific abilities: verbal reasoning, quantitative reasoning, abstract/visual reasoning, and short-term memory. Other widely used measures include the *WJ-R* and the *K-ABC* tests.

Because virtually all students in special education programs are tested with a general measure of intelligence, teachers should be familiar with these tests, their content, and their interpretation. However, the general tests of cognition are inappropriate for evaluating very young students and students with unique disabling conditions. In these situations, evaluators rely on intelligence tests designed specifically for use with the appropriate population of students.

Group Intelligence Tests

Designed to be given to more than one student at a time and often given to large groups at once, **group intelligence tests** are useful screening measures that identify students who may need follow-up assessment with an individually administered, general measure of intellectual ability. Other major advantages include the ability to test many students quickly and inexpensively. Because of these advantages, group intelligence tests remain popular in education, business, industry, and the military. However, they are not particularly useful with students who have special needs and thus are infrequently used in special education. Reviews of some of the most widely used group intelligence tests follow.

Cognitive Abilities Test (CogAT)

The *Cognitive Abilities Test (CogAT)* (Thorndike & Hagen, 1993) assesses the reasoning and problem-solving abilities of students from the 1st through the 12th grade. Consisting of subtests that measure verbal, quantitative, and nonverbal (spatial) abilities, the *CogAT* takes approximately 90 minutes to complete and produces verbal, quantitative, nonverbal, and composite scores.

Kuhlmann–Anderson Measure of Academic Potential, Eighth Edition

The *Kuhlmann–Anderson Measure of Academic Potential, Eighth Edition* (Kuhlmann & Anderson, 1982), contains verbal and nonverbal subtests for assessing the cognitive ability of students from kindergarten through grade 12. The *Kuhlmann–Anderson* yields separate verbal, nonverbal, and composite scores.

Otis–Lennon School Ability Test (OLSAT)

Perhaps the most widely used group intelligence test, the *Otis–Lennon School Ability Test (OLSAT)* (Otis & Lennon, 1996) consists of five subtests for estimating the intelligence of children from grades 1 through 12. The subtests are verbal comprehension, verbal reasoning, pictorial reasoning, figural reasoning, and quantitative reasoning. The *OLSAT* was standardized with the *Stanford Achievement Test Series (Stanford 8)* and administered with the *Metropolitan Achievement Tests, Seventh Edition (MAT7)*. Giving the *OLSAT* with the *Stanford 8* or the *MAT7* yields an achievement/ability comparison index (AAC) that describes student ability in relation to the achievement of other students with the same measured ability.

Test of Cognitive Skills, Second Edition (TCS/2)

The *Test of Cognitive Skills, Second Edition (TCS/2)* (CBT/McGraw-Hill, 1992) contains four subtests: sequences, analogies, memory, and verbal reasoning. The *TCS/2* measures the learning ability of students from grades 2 through 12 and takes approximately 50 minutes to administer. Scores are available for each subtest, and the combined scores yield an overall score called a *Cognitive Skills Index (CSI)*. *TCS/2* scores may also be used with scores from the *Comprehensive Tests of Basic Skills (CTBS)* or the *California Achievement Test* to predict achievement in later grades.

Limitations of Group Intelligence Tests

Although inexpensive and easy to administer, group intelligence tests exhibit several limitations. First of all, the multiple-choice format limits the range and variety of questions on these tests. Second, most group tests require students to bubble in their responses to multiple-choice questions on a machine-scored answer sheet. This pencil-on-paper format requires good reading skills, sophisticated test-taking know-how, and sufficient fine motor dexterity. For this reason, group tests are not suitable for students with special needs who have reading problems. For these students, a low score may reflect reading problems rather than low intelligence. Likewise, students with visual-perception problems, who have difficulty filling in computer-scored answer sheets and who often skip items, may receive low scores on group tests due to visual-processing deficits and poor test-taking skills rather than intellectual deficiencies. Because of these limitations, schools restrict the use of group tests in special education to specific situations requiring a screening test of intelligence. Therefore, assessment teams avoid making major educational decisions based on group test results.

Specialized Intelligence Tests

Although the individually administered, general tests of intelligence are used whenever possible, evaluators sometimes use specialized intelligence tests with students who have sensory impairments such as deafness and blindness, physical impairments, and disabilities such as severe mental retardation. Students with these disabilities have unique needs and characteristics that define the way they should be assessed. When evaluators fail to take these unique characteristics into account, errors in test administration, difficulties in test interpretation, and other inaccuracies in the assessment process may result. A fundamental goal of assessment in special education is to minimize these types of problems, and in most cases these special characteristics do not prevent evaluators from using a general test of intelligence, such as the *WISC-III*. However, in some situations, unusual test-taking behaviors and learning styles preclude the use of general tests. When this occurs, evaluators depend on a variety of specialized intelligence tests to reduce errors and avoid discrimination.

The characteristics displayed by students with special needs vary depending on the specific disability. For example, tests that require motor performance, such as copying block designs, may be inappropriate for students with certain physical disabilities. Likewise, tests that emphasize verbal language skills may not be appropriate for students with hearing impairments. In a similar way, students with visual-perception impairments may not perform up to their ability level on tests that require visual-reasoning ability. Students with culturally different backgrounds also must be considered in intelligence testing because failure to consider their needs, experiences, and response styles may bias testing results. Although not used on a widespread basis, the specialized intelligence tests have been developed for situations in which students cannot be properly assessed using traditional instruments and methods.

Columbia Mental Maturity Scale

The *Columbia Mental Maturity Scale, third edition (CMMS)* (Burgemeister et al., 1972), is a classic specialized test that is still used on a limited basis. The *CMMS* is a test of visual-reasoning ability that requires no verbal response and minimum motor response. Originally developed for measuring the intelligence of children with physical handicaps, the *CMMS* does not require reading, writing, or speaking skills. The scale consists of a series of 92 printed drawings on large cards and allows for a variety of responses to these test items, including pointing to the correct drawing and, for children with severe physical disabilities, using an eye-blink communication system.

Designed for children from 3 years 6 months through 9 years of age, the scale takes 15 to 20 minutes to give. The administration procedure requires the child to select the drawing that does not belong in a series of drawings illustrated on each of the 92 cards. The drawings use shape, size, missing parts, and symbols for the various visual discrimination tasks. Scores obtained from the *CMMS* include a global deviation IQ score (M = 100, SD = 16) with corresponding percentiles and stanines. An age-equivalent score, called a *maturity index score,* is also available. A national sample of 2,600 children from 25 states, stratified by gender, parental occupation, race, and geographic area, provided norms for the test. Coefficients for split-half and test-retest reliability averaged in the .80s, and correlations for concurrent validity with other intelligence tests ranged from the .30s to the .70s. Overall, the *CMMS* exhibits adequate technical characteristics.

Although the *CMMS* measures only one type of intellectual ability, it is technically adequate, well designed, and easy to administer and score. The test is especially useful with children who are nonvocal due to severe physical disabilities.

Comprehensive Test of Nonverbal Intelligence (CTONI)

The increasingly popular *Comprehensive Test of Nonverbal Intelligence (CTONI)* (Hammill et al., 1996) measures six different types of nonverbal reasoning abilities. No oral responses, reading, writing, or object manipulation are required. The *CTONI* is especially appropriate for use with individuals who are bilingual, speak a language other than English, or are socially/economically disadvantaged, deaf, language disordered, motor impaired, or neurologically impaired. Suitable for students ages 6 through 18, the *CTONI* is individually administered in less than 60 minutes. The raw scores of each subtest are translated into percentiles, age equivalents, and standard scores. Three composite scores are also provided: a nonverbal intelligence quotient, a pictorial nonverbal intelligence quotient, and a geometric nonverbal intelligence quotient. Standardized on a population of more than 2,000 students from 23 states, the *CTONI* exhibits adequate reliability and limited evidence regarding validity.

The highly useful *Comprehensive Test of Nonverbal Intelligence-Computer Administered (CTONI-CA)* (Hammill et al., 1997) is an innovative, interactive multimedia test given on a PC-compatible computer, which gives all the instructions to the person being tested in a clear, pleasant human voice. The examinee simply points the mouse and clicks on the answer. The program then automatically gives the items until a ceiling is reached, and then the other subtests are given one by one. When the testing is completed, the computer generates a report that can be viewed on the screen or printed.

Test of Nonverbal Intelligence, Third Edition (TONI-3)

The *Test of Nonverbal Intelligence, Third Edition (TONI-3)* (Brown et al., 1997) measures nonverbal intelligence and visual-reasoning ability. Useful with students who have limited language skills in reading, writing, speech, or listening, the age range of the *TONI-3* is 5 to 85 years. Consisting of sets of abstract figures and drawings, the *TONI-3* takes about 15 minutes to give. The evaluator may pantomime the simple instructions, if necessary, and the student responds by selecting the missing element from the sets of drawings, which test visual-matching ability and ability to comprehend visual analogies and progressions. The test is completely nonverbal and mostly motor free, requiring only a point, nod, or symbolic gesture to indicate response choices.

Evaluators may report *TONI-3* results using an age-based standard score (M = 100, SD = 15) or a percentile rank. Two forms of the test provide a convenient method for retesting. Standardized on a sample of over 3,000 individuals, the *TONI-3* exhibits adequate reliability. However, the manual presents limited information regarding validity.

Particularly useful with students who have limited English proficiency, speech and language problems, or physical impairments, the *TONI-3* is a specialized instrument for measuring nonverbal problem-solving ability. Although restricted in scope, the *TONI-3* represents a promising alternative to general intelligence testing in situations that require specialized instruments.

System of Multipluralistic Assessment (SOMPA)

The *System of Multicultural Pluralistic Assessment (SOMPA)* (Mercer & Lewis, 1978) is significant because the instrument made such a dramatic contribution to reducing racial and cultural bias in intelligence testing. Unlike traditional intelligence tests, the *SOMPA* is a comprehnsive system that contains nine different measures for evaluating the intellectual abilities, perceptual-motor abilities, and adaptive behavior skills of students between the ages of 5 and 11 years. The *SOMPA* estimates learning potential by considering sociocultural and health factors as an integral part of the assessment process. By including evaluation of language and cultural differences in assessing intellectual performance, the *SOMPA* attempts to minimize racial and cultural bias in classifying and placing students in special education.

The *SOMPA* consists of two major components (parent interview materials and student assessment materials) and requires administration by a team of certified professionals. A trained social worker gives the parent interview to the student's primary care giver in the home in about an hour. The parent interview includes three measures: (1) an adaptive behavior inventory, (2) a sociocultural scale, and (3) a health history inventory. A psychologist or diagnostician gives the student assessment in a school setting in about two hours. Materials in the student assessment component include measurement of physical dexterity, weight by height, visual acuity, auditory acuity, visual-motor skills, and intellectual ability (the latter determined by the *Wechsler Intelligence Scale for Children-Revised* or the *Wechsler Preschool and Primary Scale of Intelligence-Revised*).

In addition to using IQ scores in the conventional manner, the *SOMPA* scoring system accounts for social and cultural background variations by transforming WISC-R scores into a standard score referred to as *estimated learning potential (ELP)*. The ELP represents ability level in comparison with students with similar backgrounds and avoids reliance on a traditional IQ score. Use of an ELP score rather than an IQ is consistent with the views of Jane Mercer, one of the authors of the *SOMPA*, who advocates eliminating traditional IQ testing altogether because it tends to discriminate against certain students. However, other experts contend that ELP scores may not predict school performance as well as IQ scores. Furthermore, Sattler (1992) argues against using the *SOMPA* for classification and placement because of the inadequate validity of the ELP score and the lack of national norms. Although the *SOMPA* provides norms for black, Hispanic, and white students, the norms were developed in California and therefore may not represent all students in other states.

Despite these criticisms, the *SOMPA* introduced many innovations that encourage reliance on culturally sensitive measures of behavior to support or modify classification decisions made during assessment. Although not widely used today, many of the features of the *SOMPA* have been incorporated into more contemporary measures, resulting in significant reductions in the number of students, especially minority students, who are clinically diagnosed as retarded but not considered retarded in their home or community.

Universal Nonverbal Intelligence Test (UNIT)

One of the newest specialized intelligence tests, the *Universal Nonverbal Intelligence Test (UNIT)* (Bracken & McCallum, 1997) is a language-free test that requires no receptive or expressive language from the examiner or the examinee. According to McCallum and Bracken, tests like the *UNIT* are needed because of the increasing number of non-English-speaking or limited-English-proficient (LEP) students in the schools. Tests like the *UNIT* are also needed for children with hearing impairments or receptive and expressive language disabilities. Children with these impairments and those with limited English proficiency are unfairly disadvantaged when assessed by means of spoken language.

The *UNIT,* which is designed for use with children from age 5 through 17, contains six subtests in two major categories: memory and reasoning. The three memory subtests are object memory, spatial memory, and symbolic memory. The three reasoning subtests are cube design, mazes, and analogic reasoning. Completing the *UNIT* requires approximately 45 minutes; it may also be given in short form by administering only two or four subtests. The short-form versions require only 15 or 30 minutes to give and may have limited usefulness as gross screening measures. Available *UNIT* scores include a full-scale score, a memory quotient, a reasoning quotient, a symbolic quotient, and a nonsymbolic quotient. Individual subtest scores can also be obtained for each of the six subtests.

Standardized on a national sample, the initial reliability and validity data indicate that the *UNIT* displays adequate technical qualities and thus has the potential to become a valuable test in situations that require administration of a nonverbal intelligence test.

Other Specialized Tests of Intelligence

A number of other specialized tests of intelligence meet the unique needs of students with disabilities. These tests are limited in usefulness because they often have less than adequate technical characteristics and, like so many of the specialized tests, may have old publication dates. However, they do provide a means of assessing the cognitive ability of students for whom the traditional tests are inappropriate. These tests include but are not limited to the following:

- The *Goodenough-Harris Drawing Test* (Harris, 1963), which measures IQ by evaluating specific details and features of a drawing of a human figure.

- The *Pictorial Test of Intelligence (PTI)* (French, 1964), which is a nonverbal measure of aptitude for children from age 3 through 8 years that includes six subtests: picture vocabulary, form discrimination, information and comprehension, similarities, size and number, and intermediate recall.
- *Raven's Progressive Matrices* (Raven, 1983–1986), which are a series of three nonverbal picture tests of visual reasoning ability. The *Coloured Progressive Matrices* are for children from ages 5 to 11 years who have mental and physical disabilities. The *Standard Progressive Matrices* are for individuals from 6 to 80 years. The *Advanced Progressive Matrices* are for individuals from 11 years to adulthood.
- The *Slosson Intelligence Test, Revised (SIT-R)* (Slosson et al., 1991) is a measure of the cognitive ability of children from 4 through adulthood. Designed for evaluating the mental ability of individuals who are learning disabled, mentally retarded, blind, or orthopedically disabled, the *SIT-R* provides a quick estimate of general verbal cognitive ability.

The wide variety of specialized tests confirms the complexity of the concept of intelligence and also illustrates the diversity of opinion among test developers regarding methods for measuring cognitive ability. Representing attempts to make intelligence testing as fair as possible for students with unique learning characteristics and disabilities, these specialized tests provide viable alternatives, when used in appropriate situations, to the standard tests.

Intelligence Tests for Infants, Toddlers, and Preschoolers

Infants, toddlers, and preschoolers represent a special population with unique characteristics, especially language and communication, that define appropriate assessment procedures for very young children and suggest the need for specialized tests of intellectual ability. In general, specialized tests for this group of children estimate learning potential based on a relatively narrow sample of behavior, and, unfortunately, some of these tests show limited reliability and validity.

Because the behavior of very young children is less predictable and changes more rapidly than that of older students, measuring the intellectual development of infants, toddlers, and preschoolers is more difficult. For this reason, infant tests should be viewed as useful measures of development for predicting cognitive ability rather than as traditional measures of intelligence. Despite these limitations, tests of this type play an important role in identifying and serving very young students with special needs. Reviews of representative intelligence tests for infants, toddlers, and preschoolers follow.

Bayley Scales of Infant Development

The most carefully designed and widely administered infant developmental scales are the *Bayley Scales of Infant Development, Second Edition (BSID-II)* (Bayley, 1993). Designed to measure the behavior of infants from 1 month to 30 months, the *BSID-II* includes a mental scale, a motor scale, and a behavior rating scale. The mental scale measures sensory and perceptual skills, vocalizations, memory, problem solving, and early verbal communication. The motor scale measures gross and fine motor skills. The behavior scale is a rating scale completed by a primary care giver. The mental and motor scales take about 45 minutes to give, and each produces a standard score with a mean of 100 and a standard deviation of 16. Standardized using a national sample of over 1,000 infants, the *Bayley Scales* exhibit good technical characteristics. Split-half reliabilities for the mental scale range from .81 to .93 and for the motor scale from .68 to .92. Evidence supporting the construct validity of the test is available from numerous research studies with a variety of groups of infants. The *Bayley Scales of Infant Development, Second Edition* are a useful tool for early identification of infants with disabilities and have separate mental and motor tests to pinpoint individual needs.

Bayley Infant Neurodevelopmental Screener (BINS)

A complementary product to the *BSID-II* is the *Bayley Infant Neurodevelopmental Screener (BINS)* (Aylward, 1995), which was developed for use by developmental pediatricians, pediatric nurse practitioners, occupational and physical therapists, and school psychologists who screen infants from 3 to 24 months. The *BINS* consists of items that assess basic neurological development, auditory and visual reception, cognitive process, and social development. Standardized on 600 infants, the sample represents infants from Neonatal Intensive Care Unit follow-up clinics who were born prematurely or asphyxiated at birth or who have experienced intraventricular hemorrhage, apnea, patent ductus arteriosus, or seizures. The *BINS* takes 5 to 10 minutes to give and a few more minutes to score. The individual items are scored as optimal or nonoptimal. Optimal items are summed, and the total score is determined relative to the cutoff score to determine an infant's risk classification.

Extended Merrill-Palmer Scale

Because the *Extended Merrill-Palmer Scale* (Ball et al., 1978) measures both the verbal and nonverbal intelligence of children from age 3 through 5 years, it is a valuable tool for use in special education. The *Extended Merrill-Palmer Scale* evaluates intellectual behavior in two categories and four dimensions. The two categories are the content of thinking and the process of thinking, each of which category includes two dimensions: the content dimensions, which include semantic production (verbal) and figural production (nonverbal) and process dimensions, which include productive thinking (verbal) and evaluative thinking (nonverbal). Available test scores encompass a general score and four subtest scores, one for each dimension. These scores provide a profile useful in diagnosis and programming. However, the *Extended Merrill-Palmer Scale* exhibits several technical deficiencies, including a limited standardization sample, low reliability estimates, and no validity information in the test manual. These limitations make the *Extended Merrill-Palmer Scale* most useful when given as an adjunct in a comprehensive battery of tests rather than as the primary instrument. Evaluators find the nonverbal scores particularly useful with children who have language problems and the verbal scores especially valuable with children who have physical disabilities.

McCarthy Scales of Children's Abilities

The *McCarthy Scales of Children's Abilities* (McCarthy, 1972), an individual test of intelligence for children from 2½ to 8½ years of age, exhibits excellent norms and adequate reliability and validity. Like the *Merrill-Palmer Scale,* the *McCarthy Scales* provide a profile of ability across both verbal and nonverbal subtests. The six overlapping subtests are the following:

- Verbal
- Perceptual-performance
- Quantitative
- Memory
- Motor
- General cognitive skills

It takes about an hour to administer the *McCarthy Scales,* which yield standard scores (M = 50, SD = 10) for each of the six subtests and an overall standard score (M = 100, SD = 16). However, the overall score has a bottom limit of 50 and a top limit of 150. This prevents use of the instrument with children who have intellectual abilities at extremely high and low levels. The *McCarthy Scales* include a well-designed manual, complete guidelines, and adequate materials, which combine to make the *McCarthy Scales* a useful tool for evaluating young children.

McCarthy Screening Test (MST)

The *McCarthy Screening Test (MST)* (McCarthy, 1978) includes six component scales, all drawn from the *McCarthy Scales of Children's Abilities,* which predict a child's ability for success in schoolwork in the early grades. Designed to identify children who may be at risk for learning problems, the *MST* includes subtests that measure verbal memory, right-left orientation, leg coordination, draw-a-design, numeric memory, and conceptual grouping. The *MST* measures the abilities of children from age 4 through 6.6 years and takes about 20 minutes to administer. Poor performance on the *MST* may indicate that further testing for a disability is needed.

Ordinal Scales of Psychological Development

The *Ordinal Scales of Psychological Development* (Uzgiris & Hunt, 1975) measure the conceptual level of infants from 2 weeks to 2 years of age. Evaluators often use the *Ordinal Scales,* which are based on the Piagetian steps of development, for assessing children with severe and profound disabilities. The *Ordinal Scales* measure development in seven areas:

1. Visual pursuit
2. Permanence of objects
3. Means-ends relationships
4. Gestural and vocal imitation
5. Causality
6. Construction of objects in space
7. Behavior of objects

Unlike all of the other tests reviewed in this chapter, no norms exist for the *Ordinal Scales of Psychological Development.* Despite this, however, leading diagnosticians (Dunst, 1980; Langley, 1986) have documented the value of the *Ordinal Scales.*

Their value is in the flexible administration procedures that identify a student's level of conceptual development, enabling the evaluator to modify the assessment procedures to elicit optimal responses. In addition, the *Ordinal Scales* draw on concepts that readily translate into intervention strategies. When conducting a formal evaluation for classification and placement purposes, many evaluators give the *Ordinal Scales* together with a standard measure of intellectual development. Used in this way, the *Ordinal Scales* provide additional assessment data that help staffing teams make the best possible classification and placement decision. See Chapter 8 for additional information about the *Ordinal Scales*.

Wechsler Preschool and Primary Scale of Intelligence-Revised

The *Wechsler Preschool and Primary Scale of Intelligence-Revised (WPPSI-R)* (Wechsler, 1989) is designed for young children from 3 years to 7 years 3 months of age. One of the most popular tests for measuring the intelligence of young children, the *WPPSI-R* takes about 75 minutes to give. Like the *WISC-III*, the *WPPSI-R* contains a verbal scale and a performance scale. The six *WPPSI-R* verbal subtests are the following:

Information	Vocabulary
Comprehension	Similarities
Arithmetic	Sentences

The six performance subtests are as follows:

Object assembly	Mazes
Geometric design	Picture completion
Block design	Animal pegs

Available *WPPSI-R* scores include a scaled score for each subtest, a verbal IQ, a performance IQ, and a full-scale IQ. The somewhat restricted range of IQs is 41–160. Because the *WPPSI-R* is often used to identify children with mental retardation, the lower range of 41 restricts use with children suspected of having profound mental retardation.

Standardized on a sample of 1,700 children, the *WPPSI-R* displays excellent reliability and validity. Reviewers (Bracken, 1992; Braden, 1992) describe the test as technically superior and likely to be the test of choice among psychologists. Because of its popularity among practitioners and researchers, the *WPPSI-R* is considered the classic preschool intelligence test.

☑ Comprehension Checklist

Specialized intelligence tests and intelligence tests for infants, toddlers, and preschoolers further illustrate the diversity that exists in the measurement of cognitive ability. Unlike general tests of intelligence, which rely primarily on verbal language skills, the specialized tests often depend on measurement of motor performance, visual reasoning ability, and receptive language skills to predict learning potential. The availability of so many tests provides a range of options in selecting appropriate measures for meeting the unique needs of students in special education.

Guidelines for Teachers in the Use of Intelligence Tests

Knowledge of intelligence tests is useless without considering the practical consequences of such testing. Because teachers provide direct services to students on a daily basis, they tend to be especially sensitive to the functional aspects of testing. The following applied, pragmatic considerations serve as guidelines for teachers to follow in the use of intelligence tests.

- When reporting an intelligence test score, *always name the test and specify the date of testing as part of the reporting process.* This is important because each test measures intelligence somewhat differently (e.g., an IQ of 68 on one test equals an IQ of 70 on another), and test scores more than 3 years old may not be as accurate as a current score.
- Although *professionals should avoid making major educational decisions on the basis of test scores alone,* the general procedure for interpreting intelligence test scores with a mean of 100 and a standard deviation of 15 is as follows:

  Scores in the 85 to 115 range fall within one standard deviation from the mean (100 ±15) and reflect average intelligence.

  Scores in the 115 to 130 range are two standard deviations above the mean and reflect above-average intelligence.

  Scores of approximately 130 and above are more than two standard deviations above the mean and indicate superior intellectual ability.

  Scores from 70 to 85 are two standard deviations below the mean and fall into the slow-learning category.

  Very low IQs (below approximately 70 IQ points, or more than two standard deviations below the mean) indicate significant intellectual deficiency.
- Although intelligence and creativity are positively correlated, distinct differences also exist between the two traits. For this reason, *teachers should avoid making assumptions about a student's creativity based on intelligence test results.* In fact, because creativity is such a dynamic and divergent characteristic, evaluators rely on completely separate tests to measure it.
- Although the intelligence of individuals tends to remain stable throughout life, it *can change over time.* The specific factors that cause changes in intelligence are far from clear, but most experts agree that significant variations occur most frequently among those with extremely low or high levels of mental ability.
- Intelligence tests are excellent predictors of success in school, but they are *poor predictors of other behaviors such as vocational success and personal or social satisfaction.*
- Professionals must *avoid judging intelligence test results in isolation.* Instead they should consider intelligence test results along with other relevant assessment data, including achievement, family history, motivation, adaptive behavior, and sociocultural background.
- Intelligence tests play a key role in classifying and placing students in special education. However, most intelligence tests provide little information that directly translates into specific instructional objectives. Therefore, most *teachers rely on estimates of intellectual ability as a guide in establishing overall educational goals rather than for identifying specific intervention needs.*

FOCUS 7–3

Intelligence Testing and *The Bell Curve*

When *The Bell Curve: Intelligence and Class Structure in American Life* (Herrnstein & Murray, 1994) was published, intelligence testing was criticized. A basic argument of the book is that widespread intelligence testing creates a class of intellectual elites in positions of political and economic power. According to the authors, the problem is that economically and socially disadvantaged children (many of whom are from minority groups) are excluded from this elite class. *The Bell Curve* controversy raises continuing social and political arguments. As educators we need to be aware of and sensitive to these arguments because children from minority groups are overrepresented in special education classes due to low scores on intelligence tests. In a commentary on the book, Thorndike (1997) suggests that we ask what the research data say about measuring intelligence to predict academic success. Because the data show such a strong positive correlation between intelligence and academic success, we rely on intelligence testing to identify students with disabilities. However, if we eliminate intelligence tests, accurate identification would be even more difficult. Our goal as special educators should be to eliminate bias in the use of intelligence tests so that all children are treated fairly and equally.

Summary

Testing intelligence, the process of measuring the learning ability of students, is a complex component of assessment in special education. Questions concerning the proper use of intelligence testing account for much of the complexity, but even the definition of intelligence itself remains a topic of debate. Some think of intelligence as a global ability, whereas others define it as a set of specific aptitudes. The diverse array of available intelligence tests further contributes to the complex nature of the subject (see Table 7–5 on page 187). Intelligence tests include the widely used general measures of intellectual ability, such as the *WISC-III*, and a number of specialized instruments. Although this variety adds to the intricacy of the subject, it also provides a range of options to choose from in selecting a test to meet the needs of the individual student.

In addition to the complex nature of the subject, controversy surrounds intelligence testing (see Focus 7–3) and the use of IQ scores. For special educators the debate encompasses several problems, including limited predictive validity, inaccuracy of IQ scores at the extremes, and bias against culturally and linguistically different students. As a result of these issues, some critics advocate the elimination of intelligence testing altogether. However, most experts support continued use of intelligence testing and promote continued efforts to improve assessment procedures and to reduce concerns about inequality and imprecision.

Because virtually all students in special education are given one or more intelligence tests, it is imperative for teachers to be familiar with the tests and understand the implications of the test results. Special education teachers equipped with this knowledge can better serve their students by helping to ensure accuracy and fairness in the use of intelligence tests.

Chapter Review and Application

Multiple Choice

Directions: Read each item carefully. In the blank beside each item, write the letter of the best response. Each item contains only one best answer. Check your answers with the answer key at the end of the book.

_____ 1. Most intelligence testing with students who have special needs occurs during the _____ stage of assessment.
   a. screening
   b. classification and placement
   c. instructional intervention
   d. measuring progress

_____ 2. These intelligence tests usually consist of items that measure verbal and performance skills.
   a. Individually administered
   b. Group administered
   c. Tests for special populations
   d. Tests for infants, toddlers, and preschoolers

_____ 3. These pencil-on-paper intelligence tests use "bubble-in" scoring sheets.
   a. Individually administered
   b. Group administered
   c. Tests for special populations
   d. Tests for infants, toddlers, and preschoolers

_____ 4. These intelligence tests frequently consist of items that measure visual reasoning ability.
   a. Individually administered
   b. Group administered
   c. Tests for special populations
   d. Tests for infants, toddlers, and preschoolers

_____ 5. Intelligence tests are best at predicting
   a school success.
   b. vocational success.
   c. preferred learning style.
   d. student conduct and behavior.

_____ 6. Intelligence tests tend to be most accurate
   a. at extremely low levels of performance.
   b. at the midrange of performance.
   c. at extremely high levels of performance.
   d. at both extremely low and high levels of performance.

_____ 7. Most intelligence tests tend to favor students from
   a. minority groups.
   b. low socioeconomic backgrounds.

    c. rural areas.

    d. middle-class backgrounds.

_____ **8.** For the most part, group intelligence tests serve as

    a. screening tests.

    b. comprehensive diagnostic tools.

    c. specialized tests for special populations.

    d. tests for infants and toddlers.

_____ **9.** The most widely used, individually administered general test of intelligence is the

    a. *Stanford–Binet Intelligence Scale: Fourth Edition (SB4).*

    b. *Woodcock–Johnson Psychoeducational Battery-Revised (WJ-R).*

    c. *Kaufman Assessment Battery for Children (K-ABC).*

    d. *Wechsler Intelligence Scale for Children-Third Edition (WISC-III).*

_____ **10.** Which is the oldest intelligence test?

    a. *Stanford–Binet Intelligence Scale: Fourth Edition (SB4)*

    b. *Woodcock–Johnson Psychoeducational Battery-Revised (WJ-R)*

    c. *Kaufman Assessment Battery for Children (K-ABC)*

    d. *Wechsler Intelligence Scale for Children-Third Edition (WISC-III)*

_____ **11.** Which test measures both intelligence and achievement?

    a. *Stanford–Binet Intelligence Scale: Fourth Edition (SB4)*

    b. *Woodcock–Johnson Psychoeducational Battery-Revised (WJ-R)*

    c. *Wechsler Intelligence Scale for Children-Third Edition (WISC-III)*

_____ **12.** No other test provides as many scores and profiles as the _____.

    a. *Stanford–Binet Intelligence Scale: Fourth Edition (SB4)*

    b. *Woodcock–Johnson Psychoeducational Battery-Revised (WJ-R)*

    c. *Kaufman Assessment Battery for Children (K-ABC)*

    d. *Wechsler Intelligence Scale for Children-Third Edition (WISC-III)*

_____ **13.** Which intelligence test provides sociocultural percentiles, normed on a special sample of minority and nonminority students?

    a. *Stanford–Binet Intelligence Scale: Fourth Edition (SB4)*

    b. *Woodcock–Johnson Psychoeducational Battery-Revised (WJ-R)*

    c. *Kaufman Assessment Battery for Children (K-ABC)*

    d. *Wechsler Intelligence Scale for Children-Third Edition (WISC-III)*

_____ **14.** Measuring the intelligence of very young children is _____.

    a. more difficult because the behavior of infants and toddlers is less predictable and changes more rapidly

    b. about the same because the infant and toddler tests measure similar behaviors

    c. less difficult because infants and toddlers display fewer behaviors

    d. much less difficult because infants and toddlers display fewer advanced behaviors

_____ **15.** This carefully designed and widely administered test includes a mental scale, a motor scale, and a behavior rating scale.

    a. *Bayley Scales of Infant Development, Second Edition (BSID-II)*

    b. *Ordinal Scales of Psychological Development*

    c. *Wechsler Preschool and Primary Scale of Intelligence-Revised*

    d. *McCarthy Scales of Children's Abilities*

_____ **16.** This test is based on the Piagetian steps of development.
  a. *Bayley Scales of Infant Development, Second Edition (BSID-II)*
  b. *Ordinal Scales of Psychological Development*
  c. *Wechsler Preschool and Primary Scale of Intelligence-Revised*
  d. *McCarthy Scales of Children's Abilities*

Match Type of Behavior

Directions: Match the following intelligence test items with the type of behavior they measure. Select from these choices: verbal language or performance. In the blank beside each item write the best response. Use each choice more than once. Check your answers with the answer key at the end of the book.

_____ **1.** Answering general information questions such as "Who invented the telephone?"
_____ **2.** Tracing a path through mazes of increasing complexity.
_____ **3.** Defining words by asking questions such as "What is a novel?"
_____ **4.** Arranging small blocks according to visually presented designs.
_____ **5.** Solving arithmetic problems such as "If you have $12.50 and you spend $5.00, how much would you have left?"
_____ **6.** Coding by associating and copying specified symbols.
_____ **7.** Paper folding and cutting.
_____ **8.** Identifying similarities such as "What do apples and oranges have in common?"

Match Type of Intelligence Test

Directions: Match the following intelligence tests with the appropriate type of test. Select from the following types of tests: group; individually administered, general; specialized; or infant, toddler, preschool. In the blank beside each question, write the best response. You may use some choices more than once. Check your answers with the answer key at the end of the book.

_____ **1.** *Otis–Lennon School Ability Test (OLSAT)*
_____ **2.** *Wechsler Intelligence Scale for Children-Third Edition (WISC-III)*
_____ **3.** *Comprehensive Test of Nonverbal Intelligence (CTONI)*
_____ **4.** *Extended Merrill–Palmer Scales of Intelligence*
_____ **5.** *Stanford–Binet Intelligence Scale: Fourth Edition (SB4)*
_____ **6.** *Cognitive Abilities Test (CogAT)*
_____ **7.** *Universal Nonverbal Intelligence Test (UNIT)*
_____ **8.** *Ordinal Scales of Psychological Development*
_____ **9.** *Kaufman Assessment Battery for Children (K-ABC)*

True-False

Directions: Answer true or false for each of the following statements about assessing intelligence by writing "T" or "F" in the blank beside each item. Check your answers with the answer key at the end of the book.

_____ **1.** When reporting an intelligence test score, you should name the test and specify the date of testing as part of the reporting process.

____ **2.** Few if any differences exist between intelligence and creativity.

____ **3.** Most intelligence tests provide little information that directly translates into specific instructional objectives.

____ **4.** Intelligence tests are excellent predictors of school success.

____ **5.** Intelligence tests are outstanding predictors of vocational success.

____ **6.** Intelligence test scores should be judged and evaluated in isolation, without regard for other assessment data.

Short Answers

Directions: Review your understanding of the material in this chapter by answering the following short answer items. Compare your responses with the sample answers. Your responses should contain information that is similar to but not exactly the same as the information in the sample answers at the end of the book.

1. Explain three of the major issues associated with intelligence testing of students with special needs, identify which of these is of the greatest concern, and explain why.

2. List four reasons for using intelligence tests with students who have disabilities.

3. Describe three advantages and three limitations of group intelligence tests.

4. Describe the basic characteristics and uses of two intelligence tests for screening groups of children.

5. What are the advantages of test batteries like the *Woodcock–Johnson Psychoeducational Battery-Revised (WJ-R)* that include an intelligence test and an achievement test?

6. Which individually-administered general test of intelligence would you use to measure the intelligence of a 10-year-old student suspected of having a mild to moderate disability. Why would you use this particular test?

7. Which specialized test would you use to measure the intelligence of a nonverbal child suspected of having severe mental retardation? Why would you use this particular test?

8. Which preschool test would you use to measure the intelligence of a 5-year-old child suspected of having mild developmental disabilities? Why would you use this particular test?

9. Which infant test would you use to measure the intelligence of a 2-year-old? Why would you use this particular test?

References

Anastasi, A. (1988). Review of the *Stanford–Binet Intelligence Scale:* Fourth edition. In J. C. Conoley, J. J. Kramer, & J. V. Mitchell (Eds.). *The Supplement to the Ninth Mental Measurements Yearbook.* Lincoln, NE: Buros Institute of Mental Measurement of the University of Nebraska.

Aylward, G. P. (1995). *Bayley Infant Neurodevelopmental Screener (BINS).* San Antonio, TX: Psychological Corporation.

Ball, R. S., Merrifield, P., & Scott, L. (1978). *The Extended Merrill–Palmer Scale.* Chicago: Stoetling.

Bayley, N. (1993). *Bayley Scales of Infant Development* (2d ed.). San Antonio, TX: Psychological Corporation.

Bortner, M. (1985). Review of the *WISC-R*. In J. V. Mitchell (Ed.), *The Ninth Mental Measurements Yearbook*. Lincoln, NE: Buros Institute of Mental Measurement of the University of Nebraska.

Bracken, B. A. (1992). Review of the *WPPSI-R*. In J. J. Kramer & J. C. Conoley (Eds.), *The Eleventh Mental Measurements Yearbook*. Lincoln, NE: Buros Institute of Mental Measurement of the University of Nebraska.

Bracken, B. A., & McCallum, R. S., (1997). *Universal Nonverbal Intelligence Test*. Chicago: Riverside.

Braden, J. P. (1992). Review of the *WPPSI-R*. In J. J. Kramer and J. C. Conoley (Eds.), *The Eleventh Mental Measurements Yearbook*. Lincoln, NE: Buros Institute of Mental Measurement of the University of Nebraska.

———— (1995). Review of the *WISC-III*. In J. C. Conoley and J. C. Impara (Eds.), *The Twelfth Mental Measurements Yearbook*. Lincoln, NE: Buros Institute of Mental Measurement of the University of Nebraska.

Brown, L., Shervenou, R. J., & Johnsen, S. K. (1997). *Test of Nonverbal Intelligence* (3d ed.). Austin, TX: PRO-ED.

Burgemeister, B. B., Blum, L. H., & Lorge, I. (1972). *Columbia Mental Maturity Scale* (3d ed.). San Antonio, TX: Psychological Corporation.

Chen, J., & Gardner, H. (1997). Alternative assessment from a multiple intelligences theoretical perspective. In D. P. Flanagan, J. L. Genshaft, & P. L. Harrison (Eds.), *Contemporary Intellectual Assessment: Theories, Tests, and Issues*. New York: The Guilford Press, 105–21.

Cronbach, L. J. (1989). Review of the *Stanford–Binet Intelligence Scale: Fourth edition*. In J. C. Conoley & J. J. Kramer (Eds.), *The Tenth Mental Measurements Yearbook*. Lincoln, NE: Buros Institute of Mental Measurements of the University of Nebraska.

(CTB/McGraw-Hill. *Test of Cognitive Skills* (2d ed.). (1992). Monterey, CA: Author.

Cummings, J. A. (1995). Review of the *WR-J*. In J. C. Conoley & J. C. Impara (Eds.), *The Twelfth Mental Measurements Yearbook*. Lincoln, NE: Buros Institute of Mental Measurement of the University of Nebraska, 1113–16.

Detterman. D. K. (1985). Review of the *WISC-R*. In J. V. Mitchell (Ed.), *The Ninth Mental Measurements Yearbook*. Lincoln, NE: Buros Institute of Mental Measurement of the University of Nebraska.

Dunst, C. (1980). *A Clinical and Educational Manual for Use with the Uzgiris and Hunt Scales of Infant and Psychological Development*. Austin, TX: PRO-ED.

French, J. L. (1964). *Manual: Pictorial Test of Intelligence*. Chicago: Riverside Publishing.

Gardner, H. (1993). *Multiple Intelligences: The Theory in Practice*. New York: Basic Books.

Glutting, J. J. (1989). Introduction to the structure and application of the *Stanford–Binet Intelligence Scale: Fourth edition*. *Journal of School Psychology* 27, 69–80.

Hammill, D. D., Pearson, N. A., & Wiederholt, J. L. (1996). *Comprehensive Test of Nonverbal Intelligence*. Austin, TX: PRO-ED.

————(1997). *Comprehensive Test of Nonverbal Intelligence-Computer Administered*. Austin, TX: PRO-ED.

Harris, D. B. (1963). *Goodenough–Harris Drawing Test*. San Diego: Harcourt Brace Jovanovich.

Hessler, G. L. (1993). *Use and Interpretation of the WJ-R*. Itasca, IL: Riverside Publishing Company.

Herrnstein, R. J., & Murray, C. (1994). *The Bell Curve: Intelligence and Class Structure in American Life*. New York: The Free Press.

Horn, J. L. (1985). Remodeling old models of intelligence. In B. B. Wolman (Ed.), *Handbook of Intelligence: Theories, Measurements, and Applications*. New York: John Wiley and Sons.

Kaufman, A. A., & Kaufman, N. L. (1983). *Kaufman Assessment Battery for Children*. Circle Pines, MN: American Guidance Service.

Kuhlmann, F., & Anderson, R. G. (1982). *Kuhlmann–Anderson Measure of Academic Potential,* (8th ed.). Bensenville, IL: Scholastic Testing Service.

Langley, M. B. (1986). Psychoeducational assessment of visually impaired students with additional handicaps. In D. Ellis (Ed.), *Sensory Impairments in Mentally Handicapped People.* San Diego, CA: College Hill Press.

Lee, S. W. (1995). Review of the *WR-J.* In J. C. Conoley & J. C. Impara (Eds.), *The Twelfth Mental Measurements Yearbook.* Lincoln, NE: Buros Institute of Mental Measurement of the University of Nebraska, 1116–19.

Mather, N., (1991). *Instructional guide to the* WJ-R. Itasca, IL: Riverside Publishing Company.

Mather, N., & Jaffe, L. E. (1992). WJ-R *Recommendations and Reports.* Itasca, IL: Riverside Publishing Company.

McCallum, R. S., & Bracken, B. A. (1997). The universal nonverbal intelligence test. In D. P. Flanagan, J. L. Genshaft, & P. L. Harrison (Eds.), *Contemporary Intellectual Assessment: Theories, Tests, and Issues.* New York: Guilford Press, 268–80.

McCarthy, D. A. (1972). *McCarthy Scales of Children's Abilities.* San Antonio, TX: Psychological Corporation.

———(1978). *McCarthy Screening Test.* San Antonio, TX: Psychological Corporation.

McGrew, K. S. (1994). *Clinical Interpretation of the Woodcock–Johnson Tests of Cognitive Ability.* Itasca, IL: Riverside Publishing Company.

Mercer, J. R., & Lewis, J. F. (1978). *System of Multicultural Pluralistic Assessment.* San Antonio: The Psychological Corporation.

Miller-Jones, D. (1989). Culture and testing. *American Psychologist,* 44, 360–66.

Murphy, K. R., & Davidshofer, C. O. (1988). *Psychological Testing: Principles and Applications.* (2d ed.). Englewood Cliffs, NJ: Prentice-Hall.

Otis, A. S., & Lennon, R. T. (1996). *Otis–Lennon School Ability Test (7th ed.).* San Antonio, TX: The Psychological Corporation.

Raven, J. C. (1983–1986). *Raven's Progressive Matrices.* San Antonio, TX: Psychological Corporation.

Robinson, H. B., & Robinson, N. M. (1965). *The Mentally Retarded Child: A Psychological Approach.* New York: McGraw-Hill.

Roid, G. H. (August 1990). *Historical Continuity in Intelligence Assessment: Goals of the* WISC-III *Standardization,* Boston, MA: Paper presented at the Annual Meeting of the American Psychological Association. ERIC Document Reproduction Service ED #329 589.

Salvia, J., & Ysseldyke, J. E. (1991). *Assessment* (5th ed.). Boston: Houghton Mifflin.

Sandoval, J. (1995). Review of the WISC-III. In J. C. Conoley & J. J. Kramer (Eds.), *The Tenth Mental Measurements Yearbook.* Lincoln, NE: Buros Institute of Mental Measurements of the University of Nebraska.

Sattler, J. M. (1992). *Assessment of Children* (3d ed.) San Diego: Author.

Schrank, F. A., & Woodcock, R. W. (1995). *Report Writer for the WJ-R.* Itasca, IL: Riverside Publishing Company.

Slosson, R. L., Nicholson, C. L., & Hibpshman, T. H. (1991). *Slosson Intelligence Test* (rev. ed.). East Aurora, NY: Slosson Educational Publications.

Teele, S. (1997). *Teele Inventory for Multiple Intelligences.* Redland, CA: Sue Teele and Associates.

Terman, L., & Merrill, M. (1916). *Stanford–Binet Intelligence Scale.* Boston: Houghton Mifflin.

———(1937). *Stanford-Binet Intelligence Scale.* Boston: Houghton Mifflin.

———(1960). *Stanford–Binet Intelligence Scale.* Boston: Houghton Mifflin.

———(1993). *Stanford–Binet Intelligence Scale: 1992 Norms Edition.* Boston: Houghton-Mifflin Company.

Thorndike, R. L., & Hagen, E. (1993). *Cognitive Abilities Test.* Chicago: Riverside Publishing Company.

Thorndike, R. L., Hagen, E., & Sattler, J. (1986a). *Stanford–Binet Intelligence Scale* (4th ed.). Chicago: Riverside Publishing Company.

———(1986b). *Stanford–Binet Intelligence Scale:* (4th ed.). *Guide for administering and scoring.* Chicago: Riverside Publishing Company.

———(1986c). *Technical Manual: Stanford–Binet Intelligence Scale:* (4th ed.). Chicago: Riverside Publishing Company.

Thorndike, R. M. (1997). *Measurement and Evaluation in Psychology and Education* (6th ed.). Upper Saddle River, NJ: Merrill/Prentice Hall.

Uzgiris, F., & Hunt, J. (1975). *Assessment in Infancy: The Ordinal Scales of Psychological Development.* Urbana, IL: University of Illinois Press.

Wechsler, D. (1974). *Manual for the Wechsler Intelligence Scale for Children-Revised.* San Antonio, TX: Psychological Corporation.

———(1981). *Manual for the Wechsler Adult Intelligence Scale-Revised.* Cleveland: The Psychological Corporation.

———(1989). *Manual for the Wechsler Preschool and Primary Scale of Intelligence-Revised.* Cleveland: The Psychological Corporation.

———(1991). *Manual for the Wechsler Intelligence Scale for Children* (3d ed.). Cleveland: The Psychological Corporation.

———(1992). *Wechsler Individual Achievement Test.* Cleveland: The Psychological Corporation.

———(1993). *Wechsler Preschool and Primary Scale of Intelligence-Revised.* Cleveland: The Psychological Corporation.

Witt, J., and Gresham, F. (1985). Review of the WISC-R. In J. V. Mitchell (Ed.), *The Ninth Mental Measurements Yearbook.* Lincoln, NE: Buros Institute of Mental Measurement of the University of Nebraska.

Woodcock, R. J., & Muñoz-Sandoval, A. F. (1996). *Batería Woodcock–Muñoz-Revisada.* Itasca, IL: Riverside Publishing Company.

Woodcock, R. W., & Johnson, M. B. (1989). *Woodcock–Johnson Psycho-Educational Battery-Revised.* Itasca, IL: Riverside Publishing Company.

Table 7–5   Defining of Intelligence Tests

Name of Test	Type of Test	Suitable for Individuals Who Are	Brief Description of Test	Purpose of Administering Test
Batería Woodcock–Muñoz-Revisada (Batería-R) (Woodcock & Muñoz-Sandoval, 1996)	Comprehensive, individually administered general measure of intellectual ability and academic achievement	2–retirement	Parallel Spanish version of the Woodcock-Johnson–Revised	To assess cognitive abilities and achievement levels in Spanish-speaking children
Bayley Infant Neurodevelopmental Screener (BINS) (Aylward, 1995)	Infant screening test	3–24 months	Assesses basic neurological development, auditory and visual reception, verbal and motor expression, and cognitive processes	To screen infants and to obtain an estimate of the infant's risk classification
Bayley Scales of Infant Development–Second Edition (BSID-II) (Bayley, 1993)	Infant intelligence test	1–42 months	Includes a mental scale, a motor scale, and a behavior-rating scale	To identify children who have a cognitive or motor delay and to help develop intervention plans
Cognitive Abilities Test (CogAT) (Thorndike & Hagen, 1993)	Group-administered screening test	Kindergarten–12th grade	Measures cognitive functioning and problem solving, including verbal, quantitative, and nonverbal reasoning	To estimate potential for school success
Columbia Mental Maturity Scale (3d ed.) (CMMS) (Burgemeister et al., 1972)	Nonverbal test of intelligence	With physical disabilities from 3 years 6 months–9 years of age	A test of visual reasoning ability that requires no verbal response and minimum motor responses	To measure the intelligence of children
Comprehensive Test of Nonverbal Intelligence (CTONI) (Hammill et al., 1996)	Nonverbal test of intelligence	6–18 years	Measures six different types of nonverbal reasoning abilities	To estimate the nonverbal intelligence of children who are bilingual, speak a language other than English, are socially/economically disadvantaged, deaf, language disordered, motor impaired, or neurologically impaired

Table 7–5 *(continued)*

Name of Test	Type of Test	Suitable for Individuals Who Are	Brief Description of Test	Purpose of Administering Test
Extended Merrill-Palmer Scale (Ball et al., 1978)	Individually administered, general intelligence test for preschool children	3–5 years	Consists of verbal and nonverbal subtests that provide a useful profile for diagnosis and programming	To measure verbal and nonverbal intelligence
Goodenough–Harris Drawing Test (Harris, 1963)	Nonverbal intelligence test suitable for group or individual administration	3–15 years	Measures IQ by evaluating specific details and features of a drawing of a human figure	A nonverbal instrument for assessing mental maturity
Kaufman Assessment Battery for Children (K-ABC) (Kaufman & Kaufman, 1983)	Comprehensive, individually administered intelligence test	2.5–12.5 years	A general measure of intellectual ability and academic achievement	To identify learning ability and achievement
Kuhlmann–Anderson Measure of Academic Potential (8th ed.) (Kuhlmann & Anderson, 1982)	Group-administered screening test	1st–12th grade	A general measure of cognitive skills related to school learning	To estimate school learning ability
McCarthy Scales of Children's Abilities (McCarthy, 1972)	Individual test of intelligence	2.5–8.5 years	Measures cognitive and motor development and incorporates toylike materials and gamelike tasks that children enjoy	To determine a child's general intellectual level as required under IDEA legislation
McCarthy Screening Test (MST) (McCarthy, 1978)	Individually administered screening test of intellectual development	4–6.6 years	Includes six subtests predictive of a child's ability to cope with schoolwork in the early grades	To screen children for early learning difficulties
Ordinal Scales of Psychological Development (Uzgiris & Hunt, 1975)	Specialized measure of cognitive development for children with severe and profound disabilities	Functioning in the age range from 2 weeks–2 years	Measures development of visual pursuit, object permanence, means-ends relationships, gestural and vocal imitation, causality, objects in space, and behavior relating to objects	Based on the Piagetian steps of development, the scales are used extensively for assessing children with severe and profound handicaps

*Tests marked with asterisks are featured in tables in this chapter.

Table 7–5   *(continued)*

Name of Test	Type of Test	Suitable for Individuals Who Are	Brief Description of Test	Purpose of Administering Test
Otis–Lennon School Ability Test (OLSAT) (Otis & Lennon, 1996)	Group-administered screening test	1st–12th grade	Consists of five subtests: verbal comprehension, verbal reasoning, pictorial reasoning, figural reasoning, and quantitative reasoning	To estimate potential for school success
Pictorial Test of Intelligence (PTI) (French, 1964)	Nonverbal intelligence test	3–8 years	Contains subtests that measure picture vocabulary, form discrimination, information and comprehension, similarities, size and number, and intermediate recall	A picture test of intelligence
Raven's Progressive Matrices (Raven, 1983–1986)	Nonverbal intelligence test	Coloured Progressive Matrices—5 to 11, Standard Progressive Matrices—6 to 80, Advanced Progressive Matrices—11 years–adulthood	A series of three nonverbal picture tests of visual reasoning ability	To assess nonverbal abilities at three levels: easy, average, and difficult
Slosson Intelligence Test, Revised (SIT-R) (Slosson et al., 1991)	Screening test of verbal intelligence	4–adulthood	Contains six subtests: general information, similarities and differences, vocabulary, comprehension, arithmetic, and auditory memory	Designed for use as a quick estimate of general verbal cognitive ability
*Stanford–Binet Intelligence Scale (4th ed.) (Thorndike et al., 1986a)	Comprehensive, individually administered intelligence test	2–16 years	A general measure of intellectual ability with subtests for verbal reasoning, quantitative reasoning, abstract/visual reasoning, and short-term memory	To identify overall learning ability

Table 7–5   *(continued)*

Name of Test	Type of Test	Suitable for Individuals Who Are	Brief Description of Test	Purpose of Administering Test
System of Multicultural Pluralistic Intelligence (SOMPA) (Mercer & Lewis 1978)	A system for estimating learning potential by considering sociocultural and health factors as an integral part of the testing process	5–11 years	Consists of two major components (parent interview materials and student assessment materials) and includes evaluation of language and cultural differences in assessing intellectual performance	Attempts to minimize racial and cultural bias in classifying and placing students in special education
Teele Inventory for Multiple Intelligences	An informal measure of multiple intelligences	School age	Provides classroom-based measures of multiple intelligences	Designed for teachers to use in the classroom
Test of Cognitive Skills (2d ed.) (TCS/2) (CTB/ McGraw-Hilll, 1992)	Group-administered screening test	2nd–12th grade	This test consists of four subtests: sequences, analogies, memory, and verbal reasoning	To estimate potential for school success
Wechsler Adult Intelligence Scale-Revised (WAIS-R) (Wechsler, 1981)	Comprehensive, individually administered, general test of intelligence	16 years–retirement	Contains two scales, verbal and performance, which can be given separately or together	To assess general learning ability
Wechsler Intelligence Scale for Children (3d ed.) (WISC-III) (Wechsler, 1991)	Comprehensive, individually administered, general test of intelligence	6–16 years	A general measure of intellectual ability with verbal and performance subtests	To identify the global learning ability of children
Wechsler Preschool and Primary Scale of Intelligence -Revised (WPPSI-R) (Wechsler, 1989)	Comprehensive, individually administered intelligence test	3 years–7 years 3 months	Contains a verbal scale and a performance scale	To measure the intellectual abilities in young children, to classify and place young children with disabilities in special education
Woodcock–Johnson Psycho-educational Battery-Revised (WJ-R) (Woodcock & Johnson, 1989)	Comprehensive, individually administered general measure of intellectual ability and academic achievement	2 years–retirement	Broad cognitive abillity, academic achievement, and a variety of subtest and individual test scores	A valuable tool for making placement decisions and for planning individual programs

Table 7–5   (continued)

Name of Test	Type of Test	Suitable for Individuals Who Are	Brief Description of Test	Purpose of Administering Test
Universal Nonverbal Intelligence Test (UNIT) (Bracken & McCallum, 1997)	Language-free test that requires no receptive or expressive language	5–19 years	A specialized measure of intelligence with subtests for memory and reasoning	Designed for non-English-speaking or limited-English-proficient (LEP) students and also for children with hearing impairments or receptive and expressive language disabilities

CHAPTER 8

Developmental Assessment

Overview

Developmental assessment, an increasingly important topic in special education, is the process of measuring and evaluating the growth and progress of children from infancy through the primary grades. Special educators who work with young children and their families need in-depth knowledge of developmental assessment to identify and respond to the needs of their students. For other special educators, understanding developmental assessment is part of a comprehensive knowledge base in testing and evaluation.

This chapter assists you in learning the essential concepts and techniques of developmental assessment as it applies to special education. To achieve this goal, we consider the questions teachers should ask about the developmental approach and examine its principles. In addition, we investigate four types of developmental assessment instruments: screening tests, diagnostic scales, readiness tests, and specialized measures. Accompanying each type of instrument is a definition of the category, a description of representative evaluation tools, and a discussion of practical applications for special education teachers. At the conclusion of the chapter, we consider the current trends and issues in developmental assessment and review the developmental tests used most often by preschool teachers.

Objectives

After reading this chapter, you will be prepared to do the following:

- Understand the purpose and use of developmental assessment in special education.
- Use the questions teachers ask in applying the developmental approach.
- Apply the principles of developmental assessment to practical teaching situations.
- Use developmental screening tests to identify children who are potentially at risk and need follow-up assessment.
- Use diagnostic scales and developmental assessment systems.
- Use readiness tests.
- Use specialized developmental tests for infants, toddlers, and students with severe disabilities.

Description of Developmental Assessment

When Trisha Tisdale began her first year as a preschool teacher in a small rural school district, she had several questions about developmental assessment. How could she use developmental screening tests to decide what to do and where to begin instructional intervention with her new students? Which developmental assessment and intervention system should she use for developing IEPs, planning the curriculum, and measuring student progress? Should she use specialized developmental scales with the two children who have severe, multiple disabilities? Would she use any of the developmental readiness tests to determine the preparedness of her children for academic instruction? Ms. Tisdale decided to make an appointment with the coordinator for preschool programs to answer these questions.

In this chapter, you discover answers to Ms. Tisdale's questions about developmental assessment. You also learn about other ways teachers use developmental assessment in intervention programs for young children with special needs.

Developmental assessment is a specialized type of assessment for measuring the performance of young children, especially infants, toddlers, and preschoolers from birth to approximately 6 years of age. By utilizing predictable patterns that children follow as they grow, developmental assessment helps determine whether a child is following the normal sequence of skill acquisition at expected age levels. For example, the **developmental milestones** (critical skills in early childhood development), such as walking, saying one or two words, and toilet training, all occur at about the same age for most children, who normally learn these three skills at about 1 year, 1 year, and 2 years, respectively. Surprisingly, this similarity in development occurs even across cultures and social classes for children up to approximately 6 years of age. For this reason, most developmental tests assess behavior within the age range of birth through 6 years. However, some instruments measure behavior beyond the 6-year-old level, and a few tools extend even into adulthood. In addition, specialized developmental scales evaluate behavior in narrow age ranges such as 4 to 6 years of age or birth to 3 years of age.

Experts in assessment of young children have given developmental tests a special name: **developmental scales,** which are specialized tests of the performance of young children that consist of checklists of behavior arranged by skill area in chronological order. Most developmental scales measure performance in several specific skill areas, often called **developmental learning areas,** which are the skills measured by developmental scales and which make up the curriculum in educational intervention programs for infants, toddlers, and preschoolers. The traditional developmental learning areas consist of the following:

- Fine motor (small muscle) skills.
- Gross motor (large muscle) skills.
- Communication and language development.
- Social development.
- Cognitive functioning.
- Self-help skills.

Specialized developmental scales evaluate behavior in additional learning areas such as sensorimotor skills and reflexive behaviors for infants and toddlers, and, for preschool children, preacademic or readiness skills necessary for success in the first grade.

Using Developmental Assessment in the Classroom

In the classroom, teachers use developmental scales as part of the diagnostic-prescriptive process. The diagnostic component encompasses administering a developmental scale to determine current levels of performance and, more important, to identify specific skills the child has learned, has not learned, and needs to learn next. The prescriptive component uses diagnostic information to develop a prescription or individual plan specifying appropriate goals for the child. The teacher then translates the objectives into specific learning activities and lessons for everyday use. Reassessment to measure progress over time occurs after the individual prescription or intervention plan is carried out. By comparing the results of the first assessment to the follow-up assessment, the teacher obtains an accurate estimate of developmental growth. Revision of the child's individual program follows retesting. The revision process uses the reassessment data to establish new priorities for intervention, which become new or modified objectives in the individual plan. Such developmental assessment, however, should not take place in isolation but should occur as part of the overall instructional process and, in fact, is consistent with best-practice guidelines and legal mandates, including the Individuals with Disabilities Education Act (IDEA).

Provisions for Infants and Toddlers in the Individuals With Disabilities Education Act

The Individuals with Disabilities Education Act (IDEA) extends full rights to a free, appropriate public education to 3- to 5-year-old children with disabilities and encourages early intervention programs for infants and toddlers under 3 years of age and their families. A key provision of the law requires the development of a special individualized education plan (IEP) for each child. IDEA recognizes the importance of parents by replacing the IEP requirement with an **individualized family service plan** (IFSP) requirement for infants and toddlers (birth through 3 years). Similar in content to the IEP, the guidelines for the family service plan include specific requirements for parental participation and additional regulations for assessing the child and the family.

Under IDEA, each child under 3 years must receive a multidisciplinary evaluation, which includes assessment of family needs. Like the IEP, the family service plan addresses the present levels of performance as well as goals and criteria for determining attainment of objectives. However, the family service plan assesses performance in the following areas:

- Physical development.
- Cognitive development.
- Language and speech development.
- Psychosocial development.
- Self-help skills.

The law requires a statement of a family's strengths and needs related to their child and mandates a justification of the extent, if any, to which services will not be provided in a natural environment.

From this description you can see the important role of assessment in planning programs for all children with disabilities. Furthermore, IDEA mandates use of a diagnostic-prescriptive approach to assessment and intervention by requiring the following:

- Identification of present levels of performance (diagnosis).
- Development of an intervention program based on goals (prescription).
- Follow-up evaluation to determine attainment of objectives (diagnosis).
- Revision of objectives (update of the prescription).

This legislation also calls for nondiscriminatory assessment procedures (see also Focus 8–1). To ensure nondiscriminatory testing, other evaluation materials must be provided in the child's native language or other appropriate communication mode. In addition, the tests given to children with impaired sensory, manual, or speaking skills should accurately reflect the child's ability level rather than the child's impaired skills. This means that tests must be carefully selected to avoid discrimination. Obviously, for teachers to meet all of these legal mandates by themselves is difficult if not impossible. Therefore, teachers serve as members of a team that includes other professionals and parents.

The Team Approach

Because no single professional possesses all the knowledge and skills necessary to comprehensively assess a student, the **team approach** to developmental diagnosis enables professionals to combine efforts with parents to obtain the best possible assessment data for meeting the needs of the child and the family. The team approach therefore relies on the expertise of professionals from various disciplines as well as on the family. Assessment teams often consist of several professionals, including

FOCUS 8–1

Developmental Assessment and Cultural Diversity

When assessing young children, we should be aware of and sensitive to the many sociocultural differences that may influence a child's performance. The following practical guidelines, developed by McAffee and Leong (1997), are especially suited to assessing young children. The basic principle is to assume that there will be sociocultural differences in children's actions, behaviors, and responses and then to account for these differences in the assessment process. A second important guideline is to involve parents, the community, and language, cultural, and social specialists in the assessment process. We should also be sure to use a variety of assessment approaches that allow children to demonstrate their full potential. This may involve rephrasing, restating, or recasting assessment tasks in ways that might be familiar and understandable to children. It may also include changing assessment settings to ones that are more familiar to the child. When we do this, we are better able to assess the child's interests and activities by linking them to their homes and communities.

FOCUS 8–2

Arena Assessment

One innovative approach to team evaluation is arena assessment. Arena assessment uses a team of professionals from various disciplines who simultaneously evaluate a child. By conducting the evaluation together, the team makes decisions based on a collective sample of behavior, and they have opportunities to immediately talk with each other about those decisions. Because the team works together, they see all aspects of the child's development rather than separate sensory, motor, intellectual, language, and social domains. This approach has advantages for everyone involved in the process: the child, the family, and the professionals. Arena assessment avoids the problem of having to schedule separate evaluation sessions for each professional. This makes the assessment process shorter for the child, the parents, and the professionals. The parents or primary care givers have to provide information only once instead of answering the same questions in separate sessions with individual professionals. A key advantage for professionals is immediate access to the skills and knowledge of their colleagues. This helps the team make unified assessment decisions regarding what is best for the child and the family (McLean & Crais, 1996).

teachers, home intervention specialists, therapists, diagnosticians, and social workers. Although several team approaches exist, the typical approach involves each team member assessing the student in one or more learning areas. For example, the teacher may assess a child's social skills, the occupational therapist might evaluate self-help skills, the physical therapist usually appraises gross motor skills, and the speech therapist may measure performance in language and communication. Parents participate in the assessment activities as appropriate, and, after completing the assessment, the team members identify and discuss priorities for intervention. In a staff meeting, the participants establish a set of intervention goals for the child and the family. Focus 8–2 discusses an innovative approach to team evaluation.

Questions Teachers Ask About the Developmental Approach

The of use of developmental scales involves answering the following four questions:

1. What is normal development?
2. Is the child following the normal developmental pattern?
3. Why are delays in development occurring?
4. What can be done about the developmental delays?

What Is Normal Development?   Normal development is the patterns of skill acquisition that the average child follows in growing and developing. Child development specialists have found that this pattern is remarkably similar among children. These well-documented patterns constitute the standard of behavior for measuring the developmental progress of individual children.

Is the Child Following the Normal Developmental Pattern?   Although most children follow a predictable developmental pattern, some progress much faster than average, and others exhibit significant developmental delays in one or more learning areas. Developmental diagnosis uses assessment procedures to identify patterns of individual development, which includes determining the extent and nature of any deviations from normal development, identifying strengths and weaknesses within and across learning areas, and detecting splinter skills or gaps in development. **Splinter skills** are behaviors developed in isolation from related skills, such as learning to write the letters of the alphabet without understanding the meaning of the letters. **Gaps in development** are deficits in major skill areas that impede the development of higher level skills. For example, problems with the basic locomotion skill of walking may block the development of higher level locomotion skills such as running, jumping, skipping, and hopping.

Why Are Delays in Development Occurring?   After evaluators identify the presence of significant variations from normal development, they should determine the reasons for the variability. Reasons for deviation from normal development may include physical or sensory problems, such as a visual impairment that prevents a child from performing a particular skill, behavioral problems, cognitive delays, or a lack of experience and exposure. Identifying these reasons is vital in deciding the best possible approach to intervention.

What Can Be Done About Developmental Delays?   After identifying the specific delays and the reasons for the deficits, the developmental approach to intervention involves creating an intervention program to help a child learn the skills or behaviors that occur next in the normal sequence. For example, a child who demonstrates the ability to copy a vertical and a horizontal line with a crayon should next learn to copy a circle and a cross. Likewise, after children learn single words, they are ready to begin saying two- and three-word sentences. The extent to which teachers follow the normal developmental sequence in intervention depends on several factors, including the severity of the disability, the reasons for and the extent of the developmental delays, and the child's age. In general, the developmental approach works best with young children. Older students often require a functional or practical skills approach to meet their needs. **Functional skills** are practical life skills associated with independence in daily living activities.

Principles of Developmental Assessment

Originally described by Banus (1971) in a textbook for occupational therapists, the **principles of developmental assessment** are guidelines for professionals in using the developmental approach to assess the behavior and performance of young children with special needs. These principles include the following:

- Children follow a predictable sequence as they develop.
- Lower developmental skills precede higher developmental skills.
- Higher skills usually begin to emerge before lower skills drop out.
- Developmental progress depends in part on maturation.
- Critical moments exist for children as they grow.

- Children with disabilities may skip stages of development.
- Children with severe handicaps may develop abnormal patterns of development.

The Predictable Sequence of Development   Children follow a predictable pattern as they grow. For this reason test writers arrange the items on developmental scales according to this sequence. Teachers rely on this predictable sequence when they use developmental scales as a curriculum guide for designing intervention programs and arranging learning activities.

Lower Skills Precede Higher Skills   Because skills develop in a predictable pattern, lower skills must precede higher skills. For example, scribbling (a lower skill) is a prerequisite for learning to draw the basic geometric shapes (a higher skill). Likewise, learning the meanings of words receptively represents a lower skill that is necessary for learning the higher level skill of saying words expressively. Teachers rely on developmental scales, their knowledge of child development, and their experience with children to determine if a child has learned the prerequisite skills to begin learning higher level skills.

The Emergence of Higher Skills Before Lower Skills Drop Out   In concert with the lower-to-higher skills concept is the principle that lower skills need not drop out completely before higher skills begin to emerge. Many teachers and parents have experienced a classic illustration of this principle with children who crawl and creep while simultaneously learning to walk. With nondisabled children, higher level skills like walking seem to emerge naturally. However, with young children who have disabilities, higher level skills may not emerge without intervention. Special educators rely on their professional judgment and experience to decide when to introduce higher level skills, and intervention largely depends on the needs and interests of the particular child.

The Dependence of Development on Maturation   Developmental progress depends in part on maturation of the nervous system as well as psychological maturation. For this reason, teachers should not expect performance of a skill until the child demonstrates the necessary physical and psychological maturation levels for learning that particular skill.

Critical Moments in the Development of Children   The principle of the **critical moment** involves the optimal time during which a child is physically, psychologically, and emotionally ready to learn a particular skill. Other terms for this phenomenon include the **critical period** and the **teachable moment.** Developmental assessment helps professionals identify critical moments by determining mastered, emerging, and unlearned skills. When teachers attempt to introduce a new skill before the critical moment, a child may find it difficult if not impossible to learn the skill. Likewise, when teachers introduce a skill after the critical period, acquisition becomes increasingly difficult. For example, an infant reaches the critical moment for learning the eating skill of chewing at an early age (approximately 6 months). It is difficult (and dangerous due to the risk of choking on food) to introduce chewing before this age. If a child skips the chewing stage, it may become increasingly difficult to learn the skill at older ages.

Skipping of Developmental Stages by Children With Disabilities Children with disabilities often skip stages of development, which may lead to gaps in development and splinter skills. A gap in development refers to a delay or slowdown in the development of a particular skill or set of skills. A splinter skill is a skill learned in isolation from related skills. Teachers use developmental tests to identify gaps and splinter skills in need of remedial programming.

Abnormal Patterns of Development Among Children With Severe Disabilities Children with severe disabilities often fail to follow the normal sequence of development and may even develop abnormal patterns due to the severity of their disabilities. For example, children with severe physical impairments frequently retain primitive reflexes that normal infants integrate into higher level movement patterns in the first few months of life. As a result of retaining reflexive movement patterns, these children may have extreme difficulty learning to move, communicate, or perform self-help skills. For example, in the self-help skill area of eating, some children develop abnormal gag and bite reflexes due to physical impairments, which often impairs their ability to learn how to chew food.

Categories of Developmental Assessment

Like all types of assessment, developmental assessment includes several categories, each of which has a different goal and produces specific types of assessment data. These categories include screening, diagnosis, readiness testing, and specialized evaluation. Although overlap exists among these four categories, each group fulfills a different purpose. Developmental screening provides a thumbnail sketch of the overall development of young children. In contrast, developmental diagnosis furnishes in-depth information about strengths, weaknesses, and gaps in development. The readiness tests, designed to determine whether a student is ready for the typical first-grade curriculum, focus on preacademic skills and concepts. Finally, specialized evaluation includes instruments and procedures for assessing children with unique needs, including infants and children with severe and profound disabilities. Special educators may select from among several categories of developmental assessment instruments and procedures. However, in many situations, developmental assessment begins with the screening process.

Why Do We Use Developmental Assessment With Young Children With Special Needs? We use developmental assessment with young children who have special needs for several reasons: to identify young children with potential developmental delays and to suggest what to do with new students and where to begin instruction while awaiting more comprehensive developmental diagnosis. See Focus 8–3. The *Developmental Indicators for the Assessment of Learning-Third Edition (DIAL-3)* is an example of a widely used screening test. We use developmental diagnosis to identify, classify, and place infants, toddlers, and preschoolers into special education programs and services. We also use it in programming and curriculum development, including writing IEPs and developing intervention programs. The *Battelle Developmental Inventory (BDI)* is a developmental scale often used to identify children with disabilities, to aid in curriculum and program development, and to measure developmental progress.

FOCUS 8–3

Why Do We Use Developmental Assessment With Young Children Who Have Disabilities?

- To screen young children for potential developmental and learning problems
- To assist in the process of diagnosing the disabilities of children with learning problems
- To assess the readiness skills of young children with special needs
- To obtain data and information for writing individual plans and developing intervention programs
- To measure the developmental progress of young children with special needs

The following narrative illustrates how a diagnostic teacher used developmental assessment to evaluate the learning needs of J. J.

J. J., small, disheveled, and withdrawn, sat alone in a corner of the diagnostic classroom and did nothing: he did not participate, play, or even misbehave. In the meantime, he continued to fail the developmental milestones for his age group.

Curious about this unusual young child, the diagnostic teacher who was to administer a developmental test checked his records. The developmental screening test results from the Developmental Indicators for the Assessment of Learning-Third Edition (DIAL-3) *identified potential delays in development, and the social history report indicated that J. J.'s mother had died when he was an infant and that his grandmother was raising him.*

When the diagnostic teacher began testing J. J. with the Learning Accomplishment Profile (LAP), *he withdrew and, after several failed attempts, the teacher had to reschedule the testing for another day. During the next testing session, J. J. began withdrawing again. However, to avoid repeating the earlier failure, the diagnostic teacher tried popcorn and other food reinforcers as rewards for effort. Finally, J. J. began to interact, and the diagnostic teacher completed the testing successfully. For J. J. it was a positive experience. For the diagnostic teacher, it illustrated the necessity of modifying testing procedures to meet the needs of the individual student.*

Afterward, the assessment team relied on the evaluation results provided by the diagnostic teacher to support the conclusion that, although J. J. displayed some serious developmental lags, he performed many behaviors representative of his chronological age when given additional reinforcement.

After spending several weeks in the diagnostic classroom, J. J. returned to his regular preschool program (with some extra help from the staff). At age 5, J. J. was retested with the LAP. *The results showed remarkable progress, and J. J. was enrolled in a regular kindergarten program.*

✓ Comprehension Checklist

Developmental assessment measures and evaluates the growth and progress of young children. An understanding of its purpose, use, and principles helps build a comprehensive knowledge base in this increasingly important area. This information, coupled with insight into legal mandates and programming implications, serves as the basis for considering the various types of developmental instruments used in special education. Teachers use developmental assessment as a component in the diagnostic-prescriptive process.

Developmental Screening

The purpose of **developmental screening** is to identify the general performance levels of young children from birth to approximately 6 years of age. Screening alerts parents and professionals to children who may have a developmental delay or learning disability. In addition, teachers often rely on developmental screening to determine overall levels of functioning and to develop initial programming goals with new students. When professionals conduct developmental screening, they use concise, abbreviated tests and evaluation procedures that provide an overall picture of functioning rather than a detailed analysis. Although developmental screening is an efficient way to identify children with possible delays, professionals must avoid using screening to label children or diagnose developmental disabilities. Screening focuses on one question: Does a potential learning or behavior problem exist that requires further attention?

Limited Predictive Validity of Developmental Screening Tests

Compared with diagnostic assessment, developmental screening tests and procedures exhibit limited predictive validity. This is due to the short length of screening tests coupled with the instability and rapid change that characterize the behavior of young children. As a result, evaluators must interpret results from developmental screening cautiously. Although screening provides useful information regarding possible levels of performance, professionals should treat screening results as estimates rather than exact or precise measures.

Guidelines for Developmental Screening

The Illinois Association for Supervision and Curriculum Development (1990, Spring) prepared the following guidelines for developmental screening. They emphasize practical considerations in response to the needs of young children and recommend that professionals do the following:

- Rely on play as a key part of all screening activities.
- Conduct interactions with the child in a positive manner.
- Emphasize hands-on activities rather than paper-and-pencil tasks.
- Provide parents with written information about the purpose and limitations of the screening.
- Allow parents to stay with their child during screening.
- Include a parent interview as part of the screening.
- Give parents immediate feedback about the results of the screening.
- Involve parents as active members of the screening team.
- Ensure that all evaluators have experience with the children being screened.
- Certify that all screeners are specifically trained, sensitive to sociocultural issues, and knowledgeable about the limitations of screening instruments.

Although these guidelines pertain to the screening process with young children, they are applicable to assessment activities in general. The emphasis on parent participation highlights the key role of the family in the assessment process, especially with young children.

Who Uses Developmental Screening?

Many professionals use developmental screening with young children. Special education teachers rely on screening tests when they conduct initial observations and form first impressions of new students. Teachers screen new students to identify levels of performance and determine the special needs and interests of the child and the family. Intervention specialists, who serve infants and toddlers in home-based programs, employ similar screening techniques as they begin working with children and their families. Specialists, such as speech and language pathologists, occupational therapists, and physical therapists, also depend on screening to identify children who may need therapy services.

A different use of screening involves conducting group screening at day care centers and preschool kindergarten programs to identify children who are potentially at risk. Medical professionals, including pediatricians, nurses, and medical social workers, also employ developmental screening to identify children who may need to be referred for diagnostic assessment. Psychologists and educational diagnosticians also rely on screening tests as one of the initial steps in the assessment process.

Representative Developmental Screening Tests

Two representative developmental screening tests in widespread use are the *Developmental Indicators for the Assessment of Learning-Third Edition (DIAL-3)* and the *Denver II.* The *DIAL-3,* which is designed for use in group and individual settings, represents one of the leading tests of its type. Originally published in 1954, the *Denver II* was one of the first developmental screening tests and is still used today by many professionals.

The *Developmental Indicators for the Assessment of Learning-Third Edition*

The *Developmental Indicators for the Assessment of Learning-Third Edition (DIAL-3)* (Mardell-Czudnowski & Goldenberg, 1998) assesses learning in motor development, conceptual development, language skills, self-help skills, and social development. Designed for individual administration by a single evaluator or group administration by a team of professionals and paraprofessionals, it requires 30 to 45 minutes to give. The *DIAL-3* (summarized in Table 8–1) identifies children who need a complete diagnostic evaluation and is popular because it is easy to use, has well-designed administration procedures, and includes many supplemental features.

Screening teams frequently give the *DIAL-3* to all of the children in a particular site such as a day care center, a preschool program, a group of kindergarten classes, or a Headstart program. Children scoring below the cutoff level are referred for a

Table 8–1 *Developmental Indicators for the Assessment of Learning-Third Edition (DIAL-3)*

Type of Test:	Norm referenced, group or individually administered
Purpose:	A screening test of developmental learning
Content Areas:	Motor development, concept development, language skills, self-help skills, and social development
Administration Time:	30 to 45 minutes
Age Levels:	3–6 years
Suitable for:	Identifying students with potential delays who need further evaluation
Scores:	The *Dial-3* provides standard deviation and percentile cutoff points for total and subtest scores. Percentile ranks and standard scores are also provided.
In Short:	The well-designed *DIAL-3* is appropriate for individual administration by a single evaluator or group administration by a team of professionals and paraprofessionals.

complete developmental evaluation as a follow-up to the screening process. In addition, an evaluator may use the *DIAL-3* to assess children on an individual basis.

Materials for the *DIAL-3* The *DIAL-3* kit consists of a large canvas carry bag that contains a manual, score sheets, parent questionnaires, manipulatives, dials, operator's handbooks in English and Spanish, and a training packet. The well-designed materials appeal to young children, making it easy to conduct assessment in a play-like atmosphere. Optional materials include a training video and a computer-assisted scoring program.

Administration and Scoring of the *DIAL-3* When given to a group of children at a prearranged screening site, administration begins with a warm-up period for the children. After they feel comfortable, they are guided through different testing stations. A play area serves as a waiting station. The *DIAL-3* provides standard deviation and percentile cutoff points by chronological age at two-month intervals for total and subtest scores in motor, concepts, language, self-help, and social areas. Percentile ranks and standard scores are also provided. A sample from the *DIAL-3* showing decisions for the five screening areas and the *DIAL-3* total recorded on the score summary for Ray (chronological age 4-8) appears in Figure 8–1. An example of the overall screening decision recorded on the front of Ray's record form appears in Figure 8–2.

Technical Characteristics of the *DIAL-3* Standardized on a sample of 1,560 English-speaking and 650 Spanish-speaking children, the *DIAL-3* exhibits adequate technical qualities as a screening measure. The test developers conducted appropriate reliability and validity studies as part of the revision process, and additional studies using the *DIAL* and the *DIAL-R* have been conducted during the past two decades, providing further evidence of validity.

Summary of the *DIAL-3* The primary purpose of the *DIAL-3*, which is useful in a variety of settings, is to identify children with potential delays who need further

Figure 8–1   Decisions for the Five Screening Areas and the DIAL-3 Total Recorded on the Score Summary for Ray (Chronological Age, 4-8)

Score Summary

Area	Scaled Score Total	Other	Decision — Potential delay	Decision — OK
Motor	7		X	
Concepts	13			X
Language	12			X
DIAL-3 Total	32			X

Area	Raw Score Total	Other	Decision — Potential delay	Decision — OK
Self-Help Development	19			X
Social Development	23			X

Use cutoffs found in Appendix E in the manual.

Cutoffs chosen:

☐ 16 percent (1.0 SD)

☐ 10 percent (1.3 SD)

☒ 7 percent (1.5 SD)

☐ 5 percent (1.7 SD)

☐ 2 percent (2.0 SD)

Sumario de puntaje

Area	Puntaje total compensado	Otro	Decisión — Retraso potencial	Decisión — OK
Motora	7		X	
Conceptos	13			X
Lenguaje	12			X
Total del DIAL-3	32			X

Area	Puntaje base ajustado	Otro	Decisión — Retraso potencial	Decisión — OK
Desarrollo de autosuficiencia	21			X
Desarrollo social	25			X

Use los valores indicados en el apéndice E del manual.

Valores elegidos:

☐ 16 por ciento (1.0 SD)

☐ 10 por ciento (1.3 SD)

☒ 7 por ciento (1.5 SD)

☐ 5 por ciento (1.7 SD)

☐ 2 por ciento (2.0 SD)

From Mardell-Czudnowski, D. D., & Goldenberg, D. S. (1998). *Developmental Indicators for the Assessment of Learning-Third Edition (DIAL-3)*. Circle Pines, MN: American Guidance Service. Reprinted with permission of American Guidance Service, Inc.

evaluation. The instrument can be given to individuals or groups of children. The test kit includes well-designed materials for training an assessment team, making the *DIAL-3* an excellent instrument for personnel preparation, especially in assessment courses for special education students.

Denver II

The *Denver II* (Frankenburg et al., 1990) is an individually administered screening test for children from birth to 6 years of age. The *Denver II* evaluates developmental learning in personal-social, fine motor–adaptive, language, and gross motor skills; see Table 8–2 for a summary of the test. The authors initially designed the test for health care providers to screen young children in hospital settings, but professionals in many disciplines, including special educators, also use the test.

Materials for the *Denver II*   The well-designed *Denver II* test materials include a one-page score sheet and a brief manual. The *Denver II* features a compact test kit

Figure 8–2   Overall Screening Decision Recorded on the Front of the Record Form for Ray (Chronological Age, 4-8)

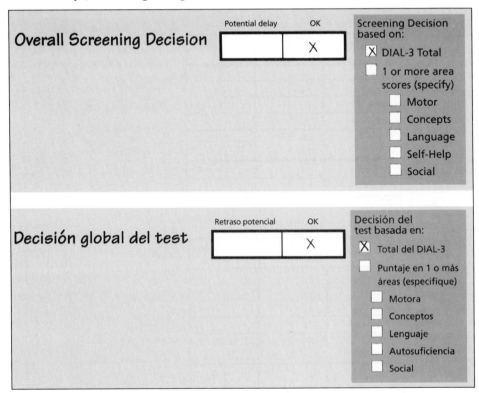

From Mardell-Czudnowski, C. D., & Goldenberg, D. S. (1998). *Developmental Indicators for the Assessment of Learning-Third Edition (DIAL-3).* Circle Pines, MN: American Guidance Service. Reprinted with permission of American Guidance Service, Inc.

Table 8–2   *Denver II*

Type of Test:	Norm referenced and individually administered
Purpose:	A screening test of developmental learning
Content Areas:	Personal-social, fine motor adaptive, gross motor, and language skills
Administration Time:	20 to 30 minutes
Age Levels:	Birth–6 years
Suitable for:	Identifying students with potential developmental delays who need further evaluation
Scores:	Uses descriptive statements, including advanced, normal, caution, delayed, and untestable, rather than number scores
In Short:	The *Denver II* no longer represents the best of the available developmental screening tests. For this reason special educators should consider using other available screening instruments.

and easy-to-follow scoring procedures. After an examiner becomes familiar with the test items, the brief manual is not needed to give the test.

Administration and Scoring of the *Denver II* Administering the *Denver II* takes 20 to 30 minutes. As with the *DIAL-3,* the evaluator uses descriptive statements to interpret performance on individual items. The *Denver II* descriptions include advanced, normal, caution, and delayed. The evaluator, who has the option of scoring some items on the basis of a report from a parent or another primary care giver, interprets overall performance by summarizing a child's performance on individual items and each subtest. The *Denver II* suggests that evaluators consider using the term *untestable* to interpret the performance of a child who refuses to perform most of the items. Unfortunately, some evaluators have relied on terms such as *untestable* to unfairly label children for whom appropriate assessment procedures were not available. Furthermore, labeling a child untestable using results from a brief screening test violates contemporary legal, ethical, and professional standards because a child's performance during a 20-minute testing session may not represent typical ability or overall behavior. Most special educators believe that the inability to test a particular child results from the lack of suitable testing procedures and that no child is untestable even though some children may be difficult to test.

Technical Characteristics of the *Denver II* Test developers standardized the *Denver II* with a sample of more than 2,000 children from Colorado. Unfortunately, establishing norms with a sample group from only one state limits the representativeness of those norms. Nevertheless, initial data on the *Denver II* indicate that the instrument exhibits appropriate validity and reliability. However, because the test is norm referenced, additional investigation is needed to establish its technical adequacy.

Summary of the *Denver II* Although the *Denver II* is substantially improved compared with the earlier edition of the test, the instrument no longer represents the best of the available screening tests for use in educational settings. In most situations, special educators should consider using other available screening instruments instead.

Other Developmental Screening Tests

Special educators may select from a number of screening tests to obtain an overview of the developmental skills of young children. Brief reviews of several of these tests follow.

AGS Early Screening Profiles The *AGS Early Screening Profiles (ESP)* (Harrison et al., 1990) measure performance in cognitive/language, motor, and self-help/social skills and survey the child's articulation, home environment, health history, and behavior. Designed to provide practical information to help make accurate screening decisions, the norm-referenced *ESP* is for children from 2 through 6 years of age and can be administered individually or to groups of children using a format in which children move from station to station. The entire instrument takes about 45 minutes to administer and offers two levels of scoring. Level I scores, which can be obtained quickly, consist of three descriptive statements—above average, average, or below average—for the three subtests. Level II scores include standard scores, normal curve equivalents, percentiles, stanines, and age equivalents for the three subtests and the total test. Level II scores also include descriptive statements of above average, average, or below average for the three subtests and the total test. The *ESP* was standardized on more than 1,000 children, and the manual provides considerable evidence regarding the reliability and validity of the instrument.

Battelle Developmental Screening Test   The *Battelle Developmental Screening Test* (Newborg et al., 1988b) is made up of 96 items taken from the 341 items in the *Battelle Developmental Inventory (BDI),* which is reviewed later in this chapter. The norm-referenced, individually administered *BDI Screening Test* covers the same five domains as the full *BDI:* personal-social, adaptive, motor, communication, and cognition. Designed for the age range from birth to 8 years, the test takes about 30 minutes to administer. Like the complete *BDI,* the *Screening Test* can be administered using direct testing, observation, or interview. As with all tests, the direct method provides the most accurate diagnostic information in most situations. The *BDI Screening Test* provides a choice of cutoff scores from three probability levels corresponding to 1, $1^1/_2$, or 2 standard deviations below the mean. The *BDI Screening Test* was standardized on a sample of 800 children. The manual reports no information regarding the reliability of the *Screening Test* and provides limited information regarding the reliability of the instrument.

Brigance Preschool Screen and Brigance Early Preschool Screen   The *Brigance Preschool Screen for Three- and Four-Year-Old Children* (Brigance, 1985) and the *Brigance Early Preschool Screen for Two-Year-Old and Two-and-One-Half-Year-Old Children* (Brigance, 1990) measure fine motor, gross motor, language, and cognitive skills. The tests yield one overall score with a total of 100 possible points. The manual recommends referring children who score below 60 points for further testing. The Brigance instruments are not norm referenced, and the manual provides no reliability or validity information. For this reason, the *Brigance Preschool Screen* and *Early Preschool Screen* should not be used to make referral decisions. The instruments are most useful as brief curriculum guides for teachers with new children because they can provide teachers with ideas of what to do and where to begin while awaiting more comprehensive assessment.

FirstSTEP: Screening Test for Evaluating Preschoolers   *FirstSTEP: Screening Test for Evaluating Preschoolers* (Miller, 1993) is an individually administered, norm-referenced screening test for children from 2 years, 9 months to 6 years, 2 months and is designed to identify preschool children who are at risk for developmental delays in the five areas mandated by IDEA: cognition, communication, motor, social-emotional, and adaptive behavior. *FirstSTEP* also provides an optional parent/teacher scale that adds information about the child's typical behavior at home and at school to the behavior observed during screening. *FirstSTEP* takes about 15 minutes to administer.

☑ Comprehension Checklist

Screening, which is one of the major categories of developmental assessment, includes an assortment of tools from which to choose. The diversity of available instruments allows professionals from a number of disciplines to use developmental screening in the important task of initially identifying children with potential disabilities. As with all assessment, the selection of a particular instrument depends on the needs of the individual child and the purpose of the screening.

Diagnostic Scales of Developmental Skills

Unlike screening tests that provide an overview of developmental learning, diagnostic scales of developmental skills produce a comprehensive, in-depth evaluation of performance. Special educators require such diagnostic information to identify young children who require special education services, to place young children into appropriate special education programs, to develop intervention objectives, and to measure progress. To meet these diverse requirements, professionals may select from a variety of diagnostic scales.

Representative Diagnostic Scales

The following reviews of three representative tests illustrate the characteristics of diagnostic scales of developmental skills. The reviews cover several of the foremost instruments, including the *Learning Accomplishment Profile,* the *Battelle Developmental Inventory,* and the *Brigance Diagnostic Inventory of Early Development.*

Learning Accomplishment Profile-Standardized Assessment

The *Learning Accomplishment Profile-Standardized Assessment (LAP-D Standardized Assessment)* was originally developed by Wilson-LeMay et al. in 1977 and standardized by Nehring et al. in 1992. The authors developed the widely used *LAP-D Standardized Assessment* (see Table 8–3) for evaluating the development of children from 6 months through 6 years of age. The instrument is useful as both a diagnostic test and a curriculum guide. Other available versions of the *LAP* include the *Learning Accomplishment Profile- Revised Edition (LAP-R)* (Sanford & Zelman, 1981), which covers a developmental age range from 36 to 72 months, and the *Early Learning Accomplishment Profile (E-LAP)* (Glover et al., 1988), which assesses the development of children from birth to 36 months.

The *LAP-D Standardized Assessment* provides an in-depth analysis of strengths and weaknesses in eight domains as follows:

1. Gross motor—Body movement
2. Gross motor—Object movement
3. Fine motor—Manipulation
4. Fine motor—Writing
5. Cognitive—Matching
6. Cognitive—Counting
7. Language—Naming
8. Language—Comprehension

As a diagnostic tool, the *LAP-D Standardized Assessment* is an effective system for determining whether a student displays age-appropriate developmental skills. It generates detailed information about preacademic skill development in writing, counting, reading, naming, and comprehension, skills preschoolers must master to succeed in kindergarten and early first grade. Diagnosticians and teachers also rely on the test to specify skills in need of remediation and to establish priorities for intervention based on the student's individual profile of strengths, weaknesses, and gaps in development.

Other Diagnostic Tests of Developmental Skills

Although the *LAP-D Standardized Assessment,* the *Battelle Developmental Inventory,* and the *Brigance Early* represent three of the most frequently used developmental scales, special educators may select from among many other instruments to obtain a test that fits the needs of their students. Brief reviews of several of these tools follow.

Carolina Curriculum for Infants and Toddlers With Special Needs, Second Edition,* and the *Carolina Curriculum for Preschoolers With Special Needs The curriculum-based *Carolina Curriculum for Infants and Toddlers with Special Needs, Second Edition* (Johnson-Martin et al., 1991) and *Carolina Curriculum for Preschoolers with Special Needs* (Johnson-Martin et al., 1990) provide intervention strategies and assessment information for children from birth through 5 years of age. These curricula cover cognition, communication, social adaption, fine motor skills, and gross motor skills. The infant and toddler curriculum, which includes 24 curriculum sequences in a checklist format, is designed for children with the developmental ages of birth to 24 months. The preschooler curriculum, which includes 25 skills sequences, is for children between the developmental ages of 2 and 5 years. Each curriculum includes an assessment log that graphically charts a child's ongoing progress. Teachers may complete these assessments using observation and direct testing with corresponding program areas for intervention.

Developmental Observation Checklist System The *Developmental Observation Checklist System (DOCS)* (Hresko et al., 1994) includes components for measuring general development, adjustment behavior, parent stress, and parent support. The general development component measures language, motor, social, and cognitive skills. The *DOCS* is designed for children from birth through 6 years of age and can be completed by parents or care givers based on their observation of the child's daily behaviors. Standardized on more than 1,400 children, available *DOCS* scores include quotients, NCEs, age equivalents, and percentiles.

Gesell Developmental Schedules The *Gesell Developmental Schedules* (revised by Knobloch & Pasamanick in 1974 and by Knobloch et al. in 1980) are the original developmental scales that were first published in 1940. The *Gesell Developmental Schedules* describe the developmental progress of children from ages 4 weeks to 6 years in gross motor, fine motor, communication, personal-social, and adaptive behavior. Gesell designed the schedules for use as criterion-based measures of child progress rather than as a tool for identifying children with disabilities.

Mullen Scales of Early Learning: AGS Edition The *Mullen Scales of Early Learning: AGS Edition* (Mullen, 1995) assess the language, motor, and perceptual abilities of children from birth to 5 years, 8 months of age. The *Mullen Scales* include subtests in gross motor, visual reception, fine motor, expressive language, and receptive language. Administration times for the *Mullen Scales* are about 15 minutes with 1-year-old infants, about 30 minutes with 3-year-old toddlers, and about 60 minutes with 5-year-old preschoolers. Available scores for this norm-referenced measure include *t*-scores, percentile ranks, and age equivalents for each scale, and standard scores and percentile ranks for the total test. The *Mullen Scales of Early Learning* include attractive test materials and optional computer scoring software that provides scoring information and furnishes a narrative report. An optional intervention report lists a number of suggestions for developmentally appropriate tasks from the *You and Your Small Wonder* books by Merle Karnes. Teachers can use these suggestions to develop learning games and to plan intervention activities.

Developmental Tests Used by Special Education Teachers

A study of developmental tests used by special education teachers in preschool programs was conducted by Johnson and Beauchamp (1987), who asked teachers what tests they used and then examined the test features important to teachers. The survey included the responses of 105 preschool special education teachers from 34 states. A summary of the results appears in Table 8–6.

Teachers gave four reasons for using a particular developmental scale, including history of use (i.e., the test was already in place), and scope, applicability, and ease of use of the test. Teachers also identified the most important test characteristics, including the scope of the test, the materials, the standardization, and the scoring and administration procedures. In a summary of the study, Johnson and Beauchamp criticized those who used outmoded tests like the *Denver Developmental Screening Test* and suggested that reliance on inappropriate tests may result from using what is available in a particular school, lack of involvement in the test selection process, and inadequate knowledge of other available tests.

☑ Comprehension Checklist

Diagnostic assessment with an individually administered developmental scale is a key component in the process of providing individualized programs for preschool children receiving special education services. Diagnosticians employ developmental scales in the process of classifying and placing young children into appropriate special education programs and services. Special education teachers, on the other hand, rely on developmental scales to develop intervention programs and to measure student progress. Professionals may select from an array of available instruments to ensure that they match the assessment instrument to the needs of the child and the family.

Table 8–6 Developmental Scales Used by Special Education Teachers

Test Name	Usage (%)
Brigance Diagnostic Inventory of Early Development	46
Learning Accomplishment Profile	39
Denver Developmental Screening Test	20
Developmental Profile	17
Teacher, district, or state developed	12
Hawaii Early Learning Profile	11
Battelle Developmental Inventory	6

Developmental Readiness Tests

The **readiness tests** are a special category of developmental scales designed to measure children's knowledge of the basic skills necessary for success in the beginning years of school. Whereas the more general developmental scales often measure behavior from birth through 6 years of age, the readiness tests usually measure the behavior of children from age 4 through 7 years. Most teachers consider readiness to include the following skills and knowledge:

- General information about oneself and the immediate environment.
- The self-help skills of basic toileting, dressing, eating, and hygiene.
- Fine motor skills consisting of manipulation, drawing, and manual dexterity.
- The relational concepts of space, time, and quantity, including the categorizing and sequencing abilities necessary for success in beginning academics.
- The gross motor skills of locomotion, catching and throwing, moving balance, and stationary balance.
- Language development, including receptive, expressive, and speech skills.
- Handwriting skills up to the level of drawing with crayons and using a primary pencil.
- Reading readiness skills such as sound discrimination, sound-letter correspondence, knowledge of letters, and knowledge of words.
- Number readiness skills associated with recognizing and printing numbers, counting, numerical sequencing, and knowledge of equivalent sets.
- The social skills of constructive play, interactive play, and following instructions.
- Classroom behavior skills necessary to play cooperatively with peers, follow directions, complete assignments independently, and participate in classroom activities.

Teachers find that children with these skills tend to be successful in the beginning school years, whereas children without them may struggle in first grade or even fail altogether. Preschool teachers use assessment information about a child's skill development to determine school readiness and to plan instruction. However, evaluation of children's readiness skills should consist of more than testing because the behavior of preschool children varies a great deal from day to day. For this reason, teachers should use other relevant assessment information in the evaluation process, including direct observation, informal assessment, teacher judgment, parent needs, family background, and other relevant information.

Representative Readiness Tests

Two representative instruments, the *Boehm Test of Basic Concepts-Revised* and the *Basic School Skills Inventory-Third Edition,* illustrate the kinds of behaviors measured by readiness tests.

Boehm Test of Basic Concepts-Revised

The *Boehm Test of Basic Concepts-Revised (Boehm-R)* (Boehm, 1986b) is a norm-referenced instrument designed for group administration to determine whether a student understands verbal instructions well enough for success in the primary grades (see Table 8–7 for a summary). Designed for children in kindergarten, Grade 1, and Grade 2, the

Boehm-R measures 50 important concepts, including more-less, first-last, and same-different. The test items, grouped into three main categories of space, time, and quantity, incorporate the concepts of following directions, understanding sequences of events, completing worksheets and tests, and performing problem-solving activities.

A version of the *Boehm-R* for even younger children is also available. The *Boehm Test of Basic Concepts-Preschool Version (Boehm-Preschool)* (Boehm, 1986a) is for early identification of basic concept deficiencies. Designed for children from 3 to 5 years of age or for older children with identified language difficulties, the *Boehm-Preschool* is useful in preschool screening programs for identifying weaknesses in basic concept comprehension. It takes only 10–15 minutes to give and to score the *Boehm-Preschool*.

Materials for the *Boehm-R* The *Boehm-R* materials include a manual, two alternate forms, and an applications booklet that measures skill in using concepts in combination, in sequences, and in making comparisons.

Administration and Scoring of the *Boehm-R* Designed for group administration, the *Boehm-R* takes about 40 minutes to give. The evaluator records the results on a class record form that provides information about the performance of each child and the entire class, including the number and percent of children answering each item correctly, the percentile rank of each child, and the average raw score. An optional error-analysis scoring procedure and a parent–teacher conference report form provide additional interpretive data.

Technical Characteristics of the *Boehm-R* The developers created norms by administering the *Boehm-R* to a national sample of children at the beginning and end of the school year. The developers also conducted a variety of reliability and validity studies with the test and completed research on the use of the test with special populations, including children with visual impairment, hearing impairment, learning disabilities, and mild mental retardation.

Table 8–7 *Boehm Test of Basic Concepts-Revised*

Type of Test:	Norm referenced, group administered
Purpose:	To determine if a student understands verbal instructions well enough for success in the primary grades
Content Areas:	Measures 50 important concepts including more-less, first-last, and same-different
Administration Time:	40 minutes
Age Levels:	Kindergarten, grade 1, and grade 2
Suitable for:	Students with mild and moderate disabilities
Scores:	A class record form provides information about the performance of each child and the entire class, including the number and percent of children answering each item correctly, the percentile rank of each child, and the average raw score.
In Short:	Teachers can use the results from the *Boehm-R* for both individual remediation and group instruction.

Summary of the *Boehm-R*   Teachers can use the results from the *Boehm-R* for both individual remediation and group instruction. The test authors recommend individualized instruction when the overall class performs well but some children score below average. They suggest group instruction when most of the children in the class score below average. Instruction should focus on items missed or omitted on the test, and, after targeting specific concepts for instruction, teachers should present each concept in a regular sequence.

Basic School Skills Inventory-Third Edition

The *Basic School Skills Inventory-Third Edition (BSSI-3)* (Hammill et al., 1998) is a norm-referenced screening test that identifies children ages 4 through 6 years who are at risk for school failure, who need more in-depth assessment, and who should be referred for additional study. The instrument assesses the skills necessary for success in beginning school. Unlike the *Boehm-R*, which measures the underlying concepts necessary for school success, the *BSSI-3* emphasizes tasks the child is asked to perform in the classroom (see Table 8–8 for a summary of the *BSSI-3*). The six subtests include daily living skills, spoken language, reading readiness, writing readiness, math readiness, and classroom behavior. Each item is written as a behavioral objective that facilitates the development of IEPs.

Materials for the *BSSI-3*   The *BSSI-3* materials include a teacher's manual, a picture book used with the inventory, and a pad of score sheets.

Administration and Scoring of the *BSSI-3*   The test authors designed the *BSSI-3* for teachers and others who see a child in the classroom on a regular basis. For this reason, it may not be appropriate for use by psychologists, counselors, and parents unless they have systematically observed the child in the classroom setting.

Summary of the *BSSI-3*   The *BSSI-3*, a classroom-based assessment tool for teachers of preacademic children, is appropriate for children from 4 through 6 years of age.

Table 8–8   *Basic School Skills Inventory-Third Edition*

Type of Test:	Norm referenced, individually administered screening test
Purpose:	To locate children who are at risk for school failure, who need more in-depth assessment, and who should be referred for additional study
Content Areas:	Daily living skills, spoken language, reading readiness, writing readiness, math readiness, and classroom behavior
Administration Time:	10 minutes
Age Levels:	4–6 years
Suitable for:	Students with mild and moderate disabilities
Scores:	Standard scores, percentiles, and age and grade equivalents for each scale
In Short:	The *BSSI-3* assesses the skills necessary for success in beginning school.

Teachers also find it suitable for older children who function in this developmental age range. The *BSSI-3* provides a quick teacher rating scale of early readiness skills.

Other Readiness Tests

Brief reviews of several other readiness tests that teachers of preacademic children have found to be useful follow.

Lee–Clark Reading Readiness Test The *Lee–Clark Reading Readiness Test* (Lee & Clark, 1962) is a norm-referenced, group-administered test for children who are finishing kindergarten or beginning the first grade. The *Lee–Clark* contains four subtests: letter matching, letter discrimination, picture vocabulary, and letter and word recognition. Teachers find this test useful as a measure of children's knowledge of the basic skills necessary for reading success in the beginning years of school.

Daberon Screening for School Readiness Test, Second Edition The *Daberon Screening for School Readiness Test, Second Edition (DABERON-2)* (Danzer et al., 1991) is a norm-referenced, group-administered measure of school readiness in children ages 4 through 6. The *Daberon-2* includes subtests for measuring body parts, color and number concepts, gross motor development, categorization, and other developmental abilities that relate to early academic success. The individually administered *Daberon-2* takes 20 to 40 minutes to give and score and can help identify children at risk for school failure. Teachers can use the instrument to identify instructional objectives and develop IEPs. The test includes a classroom summary form, a report on readiness, a summary of performance, and practical suggestions for parents.

Metropolitan Readiness Tests, Sixth Edition The norm-referenced *Metropolitan Readiness Tests, Sixth Edition (MRT 6)* (Nurss, 1995), use a colorful easel format for individualized administration. The *MRT 6* assesses literacy development in children from 4 through 7 years of age. The *MRT 6* assesses five areas:

- Visual discrimination.
- Beginning consonants.
- Sound-letter correspondence.
- Story comprehension (using a big book).
- Quantitative concepts and reasoning.

The *MRT 6* is a comprehensive, diagnostic tool that takes up to 85 minutes in four sittings to administer. It yields standard scores, percentile ranks, and stanines and includes a conference report that explains the purpose of the *MRT 6* and the results in a convenient format for teachers to use when conferring with parents.

In addition to these specialized readiness tests, many teachers find that general developmental scales such as the *DIAL-3* and the *LAP-D Standardized Assessment* contain features that make them useful for readiness testing.

☑ Comprehension Checklist

Readiness tests, which measure the skills necessary for academic success in the primary grades, represent a special category of developmental assessment tools. Teachers may select from a variety of readiness tests to obtain a tool suited to the needs of their particular students. These include both group and individually administered scales.

Specialized Developmental Assessment

Some young children in special education programs display unique needs and characteristics that call for the use of specialized developmental assessment procedures. Such children include those with the following characteristics:

- Severe to profound intellectual impairment.
- Severe language and communication deficits.
- Sensory impairments, including deafness or blindness.
- Physical disabilities.
- Severe emotional disturbance, including autism.

Students with the most severe of these disabilities may depend on others or on specialized medical equipment to maintain life functions such as breathing, eating, digestion, elimination, and circulation. In other cases, performance may be limited by inappropriate behaviors such as stereotypy (e.g., light flicking or rocking) or self-injury (e.g., head banging or hand biting). In addition, communication levels may range from little more than subtle physical movements to verbal and gestural abilities. All of these situations preclude the use of traditional developmental assessment tools and require evaluators to turn to a number of specialized developmental tests and assessment procedures. Unfortunately, a single source explaining developmental assessment for students with severe disabilities does not exist. For this reason, evaluators need to consult a variety of resources and to work with a team of professionals from an array of disciplines. The team approach helps to ensure consideration of all aspects of a child's needs in the assessment process.

Unique Areas of Assessment for Students With Severe Disabilities

When assessing students with severe disabilities, evaluators must consider unique learning areas and domains of assessment. The need for assessment in nontraditional areas is one of the reasons for difficulty in the assessment process (Florida Department of Education, 1986; Venn & Dykes, 1987). These unique areas of assessment include the following:

- Primary method of communication.
- Sensory input and intactness of motor processes.
- Medical stability.
- Fatigue.
- Extent of maladaptive behaviors.

Primary Method of Communication   Although some students with severe disabilities may exhibit normal speech, others present various speech, language, and communication deficits. At the more severe levels, the speech of some children may be unintelligible to all but the primary care givers. In other cases, children may not speak at all but may communicate by nonverbal or nonvocal means including sign language, gestures, or various body movements and vocalizations. In most situations, evaluators and teachers should collaborate with a speech, language, and communication therapist to identify and evaluate the primary response mode. After identifying the primary response mode, assessment procedures should be tailored to the individual communication skills of the child.

Sensory Input and Intactness of Motor Processes   *Sensory input and intactness of motor processes* refers to how well the child sees, hears, moves about, and performs fine motor manipulation and drawing tasks. Evaluators should assess these characteristics prior to general assessment. Because evaluators may need to use specialized assessment techniques and instruments to assess sensory and motor function, they often collaborate with specialists such as neurodevelopmental therapists, physical therapists, occupational therapists, vision teachers, or audiologists.

Medical Stability   Some medically fragile students require frequent medical care, including hospitalization. With these students, determining health and medical stability is an important consideration in the assessment process. In these cases, the participation of medical specialists as an integral part of the assessment team may be necessary.

Fatigue   Fatigue refers to stamina and attention during the assessment process. Some children with severe disabilities tire and lose concentration quickly. This may be influenced by medication, which may lower attention levels or make the student irritable or hypersensitive. Because fatigue represents a common problem with young children, the evaluator should consider this characteristic carefully as part of the assessment process. If the child lacks stamina or is inattentive, assessment may take longer to complete than if the child exhibits good stamina and is attentive.

Extent of Maladaptive Behaviors   Maladaptive behaviors exhibited by young children with severe disabilities include self-stimulation (e.g., light flicking), self-abuse (e.g., head banging), extreme noncompliance and task resistance, and other inappropriate behaviors that may interfere with the assessment process. Assessing maladaptive behavior is often necessary with young children who have severe disabilities.

Characteristics of Assessment Instruments for Students With Severe Disabilities

In addition to evaluating student characteristics, evaluators should look for several key characteristics of the assessment instruments themselves as part of the test selection process (Venn & Dykes, 1987). These characteristics include the following:

- Adaptable response modes.
- Flexible administration procedures.
- Provisions for giving partial credit.
- A wide sample of behaviors.
- Procedures for developing a positive intervention plan.

The goal is to select instruments that minimize the student's impairments and maximize the student's ability to respond. This strategy produces the best possible assessment information for developing a positive intervention plan.

Adaptable Response Modes   *Adapting the response mode* refers to modifying a test item to match the child's unique patterns of responding. For nonverbal children, verbal test items need to be modified to allow response modes such as sign language or pointing to symbols on a communication board. For children with physical impairments, the response mode for test items that require motor responses can often be modified through the use of switches or other augmentative communication aids. Likewise, modifying assessment materials by substituting a motivating stimulus for a nonmotivating one improves the chances for student success. For example, toys that produce sound, have knobs to turn, buttons to push, and attractive visuals should be substituted for dull, uninteresting toys. The goal is to maintain the child's attention with sound, motion, color, and novelty.

Flexible Administration Procedures   Although highly structured tests with specific administration procedures are necessary in certain situations, teachers generally prefer more flexible measures when they assess students prior to developing intervention programs. Flexible tests allow evaluators to modify the assessment procedures to meet the unique needs and response styles of individual students. Some tests provide specific guidelines for adapting administration procedures and test items. For example, the *Developmental Activities Screening Inventory-II* (reviewed later in this chapter) includes specific instructions for adapting the instrument when testing children who are blind or nonverbal.

Provisions for Giving Partial Credit   *Partial credit* refers to scoring that provides recognition for completing part of a task. Partial credit scoring goes beyond simple pass-fail scoring by furnishing more than two scoring criteria. Some developmental tests for special populations provide three scoring criteria:

- Pass, which indicates independence on a particular skill.
- Emerging, which denotes significant progress toward independence.
- Fail, which signifies little or no acquisition of a skill.

For example, a child may not walk independently (pass), but this skill may be emerging. With pass-fail scoring the child would fail this item. With three scoring criteria the child would receive partial credit (emerging) as an interim score between pass and fail. Some scales for special populations include more than three scoring criteria, and this enables measurement of small increments of progress in children. For example, the *Developmental Assessment for the Severely Handicapped (DASH)* (Dykes, 1980) includes a "task resistive" scoring category, which refers to situations in which a child goes beyond failing an item by refusing to even attempt a task. Using a scoring system with this criterion makes it possible to show improvement when a child begins to cooperate in learning a task.

A Wide Sample of Behaviors   The best instruments for children with severe disabilities have numerous test items that sample a wide range of behaviors. Instruments with a small number of items fail to provide an adequate sample for making accurate assessment decisions. In fact, children with severe disabilities usually fail so many items on short tests that the results show what the children cannot do rather than what they can do. In contrast, instruments with many items sample an array of behaviors, thus providing opportunities to discover emerging skills and behaviors that children can successfully perform. For this reason, teachers and evaluators prefer tests with a wide sample of behaviors.

Procedures for Developing a Positive Intervention Plan   Rather than relying on testing to confirm low levels of performance and the lack of functional skills, evaluators should use instruments that provide a means to develop a positive intervention plan. Developmental scales that include extensive information on intervention and programming make it easier to achieve this goal. Likewise, scales that contain the features just described make it easier to generate a functional and practical plan for meeting the individual and often unique learning needs of students with severe and multiple disabilities.

Specialized Developmental Assessment Instruments

The following specialized assessment instruments are tools that special education teachers and other professionals rely on to evaluate the developmental progress of young children with severe, profound, and multiple disabilities. Although similar in content to conventional developmental scales, each of these tests contains unique features that make it particularly applicable for specialized use.

Ordinal Scales of Psychological Development   *Assessment in Infancy: Ordinal Scales of Psychological Development* (Uzgiris & Hunt, 1975) measure the ability to visually follow objects, to understand means-ends relationships, to engage in gestural and vocal imitation, and to play with objects. The *Ordinal Scales* assess these abilities using criterion-referenced test items that were originally developed for use with infants but are often used with older children who have severe delays or disabilities (McCormick, 1996). The *Ordinal Scales* are based on the Piagetian sensorimotor hierarchy of conceptual development. This hierarchy represents a key curriculum element in most infant, toddler, and preschool programs. In 1980 Dunst enhanced the *Ordinal Scales of Psychological Development* by providing simplified administration and scoring procedures and adding supplemental items to make the scale clinically and educationally more useful. The Dunst manual includes procedures for profiling a child's overall pattern of sensorimotor development, identifying abilities and interests, and designing intervention activities. These scoring forms make the *Ordinal Scales* more practical to use and easier to translate into a curriculum designed to emphasize acquisition of communication and social interaction skills in functional environments.

The *Observation of Behavior in Socially and Ecologically Relevant and Valid Environments*   The *Observation of Behavior in Socially and Ecologically Relevant and Valid Environments (OBSERVE)* (Dunst & McWilliam, 1988) provides an observation system based on the Piagetian stages of development that is especially designed for children with severe, profound, and multiple disabilities. *OBSERVE* evaluates five levels of behavioral interactions: attentional, contingency, differentiated, encoded, and symbolic. McCormick (1996) indicated that *OBSERVE* enables assessment of the ongoing interactions of a child in social and nonsocial settings. Unlike traditional assessment in which the child must conform to standardized testing, *OBSERVE* matches the assessment process with the child's interaction ability and preferred response modes. This provides a more accurate measure of the child's ability to learn new behaviors than is offered by traditional testing procedures.

Developmental Activities Screening Inventory (DASI-II)   Like the *Ordinal Scales of Psychological Development,* the *Developmental Activities Screening Inventory-II (DASI-II)* (Fewell & Langley, 1984) also measures cognitive development from a Piagetian perspective. This informal, criterion-referenced scale covers an age range of birth to 5 years and is designed for use by teachers, diagnosticians, and psychologists. Skills measured by the 67 *DASI-II* items include the following:

- Sensory intactness.
- Means-ends relationships.
- Cause-effect memory.
- Seriation.
- Reasoning.

These neurological and cognitive skills are essential for young children as they grow and develop language and reasoning ability. The *DASI-II* materials include learning activities for teaching the specific skills evaluated by the test and samples of intervention programs based on *DASI-II* test results. The test can be given either verbally or visually, and each test item includes adaptation for use with children who are visually impaired. These features make the *DASI-II* ideal for use with young children who have severe, profound, and multiple disabilities. In some situations, psychologists and diagnosticians find it helpful to give the *DASI-II* to nonverbal children as a supplemental test that complements data obtained from conventional intelligence testing with instruments such as the performance subtest of the *WISC-III.*

Hawaii Early Learning Profile (HELP)   Also designed to measure Piagetian concept development, the *Hawaii Early Learning Profile (HELP)* (Furuno et al., 1988), a criterion-referenced developmental scale, includes a detailed cognitive subtest containing a variety of items. The Piagetian domains on the profile include developmental test items for concepts such as the following:

- Object permanence: The child looks for the hidden toy.
- Imitation skills: The child claps hands in imitation.
- Means-ends relationships: The child pushes the button to see the toy car go.
- Spatial concepts: The child builds with blocks.
- Cause-effect relationships: The child gives the complicated toy to an adult to make it go.

In addition to the cognitive subtest, the *HELP* includes all of the major subtests in the developmental curriculum as well as a complete description of goals and learning activities for each item on the test. Most practitioners consider the *HELP* to be especially applicable to students with severe and profound disabilities because it contains a large combination of developmental items. The *HELP* is suitable for children who are birth to 3 years of age or older with severe and profound disabilities.

Vulpé Assessment Battery   The *Vulpé Assessment Battery* (Vulpé, 1982), a comprehensive developmental scale, measures the performance of children from birth through 6 years of age. Designed as a criterion-referenced, individually administered tool, the *Vulpé Assessment Battery* provides detailed evaluation of performance in all the major developmental learning areas. In addition, it includes measures of learning in areas typically not covered on developmental scales, such as the following:

- Organizational skills.
- The environment.
- Basic senses and functions.
- Developmental reflexes.
- Muscle strength.
- Motor planning.
- Balance.

In a critical review, Venn (1987) described the *Vulpé Assessment Battery* as providing a system for evaluating the "whole" child in relation to the environment and central nervous system function. This type of diagnostic tool is appropriate for use by a wide range of professionals, including special educators, occupational therapists, physical therapists, psychologists, diagnosticians, and home intervention specialists. It also lends itself to use by an assessment team made up of professionals from these disciplines. Because of the comprehensive nature of the battery, special education teachers find it especially appropriate for young children who have severe, profound, and multiple disabilities. Vulpé wrote the scales based on extensive experience as an occupational therapist, and this professional orientation produced an instrument that is especially sensitive to the neurological and sensory-motor development of young children. First published in 1969 for a series of training seminars with practitioners who serve children with mental retardation, recent editions of the test expanded and improved the original battery.

☑ Comprehension Checklist

Like the readiness tests, these developmental scales represent a specialized type of assessment designed to meet the unique needs of preschool students with severe and profound disabilities. Because they respond to the characteristics of these children, the content of these tests centers less on preacademic skills and more on language, cognitive, and motor skills. The tests in this group also include more flexible administration procedures to meet the needs of children with sensory, motor, neurological, and intellectual deficits.

Infant Assessment

Practitioners who assess infants and toddlers face several unique challenges. First, few courses and training programs on infant-toddler assessment exist. Second, few textbooks or training manuals are available that focus on assessing infants and toddlers with disabilities. A paucity of assessment instruments compounds the problem. For these reasons, infant and toddler intervention specialists must reach out to a variety of sources to provide accurate and effective assessment. In addition to the lack of resources and information, several differences exist between traditional assessment models and those designed for infants and toddlers. These differences include team approaches that emphasize the family unit, a focus on home-based assessment in natural settings rather than a center or school-based testing, and more active participation by professionals from health-related disciplines such as physical and occupational therapy. Because of these variations from traditional evaluation, the steps in the assessment process differ somewhat from those of conventional testing. The steps include the following:

- Obtaining case history information by questionnaires and direct interviews in the home environment.
- Conducting developmental screening in the home setting.
- Completing comprehensive assessment in the natural environment, using appropriate instruments.
- Interpreting results.
- Discussing the results with the parents and other professionals.

The Case History

Even in the best circumstances, it is difficult to test very young children because they have fewer behaviors and a more restricted range of behaviors than older children, and their behavior changes quickly due to rapid growth and development. For this reason, a complete case history is one of the best sources of information about infants and toddlers and their families. Evaluators may obtain such information from questionnaires or direct interviews, and this is a necessary step prior to testing a child. According to Rossetti (1990), evaluators should include the specific information outlined in Table 8–9 in a comprehensive case history.

Developmental Assessment With Infants and Toddlers

After obtaining case history information, an evaluator or an evaluation team collects developmental assessment data. Developmental assessment with infants and toddlers, including developmental screening, represents a dynamic process in which

Table 8–9   Information in a Comprehensive Case History

Area	Specific Information
Biographical information	Date of birth Description of the problem
Medical history	Significant medical problems before, during, and soon after birth Current medical treatments Medications
Developmental history	Description of developmental milestones Areas of delay Recent developmental changes
Educational history	Description of educational interventions Parents' view of educational needs
Social history	Description of siblings Interactions with parents and siblings Behavior problems

the evaluator obtains samples of behaviors by observing in unstructured play settings. The evaluator also measures performance in more structured, testlike situations. Observing and measuring the behavior of infants and toddlers provides an estimation of a child's developmental level and better assessment information than testing in the traditional manner. This process yields information about developmental functioning across several domains of assessment, including the following:

- Language and communication.
- Fine motor development.
- Gross motor development.
- Social development.
- Reflex development.
- Organizational behavior and cognitive processes.
- Sensory skills.
- Family assessment.
- Environmental influences.

Representative Assessment Instruments for Infants and Toddlers

Two representative assessment instruments specifically for use with infants and toddlers are the *Birth to Three Assessment and Intervention System* and the *Early Learning Accomplishment Profile*. Although in some cases an assessment team may choose to rely on a more general developmental scale, such as the *Battelle Developmental Inventory (BDI)* or the *Hawaii Early Learning Profile (HELP)* (both described earlier in this chapter), a specialized test often best fits the needs of the child and the purposes of the assessment.

Birth to Three Assessment and Intervention System The *Birth to Three Assessment and Intervention System*, a developmental scale and programming guide for infants and very young children, consists of the *Birth to Three Screening Test of Learning and Language Development* (Bangs & Dodson, 1986), the *Birth to Three Checklist of Learning and Language Behavior* (Bangs, 1986a), and the *Birth to Three Intervention Manual* (Bangs, 1986b). The *Birth to Three Screening Test*, a norm-referenced tool, screens children at high risk for developmental delay. The *Birth to Three Checklist*, a criterion-referenced scale, and the *Birth to Three Intervention Manual* are a system for classroom and home-based diagnostic assessment and intervention. Parent involvement, parent training, and home instruction are key features of the *Birth to Three* intervention program. The subtests on both the screening test and the checklist include the following:

- Language comprehension.
- Language expression.
- Avenues to learning (cognitive development).
- Social and personal development.
- Motor development.

In a comprehensive review, Venn (1988) concluded that the well-organized and easy-to-follow *Birth to Three* system is best when used with infants and toddlers who have mild disabilities. Although the norms for the screening test display some weaknesses, the other technical aspects of the system are more than adequate. When used as a criterion-referenced tool, *Birth to Three* provides a complete developmental system that includes test results plus an intervention guide for developing individual programs for children and their families.

Early Learning Accomplishment Profile   The *Early Learning Accomplishment Profile (E-LAP)* (Glover et al., 1988), a criterion-referenced test, assesses the overall development of children from birth to 36 months. The developmental subtests on the *E-LAP* include the following:

- Gross motor.
- Fine motor.
- Cognitive.
- Language.
- Self-help skills.
- Social-emotional skill areas.

Because subtests measuring skills such as sensory intactness and neurological status are not included on the *E-LAP*, it is best with very young children who have mild and moderate disabilities. The *E-LAP* results include a detailed profile of strengths and weaknesses across the six subtest areas, and the materials include a set of 380 early learning activity cards. These sequenced cards contain learning activities and teaching techniques keyed to the *E-LAP* test items. Each card includes a written objective as well as suggestions for helping a child learn a particular skill. Those who rely on the *LAP-R* (which has an age range of 3 to 6 years) may find that the *E-LAP* is an excellent supplement for children who function at or below the 3-year-old age level.

☑ Comprehension Checklist

Assessment of infants and toddlers is a specialized type of developmental appraisal. With the recent growth of early intervention programs, this type of assessment has become increasingly important. The process of assessing infants and toddlers emphasizes the family unit, home-based natural settings, and a team approach that includes active participation of medical and other health professionals.

Summary

With the expansion of programs and services for young children with disabilities, developmental assessment has become an increasingly prominent area of testing in special education. Developmental assessment encompasses appraisal techniques for use with children from infancy through the early primary grades. It includes instruments and procedures for students who range in performance levels from nondisabled to mildly and severely delayed.

Recent refinements in developmental testing reflect several of the most important trends in assessment. One of these refinements, evaluating family needs in new ways, serves as an integral part of the developmental assessment process. Evaluating family needs goes beyond considering the parents to also including siblings and extended family members. Refinements in the use of the team approach, such as having the parents serve as key team members, represent another important consideration. Recognition that early assessment and intervention may either reduce the severity of or, in some cases, prevent a disability altogether is also a significant factor.

Because of the importance of developmental assessment, preschool teachers and infant intervention specialists should be thoroughly familiar with the procedures and instruments (see Table 8–10 on p. 235). For other special educators, understanding developmental assessment is one component in building a comprehensive knowledge base in appraisal techniques. This knowledge helps teachers ensure that students receive appropriate assessment designed to fit the unique needs of the child and the family.

Chapter Review and Application

Multiple Choice

Directions: Read each item carefully. In the blank beside each item, write the letter of the best response. Each question contains only one best answer. Check your answers with the answer key at the end of the book.

_____ 1. Developmental assessment is a specialized type of assessment for measuring the performance of children, especially infants, toddlers, preschoolers, and young children from which age range?
  a. 1 year to approximately 4 years of age
  b. 1 year to approximately 5 years of age
  c. birth to approximately 6 years of age
  d. birth to approximately 9 years of age

_____ 2. Skills or subjects that make up the curriculum for infants, toddlers, and preschoolers.
  a. Family Support Plan
  b. Developmental milestones
  c. Developmental learning areas
  d. Developmental scales

_____ 3. The most critical or important skills in early childhood development such as walking, talking, and toilet training.
  a. Family Support Plan
  b. Developmental milestones
  c. Developmental learning areas
  d. Developmental scales

_____ 4. Tests that measure the performance of young children, including infants, toddlers, and preschoolers.
  a. Family Support Plan
  b. Developmental milestones
  c. Developmental learning areas
  d. Developmental scales

_____ 5. This includes present levels of performance, objectives, and the family's strengths and needs related to the child.
  a. Family Support Plan
  b. Developmental milestones

    c. Developmental learning areas

    d. Developmental scales

_____ **6.** Simultaneous assessment of a child by multiple professionals from different disciplines

    a. Team assessment

    b. Developmental assessment

    c. Arena assessment

    d. Group assessment

_____ **7.** Which of the following is a developmental screening test?

    a. *Hawaii Early Learning Profile*

    b. *Basic School Skills Inventory-Third Edition*

    c. *Ordinal Scales of Psychological Development*

    d. *Denver II*

_____ **8.** Which of the following is a readiness test?

    a. *Developmental Indicators for the Assessment of Learning-Third Edition*

    b. *Basic School Skills Inventory-Third Edition*

    c. *Battelle Developmental Inventory*

    d. *Denver II*

_____ **9.** Which of the following is a comprehensive diagnostic scale?

    a. *Ordinal Scales of Psychological Development*

    b. *Battelle Developmental Inventory*

    c. *Basic School Skills Inventory-Third Edition*

    d. *Developmental Indicators for the Assessment of Learning-Third Edition*

_____ **10.** Which of the following is a specialized developmental scale for children with severe disabilities?

    a. *Ordinal Scales of Psychological Development*

    b. *Battelle Developmental Inventory*

    c. *Basic School Skills Inventory-Third Edition*

    d. *Developmental Indicators for the Assessment of Learning-Third Edition*

Match Principles of Developmental Assessment

Directions: Match the principles of developmental assessment with the examples of child behavior. Select from examples a, b, c, or d. In the blank beside each item, write the letter of the best response. Use each choice only once. Use the answer key at the end of the book to check your answers.

  a. Scribbling is a prerequisite for drawing.

  b. Children crawl and creep while simultaneously learning to walk.

  c. If an infant who is learning to eat skips the "chewing stage," it may become increasingly difficult to learn this skill at older ages.

  d. Children with physical disabilities sometimes retain reflexive movement patterns that make it difficult for them to learn higher level movement patterns.

_____ **1.** Abnormal patterns of development among children with severe disabilities.

_____ **2.** The emergence of higher skills before lower skills drop out.

_____ **3.** Critical moments in the growth and development of children.

_____ **4.** The need for lower skills before higher skills develop.

Match Descriptions of Developmental Assessment

Directions: Match the descriptions of developmental assessment with the types of developmental assessment. Select from the following types: developmental screening, developmental diagnosis, readiness testing, specialized developmental assessment. In the blank beside each item, write the type of developmental assessment that is the best answer for the statement. Use each type only once. Use the answer key at the end of the book to check your answers.

_____ **1.** Furnishes in-depth data about strengths, weaknesses, and gaps in development.

_____ **2.** Provides a thumbnail sketch of the overall development of young children.

_____ **3.** Includes instruments and procedures for assessing children with unique needs, including young children with severe and profound disabilities.

_____ **4.** Determines whether children have the prerequisite skills for success in the first-grade curriculum.

Match Developmental Tests

Directions: Match the following developmental tests with the types of tests. Select from the following: screening, diagnostic readiness, specialized (for children with severe disabilities). In the blank beside each item, write the type of developmental test that is the best answer for the statement. You may use some types more than once. Use the answer key at the end of the book to check your answers.

_____ **1.** *DIAL-3*

_____ **2.** *Boehm Test of Basic Concepts-Revised*

_____ **3.** *Vulpé Assessment Battery*

_____ **4.** *FirstSTEP*

_____ **5.** *Gesell Developmental Schedules*

_____ **6.** *Basic School Skills Inventory-Third Edition*

_____ **7.** *LAP-D*

True-False

Directions: Answer true or false for each of the following statements about assessing intelligence by writing T or F in the blanks. Use the answer key at the end of the book to check your answers.

_____ **1.** Developmental screening provides a fast, efficient way to label children and diagnose developmental disabilities.

_____ **2.** Developmental screening tests and procedures exhibit limited predictive validity.

_____ **3.** According to the guidelines for developmental screening, parents should not be allowed to stay with their child during screening.

_____ **4.** Assessment instruments for children with severe disabilities should offer a wide sample of behaviors.

_____ **5.** Assessment instruments for children with severe disabilities should have rigid, highly structured administration procedures.

_____ **6.** The best assessment instruments for children with severe disabilities use a simple pass-fail scoring protocol.

Short Answers

Directions: Review your understanding of the material in this chapter by answering the following short answer questions. After you have responded to each question, compare your responses with the sample answers. Your responses should contain information that is similar to but not exactly the same as the information in the sample answers at the end of the book.

1. What are five uses of developmental assessment? Which of these uses do you think are most directly related to the responsibilities of the special education teacher?

2. Which developmental screening test would you use if you were asked to screen a group of preschoolers: the *DIAL-3* or the *Denver II*? Why?

3. Which two of the following three scales would be appropriate for use as the developmental test in initially identifying and placing a preschooler: the *LAP-D Standardized Assessment,* the *Battelle Developmental Inventory,* or the *Brigance Early*? Why?

4. Why is the case history so important in assessing children, especially infants and toddlers with special needs, and what specific types of information should be included in a complete case history about an infant or toddler?

5. What type of assessment information is provided by the *Birth to Three Assessment and Intervention System?* In your answer describe the *Birth to Three* subtests and discuss the purposes for giving the test and using it as an intervention system.

References

Bangs, T. (1986a). *Birth to Three Checklist of Learning and Language Behavior.* Allen, TX: DLM Teaching Resources.

———(1986b). *Birth to Three Intervention Manual.* Allen, TX: DLM Teaching Resources.

Bangs, T., & Dodson, S. (1986). *Birth to Three Screening Test of Learning and Language Development.* Allen, TX: DLM Teaching Resources.

Banus, B. S. (1971). *The Developmental Therapist: A Prototype of the Pediatric Occupational Therapist.* Thorofare, NJ: Charles B. Slack.

Boehm, A. (1986a) *Boehm Test of Basic Concepts-Preschool Version (Boehm-Preschool).* San Antonio, TX: Psychological Corporation.

———(1986b). *Boehm Test of Basic Concepts-Revised.* San Antonio, TX: Psychological Corporation.

Brigance, A. H. (1985). *Brigance Preschool Screen for Three-a nd Four-Year-Old Children.* North Billerica, MA: Curriculum Associates.

———(1990). *Brigance Early Preschool Screen for Two-Year-Old and Two-and-One-Half-Year-Old Children.* North Billerica, MA: Curriculum Associates.

———(1991). *Revised Brigance Diagnostic Inventory of Early Development.* North Billerica, MA: Curriculum Associates.

Danzer, V., Gerber, M. F., Lyons, T., & Voress, J. K. (1991). *Daberon Screening for School Readiness Test* (2d ed.). Austin, TX: PRO-ED.

Dunst, C. (1980). *A Clinical and Educational Manual for Use with the Uzgiris and Hunt Scales of Infant Psychological Development.* Austin, TX: PRO-ED.

Dunst, C., & McWilliam, R. A. (1988). Cognitive assessment and multiply handicapped young children. In T. D. Wachs & R. Sheehan (Eds.), *Assessment of Developmentally Disabled Children.* New York: Plenum Press, 213–38.

Dykes, M. K. (1980). *Developmental Assessment for the Severely Handicapped.* Austin, TX: PRO-ED.

Fewell, R. R., & Langley, M. B. (1984). *Developmental Activities Screening Inventory-II.* Austin, TX: PRO-ED.

Florida Department of Education. (1986). *Assessment: Educating the Severely/Profoundly Handicapped.* Tallahassee, FL: Florida Department of Education.

Frankenburg, W., Dodds, J., Archers, P., Bresnick, B., Maschka, P., Edelman, N., & Shapiro, H. (1990). *Denver Developmental Screening Test-II.* Denver, CO: Denver Developmental Materials.

Furuno, S., O'Reilly, K., Hosaka, C., Inatsuka, T., Aleman, T., & Zeislaft, B. (1988). *Hawaii Early Learning Profile.* Palo Alto, CA: VORT.

Gesell, A. (1940). *Gesell Developmental Schedules.* Cheshire, CT: Nigel Cox.

Glover, M. E., Preminger, J. L., & Sanford, A. R. (1988). *Early Learning Accomplishment Profile.* Lewisville, NC: Kaplan School Supply Corporation.

Hammill, D. D., Leigh, J. E., Pearson, N. A., & Maddox, T. (1998). *Basic School Skills Inventory* (3d ed.). Austin, TX: PRO-ED.

Harrison, P. L., Kaufman, A. S., Kaufman, N. L., Bruininks, P. H., Rynders, J., Ilmer, S., Sparrow, S. S., & Chichetti, D. V. (1990). *AGS Early Screening Profiles.* Circle Pines, MN: American Guidance Service.

Hresko, W. P., Miguel, S. H., Sherbenour, R. J., & Burton, S. D. (1994). *The Developmental Observation Checklist System.* Austin, TX: PRO-ED.

Illinois Association for Supervision and Curriculum Development. (1990, Spring). How does your screener stack up? *Assessment Information Exchange: A Professional Service for Users of American Guidance Service Tests,* 7–11.

Johnson, L. J., & Beauchamp, K. D. (1987). Preschool assessment measures: What are teachers using? *Journal of the Division for Early Childhood,* 12, 70–76.

Johnson-Martin, N. M., Attermeier, S. M., & Hecker, B. J. (1990). *The Carolina Curriculum for Preschoolers with Special Needs.* Baltimore, MD: Paul H. Brookes.

Johnson-Martin, N. M., Jens, K. G., Attermeier, S. M., & Hecker, B. J. (1991). *The Carolina Curriculum for Infants and Toddlers with Special Needs* (2d ed.). Baltimore, MD: Paul H. Brookes.

Knobloch, H., & Pasamanick, B. (1974). *Gesell and Amatruda's Developmental Diagnosis: The Evaluation and Management of Normal and Abnormal Neuropsychological Development in Infancy and Early Childhood* (3d ed.). New York: Harper & Row.

Knobloch, H., Stevens, F., & Malone, A. F. (1980). *Manual of Developmental Diagnosis.* New York: Harper & Row.

Lee, J., & Clark, W. (1962). *Lee–Clark Reading Readiness Test.* Monterey, CA: CTB/McGraw-Hill.

Mardell-Czudnowski, C. D., & Goldenberg, D. S. (1998). *Developmental Indicators for the Assessment of Learning* (3d ed.). Circle Pines, MN: American Guidance Service.

McAffee, O., & Leong, D. (1997). *Assessing and Guiding Young Children's Development and Learning* (2d ed.). Boston: Allyn and Bacon.

McCormick, K. (1996). Assessing cognitive development. In M. McLean, D. B. Bailey, & M. Wolery (Eds.), *Assessing Infants and Preschoolers with Special Needs* (2d ed.). Upper Saddle River, NJ: Merrill/Prentice Hall, 268–304.

McLean, M., & Crais, E. R. (1996). Procedural considerations in assessing infants and preschoolers with disabilities. In M. McLean, D. B. Bailey, & M. Wolery (Eds.), *Assessing Infants and Preschoolers with Special Needs,* (2d ed.). Upper Saddle River, NJ: Merrill/Prentice Hall, 46–65.

Miller, L. J. (1993). *FirstSTEP: Screening Test for Evaluating Preschoolers.* San Antonio, TX: Psychological Corporation.

Mullen, E. M. (1995). *Mullen Scales of Early Learning: AGS Edition.* Circle Pines, MN: American Guidance Service.

Nehring, A., Nehring, E., Bruni, J., & Randolph, P. (1992). *Learning Accomplishment Profile-Diagnostic Edition.* Winston-Salem, NC: Kaplan Press.

Newborg, J., Stock, J., Wnek, L., Guidubaldi, J., & Svinicki, J. (1988a). *Battelle Developmental Inventory.* Itasca, IL: Riverside Publishing.

———(1988b). *Battelle Developmental Screening Test.* Itasca, IL: Riverside Publishing.

Nurss, J. R. (1995). *Metropolitan Readiness Tests,* (6th ed.). San Antonio, TX: Psychological Corporation.

Rossetti, L. M. (1990). *Infant-Toddler Assessment: An Interdisciplinary Approach.* Boston: Little, Brown.

Sanford, A., & Zelman, J. (1981). *Learning Accomplishment Profile* (rev. ed.). Winston-Salem, NC: Kaplan Press.

Uzgiris, F., & Hunt, J. (1975). *Assessment in Infancy: The Ordinal Scales of Psychological Development.* Urbana, IL: University of Illinois Press.

Venn, J. J. (1987). A review of the Vulpé Assessment Battery. In D. Keyser & R. Sweetland (Eds.), *Test critiques* (vol. 6). Kansas City, MO: Test Corporation of America, 622–28.

———(1988). A review of the *Birth to Three Assessment and Intervention System.* In D. Keyser & R. Sweetland (Eds.), *Test critiques* (vol. 7). Kansas City, MO: Test Corporation of America, 49–54.

Venn, J. J., & Dykes, M. K. (1987). Assessing the physically handicapped. In W. H. Berdine and S.A. Meyer (Eds.), *Assessment in Special Education* Boston: Little, Brown, 278–308.

Vulpé, S. (1969). *Home Care and Management of the Mentally Retarded Child: Assessment Battery.* Toronto: National Institute on Mental Retardation.

———(1982). *Vulpé Assessment Battery* (2d ed.). Toronto: National Institute on Mental Retardation.

Wilson-LeMay, D., Griffin, P., Sanford, A., & Maltes, S. (1977). *Learning Accomplishment Profile: Diagnostic Edition.* Winston-Salem, NC: Kaplan Press.

Table 8–10   Review of Development Tests

Name of Test	Type of Test	Suitable for Individuals Who Are	Brief Description of Test	Purpose of Administering Test
AGS Early Screening Profiles (Harrison et al., 1990)	Norm referenced screening test	2–6 years	Uses multiple domains, settings, and sources to measure cognitive, language, motor, self-help, and social skills; also surveys the child's articulation, home environment, health history, and test behavior	To provide practical information for making accurate screening decisions
Basic School Skills (3d ed.) (BSSI-3) (Hammill et al., 1998)	Norm-referenced, individually administered readiness test	4–6.5 years	Measures daily living skills, spoken language, reading, writing, mathematics, and classroom behavior	To locate children who are at high risk for school failure, who need more in-depth assessment, and who should be referred for additional testing
*Battelle Developmental Inventory (BDI) (Newborg et al., 1988a)	Norm-referenced, individually administered screening test and diagnostic scale	Birth–8 years	Measures performance in personal, social, adaptive, motor, communicative, and cognitive skills	To screen children for potential disabilities; to classify and place young children into appropriate special education programs; to develop IEPs and intervention programs; to measure progress
Battelle Developmental Screening Test (Newborg et al., 1988b)	Norm-referenced, individually administered screening test	Birth–8 years	Measures development in personal-social, adaptive, motor, communicative, and cognitive skills	To identify children with potential developmental delays or other disabilities
Birth to Three Assessment and Intervention System (Bangs & Dodson, 1986; Bangs, 1986a, 1986b)	Norm-referenced screening test, a criterion-referenced diagnostic scale, and an intervention manual	Birth–3 years	Subtests include language comprehension, language expression, avenues to learning (cognitive development), social development, personal development, and motor development	To screen children at high risk for developmental delay, to obtain a diagnostic assessment, and to develop a classroom and home-based intervention system

*Tests marked with asterisks are featured in tables in this chapter.

Table 8–10   *(continued)*

Name of Test	Type of Test	Suitable for Individuals Who Are	Brief Description of Test	Purpose of Administering Test
Boehm Test of Basic Concepts-Preschool Version (Boehm-Preschool) (Boehm, 1986a)	Norm-referenced, individually administered readiness test	3–5 years, or older children with identified language difficulties	Helps with early identification of children with basic concept deficiencies	Useful for preschool screening programs to identify weaknesses in basic concept comprehension
Boehm Test of Basic Concepts-Revised (Boehm, 1986b)	Norm-referenced readiness test, group administered	Kindergarten–grade 2	Incorporates 50 important concepts such as more-less, first-last, same-different, following directions, under-standing sequences, and problem solving	To measure a child's knowledge of the basic understanding necessary for success in the beginning years of school
Brigance Early Preschool Screen for Two-Year-Old and Two-and-One-Half-Year-Old Children (Brigance, 1990)	Criterion-referenced, individually administered developmental screen-ing test	2–2.5 years	Measures fine motor, gross motor, lan-guage, and cogni-tive skills	To measure children's basic skills in the major developmental learning areas
Brigance Preschool Screen for Three- and Four-Year-Old Children (Brigance, 1985)	Criterion referenced, individually administered	3–4 years	Measures fine motor, gross motor, lan-guage, and cogni-tive skills	To measure children's basic skills in the major developmental learning areas
Carolina Curriculum for Infants and Toddlers with Special Needs (2d ed.) (Johnson-Martin et al., 1991)	Criterion-referenced, individually administered curriculum guide and diagnostic checklist	Birth–24 months	Covers cognition, communication, social adaption, fine motor skills, and gross motor skills	Provides intervention strategies and assess-ment information, includes an assess-ment log for charting the child's ongoing progress
Carolina Curriculum for Preschoolers with Special Needs (Johnson-Martin et al., 1990)	Criterion-referenced curriculum guide and diagnostic checklist	2–5 years	Covers cognition, communication, social adaption, fine motor, and gross motor skills	Provides intervention strategies and assess-ment information, in cludes an assessment log for charting the child's ongoing progress
Daberon Screening for School Readiness Test (2d ed.) (Danzer et al., 1991)	Norm-referenced, group-administered screening level readiness test	4–6 years	Samples knowledge of body parts, color and number concepts, gross motor devel-opmental abilities re-lated to early academic success	To identify children at risk for school failure, to help develop instruc-tional objectives, and to assist in writing IEPs

Table 8–10   *(continued)*

Name of Test	*Type of Test*	*Suitable for Individuals Who Are*	*Brief Description of Test*	*Purpose of Administering Test*
Denver II (Frankenburg et al., 1990)	Norm-referenced, individually administered screening test	Birth–6 years	Measures developmental progress in personal-social, fine motor–adaptive, gross motor, and language skills	To screen young children with potential developmental delays
Developmental Activities Screening Inventory (DASI-II) (Fewell & Langley, 1984)	Criterion-referenced, individually administered screening test	Birth–5 years	Measures cognitive development from a Piagetian perspective; can be given verbally or nonverbally; includes learning activities for teaching the specific skills evaluated by the test	To measure the cognitive development of young children with severe and multiple disabilities
Developmental Assessment for the Severely Handicapped (DASH) (Dykes, 1980)	Criterion-referenced, individually administered diagnostic scale	Birth–6 years of age and older children with severe disabilities who are functioning in the developmental age range	Measures a wide sample of behaviors in all of the major learning areas, offers flexible administration procedures, includes extensive provisions for giving partial credit	To measure the developmental progress of children with severe, profound, and multiple disabilities
Developmental Indicators for the Assessment of Learning (3d ed.) *(DIAL-3)* (Mardell-Czudnowski & Goldenberg, 1998)	Norm-referenced, group or individually administered screening test	2–6 years	Measures developmental progress in motor development, concept development, and language skills	To identify young children with potential developmental delays
Developmental Observation Checklist System (DOCS) (Hresko et al., 1994)	Norm-referenced, individually administered observation checklist	Birth–6 years	Measures general development, adjustment behavior, parent stress, and parent support; the general development section includes language, motor, social, and cognitive skills	To measure child development based on parents' or care givers' observation of the child's daily behaviors

Table 8–10   *(continued)*

Name of Test	Type of Test	Suitable for Individuals Who Are	Brief Description of Test	Purpose of Administering Test
Early Learning Accomplishment Profile (E-LAP) (Glover et al., 1988)	Criterion-referenced, individually administered diagnostic scale	Birth–3 years	Evaluates gross motor, fine motor, cognitive language, self-help, and social-emotional skills	To assess overall development and to assist in developing IEP objectives and intervention activities
Gesell Developmental Schedules (revised by Knobloch & Pasamanick, 1974, and by Knobloch et al., 1980)	Criterion-referenced, individually administered diagnostic scale	4 weeks–6 years	Measures gross motor, fine motor, communication, personal-social, and adaptive behavior	Gesell designed the schedules for use as criterion-based measures of child progress
FirstSTEP: Screening Test for Evaluating Preschoolers (Miller, 1993)	Norm-referenced, individually administered screening test	2 years, 9 months–6 years, 2 months	Evaluates development in the five areas mandated by IDEA: cognition, communication, motor, social-emotional, and adaptive behavior; also provides an optional parent/teacher scale to add information about the child's typical behavior at home and at school	To identify preschool children who are at risk for developmental delays
Hawaii Early Learning Profile (HELP) (Furuno et al., 1988)	Criterion-referenced, individually administered diagnostic scale	Birth–3 years	Includes all of the major subtests in the developmental curriculum as well as a complete description of goals and learning activities for each item on the test	Especially useful with young children who have severe and profound disabilities because it contains numerous test items
Learning Accomplishment Profile-Standardized Assessment (LAP-D) (Nehring et al., 1992)	Norm-referenced, individually administered diagnostic scale	6 months–6 years	Measures developmental learning in body movement, object movement, fine motor manipulation, fine motor writing, cognitive matching, cognitive counting, language naming, and language comprehension	To assess overall development, to help write IEPs, to develop intervention programs, and to measure progress

Table 8–10 *(continued)*

Name of Test	Type of Test	Suitable for Individuals Who Are	Brief Description of Test	Purpose of Administering Test
Lee–Clark Reading Readiness Test (Lee & Clark, 1962)	Norm-referenced, group-administered reading readiness test	Kindergarten or beginning Grade 1	Measures letter matching, letter discrimination, picture vocabulary, and letter and word recognition	To measure a child's knowledge of the basic skills necessary for reading success in the beginning years of school
Metropolitan Readiness Tests (MRT 6) (Nurss, 1995)	Norm-referenced, group or individually administered readiness test	4–7 years	Assesses visual discrimination, beginning consonants, sound-letter correspondence, story comprehension (using a big book), and quantitative concepts and reasoning	To assess literacy development in prekindergarten and kindergarten children
Observation of Behavior in Socially and Ecologically Relevant and Valid Environments (OBSERVE) (Dunst & McWilliam, 1988)	Criterion-referenced, individually administered observation system	Severely disabled with profound and multiple disabilities	Evaluates five levels of behavioral interactions: attentional, contingency, differentiated, encoded, and symbolic	Enables assessment of the ongoing interactions of a child in social and nonsocial settings
Mullen Scales of Early Learning: AGS Edition (Mullen, 1995)	Norm-referenced, individually administered diagnostic scale	Birth–5 years, 8 months	Provides assessment of language, motor, and perceptual abilities with subtests in gross motor, visual reception, fine motor, expressive language, and receptive language	To develop and plan school and home-based early intervention programs for young children with developmental disabilities
Ordinal Scales of Psychological Development (Uzgiris & Hunt, 1975)	Criterion-referenced, individually administered diagnostic scale	Originally developed for use with infants but are often used with older children who have severe delays or disabilities	Measures a child's ability to visually follow objects, understand means-ends relationships, engage in gestural and vocal imitation, and play with objects	To assess the conceptual development of children with severe disabilities using the Piagetian sensorimotor hierarchy
Revised Brigance Diagnostic Inventory of Early Development (Brigance Early) (Brigance, 1991)	Criterion-referenced, individually administered diagnostic scale	Birth–6 years	A developmental checklist and curriculum guide	To write IEPs, to develop intervention programs, and to measure progress

Table 8–10   (continued)

Name of Test	Type of Test	Suitable for Individuals Who Are	Brief Description of Test	Purpose of Administering Test
Vulpé Assessment Battery (Vulpé, 1982)	Criterion-referenced, individually administered diagnostic scale	Birth–6 years with severe, profound, and multiple disabilities	Measures performance in the developmental learning areas and in organizational skills, the environment, basic sense and functions, reflexes, muscle strength, motor planning, and balance	To assess the developmental progress of young children with severe, profound, and multiple disabilities

Assessment of Perception and Motor Proficiency

Overview

Assessment of perception and motor proficiency measures visual- and auditory-processing ability as well as fine and gross motor skill development. In this chapter we investigate the concepts and techniques associated with assessing perception and motor proficiency. We study key terms, significant concepts, and important issues associated with assessment in these domains. In addition, we review practical, applied guidelines for assessing perceptual-processing ability and motor skill development. Finally, we examine the tests and evaluation procedures special educators use to identify performance levels and develop intervention programs in the areas of perception and motor proficiency. As we review each test and evaluation technique, we consider its purpose and use, materials, administration procedures, scoring and interpretation process, and technical characteristics.

Objectives

After reading this chapter, you will be prepared to do the following:

- Understand perception, motor proficiency, and perceptual-motor ability.
- Apply guidelines for assessing perception, motor proficiency, and perceptual-motor development.
- Describe the skills measured by perception and perceptual-motor development tests.
- Use representative tests of perception and perceptual-motor development.
- Identify the sensory learning modalities of children with special needs.
- Use the tests and observation procedures that assess modality preferences.
- Assess the motor development of children with special needs to identify specific deficits and develop instructional intervention programs.
- Use representative tests of fine and gross motor development.
- Discuss the role of evaluating perceptual, motor, and perceptual-motor skills in the overall process of assessment in special education.

Introduction to Assessing Perception and Motor Proficiency

The following two accounts introduce assessment of perception and motor proficiency from the perspective of special education teachers who want learn more about using assessment to meet the needs of their students. The deficits described in these accounts, a visual-processing problem and a fine motor delay, are typical of the perceptual and motor difficulties of young children with special needs.

During preplanning, Mrs. Jones was transferred to a new class for young children with learning disabilities. Included in her class were several children with severe visual- and auditory-perception problems. For example, two 6-year-old children had difficulty copying and printing certain letters correctly. Their problems included consistent reversal and occasional rotation of letters such as p, b, *and* d. *The children also exhibited difficulty learning basic reading skills. Mrs. Jones observed that the children had poor memory for visual information but good memory for auditory information. Because she had little prior experience teaching young children with these perceptual difficulties, Mrs. Jones had several questions about where to begin and what to do, including the following: What are the most common perceptual problems of young children with learning disabilities? Are there specialized tests for assessing children with perceptual problems? How important is observational assessment in identifying and developing intervention programs? What is the best way to develop IEP goals? How should she measure progress in remediating the perceptual problems of her students?*

When two children with cerebral palsy joined Mrs. Fuller's special education class, she had several questions about how to help them develop their motor proficiency to the maximum. Because she had never worked with children with severe motor disabilities, she wondered what was meant by the terms fine motor skills *and* gross motor skills *that appeared in reports in the children's cumulative folders. She was unfamiliar with the motor proficiency test that the diagnostician used to assess the children's motor development. She knew that she must first obtain some basic information about cerebral palsy and assessing motor development. She then could ask how to best develop intervention programs for her new students and write appropriate IEP objectives. This would also help her measure the progress of the students in fine motor and gross motor development.*

These two scenarios highlight many of the questions teachers have about how assessment can help them remediate their students' perceptual and motor deficits. In this chapter we discover answers to these questions and we investigate other aspects of the processes and procedures associated with evaluating the perception and motor proficiency of children with special needs.

Definition of Perception and Motor Proficiency

Perception is the process of comprehending information received by the senses. Assessment of perception involves measuring the way in which students process information from the senses, especially visual and auditory information.

In contrast to perception, which concerns sensory input, **motor proficiency** refers to movement output. Motor proficiency is the efficiency of movements controlled by the body's muscles. The two major types of motor activity are fine and gross motor movement. **Fine motor** addresses movement and response speed controlled by the small muscles of the body and includes hand and finger dexterity, drawing, and manipulation of small objects. **Gross motor,** on the other hand, refers to movement controlled by the large muscles of the body, including those that regulate walking, throwing, catching, and balancing. Assessing motor development involves measuring and evaluating motor performance to identify present levels of movement proficiency. Special educators use the results of this assessment to plan instructional intervention programs.

Although special educators often assess perception and motor ability separately, they may evaluate the two domains together, which is referred to as **perceptual-motor** and is defined as the process of integrating sensory information with corresponding body movements. A basic psychological process, coordinating perceptual input with motor output includes visual-motor, auditory-motor, and tactile-motor skills. For example, **visual-motor processing** refers to coordinating sensory information from the eyes with corresponding movements such as eye-hand coordination and visual-motor control. Likewise, **auditory-motor processing** refers to coordinating sensory information from the ears with fine and gross motor body movements. When evaluating perception, perceptual-motor performance, and motor proficiency, evaluators follow certain guidelines to ensure accuracy in the assessment.

Guidelines for Assessing Perception and Motor Proficiency

The guidelines for assessing perception and motor proficiency contain practical suggestions for accurate administration of tests and appropriate interpretation of results. These guidelines include the following:

- Screen for vision or hearing impairment.
- Exercise caution with students who have physical or sensory impairments.
- Assess older students carefully.
- Determine the need for training.
- Observe student behavior carefully.

Screening for Vision or Hearing Impairment   Prior to assessment, evaluators should rule out vision or hearing impairment as a cause of perception or motor delays because sensory disabilities such as poor visual acuity or hearing loss can affect the results of evaluations and lead to misinterpretation of results. Evaluators may screen for vision or hearing deficits in several ways as appropriate to the individual situation and the needs of the student. Screening steps may include reviewing a student's cumulative record for information about visual and hearing status, observing a student directly, or interviewing a teacher who is familiar with a student. If the screening process indicates a potential problem, the evaluator should refer the student to a specialist for evaluation. In some cases a teacher may observe sensory difficulties not detected during the screening. For example, if a teacher observes changes in visual or hearing functioning or recognizes an unusual visual or auditory behavior, the teacher should refer the student to a specialist. The referral should include a description of possible impairment and observed changes in behavior.

Exercising Caution With Students With Physical or Sensory Impairments   Because students with severe physical or sensory impairments may not be able to perform certain test items, evaluators should use perceptual and motor tests cautiously. For example, seeing complex drawings on visual-motor tests may be impossible for a student with a severe visual impairment. Likewise, a student with a hearing loss may be incapable of responding to auditory items on tests of auditory discrimination. In cases of severe physical or sensory impairment, special educators should avoid giving perceptual and motor tests altogether. In other cases, special educators should exercise caution when giving tests to students with physical and sensory disabilities and realize the possible limitations of the results.

Assessing Older Students Carefully   Many of the perceptual and motor tests are designed for young children (e.g., preschoolers and elementary students) rather than older students. For older students, the focus of instruction shifts to academic, social, and career skills rather than basic perceptual-processing and motor skills. As a result, evaluators should check the age range of tests before using them with older students.

Determining the Need for Training   Students with limited English proficiency and students from deprived backgrounds may need experience with and exposure to perceptual and motor tasks prior to assessment. Providing training ensures accuracy and fairness in the assessment process. This training usually takes the form of extended practice with examples of the behaviors measured by perceptual and motor tests. For example, if an assessment requires building with 1-inch cubes, throwing and catching bean bags, and performing dynamic balance movements such as standing on one leg and walking a balance beam, the student should practice activities like these. Likewise, if a visual-motor perception test requires copying complex geometric drawings, care should be taken to make sure that the child has been exposed to similar tasks before testing. The practice training should include correcting errors and reinforcing appropriate responses to ensure that inexperience does not mitigate assessment results. However, evaluators must avoid training and practice with actual test items.

Observing Student Behavior Carefully   Although special educators may select from a number of tests of perceptual and motor skills, no test replaces the diagnostic information an insightful teacher gathers from daily observation of and contact with a student. For this reason, special educators should rely on careful observation as a key element in identifying needs and establishing intervention programs for students with perceptual processing and motor development problems. If careful observation fails to confirm the results of testing, the test results should be carefully reviewed for accuracy.

☑ Comprehension Checklist

Understanding the meaning of the terms *perception, motor proficiency,* and *perceptual-motor performance* provides a foundation for building a knowledge base of assessment techniques in these specialized domains. *Perception* refers to processing information received by the senses, *motor proficiency* concerns movements controlled by the muscles, and *perceptual-motor performance* involves the process of integrating information received by the senses with corresponding body movements.

Perceptual-motor processes include visual-motor, auditory-motor, and tactile-motor performance. When assessing student ability in these domains, special educators should follow established guidelines to ensure the collection of accurate and effective information.

Tests of Perception and Perceptual-Motor Skills

Special educators may choose from a variety of tests of perception and perceptual-motor skills. These instruments assess levels of perceptual performance and identify deficits in perceptual skill development. Most often designed to assess a specific perceptual or perceptual-motor skill, the tests include measures of visual, auditory, and tactile perception as well as visual-motor and auditory-motor processing ability.

Why Do We Assess Perception and Perceptual-Motor Skills?

For children with perceptual and perceptual-motor deficits, assessing the extent and nature of those deficits is an essential step in the intervention and remediation process. In the initial stages assessment involves screening to identify children with potential perceptual and perceptual-motor deficits. See Focus 9–1. Once children have been screened, comprehensive assessment is used to diagnose the exact nature and extent of the deficits. Most children have specific problems in particular perceptual-processing domains rather than generalized problems in all perceptual-processing domains. The most common problems include visual-processing deficits that result in poor visual-motor integration and weaknesses in visual perception. These difficulties are significant because good visual perception is a basic process necessary for interacting with the environment. Intact visual-processing ability is also important for learning basic academic skills such as handwriting and reading.

The following account is a practical, applied illustration of why we assess perception and perceptual-motor skills. In this scenario a teacher uses assessment to help a child with an auditory-perception problem. The auditory-perception problem described in this account is one of the most common perception deficits in children.

FOCUS 9–1

Why Do We Assess the Perception and Perceptual-Motor Skills of Children With Special Needs?

- To screen children for possible perception and perceptual-motor deficits
- To obtain diagnostic data and information regarding specific perception and perceptual-motor deficits in children identified as having potential problems
- To assist in developing IEPs and more specific intervention activities for children with perception and perceptual-motor deficits
- To monitor the effectiveness of intervention programs designed to remediate perception and perceptual-motor deficits

Rossi, a quiet, 6-year-old student of average intelligence, had difficulty remembering directions, especially when the teacher gave two or more directions at once. She also had trouble remembering details in long stories read aloud and had problems repeating nursery rhymes. Her teacher observed that Rossi displayed good memory for visual information but poor memory for auditory information. To identify the nature and extent of the problem, the teacher referred Rossi for assessment by a specialist. As part of the assessment, an audiologist screened Rossi's hearing to rule out an acuity problem as a causal factor. The audiologist failed to find any significant deficits. However, when a diagnostician gave Rossi a test of auditory perception, the results indicated that she performed significantly below average in auditory memory. Her specific problems included deficits in recognition memory and memory for content and sequence. As a result of the testing, the specialist recommended some remedial intervention activities for Rossi. The teacher implemented the activities in the classroom and started to present class information using the visual and the auditory modality to accommodate Rossi's learning deficit and those of other children in the class who had similar difficulties.

Questions About the Perceptual-Motor Approach

Although experts agree about the general nature of perception and perceptual-motor development, they often disagree about the effectiveness of tests and intervention techniques in this area. Theorists suggest that perceptual-motor deficits cause academic failure and that remediating deficits improves academic performance. Unfortunately, a lack of evidence exists to support this contention. Critics point out that the perceptual-motor tests are often technically inadequate, and they question the effectiveness of the resulting intervention programs. In particular, many experts question the value of assessment and intervention with older students, who need to focus on academic and functional skills rather than basic processing skills. Despite these concerns, measuring perceptual-motor performance is one component in a comprehensive assessment battery, especially with young children with neurological deficits. With certain students, identifying perceptual and perceptual-motor deficits and developing appropriate intervention programs to remediate these deficits is part of a complete intervention program.

Representative Tests of Perception and Perceptual-Motor Development

The following sections include reviews of representative tests of perception and perceptual-motor development. Two tests, the *Developmental Test of Visual-Motor Integration* and the *Goldman–Fristoe–Woodcock Auditory Skills Test Battery,* receive detailed reviews.

Developmental Test of Visual-Motor Integration, Fourth Edition

The *Developmental Test of Visual-Motor Integration, Fourth Edition (VMI-4)* (Beery, 1997) assesses the ability of children from age 3 through 18 years to integrate visual perception with fine motor coordination. The *VMI-4* test items, which are arranged in order of increasing difficulty, consist of geometric figures that children look at and then copy (see Table 9–1). Beery developed the *VMI-4* for use by preschool teachers, primary teachers, teachers of students with disabilities, and diagnosticians. The purpose of the *VMI-4* is to prevent learning and behavioral problems through early screening identification.

The *VMI-4* also includes optional tests for assessing visual perception and motor coordination. A visual-motor imitation test for children 3 years of age or under is another optional *VMI-4* component.

VMI-4 **Materials** *VMI-4* test materials include a student response booklet, an examiner's manual, and packages of short and long forms, visual test booklets, and motor test booklets.

Administration and Scoring of *VMI-4* The *VMI-4* takes about 15 minutes to administer and score, using a pass-fail criterion for each geometric design. The short form uses 18 items to assess the visual-motor integration of children from 3 to 8 years of age. The long form, designed for children from 3 to 18 years of age, uses 27 items and can also be used with adults who have visual-motor-integration deficits. Administration time for each optional test is about 5 minutes. Results are reported as percentiles and standard score equivalents. A profile comparison of the *VMI-4* results is also available.

Technical Qualities of the *VMI-4* Beery (1997) standardized the *VMI-4* on the basis of scores from a sample group of more than 3,000 children from age 3 to 19 years. The author provides support for the reliability of the *VMI-4* on the basis of a variety of studies, including split-half reliability research that produced a median coefficient of .79, test-retest studies with a median coefficient of .81, and several investigations of interrater reliability that yielded a median coefficient of .93. The author also provided summaries of concurrent and predictive validity research taken from an earlier edition of the *VMI-4*. This research included several concurrent validity studies that produced correlations ranging from .37 to .82. Because it relies on data from the original version, the revised version of the *VMI-4* displays poor validity. However, it

Table 9–1 *Developmental Test of Visual-Motor Integration, Fourth Edition (VMI-4)*

Type of Test:	Norm-referenced screening test
Purpose:	To assess proficiency in integrating visual perception with fine motor coordination
Content Areas:	Long form: 27 items; short form: 18 items
Administration Time:	15–20 minutes
Age Levels:	Long form 3–18 years; short form 3–8 years
Suitable for:	Students who display difficulty with visual perception and fine motor coordination, including those with mild and moderate disabilities
Scores:	Percentiles and standard scores
In Short:	The *VMI-4* is a useful screening test of visual-motor skills. *VMI-4* test items include various drawing and visual discrimination tasks such as drawing within lines, making geometric patterns, and identifying shapes.

exhibits satisfactory reliability and normative data, especially in comparison with similar tests of perceptual-motor ability.

Summary   The *VMI-4,* a standardized measure of visual-motor proficiency, has value when diagnosticians and teachers use it as a screening test or as one tool in an assessment battery. However, the test, consisting of 27 geometric designs, measures a restricted sample of visual-motor ability, and for this reason special educators should use it together with other assessment data and information rather than in isolation.

Goldman–Fristoe–Woodcock Auditory Skills Test Battery

The *Goldman–Fristoe–Woodcock Auditory Skills Test Battery (GFW Battery)* (Goldman et al., 1974), a comprehensive, individually administered instrument for measuring auditory deficiencies, consists of 12 tests in four categories:

1. Auditory selective attention
2. Auditory discrimination, parts I, II, and III
3. Auditory memory
   a. Recognition memory
   b. Memory for content
   c. Memory for sequence
4. Sound-symbol relationships
   a. Sound mimicry
   b. Sound recognition
   c. Sound analysis
   d. Sound blending
   e. Sound-symbol association
   f. Reading of symbols
   g. Spelling sounds

The developers designed the battery for speech and language therapists, audiologists, diagnosticians, and reading specialists to use with individuals from age 3 years through adulthood. The instrument assists in identifying auditory problems associated with learning difficulties, particularly in reading. See Table 9–2 for a summary of the *GFW Battery.*

Test Materials for the *GFW Battery*   Test materials consist of five easel-type test kits containing all test materials, including audiocassettes, a technical manual, and a package of scoresheets.

Administration and Scoring of the *GFW Battery*   The examiner may give a single test or a cluster of tests, depending on the needs of the student and the purpose for testing. Audiocassettes help the examiner follow standardized administration procedures. The complete battery takes over an hour to administer, and individual tests take approximately 15 minutes. When the complete battery is given, the test provides an overview of auditory skills and produces age-based standard scores, percentiles, stanines, and age equivalents. The test also includes sound confusion and reading error inventories. However, the examiner's manual lacks guidelines for interpreting test results, and this limits its usefulness among professionals without formal training in developing intervention programs for students with deficits in auditory processing.

Table 9–2 *Goodman–Fristoe–Woodcock Auditory Skills Test Battery (GFW Battery)*

Type of Test:	Norm referenced
Purpose:	Measures auditory-processing skills
Content Areas:	Auditory selective attention, auditory discrimination, auditory memory, and sound-symbol relationships
Administration Time:	An hour for the complete battery and 15 minutes for each test
Age Levels:	3 years–adulthood
Suitable for:	Students who exhibit auditory processing deficits, including those with learning disabilities and speech and language impairments
Scores:	Standard scores, percentiles, stanines, and age equivalents
In Short:	The *GFW Battery* is a valuable tool for identifying auditory problems often associated with learning difficulties, and it is best used as an informal measure of auditory perception.

Technical Qualities of the *GFW Battery*   Because it was developed with a limited sample group from three states, the *GFW Battery* standardization plan produced norms that may not adequately represent students from across the nation. In addition, the test developers relied on small sample groups to examine the reliability and validity of the instrument. Although the test lacks sufficient technical qualities for use as a norm-referenced tool, it is valuable when used in a criterion-referenced manner.

Summary   The *Goldman–Fristoe–Woodcock Auditory Skills Test Battery* measures selective attention, discrimination, memory, and sound-symbol relationships. This instrument, which is useful as an informal measure of auditory deficiencies, assists in identifying auditory problems associated with learning difficulties, particularly in reading.

Other Tests of Perception and Perceptual-Motor Skills

Tests of perception and perceptual-motor skills are widely used in special education and related disciplines. Brief descriptions of other available perceptual tests follow.

Detroit Tests of Learning Aptitude-4   The *Detroit Tests of Learning Aptitude-4 (DTLA-4)* (Hammill, 1998) are comprehensive, individually administered, norm-referenced diagnostic measures of psychological aptitudes and perceptual-processing abilities in four domains: linguistic, cognitive, attention, and motor. Designed for use with students from age 6 through 17 years, the *DTLA-4* subtests include word opposites, design sequences, sentence imitation, reversed letters, story construction, design reproduction, basic information, symbolic relations, word sequences, and story sequences. *DTLA-4* scores include standard scores, percentile ranks, age equivalents, and composite scores. Testing time for the *DTLA-4* varies from 1 to 2 hours.

Detroit Tests of Learning Aptitude-Primary, Second Edition   The *Detroit Tests of Learning Aptitude-Primary, Second Edition (DTLA-P-2)* (Hammill & Bryant, 1991) are a modification of the *DTLA-3* intended for children from age 3 through 9 years. The *DTLA-P* measures abilities and deficiencies in three domains: language, attention, and motor. *DTLA-P-2* subtests include articulation, conceptual matching, design reproduction, digit sequences, draw-a-person, letter sequences, motor directions, object sequences, oral directions, picture fragments, picture identification, sentence imitation, and symbolic relations. Administration time for the *DTLA-P-2* is about 45 minutes, and available scores include standard scores, percentile ranks, age equivalents, composite scores, a total score, and a general mental ability score.

Developmental Test of Visual Perception: Second Edition   The individually administered, norm-referenced *Developmental Test of Visual Perception: Second Edition (DTVP-2)* (Hammill et al., 1993) is a revision of the *Developmental Test of Visual Perception* (Frostig et al., 1964, 1966). The *DTVP-2* is a comprehensive diagnostic instrument for assessing the visual-processing skills of children from ages 4 to 10 years. The test includes the following eight subtests:

Type of visual perception	*Description*
Eye-hand coordination	Drawing straight, curved, and diagonal lines within increasingly difficult boundaries
Copying	Copying increasingly complex figures from model drawings
Spatial relations	Reproducing model patterns by connecting dots on a blank grid of dots
Position in space	Discriminating and matching various figures that appear in rotated and reversed positions
Figure-ground	Finding geometric shapes hidden within a complex background of other shapes and forms
Visual closure	Viewing a geometric figure and then selecting the matching figure from a series of figures that all have missing parts
Visual-motor speed	Drawing special marks in selected geometric designs on a page filled with various designs
Form constancy	Identifying geometric shapes displayed in different sizes, shadings, and positions

The original *Developmental Test of Visual Perception (DTVP)* was widely used by special education teachers with young students with visual-processing deficits. Even more popular than the test itself was a companion intervention program, the *Frostig Program for the Development of Visual Perception* (Frostig & Horne, 1973), which consists of a series of worksheets for improving visual-perceptual skills. These Frostig worksheets and other similar ones remain in widespread use in special education programs for primary students. As a result, many special educators will find the 1993 edition of the *DTVP* to be a useful tool for identifying the presence and degree of visual-perception problems in children and measuring the effectiveness of intervention programs.

Kent Visual Perception Test   The *Kent Visual Perception Test (KVPT)* (Melamed, 1996) measures visual-perceptual skills using three perceptual-processing tasks: discrimination, memory, and copying (construction). The test may be given to children ages 5 through 11. The *KVPT* features a model of perceptual processing to assist in interpretation and also includes suggestions and examples of the best ways to use the test in school and in clinical and neuropsychological evaluations. *KVPT* norms were based on the performance of 741 children. In addition, a limited amount of reliability and validity data regarding *KVPT* test scores are available. The test takes about 30 minutes to administer and yields standard scores and percentile ranks for the total score and error analysis. The error-analysis procedure describes in detail a child's specific perceptual deficits.

Motor-Free Visual Perception Test, Revised   The *Motor-Free Visual Perception Test, Revised (MVPT-R)* (Colarusso & Hammill, 1996) is a screening test for measuring the visual perception of children between the ages of 4 and 11. The *MVPT-R* is especially useful with children who may have learning, cognitive, motor, or physical disabilities. The 40 test plates may be individually administered and scored in about 15 minutes. Colarusso and Hammill designed the test for teachers, psychologists, or educational specialists. *MVPT-R* scores include perceptual ages and standard scores. The *MVPT-R* assesses the following five areas of visual perception:

* Spatial relationships—the ability to orient one's body in space and to perceive the positions of objects in relation to oneself and other objects.
* Visual discrimination—the ability to discriminate dominant features in different objects.
* Figure-ground—the ability to distinguish an object from its background.
* Visual closure—the ability to identify incomplete figures when only fragments are presented.
* Visual memory—the ability to recall dominant features of one stimulus item or to remember the sequence of several items.

Test of Auditory-Perceptual Skills, Revised   The *Test of Auditory-Perceptual Skills, Revised (TAPS-R)* (Gardner, 1997) is a norm-referenced test of children's ability to perceive auditory information and is designed for use in diagnosing children from age 4 to 13 who have auditory difficulties, imperceptions of auditory modality, and language problems that could underlie learning problems. The test takes about 25 minutes to give and score and contains subtests that measure auditory number memory, auditory sentence memory, auditory word memory, auditory interpretation of directions, auditory word discrimination, and auditory processing. The test also includes a hyperactive rating scale that may help determine the effects of a child's behavior on the test results as well as in the classroom. Available *TAPS-R* scores include standard scores, scaled scores, stanines, and percentiles.

Test of Auditory-Perceptual Skills: Upper Level   The *Test of Auditory-Perceptual Skills: Upper Level (TAPS:UL)* (Gardner, 1994) is designed for children ages 12 to 18. Like the *TAPS-R*, the *TAPS:UL* assesses auditory-perceptual skills for diagnosing children and teenagers who have auditory-perceptual difficulties, imperceptions of auditory processing, or language-related learning problems.

Test of Visual Motor Integration   The *Test of Visual Motor Integration (TVMI)* (Hammill et al., 1996) is a screening test of the visual-motor abilities of children ages 4 to 17.

Children take the test by copying a series of increasingly complex geometric figures. Young children ages 4 to 8 copy up to 12 figures, and older children copy as many as 30. The *TVMI* takes about 20 minutes to administer to either individual children or groups of children. The test is scored by rating each item as either 0, 1, 2, or 3, which makes it possible to easily identify potentially severe as well as potentially superior copying skills. Normed on a sample of more than 2,000 students, *TVMI* results are reported in standard scores, percentiles, and age equivalents.

Wide Range Assessment of Visual Motor Abilities   The *Wide Range Assessment of Visual Motor Abilities (WRAVMA)* (Adams & Sheslow, 1995) is a norm-referenced measure of the visual-motor skills of children and adolescents 3 to 17 years of age. *WRAVMA* includes subtests that measure visual-motor integration (evaluated using a drawing test), visual-spatial relations (evaluated using a matching test), and fine motor (evaluated using a pegboard test). It takes about 15 to 30 minutes to administer the *WRAVMA*. Available test scores include scaled scores, standard scores, age equivalents, and percentiles.

☑ Comprehension Checklist

Assessing perception and perceptual-motor ability involves observing and measuring the way students process and respond to sensory information. Perception and perceptual-motor skills include visual and auditory perception as well as visual-motor and auditory-motor proficiency. Because of questions about the reliability and validity of assessment instruments in these domains, special educators should use tests carefully with full knowledge of their limits and imperfections.

Assessing Learning Modalities

Learning modalities are the primary or preferred sensory modes for learning new or difficult information. These sensory modes include visual, auditory, and **kinesthetic** (a combination of feeling, balance, and motion) modalities. Although children rely on all sensory modalities, they usually display preferences for learning through a primary modality. For most children, the visual mode preferred. However, the auditory and tactile modes also play an important role in learning.

Assessing learning modalities involves the use of tests but more often entails careful observation by a teacher trained to identify modality strengths and weaknesses in daily classroom behavior. Knowledgeable teachers usually identify preferred modalities by associating student behaviors with each modality. Although no one relies exclusively on one modality, most students display a primary modality. For example, student behaviors representative of visual learners include learning best by seeing and watching. In contrast, auditory learners prefer to learn by listening. Tactile learners learn best when they have an opportunity to learn by doing and through direct participation. An informal checklist for assessing modality strengths, adapted from an observation system developed by Milone (1981), appears in Figure 9–1. Teachers may use this checklist as a curriculum-based assessment tool for identifying the modality strengths of their students. After noting which of these behaviors a student typically displays in the classroom, teachers can then develop appropriate intervention activities.

Figure 9–1   Informal Checklist of Modality Strengths

Date: _____   Student: _____

Observer: _____   School & Class: _____

Directions: The observer should know the student well. Complete the checklist by placing a checkmark after each behavior the student exhibits on a consistent basis. The relative number of checks in each modality provides an indication of modality strengths.

Behavior	Visual	✔	Auditory	✔	Kinesthetic	✔
Learning style	Learns best by looking		Learns best by hearing		Learns best through through direct experience	
	Likes to watch demonstrations		Likes verbal directions		Likes hands-on involvement	
Reading	Likes word pictures, descriptions, and illustrations		Likes drama, dialogue, and plays		Likes action stories	
	Learns from photographs, diagrams, graphs, and charts		May move lips or whisper when reading		May not enjoy reading	
Memory	Remembers by writing things down and drawing		Remembers best by saying things		Remembers what happened and who did what	
	Good memory for faces		Good memory for names		Good memory for events	
Distractibility	May notice visual distractions and extra motion		May notice excessive noise and sounds		Difficulty concentrating on visual information	
	May not notice extra sounds (e.g., a noisy classroom)		May not notice visual distractions and extra motion		Difficulty concentrating on auditory information	
Behavior during periods of inactivity	Stares into space and watches something		Talks to others		Restless, squirmy	
	Doodles or draws		Talks to self or hums		Wants to move around	

Figure 9–1   *(continued)*

Behavior	Visual	✔	Auditory	✔	Kinesthetic	✔
Communication	Tends to be quiet		Enjoys talking		Uses gestures and movement when talking	
	May become impatient when listening		Likes hearing others talk		Loses interest in long conversations	
Artistic interests	Prefers visual arts		Prefers music		Prefers sculpture and hands-on exhibits	
	Likes details and components		Likes work as a whole		May show little interest in art	
Physical appearance	Tends to be neat and orderly		May mix and match clothes		May look ruffled due to activity	
	May not vary appearance		May vary appearance		May appear disheveled	
Behavior in new settings	Looks around and watches		Talks about setting and environment		Moves about environment	
	Examines details		Discusses setting and how it feels		Touches, feels, and handles	
Total number of checks	**Visual Characteristics**		**Auditory Characteristics**		**Kinesthetic Characteristics**	

Modality-Based Assessment and Instruction

According to Milone (1981), the central element of modality-based assessment and instruction is identifying and teaching to a student's learning strengths. Milone points out that, because students display various modality strengths, most group instruction should include activities that draw on all learning modalities. For example, students who prefer the auditory modality may learn spelling best when they hear and say the letters out loud. On the other hand, strong visual learners may prefer to learn by seeing the words and creating mental pictures of them. Finally, students who prefer the kinesthetic modality may learn best when they write the words on paper or on the chalkboard. Lessons incorporating activities that tap each modality respond to the modality strengths of all students regardless of their modality preference.

Learning Modality Tests

Special educators may select from among several available tests of learning modalities, including the *Learning Style Inventory,* the *Swassing–Barbe Modality Index,* and the *Kerby Learning Modality Test.* Brief reviews of each of these instruments follow.

Learning Style Inventory The *Learning Style Inventory* (Dunn et al., 1984), a criterion-referenced measure of modality preferences, consists of approximately 100 statements about how students like to learn. Students respond to each statement on the basis of their preferences for learning new or difficult information. The inventory measures the modality preferences of students from elementary age to adulthood. Administration involves having students provide true or false answers after reading each statement. The directions include instructions for the students to give their first reactions to each question, and administration takes about 20 minutes. Because the manual provides little information about the technical adequacy of the *Learning Style Inventory,* teachers and diagnosticians should use it as an informal measure of learning modalities and interpret results cautiously.

Swassing–Barbe Modality Index A criterion-referenced screening test for identifying the sensory modality preferences of elementary students, the *Swassing–Barbe Modality Index* (Swassing & Barbe, 1979a) is a component of the *Zaner–Bloser Modality Kit* (Swassing & Barbe, 1979b). The *Swassing–Barbe Modality Index (SBMI)* uses a match-to-sample task consisting of geometric shapes arranged in increasingly difficult sequences. Testing with the *SBMI* geometric shape sequences is conducted three times, once in each modality: visual, auditory, and kinesthetic. During administration, the first task involves matching a single shape; this is used as a sample item. The testing proceeds with increasingly difficult tasks until reaching the last, most complex task, which requires matching nine shapes in the correct sequence. The *SBMI* takes about 15 to 20 minutes to administer. Testing begins with the visual items, in which a student matches increasingly difficult sequences of geometric shapes from visual memory. When the student makes errors in two consecutive sequences or completes all the items, the evaluator administers the auditory subtest by reading aloud the names of the shapes in sequence from the scoresheet. The evaluator gives the final, kinesthetic subtest by having the student feel the shapes without seeing them. Scoring is based on the percentage of correctly placed shapes in each modality. Differences of five or more percentage points between modalities are educationally significant. This means that if one modality is five or more points greater than another, it is the stronger of the two. If one modality is five points greater than each of the remaining modalities, it is the dominant modality.

Kerby Learning Modality Test A criterion-referenced screening test for students from age 5 through 11 years, the *Kerby Learning Modality Test* (Kerby, 1980) measures strengths and weaknesses in visual, auditory, and motor modalities. Evaluators can give the eight subtests individually or to groups of students in about 15 minutes. The subtests include visual and auditory discrimination, visual and auditory closure, visual and auditory memory, and visual and auditory motor coordination. A standardized tool, the *Kerby Learning Modality Test* helps to identify modality preferences and to plan teaching strategies that respond to those preferences.

☑ Comprehension Checklist

Assessing learning modalities involves observing and measuring student preferences for learning new or difficult information. Most experts recognize the visual, auditory, and kinesthetic modalities as important in education, and teachers find that many students display a preference for visual learning. Although teachers usually rely on direct observation of student behavior rather than testing to identify preferred learning modalities, they may also select from among a few commercially available inventories to assess modality preferences. These inventories are best used when teachers use them as informal, criterion-based tools.

Assessing Motor Proficiency

Like sensory perception, motor development plays a central role in the process of interacting with the environment, especially in the lives of children. In fact, much of the learning that takes place with young children is directly related to movement skills and motor performance, particularly in the first few years of life when control of the environment occurs primarily through sensory-motor actions. Many specialists (Bergen & Colangelo, 1985; Connor et al., 1978; Finnie, 1975; Ward, 1984) view motor activity as the vehicle children first use to interact with and comprehend the environment. As motor skills increase, a child's environment also expands. Furthermore, rather than occurring in isolation, motor development takes place in concert with perceptual, cognitive, and affective growth. Likewise, deficits in motor skill development hinder important learning experiences related to exploration, play, cognition, and socialization. For this reason, students who manifest difficulties in motor development require assessment to identify specific deficits and to develop instructional intervention programs designed to improve movement skills.

Why Do We Assess the Motor Proficiency of Students With Disabilities?

We assess motor proficiency for several reasons. First, we use screening tests to obtain a brief survey of overall motor proficiency to identify children with potential motor disabilities. Second, we use comprehensive motor tests to obtain diagnostic evaluations that provide us with information regarding strengths, weaknesses, and gaps in gross and fine motor development. We also use comprehensive tests as curriculum guides to assist in writing IEPs and to develop age-appropriate intervention

FOCUS 9–2

Why Do We Assess the Motor Proficiency of Children With Disabilities?

- To screen children for possible deficits in motor proficiency
- To diagnose specific strengths, weaknesses, and gaps in fine and gross motor skills
- To assist in writing IEPs
- To help develop intervention programs and learning activities
- To measure student progress
- To evaluate the effectiveness of intervention programs

programs and activities. Finally, we assess motor proficiency to measure student progress and evaluate program effectiveness. See Focus 9–2.

The following account gives a practical example of why we assess the motor development of young children with special needs. In this scenario a special education teacher relies on assessment to help a child with a fine motor skill deficit, which is described as poor eye-hand coordination and delayed manual dexterity, a common motor development difficulty in children with special needs.

Ray, a 5-year-old student in a preschool class for children with learning disabilities, seemed to have significant deficits in fine motor development but appeared to function within the expected range in gross motor skill performance. Concerned about the nature and extent of Ray's fine motor problems, the teacher gave him the fine motor section of the Peabody Developmental Motor Scales and Activity Cards *to diagnose specific strengths, weaknesses, and gaps in fine motor development. The results revealed problems with eye-hand coordination and manual dexterity. More specifically, Ray had difficulty copying geometric shapes, building with blocks, and cutting with scissors. The results also showed that his performance was within expected limits for his age group on the fine motor tasks of grasping and hand use. After interpreting the assessment results, the teacher used the activity cards to write an IEP goal in fine motor development and prepare specific learning activities to help remediate Ray's deficits. Six months later, the teacher readministered the fine motor scale to measure his progress and gauge the effectiveness of the intervention program.*

Representative Tests of Motor Proficiency

From among the published tests of motor proficiency, two widely used measures are the *Bruininks–Oseretsky Test of Motor Proficiency* and the *Peabody Developmental Motor Scales and Activity Cards*. Comprehensive reviews of these instruments and brief reviews of other available motor tests follow.

Bruininks–Oseretsky Test of Motor Proficiency

The norm-referenced, individually administered *Bruininks–Oseretsky Test of Motor Proficiency* (Bruininks, 1978) measures the fine and gross motor skills of children from 4.5 to 14.5 years of age. The test includes a short form for obtaining a brief survey of general motor proficiency and a complete battery for obtaining a diagnostic evaluation of specific strengths, weaknesses, and gaps in motor development (see Table 9–3 for a summary). Designed for use by adaptive physical education teachers, physical and occupational therapists, school psychologists, and special education teachers, the *Bruininks–Oseretsky* test contains subtests that measure the following:

- Gross motor development.
  - Running speed and agility.
  - Balance.
  - Bilateral coordination.
  - Strength.
- Gross and fine motor development.
  - Upper limb coordination.

- Fine motor development.

  Response speed.

  Visual-motor control.

  Upper limb speed and dexterity.

Materials for the *Bruininks–Oseretsky Test* The *Bruininks–Oseretsky* test kit includes a test manual, a screening scoresheet, a complete battery scoresheet, and a complete set of test administration materials, which are contained in a large metal briefcase.

Administration and Scoring of the *Bruininks–Oseretsky Test* The complete battery takes about an hour to administer, whereas the short form takes about 20 minutes. Before giving the *Bruininks–Oseretsky* test, the examiner determines the arm and leg preference of the student because many subtest items require performance with the preferred limb. The examiner times a few of the items, such as response speed and upper limb speed and dexterity, with a stopwatch, but most items are not timed. For the complete battery, the examiner gives eight subtests made up of 46 items. For the short form, the examiner gives only 14 items from among the eight subtests. The manual includes clear, easy-to-follow directions for presenting each item and scoring student performance. The test kit includes most test materials, except for the large gross motor equipment such as the balance beam.

    The test produces age-equivalent scores for each of the eight subtests as well as for the composite scores. Available test scores also include standard scores, percentiles, and stanines for the gross and fine motor composites, the overall battery, and the short form.

Technical Characteristics of the *Bruininks–Oseretsky Test* The *Bruininks–Oseretsky* test standardization program included a representative sample of 800 students between

Table 9–3   *Bruininks–Oseretsky Test for Motor Proficiency*

Type of Test:	Norm-referenced and individually administered
Purpose:	A diagnostic test of motor development
Content Areas:	Gross motor and fine motor development
Administration Time:	About an hour for the complete battery and 20 minutes for the screening test
Age Levels:	4.5–14.5 years
Suitable for:	Students with deficits in motor development associated with mild, moderate, and severe disabilities, including specific learning disabilities and mental retardation
Scores:	Age-based standard scores, percentiles, stanines, and age equivalents
In Short:	The *Bruininks–Oseretsky* test includes a short form for screening and a long form for obtaining a complete picture of motor proficiency. The long form includes measures of gross and fine motor performance as well as general skill development.

3 and 18 years of age that was stratified by gender, ethnicity, community size, and geographic region. To provide evidence of validity, the developers reported findings from several studies, including an investigation of the relationship between the content of the *Bruininks–Oseretsky* test and research findings on motor development, an examination of the internal consistency of the subtests, and a factor analysis of the subtest items. However, some of the internal consistency correlations, which ranged from .56 to .81, were too low to establish the validity of the subtest scores. Likewise, some correlations from the factor analysis fell below acceptable levels. For this reason, evaluators should interpret subtest scores cautiously. In contrast to the limitations of the subtest scores, the *Bruininks–Oseretsky* test manual describes other validity studies that provided positive evidence regarding the effectiveness of the overall scores and the validity of the instrument. These studies included a review of research on motor development and the results of an investigation comparing scores from contrasting groups of disabled and nondisabled children. The investigation involved analyzing the test performance of nondisabled students and students with learning disabilities, mild retardation, and moderate to severe retardation.

The test manual includes support for the reliability of the *Bruininks–Oseretsky* test in the form of test-retest data, estimates of the standard error of measurement (SEM), and interrater reliability coefficients. The test-retest correlations for the composite scores averaged in the .80 to .90 range, and the SEM averaged 4 or 5 standard score points for the composite scores. Most of the interrater reliability correlations were between .80 and .97. Overall, these data indicate that the test has good reliability.

Summary　　The *Bruininks–Oseretsky Test of Motor Proficiency* provides examiners with an instrument for obtaining either a brief overview of motor development, using the short form, or a complete picture of motor proficiency, using the complete battery. The complete battery yields separate measures of gross and fine motor performance as well as general skill development. Consisting of enjoyable gamelike tasks, this test format encourages students to perform at their best. Teachers who use the *Bruininks–Oseretsky* test can link assessment results to specific remediation activities by using a companion curriculum guide, *Body Skills: A Motor Development Curriculum for Children* (Werder & Bruininks, 1988); this guide provides a systematic method for planning and teaching skills in body management, locomotion, body fitness, and fine motor skills.

Peabody Developmental Motor Scales and Activity Cards

The *Peabody Developmental Motor Scales and Activity Cards (PDMS)* (Folio & Fewell, 1983) is a comprehensive assessment tool and curriculum guide for children from birth to 7 years of age. The individually administered, norm-referenced developmental scales are a diagnostic tool for determining fine and gross motor skill development and developing age-appropriate intervention activities. The activity cards, contained in an indexed card file, provide 282 motor activities referenced to the *PDMS* test items. Special educators who use the scales with the activity cards have a complete system for combining diagnostic testing with instructional programming. Designed as a diagnostic instrument and instructional tool, the *PDMS* is also valuable as a parent guide for developing home programs. In addition, the instrument is useful to physical therapists, occupational therapists, and adaptive physical education teachers who need a standardized diagnostic tool to assess motor proficiency and to recommend intervention activities. The gross motor subtest consists of items in five skill categories:

1. Reflexes
2. Balance
3. Nonlocomotor (e.g., jumping, standing, and sitting)
4. Locomotor (e.g., walking and running)
5. Receipt and propulsion (e.g., throwing and catching)

The fine motor subtest includes items in four skill categories:

1. Grasping
2. Hand use
3. Eye-hand coordination
4. Manual dexterity

Materials for the *PDMS*   The *PDMS* kit includes all materials needed to give the test except for a few pieces of large equipment, such as a balance beam for measuring dynamic balance. The well-designed materials include a test manual, a scoresheet, and a set of indexed activity cards.

Administration and Scoring of the *PDMS*   Designed for individual administration, the *PDMS* produces several standardized scores, including age equivalents, percentiles, and a standard score called a *developmental motor quotient*. Evaluators may obtain these scores for overall motor development, total fine and gross motor development, and each skill cluster. The *PDMS* relies on three criteria for scoring each item rather than the usual pass-fail scoring. This three-point system has the advan-

Table 9–4   *Peabody Developmental Motor Scales and Activity Cards (PDMS)*

Type of Test:	A norm-referenced, individually administered developmental scale and curriculum guide
Purpose:	To assess motor proficiency and develop intervention programs
Content Areas:	Gross motor and fine motor development
Administration Time:	Approximately 1 hour
Age Levels:	Birth–7 years
Suitable for:	Students with motor impairment, including those with severe disabilities, sensory impairments, and mild delays
Scores:	Age equivalents, percentiles, standard scores for overall, fine, and gross motor development, and for each skill cluster
In Short:	The *PDMS* is a well-designed assessment instrument and programming guide. It produces detailed assessment data for identifying present levels of motor performance, developing intervention programs, and measuring student progress.

tage of including an "emerging" category that helps to identify developing skills and to measure the progress of students who acquire new skills at a slow rate. The *PDMS* manual provides specific guidelines for interpreting test results by providing detailed case studies that illustrate use of the instrument to diagnose motor proficiency, write IEPs, and develop instructional programs.

Technical Qualities of the *PDMS* The *PDMS* was standardized on a representative sample of 617 infants and children, following a carefully planned testing program to ensure adequate representation of the national population. The *PDMS* researchers reported two methods of estimating reliability: test-retest and interrater. These studies provide evidence from two separate perspectives to support the reliability of *PDMS* scores. The researchers reported test-retest reliability coefficients from .80 to .95 and an interrater reliability coefficient of .99. In addition, the *PDMS* manual provides evidence concerning both construct- and criterion-related validity. To establish construct validity, the developers compared the test performance of children across adjacent ages and conducted a regression analysis of age-score correlations. Evidence of criterion-related validity included correlations between the *PDMS* and the *Bayley Scales of Infant Development* (Bayley, 1969), and between the *PDMS* and the *West Haverstraw Motor Development Test* (New York State Rehabilitation Hospital, 1964). However, the correlations between the *PDMS* and the two concurrent measures fell below acceptable levels. In a detailed review, Venn (1986) concluded that the *PDMS* demonstrated adequate initial reliability and validity but suggested the need for additional data to confirm the results of this research.

Summary The *PDMS* is an excellent tool for assessing the motor development of young children. In addition to providing developmental scales and accompanying activities specifically designed for children with motor problems, the *PDMS* features an enhanced scoring system and a large number of items from which to choose. Appropriate for use with children who have severe disabilities, including sensory impairments, the *PDMS* also works well with children who display mild delays in motor development. Special educators who use the *PDMS* can obtain detailed assessment data for identifying present levels of motor performance, developing intervention programs, and measuring student progress.

Other Tests of Motor Development

Brief reviews of other available tests for measuring the motor development of children with special needs follow.

Movement Assessment Battery for Children The *Movement Assessment Battery for Children (Movement ABC)* (Henderson & Sugden, 1992) includes an assessment instrument and a program-planning guide for children. The battery includes a screening checklist; a comprehensive assessment tool that measures manual dexterity, ball skills, and static and dynamic balance; and a resource guide that offers practical remediation activities and ongoing programs, including case studies. Designed for children from 4 though 12 years of age, the *Movement ABC* takes about 30 minutes to administer. Although the *Movement ABC* provides norm-referenced percentiles by age group, the instrument is primarily designed as a criterion-referenced tool for identifying and correcting the movement difficulties of children with motor skills disabilities.

Test of Gross Motor Development   The *Test of Gross Motor Development (TGMD)* (Ulrich, 1985) measures the gross motor skills of children from 3 to 10 years of age. The *TGMD* identifies children who are significantly behind their peers in gross motor development, assists in developing instructional programs, monitors progress, and evaluates treatment. Standardized on a sample of 908 children in eight states, the reliability and validity of *TGMD* scores were examined as part of the test development process. Results from *TGMD* testing may be reported using percentiles, standard scores, or a composite quotient that expresses total gross motor developmental performance.

Multiple-Skill Tests With Motor Development Subtests   In addition to the single-skill tests of motor development, such as the *Bruininks–Oseretsky Test of Motor Proficiency* and the *Peabody Developmental Motor Scales,* special educators also rely on multiple-skill tests that include subtests for measuring motor skill development. Among the available multiple-skill tests that contain motor subtests are the *LAP-D Standardized Assessment,* the *Revised Brigance Diagnostic Inventory of Early Development,* the *Battelle Developmental Inventory,* and the *Hawaii Early Learning Profile.* Reviews of these multiple-skill tests appear in Chapter 8. Although not as detailed as the single-skill instruments, the multiple-skill tests often provide an appropriate measure of motor skill development when in-depth information is not required.

☑ Comprehension Checklist

Assessing motor proficiency involves determining levels of performance in both fine motor and gross motor development. *Fine motor* refers to small muscle movements such as hand and finger dexterity. *Gross motor* refers to large muscle movements such as walking and running. When special educators need in-depth diagnostic assessment, they usually rely on specialized tests such as the *Bruininks–Oseretsky Test of Motor Proficiency* or the *Peabody Developmental Motor Scales.* Alternatively, special educators may assess motor skill development with one of many multiple-skill tests. Regardless of the specific assessment approach, resulting data should help to identify specific motor problems and to design appropriate remediation activities.

Summary

The assessment of perceptual ability and motor proficiency includes a diverse collection of specific tests and techniques (see Table 9–5 on p. 270). This collection encompasses measures of perceptual ability, perceptual-motor performance, sensory learning modalities, and fine and gross motor development. These tests and procedures identify levels of performance as well as strengths, weaknesses, and gaps in development. Teachers use these results to write IEPs and to develop appropriate instructional objectives for students with processing deficits and motor delays.

Although evaluating perception and motor proficiency is an essential step in identifying the learning needs of certain students, many pitfalls exist, including misconceptions about the meaning of perception and motor development, questions about the reliability and validity of tests and observation procedures, and misuse of results. Fortunately, guidelines for avoiding these hazards exist, and by following them, professionals ensure accurate and effective assessment of perception and motor proficiency.

Despite the challenges associated with assessing perception and motor proficiency, those who serve students with disabilities should be well versed in the available tests and procedures and their appropriateness in given situations. For special educators, understanding the assessment of perception and motor skill development is one element of a complete knowledge base in appraisal techniques. This knowledge helps equip professionals with the necessary competencies to respond to the individual needs of students with perceptual and motor skill deficits.

Chapter Review and Application

Multiple Choice

Directions: Read each item carefully. In the blank beside each item, write the letter of the best response. Each item contains only one best answer. Check your answers with the answer key at the end of the book.

_____ 1. The preferred sensory learning modality for most children is the _____ mode.
    a. visual
    b. auditory
    c. kinesthetic

_____ 2. The kinesthetic mode consists of a combination of _____.
    a. feeling, motion, and vision
    b. feeling, vision, and hearing
    c. feeling, balance, and vision
    d. feeling, balance, and motion

_____ 3. Assessing learning modalities most often involves _____.
    a. use of norm-referenced screening tests
    b. use of norm-referenced diagnostic tests
    c. an interview with the child
    d. careful observation by a trained teacher

_____ 4. Student behaviors representative of _____ learners include learning best by seeing and watching.
    a. auditory
    b. visual
    c. tactile

_____ 5. _____ learners prefer to learn by listening.
    a. Auditory
    b. Visual
    c. Tactile

_____ 6. _____ learners learn best by doing and through direct participation.
    a. Auditory
    b. Visual
    c. Tactile

_____ **7.** Which of the following tests is the most comprehensive instrument?
  a. *Goldman–Fristoe–Woodcock Auditory Skills Test Battery*
  b. *Test of Auditory-Perceptual Skills, Revised*
  c. *Test of Auditory-Perceptual Skills, Upper Level*
  d. *Test of Visual-Motor Integration*

_____ **8.** Which of the following is a comprehensive diagnostic instrument?
  a. *Developmental Test of Visual-Motor Integration*
  b. *Test of Visual Motor Integration*
  c. *Motor-Free Visual Perception Test, Revised*
  d. *Developmental Test of Visual Perception: Second Edition*

_____ **9.** Which of the following tests has the largest age range for testing children from 4.5 to 14.5 years of age?
  a. *Bruininks–Oseretsky Test of Motor Proficiency*
  b. *Peabody Developmental Motor Scales*
  c. *Movement Assessment Battery for Children*
  d. *Test of Gross Motor Development*

_____ **10.** Which of the following tests provides 282 motor activity cards referenced to the test items?
  a. *Bruininks–Oseretsky Test of Motor Proficiency*
  b. *Peabody Developmental Motor Scales*
  c. *Movement Assessment Battery for Children*
  d. *Test of Gross Motor Development*

_____ **11.** Which of the following tests is primarily designed as a criterion-referenced tool for identifying and correcting the movement difficulties of children with motor skills disabilities?
  a. *Bruininks–Oseretsky Test of Motor Proficiency*
  b. *Peabody Developmental Motor Scales*
  c. *Movement Assessment Battery for Children*
  d. *Test of Gross Motor Development*

Match Definitions

Directions: Match the definitions in "A" through "K" with the perceptual and motor terms and concepts in items 1 through 11. Write the letter of the correct response that is the best definition in the blank beside each term or concept. Use each letter choice only once. Use the answer key at the end of the book to check your answers.

  a. Movement controlled by the large muscles of the body
  b. Coordinating sensory information from the eyes with corresponding movement activities such as eye-hand coordination and visual-motor control
  c. Integrating information received by the senses with corresponding movements of the body
  d. Walking, throwing, catching, and balance
  e. Hand and finger dexterity, drawing, and manipulating small objects
  f. Coordinating sensory information from the ears with fine and gross motor body movements
  g. Movement controlled by the small muscles of the body
  h. The efficiency of movements controlled by the muscles of the body

    i. Measurement of the way in which students process information from the senses
    j. Comprehending or giving meaning to information received by the senses
    k. Primary or preferred sensory modes for learning new or difficult information

_____ **1.** Perception
_____ **2.** Assessment of perception
_____ **3.** Learning modalities
_____ **4.** Motor proficiency
_____ **5.** Fine motor
_____ **6.** Examples of fine motor movements
_____ **7.** Gross motor
_____ **8.** Examples of gross motor movements
_____ **9.** Perceptual-motor
_____ **10.** Visual-motor processing
_____ **11.** Auditory-motor processing

Short Answers

Directions: Review your understanding of the material in this chapter by answering the following short answer items. Compare your responses to the sample answers. Your responses should contain information that is similar to but not exactly the same as that in the sample answers at the end of the book.

_____ **1.** List the five guidelines for assessing perception and motor proficiency and give a practical example that illustrates your understanding of each guideline.

_____ **2.** Your observations indicate that a child in your class has a severe auditory-processing problem. This child also displays many characteristics associated with attention deficit hyperactivity disorder (ADHD). You have decided to test the child to confirm your observations and identify specific skills in need of remediation. Which of the following tests would you use: the *Goldman–Fristoe–Woodcock Auditory Skills Test Battery* or the *Test of Auditory-Perceptual Skills, Revised?* Why would you select this test?

_____ **3.** A child with disabilities is suspected of having a visual-processing problem. Which test would you use to assess a wide variety of visual perception skills: the *Developmental Test of Visual-Motor Integration*, the *Test of Visual Motor Integration*, the *Motor-Free Visual Perception Test, Revised,* or the *Developmental Test of Visual Perception: Second Edition?* Why would you select this particular test?

_____ **4.** Which test or assessment procedure would you use to assess the learning modality preferences of a small group of children with disabilities: The *Swassing–Barbe Modality Index,* the *Kerby Learning Modality Test,* or teacher observation using the *Observable Characteristics of Modality Strength?* Why would you use this particular test or assessment procedure?

_____ **5.** For identifying appropriate intervention activities for a $5^{1}/_{2}$-year-old child, which of the following tests of motor proficiency would you select: the *Bruininks–Oseretsky Test of Motor Proficiency* or the *Peabody Developmental Motor Scales?* Why would you select this test?

References

Adams, W. & Sheslow, D. (1995). *Wide Range Assessment of Visual Motor Abilities.* Wilmington, DE: Wide Range Incorporated.

Bayley, N. A. (1969). *Bayley Scales of Infant Development.* San Antonio, TX: Psychological Corporation.

Beery, K. E. (1997). *Developmental Test of Visual-Motor Integration,* (4th ed.). Austin, TX: PRO-ED.

Bergen, A. F., & Colangelo, C. (1985). *Positioning the Client with Central Nervous System Deficits* (2d ed.). Valhalla, NY: Valhalla Rehabilitation Publications.

Bruininks, R. H. (1978). *Bruininks–Oseretsky Test of Motor Proficiency.* Circle Pines, MN: American Guidance Service.

Colarusso, R. P., & Hammill, D. D. (1996). *Motor-Free Visual Perception Test, Revised.* Austin, TX: PRO-ED.

Connor, F. P., Williamson, G. G., & Siepp, J. M. (1978). *Program Guide for Infants and Toddlers with Neuromotor and Other Developmental Disabilities.* New York: Teachers College Press.

Dunn, R., Dunn, K., & Price, G. E. (1984). *Learning Style Inventory.* Lawrence, KS: Price Systems.

Finnie, N. R. (1975). *Handling the Young Cerebral Palsied Child at Home.* New York: Dutton.

Folio, R. M., & Fewell, R. R. (1983). *Peabody Developmental Motor Scales and Activity Cards.* Allen, TX: DLM Teaching Resources.

Frostig, M., & Horne, D. (1973). *Frostig Program for the Development of Visual Perception.* Chicago: Follett.

Frostig, M., Lefever, W., & Whittlesey, J. (1966). *Administration and Scoring Manual: Marianne Frostig Developmental Test of Visual Perception.* Palo Alto, CA: Consulting Psychologists Press.

Frostig, M., Maslow, P., Lefever, W., & Whittlesey, J. (1964). *The Marianne Frostig Developmental Test of Visual Perception: 1963 Standardization.* Palo Alto, CA: Consulting Psychologists Press.

Gardner, M. F. (1994). *Test of Auditory-Perceptual Skills: Upper Level.* Austin, TX: PRO-ED.

———(1997). *Test of Auditory-Perceptual Skills, Revised.* Austin, TX: PRO-ED.

Goldman, R., Fristoe, M., & Woodcock, R. W. (1974). *Goldman–Fristoe–Woodcock Auditory Skills Test Battery.* Circle Pines, MN: American Guidance Service.

Hammill, D. D. (1998). *Detroit Tests of Learning Aptitude-4.* Austin, TX: PRO-ED.

Hammill, D. D., & Bryant, B. R. (1991). *Detroit Tests of Learning Aptitude-Primary* (2d ed.). Austin, TX: PRO-ED.

Hammill, D. D., Pearson, N. A., & Voress, J. K. (1993). *Developmental Test of Visual Perception:* (2d ed.). Austin, TX: PRO-ED.

———(1996). *Test of Visual Motor Integration.* Austin, TX: PRO-ED.

Henderson, S. H., & Sugden, D. A. (1992). *Movement Assessment Battery for Children.* San Antonio, TX: Psychological Corporation.

Kerby, M. I. (1980). *Kerby Learning Modality Test.* Los Angeles: Western Psychological Services.

Melamed, L. E. (1996). *Kent Visual Perception Test.* Austin, TX: PRO-ED.

Milone, M. N. (1981). *An Introduction to Modality-Based Instruction.* Columbus, OH: Zaner–Bloser.

New York State Rehabilitation Hospital. (1964). *West Haverstraw Motor Development Test.* West Haverstraw, NY: Author.

Swassing, R. H., & Barbe, W. B. (1979a). *Swassing–Barbe Modality Index.* Columbus, OH: Zaner-Bloser.

———(1979b). *Zaner-Bloser Modality Kit.* Columbus, OH: Zaner-Bloser.

Ulrich, D. A. (1985). *Test of Gross Motor Development.* Austin, TX: PRO-ED.

Venn, J. J. (1986). A review of the *Peabody Developmental Motor Scales and Activity Cards.* In D. Keyser & R. Sweetland (Eds.), *Test Critiques* (vol. 5). Kansas City, MO: Test Corporation of America, 310–13.

Ward, D. E. (1984). *Positioning the Handicapped Child for Function.* Chicago: Phoenix Press.

Werder, J. K., & Bruininks, R. H. (1988). *Body Skills: A Motor Development Curriculum for Children.* Circle Pines, MN: American Guidance Service.

Table 9–5   Review of Perception and Motor Proficiency Tests

Name of Test	Type of Test	Suitable for Individuals Who Are	Brief Description of Test	Purpose of Administering Test
*Bruininks–Oseretsky Test of Motor Proficiency (Bruininks, 1978)	Norm-referenced, individually administered diagnostic test including a short form and a complete battery	4.5–14.5 years	Measures fine and gross motor development including running speed and agility, balance, bilateral coordination, strength, upper limb coordination, response speed, visual-motor control, upper limb speed, and dexterity	To obtain a brief overview of motor development using the short form or a complete picture of motor proficiency using the complete battery; teachers can link assessment to remediation using a companion curriculum
Detroit Tests of Learning Aptitude-4 (Hammill, 1998)	Norm-referenced, individually administered diagnostic test	6–17 years	Measures skills in four domains: linguistic, cognitive, attention, and motor	To assess psychological aptitudes and perceptual-processing abilities
Detroit Tests of Learning Aptitude-Primary (2d ed.) (Hammill & Bryant, 1991)	Norm-referenced, individually administered diagnostic test	3–9 years	Includes subtests in articulation, conceptual matching, design reproduction, digit sequences, draw-a-person, letter sequences, motor directions, object sequences, oral directions, picture fragments, picture identification, sentence imitation, and symbolic relations	To measure abilities and deficiencies in three domains: language, articulation, and motor
Developmental Test of Visual-Motor Integration (4th ed.) (Beery, 1997)	Norm-referenced screening test	3–16 years	Includes a variety of drawing and visual discrimination tasks such as drawing within the lines, making geometric patterns, and identifying shapes	To assess proficiency in integrating visual perception with fine motor coordination
Developmental Test of Visual Perception (2d ed.) (Hammill et al., 1993)	Norm-referenced diagnostic test	4–10 years	Measures eye-hand coordination, spatial relations, position-in-space, figure-ground, visual closure, visual-motor speed, and form constancy	To assess visual processing skills, identify the presence and degree of visual perception problems, and to measure the effectiveness of intervention programs

*Tests marked with asterisks are featured in tables in this chapter.

Table 9–5 (continued)

Name of Test	Type of Test	Suitable for Individuals Who Are	Brief Description of Test	Purpose of Administering Test
*Goldman–Fristoe–Woodcock Auditory Skills Test Battery (Goldman et al., 1974)	Norm-referenced, individually administered diagnostic test	3 years–adulthood	Measures auditory selective attention, auditory discrimination, auditory memory, and sound-symbol relationships	To diagnose auditory-processing deficits
Kent Visual Perception Test (Melamed, 1996)	Norm-referenced diagnostic test	5–11 years	Measures three perceptual-processing tasks: discrimination, memory, and copying (construction)	To assess the visual-perception skills of children
Kerby Learning Modality Test (Kerby, 1980)	Criterion-referenced screening test	5–11 years	Includes subtests in visual and auditory discrimination, visual and auditory closure, visual and auditory memory, and visual and auditory coordination	To evaluate strengths and weaknesses in visual, auditory, and motor modalities
Learning Style Inventory (Dunn et al., 1984)	Criterion-referenced self-report inventory	Elementary age–adulthood	Consists of 100 true-false statements about how students like to learn	To identify preferred learning modalities
Motor-Free Visual Perception Test, Revised (Colarusso & Hammill, 1996)	Norm-referenced screening test	4–11 years	Assesses five areas of visual perception: spatial relationships, visual discrimination, figure-ground, visual closure, and visual memory	To assess the visual perception of all children but especially children with learning, cognitive, motor, or physical disabilities
Movement Assessment Battery for Children (Henderson & Sugden, 1992)	Criterion-referenced assessment instrument and programming guide	4–12 years	Measures manual dexterity, ball skills, and static and dynamic balance	To help identify and correct the movement difficulties of children with motor disabilities
*Peabody Developmental Motor Scales and Activity Cards (Folio & Fewell, 1983)	Norm-referenced, individually administered diagnostic scale and curriculum guide	Birth–7 years	Gross motor subtests include reflexes, balance, nonlocomotor, locomotor, and receipt and propulsion; fine motor subtests include grasping, hand use, eye-hand coordination, and manual dexterity	To obtain detailed assessment data for identifying present levels of motor performance, developing intervention programs, and measuring student progress

Table 9–5   *(continued)*

Name of Test	Type of Test	Suitable for Individuals Who Are	Brief Description of Test	Purpose of Administering Test
Swassing–Barbe Modality Index (Swassing & Barbe, 1979a)	Criterion-referenced screening test	Elementary grades	Uses a match-to-sample task consisting of geometric shapes arranged in increasingly difficult sequences; testing with the geometric shape sequences is conducted three times, once in each modality: visual, auditory, and kinesthetic	To identify the sensory modality learning preferences of elementary students
Test of Auditory-Perceptual Skills, Revised (Gardner, 1997)	Norm-referenced, individually administered	4–13 years	Measures auditory number memory, auditory sentence memory, auditory word memory, auditory interpretation of directions, auditory word discrimination, and auditory processing	To measure children's ability to perceive auditory information and to diagnose children with auditory difficulties
Test of Auditory-Perceptual Skills: Upper Level (Gardner, 1994)	Norm-referenced, individually administered	12–18 years	Measures auditory number memory, auditory sentence memory, auditory word memory, auditory interpretation of directions, auditory word discrimination, and auditory processing	To assess the auditory perceptual skills of older children with difficulties in auditory processing and language
Test of Gross Motor Development (Ulrich, 1985)	Norm-referenced, individually administered diagnostic test	3–10 years	Measures dynamic and static balance, locomotion, and receipt and propulsion	To identify children who are significantly behind their peers in gross motor development, to assist in developing instructional programs, to monitor progress, and to evaluate treatment
Test of Visual Motor Integration (Hammill et al., 1996)	Norm-referenced screening test	4–17 years	Asks children to copy an increasingly difficult series of geometric figures	To measure the visual-motor ability of individuals or groups of children

Table 9–5   (continued)

Name of Test	Type of Test	Suitable for Individuals Who Are	Brief Description of Test	Purpose of Administering Test
Wide Range Assessment of Visual Motor Abilities (Adams & Sheslow, 1995)	Norm-referenced, individually administered screening test	3–17 years	Measures visual-motor integration (evaluated using a drawing test), visual-spatial relations (evaluated using a matching test), and fine motor (evaluated using a pegboard test)	To assess the visual-motor skills of children and adolescents

CHAPTER 10

Assessment of Language

Overview

Assessment of language is concerned with receptive and expressive communication skills, including listening and speaking. In this chapter you study the tests that assess the language of children with disabilities. To achieve this goal we review the definition of language and the behaviors measured by language tests and procedures. We also investigate the way special educators use language assessment procedures, analyze the issues surrounding their use, and explore the ways in which teachers can link language assessment with instruction. After this introduction, we examine the range of instruments that assess language, including the most frequently used individually administered language tests. As we review each test, we consider the purpose of the instrument, the test materials, the administration and scoring procedures, and the technical characteristics. At the conclusion of the chapter, we consider procedures for assessing children who are culturally and linguistically diverse, an increasingly important topic due to the growing numbers of bilingual children in school.

Objectives

After reading this chapter, you will be prepared to do the following:

- Understand the purpose of language assessment.
- Understand current trends in the assessment of language.
- Understand the structural components of language.
- Link language assessment with classroom instruction.
- Use the tests for assessing the sounds of language (phonemes), the units of meaning (morphemes), and phrases and sentences (syntax).
- Use the tests for assessing word meanings and relationships (semantics) and the use of language in context (pragmatics).
- Use the comprehensive measures of language.
- Apply assessment procedures for bilingual students with disabilities.

The Importance of Language Assessment

Ms. Kaye has never conducted a language assessment, but because she has several children in her class with language disabilities, she is considering doing so for the first time. Before beginning she wants to know: What exactly is language assessment? Are there different kinds of language assessment? Next, she asks: Why use language assessment? Can it really make a difference in teaching and learning? How can language assessment help teachers? What can language assessment do for children?

Ms. Kaye does some research, consults some educators, and decides she'd like to try language assessment because of its purported advantages in diagnosing specific skills in need of remediation and documenting improvement over the course of a year. She gets some helpful information on how to implement language assessment in a special education classroom for preschoolers. She doesn't know, however, how to tailor the tests for her children with language deficits. None of the articles she read mentioned this, and none of her colleagues have ever dealt with language assessment in the preschool classroom. This causes her to ask: Will language assessment of her preschool children be different from that of older students? How will it meet instructional needs? What specifically can it do for children with special needs that more general assessment methods don't? Who does she talk with to find out? She decides to visit one of the district's educational diagnosticians whom she has met before, and to consult a special education teacher in another school who she knows uses language assessment with success.

In broad terms, **language** refers to any means used to receive or send messages. More specifically, language is the use of organized voice sounds and written symbols to communicate thoughts and feelings. Language occurs at expressive, receptive, and inner levels of communication. **Expressive language** refers to sending messages and to translating thoughts, ideas, and signals into vocal or motor expression (the latter includes writing and sign language or other nonvocal forms of communication). **Receptive language** consists of receiving input with the senses (usually the ears) and giving meaning to the sensory input. **Inner language** is the use of language in thinking, planning, and cognition. Often referred to as *thought within oneself,* inner language is a necessary developmental building block for receptive and expressive language. Development and use of language begin in infancy and continue throughout life. For infants the development of early communication skills provides the groundwork for later acquisition of symbolic language and serves as the basis for social and cognitive growth. For toddlers and preschoolers, language development includes learning an extensive range and variety of receptive and expressive language skills that develop in concert with cognitive, motor, and social skills. For school-age children, language is both the foundation for academic learning and the basis for organizing thought itself. For adults, language is an integral part of daily living at home, at work, and in the community. Thus, language is essential in all aspects of life.

Many students with disabilities exhibit significant language deficits. In fact, language problems are the single most common disability among school-age children. These problems may occur in both receptive (understanding messages) and expressive (sending messages) language. Speech difficulties in the form of articulation disorders represent by far the most common language deficits in children. Some students who use nonstandard English or English as a second language also have language deficits. Special educators associate specific language problems with certain disabilities. For example, students with hearing disabilities typically manifest severe speech and language deficits based on the type, severity, and age of onset of deafness. Likewise, some physical disabilities such as cerebral palsy cause characteristic speech problems. Students with mental retardation may exhibit general delays in developing language skills. The extent of the delays depends upon the severity of retardation. Because language deficits represent one of the most common learning problems of students with disabilities, special educators must understand language deficits, assessment strategies used to diagnose specific language problems, and the development and implementation of remedial intervention programs. Additional information about assessing speech and language disorders appears in Focus 10–1.

Current Trends

The current trends described next clarify the meaning and use of language assessment with students who have disabilities.

- Many tests in other domains rely on language-based items. For example, certain widely used, individually administered intelligence tests consist primarily of items requiring a student to respond verbally to an evaluator's oral questions. Likewise, most tests of social and academic skills rely heavily on a student's receptive and expressive language ability. When assessing students with language disabilities, special educators should exercise caution because a language deficit rather than lack of knowledge in a particular content area may depress test results. For example, psychologists avoid administering the verbal subtest of the *Wechsler Intelligence Scale for Children-Third Edition (WISC-III)* to students with hearing impairments because it relies primarily on language skills to measure intelligence.
- Most language tests and assessment procedures measure the development and skills of young children. Fewer measures assess the language proficiency of adolescents and adults.
- Overton (1992) considers remediation of language disorders a shared responsibility among speech clinicians and teachers. Overton suggests that speech clinicians have primary responsibility for diagnosing and guiding efforts to remediate speech disorders (articulation, voice, and fluency problems). However, teachers and clinicians must also diagnose problems and design intervention goals to improve a student's receptive, expressive, and written language skills. When clinicians and teachers use a team approach, they are better able to respond to the needs of their students.
- Interpreting assessment results includes consideration of language development in relation to general learning ability, academic achievement, and social skills.
- Carlisle and Johnson (1989) point out that students with learning disabilities frequently exhibit specific language deficits, which typically include problems with word meanings, memory, and ability to generalize.
- A student's lack of motivation and inappropriate behavior may significantly depress language performance. Outgoing students may hide language deficiencies behind disruptive behavior, whereas withdrawn students may simply refuse to display language skills up to their level of ability.
- In current practice, language assessment receives less emphasis than does assessment of academic and functional skills. Although many factors contribute to this lack of emphasis, special educators need to devote more attention to assessment and intervention in this important domain.

FOCUS 10–1

> **Understanding the Assessment of Speech and Language Disorders**
>
> *Speech Disorders*
>
> - Assessment questions arise when a parent or a teacher has difficulty understanding a child's speech.
> - The speech pathologist is the primary practitioner in the assessment process, including screening, comprehensive assessment, writing the IEP, and developing specific interventions.
> - Children with speech disabilities generally have difficulty producing the correct sounds of speech in a particular area of speech production such as articulation.
>
> *Language Disorders*
>
> - Assessment questions focus on the child's expressive language, receptive language, or inner language.
> - Expressive language is the ability to communicate with others using speech or alternative methods of communication such as sign language.
> - Receptive language is the understanding of the language of others.
> - Inner language is the use of language in thinking, planning, and other cognitive processes.

The Structural Components of Language

Language consists of both receptive and expressive elements. Receptive language (listening) decodes the meaning of messages, including written ones. Expressive language (speech) translates ideas into vocal or motor expression, including sign language and writing. In addition to these receptive and expressive elements, Wiig and Semel (1984) described language as consisting of five structural components.

Phonology Phonology is the study of the smallest units of sound in language. These units are called *phonemes*. American English includes 44 speech sounds, or phonemes. They have no meaning by themselves but contribute to word meaning. For example, the word *boy* includes three phonemes: *b, o,* and *y.*

Morphology Morphology is the study of the smallest meaningful units of language. These units are called *morphemes*. For example, the word *boy* has one morpheme, but the plural form of the word (*boys*) has two morphemes because *s* is a separate language unit.

Syntax Syntax is the way morphemes or words go together to form phrases and meaningful sentences. For example, the sentence *I am going to the store* is syntactically correct, but the sentence *I going store* is incorrect. Morphology and syntax are the two components of grammar.

Semantics   **Semantics** involves understanding and expressing word meanings and relationships, including vocabulary, synonyms, antonyms, word categories, ambiguities, and absurdities. For example, word relationships include the associations that exist between words such as *8:45* and *a quarter to nine,* and between *house* and *home.*

Pragmatics   **Pragmatics** is the use of language in context, especially during social interaction. The essence of pragmatics is the process of sharing intents, which occurs in a wide variety of settings and contexts, including those involving two people, small groups, and large groups. For example, the verbal sharing of intents includes intimate communication such as whispering in someone's ear as well as highly formal communication such as being introduced at a presidential reception. Pragmatics involves a rule system consisting of the setting, the characteristics of the participants, the topic, and the purpose of the interaction (Wiig & Semel, 1984).

Assessing language involves measuring receptive and expressive skills in these structural components. A description of the receptive and expressive aspects of the structural components of language follows.

Structural Components of Language

Component	Receptive Level	Expressive Level
Phonology	Discriminating speech sounds	Articulating speech sounds
Morphology and syntax	Understanding grammatical structure of language	Using grammar in words and sentences
Semantics and pragmatics	Understanding word meanings and contextual language cues	Using word meanings and using language in context

Why Do We Assess the Language of Children With Disabilities?

Language problems are the single most common disability among school-age children. For this reason special education teachers need a thorough grounding in the techniques associated with assessment of language. Language assessment is a necessary element of screening children with potential language disabilities who may need further assessment to determine whether they qualify for and would benefit from special education services. Language assessment is also essential in classifying and placing children with language deficits. In the classroom, teachers use language assessment to help develop IEPs, to plan instructional programs, and to develop specific learning activities for individual children and groups of children. Finally, measuring children's progress in language development also requires the use of language assessment. Focus 10–2 summarizes the reasons for assessing the language of students with special needs.

The following account illustrates one way in which language assessment helps us diagnose the language problems of a child, assists in developing remedial intervention activities, and measures the progress of a child with a language deficit.

Jeffrey was 10 years old and in the fourth grade when the child-study team recommended that he receive a comprehensive language evaluation. Although he had not received speech or language therapy or other special assistance in the primary grades, the team suspected language problems as the cause of his academic difficulties, including his failing grades in school.

FOCUS 10–2

Why Do We Assess the Language of Children With Special Needs?

- To screen children who may have language deficits
- To identify, classify, and place children with language deficits
- To help develop IEPs, plan instructional programs, and develop specific language interventions
- To measure the progress of children with language deficits

Jeffrey's teachers, puzzled by his lack of academic progress, described his classroom performance as "weak," "inconsistent," and "confused."

As part of the assessment, a speech and language pathologist gave Jeffrey several formal tests of language ability and obtained a spontaneous language sample for later analysis. The results revealed that Jeffrey's most serious difficulty involved understanding word meanings. A second difficulty concerned recalling and retrieving words. As a result of the assessment, the child-study team identified Jeffrey's language disability and arranged for him to begin receiving language therapy. The language therapist tried several intervention approaches designed to improve Jeffrey's word-finding skills, including word-finding strategies and self-cueing techniques. These approaches helped Jeffrey improve his speed and accuracy in word finding. The therapist also monitored the carryover effects of the direct intervention on Jeffrey's oral and silent reading, reading comprehension, and writing performance in the classroom. As part of the monitoring process, the therapist consulted with the classroom teacher on a regular basis. After a year of intervention, Jeffrey posted gains of about 3 years on word knowledge and word-finding skills.

Jeffrey, now in junior high school, receives assistance with school work from a professional tutor rather than a language therapist. His parents are committed to helping their son in the future by providing him with the learning aids (such as tape recorders and computers) that he will need in high school and college.

This account, based on a case study by Wiig and Semel (1984), illustrates the importance of assessment in identifying language problems and developing intervention programs. In Jeffrey's case, professionals relied on assessment to diagnose specific deficits and used the results to develop an individualized intervention plan and to monitor progress.

Linking Assessment With Instruction

Although norm-referenced tests are valuable in the instructional process, informal, curriculum-based assessment often provides the most direct link between assessment and classroom intervention. Some of the most useful curriculum-based assessment techniques include the following:

- Collecting spontaneous language samples in real-life settings.
- Analyzing the mean length of utterances (MLUs).
- Conducting developmental sentence analysis.
- Interviewing the child and the parents.

- Completing criterion-referenced checklists of specific language behaviors.
- Observing the child's language in natural settings such as the classroom, the home, or with peers.

This chapter discusses each of these assessment approaches. In many situations, these informal assessment techniques may be used along with formal, norm-referenced testing. Using informal and formal assessment together provides more accurate and more complete data for making the best possible decision regarding the language of a particular child. For example, when assessing children who are culturally and linguistically diverse, informal assessment provides valuable information that cannot be obtained through formal testing. In other situations, teachers may use one or more informal assessment techniques as part of instruction. Informal assessment helps teachers write IEPs, develop intervention programs, and measure student progress.

☑ Comprehension Checklist

Language, any means an individual uses to receive or send messages, is essential in all aspects of life. The most common disabilities among school-age children are associated with expressive and receptive language problems, which may correlate with any of the five structural components of language: phonology, morphology, syntax, semantics, and pragmatics. Although norm-referenced tests are valuable in the instructional process, informal, curriculum-based assessment often provides the most direct link between assessment and intervention.

Assessing the Sounds of Language: Phonology

Assessing phonology, the sounds of language known as *phonemes*, involves evaluating the manner in which a student uses speech sounds both receptively and expressively. All spoken languages consists of basic sounds, or phonemes. The expressive elements of oral language begin with these basic speech sounds. However, for children with disabilities, development of the sounds of language often occurs later than usual. Articulation disorders, the most common of all speech disorders, occur when a student fails to produce the phonemes of language appropriately. Phonological assessment includes evaluating a student's ability to discriminate between speech sounds when listening and to articulate these sounds when speaking. Reviews of two representative tests of phonology, the *Goldman–Fristoe Test of Articulation-Revised* and the *Goldman–Fristoe–Woodcock Test of Auditory Discrimination,* follow.

Goldman–Fristoe Test of Articulation-Revised

The *Goldman–Fristoe Test of Articulation-Revised* (Goldman & Fristoe, 1986) provides a structured method for evaluating an important element of speech: articulation of consonant sounds. Designed for children from age 2 through 16 years and beyond, the test includes the following:

- A sounds-in-words subtest to measure articulation of speech sounds.
- A sounds-in-sentences subtest to evaluate sound production in connected speech.
- A stimulability subtest to gauge the ability to correct misarticulated sounds when given a model of correct production.

Table 10–1   *Goldman–Fristoe Test of Articulation-Revised*

Type of Test:	Criterion referenced and individually administered
Purpose:	To diagnose articulation problems
Content Areas:	Sounds in words and sentences; stimulability
Administration Time:	Approximately 40 minutes
Age Levels:	2–16 years
Suitable for:	Students with articulation impairments, or as a tool for identifying such students
Scores:	Item analysis of specific articulation errors
In Short:	The *Goldman–Fristoe Test of Articulation-Revised* provides a structured tool for identifying errors in articulation, including positions in which errors occur, types of frequently occurring errors, error patterns as complexity increases, and errors in voicing.

The authors designed the Goldman–Fristoe test for speech pathologists to use before beginning therapy and for audiologists and special educators to use as a diagnostic tool. A summary of the *Goldman–Fristoe Test of Articulation-Revised* appears in Table 10–1.

Materials for the *Goldman–Fristoe Test* Goldman–Fristoe materials include an examiner's manual, a booklet of pictures used to prompt articulation of speech sounds, and a response matrix scoring form for conducting an item analysis of specific errors.

Administration and Scoring of the *Goldman–Fristoe Test* The Goldman–Fristoe test takes approximately 40 minutes to administer. The sounds-in-words subtest presents 35 pictures that prompt articulation of speech sounds in the initial, medial, and final positions. The sounds-in-sentences subtest contains two stories read while a child looks at pictures illustrating the key words in the story. The child then tells the story to the evaluator while looking at the pictures. The evaluator scores the child's skill at articulating the key words in the story. The stimulability subtest examines a child's ability to correct misarticulated sounds after the evaluator models the correct production. The evaluator uses sounds misarticulated in the sounds-in-words subtest as the basis for the stimulability subtest.

Designed as a criterion-referenced measure to identify error patterns such as the frequency of misarticulations and the positions in which misarticulations occur, the test does not yield traditional scores. Rather, it provides an item analysis of specific articulation errors. However, evaluators may obtain norm-referenced scores in the form of age percentiles for the sounds-in-words and stimulability subtests. The percentiles are a supplement to diagnostic interpretation, and evaluators should use them cautiously because of technical weaknesses in the standardization sample.

Interpretation, based on completion of a response matrix form, enables evaluators to identify various situations in which misarticulated sounds occur. Evaluators may obtain diagnostic information on articulation patterns in both words and sentences as well as a student's ability to correct misarticulations. The test provides evaluators with a system for analyzing articulation patterns in several dimensions, including positions in which errors occur, most frequently occurring errors, error patterns as complexity increases, and errors in voicing.

Evaluators may enhance Goldman–Fristoe assessment by using the instrument together with the *Khan–Lewis Phonological Analysis (KLPA)* (Khan & Lewis, 1983). Like the *Goldman–Fristoe Test of Articulation-Revised,* the *KLPA* is a criterion-referenced tool. To use the *KLPA,* evaluators first administer the sounds-in-words subtest of the *Goldman–Fristoe Test of Articulation-Revised* and then give the *KLPA,* which analyzes the use of 15 phonological processes in the speech production of young children from 2 through 5 years of age. Use of the *KLPA* involves recording the results of the sounds-in-words subtest on an analysis form that lists the most common sound changes when words are mispronounced. The evaluator then relies on the items identified from the list to pinpoint phonological deficits.

Technical Characteristics of the *Goldman–Fristoe Test*   The manual reports test-retest and interrater reliability studies as well as initial studies of the validity of the instrument. Overall, the test demonstrates adequate reliability and validity when used as a criterion-referenced measure.

The authors developed norms from data collected as part of a national speech and hearing study of 38,884 children. The study included administration of the *Goldman–Fristoe Test of Articulation-Revised* to the subjects in the sample group, and the authors calculated norms with data from this study. Because the authors initially designed the test for criterion- rather than norm-referenced use and standardized it in an unusual manner, examiners must treat the norms as a supplement to the major purpose of the test.

Summary of the *Goldman–Fristoe Test*   The *Goldman–Fristoe Test of Articulation-Revised* is a criterion-referenced assessment tool that provides a structured means for identifying errors in articulation. Easy to administer and score, it includes measures of single-word and conversational-speech production both spontaneously and after modeling.

Goldman–Fristoe–Woodcock Test of Auditory Discrimination

The *Goldman–Fristoe–Woodcock Test of Auditory Discrimination (GFW),* (Goldman, Fristoe, & Woodcock, 1976), an individually administered screening test, measures the ability to differentiate between speech sounds in quiet and noisy situations. The authors designed the *GFW* for speech, language, and hearing clinicians, and they also recommend it for use by audiologists, diagnosticians, reading specialists, and special educators. The *GFW* assesses the auditory discrimination ability of children from 4 years of age through adulthood. A summary of the *GFW* appears in Table 10–2.

Materials for the *GFW*   Goldman–Fristoe–Woodcock test materials include an easel-kit of stimulus pictures, a manual, an audiocassette, and a scoring sheet.

Administration and Scoring of the *GFW*   Requiring about 20 minutes to administer, the *GFW* uses a cassette recorder to play a $7^1/_2$-minute tape that contains the two subtests. The manual provides clear directions for administering, scoring, and interpreting results, including a discussion of problems associated with testing discrimination ability and suggestions for auditory training techniques to remediate

Table 10–2   *Goldman–Fristoe–Woodcock Test of Auditory Discrimination (GFW)*

Type of Test:	Norm referenced and individually administered
Purpose:	A screening test of auditory discrimination
Content Areas:	Auditory discrimination under noisy and quiet conditions
Administration Time:	Approximately 20 minutes
Age Levels:	4 years–adult
Suitable for:	Students with auditory discrimination deficits, including those with speech and learning disabilities, mental retardation, and hearing impairments
Scores:	Standard scores, percentiles, and error pattern analysis of specific discrimination errors
In Short:	The *GFW* is a well-designed screening test with good technical characteristics.

discrimination deficits. Evaluators may obtain both standard scores and percentiles and may also use an error pattern analysis procedure to identify specific types of listening errors for the purpose of developing intervention objectives.

Technical Characteristics of the *GFW*   Standardized on a sample group of individuals from age 3 to 84 years, the *GFW* exhibits satisfactory reliability and validity. In addition to comparing norms for the general population, evaluators may compare a child's listening ability to that of subjects from nine clinical samples, including groups with learning deficits, mental retardation, hearing impairments, and speech disabilities.

Summary of the *GFW*   The *Goldman–Fristoe–Woodcock Test of Auditory Discrimination* provides a rapid and easy method for identifying performance levels in auditory discrimination. The instrument has value as a screening test with students who display difficulty in listening.

☑ Comprehension Checklist

Assessing phonology, the sounds of language known as *phonemes,* involves measuring student proficiency in the use of speech sounds. Representative tests of phonology include the *Goldman–Fristoe Test of Articulation-Revised* and the *Goldman–Fristoe–Woodcock Test of Auditory Discrimination.* Designed primarily for use by speech clinicians, special educators also rely on these instruments to identify learning needs and develop instructional objectives for students with language problems.

Assessing Units of Meaning (Morphemes) and Phrases and Sentences (Syntax)

Morphology is the study of the smallest units of meaning in language, known as *morphemes,* which may be either free or bound. Free morphemes, meaningful when they stand alone, include words such as *run, slow,* and *teach.* Bound morphemes, meaningful only when attached to a free morpheme, include units such as *-ly* in *slowly* and the *-er* in *teacher*. Syntax, the way in which words combine to form phrases and sentences, follows a set of grammatical rules. Assessing syntax involves measuring the ability to understand the meaning of sentences and to form sentences that follow the grammatical rules. Representative tests of morphology and syntax include the *Test of Auditory Comprehension of Language-Revised* and the *Carrow Elicited Language Inventory*. Reviews of these two instruments follow along with a description of informal measures of morphology and syntax.

Test of Auditory Comprehension of Language-Revised

The *Test of Auditory Comprehension of Language-Revised (TACL-R)* (Carrow-Woolfolk, 1985) is an individually administered, norm-referenced test for assessing the language comprehension of children from 3 through 9 years of age. The *TACL-R* assesses the receptive language components of morphology, syntax, and semantics. Test items measure auditory comprehension of language in three categories: vocabulary (literal meaning of words), morphology (grammatical morphemes), and syntax (meaning from sentences). The author developed the *TACL-R* to identify children with language deficits, to measure school readiness, to plan instructional programs, and to monitor student progress. A summary of the *TACL-R* appears in Table 10–3.

Materials for the *TACL-R* *TACL-R* materials include an examiner's manual, a test booklet containing line drawings, and a scoresheet. Supplementary materials include a demonstration videotape and a computer scoring program.

Administration and Scoring of the *TACL-R* Consisting of 120 items, the *TACL-R* presents a page containing three line drawings, and an evaluator reads a word or sentence that corresponds to one of the drawings. The child responds by pointing to the drawing that shows the correct meaning of the word or sentence. The *TACL-R* requires no oral response. The *TACL-R* vocabulary items measure receptive understanding of various words and word relations such as "riding a little bicycle." Morphological items assess receptive grammatical ability by using prepositions, nouns,

Table 10–3 *Test of Auditory Comprehension of Language-Revised (TACL-R)*

Type of Test:	Individually administered, norm referenced
Purpose:	Assesses auditory comprehension ability
Content Areas:	Vocabulary, morphology, and syntax
Administration Time:	20 minutes
Age Levels:	3–9 years
Suitable for:	Students with mild and moderate disabilities, including speech and learning disabilities, emotional disturbance, mental retardation, and physical impairments
Scores:	Percentile ranks, standard scores, and age equivalents
In Short:	The *Test of Auditory Comprehension of Language-Revised* is a well-designed picture test for assessing receptive language abilities.

and verbs. Syntactical items assess understanding of the meaning of sentences that use passive and active voices and direct and indirect objects. *TACL-R* scores include percentile ranks and age equivalents. In addition, evaluators may convert percentile ranks into various standard scores, including *z*-scores, *t*-scores, quotient scores, and normal curve equivalents.

Technical Characteristics of the *TACL-R*   Standardized with a group of more than 1,000 children, the sample was designed to represent the national population in terms of family occupation, ethnic or racial background, gender, and geographic region. In estimating reliability, the author calculated 40 split-half reliability coefficients. All total score coefficients surpassed .91. The subtest coefficients were lower, but all fell within the range of .73 to .96. The manual presents several types of information to support validity, including a discussion of content validity and evidence of construct validity based on correlations between *TACL-R* scores and age. The manual also describes several criterion-related validity studies that provide evidence of the effectiveness of the instrument. Overall, the *TACL-R* demonstrates acceptable technical qualities. However, as is the case with many tests, evaluators should use the subtest scores with caution because of low reliability coefficients.

Summary of the *TACL-R*   An individually administered, norm-referenced picture test of language ability, the *Test of Auditory Comprehension of Language-Revised* measures the receptive vocabulary, morphology, and syntax abilities of students between 3 and 9 years of age. The *TACL-R* demonstrates adequate technical qualities for use as a norm-referenced tool.

Carrow Elicited Language Inventory

One of only a few available tests of expressive grammatical proficiency, the *Carrow Elicited Language Inventory (CELI)* (Carrow, 1974) is an individually administered test for children from 3 through 7 years of age. Designed to provide a systematic evaluation of grammatical ability, the *CELI* measures the following grammatical forms: 41 pronouns, 14 prepositions, 7 conjunctions, 41 articles, 9 adverbs, 5 *wh-* questions, 13 negatives, 59 nouns, 7 adjectives, 103 verbs, 8 infinitives, and 1 gerund. Although the *CELI* was developed for speech and language pathologists, all professionals with language training may use the test. However, the manual cautions against using the instrument with students who have severe speech and language disabilities. A summary of the *CELI* appears in Table 10–4.

Materials for the *CELI*   *CELI* materials consist of an examiner's manual, a matrix of error types, an item analysis form, a separate verb protocol scoresheet, and a training tape that includes samples of children's responses.

Administration and Scoring of the *CELI*   Consisting of 51 model sentences (with an average length of six words) and 1 model phrase, the *CELI* uses a procedure in which the evaluator says a stimulus sentence and the student imitates it. The underlying assumption is that correct imitation indicates knowledge of syntactic structures and incorrect imitation reflects the student's own syntactic rules. During the testing, the evaluator tapes the responses for later analysis. Although it takes 10 to 20 minutes to administer the *CELI,* analysis of the taped responses takes approximately an hour.

Table 10–4   *Carrow Elicited Language Inventory (CELI)*

Type of Test:	Individually administered, criterion referenced
Purpose:	A diagnostic test of expressive morphological and syntactic (grammatical) proficiency
Content Areas:	Expressive morphology and syntax
Administration Time:	20 minutes to administer; 60 minutes to score
Age Levels:	3–7 years
Suitable for:	Students with mild and moderate speech and language disabilities
Scores:	Uses a complex matrix that produces a detailed analysis of verb and other grammatical errors
In Short:	One of only a few tests of expressive grammatical abilities, the *CELI* is valuable as a criterion-referenced measure. However, because of weaknesses in the standardization sample, evaluators should use scores derived from the *CELI* norms with caution.

The evaluator scores the *CELI* using an error analysis procedure that includes completing a matrix of error types and a verb protocol scoresheet. When evaluators need a score to describe results, they may report a total error score and subtest error scores in the form of percentile ranks or stanines, which, however, suffer from technical deficiencies that limit their usefulness.

Technical Characteristics of the *CELI*   The *CELI* was standardized with a restricted sample of 475 white, middle-class children in Houston; the test manual discusses the limitations of the norm group, including the exclusion of children with speech and language disabilities from the sample. Because of the weaknesses of the standardization sample, evaluators should avoid using the *CELI* as a norm-referenced test.

The manual provides evidence of *CELI* reliability in the form of a test-retest coefficient of .98 based on a sample of 25 children and interrater reliability coefficients of .98 and .99 from two separate studies. The manual also describes a concurrent validity study that compares *CELI* and *Developmental Sentence Analysis* (Lee, 1974) scores. This study produced a correlation of .79. A second concurrent validity study compared the *CELI* scores of 20 children with ratings from expert clinicians. This study produced a correlation coefficient of .77. These reliability and validity data provide sufficient evidence to establish the effectiveness and accuracy of the *CELI* for use as a criterion-referenced tool.

Summary of the *CELI*   The *Carrow Elicited Language Inventory* is an individually administered test of the expressive morphological (units of meaning) and syntactical (phrases and sentences) ability of children. It is useful as a diagnostic instrument to identify children with language deficits, as a programming tool for analyzing error response patterns prior to developing an intervention program, and as a criterion-referenced measure of expressive grammatical competence.

Informal Measures for Assessing Morphology and Syntax

In addition to relying on formal testing to assess the morphology and syntax abilities of students, many evaluators also use less formal evaluation techniques—assessment of mean length of utterance and developmental sentence analysis. These less formal approaches assess the **spontaneous language** of students, which is the candid, unrehearsed verbal expression that occurs naturally in real-life situations. Assessing spontaneous language involves collecting a speech sample by tape recording for later transcription and analysis. Spontaneous language sampling displays distinct advantages over formal testing, which Wiig and Semel (1984) described in the following way:

- Spontaneous language sampling places fewer controls on the student than structured language tests.
- Students may exhibit phrases and sentences in spontaneous speech not observed during formal language testing.
- Spontaneous sampling enables the evaluator to observe language during interactions with others in natural settings.
- Spontaneous sampling enables evaluation of the words and sentences a student knows well enough to use in everyday language.

Wiig and Semel (1984) also cited limitations of spontaneous language sampling, especially in terms of the sample size. In typical situations, a spontaneous speech sample contains 50 to 100 utterances. Because this is a relatively small sample, situational variables such as the topic of conversation, the task at hand, the age of the student, and the elicitation procedures can negatively affect the quality of the samples. Larger samples consisting of 300 to 800 utterances reduce these negative influences. However, it is not always feasible to collect and analyze large samples. Therefore typical language samples tend to be less than ideal in size and usually focus on analysis of specific spontaneous measures of language.

Mean Length of Utterance   The **mean length of utterance (MLU)** is an assessment procedure for evaluating the ability to form words, phrases, and sentences. According to Brown (1973), MLU analysis is ideal for measuring the language level of young children. The MLU assessment procedure involves tape recording and later analyzing a spontaneous speech sample containing a minimum of 50 consecutive utterances. The evaluator elicits a speech sample by using stimuli such as story pictures or toys and asking open-ended questions such as "What can you tell me about this?" After transcribing the speech sample from the tape, the evaluator calculates an MLU by counting the number of morphemes produced and dividing the total by the number of utterances. For example, a toddler who says "Get ball" (2 morphemes), "Mama" (1 morpheme), "Dog woof" (2 morphemes), and "Dog" (1 morpheme) produces an MLU of 1.5 morphemes (6 ÷ 4 = 1.5), where 6 is the number of morphemes produced and 4 is the number of utterances. Although MLU analysis represents a helpful technique, it is time consuming. Brown (1973) suggests using MLUs with utterances with a maximum of four morphemes. This means that MLUs work best with young children and students with severe language delays.

Developmental Sentence Analysis   **Developmental sentence analysis** (Lee, 1974) is an assessment procedure for collecting and analyzing a speech sample to measure the ability to spontaneously produce words and sentences. Unlike the MLU procedure, which simply counts the average length of utterances, developmental sentence analysis involves examination of eight grammatical categories that represent syntactic ability:

1. Indefinite pronouns and noun modifiers
2. Personal pronouns
3. Main verbs
4. Secondary verbs
5. Negatives
6. Conjunctions
7. Interrogative reversals
8. *Wh-* questions

The administration procedure is similar to the MLU method. An evaluator tapes and later transcribes a natural language sample, using an informal interview format with pictures or other appropriate stimuli to elicit responses. Scoring the sample requires 50 consecutive sentences and produces a quantitative score called a *developmental sentence score (DSS)*. Lee (1974) defines a complete sentence as any utterance containing a noun and verb in a subject-predicate relationship such as "Mama bye bye." The evaluator assigns a point value (from 1 to 8) to each word in the sample, with developmentally advanced words receiving higher point values. For example, third-person pronouns (2 points) receive more points than first- or second-person pronouns (1 point), and plurals receive the highest pronoun point values (3 points). The evaluator calculates a developmental sentence score by totaling the number points given to the words in the sample and dividing the total by the number of sentences (50). Finally, the evaluator converts the raw score into an age-based percentile rank that shows where the score falls in relation to the 10th, 25th, 50th, and 75th percentiles.

Developmental sentence analysis is a norm-referenced procedure designed for children from 2 through 6 years of age. The author based the norms on a sample of 200 children from middle-class homes in four states. Unfortunately, this restricted sample limits the usefulness of the norms. In addition, limited reliability and no validity data exist to support the technical adequacy of the procedure. For this reason, evaluators should rely on developmental sentence analysis as an informal technique. Special educators and speech clinicians may use results from developmental sentence analysis to generate intervention objectives that respond directly to a child's expressive language strengths and weaknesses. Valuable as a measure of performance levels in expressive language as well as an instructional guide, teachers and clinicians can also use the procedure in conjunction with the interactive language development teaching method developed by Lee, Koenigsknecht, and Mulhern (1975) to remediate language problems.

✅ Comprehension Checklist

Professionals may select from among a variety of diagnostic tests and informal, clinical evaluation procedures to assess a student's grasp of morphology and syntax. Because the various techniques differ in design and purpose, the evaluator should select an appropriate procedure on the basis of individual student requirements and the purpose for conducting the assessment. Although laws and professional standards mandate use of individually administered, norm-referenced tests for making placement decisions, most teachers and clinicians prefer less formal procedures such as developmental sentence analysis for making curriculum-based instructional decisions. Regardless of the specific assessment approach, resulting data should help the teacher to place students appropriately, identify specific language problems, and design appropriate remediation activities.

Assessing Word Meanings and Relationships (Semantics) and the Use of Language in Context (Pragmatics)

Assessing semantics involves measuring receptive and expressive vocabulary skills as well as the ability to define words, categorize words, identify synonyms and antonyms, and comprehend absurdity or ambiguity. Vocabulary is the most frequently measured element of semantics.

Representative Instruments for Assessing Semantics

Instruments for assessing vocabulary include many of the intelligence tests reviewed in Chapter 4. For example, the verbal subtest of the *Wechsler Intelligence Scale for Children-Third Edition (WISC-III)* measures several types of expressive vocabulary skills, including the ability to define words. Parts of the *Stanford–Binet Intelligence Scale: Fourth Edition* also measure semantic skills such as vocabulary, absurdities, and verbal relations. Other devices for measuring receptive vocabulary include the picture tests of intelligence described in Chapter 4 and the widely used *Peabody Picture Vocabulary Test-Third Edition (PPVT-III)*, of which a detailed review follows.

Instruments for measuring other aspects of semantics as well as devices for measuring pragmatics are not as readily available. However, professionals may select from among a few commercial devices, including several informal inventories for assessing student performance in the areas of word relationships and the contextual use of language. Pragmatics, the usage of language in context, refers to understanding the structure of different forms of communication. Pragmatic rules include the following:

- Routines for taking turns in conversations.
- Use of formal versus informal conversations among supervisors, family, and peers.
- Appropriate use of verbal humor in social situations.

One of the available tests of pragmatics is the *Test of Pragmatic Skills*. A review of this instrument follows, along with a description of a series of informal checklists designed to measure pragmatic communication skills.

Peabody Picture Vocabulary Test-Third Edition

Receptive language vocabulary—the ability to understand word meanings—is an important semantic language skill. Although a number of tests include receptive language vocabulary subtests, one test, the *Peabody Picture Vocabulary Test-Third Edition*

Table 10–5 Peabody Picture Vocabulary Test-Third Edition (PPVT-III)

Type of Test:	Norm referenced, individually administered
Purpose:	A screening test of receptive language vocabulary
Content Areas:	Receptive (hearing) vocabulary
Administration Time:	Approximately 20 minutes
Age Levels:	2.5 years–adulthood
Suitable for:	Students with mild, moderate, and severe disabilities, including learning and physical disabilities, emotional disturbance, and mental retardation
Scores:	Standard score equivalents, percentiles, stanines, and age equivalents
In Short:	The *PPVT-III* is a well-written, easy-to-use test for estimating receptive language vocabulary. It exhibits excellent technical characteristics.

(Dunn & Dunn, 1997), measures this aspect of language in isolation. Perhaps the most widely used language test in special education, the *PPVT-III* is a norm-referenced screening test of receptive (hearing) vocabulary. Designed for individuals from age 2^1/$_2$ years to adulthood, the *PPVT-III* does not require reading or writing ability and is used in schools and clinics to screen children at all levels of ability. Each *PPVT-III* item consists of four simple line drawings on a page. The test is given by having the child select a drawing (from among the four choices) that best represents the meaning of each word presented orally. Because a student can select the drawing by naming the number of the drawing (1 through 4) or pointing to it, the *PPVT-III* can be used with verbal children and those who are nonverbal or nonvocal. A summary of the *PPVT-III* appears in Table 10–5.

A Spanish version of the *Peabody Picture Vocabulary Test,* the *TVIP: Test de Vocabulario en Imágenes Peabody* (Dunn et al., 1986), is available for assessing the receptive vocabulary of Spanish-speaking children and adolescents from 2^1/$_2$ to 18 years of age. The *TVIP* is designed for evaluating the language development of Spanish-speaking preschool children, screening Spanish-speaking children entering kindergarten or first grade, determining the more effective language instruction for bilingual children, and evaluating the Spanish vocabulary of older students. Based on the *Peabody Picture Vocabulary Test-Revised,* the *TVIP* contains 125 translated items to assess the vocabulary of Spanish-speaking and bilingual students. The manual is available in English and Spanish, and norms are available for both combined and separate Mexican and Puerto Rican standardization samples.

Materials for the *PPVT-III*   *PPVT-III* materials consist of separate, easel-type booklets for form IIIA and form IIIB, both containing 204 plates with four line drawings on each plate. The *PPVT-III* also includes a well-written and thorough test manual.

Administration and Scoring of the *PPVT-III*   The well-designed *PPVT-III* administration procedures make it easy for evaluators to give and score the test in 20 minutes or less. Administration involves giving several training items and a portion of the 204 test items arranged in increasing order of difficulty. A sample test plate from the *PPVT-III* administration booklet appears in Figure 10–1. Evaluators may report *PPVT-III* results using standard scores, percentiles, stanines, or age equivalents.

In the past, professionals relied on the *PPVT* as more than a screening measure of receptive language vocabulary. Because it yields a standard score with a mean of 100 and a standard deviation of 15, some evaluators employed earlier versions of the *PPVT* as a picture test of intelligence. Others used it as a more general measure of language development. However, the *PPVT-III* is a screening test rather than a diagnostic tool. As a screening test, it estimates only present levels of performance in receptive vocabulary and does not replace comprehensive diagnostic evaluation. For this reason, one should use the *PPVT-III* for screening purposes or as a single instrument in a battery of assessments that make up a comprehensive diagnostic evaluation.

Technical Characteristics of the *PPVT-III*   Standardized on a national sample of children and adults from $2^{1}/_{2}$ to 90 years of age, the *PPVT-III* norms are based on U.S. Census figures for gender, race/ethnicity, region, and education level. A variety of studies of the split-half, alternate-form, and test-retest reliability of the *PPVT-III* have established the consistency of *PPVT-III* scores. Likewise, the effectiveness of the

Figure 10–1   Sample test plate from the *Peabody Picture Vocabulary Test-Third Edition (PPVT-III)*

Training Plate D

(From Dunn, L. M., & Dunn, L. M. [1997]. *Peabody Picture Vocabulary Test-Third Edition.* Circle Pines, MN: American Guidance Service. Reprinted with permission of Lloyd and Leola Dunn.)

PPVT-III has been clearly demonstrated through numerous content, construct, and concurrent validity studies. Furthermore, many researchers use the *PPVT-III* as a criterion measure in various independent scientific studies that provide further evidence to support the excellent technical qualities of the *PPVT-III*.

Summary of the *PPVT-III* The *PPVT-III* is a well-designed, easy-to-use tool for estimating an important component of oral language: receptive language vocabulary. In addition to displaying excellent technical characteristics, the outstanding design of the *PPVT-III* makes it easy to administer, score, and interpret. A wide range of professionals including special educators, school and clinical psychologists, educational diagnosticians, counselors, and speech and language pathologists use the *PPVT-III* with children and adults at all levels of ability.

Boehm Test of Basic Concepts-Revised

The *Boehm Test of Basic Concepts-Revised (BTBC-R)* (Boehm, 1986a) assesses the receptive vocabulary development of students from kindergarten through grade 2. Designed for group or individual administration, this norm-referenced test evaluates mastery of the basic concepts essential for understanding the verbal instructions necessary for early school achievement. Containing 50 concepts, the *BTBC-R* measures understanding in three major context categories:

1. Space (e.g., top, next to, and through)
2. Quantity (e.g., first, most, and part)
3. Time (e.g., starting, after, and before)

Although it assesses both language and nonlanguage abilities, most reviewers include the *BTBC-R* in the discussion of language assessment because results from the test help special educators identify students with possible weaknesses in receptive language vocabulary and in basic concepts. A summary of the *BTBC-R* appears in Table 10–6. Information about using the *BTBC-R* as a developmental readiness

Table 10–6 *Boehm Test of Basic Concepts-Revised*

Type of Test:	Norm referenced, group administered
Purpose:	Screening test of receptive vocabulary development
Content Areas:	Relational concepts of space, quantity, and time
Administration Time:	Approximately 30–40 minutes
Age Levels:	Revised version: kindergarten–grade 2
Suitable for:	Students with mild and moderate disabilities, including learning disabilities, emotional disturbance, developmental delays, and educable mental retardation
Scores:	Percentile ranks by grade, socioeconomic level, and beginning or end of school year
In Short:	This well-designed test is a tool for measuring the basic concept development of individuals and groups of students.

test appears in Chapter 8. Teachers may also administer a supplementary applications subtest to assess understanding of concepts used in combination or in sequences, and to make comparisons. A preschool version of the test, the *Boehm Test of Basic Concepts-Preschool Version (BTBC-PV)* (Boehm, 1986b) includes 26 easier concepts and is appropriate for children from 3 to 5 years of age.

Materials for the *BTBC-R*   *BTBC-R* materials include an examiner's manual, two separate scoresheet forms, and a supplementary applications booklet.

Administration and Scoring of the *BTBC-R*   The *BTBC-R* measures understanding of relational concepts by using a picture identification task. The evaluator administers the *BTBC-R* by describing the intended concept and having the students mark the correct drawing from a row with three selections. In the supplementary applications subtest, the students follow multistep directions, make comparisons, and place objects in order. The *BTBC-R* produces percentile rank scores by grade level, socioeconomic level, and time of school year.

The *BTBC-R* manual includes information on using the test with students who have special needs, including descriptions of research studies on the concept development patterns of students with disabilities and data on the performance of children with delays in syntactic development. The information on children with syntactic delays includes a description of the reasons for errors that teachers should consider in developing intervention strategies. They include the following:

- Difficulty in focusing on key words in instructions.
- Inability to attend to syntactic features such as plural endings.
- Processing problems due to direction complexity and length.
- Poor understanding of the concept of name labels.
- Confusion between similar concepts.
- Difficulty with abstractions.
- Poor auditory memory.
- Difficulty comprehending spatial concepts because of deficits in spatial perception.

Technical Qualities of the *BTBC-R*   Standardized with a group of more than 1,500 children from kindergarten to second grade, the *BTBC-R* followed a well-designed test development plan based on a representative national sample. Split-half reliability coefficients for forms C and D ranged from .55 to .87 with a median coefficient of .77. For the applications booklet, the coefficients ranged from .72 to .82 with a median of .76. Test-retest reliability coefficients ranged from a low of .69 to a high of .88. Overall, these reliability coefficients fall below acceptable levels for some subtests.

Summary of the *BTBC-R*   Because they measure the essential skill of understanding basic concepts, the *BTBC-R* and the *BTBC-PV* serve as screening tools for evaluating skills in receptive concept development. The tests are valuable for measuring performance levels in conceptual development as well as for use as instructional guides, and teachers can use them with the *Boehm Resources Guide for Basic Concept Teaching* (Boehm, 1976), which provides practical, applied suggestions for developing instructional programs in basic concept development for individuals and groups of students.

Other Tests of Semantics and Pragmatics

A range of tests and informal assessment procedures are available to evaluate the semantic and pragmatic skills of children with special needs. Brief reviews of many of these measures follow.

Comprehensive Receptive and Expressive Vocabulary Test   The *Comprehensive Receptive and Expressive Vocabulary Test (CREVT)* (Wallace & Hammill, 1994) is a norm-referenced, individually administered test designed to identify children who are significantly below their peers in oral vocabulary proficiency. Designed for children from 4 through 18 years of age, the *CREVT* has an expressive and a receptive subtest and two equivalent forms. The *CREVT* is also available in adult and computerized formats. The *Comprehensive Receptive and Expressive Vocabulary Test-Adult (CREVT-A)* (Wallace & Hammill, 1997a) is a norm-referenced, individually administered test that takes about 30 minutes to give and score. Designed for adults from age 18 through retirement, the *CREVT-A* was standardized on more than 700 adults from 10 states. The *Comprehensive Receptive and Expressive Vocabulary Test-Computer Administered (CREVT-CA)* (Wallace & Hammill, 1997b) is an interactive multimedia test that can be given entirely on a home or office computer. During the receptive part of the test, a human voice pronounces a word while the child views six real-life pictures. The child simply points the mouse and clicks it on a picture to indicate the answer. For the expressive portion, the computer screen is turned away from the child. The computer gives the instructions orally and asks the child to define a series of words. The evaluator listens to the child's definitions and scores them using the criteria shown on the screen. When the testing is finished, the evaluator can view a comprehensive report of the results on the computer screen or print a hard copy of the report.

Expressive One-Word Picture Vocabulary Test-Revised   The norm-referenced, individually administered *Expressive One Word Picture Vocabulary Test-Revised (EOWPVT-R)* (Gardner, 1990) measures verbal expression of language by having children make word-picture associations. The *EOWPVT-R* takes about 10 minutes to give and is suitable for children from 2 through 11 years of age. Consisting of 100 black-and-white line drawings of common objects and collections of objects, the test is given by showing pictures one at a time and having the child name each picture. Results from the *EOWPVT-R* can be reported as age equivalents, standard scores, scaled scores, percentiles, or stanines. An upper extension of the original *EOWPVT*, the *Expressive One-Word Picture Vocabulary Test: Upper Extension* (Gardner & Brownell, 1983) is available for assessing the expressive vocabulary of adolescents from 12 through 15 years of age.

Expressive Vocabulary Test   The *Expressive Vocabulary Test (EVT)* (Williams, 1997) is a norm-referenced, individually administered measure of expressive vocabulary and word retrieval for Standard American English. Designed for children and adults from $2\frac{1}{2}$ to 85-plus years of age, the *EVT* takes about 25 minutes to give. Co-normed with the *PPVT-III*, the *EVT* features two types of items: labeling and synonyms. The child responds to each item with a one-word answer. All items are presented with pictures. Some of the test items include instructions to help the child do as well as possible on later items. Other test items include prompts that the evaluator can give when a child gives a close or related response. Like the *PPVT-III,* the test requires no reading or writing skills. Available scores include standard scores, percentile ranks, stanines, and age equivalents.

Oral and Written Language Scales-Listening Comprehension Scale and Oral Expression Scale   The *Oral and Written Language Scales (OWLS)-Listening Comprehension Scale and Oral Expression Scale* (Carrow-Woolfolk, 1995) are norm-referenced, individually administered measures of the receptive and expressive language of children and young adults from 3 through 21 years of age. A review of the third component of the *OWLS,* the *Written Expression Scale,* appears in Chapter 17, Assessment of Written Language. The *Listening Comprehension Scale* measures receptive language and consists of three examples and 111 items. The evaluator reads the verbal stimulus, and the child responds by selecting one of four pictures. The *Listening Comprehension Scale* takes about 15 minutes to administer. The *Oral Expression Scale* measures the understanding and use of spoken language and consists of two examples and 96 items. The evaluator reads a verbal stimulus and shows a picture or pictures, and the child responds orally by answering a question, completing a sentence, or generating one or more sentences. The *Oral Comprehension Scale* takes about 25 minutes to administer. The scales provide a variety of clinical and school-based applications for measuring language knowledge and processing skills in children and adolescents. These applications include identifying children with language deficits, designing language intervention tasks, and monitoring growth in language skills.

Receptive One-Word Picture Vocabulary Test   The norm-referenced, individually administered *Receptive One-Word Picture Vocabulary Test (ROWPVT)* (Gardner, 1985) assesses the receptive hearing vocabulary of children from 2 through 11 years of age. Designed as a companion test to the *Expressive One-Word Vocabulary Test-Revised,* the *ROWPVT* takes about 20 minutes to administer. An upper extension of the *ROWPVT,* the *Receptive One-Word Picture Vocabulary Test: Upper Extension* (Gardner & Brownell, 1987) is available for use with students from 12 to 15 years of age.

Test of Pragmatic Skills   The *Test of Pragmatic Skills* (Shulman, 1986), an individually administered, criterion-referenced instrument, enables analysis of expressive language as it occurs in structured play interactions. For example, in one of the play sessions the evaluator and the student use puppets to talk about television programs. The evaluator leads the student through each of four play sessions based on a written script. Designed for children from age 3 through 8 years, the test measures 10 different communicative intents:

1. Requesting information
2. Requesting action
3. Rejecting or denying
4. Naming or labeling
5. Answering or responding
6. Informing
7. Reasoning
8. Summoning or calling
9. Greeting
10. Closing conversation

Behavioral Observation and Rating   Because few formal tests of semantics and pragmatics exist other than picture vocabulary tests such as the *PPVT-R*, teachers often rely on direct observation and rating of verbal interaction skills for gathering assessment data on semantic and pragmatic communication skills. Wiig and Bray (1983) developed *Let's Talk for Children (LTC)*, a social communications training curriculum that includes a progress checklist for children from 3 to 8 years of age. This checklist is an informal device for identifying communication intents and social communication skills with students who are experiencing difficultly in semantic and pragmatic language development. An evaluator completes the checklist after observing a student in a natural setting such as in the classroom, at home, or with peers. Other components of the *LTC* curriculum include the following items:

- A professional's guide.
- A set of communication situation cards.
- A set of communication activity cards.
- Hand puppets and "Barney Bag."
- A home activities manual.
- A set of *Let's Talk* stickers.

Wiig (1982a) included a similar communication skills checklist in the *Let's Talk Inventory for Adolescents* and designed it for use as an informal, criterion-referenced device to measure social communication skills relevant to older students. The device measures the following communication skills:

Skill	Description
Ritualizing	Greetings, farewells, requests to repeat and clarify
Informing	Asking for and telling about names, locations, and time
Controlling	Expressing wants, making promises, giving warnings
Expressing Feelings	Expressing attitudes, reactions, and feelings including affection, apologies, and complaints

Wiig (1982b) also published *Let's Talk: Developing Prosocial Communication Skills*, a set of curriculum materials specifically for students with language delays, language disorders, or language differences. Designed for social communication training and field tested with students with language and learning disabilities, these materials include structured group interaction activities, role-playing activities, and communication card games.

☑ Comprehension Checklist

Assessment of semantics involves measuring a student's ability to understand and express word meanings and relationships. Vocabulary is the most familiar component of semantics, and assessment devices for estimating expressive vocabulary include many of the intelligence tests reviewed in Chapter 4. Devices for measuring receptive vocabulary include one of the most widely used language tests, the *PPVT-III*. Measures of other aspects of semantics, as well as devices for measuring pragmatics, the usage of language in context, are not as readily available. However, professionals may select from among several available instruments including both formal tests and informal inventories for assessing student performance in semantics and pragmatics.

Comprehensive Measures of Language

In addition to the instruments for assessing specific structural components of language, special educators may also select from a variety of comprehensive measures of language. Rather than focusing on a single construct, these measures contain separate subtests for evaluating different structural components of language. Three representative comprehensive language tests are the *Test of Language Development-Primary, Third Edition*, the *Test of Language Development-Intermediate, Third Edition*, and the *Test of Adolescent and Adult Language-3*. Detailed reviews of these tests follow along with brief reviews of other available comprehensive language tests.

Test of Language Development-Primary, Third Edition

The *Test of Language Development-Primary, Third Edition (TOLD-P:3)* (Newcomer & Hammill, 1997) is a comprehensive, norm-referenced, individually administered test of spoken language. Designed for children from 4 through 8 years of age, the *TOLD-P:3* helps to identify language disorders and to isolate particular types of language deficits in need of remediation. A summary of the *TOLD-P:3* appears in Table 10–7. The language skills evaluated by the nine *TOLD-P:3* subtests include the following:

Subtest	*Specific Skill*	*Structural Component*
Picture vocabulary	Understanding words	Semantics
Relational vocabulary	Mediating vocabulary	Semantics
Oral vocabulary	Defining words	Semantics
Grammatic understanding	Understanding sentence meaning	Syntax
Grammatic completion	Understanding sentence formation	Syntax
Sentence imitation	Repeating sentences	Syntax
Word discrimination	Noticing sound differences	Phonology
Phonemic analysis	Segmenting words into smaller units	Phonology
Word articulation	Saying words correctly	Phonology

Materials for the *TOLD-P:3*   The *TOLD-P:3* test kit contains an examiner's manual, a picture book, and a package of 25 profile/record forms in a small cardboard storage box. Computer software for scoring the *TOLD-P:3* is available as an optional item.

Administration and Scoring of the *TOLD-P:3*   Designed for individual administration, the *TOLD-P:3* takes about an hour to administer and score. Results can be reported as standard scores, percentiles, or age equivalents. Combining scores from different subtests provides scores for overall spoken language, listening, speaking, semantics, and syntax. The scoresheet includes a profile for visual presentation of results, which is useful for gauging strengths and weaknesses in various language ability areas.

Technical Characteristics of the *TOLD-P:3*   Standardized with a group of more than 1,000 students from 30 states, the *TOLD-P:3* sample included children from diverse ethnic, language, and socioeconomic backgrounds. Standardization followed a well-designed testing plan to ensure representation of the national population. The developers estimated the reliability of *TOLD-P:3* scores based on coefficient alpha and test-retest methods and used several procedures to establish validity, including relating the

Table 10–7 *Test of Language Development-Primary, Third Edition*

Type of Test:	Norm referenced, individually administered
Purpose:	Comprehensive diagnostic assessment of language abilities
Content Areas:	Picture, relational and oral vocabulary, grammatic understanding and completion, sentence imitation, word discrimination, phonemic analysis, and word articulation
Administration Time:	Approximately 1 hour
Age Levels:	4–8 years
Suitable for:	Students with mild and moderate disabilities, including speech and language impairments, learning disabilities, emotional disturbance, and educable mental retardation
Scores:	Standard scores, percentiles, and age equivalents
In Short:	This well-written diagnostic test of language ability helps to identify students with language disorders, isolate particular types of disorders, and develop individual intervention programs.

test's content to children's actual language, correlating subtests with other commonly used tests, and studying the relationship of *TOLD-P:3* scores to age, IQ, and achievement. These reliability and validity measures provide initial evidence to support the consistency and effectiveness of *TOLD-P:3* scores. Overall, the test exhibits adequate technical characteristics for use as norm-referenced instrument.

Summary of the *TOLD-P:3*   The primary version of the *Test of Language Development, Third Edition* is an individually administered, norm-referenced test for identifying children with language problems and pinpointing specific types of deficiencies. The *TOLD-P:3* displays adequate technical characteristics for use in classification and instructional programming. The instrument is well written and easy to administer and score. These positive qualities account for the popularity of the *TOLD-P:3* among speech clinicians and special educators.

Test of Language Development-Intermediate, Third Edition

The *Test of Language Development-Intermediate, Third Edition (TOLD-I:3)* (Hammill & Newcomer, 1997) is a comprehensive, norm-referenced, individually administered test of spoken language for children from 8 through 12 years of age. A summary of the *TOLD-I-3* appears in Table 10–8. The six *TOLD-I:3* subtests are as follows:

Subtest	Specific Skill	Structural Component
Sentence combining	Constructing sentences	Syntax
Picture vocabulary	Understanding word relationships	Semantics
Word ordering	Making sentences	Syntax
Generals	Understanding abstract words	Semantics
Grammatic comprehension	Understanding grammar in comprehension sentences	Syntax
Malapropisms	Correcting ridiculous sentences	Semantics

Table 10–8   *Test of Language Development-Intermediate, Third Edition*

Type of Test:	Norm referenced, individually administered
Purpose:	Comprehensive diagnostic assessment of language abilities
Content Areas:	Sentence combining, picture vocabulary, word ordering, generals, spoken language skills, grammatic comprehension, and malapropisms
Administration Time:	Approximately 1 hour
Age Levels:	8–12 years
Suitable for:	Students with mild and moderate disabilities, including speech and language impairments, learning disabilities, emotional disturbance, and educable mental retardation
Scores:	Standard scores, percentiles, and age-equivalent scores consistency
In Short:	This well-written diagnostic test of language ability is useful for identifying students with language disorders, isolating particular types of disorders, and using the results to develop intervention programs.

Materials for the *TOLD-I:3* The *TOLD-I:3* kit includes an examiner's manual, a picture book, and 25 profile/examiner record forms. An optional computer scoring system helps to score the *TOLD-I:3* and generates a multipage report.

Administration and Scoring of the *TOLD-I:3* Designed for individual administration, the *TOLD-I:3* takes about an hour to administer and score. Results can be reported as standard scores, percentiles, or age equivalents. The scoresheet includes a profile for visual presentation of results and for illustrating individual strengths and deficiencies in basic language abilities.

Technical Characteristics of the *TOLD-I:3* The *TOLD-I:3* was standardized using a sample group of more than 700 children from 19 states. Test reliability was investigated using coefficient alpha and test-retest methodology. The manual provides evidence to support the content, concurrent, and construct validity of the *TOLD-I:3*. Overall, the test exhibits adequate technical characteristics for use as a norm-referenced instrument.

Summary of the *TOLD-I:3* The intermediate version of the *Test of Language Development, Third Edition*, is an individually administered, norm-referenced test for identifying children with language problems and pinpointing individual strengths and deficiencies in basic language abilities. The well-written, easy-to-administer *TOLD-I:3* is one of the most popular tests of spoken language.

Test of Adolescent and Adult Language–3

The *Test of Adolescent and Adult Language–3 (TOAL-3)* (Hammill et al., 1994) is a norm-referenced measure of the receptive and expressive language abilities of students from age 12 through 24 years. One of only a few instruments specifically designed

Table 10–9 *Test of Adolescent and Adult Language-3 (TOAL-3)*

Type of Test:	Norm referenced, individually administered
Purpose:	An individually administered diagnostic test of language development
Content Areas:	Vocabulary (semantics) and grammar (syntax) in listening, speaking, reading, and writing
Administration Time:	1–3 hours
Age Levels:	12–24 years
Suitable for:	Students with mild and moderate disabilities, including speech and language impairments, learning disabilities, emotional disturbance, and educable mental retardation
Scores:	A total language standard score and standard scores in 10 areas: listening, speaking, reading, writing, spoken language, written language, vocabulary, grammar, receptive language, and expressive language.
In Short:	Designed for junior high and high school students, the *TOAL-3* is a comprehensive diagnostic test tha measures both expressive and receptive language abilities.

for adolescents, this test includes items that identify performance levels and determine the deficits of students with language delays. The *Test of Adolescent and Adult Language–3* is a comprehensive measure of language abilities, evaluating semantic and syntactical ability in listening, speaking, reading, and writing. A summary of the *TOAL-3* appears in Table 10–9.

Materials for the *TOAL-3* Test kit materials include an examiner's manual, 10 test booklets, 50 answer booklets, and 50 summary/profile sheets. Optional scoring software is available.

Administration and Scoring of the *TOAL-3* It takes from 1 to 3 hours to administer the *TOAL-3*. Giving the test involves using a variety of administration procedures. For example, the test employs a picture vocabulary format to measure listening vocabulary. Several subtests involve reading a series of words or sentences and having the student select from the stimulus words or sentences. In the writing vocabulary subtest, the adolescent reads a word and then writes a sentence using the word. The *TOAL-3* provides a total language standard score and standard scores in 10 composite areas: listening, speaking, reading, writing, spoken language, written language, vocabulary, grammar, receptive language, and expressive language.

Technical Characteristics of the *TOAL-3* The developers derived the *TOAL-3* test scores from the performance of a sample of more than 3,000 people from 22 states and 3 Canadian provinces. Although the sample size is more than adequate, the developers failed to provide details about the sampling plan and the method of subject selection. This lack of information makes it difficult to determine the adequacy of the standardization plan. The test manual presents information on three types of reliability (internal consistency, test-retest, and interscorer), with most coefficients falling in the .80 to .90 range, indicating scores with satisfactory accuracy. The manual also provides data to support the content, criterion-related, and construct validity of the instrument. A description of the effectiveness of the test items and subtests provides an indication of content validity. Several studies compare the test to other language tests. The construct validity of the *TOAL-3* rests primarily on data from a study showing that scores from the instrument discriminate between students with known language disabilities and those without language problems. Overall, the test presents mediocre evidence of validity.

Summary of the *TOAL-3* One of only a few tests designed specifically for junior high and high school students, the *Test of Adolescent and Adult Language–3* provides a norm-referenced measure of several important dimensions of language. This comprehensive diagnostic test evaluates semantic and syntactical ability in the areas of listening, speaking, reading, and writing.

Other Comprehensive Tests of Language Development

In addition to the tests just reviewed, brief reviews of other available comprehensive tests of language development follow. These include tests for very young children from birth to 6 or 7 years of age as well as tests for older children and adolescents.

Bankson Language Test, Second Edition The *Bankson Language Test, Second Edition (BLT-2)* (Bankson, 1990) is a norm-referenced, individually administered test of children's psycholinguistic skills. The *BLT-2* is organized into three categories that assess (1) semantic knowledge including body parts, nouns, verbs, categories, functions, prepositions, and opposites; (2) morphological/syntactical rules including pronouns, verb usage/verb tense, plurals, comparatives/superlatives, negations, and questions; and (3) pragmatics including ritualizing, informing, controlling, and imagining. Designed for children from 3 through 6 years of age, the *BLT-2* results may be reported as standard scores or percentiles. The *BLT-2* includes a long form for diagnostic purposes and a 20-item short form for use in screening.

Clinical Evaluation of Language Fundamentals–3 The norm-referenced, individually administered *Clinical Evaluation of Language Fundamentals-Third Edition (CLEF-3)* (Semel et al., 1995) measures the language skills of children and youth from 3 through 21 years of age. Consisting of 11 subtests, the *CLEF-3* measures receptive and expressive language skills in morphology, syntax, semantics, and memory. The *CLEF-3* takes about 45 minutes to administer and score and produces standard scores, percentile ranks, stanines, and normal curve equivalents. Designed to identify and diagnose language deficits and to measure child progress in developing language skills, the *CLEF-3* has very good technical qualities.

Test of Early Language Development, Second Edition The *Test of Early Language Development, Second Edition (TELD-2)* (Hresko et al., 1991) is a norm-referenced, individually administered test of the language development of children from age 2 through 7 years. The *TELD-2* provides two equivalent forms with results reported as standard scores, percentiles, NCEs, or age equivalents. The *TELD-2* identifies spoken language disorders and isolates particular types of spoken language deficits.

Utah Test of Language Development, Third Edition   The norm-referenced, individually administered *Utah Test of Language Development, Third Edition (UTLD-3)* (Mecham, 1989) measures the expressive and receptive language skills of children from 3 through 9 years of age. The *UTLD-3* takes about 45 minutes to administer and yields subtest scores in language comprehension and language expression as well as an overall total language score.

☑ Comprehension Checklist

The comprehensive tests represent a major category of language assessment. Instead of focusing on a single component, they include separate subtests for evaluating the different structural components of language. Special educators and language pathologists frequently rely on comprehensive tests to identify children with language disorders and to isolate particular types of disorders. They also use comprehensive tests to obtain an overview of language function across domains and to identify strengths, weaknesses, and gaps in skill development. Educators and clinicians use the results of comprehensive testing to develop instructional objectives that respond to the individual needs of students with language delays and disorders.

Assessing Children Who Are Culturally and Linguistically Diverse

The number of children from diverse cultures is predicted to increase to 24 million, or 37% of the school-age population, by the year 2010. **Culturally and linguistically diverse (CLD)** refers to children from minority cultures who know and use two languages. Although students speak many different languages, a majority of CLD students speak Spanish as their native language and acquire English as a second language. Unfortunately, many CLD children, especially those with disabilities, exhibit limited English proficiency. **Limited English proficiency (LEP)** refers to CLD children who display inadequate skills in understanding and speaking the English language. One of the most pressing challenges associated with educating children who are culturally and linguistically diverse is accurate assessment of disabilities (Making Assessments of Diverse Students Meaningful, 1997).

According to experts (Fantini, 1985; Figueroa, 1989), current tests and assessment procedures fail to adequately assess the needs of CLD children with limited English proficiency. One of the central problems surrounding assessment of CLD children is that few standards and guidelines exist for deciding the readiness for testing in English. Another concern is the questionable validity of current options for testing CLD students in their native language. These options include translating tests into a student's native language, using interpreters, using tests with norms in the primary language, and relying on bilingual psychologists to administer tests.

In addition to these options for testing CLD students, evaluators often rely on other practical procedures to ensure that they have all the information needed to make the best possible assessment decisions (*CEC Today,* 1997), including detailed information about a student's school history, medical and health status, and family background. Incorporating such background data into the assessment process helps

Table 10–10   Measures of Language Proficiency in Spanish and English

Measures in Spanish	Percentage of Use
Test de Vocabulario en Imágnes Peabody (TVIP)	67
Expressive and Receptive One-Word Vocabulary Test	53
Batería Woodcock de Proficiencia en el Idioma	51
Dos Amigos Verbal Language Scales	31
Measures in English	
Peabody Picture Vocabulary Test-Revised (PPVT-R)	85
Expressive and Receptive One-Word Vocabulary Test	45
Test of Language Development, Second Edition (TOLD-2)	44
Woodcock Language Proficiency Battery	35

the evaluator to respond to the individual needs of the student. To ensure that they have sufficient information for discussing all relevant aspects of a student's language, evaluators often expand the assessment protocol in other ways as well. For example, assessment may include evaluation of language proficiency in both the first language and in English. In addition, the evaluator may use informal assessment procedures such as spontaneous language sampling, which focuses on language used in interactions with others in real-life settings. In these informal situations, students usually display everyday language that includes phrases and sentences not observable during formal testing. The *Basic Inventory of Natural Language* (Herbert, 1977, 1979, 1983) is an example of an assessment system for obtaining spontaneous language samples in Spanish and 31 other languages. Designed for students from kindergarten through the 12th grade, the inventory scores a language sample in the areas of fluency, complexity, and average sentence length.

Practices for assessing language proficiency were examined in a survey of 859 school psychologists conducted by Ochoa et al. (1996). Current best-practice guidelines recommend that schools conduct their own language proficiency assessments. The study found that 62% of the school psychologists in the study usually conducted their own language proficiency assessments. The most frequently used tests were the *Test de Vocabulario en Imágenes Peabody (TVIP)* and the *Peabody Picture Vocabulary Test-Revised*. A more complete listing of the measures of language proficiency used by school psychologists appears in Table 10–10. Best-practice guidelines recommend that in addition to using formal tests, evaluators should also use informal, nonstandardized methods to obtain a comprehensive profile of a child's language proficiency. The results of the study indicated that half of the school psychologists used informal measures such as spontaneous language samples and student interviews. A detailed list of the informal language assessment methods used by school psychologists appears in Table 10–11. Although most school psychologists conduct their own language proficiency assessments, 38% rely on language proficiency information from outside sources. Because the validity of the information provided by outside sources is often questionable, experts suggest avoiding the use of outside sources in most situations, especially when the information is more than 6 months old.

Table 10–11   Informal Language Assessment Methods

Assessment Method	Percentage of Use
Informal language sample/student interview	30
Observation of student by assessment personnel	24
Parent interview	13
Parent information or report (developmental or educational history and background information)	10

FOCUS 10–3

Assessment Strategies for Children Who Are Culturally and Linguistically Diverse

Screening Strategies

- Evaluate the child's proficiency in the native language and in English.
- Refer for special education assessment only after the child has adjusted to the new culture.
- Look for indicators of language problems beyond language acquisition.

Comprehensive Assessment Strategies

- Avoid relying on outside sources of information regarding language proficiency.
- Use current language assessment data (no more than 6 months old).
- Obtain and use both formal and informal assessment information.

Although professionals have developed procedures that address concerns about evaluating children who are culturally and linguistically diverse, more needs to be done to solve the complex issues surrounding assessment of students with limited English proficiency who receive special education services. Specialists in bilingual education, special educators, and researchers are continuing to provide better assessment tests and are also developing additional insights into ways of better using currently available assessment options. A list of assessment strategies for children who are culturally and linguistically diverse appears in Focus 10–3.

Assessing Children With Severe Communication Disorders

Some children have severe communication disorders due to disabilities such as physical impairments, severe mental retardation, developmental disabilities, or severe forms of autism. For example, children with severe cerebral palsy may be nonvocal (unable to speak due to a motor disability). Similarly, some children with severe or

Assessing Children With Severe Communication Disorders

Assessment Pinpoint	Assessment Question
Ecological assessment of communication needs	What language, communication, and interaction occur in the child's every day environment?
Evaluation of met and unmet communication needs	What types of communication does the child presently use?
Appraisal of future communication needs	What types of communication will the child need to use in the future?
Team assessment and selection of a communication system	Which communication system will best meet the child's current and future needs?
Monitoring of progress in learning the system	How well is the child learning to use the system?
Data collection to verify the effectiveness of the communication system	Is the system helping to meet the child's communication needs?

profound mental retardation may be nonverbal (unable to speak due to an intellectual deficit). Many nonvocal children use aided communication systems such as communication boards (with pictures or words) or synthesized speech voice output devices. Likewise, many nonverbal children use unaided communication systems including gestures or sign language to communicate. A description of assessment strategies for children with severe communication disorders appears in Focus 10–4.

Communication systems for nonvocal or nonverbal children fall into two major categories. Aided systems require the use of some sort of device such as a communication board (with pictures, symbols, or words), a communication notebook, or an electronic communication device. An example of an electronic device is the notebook-size Touch Talker, which has a display monitor, voice output, and a pressure-sensitive keyboard. Unaided systems are those in which the child uses only hand or body motions (e.g., gestures, sign language, or fingerspelling) to communicate (Miller, 1993).

The primary assessment question with children who are nonvocal or nonverbal focuses on selecting the appropriate assistive-technology communication devices. More specifically, the Individuals with Disabilities Education Act amendments of 1997 require "functional evaluation" in selecting, acquiring, and using assistive-technology devices. The functional evaluation process should include several components.

One of the essential first steps in the functional assessment process is an ecological evaluation of the child's communication needs. Ecological assessment should produce information about the child's communication needs at home, at school, and in other environments. The next step is to identify the ways the child currently meets communication needs and to determine the child's unmet communication needs. This may lead to setting priorities for communication. The assessment and selection of a specific communication system should be addressed by a team that includes the child (when possible), the parents, a speech and language pathologist, an occupational therapist, a teacher, and other participants as necessary. The team should consider a number of factors including chronological age, imitative ability, motor control, cognitive level of functioning, and desire to communicate. In the process of selecting a communication system, the team should also consider options for meeting future communication needs. Once the team has selected a communication system, progress in learning to use the system should be monitored, and instructional planning should include regular data collection to verify the effectiveness of the chosen system (Cohen & Spenciner, 1998).

Summary

The assessment of language is a complex process, due in part to the intricate structure of language, which consists of the following components:

- Phonemes: language sounds
- Morphemes: the smallest meaningful language units
- Syntax: word formation in phrases and sentences
- Semantics: word meanings and relationships
- Pragmatics: language usage in context

The wide range and variety of tools for assessing language further contributes to the depth of the subject (see Table 10–12, p. 312). The many choices include comprehensive diagnostic tests measuring more than one structural language component, single-skill tests for evaluating individual aspects of language, and clinical procedures such as developmental sentence analysis for measuring language as it occurs in natural settings.

Language is an integral part of daily life at home, in school, and in the community. In addition, it is the foundation of academic learning and, many experts believe, serves as the basis of intellectual development. Because students with disabilities often exhibit deficits in language and poor language skills severely limit a student's potential for success, special education teachers need a working knowledge of available tests and assessment procedures. This knowledge, coupled with hands-on experience, helps special educators, speech and language pathologists, and other professionals make placement and intervention decisions that respond to the often unique language needs of their students.

Chapter Review and Application

Multiple Choice

Directions: Read each item carefully. In the blank beside each item, write the letter of the best response. Each item contains only one best answer. Check your answers with the answer key at the end of the book.

_____ **1.** Which language disabilities are by far the most common among children?
  a. Receptive language delays
  b. Auditory discrimination problems
  c. Voicing errors
  d. Articulation disorders

_____ **2.** Assessing the smallest meaningful units of language involves measuring which language component?
   a. Phonology
   b. Morphology
   c. Pragmatics
   d. Semantics

_____ **3.** Assessing the smallest units of sounds involves measuring which language component?
   a. Phonology
   b. Morphology
   c. Pragmatics
   d. Semantics

_____ **4.** Assessing the way sounds and words go together to make up phrases and meaningful sentences involves measuring which component of language?
   a. Phonology
   b. Morphology
   c. Pragmatics
   d. Syntax

_____ **5.** Assessing the use of language in context involves measuring which component of language?
   a. Phonology
   b. Morphology
   c. Pragmatics
   d. Semantics

_____ **6.** Which component of language is measured by the *Goldman–Fristoe Test of Articulation-Revised?*
   a. Phonology
   b. Morphology
   c. Pragmatics
   d. Semantics

_____ **7.** Spontaneous language sampling does which of the following?
   a. Relies on structured administration procedures
   b. Is usually conducted in a clinical setting
   c. Provides students with an opportunity to practice their language skills
   d. Enables evaluation of a student's everyday language

_____ **8.** What is the minimum number of consecutive utterances in a spontaneous language sample?
   a. 10
   b. 25
   c. 50
   d. 75

_____ **9.** Which assessment measures only receptive language?
   a. *Peabody Picture Vocabulary Test-Third Edition*
   b. *Tests of Language Development-Intermediate, Third Edition*
   c. *Carrow Elicited Language Inventory*
   d. *Let's Talk for Children*

_____ **10.** Which assessment measures communication intents and social communication skills?

    a. *Peabody Picture Vocabulary Test-Third Edition*

    b. *Tests of Language Development-Intermediate, Third Edition*

    c. *Carrow Elicited Language Inventory*

    d. *Let's Talk for Children*

Short Answers

Directions: Review your understanding of the material in this chapter by answering the following short answer questions. Compare your responses with the sample answers at the end of the book. Your responses should contain information that is similar to but not exactly the same as the information in the sample answers.

1. Review the suggestions for linking assessment with instruction that appear at the beginning of the chapter. Which three of the suggested procedures would you be most likely to use in your classroom? Why?

2. What are the three informal measures for assessing morphology and syntax described in the chapter? What advantages do they have over formal, standardized testing? Which one seems best to you? Why?

3. The *Peabody Picture Vocabulary Test-Third Edition (PPVT-III)* is one of the most widely used language tests. Why is it used so widely with children who have special needs? Would you use it in your classroom? Why or why not?

4. Which three issues surrounding the assessment of students who are culturally and linguistically diverse (CLD) do you consider to be the most critical? Why?

References

Bankson, N. W. (1990). *Bankson Language Test-2.* Austin, TX: PRO-ED.

Boehm, A. E. (1976). *Boehm Resources Guide for Basic Concept Teaching.* San Antonio, TX: Psychological Corporation.

———(1986a). *Boehm Test of Basic Concepts-Revised.* San Antonio, TX: Psychological Corporation.

———(1986b). *Boehm Test of Basic Concepts-Preschool Edition.* San Antonio, TX: Psychological Corporation.

Brown, R. (1973). *A First Language.* Cambridge, MA: Harvard University Press.

Carlisle, J. F., & Johnson, D. J. (1989). Assessment of school-aged children. In L. B. Silver (Ed.), *The assessment of learning disabilities.* Boston: Little, Brown, pp. 73–110.

Carrow, E. (1974). *Carrow Elicited Language Inventory.* Austin, TX: Learning Concepts.

Carrow-Woolfolk, E. (1985). *Test for Auditory Comprehension of Language-Revised.* Austin, TX: PRO-ED.

———(1995). *Oral and Written Language Scales: Manual for Listening Comprehension and Oral Expression.* Circle Pines, MN: American Guidance Service.

Clinical Evaluation of Language Fundamentals-3 (CLEF-3) (Semel, Wiig, & Secord, 1995).

Cohen, L. G., & Spenciner, L. J. (1998). *Assessment of Children and Youth.* New York: Longman.

Crabtree, M. (1963). *The Houston Test of Language Development.* Houston: Houston Test Company.

Critchlow, D. E. (1996). *Dos Amigos Verbal Language Scales.* Novato, CA: Academic Therapy.

Dunn, L. M., & Dunn, L. M. (1997). *Peabody Picture Vocabulary Test-Third Edition.* Circle Pines, MN: American Guidance Service

Dunn, L. M., Lugo, D. E., Padilla, E. R., & Dunn, L. E. (1986) *TVIP: Test de Vocabulario en Imágenes Peabody.* Circle Pines, MN: American Guidance Service.

Fantini, A. E. (1985). *Language Acquisition of a Bilingual Child: A Sociolinguistic Perspective.* San Diego: College Hill Press.

Figueroa, R. A. (1989). Psychological testing of linguistic-minority students. *Exceptional Children* 56, 145–53.

Gardner, M. F. (1985). *Receptive One-Word Picture Vocabulary Test.* Novato, CA: Academic Therapy.

——— (1990). *Expressive One-Word Picture Vocabulary Test-Revised.* Novato, CA: Academic Therapy.

Gardner, M. F., & Brownell, R. (1983). *Expressive One-Word Picture Vocabulary Test: Upper Extension.* Novato, CA: Academic Therapy.

——— (1987). *Receptive One-Word Picture Vocabulary Test: Upper Extension.* Novato, CA: Academic Therapy.

Goldman, R., & Fristoe, M. (1986). *Goldman–Fristoe Test of Articulation-Revised.* Circle Pines, MN: American Guidance Service.

Goldman, R., Fristoe, M., & Woodcock, R. W. (1976). *Goldman–Fristoe–Woodcock Test of Auditory Discrimination.* Circle Pines, MN: American Guidance Service.

Hammill, D. D., Brown, V. L., Larsen, S. C., & Wiederholt, J. L. (1994). *Test of Adolescent and Adult Language-3.* Austin, TX: PRO-ED.

Hammill, D. D., & Newcomer, P. L. (1997). *Test of Language Development: Intermediate* (3d ed.) Austin, TX: PRO-ED.

Herbert, C. H. (1977, 1979, 1983). *Basic Inventory of Natural Language.* Monterey, CA: Publishers Test Service.

Hresko, W. P., Reid, D. K., & Hammill, D. D. (1991). *Test of Early Language Development* (2d ed.). Austin, TX: PRO-ED.

Khan, L., & Lewis, N. (1983). *Khan–Lewis Phonological Analysis.* Circle Pines, MN: American Guidance Service.

Langdon, H. W. (1989). Language disorder or difference? Assessing the language skills of Hispanic students. *Exceptional Children* 56, 160–67.

Lee, L. L. (1974). *Developmental Sentence Analysis.* Evanston, IL: Northwestern University Press.

Lee, L. L., Koenigsknecht, R. A., & Mulhern, S. T. (1975). *Interactive Language Development Teaching.* Evanston, IL: Northwestern University Press.

Making assessments of diverse students meaningful. (1997). *CEC Today* 4 (4), 1 & 9.

Mecham, M. J. (1989). *Utah Test of Language Development.* Austin, TX: PRO-ED.

Miller, J. M. (1993). Augmentative and alternative communication. In M. E. Snell (Ed.), *Instruction of Students With Severe Disabilities* (4th ed.). Upper Saddle River, NJ: Merrill/Prentice Hall, 319–46.

Newcomer, P. L., & Hammill, D. D. (1997). *Test of Language Development-Primary* (3d ed.). Austin, TX: PRO-ED.

Ochoa, H. O., Galarza A., & Gonzalez, D. (1996). An investigation of school psychologists' assessment practices with bilingual and limited-English-proficient children. *Diagnostique* (21, 4). 17–36.

Overton, T. (1992). *Assessment in Special Education: An Applied Approach.* New York: Merrill/Macmillan.

Semel, E., Wiig, E. H., & Secord, W. (1995). *Clinical Evaluation of Language Fundamentals* (3d. ed.). San Antonio, TX: Psychological Corporation.

Shulman, B. B. (1986). *Test of Pragmatic Skills* (rev. ed.). Tucson, AZ: Communication Skill Builders.

Wallace, G., & Hammill, D. D. (1994). *Comprehensive Receptive and Expressive Vocabulary Test.* Austin, TX: PRO–ED.

———. (1997a). *Comprehensive Receptive and Expressive Vocabulary Test-Adult.* Austin, TX: PRO–ED.

———. (1997b). *Comprehensive Receptive and Expressive Vocabulary Test-Computer Administered.* Austin, TX: PRO–ED.

Wiig, E. H. (1982a). *Let's Talk Inventory for Adolescents.* Columbus, OH: Merrill.

———. (1982b). *Let's Talk: Developing Prosocial Communication Skills.* Columbus, OH: Merrill.

Wiig, E. H., & Bray, C. M. (1983). *Let's Talk for Children.* Columbus, OH: Merrill.

Wiig, E. H., & Semel, E. (1984). *Language Assessment and Intervention for the Learning Disabled* (2d ed.).
New York: Merrill/Macmillan.

Williams, K. T. (1997). *Expressive Vocabulary Test.* Circle Pines, MN: American Guidance Service.

Woodcock, R. W. (1981). *Batería Woodcock de Proficiencia en el Idioma.* Itasca, IL: Riverside Publishing.

———. (1991). *Woodcock Language Proficiency Battery-Revised.* Itasca, IL: Riverside Publishing.

Woodcock, R. W., & Muñoz–Sandoval, A. F. (1996). *Batería Woodcock–Muñoz-Revisada.* Itasca, IL: Riverside Publishing.

Table 10–12   Review of Language Tests

Name of Test	Type of Test	Suitable for Individuals Who Are	Brief Description of Test	Purpose of Administering Test
Bankson Language Test, Second Edition (BLT-2) (Bankson, 1990)	Norm referenced, individually administered	3–6 years	Organized into three general categories: semantic knowledge, morphological/ syntactical rules, pragmatics	To measure children's psycholinguistic abilities
Bateria Woodcock–Muñoz-Revisada (Woodcock & Muñoz-Sandoval, 1996)	Norm referenced, individually administered	2–90+ years	The parallel Spanish version of the *Woodcock–Johnson Pyscho-Educational Battery-Revised*	To assess cognitive abilities and achievement levels in Spanish-speaking children and adults
Bateria Woodcock de Proficiencia en el Idioma (Woodcock, 1981)	Norm referenced, individually administered	3–17 years, adults, older adults	Measures oral language, reading, and written language. All subtests taken directly from the *Woodcock–Johnson Psycho-Educational Battery.* A revised version, *Batería Woodcock–Muñoz-Revisada,* is available.	To assess cognitive abilities and achievement levels in Spanish-speaking children and adults
Boehm Test of Basic Concepts-Revised (BTBC-R) (Boehm, 1986a)	Norm referenced, group or individual administration	Kindergarten–grade 2	Contains 50 concepts for measuring understanding in three major context categories: space (e.g., top, next to, and through), quantity (e.g., first, most, and part), and time (e.g., starting, after, and before)	To evaluate mastery of the basic concepts essential for understanding the verbal instructions necessary for early school achievement
Boehm Test of Basic Concepts-Preschool Version (BTBC-PV) (Boehm, 1986b)	Norm referenced, group or individual administration	3–5 years	A preschool version of the *Boehm Test of Basic Concepts* that measures 26 basic concepts	To evaluate mastery of the basic concepts essential for understanding the verbal instructions necessary for early school achievement

*Tests marked with asterisks are featured in tables in this chapter.

Table 10–12 *(continued)*

Name of Test	Type of Test	Suitable for Individuals Who Are	Brief Description of Test	Purpose of Administering Test
Carrow Elicited Language Inventory (CELI) (Carrow, 1974)	Criterion referenced, individually administered	3–7 years	Measures the following grammatical forms: 41 pronouns, 14 prepositions, 7 conjunctions, 41 articles, 9 adverbs, 5 *wh-* questions, 13 negatives, 59 nouns, 7 adjectives, 103 verbs, 8 infinitives, and 1 gerund	To provide a systematic evaluation of grammatical ability
Clinical Evaluation of of Language Fundamentals–Third Edition (CLEF-3) (Semel et al., 1995)	Norm referenced, individually administered	3–21 years	Consists of 11 subtests that measure receptive and expressive language skills in morphology, syntax, semantics, and memory	To identify and diagnose language deficits and to measure child progress in developing language skills
Comprehensive Receptive and Expressive Vocabulary Test (CREVT) (Wallace & Hammill, 1994)	Norm referenced, individually administered	4–18 years	Includes an expressive and a receptive subtest and two equivalent forms	To identify children who are significantly below their peers in oral vocabulary proficiency
Comprehensive Receptive and Expressive Vocabulary Test-Adult (CREVT-A) (Wallace & Hammill, 1997a)	Norm referenced, individually administered	18–retirement	Includes an expressive and a receptive subtest and two equivalent forms	To identify adults who are significantly below their peers in oral vocabulary proficiency
Comprehensive Receptive and Expressive Vocabulary Test-Computer Administered (CREVT-CA) (Wallace & Hammill, 1997b)	Norm referenced, individually administered	4–18 years	An interactive multimedia test that can be given entirely on a home or office computer	To identify children who are significantly below their peers in oral vocabulary proficiency
Dos Amigos Verbal Language Scales (Critchlow, 1996)	Norm-referenced, individually administered screening test	School-age children	Consists of two separate scales, English and Spanish, each of which contains a list of 85 stimulus words and their opposites, arranged in ascending order of difficulty	To reveal the comparative development of a child's English and Spanish and to identify the child's dominant language

Table 10–12 *(continued)*

Name of Test	Type of Test	Suitable for Individuals Who Are	Brief Description of Test	Purpose of Administering Test
Expressive One-Word Picture Vocabulary Test-Revised (EOWPVT-R) (Gardner, 1990).	Norm-referenced, individually administered screening test	2–11 years	Consists of 100 black-and-white line drawings of common objects and collections of objects	To measure the verbal expression of language by having children make word-picture associations
Expressive One-Word Picture Vocabulary Test: Upper Extension (Gardner & Brownell, 1983)	Norm-referenced, individually administered screening test	12–15 years	An upper extension of the original *Expressive One-Word Picture Vocabulary Test*	To assess the expressive vocabulary by having adolescents make word-picture associations
Expressive Vocabulary Test (EVT) (Williams, 1997)	Norm-referenced, individually administered screening test	2.5–85+ years	Includes two types of items, labeling and synonyms; items are presented with pictures, and the child responds to each item with a one-word answer	To measure expressive vocabulary and word retrieval for Standard American English
*Goldman–Fristoe Test of Articulation-Revised (Goldman & Fristoe, 1986)	Criterion referenced, individually administered	2–6 years	Contains subtests for measuring articulation of speech sounds, sound production in connected speech, and the ability to correct misarticulated sounds when given a model of correct production	For speech pathologists to use before beginning therapy and for audiologists and special educators to use as a diagnostic tool
*Goldman–Fristoe–Woodcock Test of Auditory Discrimination (GFW) (Goldman et al., 1976)	Norm-referenced, individually administered screening test	4 years–adulthood	Contains three parts: a training procedure, a quiet subtest, and a noise subtest	To measure the ability to differentiate between speech sounds in quiet and noisy situations
Khan–Lewis Phonological Analysis (KLPA) (Khan & Lewis, 1983)	Criterion referenced, individually administered	2–5 years	An in-depth measure of phonological processes that assesses 15 common disorders such as initial voicing and glottal replacement	To use with the *Goldman–Fristoe Test of Articulation* to get more detailed assessment information

Table 10–12 *(continued)*

Name of Test	Type of Test	Suitable for Individuals Who Are	Brief Description of Test	Purpose of Administering Test
Oral and Written Language Scales– Listening Compre- hension Scale and Oral Expression Scale (Carrow-Woolfolk, 1995)	Norm-referenced, indi- vidually administered	3–21 years	The *Listening Com- prehension Scale* measures receptive language and con- sists of 3 examples and 111 items; the *Oral Expression Scale* measures the under- standing and use of spoken language and consists of 2 examples and 96 items	To measure language knowledge and pro- cessing skills in children and adolescents includ- ing identifying children with language deficits, designing a variety of language intervention tasks, and monitoring growth in language skills
*Peabody Picture Vocabulary Test– Third Edition (PPVT-III) (Dunn et al., 1997)	Norm-referenced, indi- vidually administered screening test	2.5 years– adulthood	Contains 204 items; each item consists of four simple line draw- ings on a page; the child selects a draw- ing (from among the four choices) that best represents the meaning of each word presented orally	To assess receptive lan- language (hearing) vocabulary
Receptive One-Word Picture Vocabulary Test (ROWPVT) (Gardner, 1985)	Norm-referenced, indi- vidually administered screening test	2–11 years	Designed as a com- panion test to the *Expressive One-Word Vocabulary Test- Revised*	To assess receptive hearing vocabulary
Receptive One-Word Picture Vocabulary Test: Upper Extension (Gardner & Brownell, 1987)	Norm-referenced, indi- vidually administered screening test	12–15 years	An upper extension of the *Receptive One-Word Picture Vocabulary Test*	To assess receptive hearing vocabulary
*Test of Adolescent and Adult Language-3 *(TOAL-3)* (Hammill et al., 1994)	Norm-referenced, indi- vidually administered comprehensive test	12–24 years	A comprehensive measure of language abilities, evaluating semantic and syntac- stic ability in listen- ing, speaking, read- ing, and writing	To identify performance levels in receptive and expressive language and to determine the deficits of students with language delays

Table 10–12 (continued)

Name of Test	Type of Test	Suitable for Individuals Who Are	Brief Description of Test	Purpose of Administering Test
*Test of Auditory Comprehension of Language-Revised (TACL-R) (Carrow-Woolfolk, 1985)	Norm-referenced, individually administered comprehensive test	3–9 years	Measures auditory comprehension of language in three categories: vocabulary (literal meaning of words), morphology (grammatical morphemes), and syntax (meaning from sentences)	To identify children with language deficits, measure school readiness, plan instructional programs, and monitor student progress
Test of Early Language Development, Second Edition (TELD-2) (Hresko et al., 1991)	Norm referenced, individually administered	2–7 years	Provides two equivalent forms with results reported as standard scores, percentiles, NCEs, or age equivalents	To identify spoken language disorders and to isolate particular types of spoken language deficits
*Test of Language Development-Intermediate, Third Edition (TOLD-I:3) (Newcomer & Hammill, 1997)	Norm-referenced, individually administered	8–12 years	Contains six subtests: sentence combining, picture vocabulary, word ordering, generals, grammatic comprehension, and malapropisms	To identify spoken language disorders and to isolate particular types of spoken language deficits
*Test of Language Development-Primary, Third Edition (TOLD-P:3) (Newcomer & Hammill, 1997)	Norm referenced, individually administered	4–8 years	Contains nine subtests: picture vocabulary, relational vocabulary, oral vocabulary, grammatic understanding, grammatic completion, sentence imitation, word discrimination, phonemic analysis, and word articulation	To identify spoken language disorders and to isolate particular types of spoken language deficits
*Test of Pragmatic Skills (Shulman, 1986)	Criterion referenced, individually administered	3–8 years	Measures 10 different communicative intents: requesting information, requesting action, rejecting or denying, naming or labeling, answering or responding, informing, reasoning, summoning or calling, greeting, and closing conversation	To analyze expressive language as it occurs in the context of structured play interactions

Table 10–12 *(continued)*

Name of Test	Type of Test	Suitable for Individuals Who Are	Brief Description of Test	Purpose of Administering Test
(TVIP) Test de Vocabluario en Imágenes Peabody (Dunn et al., 1986)	Norm referenced, individually administered	2.5–18 years	Based on the *Peabody Picture Vocabulary Test-Revised,* the *TVIP* contains 125 translated items to assess the receptive vocabulary of Spanish-speaking and bilingual students	Designed to evaluate the receptive vocabulary development of Spanish-speaking preschool children, screen Spanish-speaking children entering kindergarten or first grade, determine the more effective language instruction for bilingual children, and evaluate the Spanish vocabulary of older students
Utah Test of Language Development, Third Edition (UTLD-3) (Mecham, 1989)	Norm referenced, individually administered	3–9 years	Includes a language comprehension subtest and a language expression subtest	To measure expressive and receptive language skills
Woodcock Language Proficiency Battery-Revised (WLPB-R) (Woodcock, 1991)	Norm referenced, individually administered	2–90+ years	Includes measures of oral language, broad reading ability, basic reading skills, reading comprehension, broad written language, basic writing skills, written expression, punctuation, spelling usage, and handwriting	To measure academic achievement in oral language, reading, and written language

CHAPTER 11

Assessment of Behavior

Overview

Special educators serve many students with emotional and behavioral problems. Thus assessment of behavior represents an important component of the measurement and evaluation process. The available tests and techniques for assessing behavior help special educators identify behavior problems, and the evaluation results help them develop intervention programs. In addition, assessment of behavior encompasses other important dimensions of conduct and personality, which include the self-concept, attitudes, and interests of students.

In this chapter you learn the essential concepts and techniques associated with the assessment of behavior. To achieve this goal, we review the principles that guide special educators in assessing behavior, and we examine various tests used in the assessment process, including the following:

- Behavior rating scales.
- Behavioral observations.
- Self-concept measures.
- Methods for assessing school attitudes and interests.
- Tests of attention deficit hyperactivity disorder (ADHD).

Throughout the chapter we consider current trends and issues in measuring and evaluating behavior as related to assessment in special education.

Objectives

After reading this chapter, you will be prepared to do the following:

- Understand the principles for assessing behavior.
- Understand the specific behaviors measured by behavior rating scales and checklists.
- Use behavior rating scales and checklists.
- Conduct behavioral observations.
- Implement behavioral recording systems to assess student conduct and inappropriate behavior.
- Understand the emotions that self-concept inventories measure.
- Use representative self-concept inventories.
- Use tests to evaluate student attitudes and interests.
- Use tests and rating scales to assess attention deficit hyperactivity disorder.

The Importance of Assessing Behavior

The following account illustrates the use of assessment in identifying and placing a student with a severe behavior disorder.

David displayed extreme difficulty controlling his behavior in the regular classroom and the special education resource room. He became easily upset and was often verbally and sometimes physically aggressive. When doing classwork, David usually began a task and then quickly became distracted. When prompted to return to work, he often demonstrated his anger by tearing up his papers. He seemed unaware of the consequences of his conduct.

David's disturbing behaviors prompted his special education and regular education teachers to inquire about placing David in a program for children with severe emotional disturbance. The teachers discovered that the process involved gathering quite a bit of assessment data. For example, the coordinator of the staffing team asked David's special education and regular education teachers to complete behavior rating scales and to document attempted interventions designed to control his aggressive behavior. In addition, the teachers were asked to arrange for the school counselor to conduct two observations of David's behavior in the classroom. Furthermore, the staffing coordinator arranged for a psychologist to conduct a clinical interview with David. Finally, the staffing team used the results from these assessments, along with other relevant information, to recommend placing David in a program for students with severe emotional disturbance.

Special educators often serve students who, like David, display severe disruptive behaviors. Unfortunately, these problems, if ignored, not only interfere with the educational progress of the individual student but often impede the performance of the entire class. Therefore teachers must intervene to manage student misbehavior and disruptions. One of the essential components in the intervention process is assessment.

Assessment of behavior involves the use of several types of measurement and evaluation procedures. In the classroom, teachers usually rely on practical, applied procedures such as observation of student behavior. However, when professionals conduct assessment to determine eligibility and make placement decisions, they use more formal evaluation procedures. Because **student behavior** is a broad term that encompasses a range of nonacademic behaviors, assessment includes evaluating other aspects of social–emotional development, which include student self-concept and attitudes as well as behaviors outside the classroom. A thorough assessment, then, identifies the influence school, family, neighborhood, and community have on a child's behavior and social–emotional development.

As you can see, assessment of behavior consists of more than dealing with conduct disorders. In fact, it includes procedures for making a range of decisions about behavior associated with the **affective domain,** which refers to opinions, attitudes, and behaviors derived from emotions rather than from thought. Obviously, measuring affective behavior is more subjective than measuring cognitive skills such as problem-solving ability and math achievement or physical ability such as running speed and throwing accuracy. One of the reasons for this subjectivity is that behavior occurs within the context of complex interaction patterns among student, teacher, and peers. Furthermore, behavior disorders involve personal and emotional feelings and values about acceptable limits for behavior. Unfortunately, deciding whether a particular behavior falls beyond acceptable limits is not as clear-cut as grading a math worksheet or a spelling test. Behavior involves social, emotional, family, and community factors that make precise measurement difficult. For this reason, the procedures for assessing behavior differ in form and content from the procedures for assessing cognitive indicators. Fortunately, however, a set of principles exists for professionals to follow as a guide to assessing behavior.

Principles for Assessing Behavior

The following principles guide special educators in assessing students with behavior problems and include important considerations regarding the proper use of tests, observation procedures, and other sources of assessment information.

- Most measures of behavior do not test in the traditional sense. Instead, they provide a structured method for recording observations of behavior. These assessment procedures include behavior rating scales, behavioral observations, and self-concept inventories.
- The assessment of behavior is a dynamic process that requires a competent observer to make subjective decisions about attitudes and conduct. For example, teachers complete behavior rating scales on the basis of their professional judgment and experience coupled with their knowledge of a student's typical conduct in the classroom. Likewise, when using direct observation to measure student misbehavior, teachers rely on their experience and professional judgment to select appropriate target behaviors and measurement procedures.
- The assessment of behavior requires the evaluator to apply specific and often technical behavioral observation procedures. Accurate and effective use of these procedures requires specialized training.
- In addition to using rating scales and direct observation, special educators rely on a variety of other sources of information when assessing student behavior, including formal and informal communication with parents, peers, teachers, and students; review of school records that detail social and educational history; and the influence of social, emotional, family, and community factors.

Why Do We Assess the Behavior of Children With Special Needs?

As teachers we are trained to monitor and assess students, and student behavior is always one of our primary concerns. Sometimes we just generally keep an eye on things to make sure that the classroom is orderly, anticipate difficult situations, and keep track of how things are going. During our general observations, we may notice important behaviors or events that require attention: Juan is upset and agitated, Felicia is asleep, or two students are yelling at each other right outside the classroom door. In educational settings with children who have behavior disorders, we may look for very specific behaviors such as signs of impending verbal or physical aggression, appropriate social behavior that should be reinforced, or student attention to keep on task. We use the information gained from our observations to make assessment decisions about student behavior, especially as it affects academic performance.

FOCUS 11–1

FOCUS 11–1

Why Do We Assess the Behavior of Children With Special Needs?

- To screen for indications of emotional disturbance or behavior disorders
- To diagnose children with emotional disturbance or behavior disorders
- To develop plans for managing student behavior and improving academic performance
- To measure the effectiveness of intervention programs

We use the data in screening and diagnostic evaluation, but most important, we use it to devise plans for managing student behavior, improving academic performance, and measuring the effectiveness of intervention programs. Focus 11–1 summarizes the reasons that we assess children with special needs.

✔ Comprehension Checklist

Teachers in special education must often intervene to manage student misbehavior. One of the essential components of effective intervention is appropriate assessment. Special educators assess student behavior by a variety of tests and evaluation procedures that include behavior rating scales, behavioral observations, and self-concept inventories. Teachers also use functional assessment (see Focus 11–2), which is a specialized type of behavior assessment. When assessing student behavior, special educators must follow established principles to ensure accurate information.

Behavior Rating Scales

Special educators use behavior rating scales to evaluate the conduct of students who exhibit inappropriate behavior. **Behavior rating scales** are written questionnaires containing lists of behaviors that raters complete by assigning a rating (usually based on a scale of 1 to 5) to each item on the checklist. Raters are usually teachers, parents, or other primary care givers who are familiar with a student's typical conduct. Special educators may choose from a variety of rating scales, including instruments designed specifically for evaluating student behavior in school programs, for measuring student behavior at home and in the community, and for assessing student behavior in specialized treatment programs such as residential centers and hospital psychiatric wards.

Because they consist of checklists of behaviors rated by an evaluator, most scales take only 20 minutes or so to complete. The checklist format is easy to quickly administer and score. However, behavior scales use an indirect, pencil-on-paper type of measurement that relies on ratings from informants such as teachers and parents. Because the ratings of informants can be biased, results from rating scales may not always match the actual behavior of the student. In addition, most rating scales and checklists are

FOCUS 11–2

Using Functional Assessment of Behavior With Culturally Diverse Students

The number of minority children in the United States is increasing dramatically, with Hispanic children making up the fastest-growing group. Unfortunately, data suggest that African-American and Hispanic students tend to be overrepresented in special education programs, whereas Asian students tend to be underrepresented. Data also suggest that minority children tend to be overreferred for possible behavior problems.

Several factors may contribute to these problems. First, children from culturally diverse backgrounds may have language differences that influence how others perceive and interact with them. These differences may be interpreted as behavior problems. Second, educators may have preconceived biases toward culturally different children that may ultimately lead to referral and placement in special education programs for children with behavior problems. Consequently, children from culturally different groups are at risk for misidentification because of higher referral rates.

These factors all point to the need for assessment practices that reduce the overreferral of minority children and minimize test bias. Functional assessment is one approach that may help because it involves directly evaluating student behavior and performance under existing teaching conditions, altering instructional practices to improve student performance, and monitoring student performance on a continuous basis. Because functional assessment is direct and continuous, it minimizes bias due to cultural differences.

Specific functional assessment procedures include conducting interviews, using rating scales, collecting direct observation data, and using functional analysis. Functional analysis is a specialized element of functional assessment that involves direct manipulation of antecedent and consequent variables identified during interviews and observations. For example, a child may be observed in a series of classroom activities, some of which include significant task demands and some of which do not. If the student displays more frequent inappropriate behavior during demanding activities, the teacher can modify the task demands to see whether this reduces inappropriate behavior and thus eliminates the need for a referral.

Much more needs to be done to reduce referrals and to minimize bias in testing. One way to respond to this challenge is to develop greater awareness of the potential for using functional assessment with children from culturally diverse backgrounds who display behavior problems.

general screening measures that provide an overview of behavior problems rather than in-depth diagnostic information. For these reasons, most professionals rely on rating scales for screening and initial identification of student behavior problems rather than for developing instructional objectives.

Representative Behavior Rating Scales

Two representative behavior rating scales are the *Devereux Behavior Rating Scale-School Form* and the *Social Skills Rating System*. Detailed reviews of these instruments appear in the following sections.

Devereux Behavior Rating Scale-School Form

The norm-referenced, individually administered *Devereux Behavior Rating Scale-School Form* (Naglieri et al., 1993) is a checklist for identifying behaviors that may indicate severe emotional disturbance in children and adolescents. The 40-item *Devereux School Form* is also useful for obtaining an ongoing record of classroom behavior, measuring behavior change, facilitating communication among professionals and parents, and conducting educational research. The *Devereux School Form* is designed for students ages 5–18 years to measure behaviors that, according to experienced teachers, interfere with academic functioning and achievement. The four subscales measure the areas addressed in the federal definition of serious emotional disturbance: interpersonal problems, inappropriate behaviors and feelings, depression, and physical symptoms and fears. A summary of the *Devereux Behavior Rating Scale-School Form* appears in Table 11–1.

Materials for the *Devereux School Form*   *Devereux School Form* materials include a manual and separate scoring forms for children ages 5–12 and for adolescents ages 13–18.

Administration and Scoring of the *Devereux School Form*   Teachers, psychologists, guidance counselors, and other assessment professionals can use the *Devereux School Form*. The informants who rate the items may include teachers who have observed a student in a classroom setting, parents, or primary care givers. Teacher raters need observation time before rating a student's behavior. The length of time depends on the class size and the amount of time the student spends with a teacher. The actual rating with the scales takes only 5 to 10 minutes. The scale is scored by recording

Table 11–1   *Devereux Behavior Rating Scale-School Form*

Type of Test:	Norm referenced, individually administered
Purpose:	Identifying behaviors that may indicate severe emotional disturbance
Content Areas:	Interpersonal problems, inappropriate behaviors and feelings, depression, and physical symptoms and fears
Administration Time:	5–10 minutes
Age Levels:	5–18 years
Suitable for:	Detecting severe emotional disturbance in students
Scores:	Total scale score and subscale scores
In Short:	A useful instrument for identifying problem behaviors and measuring behavior change

the rating for each item on a profile form. Available scores include a total scale score, subscale scores, and problem item scores for identifying specific problem behaviors for treatment. The subscale scores can help in IEP and intervention program development.

Technical Characteristics of the *Devereux School Form*   The developers standardized the *Devereux School Form* with a national sample of more than 3,000 cases. The standardization study produced separate norms for males and females, and for parent and teacher raters.

Summary of the *Devereux School Form*   The *Devereux Behavior Rating Scale-School Form* is a questionnaire for rating problem behaviors and is useful for identifying students with severe emotional disturbance, comparing results across informants (i.e., teachers and parents), identifying problem behaviors in the classroom, providing an ongoing record of behavior, measuring behavior change, and providing a means for communication among professionals and parents.

Social Skills Rating System

The *Social Skills Rating System (SSRS)* (Gresham & Elliot, 1990) consists of a standardized series of questionnaires that measure the frequency and importance of behaviors that affect performance at home and in school. Designed for use with students from age 3 to 18 years, the *SSRS* includes rating forms that are completed by the teacher, the parents, and the child. The authors developed the *SSRS* to assist in planning intervention programs for students with behavior disorders, learning disabilities, or mild mental retardation, or with any student who exhibits social or behavior problems. A summary of the *SSRS* appears in Table 11–2. The *SSRS* measures behavior in three domains:

1. Social skills
   a. Cooperation
   b. Assertion
   c. Responsibility
   d. Self-control
2. Problem behaviors
   a. Externalizing problems
   b. Internalizing problems
   c. Hyperactivity
3. Academic competence
   a. Reading and mathematics
   b. Motivation
   c. Parental support
   d. General cognitive functioning

Materials for the *SSRS*   *SSRS* materials consist of a test manual, three rating forms (teacher, parent, and student versions), and an assessment and intervention planning record. The teacher and parent rating forms are available for three levels: preschool, kindergarten through grade 6, and grades 7 through 12. The student self-rating form is available at two levels: grades 3 through 6 and grades 7 through 12. The

Table 11–2   *Social Skills Rating System (SSRS)*

Type of Test:	Norm referenced, individually administered
Purpose:	Diagnostic rating of social skills and problem behaviors
Content Areas:	Social skills, problem behaviors, and academic competence
Administration Time:	Approximately 60–90 minutes to complete all scales
Age Levels:	3–18 years
Suitable for:	Students with behavior disorders, learning disabilities, mild mental retardation, or any student who exhibits social or behavior problems
Scores:	Behavior levels, standard scores, and percentiles
In Short:	The well-designed *SSRS* uses a multiple-rater system (teacher, parent, and student) to assess social skills and to provide data for developing behavior intervention programs.

assessment and intervention planning form provides a system for summarizing all information obtained from the raters and identifying problem areas in need of intervention. Optional materials include computerized scoring and reporting software that provides behavioral objectives and suggestions for intervention. The software offers eight different report options for analysis of social behavior that include an intervention narrative and a behavioral objective report. Teachers may also use the *Social Skills Intervention Guide* (Elliot & Gresham, 1991), which links intervention strategies directly to *SSRS* assessment and includes 43 lessons with skills grouped around cooperation, assertion, responsibility, empathy, and self-control.

Administration and Scoring of the *SSRS*   Rather than a test given to a child by an evaluator, the *SSRS* is a set of rating scales completed by the child, the teacher, and the parent to measure social skill development. It takes 10 to 25 minutes for respondents to complete their scale and about 5 minutes for the evaluator (usually the teacher or psychologist) to score each scale. The *SSRS* relies on a three-point rating system (0 for never, 1 for sometimes, and 2 for very often) for all scales except the academic competence scale, which uses a five-point system. Scoring involves converting the raw scores from each questionnaire into standard scores, percentiles, and behavior levels. The manual includes detailed illustrations and sample cases that explain the scoring process and the procedures for identifying strengths and weaknesses. The evaluator interprets student performance on the basis of norm-group comparisons and individual score patterns. The manual also provides sample profiles and a list of assessment questions to aid in the interpretation of results.

Technical Characteristics of the *SSRS*   The *SSRS* was standardized with a national sample of more than 4,000 students, including students from racial and ethnic minority groups and students with disabilities. The manual reports average internal consistency coefficients ranging from .90 to .95 for the three major content areas and average coefficients for the individual subtests from .51 to .92. Average test-retest reliability coefficients of teacher and parent ratings were in the .80s, and student rating coefficients were .68. The manual also includes extensive information describing the content and concurrent validity of the *SSRS*. Overall, the *SSRS* exhibits good technical characteristics.

Summary of the *SSRS*   The *Social Skills Rating System* is a well-designed instrument for assessing the social skill development of students from 3 to 18 years of age. It uses a multiple-rater system (teacher, parent, and student) to provide data for assessing children with problem behaviors and for developing IEPs and intervention programs. The *SSRS* evaluates a broad range of behaviors that affect teacher-student relationships, peer acceptance, and academic performance. The three rating forms—teacher, parent, and student—give a comprehensive picture across school, home, and community settings.

Other Behavior Rating Scales

The use of behavior rating scales is widely accepted in special education and related disciplines. Brief descriptions of other available behavior rating scales follow.

Adjustment Scales for Children and Adolescents   The norm-referenced, individually administered *Adjustment Scales for Children and Adolescents (ASCA)* (McDermott, 1993) provide comprehensive assessment of behavior problems, psychopathology, and styles of healthy adjustment. Designed for children ages 5–17, the *ASCA* takes about 20 minutes to administer. The *ASCA* contains 97 problem behavior pinpoints and 26 positive behavior indicators, each presented in one of 29 specific situations involving authority, peers, smaller or weaker youths, recreation, learning, or confrontation. The specific behavior syndromes assessed by the *ASCA* are the following:

- Attention-deficit hyperactive.
- Solitary aggressive (provocative).
- Solitary aggressive (impulsive).
- Oppositional defiant.
- Diffident.
- Avoidant.
- Delinquent.
- Lethargic.

Standardized on a sample of 1,400 children, the *ASCA* provides separate forms designed specifically for male and female children and produces two composite overall adjustment scores and percentiles for the eight behavior syndromes just listed.

Behavior Assessment System for Children   The norm-referenced, individually administered *Behavior Assessment System for Children (BASC)* (Reynolds & Kamphaus, 1992) consists of a set of instruments for evaluating the behaviors, thoughts, and emotions of children and adolescents from 4 through 18 years of age. The three core instruments in the system are a teacher rating scale, a parent rating scale, and a self-report of personality. The system also includes a tool for collecting a structured developmental history and a form for directly observing a child's behavior in the classroom. The system gives a comprehensive picture of the child by providing teacher, parent, and child self-report ratings of behavior along with data from directly observed classroom behavior and information from a developmental history. The *BASC* measures numerous aspects of behavior and personality including positive, adaptive behaviors as well as negative, problematic dimensions. It also provides assessment data linked to ADD and ADHD.

The parent rating scale measures adaptive and problem behavior in community and home settings, contains 130 items, and takes 10–20 minutes to complete. A Spanish translation of the parent rating scale is available. The teacher rating scale measures adaptive and problem behavior in the school setting, contains 130 items, and takes 10–20 minutes to complete. The self-report personality measure assesses children's thoughts and feelings about themselves and their environment using 170 true-false questions that take about 30 minutes to complete.

Optional *BASC* materials include two computerized software packages. The basic software program calculates all scale and composite scores, displays them in table and profile formats, prints a report, and generates a narrative profile. The "plus" software includes all of the basic features plus on-line administration and an extended analysis program that identifies target behaviors for intervention.

Behavior and Emotional Rating Scale The norm-referenced, individually administered *Behavior and Emotional Rating Scale (BERS)* (Epstein & Sharma, 1997) helps measure the personal strengths of children from 5 through 18 years of age. Designed for use in schools, mental health clinics, and child welfare agencies, the *BERS* contains 52 items for measuring five aspects of a child's strength: interpersonal strength, involvement with family, intrapersonal strength, school functioning, and affective strength. Teachers, parents, counselors, or others who know the child can complete the scale in about 10 minutes. The *BERS* was normed using a sample of more than 2,000 children without disabilities and 800 children with emotional and behavioral disorders. Separate norms are available for children diagnosed with emotional and behavioral disorders. It is useful in evaluating children as part of the prereferral process and in placing children in specialized services. It can also help in developing IEP goals and creating intervention programs.

Behavior Rating Profile-2 The *Behavior Rating Profile-2 (BRP-2)* (Brown & Hammill, 1990) is a norm-referenced measure for obtaining information about a child's behavior in a variety of settings. Designed for students from 6 to 18 years of age, the profile consists of scales completed by the student, the parent, and the teacher. Completed by the student's classmates, a **sociogram** is an assessment technique for measuring social acceptance and peer popularity by having students rate each of their classmates in a nonobtrusive manner for the purpose of analyzing the group structure in a classroom and identifying the popularity of individual students. The *BRP-2* uses an ecological approach that measures differences in ratings among teachers, parents, and classmates. **Ecological assessment** considers both student and environmental characteristics (such as the classroom setting, the community, and the family situation) in the evaluation process. In ecological assessment, the evaluator analyzes student behavior within the context of the environment, setting, or situation in which the behavior occurs.

Child Behavior Checklist for Ages 4–16 The *Child Behavior Checklist (CBCL/4–16)* (Achenbach, 1981) is a norm-referenced measure of behavior problems in the form of a checklist completed by an evaluator during an interview with a parent or primary care giver. The *CBCL* provides separate checklists for three age groups: 4–5, 6–11, and 12–16 years.

Child Behavior Checklist for Ages 2–3 The *Child Behavior Checklist for Ages 2–3 (CBCL/2–3)* (Achenbach, 1986) is an adaptation of the original *Child Behavior Checklist* (Achenbach, 1981) for very young children.

Comprehensive Behavior Rating Scale for Children The *Comprehensive Behavior Rating Scale for Children (CBRSC)* (Neeper et al., 1990) is a norm-referenced, individually administered measure of children's classroom behavior. Designed for students from 6 to 14 years of age, the scale addresses cognitive as well as emotional and behavioral dimensions. The 70-item scale takes 10 to 15 minutes to complete and provides *t*-scores and percentiles for the total sample, for gender, and for ages. The *CBRSC* includes nine subscales: inattention/disorganization, reading problems, cognitive deficits, oppositional-conduct disorder, motor hyperactivity, anxiety, sluggish tempo, social competence, and daydreaming. The *CBRSC* provides useful information for diagnosis and for developing intervention plans for children having school problems.

Draw a Person: Screening Procedure for Emotional Disturbance The *Draw a Person: Screening Procedure for Emotional Disturbance (DAP:SPED)* (Naglieri et al., 1991) is a norm-referenced screening test that helps identify children and adolescents with potential emotional problems that require further evaluation. Designed for use with individuals or groups of children from 6 to 17 years of age, the *DAP:SPED* rates drawings of a man, a woman, and the self. Normed on a sample of 2,260 children, the *DAP:SPED* was developed using the extensive literature on human figure drawing. The *DAP:SPED* is easy to administer and fast to score.

☑ Comprehension Checklist

Special educators use a variety of behavior rating scales and checklists for evaluating student conduct. Designed to provide an overall measure of general levels of student behavior, most scales take only a few minutes to rate and score. Special educators rely on the scales for screening and identification of students with behavior problems as well as for measuring student progress over time. Available scales and inventories include instruments designed for use in schools, at home, and in specialized treatment centers.

Behavioral Observation

Unlike rating scales that measure student behavior indirectly, using pencil-on-paper checklists, behavioral observation relies on direct observation. A trained teacher or paraprofessional conducts **behavioral observation** by recording student actions, using specific techniques to ensure accurate measurement. *Direct observation* refers to firsthand recording of actual student behavior as it occurs in the classroom or other setting. Although special educators most frequently use behavioral observations to measure inappropriate student conduct, they use the same procedures to assess cognitive behaviors, including academic achievement. Unlike behavior rating scales that provide screening information, behavioral observations provide in-depth diagnostic results useful for developing intervention programs and documenting changes in student conduct.

In most situations, special educators rely on direct behavioral observation as the assessment procedure of first choice for measuring inappropriate behavior such as acting out, noncompliance, aggressive behavior, stereotypy, and self-injurious behavior. Although most special educators have experience with conduct problems such as acting out, noncompliance, and aggression, they may not be as familiar with stereotypy and self-injurious behavior. Gast and Wolery (1987) define **stereotypy,** also referred to as *stereotypic* or *self-stimulatory behavior,* as idiosyncratic, highly consistent, repetitive, rhythmic movements of the body or body parts. Examples include head weaving, rocking, arm and finger flapping, posturing, and mouthing hand or objects. Students with severe disabilities, including autism, childhood schizophrenia, severe and profound mental retardation, and blindness sometimes exhibit various types of stereotypy. Likewise, students with severe disabilities sometimes exhibit self-injurious behavior. Gast and Wolery describe **self-injurious behavior (SIB)** as responses that result in physical damage to the student exhibiting the behavior. Although self-injurious behavior takes many forms, common examples include hitting one's head or banging it on objects (head banging), biting parts of the body (most often the hand), hair pulling, scratching, and eye poking.

When special educators need to assess students with behavior problems, including severe disorders such as SIB as well as milder forms of inappropriate behavior such as noncompliance, they often rely on direct behavioral observation rather than indirect forms of evaluation. Direct observation uses a practical, applied type of measurement in which an observer watches the actual behavior as it occurs. As a result, behavioral observation provides practitioners with authentic assessment data for realistically defining the intensity of a problem, developing intervention programs that respond directly to a specific problem, and evaluating genuine student progress. Behavioral observation, however, is not a single type of procedure; rather, it includes a spectrum of both informal and formal observation and measurement techniques.

Informal Observation of Behavior

Informal observation involves gathering information about behavior in a casual, unsystematic manner. Teachers usually document informal observations by writing descriptions of specific events after they occur. This documentation is usually a brief log of incidents. Sometimes, however, informal documentation consists of subjective impressions about the causes of and solutions to a behavior problem. Subjective assessment may also involve estimating the frequency or duration of a behavior without any supporting data. Because of its unstructured nature, informal observation frequently produces unsatisfactory results. Overton (1992) described several of the problems with informal observation. They include the following:

- Inaccuracies due to observation of unrepresentative behaviors.
- Unreliability because observers rely on personal definitions of behavior rather than precise or stable definitions.

- Bias resulting from the subjective nature of most unsystematic observations.
- Difficulty in independently verifying subjective information.

As a result of the inadequacies of informal assessment, experts in behavioral measurement advocate the use of more formal, systematic observations of behavior and, to accomplish this, special educators may select from among a range of observation procedures.

The Behavioral Observation Process

The process of conducting formal, systematic observations includes the following:

- Identifying a target behavior in an observable manner.
- Selecting a procedure for measuring the target behavior, including setting up a data collection system.
- Observing the target behavior and collecting data.
- Recording the results on a graph.
- Interpreting and applying the results.

By following these steps, special educators help to ensure the collection of accurate observations. One of the keys to successful behavioral observation is selecting an appropriate measurement procedure, the most common of which include anecdotal recording, event recording, duration recording, partial interval recording, and momentary time sampling.

Anecdotal Recording   Anecdotal recording is a behavioral assessment method that is especially helpful in understanding why a behavior occurs. Overton (1992) defined **anecdotal recording** as systematic observation of behavior in which the observer writes down the behaviors and interactions that occur during a specific time interval. Typical time intervals include an academic period such as a math class or a nonacademic time such as lunch or recess. With anecdotal recording, observers write down their observations of the problem behavior during specified observation periods and document the event that precedes the behavior (the antecedent) and the event that follows the behavior (the consequence). Observers record their observations on a recording form. Before the actual recording begins, however, the observer selects one or more target behaviors to observe and plans the observation sessions. In most situations, the observer needs to obtain at least two or three separate samples of behavior to provide enough information for making accurate decisions. A sample anecdotal recording form appears in Figure 11–1.

Compared with other forms of behavioral observation, anecdotal recording displays several advantages (Sulzer-Azaroff & Reese, 1982). Because the procedure includes the antecedents, the behavior itself, and the consequences, it enables an evaluator to analyze the sequence of behaviors within the context of surrounding events. This analysis is especially helpful in the initial stages of identifying and evaluating behavior problems. Anecdotal recording also helps teachers select the most important behaviors to target for intervention and points out other relevant aspects of the setting in which the behavior occurs. Although anecdotal recording does not provide quantitative data suitable for graphing, it is a valid means of documenting the extent and nature of one or more problem behaviors.

Figure 11–1   Anecdotal Recording Form

Student _____	Date _____
Observer _____	Setting _____
Starting time of observation _____	Ending time _____
Total observation time _____	

Antecedent (who, what, where, when)	Behavior (include estimated frequency and/or duration)	Consequence (what occurred next?)

Event Recording   Another type of behavioral assessment, event recording, has the advantage of providing quantitative data. **Event recording** involves counting the number of occurrences of a target behavior during a specified period of time. To employ event recording successfully, the observer must be able to identify the beginning and end of each occurrence of a target behavior; like all forms of behavioral assessment, this method requires use of a recording form (see Figure 11–2). Event recording is best for documenting discrete behaviors of short duration, such as the number of aggressive acts during the school day or the frequency of talking out during a 50-minute class period. It is also useful for assessing academic and self-help skills, using recording forms like these in Figure 11–3. However, event recording is a poor measure of nondiscrete behaviors of relatively long duration, such as temper tantrums. To record nondiscrete behaviors as accurately as possible, special educators rely on another form of behavioral assessment: duration recording.

Figure 11–2   Event Recording Form

Student *Jennifer Wilson*

Observer *Ruth Herndon*

Setting *Community-Based Work Site*

Target behavior *Talking out*

Target observed

	Mon	Tues	Wed	Thurs	Fri
8:30–9:30					
9:30–10:30					
10:30–11:30					
Total					

Figure 11–3 Other Event Recording Forms

Student _____

Observer _____

Setting _____

Observation setting _____

Observation dates _____

Day	M	T	W	T	F	
Time						Total
Date						

Target observer _____

Observer _____

Observation setting _____

Observation dates _____

Student	Morning Recess	After Lunch	Afternoon Recess

Duration Recording   Certain behaviors are relatively continuous and do not occur as discrete events. These include temper tantrums, crying, sustained conversation, and stereotypy. They also include behaviors such as off-task and out-of-seat. One method for accurately measuring such sustained behaviors is **duration recording,** the total time that a target behavior occurs during a given time period. To obtain accurate duration-recording data, the observer usually uses a stopwatch to measure the total time a student spends engaged in a target behavior during a set time period. A sample form for conducting duration recording appears in Figure 11–4.

Partial Interval Recording   Although it is possible to use duration recording to measure behaviors such as on-task and off-task accurately, observers often prefer to use another form of behavioral observation—partial interval recording—because this procedure enables measurement of more than one target behavior during each observation period (e.g., off-task, talking-out, and out-of-seat). **Partial interval recording** involves dividing a time period into brief intervals (e.g., a 1-minute period into 10-second intervals, or a 10-minute period into 1-minute intervals) and observing

Figure 11–4   Duration Recording Data Collection Form

Student _____   Date _____

Observer _____

Target behavior _____

Observation setting _____

Time observed _____

Number of Occurrences	Duration of Occurrences		Number of Occurrences	Duration of Occurrences
1			6	
2			7	
3			8	
4			9	
5			10	

Total duration time _____

Comments

_____

_____

_____

whether a target behavior occurs during the interval. A sample form for this pro-cedure appears in Figure 11–5. Unfortunately, partial interval recording requires observation throughout each interval, which makes the technique difficult for teachers to use in the classroom. As a result, teachers often employ an alternative recording method—momentary time sampling—because it does not require con-tinuous observation.

Momentary Time Sampling   Because it does not require continuous observation, momentary time sampling is the preferred option for teachers and other observers who must record behavior while they are involved in other activities. **Momentary time sampling** involves recording the occurrence or nonoccurrence of one or more target behaviors at the end of specified time periods (e.g., at the end of every 5 min-utes or at the end of every minute). By recording whether a student is off-task at the end of every 5 minutes during a 50-minute class period, for example, the observer obtains a sample indicating the percentage of time in which the target behavior oc-curred. If a student were off-task during 6 of 12 time samples, the behavior occurred in 50% of the samples during that particular period. When teachers use momentary time sampling daily for a period of time (e.g., 2 weeks), they can obtain an estimate of

Figure 11–5 Partial Interval Data Collection Form

Student _____   Date _____

Observer _____

Target behavior _____

Observation setting _____

Starting time _____ Ending time _____ Total time _____

Minutes	Seconds	Data		Minutes	Seconds	Data
	20				20	
1	20			6	20	
	20				20	
	20				20	
2	20			7	20	
	20				20	
	20				20	
3	20			8	20	
	20				20	
	20				20	
4	20			9	20	
	20				20	
	20				20	
5	20			10	20	
	20				20	

Key	X = occurrence, – = nonoccurrence

Observation Summary

# of occurrences _____   % of occurrences _____

# of nonoccurrences _____   % of nonoccurrences _____

the amount of time a student spends in off-task behavior. An example of a momentary time sampling recording form appears in Figure 11–6.

Reporting Methods   Observers may report the results of behavioral observations by one of several different methods. The goal is to summarize results accurately in a manner that best describes student behavior. Often simple methods such as reporting the number of times a problem behavior occurs (e.g., the number of talk-outs in a

Figure 11–6   Momentary Time-Sampling Data Collection Form

Student's name _____   Date _____

Observer's name _____

Target behavior _____

Observation setting _____

Time Intervals	Occurrence	Nonoccurrence
10:00		
10:10		
10:20		
10:30		
10:40		
10:40		

Observation Summary

# of occurrences _____   % of occurrences _____

# of nonoccurrences _____   % of nonoccurrences _____

class period) or documenting percentage of time a behavior occurs (e.g., percentage of off-task behavior during a class period) are efficient ways to communicate results. However, the most common reporting technique relies on graphs to display the results of behavioral observations. Graphing involves plotting behavioral observation results, usually on a line or bar chart. Because graphs visually illustrate behavior, they help professionals appraise student performance and facilitate decision making (Wolery et al., 1988). Two graphs illustrating simple behavioral observation data appear in Figure 11–7.

Other Behavioral Assessment Systems   In addition to designing their own behavioral observation systems, special educators may select from among several commercially available systems, which include programs for directly observing and systematically documenting student behavior, as well as programs for measuring interactions between and among students, peers, and teachers. Formal observation systems include the *Time Sample Behavior Checklist* (Paul, 1987), the *Timeout Assessment* (Roberts, 1982), the *Daily Child Behavior Checklist* (Furey & Forehand, 1983), and the *Structured Observation System* (Budd & Fabry, 1984).

Many textbooks and manuals provide comprehensive reviews of behavioral observation techniques. Alberto & Troutman (1998), for example, published an excellent introduction to behavioral techniques that contains valuable information for teachers on assessing the behavior of students with disabilities. Their text focuses

Figure 11–7 Graphs Displaying Simple Behavioral Assessment Data

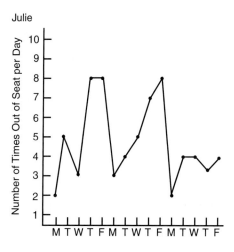

Julie

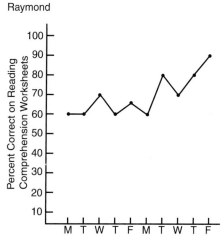

Raymond

on teaching new skills and managing inappropriate behaviors, both academic and social. Another excellent resource is the *Dictionary of Behavioral Assessment Techniques* by Hersen and Bellack (1988), which provides a comprehensive overview of the available behavioral assessment procedures, including reviews of the major tests and systems.

✔ Comprehension Checklist

Behavioral observations refer to firsthand observation and objective recording of actual student behavior as it occurs. Special educators may select from among several types of behavioral observation procedures, including relatively simple observation techniques such as anecdotal, event, and duration recording, and more complex partial-interval recording and momentary time-sampling approaches. Regardless of the specific technique, however, the goal is to employ behavioral observation as the basis for objectively identifying the extent of a problem, as a guide to establishing an intervention program, and as a tool for measuring student progress. Observers most often summarize results from behavioral observations with graphs to illustrate results.

Measures of Self-Concept, Attitudes, and Interests

Special educators must consider many facets of behavior in the assessment process. In addition to evaluating student conduct by rating scales and behavioral observations, special educators must also assess other aspects of behavior and personality, including self-concept, attitudes, and interests.

Measuring Self-Concept

Self-concept is defined as students' feelings about themselves in various life situations. Wylie (1990) published a comprehensive review of self-concept testing procedures and research. In the review Wylie points out that research studies have related self-concept to achievement, ethnic and cultural background, and social development. However, she also emphasized that although self-concept is an important dimension of personality and behavior, measuring it presents problems because of the low reliability and validity of the tests.

When evaluating complex behaviors such as self-concept, special educators should rely on multiple sources of assessment information, including interviews with students, parents, and professionals; formal and informal interactions with students; and direct observation of student behavior. In addition to these sources of information, special educators can gain valuable insight by administering one of several available inventories. Following is a review of a representative self-concept inventory, the *Piers–Harris Children's Self-Concept Scale,* along with a listing and brief description of other available self-concept measures.

Piers–Harris Children's Self-Concept Scale

The *Piers–Harris Children's Self-Concept Scale* (Piers, 1984) is norm-referenced scale designed to measure the way students feel about themselves. Consisting of 80 questions that students answer about themselves, the scale measures the self-concept of students from 8 to 18 years of age. Evaluators can use the scale to identify students with special needs, to aid in individual assessment, and to do research. The developers arranged the items on the scale in six subtest areas: behavior, intellectual and school status, physical appearance and attributes, anxiety, popularity, and happiness and satisfaction. A summary of the *Piers–Harris Children's Self-Concept Scale* appears in Table 11–3.

Materials for the *Piers–Harris Scale*   *Piers–Harris Scale* materials include a four-page scoring booklet, a test manual, and a scoring key for hand-scoring student responses on the booklet. Computerized administration and scoring with groups of students requires other materials, including scannable answer sheets.

Administration and Scoring of the *Piers–Harris Scale*   Administration involves having students respond, with either a yes or a no, to 80 statements such as "I am

Table 11–3 *Piers–Harris Children's Self-Concept Scale*

Type of Test:	Norm referenced, individually or group administered
Purpose:	Assesses self-concept
Content Areas:	Behavior, intellectual and school status, physical appearance and attributes, anxiety, popularity, and happiness and satisfaction
Administration Time:	15–20 minutes
Age Levels:	8–18 years
Suitable for:	Assessing the self-concept of students with mild and moderate disabilities, including attention deficit disorders, learning disabilities, and emotional disturbance
Scores:	Percentiles, stanines, and *t*-scores
In Short:	Although it exhibits the technical problems common among tests of this type, the *Piers–Harris* is a well-designed screening instrument useful for identifying students with self-concept problems.

smart," "I forget what I learn," and "I have a pleasant face." The test is suitable for individual or group administration and is administered in one of three ways: having students circle their responses in a four-page booklet, having students complete a scannable answer sheet, or having students use a microcomputer program. Designed for students from ages 8 to 18 years, the *Piers–Harris Scale* requires a third-grade reading level. However, the evaluator may read the test items out loud to students with reading skills below the third-grade level. Although professionals or paraprofessionals with training on the *Pier–Harris Scale* may administer the instrument, only professionals with training in assessment should interpret the results. The evaluator scores student responses to indicate both general and specific self-concept in behavior, intellectual and school status, physical appearance and attributes, anxiety, popularity, and happiness and satisfaction. Available scores include percentiles, stanines, and *t*-scores.

Technical Characteristics of the *Piers–Harris Scale*   Because it was standardized on a group of 1,183 students between the ages of 8 to 18 who were attending public school in Pennsylvania, the *Piers–Harris Scale* has limited generalizability. In addition to the initial sample, the test developers used a sample of 485 public school students to establish the cluster scale scores. Unfortunately, not enough information is available to determine the adequacy of either sample group, and, as a result, the norms are less than adequate.

The *Piers–Harris* manual provides reliability data in the form of test-retest reliability coefficients ranging from .42 to .96 and internal consistency estimates ranging from .88 to .93. Like all measures of self-concept, a number of problems affect the validity of the *Piers–Harris Scale*. The manual includes information concerning several validity issues related to assessing self-concept. **Faking,** a common validity problem with tests of this type, refers to attempts by students to distort the test results in a positive direction. Although it is acceptable and normal for students to display a

disorders. Separate norms are available for males and females. The test is best used as a screening instrument.

Brown Attention-Deficit Disorder Scales   The criterion-referenced, individually administered *Brown Attention-Deficit Disorder Scales (Brown ADD Scales)* (Brown, 1996) provide a way to quickly screen for indications of ADD in adolescents and adults. Consisting of 40 self-report items, the *Brown ADD Scales* can be administered in 20 to 40 minutes. One form of the *Brown ADD Scales* is for adolescents age 12–18, and the other is for adults. Results from the scales indicate whether a student would benefit from a full evaluation for the disorder. The *Brown ADD Scales* identify the following clusters often associated with ADD:

- Activating and organizing to work.
- Sustaining attention and concentration.
- Sustaining energy and effort.
- Managing affective interference.
- Utilizing working memory and accessing recall.

Although screening for ADD using a tool like the *Brown ADD Scales* is an important first step in the assessment process, a full evaluation is required to diagnose ADD. The *Brown ADD Scales* include a form for conducting a full evaluation that meets the diagnostic criteria for ADD. The *Brown ADD Diagnostic Form* gives a set of procedures, tools, and worksheets to use in this process. Like the *Brown ADD Scales,* there are two diagnostic forms, one for adolescents and one for adults. The *Brown ADD Diagnostic Forms* include the following items:

- Protocol and record form for conducting a semistructured clinical interview.
- Scoring summary.
- Mulitrater evaluation form for complete *DSM-IV* ADHD criteria.
- Worksheet for analysis of IQ subtest data relevant to ADD.
- Screener for co-morbid disorders.
- IQ test summary form.
- Overall diagnostic summary form.

The *Brown ADD Scales* and the included *Brown ADD Diagnostic Form* are useful for assessing attention-deficit disorders in adolescents and adults.

Children's Attention & Adjustment Survey (CAAS)   The norm-referenced, individually administered *Children's Attention & Adjustment Survey (CAAS)* (Lambert & Sandoval, 1990) helps screen for specific behavior problems related to hyperactivity and attention problems. The *CAAS* includes four scales: inattentiveness, impulsivity, hyperactivity, and conduct problems/aggressiveness. The *CAAS* uses two forms: a home form, which is completed by the parent or primary care giver, and a school form, which the teacher completes. Designed for children ages 5–13, the CAAS takes about 10–15 minutes per form to administer. Test results include a standard score and a percentile for each scale.

Conners Continuous Performance Test Computer Program 3.0   The *Conners Continuous Performance Test Computer Program 3.0* (Conners, 1997a) assesses individuals age 3 to adult suspected of having attention problems. The *Conners CPT Computer Program* administers the protocol directly using the computer screen and keyboard or mouse. The student takes the test by pressing the spacebar or mouse button following presentation of specific letters on the computer screen. A standard mode of presentation controls the number of trials, target letters presented, and intervals between the presentation of the letters. It takes 14 minutes to administer, and the results can be accessed immediately. Test results are compared with population norms and a reference group of individuals diagnosed with ADHD. Results include graphs of reaction time, number of errors, risk taking, sensitivity, and number of target hits.

Conners Rating Scales-Revised The norm-referenced, individually administered *Conners Rating Scales-Revised (CRS-R)* (Conners, 1997b) includes a parent rating scale, a teacher rating scale, and a student self-report form. The *CRS-R* includes a short and a long form, both of which are designed to screen children and adolescents who are at risk for ADHD and may need further diagnostic evaluation. Norms are available for children and adolescents aged 3 to 17 on the parent and teacher rating scales. Both scales correspond with symptoms used in the *DSM-IV* as criteria for ADHD. A hyperactivity index is also included in the long form of the parent and teacher rating scales.

Test of Variables of Attention The *Test of Variables of Attention (TOVA)* (Greenberg, 1993) is a norm-referenced, individually administered test for screening children and adults for attention-deficit disorder (ADD). Designed for individuals from age 4 to retirement, the *TOVA* is a computer-based test that consists of gamelike tasks. The test, which is taken on a computer, requires the student to press a microswitch whenever a "correct" stimulus is presented during a 22½ minute continuous visual performance test. The computer records the student's reactions for analysis and interpretation. Measured variables include omission errors (inattention), commission errors (impulsivity), reaction time, variability, postcommission reaction time, and anticipatory and multiple responses. The *TOVA* is useful in the school as a screening tool and should be used in conjunction with classroom behavior rating. It may be used to measure attention in individuals with neurological injuries and disorders as one tool in a comprehensive assessment battery. It can also identify responses to medication, determine optimal medication dosage, and monitor dosages by gauging reaction to medication over time. The instrument takes 25–30 minutes to administer. Test data are analyzed by the computer program.

☑ Comprehension Checklist

Teachers most often assess children and adolescents with ADD or ADHD to develop plans to manage behavior and academic performance. To achieve this goal teachers rely on both subjective and objective measures. The former include behavior rating scales and other tests that provide reliable data regarding the nature and severity of a child's attention and activity disorders. The objective measures include a variety of direct observation techniques that help pinpoint the problem and measure the effectiveness of interventions.

Summary

When special educators assess behavior, they use a wide range of measurement techniques and assessment instruments (see Table 11–4, p. 351). This makes the process of assessing behavior complex and challenging. In the classroom and other instructional settings, teachers most often use practical, applied assessment procedures such as observation of student behavior. However, when professionals determine student eligibility for special education services and make placement decisions, they rely on more formal, norm-referenced instruments to evaluate behavior. Although assessment of behavior focuses on measuring student conduct and misconduct, it also encompasses appraisal of other affective behaviors, including self-concept, attitudes, and interests, which further complicates the assessment process.

Despite the difficulties associated with assessing behavior, those who serve students with disabilities should be well versed in the available procedures and their appropriateness in given situations. Assessment of behavior greatly affects the potential for success of students with disabilities. For this reason, it is imperative to understand assessment of behavior, select appropriate measurement procedures, and conduct assessment accurately. Assessment of behavior gives special educators an essential tool for providing the best possible educational services to students with behavior problems.

Chapter Review and Application

Multiple Choice

Directions: Read each item carefully. In the blank beside each item, write the letter of the best response. Each question contains only one best answer. Check your answers with the answer key at the end of the book.

_____ 1. Which assessment relies on firsthand recording of actual student behavior as it occurs in the classroom or other settings?
   a. Self-concept inventories
   b. Behavior rating scales
   c. Direct observation of behavior
   d. Interest and attitude scales

_____ 2. Which assessment relies on written questionnaires containing lists of behaviors that raters complete by assigning a rating (usually based on a scale of 1 to 5)?
   a. Self-concept inventories
   b. Behavior rating scales
   c. Direct observation of behavior
   d. Interest and attitude scales

_____ 3. Which assessment measures children's feelings about themselves in various life situations?
   a. Self-concept inventories
   b. Behavior rating scales

      c. Direct observation of behavior

      d. Interest and attitude scales

_____ **4.** Which assessment has students respond to a series of statements describing people in various activities?

      a. Self-concept inventories

      b. Behavior rating scales

      c. Direct observation of behavior

      d. Interest and attitude scales

_____ **5.** Which assessment measures behaviors such as inattention, impulsivity, sustaining attention and concentration, sustaining energy and effort, and managing affective interference?

      a. Behavior rating scales

      b. Behavioral observation

      c. Self-concept inventories

      d. ADHD checklists

_____ **6.** Which assessment is best for assessing interpersonal problems, inappropriate behaviors and feelings, depression, and physical symptoms and fears?

      a. Behavior rating scales

      b. Behavioral observation

      c. Self-concept inventories

      d. ADHD checklists

_____ **7.** Which assessment is best for assessing intellectual and school status, physical appearance and attributes, anxiety, popularity, and happiness and satisfaction?

      a. Behavior rating scales

      b. Behavioral observation

      c. Self-concept inventories

      d. ADHD checklists

_____ **8.** Which assessment is best for measuring acting out, noncompliance, aggressive behavior, stereotypy, and self-injurious behavior?

      a. Behavior rating scales

      b. Behavioral observation

      c. Self-concept inventories

      d. ADHD checklists

_____ **9.** Which assessment uses a child's self-report?

      a. Behavioral observation

      b. Behavior rating scales

      c. Self-concept inventories

      d. Continuous performance test

_____ **10.** Which assessment uses an informant who knows the child well, such as a teacher or a parent?

      a. Behavioral observation

      b. Behavior rating scales

      c. Self-concept inventories

      d. Continuous performance test

Short Answers

Directions: Review your understanding of the material in this chapter by answering the following short answer questions. Compare your responses to the sample answers. Your responses should contain information that is similar to but not exactly the same as the information in the sample answers at the end of the book.

1. In what ways do instruments for assessing behavior and conduct differ from those for assessing behaviors in other domains such as academic achievement? What are the reasons for these differences?

2. What are behavior rating scales? Why are they primarily used for screening and initial identification of student behavior problems rather than for developing intervention objectives and programs?

3. What is ecological assessment? How can it help teachers expand their insight into the behavior problems of students with special needs? What are the procedures for conducting ecological assessment?

References

Achenbach, T. M. (1981). *Child Behavior Checklist for Ages 4–16.* San Antonio, TX: Psychological Corporation.
———(1986). *Child Behavior Checklist for Ages 2–3.* San Antonio, TX: Psychological Corporation.
Alberto, P. A., & Troutman, A. C. (1998). *Applied Behaviors for Teachers* (5th ed.). Upper Saddle River, NJ: Prentice-Hall.
American Psychiatric Association. (1994). *Diagnostic and Statistical Manual of Mental Disorders* (4th ed.). Washington, DC: Author.
Battle, J. (1992). *Culture-Free Self-Esteem Inventories.* (2d ed.). Austin, TX: PRO-ED.
Bracken, B. A. (1992). *Multidimensional Self Concept Scale.* Austin, TX: PRO-ED.
Brown, L., & Alexander, J. (1990). *Self-Esteem Index.* Austin, TX: PRO-ED.
Brown, L. L., & Hammill, D. D. (1990). *Behavior Rating Profile-2 (BRP-2).* Austin, TX: PRO-ED.
Brown, T. E. (1996). *Brown Attention-Deficit Disorder Scales.* San Antonio: TX: Psychological Corporation.
Budd, K .S., & Fabry, P. L. (1984). Behavioral assessment in applied parent training: Use of a structured observation system. In R. F. Dangel & R. A. Polster (Eds.), *Parent Training: Foundation of Research and Practice.* New York: Guilford Press, 417–42.
Burks, H. F. (1977). *Burks Behavior Rating Scales.* Los Angeles: Western Psychological Services.
Carroll, J. L. (1986). A review of the *Devereux Elementary School Behavior Rating Scale-II.* In D. Keyser & R. Sweetland (Eds.), *Test Critiques* (vol. 5). Kansas City, MO: Test Corporation of America, 104–8.
Conners, C. K. (1997a). *Conners Continuous Performance Test Computer Program 3.0.* Austin, TX: PRO-ED.
———(1997b). *Conners Rating Scales-Revised.* Austin, TX: PRO-ED.
Coopersmith, S. (1981). *Coopersmith Self-Esteem Inventories.* Palo Alto, CA: Consulting Psychologists Press.
Drummond, R. J. (1996). *Appraisal Procedures for Counselors and Helping Professionals* (3d ed.). Upper Saddle River, NJ: Prentice-Hall.

Elliot, S. N., & Gresham, F. M. (1991) *Social Skills Intervention Guide.* Circle Pines, MN: American Guidance Service.

Epstein, M. H., & Sharma, J. M. (1997). *Behavior and Emotional Rating Scale.* Austin, TX: PRO-ED.

Estes, T. H., Estes, J. J., Richards, J. C., & Roettger, D. (1982). *Estes Attitude Scales (EAS).* Austin, TX: PRO-ED.

Furey, W., & Forehand, R. (1983). The Daily Child Behavior Checklist. *Journal of Behavioral Assessment* 5, 345–55.

Gast, D. L., & Wolery, M. (1987). Severe maladaptive behaviors. In M. Snell (Ed.), *Systematic Instruction of Persons With Severe Handicaps* (3d ed.). New York: Merrill/Macmillan, 300–32.

Gilliam, J. (1995). *Attention-Deficit/Hyperactivity Disorder Test.* Austin, TX: PRO-ED.

Greenberg, L. (1993). *Test of Variables of Attention.* Circle Pines, MN: American Guidance Service.

Gresham, F. M., & Elliot, S. N. (1990). *Social Skills Rating System.* Circle Pines, MN: American Guidance Service.

Hersen, M., & Bellack, A. S. (1988). *Dictionary of Behavioral Assessment Techniques.* New York: Pergamon.

Jones, V. F., & Jones, L. S. (1981). *Responsible Classroom Discipline: Creating Positive Learning Environments and Solving Problems.* Boston: Allyn & Bacon.

Kaufmann, J. M. (1993). *Characteristics of Emotional and Behavioral Disorders of Children and Youth* (5th ed.). Upper Saddle River, NJ: Merrill/Prentice-Hall.

Lambert, N., & Sandoval, J. (1990). *Children's Attention & Adjustment Survey.* Circle Pines, MN: American Guidance Service.

McDermott, P. (1993). *Adjustment Scales for Children and Adolescents.* Phoenix, AZ: Ed & Psych Associates.

Naglieri, J. A., LeBuffe, P. A., & Pfeiffer, S. I. (1993). *Devereux Behavior Rating Scale-School Form.* San Antonio, TX: Psychological Corporation.

Naglieri, J. A., McNeish, T. J., & Achilles, N. B. (1991). *Draw a Person: Screening Procedure for Emotional Disturbance.* Austin, TX: PRO-ED.

Neeper, R., Lahey, B. B., & Frick, P. J. (1990). *Comprehensive Behavior Rating Scale for Children.* San Antonio, TX: Psychological Corporation.

Overton, T. (1992). *Assessment in Special Education: An Applied Approach.* New York: Merrill/Macmillan.

Paul, G. L. (1987). *Observation Assessment Instrumentation for Service and Research—The Time Sample Behavior Checklist: Assessment in Residential Treatment Settings,* (part 4). Champaign, IL: Research Press.

Piers, E. V. (1984). *Piers–Harris Children's Self-Concept Scale.* Los Angeles: Western Psychological Services.

Reynolds , C. R., & Kamphaus, R. W. (1992). *Behavior Assessment System for Children.* Circle Pines, MN: American Guidance Service.

Roberts, M. W. (1982). Resistance to timeout: Some normative data. *Journal of Behavioral Assessment* 4, 237–46.

Shea, T. M., & Bauer, A. M. (1990). *Parents and Teachers of Children With Exceptionalities* (2d ed.). Boston: Allyn & Bacon.

Spivak, G. (1982). *Devereux Elementary School Behavior Rating Scale-II.* Devon, PA: Devereux Foundation.

Spivak, G., & Spotts, J. (1966). *Devereux Child Behavior Rating Scale.* Devon, PA: Devereux Foundation.

Spivak, G., Spotts, J., & Haimes, P. E. (1967). *Devereux Adolescent Behavior Rating Scale.* Devon, PA: Devereux Foundation.

Assessment of Adaptive Behavior

Overview

Adaptive behavior is the ability to adjust to personal and social demands in the environment. When we assess adaptive behavior, we measure behaviors such as personal self-sufficiency, independence in the community, and social responsibility. In this chapter you have the opportunity to develop an understanding of the procedures for assessing adaptive behavior. To achieve this goal we review the meaning of the term and consider the types of behaviors measured by adaptive behavior scales. We investigate the way special educators use adaptive behavior scales and analyze the issues surrounding their use. After this introduction we examine the range of instruments for assessing adaptive behavior, including the most frequently used individually administered scales and inventories. As we review each scale, we consider the purpose and use of the instrument, the test materials, the administration and scoring procedures, and the technical characteristics.

Objectives

After reading this chapter, you will be prepared to do the following:

- Define *adaptive behavior*.
- Understand the range of behaviors measured by adaptive behavior scales.
- Understand the role of the informant in assessing adaptive behavior.
- Understand the way special educators use adaptive behavior scales.
- Use adaptive behavior scales and inventories with children and youth who have special needs.

Description of Adaptive Behavior and Its Assessment

Perhaps the best way to introduce assessment of adaptive behavior is through the eyes of a beginning special education teacher.

When asked by the school psychologist to rate the adaptive behavior of one of his students, Mr. Ohchoyo had many questions. Mr. Ohchoyo remembered studying adaptive behavior in school, but he had never actually used an adaptive behavior scale. The psychologist explained that rating scales, rather than tests, were used to assess adaptive behavior. This prompted Mr. Ohchoyo to ask the psychologist questions such as, What behaviors would Mr. Ohchoyo rate? How accurate is teacher rating of adaptive behavior? And what is the difference between adaptive behavior and intelligence? The psychologist understood Mr. Ohchoyo's concerns and patiently explained adaptive behavior and its assessment.

In this chapter you will discover the answers to these assessment questions. You will also investigate other aspects of assessing the adaptive behavior of children with special needs, beginning with a definition of adaptive behavior and a description of its assessment.

Adaptive behavior is the ability to adjust to personal and social demands in the environment, especially to changes in the environment. When professionals evaluate adaptive behavior, they use scales that sample behaviors related to personal self-sufficiency, independence in the community, and personal-social responsibility. Because such behavior changes as one ages, adaptive behavior scales include a range of items for measuring skill development at each age level. For example, with young children, **personal self-sufficiency** refers to the ability to perform self-help skills such as dressing, eating, hygiene, and toileting. With older children, however, personal self-sufficiency encompasses a wide range of daily living skills, such as selecting and caring for appropriate clothing and eating independently in cafeterias and restaurants. **Community independence** refers to autonomy in the community, which for young children includes playing at school, at home, and in the yard with minimal supervision. For teenagers and adults, community independence includes self-reliance in the community as related to work, recreation, and leisure activities. **Personal-social responsibility** encompasses behaviors such as trustworthiness, commitment, appropriate socialization, proper interpersonal interaction, and self-direction. For young children, personal-social responsibility refers to behaviors such as complying with parents, getting along with siblings, and playing constructively. For older children, personal-social responsibility includes behaviors such as taking care of personal items, making friends at school, and completing schoolwork.

Indirect Measurement of Adaptive Behavior

Because they assess personal and social skills, adaptive behavior scales use a distinctive type of indirect measurement that focuses on performance over time rather than one-time performance on a test. Unlike standardized tests that an evaluator gives to a student during a testing session, adaptive behavior scales rely on information from an informant who is familiar with the student and is usually a teacher or parent who knows the student's typical performance in real-life settings. With adaptive behavior, a student's ability to perform a particular skill is insufficient if the student fails to use the skill as needed. For example, a student may have the ability to manage money but may not do so on a regular basis. In this case the student's adaptive behavior is insufficient.

Evaluators must rely on indirect measurement to assess adaptive behavior because, in most instances, they are unable to directly observe the typical behavior of a student in real-life settings. An evaluator would need an extended period of time to directly assess behaviors such as eating in restaurants, hygiene skills, social interaction patterns, and mobility skills in the home, the school, and the community. Therefore, in place of direct observation, evaluators rely on the observations of an informant who knows a student well.

The Role of the Informant in Assessing Adaptive Behavior

One of the keys to successful use of adaptive behavior scales is the **informant,** who provides the information required to rate the items on a scale. The informant is usually a teacher, parent, grandparent, teacher aide, or another primary care giver. Because the informant is so important in the process of assessing adaptive behavior, the evaluator must judge the accuracy of an informant's responses (Sattler, 1992). Most informants provide reliable information, and the best informants give highly accurate, balanced, and clear information. Credible informants make it easy to rate precisely. However, some informants give biased or distorted answers. When evaluators have serious doubts about the validity of a set of responses, they must gather additional information by interviewing another informant, which enables an evaluator to compare responses for consistency. Sattler suggested that discrepancies among respondents result from the following:

- Student behavior that varies in different settings.
- Unreliable informant information.
- Differences in informant interpretation of student behavior.
- Differences in informant familiarity with a student.
- Biased or prejudiced informant attitudes.

The use of multiple sources provides a better profile of adaptive behavior, and for this reason, evaluators should attempt to conduct more than one interview whenever possible. For example, teachers can provide information from observations of student behavior in an educational setting. Parents, on the other hand, can supply information about at-home behaviors such as sleeping, leisure activities, and eating. See Focus 12–1 for additional information about the role of the informant.

Controversial Aspects of Measuring Adaptive Behavior

Controversial aspects of measuring adaptive behavior (Beirne-Smith et al., 1994) include arguments about the concept itself and debate over more practical concerns. The conceptual argument centers around disagreement over the specific definition of the term, which occurs because the concept encompasses so many different behaviors across a wide age span (infancy to retirement). More practical concerns address the reliability of informant data, and racial and ethnic bias. In an attempt to control for possible sources of bias, Mercer (1977) developed a comprehensive system of multipluralistic assessment designed to minimize bias against students from minority

FOCUS 12–1

The Role of the Informant in Assessing Adaptive Behavior

- The informant is usually a teacher or parent who knows the child's typical performance in real-life settings.
- Teachers can provide information from observations of child behavior in an educational setting.
- Parents can supply information about at-home behaviors such as sleeping, leisure time activities, and eating.
- The evaluator must judge the accuracy of an informant's responses.
- More than one informant should be interviewed whenever possible.
- When evaluators doubt the validity of a set of responses, they must gather additional information by interviewing another informant.

groups. This system (explained in greater detail in Chapter 9) consists of a complete program that is especially sensitive to language and cultural factors. The system contains valuable features, including sociocultural scales, health history inventories, and norms for black, Hispanic, and white children. Rather than emphasizing a student's intelligence test score, the system emphasizes comprehensive evaluation of adaptive behavior. Evaluators measure adaptive behavior with a unique inventory, the *Adaptive Behavior Inventory for Children*, which is a component of the *System of Multicultural Pluralistic Assessment* (Mercer & Lewis, 1977b, 1977c). This inventory includes measures of student role performance in the family, the community, and the peer group; the nonacademic aspects of school; and the earner or consumer role. The system of multipluralistic assessment is one response to the persistent problem of bias in evaluation.

Why Do We Assess the Adaptive Behavior of Children With Special Needs?

We assess the adaptive behavior of children with special needs for several reasons. Adaptive behavior scales provide us with an accurate measure of a child's ability to adjust to the personal and social demands in the environment and to changes in these demands. In fact, the most significant characteristic of children with deficits in adaptive behavior is the difficulty they have in adjusting to changes in the environment. For example, *Vineland Social Maturity Scales* measure the functional communication skills, practical daily living skills, and applied socialization skills. Children with deficits in adaptive behavior have difficulty learning these skills, especially in new situations. For this reason, we use norm-referenced adaptive behavior scales, along with other assessment information, to identify students with disabilities, determine eligibility for special education services, and make placement decisions. Assessing adaptive behavior is especially important in diagnosing mental retardation, which is defined as subaverage intellectual functioning that exists concurrently with significant deficits in adaptive behavior. Special educators also use data from adaptive behavior scales to help write IEPs and develop intervention programs, most often for children with severe and multiple disabilities who require intensive instruction in personal, social, and occupational skill development. Specialized adaptive behavior scales are available for students with specific disabilities, including learning disabilities, profound mental retardation, and trainable mental retardation. Finally, we continue to assess the adaptive behavior over time to measure child progress in adjusting to changes in the environment and learning new adaptive behavior skills.

The following vignette describes how a staffing team used results from an adaptive behavior assessment to help make a difficult placement decision.

Jimmy was a streetwise child with a history of defiant, aggressive, and disobedient behavior. Because of poor academic skills, immature social behavior, and small stature, Jimmy's school retained him in a primary classroom (grades 1 and 2) for students with mild and moderate mental retardation instead of promoting him into a classroom for students his age (grades 3, 4, and 5). However, when he reached age 10, the school moved him to the class for older students. At first, Jimmy appeared motivated and cooperative, but he made little academic progress. As the year progressed, he became frustrated and often refused to participate in class activities or to complete assigned work. He also began to behave aggressively by threatening peers and disrupting class.

As a result of these problems, Jimmy's teacher met with a staffing team to discuss possible placement in a different program. When the staffing team decided to reevaluate him, the teacher completed the classroom edition of the Vineland Adaptive Behavior Scales. *Jimmy received an overall standard score of 60 on the* Vineland Scales, *with a subtest score of 64 on the social domain. In contrast, he received a standard score of 40 on an intelligence test (the* WISC-III). *Although the intelligence test score may have qualified him for placement in a program for students with severe retardation, the staffing team recommended keeping Jimmy in his present placement because of his relatively high adaptive behavior (as measured by the* Vineland Scales) *and his good verbal skills. However, the team agreed to continue to monitor his progress and asked his teacher to complete a follow-up adaptive behavior evaluation before the end of the school year.*

This true story illustrates one important use of adaptive behavior scales. A summary of all the reasons for assessing adaptive behavior appears in Focus 12–2.

FOCUS 12–2

Why Do We Assess the Adaptive Behavior of Children With Special Needs?

- To measure a child's ability to adjust to the environment and to changes in the environment
- To diagnose mental retardation
- To identify students with disabilities, determine eligibility for special education services, and make placement decisions
- To help write IEPs and develop intervention programs, most often for children with severe and multiple disabilities who require intensive instruction in personal, social, and occupational skill development
- To measure a child's progress in adjusting to the environment and learning adaptive behavior skills

☑ Comprehension Checklist

Adaptive behavior is the ability to adjust to the environment, especially to changes in the environment. Adaptive behavior skills include personal self-sufficiency, independence in the community, and personal-social responsibility. These behaviors focus on the practical knowledge needed to live independently as an adult, including daily living skills, vocational skills, social skills, applied academic skills, and community survival skills. Special educators assess adaptive behavior with scales and inventories instead of traditional standardized tests.

Adaptive Behavior Scales

Adaptive behavior scales are completed by a professional, such as a teacher who knows the student well or an evaluator who interviews a parent or other primary care giver. These scales measure performance with a checklist of items arranged by age in a developmental sequence. Detailed reviews of several representative scales of adaptive behavior follow, accompanied by brief reviews of other available instruments.

Vineland Adaptive Behavior Scales

The *Vineland Adaptive Behavior Scales* (Sparrow et al., 1984a, b) are one of the most widely used instruments for evaluating adaptive behavior. The current scales are a revision of the original *Vineland Social Maturity Scale* (Doll, 1965). The Vineland subscales measure communication, daily living skills, socialization, and motor skills. They also provide an optional maladaptive behavior subscale for evaluating inappropriate behaviors.

There are three separate versions of the scales: a survey form, an expanded form, and a classroom edition. The survey form (Sparrow et al., 1984b) is derived from the original Vineland scale and contains 297 items, which special educators use as a screening measure to obtain an overview of adaptive behavior. The expanded form (Sparrow et al., 1984a) contains 577 items, including the items from the survey edition, and is a comprehensive diagnostic instrument that provides in-depth information across a large sample of behaviors. The classroom edition (Harrison, 1985) contains 244 items for measuring adaptive behavior in the classroom and school setting.

The age range of the survey and expanded forms is birth through 18 years. Evaluators can also assess adults with severe disabilities with either of these forms. The classroom edition measures the adaptive behavior of students from 3 through 12 years of age. Special educators normally use the norm-referenced, standardized *Vineland Scales* in identifying and placing students with mental retardation. However, they also use them to obtain evaluation data for programming and intervention purposes. A summary of the *Vineland Scales* appears in Table 12–1.

Materials for the *Vineland Adaptive Behavior Scales*   The *Vineland Scales* materials include three manuals and three scoring booklets: one each for the survey form, the expanded form, and the classroom edition. The well-written manuals are 200 to 300 pages in length, and the carefully designed scoring sheets are 8 to 16 pages long.

Table 12–1 *Vineland Adaptive Behavior Scales*

Type of Test:	Norm referenced, individually administered
Purpose:	Assesses personal and social skills
Content Areas:	Communication, daily living skills, socialization, and motor skills
Administration Time:	20 to 60 minutes to give the survey form and classroom edition; 60 to 90 minutes to give the expanded form; scoring takes 10 to 15 minutes
Suitable for:	Students with mild, moderate, and severe disabilities, including mental retardation, emotional disabilities, visual impairments, and hearing impairments, as well as adults with mental retardation
Age Levels:	Interview editions (survey and expanded forms): Birth–18 years Classroom edition: 3–12 years
Scores:	Standard scores, percentile scores, stanines, and age equivalents. Regular norms plus supplementary norms based on samples from adults with mental retardation, children with emotional disabilities, children with visual impairments, and children with hearing impairments
In Short:	Special educators use the *Vineland Adaptive Behavior Scales* to identify and place students with disabilities and to obtain evaluation data for developing intervention programs.

The expanded form also includes a detailed score summary and profile booklet. Optional materials include an audiocassette tape of a model interview process, a report to the parents, and a Spanish edition of the survey form. Evaluators may also obtain optional computer software for scoring and developing profiles.

Administration and Scoring of the *Vineland Adaptive Behavior Scales*   Evaluators give the *Vineland Scales* in the form of a general interview rather than as an item-by-item questioning procedure. The interviewer establishes rapport with the child's parent, teacher, or other primary care giver (who knows the child well) as the respondent and introduces the *Vineland Scales* before starting the interview. The interviewer begins by having the respondent discuss the behavior related to specific subtests in a general way. If the respondent does not provide enough information during the general discussion, the interviewer then uses probing questions to obtain information for scoring specific items and may need further probes to score some items. For example, he or she may say, "Give me some examples of how John uses the telephone." If the respondent fails to provide sufficient information to score each item relating to telephone skills, the interviewer probes for further information.

The survey form and classroom edition take 20 to 60 minutes to give. The expanded form takes from 60 to 90 minutes to give. Scoring the *Vineland Scales* takes

10 to 15 minutes. The authors designed the scales for use by psychologists, social workers, and other professionals (including special educators) who have graduate degrees and specific training in assessment. Professionals who use the *Vineland Scales* need to have an understanding of individuals with disabilities as well as training in interview techniques. The authors also require evaluators to study the *Vineland Scales* and practice giving them as part of the qualification process.

The *Vineland Scales* use three criteria for scoring each item. A score of 2 indicates an activity that a student usually performs. A score of 1 denotes an activity that a student performs sometimes. A score of 0 reflects an activity that a student never performs. In scoring, the evaluator counts individual item scores to obtain raw scores for each subdomain and for the total test. The evaluator then converts the raw scores into one of several derived scores, which include standard scores with a mean of 100 and a standard deviation of 15, percentile scores, stanines, and age equivalents. The evaluator may also complete a score profile graph, which appears with a sample scoring sheet in Figure 12–1. In addition to the regular norms, the *Vineland Scales* provide supplementary norms from four sample groups: adults with mental retardation, children with emotional disabilities, children with visual impairments, and children with hearing impairments.

The *Vineland* manuals provide detailed information on interpreting results, including sample case studies. The evaluator begins the interpretation process by identifying a student's general level of functioning in adaptive behavior. Next, the evaluator analyzes the subtest scores and then compares results with scores from supplementary norm groups. Finally, the evaluator interprets results from the maladaptive behavior subtest.

Evaluators then use more specific interpretation procedures, which are based on the reasons for giving the *Vineland Scales*. For example, if these scales are to diagnose mental retardation, interpretation focuses more on the standardized test scores. If given to provide information for planning an individual program, interpretation focuses on the content in the subtests. When interpreting results from the expanded form, the *Vineland Scales* provide program planning profiles in the scoring booklet.

Technical Characteristics of the *Vineland Adaptive Behavior Scales*   The interview editions (i.e., the survey and expanded forms) of the *Vineland Scales* were standardized on a national sample of more than 3,000 individuals and include smaller supplementary samples of individuals with disabilities. The authors standardized the classroom edition with a sample of approximately 3,000 students from ages 3 to 12 years. The manuals describe several types of studies conducted to investigate the consistency of *Vineland* scores, including split-half, test-retest, and interrater reliability. These studies provide sufficient data to establish the reliability of the instruments. The manuals also include information supporting the construct validity, the content validity, and the criterion-related validity of the *Vineland Scales*. Overall, these *Vineland Scales* present ample evidence of test validity.

Summary of the *Vineland Adaptive Behavior Scales*   The V*ineland Adaptive Behavior Scales* assess personal and social skills in communication, daily living activities, socialization, and motor proficiency and include an optional maladaptive behavior

Figure 12–1 Scoring Sheet from the *Vineland Adaptive Behavior Scales*

Vineland Adaptive Behavior Scales:
CLASSROOM EDITION

Child's name *Tommy*
Chronological age *12-5-7*   Questionnaire date *5-10-84*
Richard Anderson
Name of person completing score summary and profile
Position *Psychologist*
Sex *M*

Before beginning the score summary, read Chapter 5 in the manual.

SCORE SUMMARY

SUBDOMAIN	Raw Score	Standard Score X=100, SD=15 Tables B.1 and B.2	Band of Error 90% Confidence Table B.3	Nat'l %ile Rank Table B.4	Stanine Table B.4	Adaptive Level Tables B.5 and B.6	Age Equivalent Tables B.7 and B.8
Receptive	20					Adeg	12-0
Expressive	52					Mod Lo	7-2
Written	46					Adeg	18-9
COMMUNICATION DOMAIN SUM	118	96	± 7	39	5	Adeg	11-6
Personal	70					Adeg	12-3
Domestic	30					Adeg	12-6
Community	70					Adeg	11-0
DAILY LIVING SKILLS DOMAIN SUM	170	99	± 5	47	5	Adeg	12-3
Interpersonal Relationships	27					Adeg	6-3
Play and Leisure Time	15					Lo	3-5
Coping Skills	21					Adeg	6-3
SOCIALIZATION DOMAIN SUM	63	78	± 6	7	2	Mod Lo	5-5
Gross *(for ages to 5-11-30)*							
Fine							
MOTOR SKILLS DOMAIN SUM			±				
SUM OF DOMAIN STANDARD SCORES	273						
ADAPTIVE BEHAVIOR COMPOSITE		89	± 4	23	4	Adeg	9-9

(See Chapter 5 in the manual to graph scores.)

SCORE PROFILE

	Standard Score ± Band of Error	20 30 40 50 60 70 80 90 100 110 120 130 140 150 160
COMMUNICATION DOMAIN	96 ± 7	
DAILY LIVING SKILLS DOMAIN	99 ± 5	
SOCIALIZATION DOMAIN	78 ± 6	
MOTOR SKILLS DOMAIN	±	
ADAPTIVE BEHAVIOR COMPOSITE	89 ± 4	

percentile rank: 1 2 5 9 16 25 37 50 63 75 84 91 95 98 99
−5SD −4SD −3SD −2SD −1SD MEAN +1SD +2SD +3SD +4SD

(From Harrison, P. L. [1985]. *Vineland Adaptive Behavior Scales: Classroom Edition Manual*. Circle Pines, MN: American Guidance Service. Reprinted with permission of American Guidance Service, Inc.)

scale. The three versions of the *Vineland Scales* are a survey form, an expanded form, and a classroom edition. Special educators use these norm-referenced, standardized tools to identify students with mental retardation and to obtain evaluation data for planning intervention programs.

AAMR Adaptive Behavior Scales-School, Second Edition

The *AAMR (American Association on Mental Retardation) Adaptive Behavior Scales-School, Second Edition (ABS-S:2)* (Lambert et al., 1993) measures the adaptive behavior of children and youth from 3 through 18 years of age. Designed to assess the current functioning of children who are being evaluated for evidence of mental retardation, the *ABS-S:2* also helps to assess the adaptive behavior of children with autism and to differentiate between children with behavior disorders who require special education services and those who can be educated in regular education programs. A summary of the *ABS-S:2* appears in Table 12–2. A residential and community edition, the *AAMR Adaptive Behavior Scales-Residential and Community, Second Edition (ABS-RC:2)* (Nihira et al., 1993) is also available. The *ABS-RC:2* measures the behavior of adults from 18 through 80+ years of age.

The school version of the scale is divided into two parts. Part one measures personal independence in nine behavior domains:

Independent functioning   Prevocational/vocational activity
Physical development   Self-direction
Economic activity   Responsibility
Language development   Socialization
Numbers and time

Part two evaluates maladaptive behaviors in seven domains:

Social behavior   Self-abusive behavior
Conformity   Social engagement
Trustworthiness   Disturbing interpersonal behavior
Stereotyped and hyperactive behavior

Materials for the *ABS-S:2*   *ABS-S:2* materials include an evaluator's manual, a package of 25 examination booklets, a package of 25 profile/summary forms, and an optional software scoring and report system.

Table 12–2   *AAMR Adaptive Behavior Scales-School: 2 (ABS-S:2)*

Type of Test:	Norm referenced, individually administered
Purpose:	Assesses social competence with emphasis on independence in daily living and social skill development
Content Areas:	Personal independence and social maladaption
Administration Time:	30–45 minutes
Age Levels:	3–18 years
Suitable for:	Children being evaluated for mental retardation, autism, and behavior disorders
Scores:	Standard scores and percentiles
In Short:	The *ABS-S:2* is a comprehensive measure of adaptive behavior that provides considerable diagnostic and instructional information.

Administration and Scoring of the *ABS-S:2* It takes 30 to 45 minutes to give the *ABS-S:2*, and evaluators may administer it by either a first-person or third-party approach. With the first-person method, the evaluator has a professional, such as a teacher who knows the student well, rate the behaviors on the scale. With the third-party approach, the evaluator completes the scale by interviewing a parent or primary care giver familiar with the student. Available *ABS-S:2* scores include standard scores and percentiles.

Technical Characteristics of the *ABS-S:2* The *ABS-S:2* sample consisted of more than 2,000 children and youth with developmental disabilities and more than 1,000 students without disabilities gathered from 31 states. The examiner's manual also provides evidence of the reliability and validity of the instrument. This information indicates that the *ABS-S:2* scores are consistent and effective.

Summary of the *ABS-S:2* The *AAMR Adaptive Behavior Scales-School, Second Edition* is a comprehensive measure of adaptive behavior that provides useful information for making diagnostic and instructional decisions.

Adaptive Behavior Inventory

The *Adaptive Behavior Inventory (ABI)* (Brown & Leigh, 1986) is a norm-referenced measure of adaptive behavior. Designed for use by classroom teachers and other professionals who know a student well, the inventory consists of subtests that measure self-care, communication, social, academic, and occupational skills. The authors developed the *ABI* for use with students (6 to 18 years old) who are mentally handicapped and for students (5 to 18 years old) who are not mentally handicapped. The *ABI* includes two forms: a short form containing 50 items and a long form consisting of 150 items. A summary of the *ABI* appears in Table 12–3.

Materials for the *ABI* The *ABI* consists of a test manual, a scoresheet for the short form, and a profile and scoresheet for the long form.

Table 12–3 *Adaptive Behavior Inventory (ABI)*

Type of Test:	Norm referenced, individually administered
Purpose:	Provides a functional assessment of adaptive behavior
Content Areas:	Self-care, communication, social, academic, and occupational skills
Administration Time:	Approximately 25 minutes
Age Levels:	5–18 years
Suitable for:	Measuring the adaptive behavior of students who are mentally disabled
Scores:	Standard scores and percentiles for each subtest and for the total test
In Short:	The *ABI* is designed for use by classroom teachers and other professionals who know a student well. However, weak technical characteristics limit the validity of the *ABI* norms.

Administration and Scoring of the *ABI* The *ABI* takes about 25 minutes to complete and consists of rating each of the items on the scale. The *ABI* produces the following scores: standard scores, standard errors of measurement, and percentile ranks. These scores are available for each subtest and for the total test. The evaluator can compare individual results to intelligence scores from a sample of nondisabled students or from a sample of students with mental retardation. The evaluator may also compile a brief profile of results as part of the scoring procedure.

Technical Characteristics of the *ABI* The developers standardized the *ABI* with two samples of students, including a group of 1,296 students without disabilities and a separate group of 1,076 students with mental retardation. The manual describes the characteristics of these students but fails to adequately delineate the procedures used to select the students for each sample, which limits the validity of the *ABI* norms.

   The manual provides data concerning the internal consistency, test-retest reliability, and concurrent validity of the instrument, which provides an initial indication that *ABI* scores are consistent and effective. However, more research is needed to support use of the *ABI* as a tool for diagnosing and placing students in special education programs.

Summary of the *ABI* The *Adaptive Behavior Inventory* is a norm-referenced measure of adaptive behavior designed for use by classroom teachers and other professionals who know a student well. The *ABI* contains subtests that measure five different skill clusters and includes a short form with 50 items and a long form with 150 items. Unfortunately, weak technical characteristics limit the usefulness of the *ABI* norms.

Pyramid Scales

Unlike most scales of adaptive behavior, the *Pyramid Scales* (Cone, 1984) are criterion referenced rather than norm referenced. Cone developed the scales for use by teachers and diagnosticians in program planning, individual program development, and progress measurement. The scales are useful with children and adults and are appropriate for students with moderate, severe, or profound disabilities. A summary of the *Pyramid Scales* appears in Table 12–4. A list of the skill clusters and subtests in the *Pyramid Scales* follows.

Sensory Skill Cluster	*Primary Skill Cluster*	*Secondary Skill Cluster*
Tactile	Gross motor	Recreation and leisure
Auditory	Eating	Writing
Visual responsiveness	Fine motor	Domestic behavior
	Toileting	Reading
	Dressing	Vocational
	Social interaction	Time
	Washing and grooming	Money
	Receptive language	Numbers
	Expressive language	

Materials for the *Pyramid Scales* The manual for the *Pyramid Scales* includes information about the development of the instrument, directions for scoring, and a discussion of interpretation procedures. The scoring form includes a useful profile for illustrating student performance on the subtests.

Table 12–4 *Pyramid Scales*

Type of Test:	Criterion referenced, individually administered
Purpose:	Provides a functional measure of adaptive behavior for program planning and development
Content Areas:	Sensory, primary, and secondary skill clusters
Administration Time:	Approximately 1 hour
Age Levels:	Childhood–adulthood
Suitable for:	Children and adults with moderate, severe, and profound mental retardation
Scores:	Percent correct scores for each subtest
In Short:	The *Pyramid Scales* are useful for planning and developing individual programs and measuring individual progress.

Administration and Scoring of the *Pyramid Scales*   The *Pyramid Scales* have three administration options. The manual recommends that evaluators use a structured interview with an informant who is familiar with the student. However, an informant can complete the scales by reading and then rating them without an interviewer. Finally, an evaluator can rate the items on the basis of direct observation of a student's behavior. Because it is a criterion-referenced instrument, evaluators can use the scales in a flexible manner to meet the needs of a particular student. For example, special educators in preschool programs may use only the sensory and primary subtests, whereas those in high school programs may use only the secondary subtests.

The scales use a four-point scoring system, and raw scores convert into percent-correct scores for each subtest. For example, a student may complete 50% of the items correctly in the numbers subtest and only 15% of the items in the time subtest. An evaluator plots the percent-correct scores on a graph to illustrate performance across all 20 subtests.

Technical Characteristics of the *Pyramid Scales*   The *Pyramid Scales* have undergone several field tests, revisions, reliability studies, and validity studies. Technically, the scales are a more-than-adequate, criterion-referenced tool, few of which have received as much technical study as these scales.

Summary of the *Pyramid Scales*   The criterion-referenced *Pyramid Scales* measure the adaptive behavior of children and adults. Consisting of items that measure sensory, primary, and secondary skills, the author designed the scales for use in programs that serve students with severe disabilities.

Other Adaptive Behavior Scales

Brief reviews of other available adaptive behavior scales follow. These include a screening instrument, two comprehensive scales, and a scale designed for use with adolescents.

Adaptive Behavior Evaluation Scale   The norm-referenced, individually administered *Adaptive Behavior Evaluation Scale (ABES)* (McCarney, 1987) is a screening instrument for measuring the adaptive behavior of children ($4^1/_2$ through 21 years of age) with mental retardation. The *ABES* includes a school rating form and a parent rating form. The *ABES* school rating form consists of 60 items arranged into three subscales: environmental/interpersonal behaviors (37 items), self-related behaviors (13 items), and task-related behaviors (10 items). The parent rating form contains 52 items organized into three subscales: social responsibility, self-care, and personal independence.

Adaptive Behavior Inventory for Children   The norm-referenced, individually administered *Adaptive Behavior Inventory for Children (ABIC)* (Mercer & Lewis, 1977) is designed for use with children from 5 through 11 years of age. The behaviors measured by the *ABIC* include the child's role performance in the family, community, peer group, and nonacademic settings. The instrument also assesses earner/consumer behaviors and self-maintenance. The *ABIC* manual has been translated into Spanish. The same administration form is used for English and Spanish.

Responsibility and Independence Scale for Adolescents   The *Responsibility and Independence Scale for Adolescents (RISA)* (Salvia et al., 1990) measures the adaptive behavior of youth from 12 through 19 years of age. The *RISA,* a norm-referenced, individually administered scale, assesses adaptive behaviors related to social expectations, responsibility, and independence. The 136 items on the scale are organized into nine functional areas: self-management, social maturity, social communication, domestic skills, money management, citizenship, personal organization, transportation skills, and career skills.

The *RISA* is administered in a standardized interview format to a respondent who is familiar with the adolescent.

Scales of Independent Behavior-Revised   The norm-referenced, individually administered *Scales of Independent Behavior-Revised (SIB-R)* (Bruininks et al., 1996) provide a comprehensive assessment of adaptive and maladaptive behavior. Designed for individuals from infancy to retirement, the full *SIB-R* scales take about an hour to administer. The short form and the early development form take only about 20 minutes to give. A special version of the *SIB-R Short Form* for use with individuals who have visual impairments is available. The *SIB-R Short Form for the Visually Impaired* (Knowlton et al., 1997) contains 40 items and is a suitable screening test of adaptive behavior. The full *SIB-R* includes 14 adaptive behavior subtests and 8 problem behavior subtests organized into the following categories:

Adaptive Behavior Clusters

Social Interaction and Communication Skills

Social interaction
Language comprehension
Language expression

Personal Living Skills

Eating and meal preparation
Toileting
Dressing
Personal self-care
Domestic skills

Motor Skills

Gross motor
Fine motor

Community Living Skills

Time and punctuality
Money and value
Work skills
Home/community orientation

Problem Behavior Clusters

Internalized Maladaptive

Hurtful to self
Unusual or repetitive habits
Withdrawal or inattentive behavior

Externalized Maladaptive

Hurtful to others
Destructive to property
Disruptive behavior

Asocial Maladaptive

Socially offensive behavior
Uncooperative behavior

☑ Comprehension Checklist

When students require assessment in adaptive behavior, evaluators may select from among a variety of scales and inventories. Because the various instruments differ in design and purpose, special educators should select an appropriate tool on the basis of individual student requirements and the purpose for conducting the assessment. However, laws and professional standards require that evaluators use norm-referenced scales for making placement decisions. On the other hand, most teachers prefer to use less formal, more flexible scales for making curriculum-based instructional decisions.

Summary

Adaptive behavior is the ability to adjust to the personal and social demands in the environment, especially to changes in the environment. Special educators use adaptive behavior scales to obtain assessment information regarding student performance in personal self-sufficiency, independence in the community, and personal-social responsibility. Adaptive behavior focuses on assessing typical performance in real-life settings rather than on ability to perform in a testing situation. For this reason, adaptive behavior scales consist of checklists of items arranged by age. Informants usually provide the information necessary for measuring adaptive behavior, and, whenever possible, evaluators should use more than one informant to obtain a comprehensive picture of behavior as it occurs in different settings.

Most adaptive behavior scales are norm-referenced instruments that special educators use along with other tests and assessment information to identify students with disabilities, determine eligibility for special education services, and make placement decisions. Because mental retardation is defined in part as resulting from deficits in adaptive behavior, assessment plays a major role in classifying students as mentally retarded. Special educators also use results from adaptive behavior scales to formulate instructional programs focusing on personal, social, and occupational skill development. Refer to Table 12–5 (p. 375) for a summary of adaptive behavior scales.

Although test authors are refining the process of assessing adaptive behavior, additional improvements are needed. All of the existing scales exhibit some weaknesses, especially in technical characteristics. Despite these problems, special educators rely on assessment of adaptive behavior to provide important information about student performance in daily life.

Chapter Review and Application

Multiple Choice

Directions: Read each item carefully. In the blank beside each item, write the letter of the best response. Each question contains only one best answer. Check your answers with the answer key at the end of the book.

_____ 1. Which term refers to the ability to adjust to the environment?
    a. Personal self-sufficiency
    b. Community independence
    c. Personal-social responsibility
    d. Adaptive behavior

_____ 2. Which term refers to behaviors such as trustworthiness, commitment, and self-direction?
    a. Personal self-sufficiency
    b. Community independence
    c. Personal-social responsibility
    d. Adaptive behavior

_____ 3. Which term, when assessing young children, encompasses playing at school, at home, and in the yard with minimal supervision?
    a. Personal self-sufficiency
    b. Community independence
    c. Personal-social responsibility
    d. Adaptive behavior

_____ 4. Adaptive behavior is especially important in diagnosing which of the following?
    a. Mental retardation
    b. Learning disabilities
    c. Physical impairments
    d. Emotional disturbance

_____ 5. Adaptive behavior scales measure and rely on all of the following *except*
    a. typical performance over time
    b. performance during testing
    c. performance as reported by an informant

_____ 6. An informant is always which of the following?
    a. a teacher or psychologist.
    b. a parent or other primary care giver.
    c. the person who provides the information necessary to rate the items.
    d. the person who rates the items.

_____ 7. When evaluators have serious doubts about the validity of an informant's responses, they should do which of these?
    a. Invalidate the interview and start over
    b. Adjust for the inaccuracies in scoring particular items
    c. Rate the behaviors more evenly
    d. Use multiple informants

____ **8.** When administering the *Vineland Adaptive Behavior Scales,* the interview should be conducted in which of the following ways?
  a. On an item-by-item basis
  b. Like a standardized test
  c. In an open-ended, casual format

____ **9.** Which adaptive behavior scale is criterion referenced?
  a. *Vineland Adaptive Behavior Scales*
  b. *AAMD Adaptive Behavior Scale*
  c. *Pyramid Scales*
  d. *Adaptive Behavior Inventory*

____ **10.** Which adaptive behavior scale contains three separate versions: a survey form, an expanded form, and a classroom edition?
  a. *Vineland Adaptive Behavior Scales*
  b. *AAMR Adaptive Behavior Scale*
  c. *Pyramid Scales*
  d. *Adaptive Behavior Inventory*

____ **11.** Which adaptive behavior scale provides norms from regular classes, classes for students with educable mental retardation, and classes for students with trainable mental retardation?
  a. *Vineland Adaptive Behavior Scales*
  b. *AAMR Adaptive Behavior Scale*
  c. *Pyramid Scales*
  d. *Adaptive Behavior Inventory*

True-False

Directions: Answer true or false for each of the following statements about assessing adaptive behavior by writing T or F in the blank beside each item. Use the answer key in the back of the book to check your answers.

____ **1.** A majority of the adaptive behavior scales measure student performance through direct observation.

____ **2.** Experts suggest that evaluators should avoid using multiple informants when assessing adaptive behavior.

____ **3.** Adaptive behavior encompasses many different behaviors across a wide age span.

____ **4.** Identifying deficits in adaptive behavior is a required step in the process of classifying students as mentally retarded.

____ **5.** Adaptive behavior assesses typical performance in real-life settings and performance on standardized tests.

Short Answers

Directions: Review your understanding of the material in this chapter by answering the short answer items below. Compare your responses with the sample answers. Your responses should contain information that is similar to but not exactly the same as the information in the sample answers at the end of the book.

1. Define the term *adaptive behavior* and describe the types of behaviors and the age range measured by adaptive behavior scales.

2. Most adaptive behavior scales use an informant to gather information for measuring adaptive behavior. During an interview, informants sometimes give biased or distorted answers, and discrepancies can occur among informants. What is an informant? What are some of the reasons for inaccurate responses? What can the evaluator do to obtain balanced and reliable information?

3. The *Vineland Adaptive Behavior Scales* are one of the most widely used instruments for evaluating adaptive behavior. Describe the purpose, content, and age range of these scales and their use in special education.

References

Beirne-Smith, M., Patton, J. R., & Payne, J. S. (1994). *Mental Retardation* (4th ed.). New York: Merrill/Macmillan.

Brown, L., & Leigh, J. E. (1986). *Adaptive Behavior Inventory.* Austin, TX: PRO-ED.

Bruininks, R. H., Woodcock, R. W., Weatherman, R. E., & Hill, B. K. (1996). *Scales of Independent Behavior-Revised.* Itasca, IL: Riverside Publishing.

Cone, J. D. (1984). *Pyramid Scales.* Austin, TX: PRO-ED.

Doll, E. A. (1965). *Vineland Social Maturity Scale.* Circle Pines, MN: American Guidance Service.

Harrison, P. L. (1985). *Vineland Adaptive Behavior Scales: Classroom Edition Manual.* Circle Pines, MN: American Guidance Service.

Knowlton, M., Lee, I., Bruininks, R. H., Woodcock, R. W., Weatherman, R. E., & Hill, B. K. (1997). *SIB-R Short Form for the Visually Impaired.* Itasca, IL: Riverside Publishing.

Lambert, N. M., Nihira, K., & Leland, H. (1993). *AAMR Adaptive Behavior Scales-School* (2d ed.). Austin, TX: PRO-ED.

McCarney, S. B. (1987). *Adaptive Behavior Evaluation Scale.* Columbia, MO: Hawthorne Educational Services.

Mercer, J. R. (1977). *System of Multicultural Pluralistic Assessment: Technical Manual.* San Antonio, TX: Psychological Corporation.

Mercer, J. R., & Lewis, J. F. (1977a). *Adaptive Behavior Inventory for Children.* San Antonio, TX: Harcourt Brace Educational Measurement.

————. (1977b). *System of Multicultural Pluralistic Assessment: Parent Interview Manual.* San Antonio, TX: Psychological Corporation.

————. (1977c). *System of Multicultural Pluralistic Assessment: Student Assessment Manual.* San Antonio, TX: Psychological Corporation.

Nihira, K., Leland, H., & Lambert, N. M. (1993). *AAMR Adaptive Behavior Scales -Residential and Community* (2d ed.). Austin, TX: PRO-ED.

Salvia, J., Neisworth, J., & Schmidt, M. (1990). *Responsibility and Independence Scale for Adolescents.* Itasca, IL: Riverside Publishing.

Sattler, J. M. (1992). *Assessment of Children* (3d ed.). San Diego: Author.

Sparrow, S. S., Balla, D. A., & Cicchetti, D. V. (1984a). *Vineland Adaptive Behavior Scales: Expanded Form Manual* (interview ed.). Circle Pines, MN: American Guidance Service.

————. (1984b). *Vineland Adaptive Behavior Scales: Survey Form Manual* (interview ed.). Circle Pines, MN: American Guidance Service.

Table 12–5   Review of Adaptive Behavior Scales

Name of Test	Type of Test	Suitable for Individuals Who Are	Brief Description of Test	Purpose of Administering Test
*AAMR (American Association on Mental Retardation) Adaptive Behavior Scales-School, Second Edition (ABS-S:2) (Lambert et al., 1993)	Norm-referenced, individually administered comprehensive scale	3–18 years	Includes subscales for measuring personal independence and social maladaption	To assess social competence with emphasis on independence in daily living and social skill development, to assess children who are being evaluated for mental retardation, to assess the adaptive behavior of children with autism, and to differentiate children with behavior disorders who require special education services from those who can be served in regular education
AAMR Adaptive Behavior Scales-Residential and Community, Second Edition (ABS-RC:2) (Nihira et al., 1993)	Norm-referenced, individually administered comprehensive scale	18–80+ years	A residential and community edition for adults with mental retardation	To assess social competence with emphasis on independence in daily living and social skill development
Adaptive Behavior Evaluation Scale (ABES) (McCarney, 1987)	Norm-referenced, individually administered screening instrument	4.5–21 years	Includes a school rating form and a parent rating form	To measure the adaptive behavior of children with mental retardation
Adaptive Behavior Inventory (ABI) (Brown & Leigh, 1986)	Norm referenced, individually administered; includes a screening form and a comprehensive form	5–18 years	Self-care, communication, social, academic, and occupational skills	To provide a functional assessment of adaptive behavior
Adaptive Behavior Inventory for Children (ABIC) (Mercer & Lewis, 1977)	Norm referenced, individually administered, comprehensive scale	5–11 years	Includes measures of role performance in the family, community, peer group, and nonacademic settings; also assesses earner/consumer behaviors and self-maintenance	To comprehensively measure the adaptive behavior of children

*Tests marked with asterisks are featured in tables in this chapter.

Table 12–5   *(continued)*

Name of Test	Type of Test	Suitable for Individuals Who Are	Brief Description of Test	Purpose of Administering Test
Responsibility and Independence Scale for Adolescents (RISA) (Salvia et al., 1990)	Norm-referenced, individually administered comprehensive scale	12–19 years	Includes 136 items for assessing adaptive behavior in 9 functional areas: self management, social maturity, social communication, domestic skills, money management, citizenship, personal organization, transportation skills, and other skills	To assess the adaptive behavior associated with social expectations, responsibility, and independence
Pyramid Scales (Cone, 1984)	Criterion-referenced, individually administered comprehensive scale	Children and adults	Includes subscales for measuring sensory, primary, and secondary skills	For use by teachers and diagnosticians in program planning, individual program development, and progress measurement
Scales of Independent Behavior-Revised (SIB-R) (Bruininks et al., 1996)	Norm referenced, individually administered; includes a screening form and a comprehensive form	Infancy to retirement	Includes 14 adaptive behavior subscales and 8 problem behavior subscales	Comprehensive assessment of adaptive and maladaptive behavior
SIB-R Short Form for the Visually Impaired (Knowlton et al., 1997)	Norm-referenced, individually administered screening instrument	Infancy to retirement	Contains 40 items and is suitable for use as a screening test of adaptive behavior	A special version of the *SIB-R Short Form* for use with individuals who have visual impairments
*Vineland Adaptive Behavior Scales (Sparrow et al., 1984a, b)	Norm referenced, individually administered; includes a screening form and a comprehensive form	Birth–18 years	Includes subscales for measuring communication, daily living skills, socialization, motor skills, and an optional subscale for assessing maladaptive behavior	To assist in identifying and placing students with mental retardation and to obtain evaluation data for programming and intervention purposes
*Vineland Adaptive Behavior Scales: Classroom Edition (Harrison, 1985)	Norm-referenced, individually administered comprehensive scale	3–12 years	Contains 244 items for measuring adaptive behavior in the classroom and the school setting	To assist in identifying and placing students with mental retardation and to obtain evaluation data for programming and intervention purposes

C H A P T E R   1 3

Assessment of Career and Vocational Skills

Overview

The process of assessing career and vocational skills involves measuring and evaluating work-related behaviors as well as competencies in social interaction, functional academics, and activities of daily living. Special educators who teach adolescents with disabilities need in-depth knowledge of the procedures of career and vocational assessment. For special educators who teach younger students, understanding the basics of career and vocational assessment is a necessary element in building a comprehensive knowledge base in assessment.

This chapter assists you in learning the essential concepts and techniques of career and vocational assessment. To achieve this goal, we will consider the meaning of the terms *career* and *vocational assessment* and investigate various tests for assessing career and vocational skills, including the following:

- Written tests.
- Work samples.
- Situational and on-the-job assessment.
- Task analysis.

For each type of assessment we examine the definition of the category, representative tests and evaluation procedures, and practical applications useful for special education teachers. Throughout the chapter we focus on why we assess the career and vocational skills of students with disabilities and how teachers can utilize this type of assessment in instructional programs.

Objectives

After reading this chapter, you will be prepared to do the following:

- Understand the terms *career* and *vocational assessment.*
- Understand the four stages of career education.
- Use assessment data in planning transition services.
- Administer written tests for assessing career and vocational skills.
- Use work samples to assess career and vocational skills.
- Conduct situational and on-the-job assessment procedures.
- Use task analysis to assess career and vocational skills.

An Introduction to Career and Vocational Assessment

The following narrative illustrates how to begin career and vocational assessment, and also shows the value of assessing career and vocational skills.

When Barry Schwartz started thinking about teaching vocational and career skills to his teenagers with disabilities, he went to his program coordinator for information about where to begin. The coordinator suggested he begin by assessing the career and vocational skills of the students; then he could see what career and vocational skills the students needed to develop. First he needed to know the most appropriate assessment to use. The coordinator showed him what was available and helped him select an assessment. After studying the instrument, Mr. Schwartz administered it to his students and used the results to develop transition services and learning activities for each student.

Definitions of Career and Vocational Assessment

Career assessment encompasses evaluation of a broad range of practical life skills that are part of living and working as an adult. Career skills include social behaviors, functional academics, and daily living activities necessary for success on the job and in the community. Special educators usually begin to assess and teach career-related competencies in the elementary grades. Unlike the broad range of career skills, **vocational assessment** has a more specific connotation. It refers to the particular skills necessary for success in specific jobs, professions, or trades. Because vocational skills are limited to particular job skills, special and vocational educators usually begin to assess and teach vocational skills when students reach high school.

Stages of Career Development

Brolin (1986) described a comprehensive model to explain the role of career education in preparing students with the wide variety of practical skills necessary for success in postschool activities. The model includes four stages: career awareness, career exploration, career preparation, and placement and follow-up (see Focus 13–1). In the elementary grades, career education focuses on career awareness. During this stage, students learn the value of working and develop academic and social skills necessary for career success. Assessment of career awareness includes measuring and evaluating students' knowledge of various jobs and their understanding of the meaning of work. In the middle grades, the focus of career education shifts to career exploration, and students begin to experience particular types of work. Assessment in this stage involves measuring student interests and aptitudes for specific jobs, occupations, and professions. In high school, the emphasis changes to career preparation, during which students select a specific job as a career goal and begin to learn the skills necessary for success in that job. In this stage, special educators emphasize vocational assessment and training. In the final stage, placement and follow-up, special educators coordinate their efforts with other agencies to ensure that students make a successful transition from education to the adult world of living and working in the community. Assessment involves identifying transition issues and needs, establishing future goals, and identifying the agencies that will participate in reaching these goals.

FOCUS 13–1

Assessment in the Stages of Career Education

Stage of Career Education	*Assessment Question*
Career Awareness	Does the student have an understanding of the meaning of work and knowledge of a variety of jobs?
Career Exploration	What are the student's job interests and aptitudes?
Career Preparation	What are the student's specific job goals? What skills does the student need to reach these goals?
Placement and Follow-Up	What are the student's transition issues and needs? What are the student's future goals? Which agencies will participate in reaching these goals?

Transition Services

The Individuals with Disabilities Education Act (IDEA) defines **transition services** as a coordinated set of activities designed to facilitate movement from school to postschool activities, which include postsecondary education, vocational training, integrated employment (including supported employment), continuing and adult education, adult services, independent living, and community participation. IDEA requires the inclusion of a statement describing needed transition services in the IEPs of all students, beginning at age 14 years and annually thereafter. The statement must include a description of interagency responsibilities or linkages necessary to ensure a successful transition. To write appropriate statements, special educators must assess students' needs for transition services. The assessment process requires special educators to collaborate with other professionals from agencies and institutions (e.g., vocational rehabilitation) to identify suitable postschool services and to develop linkages so that students can access those services.

The addition of transition services to the IEPs of older students points out the current emphasis on **functional assessment** in career and vocational evaluation. Special educators use functional assessment to evaluate student performance in real-life, natural settings to identify proficiency in performing practical, applied skills (Clark & Kolstoe, 1990). For high school students, this means assessing performance at home, at school, on the job, and in the community. According to Clark and Kolstoe, functional assessment not only recognizes the importance of academics and specific job competencies but also includes daily living, personal-social development, and community-based skills as equally important learning domains.

Transition Planning Inventory

The *Transition Planning Inventory (TPI)* (Clark & Patton, 1997) is a criterion-referenced, individually administered instrument for identifying and planning for the transition needs of students with disabilities. The *TPI* kit includes an administration and resource guide and packages of 25 profile and assessment recommendation forms, school forms, home forms, and student forms. The administration and resource guide includes a planning notes form, which is the key assessment and individualized planning document, and a list of more than 600 transition goals correlated to each planning statement.

The recommended procedure for using the *TPI* includes the following:

- Having students, parents/guardians, and school-based personnel complete the appropriate inventory form.
- Collecting the completed forms and profiling the results on the profile form.
- Conducting a meeting to discuss the student's transition needs.
- Completing the planning notes form at the meeting that specifies additional assessment (if needed), IEP goals that need to be written, linkage activities with postschool agencies, and services that will be required after graduation.

Why Do We Assess the Career and Vocational Skills of Students With Disabilities?

With the current emphasis on transition planning, more and more attention is being given to the assessment of career and vocational skills, especially with teenagers who have special needs (see Focus 13–2). In the case of career and vocational skills, we conduct assessment to help identify the instructional needs of students in skill areas required for successful personal development and employment. The goal is to utilize efficient, comprehensive, and accurate assessments that respond to the specific needs of the students. We do this to evaluate what the student knows and can do so that interests, aptitudes, strengths, and weaknesses can be identified. Assessment in community-based settings is an important part of evaluating these skills because students receive training experiences in the community. The most effective assessments, especially during the transition phase, include the participation of the student, parents, and service providers who will be involved in the transition process.

FOCUS 13–2

Why Do We Assess the Career and Vocational Skills of Students With Disabilities?

- To identify instructional needs in skill areas required for successful personal development and employment
- To evaluate what the student knows and can do
- To identify occupational interests, aptitudes, strengths, and weaknesses

The following true story illustrates how assessment of vocational and career skills meets the needs of a student with a severe disability.

Nancy attended a special school for students labeled as trainable mentally retarded. During her senior year, the school began a supported employment program (a specialized type of job training and placement service) for the graduating students. When she enrolled in the program, her job coach gave her a picture interest inventory and interviewed her parents and teachers to identify her vocational interests. Later, the job coach matched Nancy's interests and aptitudes with a job opening as a kitchen helper in a nursing home. As part of the process of placing Nancy in this job, the job coach provided intensive, one-on-one, on-the-job training that included the use of task analytic assessment to help Nancy learn the most difficult jobs in the kitchen. The job coach also arranged for the kitchen supervisor to provide weekly evaluations of Nancy's performance. Gradually, as Nancy learned to complete her job tasks more independently, the job coach decreased the level of supervision. After 3 weeks of intensive training and 3 months of follow-along training, Nancy learned to perform all aspects of her job without assistance from the job coach. At this point, the job coach stopped helping her directly but continued to provide follow-up services as necessary. These included periodic evaluations to ensure that she continued to work at acceptable performance levels.

The following narrative, based on a case study by Hasazi and Cobb (1988), chronicles the use of vocational and career assessment to help meet the needs of a student with a learning disability.

During the summer before he entered 11th grade, Robert, a student with a learning disability, enrolled in a career exploration class at a regional vocational center. To assess his vocational interests and aptitudes, the vocational teacher used work samples based on actual jobs that provided simulated experience with various types of work. Robert performed especially well on the work sample, which consisted of printing tasks associated with work in commercial print shops. In fact, he enjoyed the printing experience so much that in the fall he enrolled in a printing program at the regional center. At his individualized education plan (IEP) meeting at the end of his junior year, Robert and his parents decided that a printing career was an appropriate goal. The IEP team developed a transition plan that included work experience in a local print shop during his senior year. When he began his work placement during the spring semester, the work experience specialist from the school accompanied him to the work site. The specialist conducted on-the-job assessment to monitor his work daily for the first week and then gradually decreased the monitoring visits to once a week.

Upon graduation, a placement specialist from the state vocational rehabilitation agency placed Robert in a job with a local printing company. The work experience specialist from the school provided him with a follow-up evaluation 6 months after graduation to assess his employment status and coordinate appropriate referrals if necessary.

These vignettes illustrate the role of assessment in providing career and vocational services to students with disabilities.

☑ Comprehension Checklist

Career assessment is a broad term that includes vocational competencies as well as social behaviors, functional academics, and daily living skills. *Vocational assessment* is a specific term that refers to measuring and evaluating student accomplishment of the competencies necessary for success in particular jobs, professions, or trades. Special educators begin to assess and teach career skills in the elementary grades, and this continues in later grades. However, in the later grades (especially high school) special educators emphasize preparing students with specific vocational skills. The law requires that the IEP of each 16-year-old student include a statement describing needed transition services. Furthermore, the IEP writing team must update the transition statement each year as part of the annual IEP writing process. In order that special educators assess student needs for transition services appropriately, they must establish links with the agencies that provide postschool services.

Written Tests of Vocational and Career Skills

Special educators rely on a variety of relatively inexpensive and easy-to-administer written tests to assess career and vocational skills. A primary advantage of written tests is that evaluators can administer and score them efficiently in short time periods. Like all assessment procedures, however, written tests have certain limitations. The major drawback is that, in some cases, written test results differ from assessment results derived from observation of actual student performance in real work situations. Because of this limitation, special educators should avoid using written test results as the sole criterion for making career and vocational placement decisions; they should also keep in mind the inherent weaknesses of pencil-on-paper testing.

Despite limitations, written tests are useful for assessing many career and vocational behaviors. These tests include rating scales, checklists of skills, and inventories for assessing vocational interests, prevocational skills, and employability skills. From this assortment, the special educator selects a particular instrument based on the student's needs and the reason for testing.

Vocational Interest Inventories

Vocational interest inventories are specialized tests for assessing the job and career preferences of individuals and groups of students. Teachers use vocational interest inventories to assist in developing career awareness and career exploration activities based on the student's job interests. Similarly, vocational evaluators use interest inventories as a component in comprehensive assessment of work potential. In addition, job placement specialists often rely on interest inventories to identify potential for success in specific jobs, trades, or professions. Reviews of two representative inventories, the *Reading Free Vocational Interest Inventory* and the *Wide Range Interest-Opinion Test,* follow, along with brief reviews of other available inventories.

Reading Free Vocational Interest Inventory-Revised

The *Reading Free Vocational Interest Inventory-Revised* (Becker, 1981, 1988) is a picture test of vocational interests. Evaluators administer the inventory by having students choose a preferred activity from 55 sets of three pictures. Becker designed this norm-referenced, group-administered test for students with intellectual and learning disabilities who display limited reading ability or language problems. The author recommends that evaluators use inventory results for vocational planning and placement and as a guide for developing instructional objectives and activities. A summary of the *Reading Free Vocational Interest Inventory-Revised* appears in Table 13–1. The inventory contains the following 11 interest areas:

1. Automotive
2. Building trades
3. Clerical
4. Animal care
5. Food service
6. Patient care
7. Horticulture
8. Housekeeping
9. Personal service
10. Laundry service
11. Materials handling

Materials for the *Reading Free Vocational Interest Inventory-Revised* Inventory materials include a revised manual published in 1988, a test booklet containing 55 test plates, a scoresheet, and a student profile graph.

Administration and Scoring of the *Reading Free Vocational Interest Inventory-Revised* The inventory is quick and easy to administer and score. Evaluators administer the inventory by presenting the series of 55 test plates (each containing three line drawings) to students, who circle the drawing they like best from each plate. Administration takes about 20 minutes, and scoring involves converting raw scores into *t*-scores, percentiles, and stanines. Evaluators also complete a student profile form that shows vocational interests across 11 job areas. However, because it is a group screening test, the results lack sufficient detail for identifying specific interests.

Table 13–1   *Reading Free Vocational Interest Inventory-Revised*

Type of Test:	Norm referenced
Purpose:	A group screening test of vocational interests
Content Areas:	11 vocational interest areas
Administration Time:	20 minutes
Age Levels:	Students, ages 13–22 years, and sheltered workshop employees, ages 17–59 years
Suitable for:	Students and adults with learning disabilities and mental retardation who display limited reading ability or language impairment
Scores:	Percentiles, *t*-scores, and stanines
In Short:	The *Reading Free Vocational Interest Inventory-Revised* is best when used as a screening measure rather than as a diagnostic tool.

Technical Characteristics of the *Reading Free Vocational Interest Inventory*   The inventory was standardized with a sample group of more than 8,000 public school students (grades 7 through 12) with learning disabilities and mental retardation and with more than 2,000 adults (ages 17 to 59 years) with mental retardation from sheltered workshops and vocational training centers. However, the manual includes only a brief description of the process the author used to identify the sample group participants, and this lack of information is a major weakness in the standardization plan. In terms of reliability, the test manual reports test-retest coefficients in the .70s and .80s, with standard errors of measurement of one or two points. The manual also reports an internal consistency coefficient of .82. On the question of validity, the author provides support for content validity based on the use of study teams to select the line drawings in the administration manual, which also reports results from a concurrent validity study that compared inventory scores with scores from the *Geist Picture Interest Inventory-Revised* (Geist, 1964), and results from a criterion-related validity study that showed a positive relationship between inventory scores and job occupations with individuals who were mentally retarded. Overall, the inventory displays satisfactory reliability and validity but inadequate norms.

Summary of the *Reading Free Vocational Interest Inventory-Revised*   The *Reading Free Vocational Interest Inventory-Revised,* a picture test of vocational interests, is a norm-referenced group screening test. The author developed the test specifically for students with mental retardation and learning disabilities. However, because of technical weaknesses in the standardization plan, special educators should use the inventory as a rough screening measure rather than as a diagnostic tool.

Wide Range Interest-Opinion Test

Like the *Reading Free Vocational Interest Inventory-Revised,* the *Wide Range Interest-Opinion Test (WRIOT)* (Jastak & Jastak, 1979) is a picture test that measures vocational interests with a series of line drawings showing people in various work-related situations. The authors designed the line drawings to measure both work interests (such as mechanics, social services, and sales) and work attitudes (including risk and ambition). They recommend the test for use in career and vocational planning, including counseling, employee selection, and coordinating instruction with student interests. Evaluators administer the *WRIOT* by having students indicate their preferences from among various drawings. The drawings that a student likes best and least serve as the basis for determining vocational interests at three levels: self-projected ability, aspiration level, and social conformity. The *WRIOT,* which is designed for use with individuals from age 5 years through adulthood, does not require students to have reading skills or verbal language ability. This makes the test suitable for students who are nonreaders, nonverbal, or nonvocal. A summary of the *WRIOT* appears in Table 13–2.

Materials for the *WRIOT*   *WRIOT* materials include a test manual, a test booklet containing 154 test plates, and a scoring form. Evaluators may obtain supplemental materials, including a filmstrip for use in place of the test plates and computer software to assist with scoring and reporting results.

Table 13–2   *Wide Range Interest-Opinion Test (WRIOT)*

Type of Test:	Norm referenced
Purpose:	A screening test of vocational interests
Content Areas:	18 vocational interest areas and 8 vocational attitudes
Administration Time:	Approximately 40 minutes
Age Levels:	5 years–adult
Suitable for:	Students with mild, moderate, and severe disabilities, including learning disabilities, emotional disturbance, and mental retardation, physical disabilities, and hearing impairments
Scores:	Percentiles, *t*-scores, standard scores, stanines, and scaled scores
In Short:	The *WRIOT* is suitable for use as a gross screening measure but technical deficiencies limit the validity of the norms.

Administration and Scoring of the *WRIOT*   Designed for group or individual administration, evaluators give the *WRIOT* by presenting a series of test plates (each containing three line drawings) to students, who select the drawings they like best and least from each plate. Administration takes about 40 minutes, and scoring consists of graphing test results (in the form of *t*-scores) on a report form that displays student likes and dislikes in 18 interest clusters and 8 attitude clusters across an occupational range that includes both unskilled labor and highly skilled jobs requiring extensive training.

Technical Characteristics of the *WRIOT*   The authors standardized the *WRIOT* on a sample of 9,184 subjects from age 5 through 35 years and older. Unfortunately, the manual fails to report details concerning the subject selection process or the characteristics of the participating subjects. In a detailed review of the test, Organist (1985) concluded that, because it fails to provide sufficient information about the standardization process, the *WRIOT* has inadequate norms. Likewise, Organist noted that the *WRIOT* manual includes few data concerning reliability and validity. In terms of reliability, the manual includes a description of one split-half reliability study, based on scores from 300 people, that yielded coefficients ranging from .82 to .95. The manual also reports scores from a concurrent validity study, based on a sample group of 100, that yielded correlations below acceptable levels. Although these two studies produced some initial data for judging technical adequacy, they fail to provide enough information to support use of the test as a norm-referenced measure.

Summary of the *WRIOT*   The *Wide Range Interest-Opinion Test* consists of a series of drawings depicting people performing various jobs. Evaluators present the drawings to students, who indicate their vocational preferences by selecting drawings they like and dislike. This selection process yields information about vocational interests and attitudes that an evaluator graphs on the *WRIOT* scoring form. The *WRIOT* has the advantage of taking less than an hour to administer and score, and evaluators may give it to students who are nonreaders. However, the *WRIOT* displays technical weaknesses. For this reason, evaluators should use caution when interpreting *WRIOT* scores. Although the instrument may be adequate as a gross screening measure to obtain a general idea of vocational interests and opinions, it lacks the necessary technical qualities to serve as a norm-referenced interest inventory.

Other Available Interest Inventories

Brief reviews of other available interest inventories follow. These inventories include group-administered instruments as well as tools for specific populations such as students with learning disabilities.

Career Interest Inventory   The norm-referenced, group-administered *Career Interest Inventory (CII)* (1990) provides information about students' educational goals, interest in a variety of school subjects and school-related activities, and interest in various occupations. The *CII* helps students explore educational and occupational alternatives, learn about careers, and set goals for the future. Designed for students from grade 7 through 12 and adults, the *CII* includes two levels. Level 1, for students in grades 7 through 9, helps students select courses to take and careers to begin exploring. Level 2, for students in grades 10–12, helps students explore postsecondary educational and career alternatives. The *CII* takes about 30 minutes to administer to a group of students. Results include an individual student report and a counselor's report for each student. The *CII* was standardized with the *Differential Aptitude Tests, Fifth Edition*. This enables comparison of aptitude with interest when the two tests are given together.

Career Inventories for the Learning Disabled   The *Career Inventories for the Learning Disabled (CILD)* (Weller & Buchanan, 1983) were designed for use by special education teachers, vocational counselors, psychologists, and educational diagnosticians who serve children and adults with learning disabilities. The criterion-referenced, individually administered *CILD* contains three inventories. The attributes inventory assesses a person's dominant personality characteristics. The ability inventory provides a profile of the person's auditory, visual, and motor abilities. The interest inventory measures an individual's interests coinciding with his or her personality attributes and abilities. The attributes and abilities inventories are completed by the evaluator after a period of observation. The interest inventory is completed by the student. The age range of the *CILD* is 6 years through adulthood.

Occupational Aptitude Survey and Interest Schedule, Second Edition   The norm-referenced *Occupational Aptitude Survey and Interest Schedule, Second Edition (OASIS-2)* (Parker, 1991) can be given individually or to groups of up to 10 students. Teachers, counselors, and other professionals can administer the *OASIS-2* in about 45 minutes to students in grades 8 through 12 who are disabled, disadvantaged, or nondisabled. The aptitude survey measures general ability, verbal aptitude, numerical aptitude, spatial aptitude, perceptual aptitude, and manual dexterity. The 240- item interest schedule measures 12 interest areas related to occupations including artistic, scientific, nature, protective, mechanical, industrial, business detail, selling, accommodating, humanitarian, leading-influencing, and physical performing. An optional *OASIS-2* interpretation workbook is available to help students understand their scores and identify what they should consider in career planning. This self-administered workbook matches aptitudes and interests with more than 250 jobs.

Assessment of Prevocational and Employability Skills

Students need to acquire certain prevocational and employability skills to ensure success on the job and in the community. **Prevocational skills** are the personal, social, and applied academic skills necessary for success on any job. Likewise, **employability skills** are generic skills important to qualify for entry-level jobs in the workplace regardless of the particular occupation or profession. Special educators use written tests of prevocational and employability skills to identify student performance levels, and results from these tests serve as guides for developing instructional objectives. Reviews of several representative tests of prevocational and employability skills appear in the following sections.

Brigance Diagnostic Inventory of Essential Skills   The criterion-referenced, individually administered *Brigance Diagnostic Inventory of Essential Skills* (Brigance, 1987) covers academic skill areas and life skills. The former includes reading/language arts, math, and study skills. Life skill subtests include food and clothing, money and finance, travel and transportation, and communication and telephone skills. The *Inventory of Essential Skills* also includes rating scales for measuring health and attitude, responsibility and self-discipline, job interview preparation, communication, and auto safety. Inventory materials include a student record book that records competency levels and defines instructional objectives and a class record book that provides a matrix of skills assessed, skills mastered, and objectives for a group of up to 15 students. The inventory is widely used to assess secondary level students and adult learners with special needs.

Brigance Diagnostic Life Skills Inventory   The *Brigance Diagnostic Life Skills Inventory* (Brigance, 1994) is a criterion-referenced tool for assessing listening, speaking, reading, writing, comprehending, and computing skills in nine life skills areas: speaking and listening, functional writing, words on common signs and warning labels, telephone skills, money and finance, food, clothing, health, and travel and transportation. The inventory, designed for use as both an assessment tool and a curriculum guide, provides sequenced activities for instructional programs that focus on teaching functional life skills. The *Life Skills Inventory* is useful in secondary special education, vocational education, ESOL programs, and adult education programs. Inventory materials include a learner record book that provides for ongoing record keeping and a program record book that tracks up to 15 students. Goals and objectives software for writing IEPs is available as an optional item.

Employability Assessment Instrument   The *Employability Assessment Instrument* (East Central Ohio Special Education Regional Resource Center, 1981), a criterion-referenced rating scale, measures 21 job readiness skills in five domains. A list of the skills by domain appears in Table 13–3. The authors developed the *Employability Assessment Instrument* as an informal tool for special educators to use with students who display

Table 13–3   Skills Measured by the *Employability Assessment Instrument*

Social Skills	Time Factors	Performance Skills	Tolerance	Academic
Self-expression	Pace	Simultaneity	Repetitiveness	Reading level
Sociability	Attendance	Accuracy	Perseverance	Math skills
Work independence	Timing	Dexterity	Stamina	Writing skills
Appearance		Choices		
Teamwork		Direction		
		Memory		
		Caution		

little potential for vocational success. The scale, which uses a 1- to 10-point rating system, takes 20 to 30 minutes to complete. The evaluator records the ratings on the profile form and matches a student's individual profile to profiles of employability skills needed for success in 55 jobs. Special educators may also use a companion guide, the *Employability Curriculum* (Burrell & Talarico, 1981), with the *Employability Assessment Instrument.*

Life-Centered Career Education (LCCE) Knowledge and Performance Batteries   The criterion-referenced, individually administered *Life-Centered Career Education (LCCE) Knowledge and Performance Batteries* (Brolin, 1992a) are curriculum-based assessment instruments for measuring the career education knowledge and skills of students with disabilities. The batteries are designed for use with high school students, especially those in educable mentally handicapped and learning disabilities programs. The *Knowledge Battery* contains 200 multiple choice questions that evaluate daily living, personal-social, and occupational skills and takes about 4 hours to administer. The *Performance Battery* contains open-ended questions, role-playing scenarios, card sorts, and activities in which students perform applied tasks such as making meals, using a telephone directory, and filling out credit applications. The 105 items on the *Performance Battery* measure a variety of skills required for success in daily living, personal-social adjustment, and occupational endeavors. The *LCCE Batteries* are linked directly with the *Life-Centered Career Education Curriculum Program* (Brolin, 1992b).

Prevocational Assessment and Curriculum Guide   The *Prevocational Assessment and Curriculum Guide* (Mithaug et al., 1978) is a criterion-referenced checklist of the skills that are important for functioning independently in vocational settings. The authors designed the checklist for use in school-based vocational training settings, sheltered workshops, and work activity centers. Designed for students with severe disabilities, the checklist measures attendance or endurance, independence, production, learning, behavior, communication skills, social skills, and self-help skills. Teachers and supervisors in vocational settings can use the checklist to determine prevocational skill performance levels and to identify relative strengths and weaknesses. Results from the checklist provide teachers with valuable information for designing instructional programs and measuring student progress.

Social and Prevocational Information Battery-Revised   The *Social and Prevocational Information Battery-Revised (SPIB-R)* (Halpern & Irvin, 1986) is a norm-referenced test of the skills necessary for success in postschool activities. The authors designed the test for use with high school students who have mild mental retardation. The *SPIB-R* includes nine subtests:

1. Job search skills
2. Job-related skills
3. Banking
4. Budgeting
5. Purchasing
6. Home management
7. Physical health care
8. Hygiene and grooming
9. Functional signs

An evaluator administers the *SPIB-R* by reading the items to the student, who marks the answers in a response booklet.

Work Personality Profile   The *Work Personality Profile (WPP)* (Bolton & Roessler, 1986) is a behavior rating scale for use in work evaluation centers and employment settings. The *WPP* assesses basic capabilities necessary for successful employment, including the following:

- Aceptance of the work role.
- Ability to profit from instruction or correction.
- Work persistence.
- Work tolerance.
- Amount of supervision required.
- Teamwork.
- Ability to socialize with co-workers.
- Social communication skills.

The *WPP* contains 58 items that the evaluator rates on a four-point scale. The scale takes about 10 minutes to complete, but evaluators must first observe a student in a work situation for at least a week. A parallel self-assessment instrument, the *Work Personality Profile-Self Report (WPP-SR)* (Bolton & Roessler, 1992) is also available. Related employability assessment materials include the *Work Performance Assessment (WPA)* (Roessler et al., 1987) and the *Job Seeking Skills Assessment (JSSA)* (Hinman et al., 1988). The *WPA* is a work simulation procedure for evaluating a student's response to typical on-the-job supervisory behaviors. The *JSSA* assesses the ability to complete job application forms and to respond appropriately during employment interviews.

☑ Comprehension Checklist

Special educators rely on a variety of **written tests** to assess vocational interests, prevocational skills, employability skills, and related career behaviors. Written tests, which are relatively inexpensive and easy to give, enable evaluators to complete administration and scoring efficiently in short time periods. However, written tests have limited ability to predict performance in actual vocational and career situations. For this reason, special educators usually avoid exclusive use of written tests. Instead, they frequently use written tests together with other, more direct assessment procedures such as work samples and situational assessments.

Work Samples

In response to the many deficiencies of written testing, vocational evaluation specialists developed the work sample approach for assessing vocational and career skills (Rotatori, 1990). **Work samples** are tasks, materials, tools, and equipment taken from real jobs or job clusters and used to measure vocational interest and potential. Because they are based on actual jobs, work samples provide students with simulated experiences of various types of work. Special educators later adapted the original work sample approach for use in school-based programs. This practical, hands-on approach enables professionals to evaluate student job interests and occupational aptitudes by performance on a variety of work samples rather than by answers to questions on a written test. With most work samples, evaluators use production rates as the criterion for judging performance. Production rates are the number of units produced in a specific time period or the speed of task completion. Standardized work sample systems provide norms based on the average production rates of typical workers in competitive employment. During work sample assessment, the evaluator compares a student's production rate to the average production rate of the workers in the norm sample group.

Commercial Work Sample Systems

Evaluators may select from a number of well-developed commercial work sample systems. Most commercial work samples are expensive and require a large area to use. For this reason, most work sample systems are located in work evaluation centers rather than individual classrooms. Brief summaries of the foremost commercial work samples appear in the following sections.

Valpar Component Work Sample System   The *Valpar Component Work Sample System* (Brandon et al., n.d.) contains 24 work samples designed for use by individuals from age 14 years through adulthood. Because it takes about 8 hours to administer all 24 samples, an evaluator may select particular samples from the complete set, depending on the needs of the individual student. *Valpar* work samples include the following:

1. Small tools
2. Size discrimination
3. Numerical sorting
4. Upper extremity range of motion
5. Whole body range of motion
6. Trilevel measurement
7. Eye-hand-foot coordination
8. Electronic soldering and inspection
9. Clerical comprehension
10. Independent problem solving
11. Multilevel sorting
12. Simulated assembly
13. Money handling
14. Integrated peer performance
15. Electrical circuitry and print reading

16. Drafting
17. Prevocational readiness battery
18. Conceptual understanding
19. Dynamic physical capacities
20. Physical capacities and mobility
21. Mechanical assembly/alignment
22. Mechanical reasoning
23. Fine finger dexterity
24. Independent perceptual screening

Each self-contained sample contains all necessary materials. Students complete some of the small samples at a desk or on a table. Other samples take up a large amount of space and require a separate workstation or work area.

Test Orientation and Work Evaluation in Rehabilitation   The *Test Orientation and Work Evaluation in Rehabilitation (TOWER)* (International Center for the Disabled, n.d.) work sample system measures 14 job skills:

1. Clerical
2. Drafting
3. Drawing
4. Electronics assembly
5. Jewelry manufacturing
6. Leather goods
7. Lettering
8. Machine shop
9. Mail clerk
10. Optical mechanics
11. Pantograph engraving
12. Sewing machine operation
13. Welding
14. Workshop assembly

The complete *TOWER* system takes 2 weeks to complete, but evaluators can use components of the system separately. The authors took the *TOWER* work samples from actual tasks of various real jobs. The *TOWER* system enables evaluators to provide students with a wide range of vocational exploration activities.

Singer Career System   The *Singer Career System* (Singer Educational Division, n.d.) consists of more than 30 work samples that use actual tools and materials from real jobs. A slide or tape machine, rather than an evaluator, presents the instructions for completing the work samples, each of which takes about 2 hours to complete. Students work at their own pace.

Philadelphia Jewish Employment and Vocational Service Work Sample System   The *Philadelphia Jewish Employment and Vocational Service Work Sample System (JEVS)* (Jewish Employment and Vocational Service, n.d.) consists of 28 work samples in 10 job groups. The work samples include tasks such as nut, bolt, and washer assembly; tile sorting; hardware assembly; proofreading; adding machine use; pipe assembly; blouse making; and drafting.

Vocational Information and Evaluation Work Samples   Mandelbaum et al. (n.d.) de-signed the *Vocational Information and Evaluation Work Samples (VIEWS)* for individuals with mild to severe mental retardation. The *VIEWS* contains 16 work samples that measure elemental work, clerical work, machine work, and crafts.

Talent Assessment Program   The *Talent Assessment Program (TAP)* (Nighswonger, n.d.) is a work sample system that stresses evaluation of perception, dexterity, tactile dis-crimination, and retention of details. The *TAP* contains 10 different tests, including fine dexterity with and without tools, gross dexterity with and without tools, flow-chart visualization, and retention of structural and mechanical detail. Because an evaluator administers the *TAP* directly, reading is not required.

Noncommercial Work Samples

Instead of using commercial work samples such as those just described, most special education teachers develop their own noncommercial work samples. Many teachers design and make their own samples for assessing student interests and aptitudes and for use as work activities in learning centers. Noncommercial work samples give students hands-on experience with tasks associated with real jobs; they are usually inexpensive, and teachers can individualize them to meet the particular interests of students. Examples of typical noncommercial work samples include the following:

- Simple assembly tasks such as packaging and parts assembly.
- Clerical tasks such as collating, folding, and stapling.
- Maintenance and sanitation jobs such as janitorial and laundry services.
- Jobs associated with running small businesses, such as a school supply store or the making and selling of craft items.

☑ Comprehension Checklist

The work sample approach provides assessment data not available from written tests. Work samples include commercially available systems and noncommercial, teacher-made job tasks. Although work samples are valuable assessment and teaching tools, they only simulate real work environments. As a result, they measure a restricted sample of the behaviors necessary for success on actual jobs. For this reason, special educators are beginning to rely more frequently on situational and on-the-job assess-ment procedures to obtain evaluation data that are as realistic as possible.

Situational and On-the-Job Assessment

Situational assessment is not a single specific procedure. Instead, it includes a variety of techniques for assessing student performance in functional settings. **Situational assessment** is the use of systematic observation to evaluate work- and career-related per-formance on the job or in real or simulated environments such as vocational training settings, simulated workstations, job tryouts in the community, and other community-based settings. Specialists in vocational rehabilitation initially developed situational sessment as a tool for evaluating student performance in structured vocational set-tings such as work evaluation centers and sheltered workshops (Gaylord-Ross, 1988).

In these settings, situational assessment consists of a 20- to 30-day evaluation of performance on actual jobs. During this period, the evaluator assesses specific work skills and work-related behaviors. Specific work skills include the amount of training needed to learn new tasks, production rates, and accuracy of work performed. Work-related behaviors include social skills, tolerance, and motivation. In recent years, special educators and other professionals have adapted traditional situational assessment for use in measuring and evaluating student vocational and career-related skills in many different work and community-based settings (Bigge, 1988; Falvey, 1986; Sailor et al., 1986; Sailor & Guess, 1983). Situational assessment is ideal for use in community-based instructional programs that occur "on location" at the workplace or in other places such as the shopping mall, bus stop, grocery store, post office, drugstore, public library, and park.

Advantages and Disadvantages of Situational Assessment

In comparison with other assessment techniques, situational assessment offers both advantages and disadvantages. Clark and Kolstoe (1990) described the following benefits and drawbacks. The beneficial aspects include the following:

- Assessing students in real-life settings rather than in artificial testing situations.
- Assessing students when they are engaged in real jobs and participating in real community-based activities.
- Avoiding the worry and fear produced by formal testing.
- Providing authentic information about student performance (what a student actually *does* instead of what he or she *can do*).
- Improving instructional planning by producing genuine assessment results that relate more directly to the curriculum.

Drawbacks include the following:

- Problems with generalizing results obtained in one situation to other situations.
- Validity that depends on the use of accurate and appropriate data collection procedures.
- Difficulty in controlling bias resulting from evaluator errors in observing, recording, and interpreting behavior.

On-the-Job Assessment

On-the-job assessment is a specific type of situational evaluation for measuring vocational behavior in actual work settings. Although even the experts have difficulty separating various types of on-the-job assessment, most distinguish between on-the-job tryouts and job-site evaluations. On-the-job tryouts place students in jobs for experience. In contrast, placement specialists use job-site evaluations for assessing the performance of individuals on actual competitive jobs. Gaylord-Ross (1988) described the typical characteristics of on-the-job tryouts as situations in which the following occur:

- Students are not paid.
- Job placement is for training students.
- Job placement is for experience rather than employment.

- The student is an addition to the work force, not a replacement.
- Both the employer and education personnel assess student performance.

Hursh and Kerns (1988) described the usual characteristics of job-site evaluation as consisting of the following:

- Placement in an actual competitive job in the community.
- Having the employer supervise the student.
- Providing additional training, supervision, and evaluation to ensure that the student performs the job in a satisfactory manner.

Regardless of the specific type of job placement in the community, on-the-job assessment has the potential of providing a realistic evaluation of student performance by enabling the evaluator to determine whether a student can perform successfully in the workplace.

Evaluation Procedures in Situational and On-the-Job Assessment

When special educators conduct situational and on-the-job assessment, they rely on more than one evaluation procedure. In some situations they may use written tests, usually in the form of checklists and scales, to evaluate student behavior and measure student performance. In other situations they may use behavioral observation techniques. Special educators also rely on task analysis, an instructional method and assessment procedure that is an ideal situational assessment tool. Often special educators use a combination of evaluation procedures rather than relying exclusively on one method. Brief descriptions of procedures for using written tests and behavioral observations in situational assessment appear in the following sections, followed by a more detailed discussion of task analysis.

Written Tests   For special educators, written tests, usually rating scales and checklists, are valuable tools for assessing student performance on the job, in the community, and in other career-oriented instructional settings. Often teachers working by themselves or as part of a professional team develop their own rating scales and checklists for specific situations. For example, if students are frequently placed in a particular business or specific setting in the community, then the best assessment tool may be a checklist of skills or rating scale of behaviors that the teacher develops for that situation. When teachers develop their own instrument, they can include items that are unique to each situation, thus helping to ensure that the instrument reflects a student's particular learning needs. Teachers may also use commercial instruments such as the *Vocational Integration Index* as part of on-the-job assessment.

Vocational Integration Index   The *Vocational Integration Index (VII)* (Parent et al., 1992) is a criterion-referenced, individually administered instrument for special educators, rehabilitation professionals, employment specialists, and consumers. The *VII* is designed to identify and choose integrated employment opportunities that are compatible with the personal and social preferences of workers with disabilities. The index consists of two scales and a manual. The *Job Scale* evaluates a job site to determine available opportunities for vocational integration. The *Consumer Scale* assesses the degree to which a worker with a disability takes advantage of integration opportunities and identifies ways to enhance the worker's job satisfaction. Each scale contains 32 items that pinpoint characteristics of the company, the work area, the employees, and the benefits relating to employee integration. The index was field tested in 56 programs with more than 600 workers with disabilities.

Behavioral Observation   The behavioral observation techniques for assessing student behavior described in Chapter 11 are also useful for assessing student performance on the job and in the community. For example, anecdotal recording helps the special educator to analyze problem behaviors or skill deficiencies within the context of surrounding events. It also helps special educators isolate relevant aspects of the situation or setting that influence the problem behavior. Therefore, when teachers need to identify why a student is experiencing difficulty in a specific work- or community-based situation, they often use anecdotal recording procedures. Special educators also use more complex approaches, such as partial-interval recording and momentary time-sampling procedures, as situational assessment tools. These behavioral observation techniques provide task-specific assessment data for helping students learn especially difficult jobs.

Task Analysis

For special educators, **task analysis** is a valuable curriculum-based assessment procedure and a useful instructional technique. Business and industry originated the term to describe the process of breaking down a job into its component parts. In business and industry, task analysis enables worker specialization and increases production efficiency, especially in assembly line work (Sailor & Guess, 1983). Gold (1975) first introduced an adapted version of task analysis for training students with severe disabilities and defined task analysis as breaking down a difficult task into small steps. More recently, Mercer and Mercer (1998) described task analysis as dividing a learning project into parts to determine needed skills, especially those that are prerequisites for performing the complete project. The analysis process helps students learn demanding vocational and career-related tasks more quickly and easily. Special educators also use task analysis to teach a variety of life management skills, including self-help skills and activities of daily living, and to teach functional academics.

Developing a Task Analysis

Developing a task analysis involves the following steps:

- Analyze the content of a task to identify the separate steps.
- Evaluate the process of a task to determine appropriate teaching strategies.
- Prepare a data collection form to measure student progress.
- Begin instruction.
- Revise the task analysis on the basis of progress data (as necessary).

Measuring and Reporting Progress

Teachers may report the results of task analysis in several ways. The goal is to summarize results accurately in a manner that best describes student performance.

Simply reporting the number of steps in a task a student has mastered (e.g., 9 of 10 steps performed correctly) is an efficient way to communicate results. However, when teachers need a more formal report of progress, they often use graphs to illustrate student performance. Teachers graph the results of task analysis by taking assessment information from a data collection form and plotting it on a line or bar chart. Because graphs visually illustrate behavior, they help teachers assess student performance and facilitate communicating assessment information with others. One type of data collection system enables teachers to display student performance data as a graph on the form itself, an example of which appears in Figure 13–1. The form lists the steps in the task from last to first. Each time a student performs a step correctly, the teacher draws a line through the number on the data sheet that represents that step. After each trial, the teacher circles the number that shows the total number of steps completed correctly. After a series of trials, the

Figure 13–1 Task Analysis Data Collection Form

Data Collection Form

Task: Photopying

Student: Jason

Teacher: Ms. Jones

Dates

Steps	4/21	4/22	4/25	4/27	4/28	4/29	5/1	5/2	5/3	5/8	5/9	5/10
_____	15	15	15	15	15	15	15	15	15	15	15	15
_____	14	14	14	14	14	14	14	14	14	14	14	14
_____	13	13	13	13	13	13	13	13	13	13	13	13
_____	12	12	12	12	12	12	12	12	12	12	12	12
_____	11	11	11	11	11	11	11	11	11	11	11	11
10. Take copies back	10	10	10	10	10	10	10	10	10	10	10	10
9. Remove copies	9	9	9	9	9	9	9	9	9	9	9	9
8. Repeat 3–7 for each page	8	8	8	8	8	8	8	8	8	8	8	8
7. Remove original	7	7	7	7	7	7	7	7	7	7	7	7
6. Start machine	6	6	6	6	6	6	6	6	6	6	6	6
5. Set quantity	5	5	5	5	5	5	5	5	5	5	5	5
4. Align paper	4	4	4	4	4	4	4	4	4	4	4	4
3. Place paper	3	3	3	3	3	3	3	3	3	3	3	3
2. Go to machine	2	2	2	2	2	2	2	2	2	2	2	2
1. Get originals	1	1	1	1	1	1	1	1	1	1	1	1

Notes and Comments _____

_____

teacher connects the circles to form a line graph showing student performance across multiple trials.

Special educators may select from a variety of task analysis procedures and data collection forms. In addition, they may develop their own variations of task analysis. Examples of different types of task analysis data collection forms appear in Figure 13–2.

Figure 13–2   Other Examples of Task Analysis Data Collection Forms

Task Analysis Data Collection Form

Name of Task   Clean classroom sink

Student   Larry   School   Pinewood Elementary

Teacher   Donna Jones   Criterion   3/3 correct trials

Description   Steps for cleaning classroom sink

Trials	Date	Get materials	Wet surface	Apply cleaner	Rub with rag	Rinse surface	Rinse rag	Put materials away						Trial Time
1	4/19	+	−	−	+	−	−	−						14 min.
2	4/20	+	−	−	+	−	−	+						14 min.
3	4/21	+	+	−	+	−	−	+						12 min.
4	4/22	+	+	+	+	−	−	+						11 min.
5	4/23	+	+	+	+	−	+	+						10 min.
6	4/27	+	+	+	+	−	−	+						11 min.
7	4/28	+	+	+	+	−	+	+						10 min.
8	4/29	+	+	+	+	−	+	−						11 min.
9	4/30	+	+	+	+	+	+	+						8 min.
10														
11														
12														
13														
14														
15														

Notes _____

Figure 13–2 *(continued)*

Task Analysis Data Sheet

Name of Task *Operating Paper Cutter*

Student: *Julie*

Teacher: *Jim Wilson*

Description _____

_____

Criterion *4/4 correct trials*

Scoring Code

3 – Without Assistance
2 – Verbal Help
1 – Modeling/Demonstration
0 – Physical Assistance

Date

Step	5-1	5-2	5-3	5-7	5-8	5-9						
1. Pick up paper	2	3	3	3	3	3						
2. Place paper	2	2	2	2	2	3						
3. Raise cutting arm	1	1	3	3	3	3						
4. Slide paper to mark	0	1	2	2	2	3						
5. Hold paper	0	1	2	2	3	3						
6. Lower cutting arm	0	0	2	2	3	3						
7. Remove and place paper	1	1	2	2	3	3						
8.												
9.												
10.												
11.												
12.												
13.												
14.												
15.												

Comments _____

_____

☑ Comprehension Checklist

When special educators use situational assessment, they rely on various assessment techniques, including checklists, observations, and task analysis. Because it can occur on the job, in the community, or at home, situational assessment offers a way to measure and evaluate students engaged in authentic activities in functional environments. However, as with all forms of assessment, special educators should carefully plan and skillfully conduct situational assessment to avoid pitfalls that lead to misleading assessment information.

Summary

Assessing career and vocational skills involves measuring and evaluating work skills as well as competencies in social interaction, functional academics, and daily living activities. More specifically, career assessment encompasses evaluation of the practical life skills needed for postschool success. *Vocational assessment,* a more restrictive term, refers to the appraisal of skills required for particular jobs. Special educators have at their disposal a variety of tests for evaluating career and vocational performance (see Table 13–4 on p. 405). These include written tests, work samples, and situational and on-the-job assessment techniques.

Because of the importance of career and vocational assessment with older students, high school teachers should be thoroughly familiar with the available tests. For other special educators, understanding career and vocational assessment is one part of a complete knowledge base of appraisal techniques in special education. This knowledge helps teachers ensure that, when students leave school, they are well prepared to make a successful transition into postschool activities.

Chapter Review and Application

Multiple Choice

Directions: Read each item carefully. In the blank beside each item, write the letter of the best response. Each item contains only one best answer. Check your answers with the answer key at the end of the book.

_____ 1. Which term encompasses the broadest range of skills?
    a. Vocational assessment
    b. Career assessment
    c. Career preparation
    d. On-the-job assessment

_____ 2. Which term is the most specific?
    a. Vocational assessment
    b. Career assessment
    c. Prevocational skills
    d. Employability skills

_____ 3. Which is the first stage in the process of career development?
    a. Preparation
    b. Exploration
    c. Awareness
    d. Placement

_____ 4. Special educators usually begin to assess and teach career development in the which of the following?
    a. Elementary grades
    b. Middle school grades
    c. High school grades
    d. Junior and senior years of high school

     5. IDEA requires the inclusion of a statement describing needed transition services in the IEPs of all students, beginning at which age?
       a. 14
       b. 15
       c. 16
       d. 17

     6. Most written tests in the career and vocational domain measure which of the following?
       a. Personal and social development
       b. On-the-job skills
       c. Specific occupational skills
       d. Vocational interests

     7. What competencies are measured when we assess social skills, time factors (e.g. attendance), performance skills, and tolerance?
       a. Vocational interests
       b. Specific vocational skills
       c. Employability skills
       d. Career placement skills

     8. Which of the following do work samples rely on?
       a. Task analysis
       b. On-the-job assessment
       c. Direct observation
       d. Simulated tasks from real jobs

     9. The *Singer Career System* and the *Talent Assessment Program* are examples of which of the following?
       a. Vocational interest inventories
       b. Task analytic assessment systems
       c. Situational assessment tools
       d. Work samples

     10. Which of the following describes task analysis?
       a. A type of norm-referenced testing
       b. A curriculum-based assessment procedure
       c. A criterion-referenced test
       d. A rating scale

Short Answers

Directions: Review your understanding of the material in this chapter by answering the following short answer items. Compare your responses with the sample answers. Your responses should contain information that is similar to but not exactly the same as the information in the sample answers at the end of the book.

1. What is the difference between the meaning and usage of the terms *career assessment* and *vocational assessment*?
2. What are transition services? Why are they important for students with disabilities? When should they begin? What is functional assessment, and why is it emphasized in identifying needed transition services, in transition planning, and in providing transition services?

3. What are the purpose, uses, and limitations of written tests for measuring vocational interests, prevocational skills, and employability skills? What are three different written tests that you would consider using to assess these career and vocational skills? How would you use each test?

4. What are situational and on-the-job assessment procedures? How have special educators adapted traditional situational assessment? What do you consider to be the most significant benefits and drawbacks of situational and on-the-job assessment? Why?

5. Construct a simple progress graph using the data from one of the task analysis data collection forms that appear in Figures 13–1 or 13–2. Discuss ways in which the graph helps document student performance and facilitates communicating assessment information to others.

References

Becker, R. L. (1981, 1988). *Reading Free Vocational Interest Inventory-Revised.* Columbus, OH: Elbert.

Bigge, J. (1988). *Curriculum-Based Instruction for Special Education Students.* Mountain View, CA: Mayfield.

Bolton, B., & Roessler, R. (1986). *Work Personality Profile.* Fayetteville, AK: Research and Training Center in Vocational Rehabilitation.

————. (1992). *Work Personality Profile-Self-Report.* Fayetteville, AK: Research and Training Center in Vocational Rehabilitation.

Brandon, T., Balton, D., Rup, D., & Raslter, C. (n.d.). *Valpar Component Work Sample System.* Tuscon, AZ: Valpar Corporation.

Brigance, A. (1987). *Brigance Diagnostic Inventory of Essential Skills.* North Billerica, MA: Curriculum Associates.

————. (1994). *Brigance Diagnostic Life Skills Inventory.* North Billerica, MA: Curriculum Associates.

Brolin, D. E. (1986). *Life-Centered Career Education: A Competency-Based Approach* (rev. ed.). Reston, VA: Council for Exceptional Children.

Brolin, D. (1992a). *Life-Centered Career Education Knowledge and Performance Batteries.* Reston, VA: Council for Exceptional Children.

————. (1992b). *Life-Centered Career Education Curriculum Program.* Reston, VA: Council for Exceptional Children.

Burrell, L. P., & Talarico, R. L. (1981). *Project Employability: Employability Curriculum.* Dover, OH: East Central Ohio Special Education Regional Resource Center (ERIC Document Reproduction Service No. ED 215 524).

Career Interest Inventory. (1990). San Antonio, TX: Harcourt Brace.

Clark, G. M., & Kolstoe, O. P. (1990). *Career Development and Transition Education for Adolescents with Disabilities.* Boston: Allyn & Bacon.

Clark, G. M., & Patton, J. R. (1997). *Transition Planning Inventory.* Austin, TX: PRO-ED.

East Central Ohio Special Education Regional Resource Center. (1981). *Project Employability: Employability Assessment Instrument.* Dover, OH: Author. (ERIC Document Reproduction Service No. ED 215 523).

Falvey, M. A. (1986). *Community-Based Curriculum: Instructional Strategies for Students With Severe Handicaps.* Baltimore, MD: Paul H. Brookes.

Gaylord-Ross, R. (Ed.). (1988). *Vocational Education of Persons With Handicaps.* Mountain View, CA: Mayfield.

Geist, H. (1964). *Geist Picture Interest Inventory-Revised*. Los Angeles, CA: Western Psychological Services.

Gold, M. (1975). *Try Another Way Training Manual*. Champaign, IL: Research Press.

Halpern, A., & Irvin, L. K. (1986). *Social and Prevocational Information Battery-Revised (SPIB-R)*. Monterey, CA: CTB/McGraw-Hill.

Hasazi, S. B., & Cobb, R. B. (1988). Vocational education of persons with mild handicaps. In R. Gaylord-Ross (Ed.), *Vocational Education of Persons With Handicaps*. Mountain View, CA: Mayfield, 331–54.

Hinman, S., Means, B., Parkerson, S., & Odeneahl, B. (1988). *Job Seeking Skills Assessment*. Fayetteville, AK: Research and Training Center in Vocational Rehabilitation.

Hursh, N. C., & Kerns, A. F. (1988). *Vocational Evaluation in Special Education*. Boston: College Hill Press.

International Center for the Disabled. (n.d.). *TOWER System*. New York: ICD Rehabilitation and Research Center, International Center for the Disabled.

Jastak, J., & Jastak, S. (1979). *Wide Range Interest-Opinion Test (WRIOT)*. Wilmington, DE: Jastak Associates.

Jewish Employment and Vocational Service (n.d.). *Philadelphia Jewish Employment and Vocational Service Work Sample System*. Philadelphia: Author.

Johansson, C. B. (1986). *Career Assessment Inventory-Enhanced*. Minneapolis, MN: NCE Interpretive Scoring Systems.

Mandelbaum, B. L., Rosen, G., & Miller, M. (n.d.). *Vocational Information and Evaluation Work Samples*. Philadelphia: Vocational Research Institute.

Mercer, C. D., & Mercer, A. R. (1998). *Teaching Students With Learning Problems* (4th ed.). Upper Saddle River, NJ: Merrill/Prentice-Hall.

Mithaug, D., Mar, D., & Stewart, J. (1978). *The Prevocational Assessment and Curriculum Guide*. Seattle: Exceptional Education.

Nighswonger, W. (n.d.). *Talent Assessment Program*. Jacksonville, FL: Talent Assessment.

Organist, J. E. (1985). A review of the *Wide Range Interest-Opinion Test*. In D. J. Keyser & R. C. Sweetland (Eds.), *Test Critiques* (vol. 8). Kansas City, MO: Test Corporation of America, 673–76.

Parent, W. S., Kregel, J., & Wehman, P. (1992) *Vocational Integration Index*. Stoneham, MA: Andover Medical Publishers.

Parker, R. M. (1991). *Occupational Aptitude Survey and Interest Schedule* (2d ed.). *(OASIS-2)*. Austin, TX: PRO-ED.

Roessler, R., Hinman, S., & Lewis, F. (1987). *Work Performance Assessment*. Fayetteville, AK: Research and Training Center in Vocational Rehabilitation.

Rotatori, A. F. (1990). *Comprehensive Assessment in Special Education: Approaches, Procedures, and Concerns*. Springfield, IL: Charles C. Thomas.

Sailor, W., & Guess, D. (1983). *Severely Handicapped Students: An Instructional Design*. Boston: Houghton Mifflin.

Sailor, W., Halvorsen, A., Anderson, J., Goetz, L., Gee, K., Doering, K., & Hunt, P. (1986). Community intensive instruction. In R. H. Horner, L. H. Meyer, and H. D. Fredericks (Eds.), *Education of Learners With Severe Handicaps: Exemplary Service Strategies*. Baltimore, MD: Paul H. Brookes, 251–88.

Singer Educational Division. (n.d.). *Singer Career System*. Rochester, NY: Singer Educational Division, Career Systems.

Weller, C., & Buchanan, M. (1983). *Career Inventories for the Learning Disabled*. Novato, CA: Academic Therapy.

Table 13–4   Review of Career and Vocational Assessment Instruments

Name of Test	Type of Test	Suitable for Individuals Who Are	Brief Description of Test	Purpose of Administering Test
Brigance Diagnostic Inventory of Essential Skills (Brigance, 1987)	Criterion-referenced, individually administered functional skills inventory	Secondary-level students and adult learners with special needs	Includes inventories for measuring academic and life skills and a rating scale for evaluating health and attitude, responsibility and self-discipline, job interview preparation, communication, and auto safety	To assess the functional academic skills and the life skills of secondary students with special needs
Brigance Diagnostic Life Skills Inventory (Brigance, 1994)	Criterion-referenced, individually administered life skills inventory	High school students–adulthood	Measures nine life skills areas: speaking and listening, functional writing, words on common signs and warning labels, telephone skills, money and finance, food, clothing, health, and travel and transportation	To use as both an assessment tool and a curriculum guide with sequenced activities for instructional programs that teach functional life skills
Career Interest Inventory (CII) (1990)	Norm-referenced, group-administered interest inventory	Grades 7–12 and adults	Includes two levels: level 1, for students in grades 7 through 9, helps students select courses to take and careers to begin exploring; level 2, for students in grades 10–12, helps students explore postsecondary educational and career alternatives	To provide information about students' educational goals, interest in a variety of school subjects and school-related activities, and interest in various occupations
Career Inventories for the Learning Disabled (CILD) (Weller & Buchanan, 1983)	Criterion-referenced, individually administered interest inventory	6 years–adulthood	Measures attributes (dominant personality characteristics) and ability (auditory, visual, and motor) using a rating scale and occupational interests usingan inventory completed by the student	To assess the career interests, attributes, and abilities of students with learning disabilities

*Tests marked with asterisks are featured in tables in this chapter.

Table 13–4 (contin

Name of Test	Type of
Employability Assessment Instrument (East Central Ohio Special Education Regional Resource Center, 1981)	Criterion-refe dividually adr rating scale
Life Centered Career Education (LCCE) Knowledge and Performance Batteries (Brolin, 1992a)	Criterion-refer dividually adm curriculum-bas ment instrume
Philadelphia Jewish Employment and Vocational Service Work Sample System (JEVS) (Jewish Employment and Vocational Service, n.d.)	Criterion-refere dividually admi work samples

Table 13–4 (continued)

Name of Test	Type of Test	Suitable for Individuals Who Are	Brief Description of Test	Purpose of Administering Test
Singer Career System (Singer Educational Division, n.d.)	Criterion-referenced, individually administered work samples	High school–adult	Consists of more than 30 work samples that use actual tools and materials from real jobs. A slide or tape machine, rather than an evaluator, presents the instructions for completing each work sample.	To evaluate job interests and occupational aptitudes by assessing performance on a variety of work samples
Social and Prevocational Information Battery-Revised (SPIB-R) (Halpern & Irvin, 1986)	Norm-referenced, individually administered inventory	High school students who have mild mental retardation	Includes nine subtests for measuring job search skills, home management, job-related skills, physical health care, banking, hygiene and grooming, budgeting, functional signs, and purchasing	To assess the skills necessary for success in postschool activities
Talent Assessment Program (TAP) (Nighswonger, n.d.)	Criterion-referenced, individually administered work samples	High school–adult	Contains 10 different tests, including fine dexterity without tools, gross dexterity without tools, fine dexterity with tools, gross dexterity with tools, flowchart visualization, and retention of structural and mechanical detail	To evaluate perception, dexterity, tactile discrimination, and retention of details using a variety of work samples
Test Orientation and Work Evaluation in Rehabilitation (TOWER) (International Center for the Disabled, n.d.)	Criterion-referenced, individually administered work samples	High school–adult	Measures 14 job skills: clerical, machine shop, drafting, mail clerk, drawing, optical mechanics, electronics assembly, pantograph engraving, jewelry manufacturing, sewing machine operation, leather goods, welding, lettering, and workshop assembly	To provide students with a wide range of vocational exploration activities

Table 13–4 *(continued)*

Name of Test	Type of Test	Suitable for Individuals Who Are	Brief Description of Test	Purpose of Administering Test
Transition Planning Inventory (TPI) (Clark & Patton, 1997)	Criterion-referenced, individually administered assessment and transition planning curriculum guide	Teenagers with disabilities	Includes an administration and resource guide and packages of 25 profile and assessment recommendation forms, school forms, home forms, and student forms. The administration and resource guide includes a planning notes form, an individualized planning document, and more than 600 transition goals.	To identify and plan for the transition needs of students with disabilities
Valpar Component Work Sample System (Brandon et al., n.d.)	Criterion-referenced, individually administered work samples	14 years–adulthood	Contains 24 work samples	To evaluate job interests and occupational aptitudes using worklike tasks administered under specific instructions
Vocational Information and Evaluation Work Samples (VIEWS) (Mandelbaum et al., n.d.)	Criterion-referenced, individually administered work samples	High school students and adults with mild to severe mental retardation	Contains 16 work samples that measure elemental work, clerical work, machine work, and crafts	To assess occupational interests and aptitudes using standardized work samples
Vocational Integration Index (VII) (Parent et al., 1992)	Criterion-referenced, individually administered rating scale	High school students and adults with severe disabilities	Consists of two scales: the *Job Scale* evaluates a job site to determine available opportunities for vocational integration; the *Consumer Scale* assesses the degree to which a worker with a disability takes advantage of integration opportunities and identifies ways to enhance worker job satisfaction	To identify and choose integrated employment opportunities that are compatible with the personal and social preferences of workers with disabilities

Table 13–4   (continued)

Name of Test	Type of Test	Suitable for Individuals Who Are	Brief Description of Test	Purpose of Administering Test
*Wide Range Interest Opinion Test (WRIOT) (Jastak & Jastak, 1979)	Norm-referenced, group- or individually administered screening test of vocational interest	5 years–adult	Picture test that measures vocational interests using a series of line drawings that show people in various work-related situations	To measure both work interests (such as mechanics, social services, and sales) and work attitudes (including risk and ambition) for use in vocational planning, including counseling, employee selection, and coordinating instruction with student interests
Work Personality Profile (WPP) (Bolton & Roessler, 1986); *Work Personality Profile-Self-Report (WPP-SR)* (Bolton & Roessler, 1992)	Criterion-referenced, individually administered behavior rating scales	High school–adult	Measures the following capabilities: acceptance of the work role, ability to profit from instruction or correction, work persistence, work tolerance, amount of supervision required, teamwork, ability to socialize with co-workers, and social communication skills	For use in work evaluation centers and employment settings to assess the basic capabilities necessary for successful employment

CHAPTER 14

Overview of Assessing
Academic Achievement

Overview

Assessing achievement is a central aspect of evaluation in special education. Achievement is the measurement of student performance after instruction and includes reading, mathematics, spelling, writing, and scholastic subjects in the school curriculum. This chapter helps you develop your knowledge and skills in this critical element of assessment. To realize this goal you learn the definition of achievement and the types of behaviors measured by achievement tests. You consider the ways in which special educators use achievement tests to meet student needs and investigate current issues surrounding their use. After this introduction you examine the various achievement tests themselves, including the most widely used, individually administered tests. As you learn about each one, you will consider the purpose of the instrument, the administration and scoring procedures, and the technical characteristics.

Objectives

After reading this chapter, you will be prepared to do the following:

- Define the term *academic achievement*.
- Understand the types of behaviors measured by achievement tests.
- Use achievement tests designed for children with special needs.
- Use group tests of achievement.
- Conduct assessment using the individually administered, multiple-skill achievement tests.
- Define the term *individually administered single-skill tests of achievement*.
- Define the term *curriculum-based assessment of academic achievement*.

Assessing the Academic Achievement of Students With Special Needs

Ms. Wan, a first-year special education teacher in an inclusion classroom, has never assessed the academic achievement of students with special needs, but she is very interested in learning about this type of assessment. She would like to know if achievement testing will help her, and wonders how she can find out more about the various achievement tests. She also asks herself several questions: What are the different kinds of achievement tests? What test is best for her students? Can achievement testing help her develop better IEPs? Can it improve her instructional program? What can it do for her students? Can she use it in an inclusion class team-teaching situation?

After doing some reading on achievement testing, Ms. Wan decides to give it a try. She hopes that the testing will provide diagnostic information for developing the best possible instructional programs. As she continues to investigate various aspects of achievement testing, she discovers that some tests are written specifically for teachers like her, including the Peabody Individual Achievement Test-Revised *and the* Brigance Diagnostic Inventories. *She decides to try out these instruments with two of her most difficult students. This practice will allow her to find out for herself what achievement testing can do.*

The Range of Achievement Tests

This chapter introduces you to the wide range of tests and evaluation procedures for assessing the achievement of students with disabilities. The goal is to help you develop an understanding of achievement tests, their meaning, use, and interpretation.

After a brief introduction, you will begin with **multiple-skill achievement tests,** which are the backbone of achievement testing in special education. Multiple-skill tests contain subtests that measure student proficiency in several domains and are useful for obtaining an overview of performance across multiple academic subjects. For example, most multiple-skill tests include reading, mathematics, and spelling subtests. Later you will examine the **single-skill achievement tests,** which are useful for gathering in-depth diagnostic information about student performance in a single domain and contain subtests for evaluating specific skills in that domain. For example, the single-skill tests of mathematics achievement include subtests for assessing content, operations, and applications. In addition, you will investigate curriculum-based assessment, an evaluation approach that measures educational success based on student progress in the local school curriculum rather than in relation to scores on standardized, norm-referenced tests. Curriculum-based assessment involves using class tests, homework assignments, classwork, and teacher impressions to make assessment decisions. When teachers use curriculum-based assessment, they integrate measurement practices from various sources, including behavioral observation, classroom instruction, and traditional psychometrics.

As you can see, the great variety of achievement tests demands an understanding of testing, interpreting tests, and decision making across many different subjects. However, the goal of all achievement testing remains the same: to obtain information designed to meet the individual and often unique academic learning needs of students.

Achievement Tests Defined

Achievement tests measure student learning in the academic subjects that make up the regular school curriculum, including reading, spelling, written expression, mathematics, general information, and specific subjects such as social studies, history, and science. These academic areas can be subdivided into specific skill clusters. For example, reading includes word identification, word attack, word comprehension, passage comprehension, and oral reading.

Achievement testing is characterized by a diverse array of tools and techniques. In fact, no other area of assessment in special education includes such a wide range of evaluation procedures across such an extended age range. The age range of achievement testing begins at kindergarten and extends through high school into college and adulthood. The tools used to measure achievement include group tests, individually administered tests, and curriculum-based appraisal procedures. Given this wide assortment, the special educator selects a particular instrument or technique on the basis of the student's needs and the reasons for the evaluation.

Why Do We Assess the Achievement of Children With Special Needs?

Special educators assess the achievement of children with special needs for several reasons, including screening, identifying, and placing students; planning instruction and intervention; developing IEPs; evaluating student progress; and monitoring program effectiveness (see Focus 14–1). Although overlap occurs among these purposes, different tests and techniques exist for each function. When screening students, for example, teachers and diagnosticians use screening tests designed to facilitate initial identification of those who may have problems in one or more academic learning areas. Reviews of several of the most frequently used screening tests appear in this chapter. Identification and placement, on the other hand, rely heavily on formal, standardized, diagnostic achievement tests, which are featured in this chapter. A major element in the process of identifying and placing students in special

FOCUS 14–1

Why Do We Assess the Achievement of Students With Special Needs?

- To screen students who may have deficits in achievement
- To identify, classify, and place students with deficits in achievement
- To determine strengths and weaknesses in academic achievement
- To plan instructional programs and develop intervention activities
- To develop IEPs
- To evaluate student progress
- To monitor program effectiveness

education involves interpreting the results from these tests. The staffing team uses the achievement test results, along with other test scores and evaluation information, to make a placement decision. Although teachers often use these formal tests in instructional planning and intervention, they rely primarily on less formal, curriculum-based assessment techniques in which the teacher selects from a series of assessment strategies that lead directly to the development of instructional objectives. Likewise, special education teachers and educational diagnosticians select from a variety of both formal and informal appraisal techniques for evaluating student progress and monitoring program effectiveness.

Formal, Standardized Testing Versus Informal, Curriculum-Based Assessment

This chapter focuses on formal, standardized tests of academic achievement. In-depth discussion of informal, curriculum-based tests for assessing achievement occurs in later chapters, especially Chapters 15, 16, 17, and 18. Although the formal, standardized tests considered in this chapter share many characteristics with informal, tests, significant differences exist between the two types. The most notable differences are summarized in Focus 14–2.

A comparative review of the two types of testing reveals that each is best in certain situations (Linn & Gronlund, 1995). The careful design and development of formal, standardized achievement tests such as those reviewed in this chapter make them especially valuable for the following instructional purposes:

- Identifying, classifying, and placing students with special needs.
- Evaluating general progress in basic academic skills and overall scholastic competencies.
- Measuring student progress over long periods of time, such as a year or a period of years.
- Identifying overall strengths and weaknesses in broad subject areas.

FOCUS 14–2

Differences Between Formal and Informal Tests of Academic Achievement

Test Characteristic	Formal, Standardized Achievement Tests	Informal, Curriculum-Based Achievement Tests
Content	Standardized, inflexible	Nonstandard, flexible
Item Quality	Usually high	Unknown but often low
Reliability and Validity	Usually high	Unknown but often low
Administration and Scoring	Standardized, precise	Nonstandard, adjustable
Interpretation	Scores can be compared.	Score comparisons are limited

- Identifying significant discrepancies between academic achievement and intellectual aptitude.
- Comparing achievement levels among children, classes, programs, and schools.

In contrast, the inflexibility in standardized testing makes it less useful in situations in which informal testing is ideal, such as the following:

- Evaluating progress in learning specific skills that may be unique to an individual student, class, program, or school.
- Measuring daily and short-term progress.
- Evaluating the value of particular educational interventions in response to the individual and often unique learning problems of children with special needs.
- Situations that require informal flexible assessment.
- Connecting assessment of achievement with classroom instruction.

These two types of testing of actually complement each other, and both are necessary in educational programs for children with special needs. Each type of testing produces useful data regarding academic achievement. In fact, teachers should use both formal and informal assessment in planning and implementing educational programs for children with special needs.

Group Tests

Given to groups of students rather than individually, **group tests** differ in format and content from individual tests. Often referred to as *survey test batteries* because they consist of a series of subtests, these tests are really brief screening tests that give an overview of achievement rather than specific diagnostic information. Used most often at the elementary school level, the batteries usually include subtests that measure the basic skills of reading , language, mathematics, and study skills. Study skills include library and reference skills and reading maps, graphs, and tables. In addition, some tests include content-oriented subtests for evaluating listening comprehension, science, and social studies. Some tests also include a written expression subtest that requires students to write a brief essay. However, most schools test basic skills only because the content-oriented subtests become outdated quickly and may not match with the objectives in the local school curriculum (Linn & Gronlund, 1995).

High schools use group achievement tests less frequently because the wide range of classes and the variability in content make it hard to identify a common core of skills that can be measured on a test. For this reason, most high school tests measure the same basic skills of reading, mathematics, language, and study skills as the elementary tests. This provides continuous measurement of these same skills across grade levels K–12 (Linn & Gronlund, 1995).

Almost all group tests rely on a multiple-choice format and are usually brief and often machine scored. Individual tests, on the other hand, sample a greater range of behaviors, and evaluators usually score them by hand rather than by machine. When developers write test questions for group tests, they limit the items to content that fits on machine-scored, multiple-choice response sheets. This format makes most group tests screening-level instruments that identify the average of the group. In contrast, individual diagnostic tests provide in-depth information that translates into instructional objectives. For these reasons, special educators rely most often on individual tests rather than group testing. However, despite their limitations in special education, the group tests are widely used. Some of the foremost group tests of achievement are the following:

- *California Achievement Tests, Fifth Edition (CAT/5)* (CTB/McGraw Hill, 1992).
- *Comprehensive Test of Basic Skills (CTBS)* (CTB/McGraw Hill, 1981).
- *Iowa Tests of Basic Skills (ITBS)* (Hoover et al., 1993).
- *Metropolitan Achievement Tests, Seventh Edition (MAT7)* (Balow et al., 1992).
- *Science Research Associates (SRA) Achievement Series* (Science Research Associates, 1985).
- *Stanford Achievement Test Series, Ninth Edition (SAT9)* (Psychological Corporation, 1996) consisting of the following:

  Stanford Early School Achievement Test (SESAT).

  Stanford Achievement Test Series (SAT).

  Test of Academic Skills (TASK).

☑ Comprehension Checklist

Assessing achievement refers to evaluating the academic performance of students in subjects such as reading, writing, and mathematics. Special educators may select from a wide range of evaluation procedures. In many cases, assessing achievement entails giving a standardized test, but teachers and diagnosticians also rely on one of the many informal appraisal techniques that identify appropriate instructional objectives for individuals and small groups of students.

Individually Administered Multiple-Skill Achievement Tests

The individually administered multiple-skill achievement tests provide overall evaluation of performance across the major academic skills in the school curriculum. These tests, often referred to as *achievement batteries* or *survey batteries,* are popular for several reasons, including the following:

- Coordination among subtests such as reading, math, and spelling.
- Reduction of errors due to common administration and scoring across subtests.
- Cost savings through the use of one test to assess achievement in multiple subjects.
- Time savings by using one test to evaluate achievement in all subject areas.
- Comparison of performance across subject areas through the use of common norms (Kubiszyn & Borich, 1990).

Although multiple-skill achievement tests exhibit many advantages over other tests, they also display certain disadvantages, including the following:

- Low reliabilities among subtests, reducing the validity of comparisons across subject areas.
- Emphasis on broad coverage of many subject areas rather than in-depth coverage of one or more areas.

- Limitations on the amount of specific diagnostic information available (Kubiszyn & Borich, 1990).

Most special educators find that the advantages of multiple-skill tests outweigh the disadvantages. Therefore, special educators frequently use them to determine the overall achievement levels of students. From among the large number of available multiple-skill achievement test batteries, teachers and diagnosticians rely on several tests most often. Reviews of each of these widely used instruments follow, beginning with the *Wide Range Achievement Test-3*.

Wide Range Achievement Test-3

The *Wide Range Achievement Test-3 (WRAT3)* (Wilkinson, 1993) is a norm-referenced, individually administered screening instrument. Measuring achievement in sight reading, spelling, and arithmetic from kindergarten through adulthood, the *WRAT3* takes about 20 minutes to give and score. The reading subtest evaluates sight reading ability associated with recognizing and naming letters and pronouncing printed words. The arithmetic subtest measures skills in rote counting, reading numerals, solving oral problems, and written computation. The spelling subtest assesses the ability to write dictated letters and words and one's own name.

Although it is a screening test rather than a comprehensive diagnostic tool, the *WRAT3* manual implies that the instrument is suitable for making diagnostic decisions. For this reason, evaluators may mistakenly employ the test to identify deficits such as learning disabilities. Because the *WRAT3* contains major content gaps, using it as a diagnostic tool may lead to invalid conclusions about student performance. For example, the reading subtest, which consists of 42 words that the examinee reads aloud, fails to measure reading comprehension skills. Likewise, the arithmetic subtest, consisting of only 40 problems, fails to adequately cover the domain of arithmetic. The limited sample of ability measured by the test represents a major flaw, and, for this reason, evaluators should use *WRAT3* results with extreme caution. A summary of the *WRAT3* appears in Table 14–1.

Table 14–1   *Wide Range Achievement Test-3 (WRAT3)*

Type of Test:	Norm referenced, individually administered
Purpose:	A screening test of academic achievement
Content Areas:	Reading recognition, arithmetic, and spelling
Administration Time:	Approximately 20 minutes
Age Levels:	Kindergarten through adulthood
Suitable for:	Students with mild disabilities, including learning disabilities and behavior disorders
Scores:	Grade equivalents, standard scores, percentiles, and absolute scores
In Short:	Although quick and easy to administer, the *WRAT3* suffers from questionable norms and other inferior technical qualities that limit its usefulness.

Materials for the *WRAT3*   The *WRAT3* provides concise and easy-to-use materials. Available separately or in a starter set, the materials include 25 blue test forms, 25 tan test forms, 25 profile/analysis forms, a manual, and plastic reading and spelling cards.

Administration and Scoring of the *WRAT3*   Designed for individual administration, the *WRAT3* includes two alternate, equivalent forms that enable evaluators to give the second form if later testing is necessary. The *WRAT3* can be given and scored in about 20 minutes. Evaluators may convert raw scores into standard scores, percentiles, or absolute scores. Absolute scores, which identify the difficulty level of each item on an interval scale, are most suitable for use in research studies such as pre- and posttesting and establishing local norms. Unlike most contemporary tests, the *WRAT3* also provides grade scores even though these are not as precise or informative as other available scores.

Technical Characteristics of the *WRAT3*   Critical reviews (Mabry, 1995; Ward, 1995) raise serious questions about the adequacy of the *WRAT3*. Mabry listed numerous weaknesses, including inadequate test content, discrepancies between test forms, inappropriate scoring procedures, inferior reliability, and unsatisfactory validity. For these reasons, Mabry characterized the inflated descriptions of the diagnostic uses of the test that appear in the *WRAT3* manual as "sheer nonsense" and "ludicrous" (pp. 1108–9). Ward described the *WRAT3*, originally published 60 years ago, as outdated and lacking adequate psychometric qualities. Ward concluded that major problems with the *WRAT-R*, the previous version of the test, were not resolved in revision. Ward cited failure to identify the test construct and to provide evidence of construct validity as the most significant problems. *Construct validity* refers to the soundness of the items that make up the test. Because tests with poor construct validity may not measure what they are supposed to measure, resulting test scores may not be valid.

Summary of the *WRAT3*   Although quick and easy to administer, the *WRAT3* suffers from questionable norms and other inferior technical qualities. Inadequate test content coupled with a lack of sufficient items to identify deficits in learning makes the *WRAT3* useful only as a rough screening measure. For this reason, evaluators should use the test cautiously, if at all.

Peabody Individual Achievement Test-Revised

In contrast to the narrow range of skills measured by the *WRAT3*, the *Peabody Individual Achievement Test-Revised (PIAT-R)* (Markwardt, 1998) assesses a wide range of academic ability across all major subjects of the school curriculum. Special educators frequently rely on this test, which is norm referenced and individually administered, to provide a clear overview of scholastic achievement and to assist in selecting more precise diagnostic tools for follow-up evaluation. The test consists of six subtests:

1. General information
2. Reading recognition
3. Reading comprehension

4. Mathematics
5. Spelling
6. Written expression

   The general information subtest measures general knowledge, and the reading recognition subtest surveys the ability to recognize printed letters and to read words. In the reading comprehension subtest, the student reads a sentence and then selects from four choices the one answer that best represents the sentence. The mathematics subtest consists of math tasks ranging from recognizing numbers to geometry and trigonometry. A summary of the *PIAT-R* appears in Table 14–2.

Materials for the *PIAT-R* The *PIAT-R* materials include four test plate booklets, a manual, a test record, and a written expression booklet. The test plate booklets, which are organized in easel-kit fashion, provide a convenient and motivating way to present the test items. Scoring the *PIAT-R* is much easier with the optional Assist software that converts raw scores into derived scores and provides subtest comparisons. The Assist report options include a score summary report, profiles for standard scores and grade and age equivalents, and a personalized narrative report.

Administration and Scoring of the *PIAT-R* Designed for individual administration to students from kindergarten through high school, the complete *PIAT-R* takes about 1½ hours to administer and score. The *PIAT-R* produces a total test score, a total reading score, and scores for each subtest. These scores include age- and grade-based standard scores, age- and grade-equivalent scores, percentiles, normal curve equivalents, and stanines. The score sheet includes a profile for visual presentation of results. A sample *PIAT-R* scoring form and scoring profile appear in Figure 14–1.

Table 14–2 *Peabody Individual Achievement Test-Revised (PIAT-R)*

Type of Test:	Norm referenced
Purpose:	A screening test of academic achievement
Content Areas:	General information, reading recognition, reading comprehension, mathematics, spelling, and written expression
Administration Time:	Approximately 60 minutes
Age Levels:	Grades K–12
Suitable for:	Students with mild and moderate disabilities, including learning disabilities, behavior disorders, educable mental retardation, sensory impairments, and physical disabilities
Scores:	Age- and grade-based standard scores, age- and grade-equivalent scores, percentiles, normal curve equivalents, and stanines
In Short:	The well-designed *PIAT-R* is a wide-range screening test of academic achievement that measures performance in the major subjects of the school curriculum. The test includes attractive materials and appropriate techinical characteristics.

Figure 14–1 Sample Forms from the *Peabody Individual Achievement Test-Revised*

Norms Used: ☑ Updated ☐ Original

Grade Placement _2.9_
Chronological Age _7-9_

	RAW SCORES ① (68% confidence)	Grade Equivalents / Age Equivalents ② (68% confidence)	DERIVED SCORES — Standard Scores ③ (68% confidence)	Percentile Ranks ④ (68% confidence)
General Information (−SEM / Raw Score / +SEM)	60 / 63 / 66	10-5 / 10-9 / 11-1	127 / 131 / 135	96 / 98 / 99
Reading Recognition	37 / 39 / 41	8-0 / 8-2 / 8-2	102 / 104 / 106	55 / 61 / 66
Reading Comprehension	43 / 46 / 49	8-2 / 8-5 / 8-7	105 / 108 / 111	63 / 70 / 77
TOTAL READING [1]	81 / 85 / 89	8-1 / 8-2 / 8-4	103 / 105 / 107	58 / 63 / 68
Mathematics	34 / 36 / 38	8-8 / 8-10 / 9-0	107 / 111 / 115	68 / 77 / 84
Spelling	33 / 35 / 37	7-4 / 7-6 / 7-8	92 / 95 / 98	30 / 37 / 45
TOTAL TEST [2]	213 / 219 / 225	8-6 / 8-7 / 8-8	106 / 108 / 110	66 / 70 / 75

Standard Scores — Grade (G.2) ☐ / Age (G.4) ☑, F W S (circle one)

Raw Score SEM Values by Confidence Level

General Information
Grade / Age	68%	90%	95%
K - 7 / 5 - 13	③	5	6
8 - 12 / 14 - 18+	②	3	4

Reading Recognition
Grade / Age	68%	90%	95%
K - 12 / 5 - 18+	②	3	4

Reading Comprehension
Grade / Age	68%	90%	95%
/ 5 - 6		7	8
K - 12 / 7 - 18+	④	5	6

Mathematics
Grade / Age	68%	90%	95%
K - 4 / 5 - 9	②	3	4
5 - 12 / 10 - 18+	③	5	6

Spelling
Grade / Age	68%	90%	95%
K - 6 / 5 - 17	②	3	4
7 - 12 / 18+	③	5	6

TOTAL TEST [2]
Grade / Age	68%	90%	95%
K - 8 / 5 - 14	⑥	10	12
9 - 12 / 15 - 18+	⑤	8	10

Written Expression
☐ Level I
☑ Level II, Prompt Ⓐ B (circle one)
Raw Score _28_
Grade-based Stanine (Levels I and II) (Table G.6 or G.7) _5_ ⑤
Developmental Scaled Score (Level II only) (Table G.8) _5_ ⑥

WRITTEN LANGUAGE COMPOSITE
Spelling Raw Score _35_   Written Expression Raw Score _28_
Scaled Score _3_ + _5_ = Scaled Score Sum _8_ (Table I.1 or I.7)
Standard Score ☐ Grade (Table I.2 or I.8) / ☑ Age (Table I.3 or I.9) — 68% confidence (Table I.4 or I.10): _92_ / _95_ / _98_ (−SEM / +SEM)
Percentile Rank (Table G.5): _30_ / _37_ / _45_ (−SEM / +SEM)

[1] The Total Reading composite raw score is the sum of the Reading Recognition and Reading Comprehension subtest raw scores.
[2] The Total Test composite raw score is the sum of the General Information, Reading Recognition, Reading Comprehension, Mathematics, and Spelling subtest raw scores. Do not include the total Reading Composite raw score.
[3] Values to be used in the standard score confidence intervals are given in Appendix H of the manual.

Figure 14–1 *(continued)*

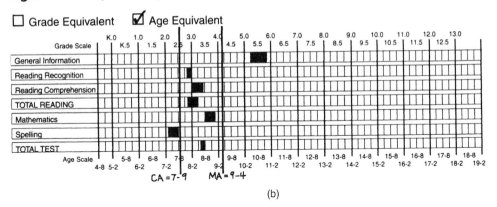

☐ Grade Equivalent ☑ Age Equivalent

(b)

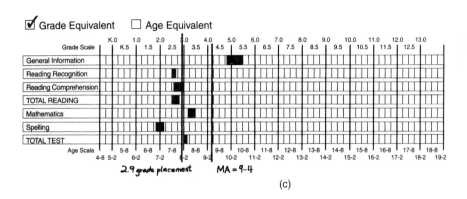

☑ Grade Equivalent ☐ Age Equivalent

(c)

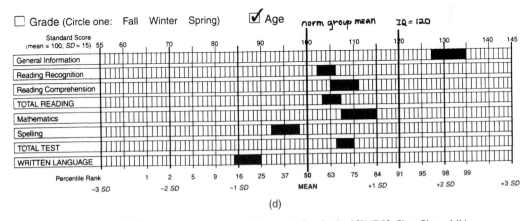

☐ Grade (Circle one: Fall Winter Spring) ☑ Age

(d)

From Markwardt, F. C. [1998]. *Peabody Individual Achievement Test-Revised [PIAT-R]*. Circe Pines, MN: American Guidance Service. Reprinted with permission of American Guidance Service, Inc.

The manual provides a clear description of administration, scoring, and interpretation procedures, including a special form for reporting results to parents. The author indicates that the evaluator may send the report form to parents if a meeting is not possible. When reviewing the *PIAT-R*, Costenbader and Adams (1991) questioned the appropriateness of sending a technical report instead of meeting directly with parents. The reviewers also noted that the *PIAT-R* manual suggests using the instrument for both screening and comprehensive diagnostic programming; however, because it contains relatively few items, the *PIAT-R* is best when used as a wide-range survey test.

Technical Characteristics of the *PIAT-R*   Following a well-designed testing plan to ensure representation of the national population, the most recent version of the *PIAT-R* incorporates a 1997 normative update based on a sample of over 3,000 people. These norms allow for comparison (including score equating) with three other major achievement batteries: the *K-TEA: Kaufman Test of Educational Achievement*, the *KeyMath-R: KeyMath Diagnostic Test of Arithmetic*, and the *WRMT-R: Woodcock Reading Mastery Test-Revised*. Ten years separate the original *PIAT-R* norms and the updated norms. The *PIAT-R* developers used several methods of estimating the reliability of the scores, including split-half, test-retest, and item-response theory. Using a variety of reliability measures provides evidence from different perspectives to support the consistency of *PIAT-R* scores. In terms of validity, the manual provides extensive evidence pertaining to the content, criterion-related, and construct validity of the test. Reviewers of the earlier version of the *PIAT-R* (Costenbader & Adams, 1991; Williams & Vincent, 1989) concluded that the *PIAT-R* is a carefully designed and well-constructed instrument with more than adequate technical and psychometric properties. The updated norms provide even further evidence of the high quality of this instrument. Furthermore, the test exhibits superior technical characteristics in comparison with most other multiple-skill screening tests of academic achievement.

Summary of the *PIAT-R*   The *PIAT-R* provides an excellent starting point for the formal evaluation process. It gives an overview of general achievement and indicates areas that may need further assessment. A well-written and highly useful screening test, the *PIAT-R* includes attractive materials and excellent technical characteristics, which account for its popularity among special educators.

Kaufman Test of Educational Achievement

The *Kaufman Test of Educational Achievement (K-TEA)* (Kaufman & Kaufman, 1998) is both a screening test and a comprehensive diagnostic test of student achievement. The *K-TEA* measures the academic performance of students from grade 1 through grade 12 and is designed for diagnosticians, special education teachers, and psychologists. The *K-TEA* includes two forms: the short form, which is a brief screening test, and the comprehensive form, which gives a complete measure of achievement across all of the basic scholastic subjects. A summary of the *K-TEA* appears in Table 14–3. The *K-TEA* subtests include the following:

Reading decoding	Letter recognition and pronunciation of words
Reading comprehension	Beginning items measure literal comprehension (e.g., "Show me your elbow"), and later items measure inferential comprehension and require oral answers to questions about a paragraph read silently

Table 14–3 *Kaufman Test of Educational Achievement (K-TEA)*

Type of Test:	Norm referenced
Purpose:	Screening and diagnosis of academic achievement
Content Areas:	Reading decoding, reading comprehension, spelling, mathematics computation, and mathematics applications
Administration Time:	Approximately 1 hour
Age Levels:	Grades K–12
Suitable for:	Students with mild and moderate disabilities, including learning disabilities, behavior disorders, educable mental retardation, sensory impairments, and physical disabilities
Scores:	Standard scores, age equivalents, grade equivalents, percentiles, stanines, and normal curve equivalents
In Short:	The well-designed *K-TEA* provides a complete system for measuring academic achievement.

Spelling	Students write orally presented words on a spelling sheet
Mathematics computation	Students solve problems on a mathematics computation worksheet that includes computation skills, measurement, and algebra
Mathematics applications	Includes fractions, decimals, money, estimation, two-step problems, and real-world problems

Materials for the *K-TEA*   The regular edition of the complete *K-TEA* test kit includes two test plate easels, two manuals, two packages of score sheets, two sample reports to parents, and two storage boxes. Optional computer software for the comprehensive form converts raw scores to derived scores, analyzes errors, and provides a narrative report with reading decoding/spelling word lists, math problem lists, and teaching objectives.

Administration and Scoring of the *K-TEA*   The *K-TEA* comprehensive form takes an average of one hour to give, and, although the administration and scoring process is complex, it is well organized. Available *K-TEA* scores include standard scores, age equivalents, grade equivalents, percentiles, stanines, and normal curve equivalents, which evaluators may obtain for each subtest and the total test. The developers normed the test during both the fall and spring, resulting in two sets of tables for each score. This feature facilitates measuring student progress at the beginning and the end of an academic year. The test also includes a score profile and an extensive error analysis summary for each subtest. The profile and summaries simplify the process of identifying error patterns and determining strengths and weaknesses.

Technical Characteristics of the *K-TEA*   The norms for the *K-TEA* were updated in 1997 using a group of more than 3,000 students. This normative update followed a well-designed development plan, resulting in norms that represent students from across the nation. The manual reports very good split-half and test-retest measures of reliability and also presents both construct and concurrent validity data to demonstrate the effectiveness of the *K-TEA* as an assessment instrument. The authors used a multistage approach to obtain construct validity data and correlated the *K-TEA* with other tests. In summary, the *K-TEA* displays very good technical qualities.

Summary of the *K-TEA*   The *K-TEA,* an excellent test for comprehensively evaluating scholastic achievement, provides useful information concerning performance levels, academic strengths, and areas needing remediation. The test incorporates several advanced features, including an error analysis summary, a parent report, and a computer software program. Evaluators who use the *K-TEA* can obtain detailed information for making placement decisions, developing instructional objectives, and measuring student progress.

Wechsler Individual Achievement Test

Like the *K-TEA,* the *Wechsler Individual Achievement Test (WIAT)* (Wechsler, 1992) is both a screening test and a comprehensive diagnostic test of student achievement. Designed for students from 5 through 19 years of age, the *WIAT* is correlated with the *Wechsler Intelligence Scale for Children-Third Edition (WISC-III).* This link helps special educators and psychologists compare achievement and intelligence test scores and evaluate differences between them. The authors designed the *WIAT* for assessing and reevaluating students, answering academic questions about students, and planning individual instructional intervention programs for students. A summary of the *WIAT* appears in Table 14–4. The eight *WIAT* subtests are as follows:

Basic reading	Measures decoding and sight reading ability with test items from the stimulus book
Reading comprehension	Requires verbal responses to orally presented questions based on printed passages (some passages have pictures)
Mathematical reasoning	Presents mathematical problems orally and also in print in the stimulus booklet
Numerical operations	Presents numerals and equations orally, including addition, subtraction, multiplication, division, fractions, and algebra
Listening comprehension	Evaluates comprehension ranging from details to inferential conclusions
Oral expression	Measures the ability to orally respond to words, scenes, directions, and sequential tasks with pictures and verbal directions
Spelling	Requires written responses to dictated letters, sounds, and words
Written expression	Measures writing skills directly

Materials for the *WIAT*   The complete *WIAT* kit includes a manual, two easel-type stimulus booklets, and a package each of scoring forms, student response booklets, and screener score sheets. An optional software program produces profile reports for the *WIAT* and the *WISC-III.* The *WIAT* developers designed the test materials to make administration as easy as possible and to hold children's interest. The easel-type test booklets are easy to manage and contain colorful drawings.

Table 14–4   *Wechsler Individual Achievement Test (WIAT)*

Type of Test:	Norm referenced
Purpose:	A screening and diagnostic test of academic achievement
Content Areas:	Screening subtests: basic reading, mathematics reasoning, and spelling
	Diagnostic subtests: basic reading, reading comprehension, mathematics reasoning, numerical operations, listening comprehension, oral expression, spelling, and written expression
Administration Time:	Screening test, 30 minutes; diagnostic test, 90–120 minutes
Age Levels:	5–19 years
Suitable for:	Students with specific learning disabilities, attention-deficit and hyperactivity disorders, behavior disorders, educable mental retardation, hearing impairment, and giftedness
Scores:	Standard scores by age and grade with fall, winter, and spring tables; percentile ranks by age and grade; and equivalent scores by age and grade
In Short:	The well-designed *WIAT* includes screening and diagnostic tests of scholastic achievement. A key feature is the match between the *WIAT* and the *WISC-III*.

Administration and Scoring of the *WIAT* Designed for individual administration, the complete *WIAT* takes 90 to 120 minutes to administer and score. Evaluators can give the brief screening version in about 30 minutes. The manual provides a clear description of administration, scoring, and interpretation procedures. One of the *WIAT* stimulus booklets, which examiners can use to screen students, contains the basic reading, mathematical reasoning, and spelling subtests. The complete *WIAT* includes these screening subtests along with five other subtests. The *WIAT* produces subtest scores; composite scores for reading, mathematics, language, and writing; a total test score; and a screening test score. Evaluators can report these scores as age- and grade-based standard scores, equivalent scores by age and grade, or percentiles. Examples of completed record forms for the *WIAT Screener* and the *WIAT Comprehensive Battery* appear in Figure 14–2.

Technical Characteristics of the *WIAT* Standardized with a representative sample of 4,252 students, the well-designed *WIAT* development plan produced high-quality national norms. To link the *WIAT* to the *WISC-III* for ability and achievement comparisons, the developers gave both tests to a subset sample of students. In addition, the developers correlated *WIAT* scores with scores from several other achievement tests, including the *Wide Range Achievement Test-Revised*, the *Kaufman Test of Educational Achievement*, the *Woodcock–Johnson Psycho-Educational Battery-Revised*, and the *Peabody Picture Vocabulary Test-Revised*. They also administered the *WIAT* to sample groups of students with the following exceptionalities: gifted, mental retardation, learning disabilities, emotional disturbance, attention-deficit hyperactivity disorder, and hearing impairment. These data provide evidence to support the validity of the *WIAT* as a diagnostic test of achievement for diagnosing academic difficulties.

Figure 14–2 Examples of Complete Record Forms for the *WIAT Screener* and the *WIAT Comprehensive Battery*

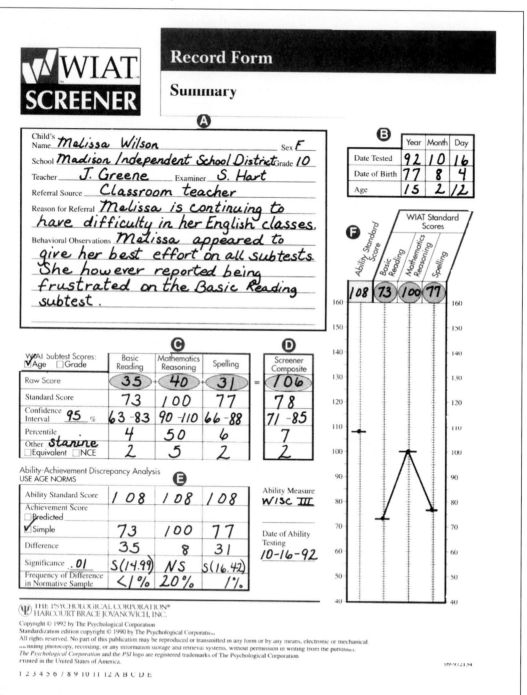

Figure 14–2 *(continued)*

WIAT
WECHSLER
INDIVIDUAL
ACHIEVEMENT
TEST

Record Form
Summary

Ⓐ

Child's Name _Melissa Wilson_　　　Sex _F_

School _Madison Independent School District_　Grade _10_

Teacher _J. Greene_　Examiner _S. Hart_

Referral Source _Classroom teacher_

Reason for Referral _Despite student and teacher efforts, Melissa continues to have great difficulty in English classes._

Behavioral Observations _Melissa appeared to give her best effort on all subtests. She however reported being frustrated on the Basic Reading and Reading Comprehension subtests._

Ⓑ

	Year	Month	Day
Date Tested	92	10	16
Date of Birth	77	8	4
Age	15	2	12

Ⓒ WIAT Subtests — ☑Age ☐Grade

	Raw Scores			Standard Score	Confidence Interval 95%	Percentile	Other ☑Equivalent ☐NCE
Basic Reading	35			73	63-83	4	9:9
Mathematics Reasoning		40		100	90-110	50	15:0
Spelling			31	77	66-88	6	10:3
Reading Comprehension	17			71	59-83	3	8:6
Numerical Operations		37		106	94-118	66	15:6
Listening Comprehension			28	104	91-117	61	16:3
Oral Expression			29	104	95-113	61	16:0
Written Expression			14	86	74-98	18	10:3

Ⓓ Composites — ☑Age ☐Grade

	Reading	Mathematics	Language	Writing	Total Composite
Sum of Raw Scores	52 +	77 +	57 +	45 =	231
Standard Score	65	103	105	77	82
Confidence Interval 95%	56-74	94-112	95-115	68-86	76-88
Percentile	1	58	63	6	12
Other ☑Equivalent ☐NCE	9:3	15:3	17:0	10:3	11:9

Figure 14–2 *(continued)*

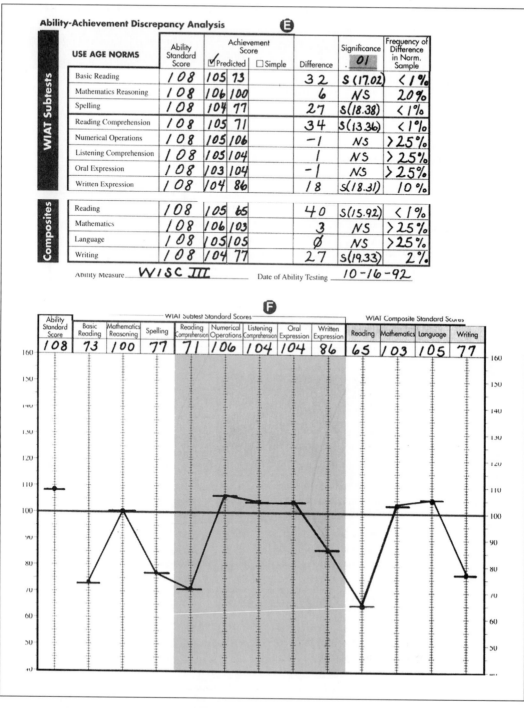

Weshler, D. [1992]. *Wechsler Individual Achievement Test.* San Antonio, TX: Psychological Corporation. Reprinted with permission of the Psychological Corporation.

Summary of the *WIAT* As a comprehensive measure of student achievement, the *WIAT* is a well-designed instrument with materials that are both easy to manage and appealing to students. Because the *WIAT* is matched to the *WISC-III*, evaluators can examine the amount of discrepancy between achievement and ability scores by comparing scores from the two tests.

Brigance Diagnostic Inventories

The *Brigance Diagnostic Inventories* are individually administered, criterion-referenced measures of academic achievement. The four separate tests that make up the series include the *Comprehensive Inventory of Basic Skills* (Brigance, 1983) for kindergarten to grade 9, the *Inventory of Basic Skills* (Brigance, 1977a) for kindergarten to grade 6, the *Assessment of Basic Skills-Spanish Edition* (Brigance, 1977b) for kindergarten to grade 6, and the *Inventory of Essential Skills* (Brigance, 1981) for grades 4 to 12. Unlike traditional norm-referenced, multiple-skill tests, these criterion-referenced inventories consist of item pools covering a wider range of content than most standardized tests. With norm-referenced tests, evaluation must follow standardized administration procedures; however, informal tools like the *Brigance Diagnostic Inventories* need not follow a rigid administration formula. Instead, the teacher may assess behavior flexibly in direct response to a student's needs and the reasons for testing. With the *Brigance* and similar measures, the teacher may give the complete inventory or parts of it as needed. This flexibility allows the inventories to serve as curriculum guides that produce instructional objectives rather than as traditional tests that produce test scores. Instead of test score results, the inventories provide assessment information that translates directly into remediation activities for individuals and small groups of students. The inventories include instructional objectives for each test item. Teachers may select objectives that meet a student's intervention needs and include those objectives on the IEP.

The *Comprehensive Inventory of Basic Skills,* the newest tool in the series, measures student achievement from kindergarten through grade 9 in 22 skill areas. The *Inventory of Basic Skills,* the first inventory in the series, measures the academic achievement of students from kindergarten through grade 6 in 14 skills areas. The *Assessment of Basic Skills-Spanish Edition,* designed for bilingual special education, migrant, and other bilingual programs, contains 10 subtests for kindergarten through grade 8. The *Inventory of Essential Skills,* designed for grade 6 through adult, includes subtests for assessing academic as well as practical skills. A listing of the subtests of each instrument appears in Table 14–5.

Materials for the *Brigance Inventories* Each inventory in the *Brigance* series includes a diagnostic test, individual student record books, an optional class record book, and IEP objective forms. Teachers can use the student record books to measure student progress over time, identify remediation activities in a planned sequence, and share progress with parents and other professionals. Supplementary materials include IEP software programs in Apple II, PC-DOS, Macintosh, and Windows versions. The software includes goals taken directly from the inventories. In addition, goals may be written by the teacher or by other members of the IEP team. Other supplemental materials include the *Brigance Prescriptive Readiness Strategies and Practice* (Brigance, 1985), the *Brigance Prescriptive Word Analysis: Strategies and Practice, Volumes I and II* (Brigance, 1987), and the

Table 14–5   Subtests of the *Brigance Diagnostic Inventories*

Comprehensive Inventory of Basic Skills	
Readiness	Writing
Speech	Math grade placement
Word recognition	Numbers
Oral reading	Number facts
Reading comprehension	Whole number computation
Listening	Fractions and mixed numbers
Functional word recognition	Decimals
Word analysis	Percents
Reference skills	Word problems
Graphs and maps	Metrics
Spelling	Math vocabulary

Inventory of Basic Skills	
Readiness	Spelling
Word recognition	Reference skills
Reading	Math placement
Word analysis	Numbers
Vocabulary	Operations
Handwriting	Measurement
Grammar and mechanics	Geometry

Assessment of Basic Skills—Spanish Edition	
Readiness	Word analysis
Speech	Listening
Functional word recognition	Writing and alphabetizing
Oral reading	Numbers and computation
Reading comprehension	Measurement

Inventory of Essential Skills	
Reading	Food and clothing
Language arts	Money and finance
Health and attitude	Travel and transportation
Job interview behavior	Communication
Auto safety	Telephone skills
Responsibility and self-discipline	

Brigance Prescriptive Study Skills: Strategies and Practice (Brigance, 1988). These remedial materials include reproducible pages with hundreds of teaching activities.

Administration and Scoring of the *Brigance Inventories* For each subtest, the *Brigance Diagnostic Inventories* provide a criterion-referenced score and the percent of items passed. They also produce estimated grade levels of performance in reading and mathematics, but evaluators should use these approximate scores cautiously. Giving a complete inventory may take several hours, and for this reason, evaluators should complete the assessment over a few sittings rather than one long session.

Technical Characteristics of the *Brigance Inventories* Although the *Brigance Inventories* display excellent face validity and measure important skills, the manual fails to include any technical information about reliability and validity. As a result, the inventories fall below minimum standards for their intended use as criterion-referenced tools. In a lengthy review, Robinson and Kovacevich (1989) concluded that, because the author provided no documentation of test development, the inventories are not tests at all. The problem, according to Robinson and Kovacevich, is that the author and publisher identified the inventories as tests rather than as item pools designed for use as checklists of skills and informal directories of teaching activities. However, when viewed as item pools rather than as tests, special educators can use the inventories as valuable curriculum planning devices that are especially useful for identifying appropriate instructional intervention activities.

Summary of the *Brigance Diagnostic Inventories* The *Brigance Diagnostic Inventories* consist of a series of informal checklists of academic achievement that provide content and features not available in traditional tests. These features include flexible administration, numerous items, and IEP objectives for each skill. Although not appropriate for making placement decisions, special educators can rely on these inventories to obtain specific information for curriculum planning and implementation. A summary of the *Brigance Diagnostic Inventories* appears in Table 14–6.

Table 14–6   *Brigance Diagnostic Inventories*

Type of Test:	Criterion referenced
Purpose:	A set of four diagnostic tests of academic achievement
Content Areas:	*Inventory of Basic Skills* 22 subtests *Inventory of Basic Skills* 14 subtests *Assessment of Basic Skills-Spanish Edition* 10 subtests *Inventory of Essential Skills* 14 subtests
Administration Time:	Flexible, but as long as several hours, depending on the number of subtests given
Age Levels:	*Comprehensive Inventory of Basic Skills* Grades K–9 *Inventory of Basic Skills* Grades K–6 *Assessment of Basic Skills-Spanish Edition* Grades K–6 *Inventory of Essential Skills* Grades 4–12
Suitable for:	Students with mild and moderate disabilities, including learning disabilities, behavior disorders, educable mental retardation, sensory impairments, and physical disabilities
Scores:	Rather than producing traditional test scores, the inventories yield instructional objectives and intervention activities.
In Short:	The *Brigance Diagnostic Inventories* are a set of informal, criterion-referenced checklists of academic achievement. The inventories provide content and features not available in traditional tests, including item pools that cover a wider range of content than most standardized tests.

Other Individually Administered Multiple-Skill Achievement Tests

Brief reviews of other available individually administered multiple-skill achievement tests follow. These tests include screening instruments as well as achievement tests for adolescents and adults.

Basic Achievement Skills Individual Screener

The *Basic Achievement Skills Individual Screener (BASIS)* (Sonnenschein, 1983) measures skills in reading, mathematics, spelling, and writing. Designed for students from first grade through adulthood, the norm-referenced *BASIS* screening test takes approximately 1 hour to administer. The purpose for administering the *BASIS* is to obtain an overall picture of student performance in the basic academic skills.

Diagnostic Achievement Battery-2

The *Diagnostic Achievement Battery-2 (DAB-2)* (Newcomer, 1990) is a norm-referenced, individually administered achievement test that measures listening, speaking, reading, writing, and mathematics. Designed for students from 6 through 14 years of age, the *DAB-2* was standardized using data from the original 1983 norm sample along with data from the 1990 version of the test. Because this standardization procedure is questionable, the *DAB-2* is best used as a screening instrument to obtain a general idea of overall achievement rather than as a diagnostic tool for placement or intervention decisions.

Diagnostic Achievement Test for Adolescents, Second Edition

The *Diagnostic Achievement Test for Adolescents, Second Edition (DATA-2)* (Newcomer & Bryant, 1993) is a norm-referenced, individually administered achievement test for students in grades 7 through 12. The subtests of the *DATA-2* measure receptive vocabulary, receptive grammar, expressive grammar, expressive vocabulary, word identification, reading comprehension, math calculations, math problem solving, spelling, and writing composition. The *DATA-2* also includes supplemental subtests for measuring science, social studies, and reference skills. An optional computer scoring system is available to quickly score the *DATA-2* and to generate a scoring summary report.

Quick-Score Achievement Test

The *Quick-Score Achievement Test (Q-SAT)* (Hammil et al., 1987) is an individually administered screening test of academic achievement for students from grade 1 through grade 12. Its purpose is to identify students with potential academic deficits who may need more comprehensive assessment. The *Q-SAT* includes subtests for measuring reading, writing, arithmetic, and factual information. Two equivalent *Q-SAT* forms enable retesting of students with a different version of the test.

Scholastic Abilities Test for Adults

The *Scholastic Abilities Test for Adults (SATA)* (Bryant et al., 1991) is a norm-referenced screening test of academic achievement. Designed to meaure the scholastic abilities of adults from 16 through 70 years of age, the *SATA* was normed on more than 1,000 people in 17 states. It measures aptitude and achievement and enables an aptitude-achievement discrepancy analysis for identifying adults who may have learning disabilities.

Woodcock–Johnson Psycho-Educational Battery-Revised, Tests of Achievement

The *Woodcock–Johnson Psycho-Educational Battery-Revised, Tests of Achievement (WJ-R ACH)* (Woodcock & Johnson, 1989) is an individually administered diagnostic test of achievement. The *WJ-R ACH* includes subtests for measuring letter-word identification, passage comprehension, calculation, applied problems, dictation, writing samples, science, social studies, and humanities. It also includes supplemental subtests for assessing word attack, reading vocabulary, qualitative concepts, proofing, writing fluency, spelling, usage, and handwriting. Designed for use with individuals from ages 2 through adulthood, the complete *Woodcock–Johnson Battery* also includes a test of cognitive ability. A complete review of the *WJ-R* appears in Chapter 7. A Spanish edition of the *Woodcock–Johnson Psycho-Educational Battery, Batería Woodcock-Muñoz-Revisada* (Woodcock & Muñoz-Sandoval, 1996), is also available. The *Batería Woodcock* is normed on more than 800 Spanish-speaking students from five countries.

☑ Comprehension Checklist

The multiple-skill achievement tests represent a major element of assessment in special education. Evaluators assess virtually all students with mild or moderate disabilities by using at least one of these instruments; furthermore, diagnosticians and teachers repeatedly measure the achievement of some students with these tests. Fortunately, special educators may select from a variety of well-designed, multiple-skill achievement tests to conduct these evaluations. Although the multiple-skill tests serve many purposes, they fail to meet all of the assessment needs of students with mild and moderate disabilities. In some situations, students require more in-depth diagnostic evaluation. When this need occurs, special educators often prefer to use a single-skill achievement test or assessment procedure.

Summary

Assessing achievement, the process of evaluating student learning as a result of instruction, represents one of the most diverse elements of assessment in special education. Scholastic achievement encompasses appraisal techniques for students from kindergarten through adulthood and includes three major strands: reading, mathematics, and written language. These strands contain a wide range of skills across extended age levels, which accounts for much of the diversity in achievement testing.

Another factor, the large assortment of tests and procedures for measuring achievement, also contributes to the diversity in achievement testing (see Table 14–7 on p. 440). Special educators require a variety of measures because generic assessment models fail to meet unique academic needs and learning styles. Therefore, a blend of tools and techniques, including norm- and criterion-referenced tests, multiple- and single-skill tests, and curriculum-based appraisal techniques, provide data for educational decision making. This chapter focused on the widely used multiple-skill tests. The following three chapters provide in-depth coverage of single-skill tests and curriculum-based assessment.

In addition to diversity, another notable aspect of achievement is its importance in schools, where academics receive the highest priority, sometimes to the exclusion of other vital educational programs and services. At the same time, most students with special needs encounter significant difficulties in learning academic subjects. Because of the diverse nature and importance of academic achievement, special educators need a working knowledge of available tests so that they can select appropriate tools and conduct skillful evaluations. This knowledge, coupled with hands-on experience, helps teachers and other professionals make the best possible assesssment decisions that respond to the academic needs of their students.

Chapter Review and Application

Multiple Choice

Directions: Read each item carefully. In the blank beside each item, write the letter of the best response. Each question contains only one best answer. Check your answers with the answer key at the end of the book.

_____ 1. Tests for assessing academic performance are called _____ tests.
    a. intelligence
    b. aptitude
    c. behavior
    d. achievement

_____ 2. The most appropriate achievement tests for making classification decisions are _____.
    a. criterion referenced and individually administered
    b. norm referenced regardless of administration procedures
    c. norm referenced and individually administered
    d. norm referenced and group administered

_____ 3. Joe, who is learning disabled, struggles in math. Which is the best test to diagnose his strengths, weaknesses, and instructional needs?
    a. Single-skill
    b. Multiple-skill
    c. Screening

_____ 4. The type of assessment that measures educational success in the local school curriculum is _____.
    a. multiple subject
    b. norm-referenced
    c. curriculum-based
    d. standardized

_____ **5.** The individually administered multiple-skill screening test of achievement that covers the greatest range and variety of content is the _____.
   a. *PIAT-R*
   b. *WRAT-3*
   c. *Brigance Diagnostic Inventory*

_____ **6.** The *Wechsler Individual Achievement Test (WIAT)* is an example of a _____ achievement test.
   a. multiple-skill
   b. single-skill
   c. curriculum-based
   d. criterion-referenced

_____ **7.** Which multiple-skill test is individually administered and criterion-referenced?
   a. *Brigance Diagnostic Inventories*
   b. *Kaufman Test of Educational Achievement*
   c. *Peabody Individual Achievement Test-Revised*
   d. *Wechsler Individual Achievement Test*

_____ **8.** The *PIAT-R* is a _____ test.
   a. criterion-referenced
   b. curriculum-based
   c. screening
   d. diagnostic

_____ **9.** The *PIAT-R* is best with students who are _____.
   a. gifted
   b. severely disabled
   c. mild to moderately disabled
   d. hearing impaired

_____ **10.** Which achievement test is designed for both screening- and diagnostic-level assessment?
   a. *PIAT-R*
   b. *WIAT*
   c. *WRAT-3*

Short Answers

Directions: Review your understanding of the material in this chapter by answering the following items. Compare your responses with the sample answers at the end of the book. Your responses should contain information that is similar to but not exactly the same as the information in the sample answers.

1. Compare and contrast the group tests of achievement and the individually administered multiple-skill tests of achievement. Which type of test is best with children who have special needs? Why?
2. Obtain copies of the *Peabody Individual Achievement Test-Revised (PIAT-R)* and the *Wide Range Achievement Test-3 (WRAT-3)*. Review the test items. How are they similar? How are they different? When would it be appropriate to use each test?
3. Compare the subtests of two diagnostic-level multiple-skill tests of academic achievement. What are the similarities and differences?

4. Mr. Smith suspects that Simone is significantly behind her peers in academic achievement. What multiple-skill test do you think Mr. Smith should use to assess her achievement? Why?
5. Discuss the purposes and uses of standardized norm-referenced testing and curriculum-based, criterion-referenced assessment of academic achievement.

References

Balow, I. H., Prescott, G. A., Hogan, T. R., & Farr, R. C. (1992). *Metropolitan Achievement Tests* (7th ed.). San Antonio, TX: Psychological Corporation.

Brigance, A. H. (1977a). *Brigance Diagnostic Inventory of Basic Skills.* North Billerica, MA: Curriculum Associates.

———. (1977b). *Brigance Assessment of Basic Skills-Spanish Edition.* North Billerica, MA: Curriculum Associates.

———. (1981). *Brigance Diagnostic Inventory of Essential Skills.* North Billerica, MA: Curriculum Associates.

———. (1983). *Brigance Diagnostic Comprehensive Inventory of Basic Skills.* North Billerica, MA: Curriculum Associates.

———. (1985). *Brigance Prescriptive Readiness Strategies and Practice.* North Billerica, MA: Curriculum Associates.

———. (1987). *Brigance Prescriptive Word Analysis: Strategies and Practice* (vol. I and II). North Billerica, MA: Curriculum Associates.

———. (1988). *Brigance Prescriptive Study Skills: Strategies and Practice.* North Billerica, MA: Curriculum Associates.

Bryant, B. R., Patton, J. R., & Dunn, C. (1991). *Scholastic Abilities Test for Adults.* Austin, TX: PRO-ED.

Costenbader, V. K., & Adams, J. W. (1991). A review of the psychometric and administrative features of the *PIAT-R:* Implications for the practitioner. *Journal of School Psychology* 29, 219–28.

CTB/McGraw Hill. (1981). *Comprehensive Test of Basic Skills.* Monterey, CA: Author.

———. (1992). *California Achievement Tests* (5th ed.). Monterey, CA: CTB/Macmillan/McGraw-Hill.

Hammil, D. D., Ammer, J. J., Cronin, M. E., Mandlebaum, L. H., & Quinby, S. S. (1987). *Quick-Score Achievement Test.* Austin, TX: PRO-ED.

Hoover, H. D., Hieronymus, A. N., & Linquist, E. F. (1993). *Iowa Tests of Basic Skills.* Itasca, IL: Riverside Publishing Company.

Kaufman, A. S., & Kaufman, N. L. (1998). *Kaufman Test of Educational Achievement (K-TEA).* Circle Pines, MN: American Guidance Service.

Kubiszyn, T., & Borich, G. (1990). *Educational Testing and Measurement: Classroom Application and Practice* (3d ed.). Glenview, IL: Scott, Foresman.

Linn, R. L., & Gronlund, N. E. (1995). *Measurement and Assessment in Teaching* (7th ed). Upper Saddle River, NJ: Merrill/Prentice Hall.

Mabry, L. (1995). A review of the *Wide Range Achievement Test-3.* In J. C. Conoley and J. C. Impara (Eds.), *The Twelfth Mental Measurements Yearbook.* Lincoln, NE: Buros Institute of Mental Measurements, 1108-10.

Markwardt, F. C. (1998). *Peabody Individual Achievement Test-Revised (PIAT-R).* Circle Pines, MN: American Guidance Service.

Newcomer, P. (1990). *Diagnostic Achievement Battery-2.* Austin, TX: PRO-ED.

Newcomer, P., & Bryant, B. R. (1993). *Diagnostic Achievement Test for Adolescents* (2d ed.). Austin, TX: PRO-ED.

Psychological Corporation. (1996). *Stanford Achievement Test Series* (9th ed.). San Antonio, TX: Author.

Robinson, J. H., & Kovacevich, D. A. (1989). A review of the *Brigance Inventories.* In D. Keyser & R. Sweetland (Eds.), *Test Critiques* (vol. 4). Kansas City, MO: Test Corporation of America, 79–98.

Science Research Associates. (1985). *Science Research Associates Achievement Series.* Monterey, CA: CTB/Macmillan/McGraw-Hill.

Sonnenschein, J. L. (1983). *Basic Achievement Skills Individual Screener.* San Antonio, TX: Harcourt Brace Educational Measurement.

Ward, A. W. (1995). A review of the *Wide Range Achievement Test-3.* In J. C. Conoley and J. C. Impara (Eds.), *The Twelfth Mental Measurements Yearbook.* Lincoln, NE: Buros Institute of Mental Measurements, 1110-11.

Wechsler, D. (1992). *Wechsler Individual Achievement Test.* San Antonio, TX: Psychological Corporation.

Wilkinson, G. S. (1993). *Wide Range Achievement Test-3.* Wilmington, DE: Wide Range, Inc.

Williams, R. E., & Vincent, K. R. (1989). A review of the *Peabody Individual Achievement Test-Revised.* In D. Keyser & R. Sweetland (Eds.), *Test critiques* (vol. 8) Kansas City, MO: Test Corporation of America, 557–62.

Woodcock, R. W. & Johnson, M. B. (1989). *Woodcock–Johnson Psycho-Educational Battery-Revised, Tests of Achievement.* Itasca, IL: Riverside Publishing Company.

Woodcock, R. J., & Muñoz-Sandoval, A. F. (1996). *Batería Woodcock–Muñoz-Revisada.* Itasca, IL: Riverside Publishing Company.

Table 14–7   Review of Multiple-Skill Achievement Tests

Name of Test	Type of Test	Suitable for Individuals Who Are	Brief Description of Test	Purpose of Administering Test
Basic Achievement Skills Individual Screener (BASIS) (Sonnenschein, 1983)	Norm-referenced, individually administered screening test	First grade– adulthood	Measures skills in reading, mathematics, spelling, and writing	To obtain an overall picture of student performance in the basic academic skills
Batería Woodcock– Muñoz-Revisada (Woodcock & Muñoz-Sandoval, 1996)	Spanish-language version of the Woodcock– Johnson-Revised	2–adulthood	Measures letter-word identification, passage comprehension, calculation, applied problems, dictation, writing samples, science, social studies, humanities, word attack, reading vocabulary, qualitative concepts, proofing, writing fluency, spelling, usage, and handwriting	To obtain a comprehensive diagnostic assessment of academic achievement
*Brigance Diagnostic Inventories (Brigance, 1977ab, 1981, 1983)	Informal, criterion-referenced checklists	Grades K–9	Includes 4 inventories: the Comprehensive Inventory of Basic Skills, the Inventory of Basic Skills, the Assessment of Basic Skills-Spanish Edition, and the Inventory of Essential Skills	To provide content and features not available in traditional tests, including item pools that cover a wider range of content than most standardized tests
California Achievement Tests, Fifth Edition (CAT/5) (CTB/McGraw Hill, 1992)	Group-administered screening test of achievement	Grades K–12	Measures reading, language, spelling, mathematics, study skills, science, and social studies	To measure achievement in the basic skills from kindergarten through grade 12
Comprehensive Test of Basic Skills (CTBS) (CTB/McGraw Hill, 1992)	Group-administered screening test of achievement	Grades K–12	Measures cognitive processes and academic achievement	To assess achievement in the basic skills commonly found in state and district curricula
Diagnostic Achievement Battery-2 (DAB-2) (Newcomer, 1990)	Norm-referenced, individually administered screening test of achievement	6–14 years	Measures listening, speaking, reading, writing, and mathematics	To obtain a general idea of overall achievement

*Tests marked with asterisks are featured in tables in this chapter.

Table 14–7   *(continued)*

Name of Test	Type of Test	Suitable for Individuals Who Are	Brief Description of Test	Purpose of Administering Test
Diagnostic Achievement Test for Adolescents, Second Edition (DATA-2) (Newcomer & Bryant, 1993)	Norm-referenced, individually administered achievement test	Grades 7–12	Measures receptive vocabulary, receptive grammar, expressive grammar, expressive vocabulary, word identification, reading comprehension, math calculation, math problem solving, spelling, writing composition, science, social studies, and reference skills	To assess the achievement levels of adolescents in basic scholastic skills and in content areas
Iowa Tests of Basic Skills (ITBS) (Hoover, et al., 1993)	Group-administered screening test of achievement	Grades K–9	Measures reading, language, and mathematics	To assess student progress in the basic academic skills
Kaufman Test of Educational Achievement (K-TEA) (Kaufman & Kaufman, 1998)	Individually administered screening and diagnostic test of academic achievement	Grades K–12	Measures reading decoding, reading comprehension, spelling, mathematics computation, and mathematics applications	To provide a complete system for measuring academic achievement
Metropolitan Achievement Tests, Seventh Edition (MAT7) (Balow et al, 1992)	Group-administered screening test of achievement	Grades K–12	Measures achievement in basic skill reas covering a broad range of objectives in reading, math, and language	To assess the basic academic skills in the school curriculum
Peabody Individual Achievement Test-Revised (PIAT-R) (Markwardt, 1998)	Individually administered, norm-referenced screening test of achievement	Grades K–12	Measures general information, reading recognition, reading comprehension, mathematics, spelling, and written expression	To conduct wide-range screening of academic achievement in the major subjects of the school curriculum
Quick-Score Achievement Test (Q-SAT) (Hammil et al, 1987)	Individually administered screening test of academic achievement	Grades 1–12	Measures reading, writing, arithmetic, and factual information	To identify students with potential academic deficits who may need more comprehensive assessment

Table 14-7   *(continued)*

Name of Test	Type of Test	Suitable for Individuals Who Are	Brief Description of Test	Purpose of Administering Test
Scholastic Abilities Test for Adults (SATA) (Bryant et al., 1991)	Norm-referenced, individually administered screening test of academic achievement	16–70 years	Includes measures of aptitude and achievement	To measure the scholastic abilites of adults and to help identify adults who may have learning disabilities
Science Research Associates (SRA) Achievement Series (Science Research Associates, 1985)	Group-administered screening test of achievement	Grades K–12	A battery of tests in basic academic curriculum areas	To survey students' general academic achievement
Stanford Achievement Test Series, Ninth Edition (SAT9) (Psychological Corporation, 1996)	Group-admininstered screening tests of achievement	Grades K–13	Includes the *Stanford Early School Achievement Test (SESAT),* the *Stanford Achievement Test Series (SAT),* and the *Stanford Test of Academic Skills (TASK)*	To assess basic academic skills
*Wechsler Individual Achievement Test (WIAT) (Wechsler, 1992)	Norm-referenced, individually administered screening and diagnostic test of academic achievement	5–19 years	Screening subtests: basic reading, mathematics reasoning, and spelling; diagnostic subtests: basic reading, reading comprehension, mathematics reasoning, numerical operations, and listening	To screen and diagnose academic achievement; a key feature is the match between the *WIAT* and the *WISC-III*
*Wide Range Achievement Test-3 (WRAT3) (Wilkinson, 1993)	Norm-referenced, individually administered screening test of academic achievement	Kindergarten–adulthood	Measures reading recognition, arithmetic, and spelling	To screen the academic achievement of children and youth
Woodcock–Johnson Psycho-Educational Battery-Revised, Tests of Achievement (WJ-R ACH) (Woodcock & Johnson, 1989)	Norm-referenced, individually administered diagnostic test of achievement	2 years–adulthood	Measures letter-word identification, passage comprehension, calculation, applied problems, dictation, writing samples, science, social studies, humanities, word attack, reading vocabulary, qualitative concepts, proofing, writing fluency, spelling, usage, and handwriting	To obtain a comprehensive diagnostic assessment of academic achievement

Assessment of Reading
Achievement

Overview

In this chapter you will investigate tests and curriculum-based measurement procedures for assessing reading achievement. Reading, a complex process of understanding printed or written material, requires many skills and perceptual processes. Teachers, parents, and students place a high value on learning to read, and it represents the most important academic skill in the school curriculum. During the early grades, students with reading deficits experience difficulty because most of the curriculum focuses on emerging literacy and other language-based skills. In the later grades, poor readers have problems because mastery of most subjects requires well-developed reading skills. Because it is such an important skill, more tests and measurements have been devised to assess reading skills than any other academic subject. This chapter enables you to develop your knowledge and skills in this key scholastic domain. Your study of each test and curriculum-based procedure includes consideration of its purpose, administration, scoring, and interpretation. Your review of each assessment will also include consideration of the diagnostic uses, educational implications, and practical applications of the instrument.

Objectives

After reading this chapter, you will be prepared to do the following:

- Understand the term reading achievement.
- Understand the types of behaviors measured by reading tests.
- Use the individually administered screening tests of reading ability.
- Use the individually administered diagnostic reading tests.
- Use informal reading inventories.
- Construct teacher-made informal reading inventories.
- Use clinical observation to assess reading performance.
- Develop diagnostic checklists to assess oral reading, silent reading, and reading comprehension.
- Use miscue analysis to evaluate reading performance.
- Use cloze procedures to evaluate reading performance.

The Importance of Assessing Reading

The following narrative illustrates some of the most common questions teachers have about assessing the reading achievement of children with special needs and also shows how to begin incorporating reading assessment into the curriculum.

Mrs. Sciarratta, a special education teacher of students with mild and moderate disabilities, has never assessed reading before. Because she knows that doing so is an essential part of reading instruction, she wonders if reading assessment could be used in her class. Her questions about reading include the following: What are the different kinds of reading assessments? Why should she consider assessing reading? Will it help improve the reading levels of her students? She is especially interested in learning about reading assessment for the students who are having the most difficulty in reading.

In order to obtain answers to her questions, Mrs. Sciarratta reviews some reading tests (obtained from the district's resource center) and does some investigation of curriculum-based assessment. She gets some helpful information from this research about how to begin to use reading assessment with students who have disabilities. Finally she decides the best way to learn about reading assessment is to try it in her classroom. She hopes that her efforts will result in increased student achievement in reading. She doesn't know, however, how to tailor assessment to her students with the most severe reading problems. None of the research she found mentioned this, and none of her colleagues have ever dealt with reading assessment in this way. She wonders if assessing the most difficult students differs from assessing "typical" students. She decides to incorporate some reading assessment into the reading curriculum. Specifically, she plans to try out a norm-referenced, individually administered diagnostic reading test and experiment with a couple of curriculum-based reading assessments. She also decides to consult with a reading specialist at the local university who has done some practical research on reading assessment with children who have special needs.

Definition of Reading

Composed of many complex skills, reading is understanding the meaning of printed or written material. Reading readiness, for example, encompasses prerequisite skills such as letter and shape recognition, left-to-right sequencing, and top-to-bottom progression. Beyond the readiness level, further reading skills include the following:

- Reading recognition, a word-attack skill involving correctly pronouncing words out loud.
- Reading comprehension, a skill consisting of understanding and attaching meaning to written material.
- Silent reading, which is characterized by lack of speech or sound and which relies on special skills assessed separately from the other types of reading.

Scholastic success as well as success in most vocational settings requires reading proficiency; therefore, it is unfortunate that so many students who receive special education services exhibit deficits in this area. In fact, experts consider reading difficulties as the most common academic learning problem. For this reason, special educators should possess a thorough understanding of methods for assessing and teaching reading.

Guidelines for Assessing Reading

The International Reading Association (1992) has developed standards for reading professionals that include general guidelines for the assessment of reading. More specific assessment standards for both reading and writing have been prepared by the International Reading Association and the National Council of Teachers of English (1994). Designed for teachers, teacher educators, and education agencies, these standards emphasize the importance of reading assessment as a continuing and essential part of reflective teaching and learning. More specifically, the standards recognize that assessment must account for the complexities of reading, writing, and language and must be based on a range of authentic literacy tasks using a variety of reading materials. The standards encourage teachers and reading specialists to use multiple measures of student progress for informing instruction, including norm- and criterion-referenced tests, inventories, portfolio assessment, observations, anecdotal records, and journals. The standards also emphasize the importance of authentic assessment practices that are sensitive to multiple literacies by taking into account linguistic and cultural differences. Finally, the standards point out the need for up-to-date knowledge about the characteristics and appropriate application of widely used and evolving approaches for assessing reading.

Because they serve as a guide for making decisions about assessing the teaching and learning of reading and writing and because most of the standards are applicable to assessment in general, the complete list of standards from the International Reading Association and the National Council of Teachers of English (1994) follows.

Standards for the Assessment of Reading and Writing

- The interests of the student are paramount in assessment.
- The primary purpose of assessment is to improve teaching and learning.
- Assessment must reflect and allow for critical inquiry into curriculum and instruction.
- Assessments must recognize and reflect the intellectually and socially complex nature of reading and writing and the important roles of school, home, and society in literacy development.
- Assessment must be fair and equitable.
- The consequences of an assessment procedure are the first and most important consideration in establishing the validity of the assessment.
- The teacher is the most important agent of assessment.
- The assessment process should involve multiple perspectives and sources of data.
- Assessment must be based in the school community.
- All members of the educational community—students, parents, teachers, administrators, policy makers, and the public—must have a voice in the development, interpretation, and reporting of assessment.
- Parents must be involved as active, essential participants in the assessment process (pp. 4–5).

Why Do We Assess the Reading Achievement of Children With Special Needs?

Special educators assess the reading achievement of children with special needs for several reasons. The overall goal of reading assessment is to inform the teaching and learning process. More specifically, reading assessment helps screen students who may have deficits in reading, identify and place students with reading disabilities, plan reading instruction and intervention programs, identify present levels of reading performance, develop IEP goals and objectives in reading, assess student progress in reading, and monitor the effectiveness of reading programs (see Focus 15–1). Different reading tests and curriculum-based assessment techniques exist for each of these purposes. Screening students with potential reading problems is an essential first step in the assessment process, and specially developed screening tests exist for this purpose. In contrast, identification and placement of students with reading disabilities relies on formal, standardized, diagnostic reading tests. Although teachers often use formal tests in instructional planning and intervention with students, most rely primarily on less formal, curriculum-based reading assessment techniques in which the teacher selects from a series of assessment strategies that are directly linked with instructional intervention.

The following narrative illustrates one of the many reasons for assessing the reading achievement of students with special needs.

Timmy, a bright, outgoing, husky 10-year-old, worked at many of his school assignments with enthusiasm but often became frustrated with reading tasks. As a result, he sometimes misbehaved in class.

Timmy's teacher thought he was an intelligent student who just didn't try hard enough, especially in reading, and she was frustrated with Timmy's misbehavior. The baffled and discouraged teacher decided to refer Timmy to the child-study team, who assigned a diagnostician to give Timmy an individually administered diagnostic test of achievement. The results indicated that he performed much lower in reading than in math and general information. More specifically, the results suggested a particular weakness in reading recognition. When the child-

---

FOCUS 15–1

Why Do We Assess the Reading Achievement of Students With Special Needs?

- To screen students who may have deficits in reading
- To identify and place students with reading disabilities
- To plan reading instruction and intervention programs
- To identify present levels of reading performance
- To develop IEP goals in reading
- To assess student progress in reading
- To monitor the effectiveness of reading programs

study team reviewed the results with the teacher, she realized that Timmy's poor performance in class may have been due to a reading problem rather than lack of effort.

The child-study team recommended further assessment, and the teacher worked with the diagnostician to identify the specific nature of the problem so they could provide special assistance for Timmy. The special assistance included use of an assessment procedure called miscue analysis, *which pinpointed Timmy's problems in reading recognition. In Timmy's case the miscue analysis revealed a consistent pattern of visual closure errors in which Timmy seemed to see only parts of some words rather than whole words. The problem was particularly evident with compound words such as* birthday, something, *and* baseball. *When the teacher gave Timmy special help with syllables and whole words, his reading recognition skills began to improve.*

☑ Comprehension Checklist

Reading, a complex process involving many skills, is the most important academic subject in the elementary school curriculum, and in later grades, most subjects require well-developed reading skills. Therefore, it is unfortunate that most experts cite reading difficulties as the most common academic learning problem. Because it is so complex and important, more tests have been developed for assessing reading than any other academic skill. When teachers assess reading, they should follow the standards developed by the International Reading Association, which highlight reading assessment as an essential part of reflective teaching and learning.

Norm-Referenced Reading Tests

Special educators who wish to conduct formal assessment of reading skills with standardized instruments may select from a number of norm-referenced screening and diagnostic tests. These include the multiple-skill tests reviewed in the previous chapter as well as a variety of single-skill tools. Both the multiple- and single-skill measures are available at the screening and diagnostic levels of assessment; however, the single-skill diagnostic instruments provide the most in-depth assessment information. For this reason, special educators often use single-skill diagnostic tests when they need detailed information to identify specific reading problems, develop instructional objectives, and create intervention activities. Because they produce standardized scores, norm-referenced reading tests are also useful in classifying and placing students in reading programs and special education programs. Reviews of representative reading tests follow, beginning with screening tests and followed by diagnostic tests.

Test of Early Reading Ability-2 (TERA-2)

The *Test of Early Reading Ability-2 (TERA-2)* (Reid et al., 1989) is a screening test of reading for children from 3 to 9 years of age. The *TERA-2* assesses contextual meaning (such as awareness of print in the environment), the alphabet (including naming letters and oral reading), and print conventions (such as book handling

Table 15–1   *Test of Early Reading Ability-2*

Type of Test:	Norm referenced
Purpose:	Screening early reading ability
Content Areas:	Contextual meaning, the alphabet, and the conventions of print
Administration Time:	20–30 minutes
Age Levels:	3–9 years
Suitable for:	Students with mild and moderate disabilities, including learning disabilities, behavior disorders, educable mental retardation, physical impairments, and hearing impairments
Scores:	Standard scores, percentile ranks, and NCEs
In Short:	*TERA-2* is useful for measuring emerging reading ability, especially print conventions.

and reading from left to right). By including a complete subtest for evaluating the conventions of print, the *TERA-2* responds to contemporary reading theory and research, which emphasizes the importance of print conventions in emerging literacy. The *TERA-2* also includes two alternate, equivalent forms so that evaluators can test with one form, implement an intervention program, and measure progress by retesting with the other form. A summary of the *TERA-2* appears in Table 15–1.

A specialized version of the *TERA*, designed for children with moderate to profound hearing loss, is also available. This version, called the *Test of Early Reading Ability-Deaf or Hard of Hearing (TERA-D/HH)* (Reid et al., 1991), can be given using simultaneous communication or American Sign Language. Although specialized instruments like the *TERA-D/HH* are important, significant reliability and validity problems limit the usefulness of this version of the test (Rothlisberg, 1995, & Toubanos, 1995). For this reason, the *TERA-D/HH* should be used cautiously until further study demonstrates the reliability of the scores and the validity of the test itself.

Materials for the *Test of Early Reading Ability-2*   The *TERA-2* is available as separate items or in kit form. The complete kit includes a manual, an administration/picture book, and profile/examiner scoring sheets for Form A and Form B.

Administration and Scoring of the *Test of Early Reading Ability-2*   It takes 20–30 minutes to give the *TERA-2* screening test. Evaluators can report performance using standard scores, percentiles, or normal curve equivalents.

Technical Characteristics of the *Test of Early Reading Ability-2*   The *TERA-2* was standardized on a representative national sample of 1,454 children, with norms for every 6-month interval from age 3 through 9. Both Beck (1992) and Hiltonsmith (1992) reviewed the *TERA-2* and concluded that the instrument displays adequate technical qualities for use as a screening device and as a starting point for instructional design. Beck and Hiltonsmith indicated that *TERA-2* scores display appropriate reliability. Although more validity research needs to be done, the initial validity studies are adequate.

Summary of the *Test of Early Reading Ability-2* The *Test of Early Reading Ability-2* is a screening test for identifying young children from 3 to 9 years of age who may be at risk for learning to read. Consisting of three subtests that measure contextual meaning, alphabet, and print conventions, the *TERA-2* includes two alternate forms for testing and retesting and is notable because it provides a complete subtest for assessing print conventions.

Slosson Oral Reading Test-Revised (SORT-R)

A measure of the ability to pronounce words at different levels of difficulty, the *Slosson Oral Reading Test-Revised (SORT-R)* (Slosson & Nicholson, 1990) is a screening test of word recognition skills. Originally published in 1963, this individually administered, norm-referenced test consists of 10 groups of 20 words. Each group represents a grade level, beginning with preschool and going to grades 9–12. A summary of the *SORT-R* appears in Table 15–2.

Materials for the *Slosson Oral Reading Test-Revised* The attractively designed test materials consist of a spiral-bound flipcard booklet containing the word lists, a manual, and a package of scoring sheets. The complete kit also includes a large-print edition of the word list booklet.

Administration and Scoring of the *Slosson Oral Reading Test-Revised* The *SORT-R* takes 3–5 minutes to administer and score. A basal level is established when a student reads all 20 words in a group. A ceiling is reached when a student fails to correctly read all 20 words in a group. The evaluator presents the word groups using a word list flipcard booklet. Students have 5 seconds to pronounce a word, but the evaluator may extend this limit if the student has a speech or visual impairment.

The test is easy to administer and score. The scoring sheet includes the essential administration and scoring procedures, making it unnecessary for the evaluator to refer to the manual. Available scores include grade and age equivalents, standard

Table 15–2 *Slosson Oral Reading Test-Revised (SORT–R)*

Type of Test:	Norm referenced
Purpose:	To assess word recognition ability
Content Area:	Word recognition
Administration Time:	3–5 minutes
Age Levels:	Preschool through high school
Suitable for:	Students with mild and moderate disabilities, including learning disabilities, behavior disorders, educable mental retardation, and physical impairments
Scores:	Grade and age equivalents, standard scores, *t*-scores, and NCEs
In Short:	A screening test for quickly determining a student's word recognition ability

scores, *t*-scores, and NCEs. Unfortunately, the test encourages evaluators to use inferior age and grade equivalent scores rather than the more precise scores such as percentiles, standard scores, or NCEs.

Technical Characteristics of the *Slosson Oral Reading Test-Revised*   The *SORT-R* was co-normed with the *Slosson Intelligence Test* using a sample of 1,331 students. Although it contains new norms and new scoring options, the *SORT-R* has the same word lists as the original 1963 test (Westby, 1995). In a critical review of the instrument, Westby concluded that the *SORT-R* was a valid and reliable tool for quickly identifying word recognition levels. A review by Shaw and Swerdlik (1995) provided a contrasting view of the technical qualities of the *SORT-R*. They found that, although the test displayed adequate reliability, the norms were inadequate and the validity was less than satisfactory. Problems with the norms centered around insufficient information about the characteristics of the sample group. Validity weaknesses were due to a lack of important details about validity studies in the manual and validity estimates that were based on outdated studies using the 1963 edition of the test.

Summary of the *Slosson Oral Reading Test-Revised*   The *Slosson Oral Reading Test-Revised (SORT-R),* an attractively designed and easy-to-use screening test, takes no more than 5 minutes to give and score. This makes the instrument a useful tool for quickly determining a student's word recognition ability; however, technical limitations make the instrument valid for use only in initial screening. Because it measures only one aspect of reading achievement, word calling ability, evaluators should avoid using the *SORT-R* to measure overall reading ability or to identify students with reading disabilities.

Slosson Test of Reading Readiness (STRR)

The *Slosson Test of Reading Readiness (STRR)* (Perry & Vitali, 1991) is an individually administered, norm-referenced prereading inventory for assessing a child's readiness to begin formal reading instruction. Designed to identify children who are at risk of failure in reading, the *STRR* is a screening tool for kindergarten and first-grade students. The *STRR* contains eight subtests: recognition of capital letters, recognition of lowercase letters, matching capital and lowercase letters, visual discrimination (matching word forms), auditory discrimination (rhyming), auditory discrimination (recognition of beginning sounds), sequencing, and opposites. A summary of the *STRR* appears in Table 15–3.

Materials for the *Slosson Test of Reading Readiness*   *STRR* materials consist of a manual, a test stimulus booklet, scoring booklets in packets of 50, and a letter to parents in packets of 50. The materials are available in a complete kit or as individual items.

Administration and Scoring of the *Slosson Test of Reading Readiness*   It takes about 15 minutes to give the *STRR*. Teachers, assessment specialists, and paraprofessionals, all with appropriate training, can administer the instrument. Although *STRR* administration procedures are quick and easy, scoring procedures are confusing and complicated (Hanna, 1995). For example, scoring criteria for specific items are inadequately detailed, and the scoring procedures change in the various subtests, making it difficult to calculate accurate raw scores. Although evaluators can report test results

Table 15-3 *Slosson Test of Reading Readiness*

Type of Test:	Norm referenced
Purpose:	A screening test of a child's readiness to begin formal reading instruction
Content Areas:	Eight subtests: recognition of capital letters, recognition of lowercase letters, matching capital and lowercase letters, visual discrimination (matching word forms), auditory discrimination (rhyming), auditory discrimination (recognition of beginning sounds), sequencing, and opposites
Administration Time:	About 15 minutes
Age Levels:	Kindergarten and first grade
Suitable for:	Students with mild and moderate disabilities, including learning disabilities, behavior disorders, educable mental retardation, and physical impairments
Scores:	Scaled scores (M = 100, SD = 16) and criterion-referenced pass/fail tables for the subtests and total score
In Short:	A gross screening measure of a child's readiness to read, the *STRR* suffers from technical deficiencies and confusing scoring procedures.

using a norm-referenced scaled score with a mean of 100 and a standard deviation of 16, the test fails to provide more useful percentile scoring capabilities. In addition to the scaled score, the test provides criterion-referenced pass/fail tables for the subtests and total score.

Technical Characteristics of the *Slosson Test of Reading Readiness*   Critical reviews by Hanna (1995) and Sawyer (1995) identified major technical weaknesses in the *STRR*. Hanna criticized the standardization, which was based on imprecise selection methods and an undefined norm sample group. Although the test has adequate reliability and validity coefficients, Hanna found that these coefficients were derived from inappropriate methodology using poorly described procedures. Sawyer found the *STRR* adequate for testing standard reading skills such as letter recognition, word attack, and phonics but deemed it unsuitable for testing more contemporary skills, including language and meaning variables, exposure to books, knowledge of print concepts, and the ability to segment spoken language.

Summary of the *Slosson Test of Reading Readiness*   The *Slosson Test of Reading Recognition (STRR)* is a gross screening measure of a child's readiness to read. Designed for kindergarteners and first graders who are at risk of failure in reading programs, the test takes about 15 minutes to give. Unfortunately, technical problems and confusing scoring procedures limit the usefulness of the test.

Woodcock Reading Mastery Tests-Revised (WRMT-R)

Foremost among the diagnostic reading tests are the *Woodcock Reading Mastery Tests-Revised (WRMT-R)* (Woodcock, 1998). The *WRMT-R*, a major revision of the original

Table 15–4   *Woodcock Reading Mastery Tests-Revised (WRMT-R)*

Type of Test:	Norm referenced and individually administered
Purpose:	To diagnose reading achievement
Content Areas:	Visual-auditory learning, letter identification, word identification, word attack, and word and passage comprehension
Administration Time:	10–30 minutes per subtest
Age Levels:	5 years–retirement
Suitable for:	Students with mild disabilities, including learning disabilities, behavior disorders, sensory impairments, and physical disabilities
Scores:	Age and grade percentile ranks, standard scores (M = 100, SD = 15), normal curve equivalents, and age and grade equivalents
In Short:	A well-designed, single-skill diagnostic test, the *WRMT-R* includes features usually not available on multiple-skill tests. These features include an error analysis procedure and five interpretive profiles.

Woodcock Reading Tests (Woodcock, 1973), serves as a diagnostic tool for assessing the reading skills of students from kindergarten through college and into adulthood. Woodcock designed the tests for educational diagnosticians, reading specialists, and special education teachers. A summary of the *WRMT-R* appears in Table 15–4. The *WRMT-R* is available in two different forms. Form H contains four reading achievement subtests and is the shorter version. Form G, the complete battery, includes the four reading achievement subtests plus the three readiness subtests listed as follows:

- Reading achievement subtests.
  Word identification.
  Word attack.
  Word comprehension (antonyms, synonyms, analogies).
  Passage comprehension.
- Readiness subtests.
  Visual-auditory learning.
  Letter identification.
  Supplementary letter checklist.

Materials for the *WRMT-R*   *WRMT-R* materials include Form G and Form H test books, Form G and Form H test record forms, sample summary record forms, a pronunciation guide cassette, a sample report to parents, an examiner's manual, and a storage box. The *WRMT-R* also includes an optional computer software program that provides a complete array of test scores and profiles, an aptitude-achievement discrepancy analysis report, and a narrative report. The discrepancy analysis report facilitates the identification of students with specific reading disabilities by comparing aptitude (measured with an intelligence test) to reading achievement (measured by the *WRMT-R*).

Administration and Scoring of the *WRMT-R* The *WRMT-R* manual provides a thorough description of the complex administration, scoring, and interpretation procedures. It takes from 10 to 30 minutes to administer each subtest. The subtests combine to form the following clusters:

- Readiness.
- Basic skills.
- Reading comprehension.
- Total reading, full scale.
- Total reading, short scale (for a quick 15-minute screening).

For each of these clusters, derived scores include age- and grade-based percentile ranks, standard scores (M = 100, SD = 15), normal curve equivalents (NCEs), age equivalents, and grade equivalents. In addition, the test provides advanced scoring and interpretation procedures such as relative performance index scores, an instructional level profile, and a percentile rank profile. The complexity of *WRMT-R* scoring makes the time needed to prepare a student's scores much longer than with other tests. Cohen and Cohen (1994) indicated that the first-time evaluator needs about an hour to score the *WRMT-R;* experienced evaluators need about 30 minutes. Optional computer software, the *WRMT-R Automated System for Scoring and Interpreting Standardized Tests (ASSIST),* greatly reduces scoring time.

Technical Characteristics of the *WRMT-R* The *WRMT-R,* standardized with a sample of more than 3,000 students, followed a detailed and precise standardization plan that ensured development of representative norms. The *WRMT-R* reports very good reliability data along with numerous studies to support both the content and concurrent validity of the test. Overall, the *WRMT-R* displays excellent technical qualities.

In a comprehensive review of the *WRMT-R,* Cohen and Cohen (1994) described the many advanced diagnostic features of the test that, in some ways, make the instrument more complicated and time consuming to administer, score, and interpret than most tests. However, because it was designed for prescriptive remediation rather than for simple screening, Cohen and Cohen indicated that the clinical value of the *WRMT-R* should take precedence over concerns about administration and scoring convenience.

Summary of the *WRMT-R* The *WRMT-R* is suitable for use as a formal diagnostic tool to make placement decisions and as a guide to create instructional objectives and remedial intervention activities. The *WRMT-R* includes diagnostic features usually not available on multiple-skill tests, such as an error analysis procedure for identifying specific strengths and weaknesses and five interpretive profiles enabling examiners to interpret test scores in a variety of ways. The *WRMT-R* also measures reading vocabulary in four areas: general, science-mathematics, social studies, and humanities. These features illustrate the benefits derived from a well-designed, single-skill diagnostic test like the *WRMT-R.*

Gates–McKillop–Horowitz Reading Diagnostic Tests

Less formal than the *WRMT-R,* the *Gates–McKillop–Horowitz Reading Diagnostic Tests* (Gates et al., 1981) are a comprehensive battery for assessing skill development and

Table 15–5   *Gates–McKillop–Horowitz Reading Diagnostic Tests*

Type of Test:	Norm referenced
Purpose:	To diagnose reading achievement
Content Areas:	Oral reading, flash words, untimed words, knowledge of word parts: word attack, recognizing the visual form of sounds, auditory blending, auditory discrimination, and written expression
Administration Time:	60–90 minutes
Age Levels:	Grades 1–6
Suitable for:	Students with mild disabilities, including learning disabilities, behavior disorders, sensory impairments, and physical disabilities
Scores:	Grade scores for four subtests and interpretation guidelines
In Short:	Although it is a valuable criterion-referenced tool for developing instructional remediation activities, the *Gates–McKillop–Horowitz* has technical weaknesses that limit its usefulness as a norm-referenced diagnostic reading test.

reading difficulties among students from grades 1 through 6. A summary of the *Gates–McKillop–Horowitz* appears in Table 15–5. Designed as an instructional tool rather than a placement test, the *Gates–McKillop–Horowitz Reading Diagnostic Tests* measure the following reading behaviors:

- Oral reading.
- Words: flash.
- Words: untimed.
- Knowledge of word parts: word attack.
- Recognition of the visual form of sounds.
- Auditory blending.
- Auditory discrimination.
- Written expression.

The word attack subtest contains six separate components:

- Syllabification.
- Recognition and blending of common word parts.
- Reading words.
- Giving letter sounds.
- Naming capital letters.
- Naming lowercase letters.

The written expression subtest includes spelling and an informal writing sample.

Materials for the *Gates–McKillop–Horowitz*   *Gates–McKillop–Horowitz* materials include a manual, a booklet of test plates, and scoring sheets.

Administration and Scoring of the *Gates–McKillop–Horowitz* Designed for individual administration, the entire test takes about 60 to 90 minutes to give. However, the evaluator may administer only certain subtests, depending on the purpose for testing and the student's needs. The test contains straightforward administration procedures, but the scoring procedures are confusing and inconvenient.

Technical Characteristics of the *Gates–McKillop–Horowitz* Although norm tables for the *Gates–McKillop–Horowitz* appear in the manual, the authors provide no information about the size or characteristics of the sample group. Likewise, the manual supplies limited reliability and validity information, and the available data fail to establish the test as accurate or effective. For these reasons, those who use the test should avoid the test scores altogether and instead concentrate on the interpretative value of the instrument as an informal diagnostic tool.

Summary of the *Gates–McKillop–Horowitz* The usefulness of the *Gates–McKillop–Horowitz Reading Diagnostic Tests*, which were designed as a norm-referenced diagnostic tool, is limited by technical shortcomings. However, special educators and diagnosticians may find practical value in the test by using it as a criterion-referenced tool to guide in the development of instructional remediation activities.

Diagnostic Reading Scales (DRS-81)

Like the *Gates–McKillop–Horowitz*, the *Diagnostic Reading Scales (DRS-81)* (Spache, 1981) are best when used as informal diagnostic tools. Spache designed the *DRS-81* for practitioners to use in pinpointing the individual strengths and weaknesses of students from grades 1 to 7. A summary of the *DRS-81* appears in Table 15–6. The *DRS-81* contains the following three subtests:

- A measure of oral reading errors derived from student performance on three graded word lists.

Table 15–6 *Diagnostic Reading Scales (DRS-81)*

Type of Test:	Criterion referenced
Purpose:	To diagnose reading achievement
Content Areas:	Oral reading, silent reading comprehension, and auditory comprehension
Administration Time:	Approximately 1 hour
Age Levels:	Grades 1–7
Suitable for:	Students with mild and moderate disabilities, including learning disabilities, behavior disorders, educable mental retardation, and physical impairments
Scores:	Three reading levels: instructional, independent, and potential
In Short:	The *DRS-81* is helpful when teachers use it as an informal diagnostic reading test.

- An estimate of silent reading comprehension based on 22 reading passages.
- A subscale of auditory comprehension consisting of 12 phonics and word analysis tests.

Materials for the *DRS-81*   The *DRS-81* materials consist of an examiner's manual, a technical manual, a student reading book, a written expression booklet, and a package of scoring booklets. A cassette tape provides models for administration, scoring, and interpretation.

Administration and Scoring of the *DRS-81*   An evaluator can give and score the *DRS-81,* which is designed for individual administration, in about an hour. No norms exist for the test, and for this reason it lacks traditional scores. Instead, the test provides estimates of three reading levels for each student: an instructional level, an independent level, and a potential level. *Instructional level* refers to the appropriate reading group placement for a student based on oral reading and comprehension skills. *Independent level* refers to silent reading ability; *potential level* estimates the ability to achieve in reading. The manual and cassette clearly describe the procedures for administering the test, identifying the three reading levels, and interpreting the results.

Technical Characteristics of the *DRS-81*   The manual fails to adequately describe the sample groups used for standardizing the instrument. Likewise, the manual provides limited evidence to support the reliability and validity of the test. Overall, these poor technical qualities represent the greatest weakness of the *DRS-81.*

Summary of the *DRS-81*   Unfortunately, the technical inadequacies of the *DRS-81* limit its usefulness as a formal diagnostic test; therefore, evaluators should use the reading level estimates with caution. When used as an informal diagnostic tool, the test provides valuable information regarding student performance in oral reading, silent reading comprehension, and auditory comprehension.

Gray Oral Reading Tests, Third Edition (GORT-3)

The *Gray Oral Reading Tests, Third Edition (GORT-3)* (Wiederholt & Bryant, 1994) measure the oral reading proficiency of students from ages 7 through 18. Designed to identify students who are significantly behind in reading proficiency and who may benefit from interventions, the *GORT-3* also helps to pinpoint reading strengths and weaknesses and to document student progress in reading. The standardized, individually administered *GORT-3* provides two alternate, equivalent forms, each containing 13 passages arranged by level of difficulty with five comprehension questions for each passage. A summary of the *GORT-3* appears in Table 15–7.

The *Gray Oral Reading Test* is also available in a diagnostic edition, the *Gray Oral Reading Tests-Diagnostic (GORT-D)* (Wiederholt and Bryant, 1991), which was designed as a supplement to the *GORT-3* for students who have difficulty reading continuous print. Consisting of seven subtests, the *GORT-D* is organized using three cue systems: meaning cues, function cues, and graphic/phonemic cues. An optional computerized program available for the *GORT-D* produces a multiple-page printout describing each subtest and reporting individual student performance.

Table 15–7 *Gray Oral Reading Tests, Third Edition*

Type of Test:	Norm referenced
Purpose:	Measuring growth in oral reading and diagnosing oral reading problems
Content Areas:	Oral reading proficiency and oral reading comprehension
Administration Time:	About 30 minutes
Age Levels:	7 through 18
Suitable for:	Students with mild and moderate disabilities, including learning disabilities, behavior disorders, educable mental retardation, and physical impairments
Scores:	Standard scores, percentiles, grade equivalents, and miscue analysis
In Short:	Designed to identify students who are significantly behind in reading proficiency and who may benefit from interventions, the *GORT-3* also helps to pinpoint reading strengths and weaknesses and to document student progress in reading.

Materials for the *Gray Oral Reading Tests, Third Edition*   The complete *GORT-3* kit consists of an examiner's manual, a student book, 25 Form A scoring forms, and 25 Form B scoring forms. The *GORT-3* test items are also available separately.

Administration and Scoring of the *Gray Oral Reading Tests, Third Edition*   It takes about 30 minutes to administer and score the *GORT-3*. The scoring procedure involves obtaining a "Passage Score" derived from the student's reading rate and reading errors and an oral reading comprehension score derived from student responses to the comprehension questions. The passage and the oral reading comprehension scores can be reported using standard scores, percentiles, or grade equivalents. The *GORT-3* also produces a total score for oral reading. The *GORT-3* manual includes a miscue analysis scoring system that helps the evaluator acquire assessment information pertaining to meaning similarity, function similarity, graphic/phonetic similarity, and self-correction.

Technical Characteristics of the *Gray Oral Reading Tests, Third Edition*   Standardized on a population of 1,485 students from 18 states, the *GORT-3* meets the generally accepted reliability and validity criteria. The only significant technical limitation is the lack of normative data stratified by race, ethnicity, and social and economic status (SES). For this reason the adequacy of the *GORT-3* with minority and low SES students cannot be determined (King, 1995).

Summary of the *Gray Oral Reading Tests, Third Edition*   The *Gray Oral Reading Tests, Third Edition,* measure reading proficiency using 13 reading passages with accompanying comprehension questions. Norm-referenced and individually administered, the *GORT-3* displays adequate technical qualities for measuring growth in oral reading and diagnosing oral reading difficulties.

Test of Reading Comprehension, Third Edition (TORC-3)

The *Test of Reading Comprehension, Third Edition (TORC-3)* (Brown et al., 1995) is the most recent revision of the *TORC,* originally published in 1978 and revised in 1986. Reading teachers, special educators, and diagnosticians can use the *TORC-3* to measure the silent reading comprehension of individuals and groups of students from age 7 through 17. A summary of the *TORC-3* appears in Table 15–8. The test includes eight subtests grouped into general reading comprehension and diagnostic supplements. The general reading comprehension core includes the following four subtests:

- General vocabulary, which measures understanding of sets of vocabulary items all related to the same general concept.
- Syntactic similarities, which measures understanding of meaningfully similar but syntactically different sentence structures.
- Paragraph reading, which measures the ability to answer questions related to story-like paragraphs.
- Sentence sequencing, which measures the ability to build relationships among sentences.

The four diagnostic supplements provide a more comprehensive evaluation of various comprehension abilities. The supplements include three measures of content area vocabulary in mathematics, social studies, and science, and a measure of the understanding of written directions commonly found in schoolwork (subtest 8).

Materials for the *TORC-3*   The complete *TORC-3* kit, which is packaged in a storage box, includes an examiner's manual, 50 answer sheets and subtest 8 forms, 50 profile/examiner record forms, and 10 student booklets. The individual items may be ordered separately.

Table 15–8   *Test of Reading Comprehension-Third Edition*

Type of Test:	Norm referenced
Purpose:	A measure of silent reading comprehension
Content Areas:	General vocabulary, syntactic similarities, paragraph reading, sentence sequencing, and understanding written directions
Administration Time:	Approximately 30 minutes
Age Levels:	7 through 17
Suitable for:	Students with mild and moderate disabilities, including learning disabilities, behavior disorders, educable mental retardation, and physical impairments
Scores:	Standard scores, percentiles, age scores, and grade scores
In Short:	The *TORC-3* is a useful tool for reading teachers, special educators, and diagnosticians to assess the understanding of written language.

Administration and Scoring of the *TORC-3* It takes about 30 minutes to test with the *TORC-3*. The evaluator can administer individual subtests or all eight subtests depending on the needs of the student and reasons for testing. Available *TORC-3* scores include standard scores, percentiles, a composite reading comprehension quotient, grade equivalents, and age equivalents.

Technical Characteristics of the *TORC-3* The *TORC-3* was standardized on a sample of 1,962 students from 19 states. Information about the sample relative to geographic region, gender, residence, race, ethnicity, and disabling condition is reported. The *TORC-3* manual also discusses studies showing the absence of gender and racial bias and research to support the reliability and validity of the instrument, which includes investigations of test-retest reliability, criterion-related validity, and content validity.

Summary of the *TORC-3* The *Test of Reading Comprehension, Third Edition* provides a method for assessing the understanding of written language with students from ages 7 to 17. Consisting of eight subtests, the *TORC-3* is suitable for use with individuals and groups.

☑ Comprehension Checklist

When special educators need to assess reading achievement and performance using formal tests, they may select from a wide range and variety of suitable instruments that include screening tests as well as comprehensive diagnostic tools. The screening tests provide an overview of reading performance; the diagnostic instruments provide detailed assessment information for identifying specific reading problems, developing instructional objectives, and creating intervention activities.

Informal Reading Inventories

Diagnosing reading disabilities is best accomplished with standardized tests such as those just described. When planning intervention, however, most teachers prefer to use **informal reading inventories.** Teachers find that assessment information from informal reading inventories translates more directly into daily instruction than do scores from standardized tests. Most informal inventories contain graded word lists for testing word recognition ability and graded reading passages for evaluating oral reading, silent reading, and comprehension.

Teachers may select from among several commercially available informal reading inventories. Brief descriptions of representative inventories follow. Because some teachers prefer to develop their own informal reading inventories, a step-by-step description of how to construct them is also included.

Analytical Reading Inventory, Fourth Edition

The informal, criterion-referenced *Analytical Reading Inventory, Fourth Edition* (Woods & Moe, 1989) provides graded word lists for primer through sixth grade and graded passages for primer through ninth grade. Consisting of three equivalent forms, the inventory measures silent reading, listening skills, and comprehension and also provides graded expository passages for social studies and science. The thorough *Analytical Reading Inventory* manual provides detailed information about inventory design, including descriptions of pilot study research and reliability research. In addition, the instrument provides a helpful system for quantitative analysis of decoding errors.

Basic Reading Inventory, Third Edition

The *Basic Reading Inventory, Third Edition* (Johns, 1985), is a criterion-referenced measure of reading ability consisting of graded word lists and graded passages. Designed for students from preprimer through eighth grade, the test provides three equivalent forms. Results derived from the test include independent, instructional, and frustration reading levels. Strengths and weaknesses in word attack, comprehension, and listening are also measured.

Ekwall Reading Inventory, Second Edition

The *Ekwall Reading Inventory, Second Edition* (Ekwall, 1986), is an informal, criterion-referenced inventory designed to check word knowledge and word analysis skills. Consisting of a graded word list, graded reading passages, and a phonics survey, the test measures the reading ability of students from preprimer to ninth grade. The inventory determines independent, instructional, and frustration reading levels as well as word analysis skills, reader characteristics, reading rate, comprehension, and phonics skills.

Formal Reading Inventory

Unlike the other reading inventories that are criterion-referenced, the *Formal Reading Inventory (FRI)* (Wiederholt, 1986) is a norm-referenced tool. Standardized on 1,737 students in grades 1 through 12 in 12 states, the *FRI* provides reading specialists, special educators, and diagnosticians with a method for assessing silent reading comprehension and oral reading miscues. The inventory includes four equivalent forms, each of which has 13 developmentally sequenced passages with five literal, inferential, critical, and affective multiple-choice questions following each story. Forms A and C assess silent reading; forms B and D evaluate oral reading ability. When giving forms B and D, the evaluator records miscues on a separate worksheet. The oral miscues relate to meaning similarity, function similarity, graphic/phonemic similarity, multiple sources, and self-correction.

Classroom Reading Inventory, Sixth Edition

The *Classroom Reading Inventory, Sixth Edition* (Silvaroli, 1990), is an informal, criterion-referenced measure of reading ability that includes graded word lists, graded passages, comprehension questions, and a graded spelling survey. The inventory also measures the silent reading and listening skills of students from preprimer through grade eight. Four forms of the test are available, and two of these contain material of special interest to teenagers and adults.

New Sucher–Allred Reading Placement Inventory

The *New Sucher–Allred Reading Placement Inventory* (Sucher & Allred, 1981) identifies the reading levels of preprimer through ninth grade students using 12 graded word lists and 12 graded passages. The inventory provides two equivalent forms, a measure of listening skills, and comprehension questions to accompany the grade level passages.

Standardized Reading Inventory

The criterion-referenced *Standardized Reading Inventory* (Newcomer, 1986) assesses reading ability using 10 word lists and 10 graded reading passages for each of its two equivalent forms. Designed for students from the preprimer level to eighth grade, the inventory provides information about word recognition skills and reading comprehension at independent, instructional, and frustration levels.

Teacher-Made Reading Inventories

Teachers often assess student reading levels by developing their own informal reading inventories using graded materials from the classroom (Bond et al., 1989; Harris & Sipay, 1985; Mercer & Mercer, 1998). Teacher-made informal reading inventories have the advantage of reflecting the reading material used in the classroom and the local school, providing a direct link between evaluation and instruction.

Informal reading inventories identify three different reading levels: independent, instructional, and frustration. At the independent level, students read by themselves with accuracy rates of 98–100% in word recognition and 90–100% in answering comprehension questions. When reading material at the independent level, students are self-reliant and can read for enjoyment. Library books and seat work instructions should be at the independent level. The *instructional level* refers to reading that students can accomplish with teacher assistance. At this level, students recognize 95% of the words and comprehend at least 75% of the material. Reading instruction in the classroom should be geared to this level. The *frustration level* refers to material that is too difficult for the student to read. At the frustration level recognition of words is 90% or below, and comprehension falls below 50%. In teaching situations, teachers should avoid asking students to read at the frustration level.

The process of constructing informal reading inventories involves preparing passages of increasing difficulty, usually from a basal reading series. The specific steps in this process appear in Focus 15–2. Because programs and materials differ significantly, teachers may modify these procedures depending on the reading program they use with their students. Although developing an inventory takes time and effort, teacher-made reading inventories have the advantage of reflecting the reading material used in the classroom. Further, teacher-made inventories directly connect assessment with the instructional emphasis, vocabulary content, and level of difficulty in the instructional program.

FOCUS 15–2

How to Construct an Informal Reading Inventory

The steps in the process of developing a teacher-made inventory are these:

1. With primary children, teachers should select passages of about 50 words for each grade level of difficulty to be assessed. With secondary students, each passage should be 150–200 words in length.
2. Most teachers limit the selection of passages to a specific range (e.g., five levels: two levels below the student's grade level, one at the grade level, and two levels above).
3. To determine a student's independent reading level, assessment should begin below the student's grade level. The teacher needs two copies of each passage. As the student reads aloud from one copy, the teacher records errors on the other copy and then asks three to five comprehension questions about the passage.
4. Teachers should record the percentage of words read accurately in each passage (by dividing the number of words read accurately by the number of words in the passage) and the percentage of comprehension questions answered correctly (by dividing the number of correct answers by the number of questions).
5. After establishing the student's independent level, the assessment continues with the student reading increasingly difficult graded passages to determine an instructional level and a frustration level. During assessment, teachers should stop testing as soon as they clearly establish the frustration level.
6. Teachers may modify these procedures to assess specific skills such as word attack skills, oral reading performance, and comprehension ability.

☑ Comprehension Checklist

Informal reading inventories consist of graded word lists and graded reading passages. These inventories provide valuable assessment information for planning interventions with students who have reading disabilities. Most inventories measure word recognition ability, oral reading, silent reading, and comprehension at three levels: independent, instructional, and frustration. Teachers may select from among several commercially available reading inventories or may develop their own teacher-constructed inventories using graded materials from the classroom.

Curriculum-Based Reading Assessment

In addition to the developing their own informal reading inventories, special education teachers and diagnosticians use many other informal, curriculum-based assessment strategies to measure reading performance and develop instructional objectives and activities. With curriculum-based assessment, teachers use student work such as class papers, homework, and class tests to evaluate reading skill and development. Curriculum-based assessment also allows teachers to conduct evaluation as part of the ongoing learning activities in the classroom. This links assessment directly to the curriculum and makes evaluation less time consuming than formal testing.

Teachers should also link informal, curriculum-based reading assessment with more formal, standardized reading test scores. In fact, the two types of assessment actually complement each other. Most teachers use formal testing along with curriculum-based assessment when making staffing and placement decisions. In other words, informal and formal testing can often be used together to obtain a complete picture of a student's strengths and weaknesses. In addition, teachers can use curriculum-based assessment data and information to support scores obtained from standardized, norm-referenced tests.

Like all appraisal procedures, curriculum-based assessment of reading has drawbacks. One problem is conducting curriculum-based reading assessment in ways that produce reliable and valid results. In actual operation, many curriculum-based procedures, especially the observational techniques, lack the precision necessary to accurately measure the complexities associated with reading. This occurs in part because reading is an interactive process, and it is difficult to isolate individual skills. Reading comprehension, for example, must be inferred because it is an internal process that cannot be directly observed. Furthermore, different approaches to teaching reading require somewhat different assessment procedures. The challenge confronting educators is to refine curriculum-based assessment in ways that overcome these limitations.

Despite these difficulties, curriculum-based assessment has many advantages. The primary advantage is the ability to evaluate student performance in direct relation to what has been taught within the curriculum. This allows the teacher to make educational decisions on the basis of actual reading behavior. Teachers have a special interest in this type of assessment because it connects evaluation with instruction in ways that inform the teaching and learning process. Specific curriculum-based techniques include clinical observation, diagnostic checklists, miscue analysis, and cloze procedures.

Clinical Observation

Observing students is a key element of informal reading assessment. Observing students, sometimes referred to as **clinical observation,** involves directly and systematically observing students in different reading situations. Observation gives teachers an impression of students' reading abilities, their awareness of books, and their social development. Notes from impressions formed during observations can be written and kept along with other assessment data to provide evidence of progress. Although observation is part of all types of informal and formal assessment, it is essential in specific situations. For example, observation is the best way to assess behaviors such as student motivation and attention, two important factors in reading success. When used as an assessment procedure, teachers should observe student reading performance over a period of time and in different situations, including oral reading, silent reading, casual reading, seat work, small-group instruction, and class testing. More specifically, Booth et al. (1994) recommended two useful techniques for teachers to use in the classroom: observation at a distance and close-in observation.

Figure 15–3   Diagnostic Checklist of Reading Comprehension

Student _____   Teacher _____

Grade Level of Passage _____   Date _____

Reading Comprehension Behavior	Observations			Comments
	1	2	3	
1. Answers factual questions about the passage				
2. Classifies, categorizes, & summarizes				
3. Makes inferences & predictions based on the passage				
4. Answers valuative questions about the passage				
5. Critically analyzes the passage				
6. Other notable behaviors (specify)				

Notes _____

_____

_____

Figure 15–4   Group Comprehension Matrix

	Sally	Ron	Jim	Tom
Makes predictions about story	+	−	+	−
Participates in discussion	+	−	+	−
Answers questions on all levels	−	−	−	+
Determines word meanings in context	−	−	−	s
Reads smoothly	s	+	−	s
Is able to retell selection in own words	+	s	s	+
Has good comprehension after silent reading	−	+	s	−
Is able to read inferentially	+	+	+	−
Possesses background knowledge	−	+	+	−

Comments _____

_____

_____

_____

Scoring key: + = yes, s = sometimes, − = no.

In oral reading, teachers use miscue analysis to measure and evaluate common student mistakes. Luftig (1989) identified four typical oral reading errors:

1. Mispronunciations: "complis" instead of "complex."
2. Omissions: "reading is process" instead of "reading is a process."
3. Insertions: "on a the table" instead of "on the table."
4. Repetitions: "What, what's the matter?" instead of "What's the matter?"

Miscue analysis reveals whether a student makes one or more of these mistakes in oral reading persistently or in a random fashion. Identifying patterns leads directly to developing intervention goals and activities.

The miscue analysis process begins with identifying a suitable group of reading passages. Appropriate passages may be selected from class textbooks and reading materials of interest to a student. The passages should be at or near the student's current reading level. Next, as the student reads, the teacher records the errors on a copy of the passage. The teacher then analyzes the performance to identify the patterns of errors and chronic errors. Finally, the teacher summarizes the results, providing a basis for developing instructional objectives and intervention activities.

For example, in Figure 15–5, Pamela's oral reading sample indicates a consistent error in omitting endings of words. In this example, Pamela omitted endings such as *-ed, -ing,* and *-a* in oral reading. The sample passage contains 55 words, and Pamela made 6 errors. This calculates into an error rate of approximately 11% (6/55 = 11%). Error rates of 10% and higher indicate that the passage is too difficult and frustrating for the student. When this happens, the evaluator should repeat the analysis procedure with an easier passage to establish the student's *instructional level,* which refers to passages read with at least 95% accuracy. In the sample passage, the student needs assistance with ending sounds and units. The teacher may attempt one of several interventions to help with this problem, including visual discrimination exercises focusing on recognizing whole words and special instruction to help Pamela build skills with syllables and whole words.

Figure 15–5   Miscue Analysis of Pamela's Oral Reading

kitty   Susan
A big, gray kitten named Susana ran away from her mother.

play
She found a ball. She played with it. A big dog came

run   want
running by. She was afraid and wanted to go home, but she
did not know the way. Her mother had been looking for her.

Susan
When she found Susana she took her home.

Cloze Procedures

Another useful group of curriculum-based assessment techniques, the **cloze procedures,** consists of informal tests of word prediction abilities for measuring comprehension skills and the way students use cues to identify words. Like miscue analysis, the cloze procedures enable teachers to determine a student's reading level using a textbook or some other readily available reading material. The most common cloze procedure, visual cloze (Bormuth, 1968), involves selecting a brief passage (about 250 words) and altering it by deleting every fifth word of the text, leaving the first and last sentences intact. The student reads the altered passage aloud and orally fills in the blanks. When a student correctly completes between 44% and 57% of the missing words, the text is considered appropriate for instruction. When a student supplies less than 44% of the words, the passage is too difficult. Likewise, when a student furnishes more than 57% of the words, the passage is too easy for use in reading instruction. Take, for example, the following passage:

"Dodger was a big brown dog with long ears and a short tail. Dodger loved to play in the yard but sometimes he would go under the fence and run away."

This would become

"Dodger was a big _____ dog with long ears _____ a short tail. Dodger _____ to play in the _____ but sometimes he would _____ under the fence and _____ away."

In this example, the passage occurs at the instructional level for students who correctly supply three of the six missing words.

Auditory cloze (Sattler, 1992) refers to a related cloze procedure. With auditory cloze, the student inserts the correct word to complete sentences spoken by the evaluator. Appropriate for use with young children, auditory cloze serves as a good beginning task because it does not require reading ability.

Sattler (1992) suggested several methods for modifying cloze procedures to provide additional assessment of word prediction abilities. One of the modifications, visual cloze with alternatives, involves having the student select the correct word from two choices (e.g., "Dodger can run after the _____ [mall/ball]"). With visual cloze the student may complete the blank with any word. In contrast, visual cloze with alternatives relies more heavily on the ability to read the sentence as well as the alternative choices. Another modification, cloze with initial grapheme, consists of giving the student the initial grapheme of the missing word ("The cat ran up the t_____ [tree]"). This modification is more difficult than traditional cloze because it limits the range of appropriate answers to words that match the initial grapheme.

☑ Comprehension Checklist

When teachers conduct curriculum-based assessment, a type of informal, authentic evaluation, they use regular classroom materials and instructional activities to evaluate student reading performance. Curriculum-based techniques include use of clinical observations, diagnostic checklists, miscue analysis, and cloze procedures. Because it leads directly to developing instructional objectives, this type of assessment is of special interest to teachers. Like all appraisal procedures, curriculum-based assessment of reading has drawbacks related to producing reliable and valid results. The challenge is to refine curriculum-based assessment in ways that overcome these limitations. Despite the difficulties, curriculum-based assessment has many advantages, including the ability to evaluate student performance in direct relation to what has been taught within the curriculum. This direct relationship allows the teacher to make educational decisions on the basis of actual reading behavior. Additional curriculum-based assessment procedures for evaluating reading appear in Chapter 18, which discusses portfolio assessment, and in Chapter 19, which focuses on assessment in inclusive settings.

Summary

Reading consists of several complex behaviors necessary to recognize and comprehend written words and passages. Reading recognition involves translating the printed word into spoken counterparts, and reading comprehension concerns understanding written content. With most students, reading assessment begins with screening followed by more formal diagnostic evaluation of specific reading problems. In addition to norm-referenced testing, assessment often involves use of curriculum-based appraisal procedures. When special educators need a norm-referenced instrument, they may select from either multiple-skill or single-skill tools, depending on the student's reading difficulties and the reasons for testing. However, when special education teachers require a direct link between assessment and classroom instruction, they rely on curriculum-based measures that directly match instruction. In all cases, the evaluator should select the test or assessment procedure that best meets a student's individual needs (see Table 15–9 on p. 477).

Chapter Review and Application

Multiple Choice

Directions: Read each item carefully. In the blank beside each item, write the letter of the best response. Each question contains only one best answer. Check your answers with the answer key at the end of the book.

_____ 1. Which of the following is a norm-referenced, diagnostic reading test?
   a. *Classroom Reading Inventory*
   b. *Woodcock Reading Mastery Test-Revised*
   c. *Test of Early Reading Ability-2*

_____ 2. Which of the following is a norm-referenced screening test of reading?
   a. *Classroom Reading Inventory*
   b. *Woodcock Reading Mastery Test-Revised*
   c. *Test of Early Reading Ability-2*

_____ 3. What are reading tests that consist primarily of graded word lists and graded passages called?
   a. Norm-referenced, single-skill diagnostic reading tests
   b. Criterion-referenced, single-skill screening tests of reading
   c. Informal reading inventories

_____ 4. "Dodger is a large, _____ dog with big ears _____ a short tail." This is an example of _____.
   a. performance measurement
   b. miscue analysis
   c. clinical observation
   d. cloze

_____ 5. If a student misreads more than 10% of the words in an oral reading passage, the passage is _____.
   a. too easy
   b. at the student's instructional level
   c. too difficult

_____ 6. Which approach to reading assessment focuses on analysis of performance on overall and subtest scores?
   a. Norm referenced
   b. Informal inventories
   c. Curriculum based

_____ 7. Which approach to reading assessment focuses on techniques such as miscue analysis, clinical observations, and checklists?
   a. Norm referenced
   b. Informal inventories
   c. Curriculum based

_____ 8. When students say "complis" instead of "complex" and "on a the table" instead of "on the table," what type of errors are they making?
   a. Listening
   b. Word recognition
   c. Oral reading

_____ 9. Which curriculum-based assessment technique involves informally testing word prediction abilities to measure comprehension skills and the way students use cues to identify words?
   a. Cloze
   b. Miscue analysis
   c. Clinical observation

_____ 10. What type of test is the _Test of Reading Comprehension-Third Edition (TORC-3)_?
   a. Curriculum based
   b. Norm referenced
   c. Criterion referenced
   d. Screening

Short Answers

Directions: Review your understanding of the material in this chapter by answering the following short answer items. Compare your responses with the sample answers at the end of the book. Your responses should contain information that is similar to but not exactly the same as the information in the sample answers.

1. What are the three approaches for assessing reading achievement discussed in the chapter? What are the primary uses of each approach?

2. How does curriculum-based assessment of reading connect assessment with classroom reading instruction? Why is this connection between assessment and instruction important?

3. What specific curriculum-based assessment techniques for evaluating reading are described in the chapter? Which of these would you prefer to use? Why?

4. Ms. Marisol suspects that Angelina is significantly behind her peers in reading achievement. She would like an in-depth, diagnostic assessment of Angelina's present levels of performance, strengths, and weaknesses in reading to help decide if Angelina should receive special help. What norm-referenced, individually administered diagnostic reading test do you think Ms. Marisol should use to obtain this assessment. Why?

References

Beck, M. D. (1992). Review of the *Test of Early Reading Ability-2.* In J. J. Kramer and J. C. Conoley (Eds.), *The Eleventh Mental Measurements Yearbook.* Lincoln, NE: Buros Institute of Mental Measurements, 942–44.

Bond, G. L., Tinker, M. A., Wasson, B. A., & Wasson, J. B. (1989). *Reading Difficulties: Their Diagnosis and Correction* (6th ed.). Englewood Cliffs, NJ: Prentice Hall.

Booth, D., Swartz, L., & Zola, M. (1994). *Classroom Voices: Language-Based Learning in the Elementary School.* Toronto: Harcourt, Brace, Canada.

Bormuth, J. R. (1968). The cloze readability procedure. *Elementary English* 45, 429–36.

Brown, V. L., Hammill, D. D., & Wiederholt, J. L. (1995). *Test of Reading Comprehension* (3d ed.). Austin, TX: PRO-ED.

Cohen, S. H., & Cohen, J. (1994). Review of the *Woodcock Reading Mastery Tests-Revised.* In D. J. Keyser and R. C. Sweetland (Eds.), *Test Critiques* (vol. X). Austin, TX: PRO-ED.

Ekwall, E. E. (1986). *Ekwall Reading Inventory* (2d ed.). Boston, MA: Allyn and Bacon.

Gates, A.I., McKillop, A.S., & Horowitz, R. (1981). *Gates–McKillop–Horowitz Reading Diagnostic Tests.* New York: Teachers College Press.

Hanna, G. S. (1995). Review of the *Slosson Test of Reading Readiness* (rev. ed.) In J. C. Conoley and J. C. Impara (Eds.), *The Twelfth Mental Measurements Yearbook.* Lincoln, NE: Buros Institute of Mental Measurements, 960–61.

Hargrove, L. J., & Poteet, J. A. (1984). *Assessment in Special Education: The Education Evaluation.* Englewood Cliffs, NJ: Prentice-Hall.

Harris, A. J., & Sipay, E. R. (1985). *How to Increase Reading Ability: A Guide to Developmental and Remedial Methods.* New York: Longman.

Hiltonsmith, R. W. (1992). Review of the *Test of Early Reading Ability-2.* In J. J. Kramer and J. C. Conoley (Eds.), *The Eleventh Mental Measurements Yearbook.* Lincoln, NE: Buros Institute of Mental Measurements, 944–46.

International Reading Association. (1992). *Standards for Reading Professionals.* Newark, DE: Author.

International Reading Association and the National Council of Teachers of English. (1994). *Standards for the Assessment of Reading and Writing.* Newark, DE: Author.

Johns, J. L. (1985). *Basic Reading Inventory* (3d ed.). Dubuque, IA: Kendall/Hunt Publishing Company.

King, J. D. (1995). Review of the *Gray Oral Reading Test,* (3d. ed.). In J. C. Conoley and J. C. Impara (Eds.), *The Twelfth Mental Measurements Yearbook.* Lincoln, NE: Buros Institute of Mental Measurements, 422–23.

Luftig, R. L. (1989). *Assessment of Learners With Special Needs*. Boston: Allyn and Bacon.

Mercer, C., & Mercer, A. (1998). *Teaching Students With Learning Problems* (5th ed.). Upper Saddle River, NJ: Merrill/Prentice Hall.

Newcomer, P. L. (1986). *Standardized Reading Inventory*. Austin, TX: PRO-ED.

Perry, L. A., & Vitali, G. J. (1991). *Slosson Test of Reading Readiness*. East Aurora, NY: Slosson Educational Publications.

Reid, D. K., Hresko, W. P., & Hammill, D. D. (1989). *Test of Early Reading Ability* (2d ed.). Austin, TX: PRO-ED.

Reid, D. K., Hresko, W. P., Hammill, D. D., & Wiltshire, S. (1991). *Test of Early Reading Ability-Deaf or Hard of Hearing*. Austin, TX: PRO-ED.

Rothlisberg, B. A. (1995). Review of the *Test of Early Reading Ability-Deaf or Hard of Hearing*. In J. C. Conoley and J. C. Impara (Eds.), *The Twelfth Mental Measurements Yearbook*. Lincoln, NE: Buros Institute of Mental Measurements, 1049–51.

Sattler, J. M. (1992). *Assessment of Children* (3d ed.). San Diego: Author.

Sawyer, D. J. (1995). Review of the *Slosson Test of Reading Readiness* (rev. ed.) In J. C. Conoley and J. C. Impara (Eds.), *The Twelfth Mental Measurements Yearbook*. Lincoln, NE: Buros Institute of Mental Measurements, 961–62.

Shaw, S. S., & Swerdlik, M. E. (1995). Review of the *Slosson Oral Reading Test* (rev. ed.). In J. Conoley and J. C. Impara (Eds.), *The Twelfth Mental Measurements Yearbook*. Lincoln, NE: Buros Institute of Mental Measurements, 958–59.

Silvaroli, N. J. (1990). *Classroom Reading Inventory* (6th ed.). Dubuque, IA: Wm C. Brown.

Slosson, R. L., & Nicholson, C. L. (1990). *Slosson Oral Reading Test* (rev. ed.). East Aurora, NY: Slosson Educational Publications.

Smith, T., Finn, D., & Dowdy, C. (1993). *Teaching Students With Mild Disabilities*. Fort Worth, TX: Harcourt Brace Jovanovich.

Spache, G. D. (1981). *Diagnostic Reading Scales*. Monterey, CA: CTB/McGraw-Hill.

Sucher, F., & Allred, R. A. (1981). *New Sucher–Allred Reading Placement Inventory*. Oklahoma City: Economy.

Toubanos, E. S. (1995). Review of the *Test of Early Reading Ability—Deaf or Hard of Hearing*. In J. C. Conoley and J. C. Impara (Eds.), *The Twelfth Mental Measurements Yearbook*. Lincoln, NE: Buros Institute of Mental Measurements, 1051–53.

Westby, C. E. (1995). Review of the *Slosson Oral Reading Test* (rev. ed.). In J. C. Conoley and J. C. Impara (Eds.), *The Twelfth Mental Measurements Yearbook*. Lincoln, NE: Buros Institute of Mental Measurements, 959–60.

Wiederholt, J. L. (1986). *Formal Reading Inventory*. Austin, TX: PRO-ED.

Wiederholt, J. L., & Bryant, B. R. (1991). *Gray Oral Reading Tests, Diagnostic*. Austin, TX: PRO-ED.

———— (1994). *Gray Oral Reading Tests* (3d ed.). Austin, TX: PRO-ED.

Wisconsin State Reading Association. (1990). *Toward an Ecological Assessment of Reading Progress*. Milwaukee, WI: Author.

Woodcock, R. (1973). *Woodcock Reading Mastery Tests*. Circle Pines, MN: American Guidance Service.

————. (1998). *Woodcock Reading Mastery Tests* (rev. ed.). Circle Pines, MN: American Guidance Service.

Woods M. L., & Moe, A. J. (1989). *Analytical Reading Inventory* (4th ed.). New York: Merrill/Macmillan.

Zigmond, N., Vallecorsa, A., & Silverman, R. (1983). *Assessment for Instructional Planning in Special Education*. Englewood Cliffs, NJ: Prentice-Hall.

Table 15–9 Review of Reading Achievement Tests

Name of Test	Type of Test	Suitable for Individuals Who Are	Brief Description of Test	Purpose of Administering Test
Analytical Reading Inventory, Fourth Edition (Woods & Moe, 1989)	Criterion-referenced, individually administered, informal reading inventory	Primer– grade 9	Measures silent reading, listening, & comprehension; includes expository passages in social studies & science	To pinpoint reading strengths & weaknesses
Classroom Reading Inventory, Sixth Edition (Silvaroli, 1990)	Criterion-referenced, individually administered reading inventory	Preprimer– grade 8	Includes graded word lists, graded passages, comprehension questions, & a graded spelling survey	To assess silent reading & listening skills
*Diagnostic Reading Scales (DRS-81) (Spache, 1981)	Criterion-referenced, individually administered reading inventory	Grades 1–7	Measures oral reading, silent reading, reading comprehension, & auditory comprehension	An informal diagnostic tool for assessing current levels of reading performance
Ekwall Reading Inventory, Second Edition (Ekwall, 1986)	Criterion-referenced, individually administered reading inventory	Preprimer– grade 9	Helps to determine independent, instructional, & frustration reading levels, as well as word analysis skills, reader characteristics, reading rate, comprehension, & phonics	To check word knowledge & word analysis skills
Formal Reading Inventory (Wiederholt, 1986)	Norm-referenced, individually administered reading inventory	Grades 1–12	Includes developmentally sequenced reading passages with multiple-choice questions for each passage	To assess silent reading, comprehension, & oral reading miscues
*Gates–McKillop– Horowitz Reading Diagnostic Tests (Gates et al., 1981)	Norm-referenced, individually administered diagnostic reading test	Grades 1–6	Measures oral reading, flash words, untimed words, word attack, recognition of the visual form of sounds, auditory blending, auditory discrimination, & written expression	An informal measure designed to diagnose reading achievement & pinpoint strengths & weaknesses

*Tests marked with asterisks are featured in tables in this chapter.

Table 15–9 *(continued)*

Name of Test	Type of Test	Suitable for Individuals Who Are	Brief Description of Test	Purpose of Administering Test
*Gray Oral Reading Tests, Third Edition (GORT-3) (Wieder-holt & Bryant, 1994)	Norm-referenced, individually administered reading test	7–18 years	Measures oral reading proficiency & oral reading comprehension	To measure growth in oral reading and to diagnose oral reading problems
New Sucher–Allred Reading Placement Inventory (Sucher & Allred, 1981)	Criterion-referenced, individually administered reading inventory	Preprimer–grade 9	Includes graded word lists & graded passages	To assess oral reading, listening skills, & reading comprehension
*Slosson Oral Reading Test-Revised (SORT-R) (Slosson & Nicholson, 1990)	Norm-referenced, individually administered screening test	Pre-K–high school	Measures word recognition skills	To screen word recognition ability
*Slosson Test of Reading Readiness (STRR) (Perry & Vitali, 1991)	Norm-referenced, individually administered prereading screening test	Grades K–1	Measures recognition of capital letters & lowercase letters; matching capital letters, lowercase letters, & word forms; rhyming; recognition of beginning sounds; sequencing; & opposites	To measure a child's readiness to begin formal reading instruction
Standardized Reading Inventory (Newcomer, 1986)	Norm-referenced, individually administered reading inventory	Preprimer–grade 8	Includes graded word lists & graded reading passages	To assess word recognition skills & reading comprehension
*Test of Early Reading Ability-2 (TERA–2) (Reid, et al., 1989)	Norm-referenced screening test of reading	3–9 years	Measures contextual meaning, the alphabet, & the conventions of print	To screen early reading ability & to measure emerging reading skills
*Test of Reading Comprehension-Third Edition (TORC-3) (Brown, et al., 1995)	Norm-referenced, individually administered diagnostic reading test	7–17 years	Measures general vocabulary, syntactic similarities, paragraph reading, sentence sequencing, & understanding written directions	To measure silent reading comprehension
*Woodcock Reading Mastery Tests-Revised (WRMT-R) (Woodcock, 1998)	Individually administered, norm-referenced diagnostic test of reading achievement	5 years–retirement	Measures visual-auditory learning, letter identification, word identification, word attack, word & passage comprehension	To diagnose reading achievement

Assessment of Mathematics Achievement

Overview

In this chapter you will investigate the assessment of student achievement in mathematics. Your investigation includes review of formal standardized tests and informal curriculum-based measurement procedures. You will learn that standardized tests are most helpful for identifying overall math achievement levels and for determining the scope and sequence in mathematics instruction. Your study of standardized instruments includes in-depth review of the *KeyMath Revised: A Diagnostic Inventory of Essential Mathematics,* which was specifically designed for use in special education. You will also discover that most teachers prefer curriculum-based measurement because it is more selective and pinpoints skills that require remediation. Your study of curriculum-based measurement will include detailed review of procedures such as error pattern analysis, diagnostic interviews, and performance measurement that teachers use to guide instructional planning. Careful use of these assessment procedures links assessment with instruction and helps teachers identify exactly what students need to know.

Objectives

After reading this chapter, you will be prepared to do the following:

- Understand the types of behaviors measured by mathematics achievement tests.
- Discuss the use of mathematics achievement tests in special education.
- Use the individually administered diagnostic tests of mathematics proficiency.
- Use curriculum-based procedures for assessing mathematics skills.
- Use error pattern analysis procedures for evaluating mathematics skills.
- Use diagnostic interviews to assess mathematics achievement.
- Use performance measurement to assess mathematics achievement.
- Use performance rate assessment of mathematics skills.

The Importance of Assessing Mathematics

The following narrative shows many of the questions teachers have about assessing mathematics and mentions some of the most widely used math tests and curriculum-based assessment techniques.

Ms. White teaches students with mild and moderate disabilities. She has never assessed mathematics before, but because she will be teaching middle school math next year, she is wondering what type of math assessment to use with her class. Her questions about math assessment include these: What are the different kinds of tests and assessment procedures? What math assessments are specifically designed for students with special needs? Why should she use math assessment? Can math assessment really help, or will it take away valuable instructional time? Will math assessment improve the teaching and learning process?

Ms. White consults with some other teachers and does some reading. She discovers standardized math tests developed specifically for students with special needs like the KeyMath Revised: A Diagnostic Inventory of Essential Mathematics. *She also learns about error pattern analysis and other curriculum-based assessment techniques that help link assessment with classroom instruction. She decides to try the* KeyMath *and the error pattern analysis procedure to discover if these assessments will help her meet the instructional needs of her students.*

Defining Mathematics Assessment

Mathematics—the ability to understand numerical patterns, groupings, and correlations—is a basic subject in the academic curriculum. Although it does not permeate the school curriculum like reading, many students with disabilities encounter difficulty in mathematics. Developing math skills is a cumulative process in that students must master lower skills before learning higher level skills. For this reason, students in the early grades who fail to learn basic math skills also experience problems in later grades with higher level math and more applied math. In addition to becoming increasingly difficult, mathematics includes numerous concepts and skills. As a result, many students with special needs require diagnostic assessment and intensive remedial instruction in mathematics.

Behaviors Measured by Mathematics Tests

Assessing student proficiency in mathematics involves measuring numerous concepts and skills. Connolly (1998) grouped mathematics skills as follows:

- Content including numeration, fractions, algebra, and geometry.
- Operations consisting of counting, computation, and reasoning.
- Applications such as measurement, problem solving, money, and time.

Because of the complex, abstract nature of mathematics, many students in special education require repeated practice and comprehensive instruction to master even basic math operations. The need for intensive instruction limits the ultimate achievement level of many students, especially in math content. In addition, some students, particularly those with severe disabilities, need more of a functional mathematics curriculum emphasizing practical applications such as measurement, money, and time skills.

Because students who leave school without adequate math skills often find it difficult to succeed in vocations and survive in daily life, special educators need techniques that assess and remediate math deficiencies. Like most areas of academic assessment, appraisal in mathematics includes both formal and informal techniques. Formal assessment relies on standardized tests, whereas informal, curriculum-based assessment (such as error pattern analysis and performance rate scoring) relies on evaluation of student performance on class assignments and other easily available work samples.

Why Do We Assess the Mathematics Achievement of Students With Special Needs?

We assess the mathematics achievement of students with special needs to screen, identify, and place students, plan instruction and intervention for students, develop IEPs, evaluate student progress, and monitor program effectiveness (see Focus 16–1). Although some overlap occurs among these purposes, specialized math tests and assessment techniques are available for each function. For example, screening tests identify students who may have such severe problems in mathematics that further assessment is needed to determine whether a disability exists. Likewise, comprehensive, norm-referenced diagnostic tests identify students with math disabilities and help place them in appropriate programs. Detailed reviews of representative norm-referenced tests appear in this chapter. Although teachers use norm-referenced tests for instructional planning purposes, they rely more often on less formal, curriculum-based assessment techniques in which they select from a variety of appraisal strategies, all of

FOCUS 16–1

Why Do We Assess the Mathematics Achievement of Students With Special Needs?

- To screen children
- To determine eligibility for special services
- To diagnose math disabilities
- To identify overall math achievement levels
- To compare math achievement levels among children
- To determine the scope and sequence in mathematics instruction
- To identify strengths, weaknesses, and gaps in development
- To help create appropriate objectives and remedial activities
- To assist in developing IEPs
- To assess progress in meeting IEP goals
- To discover what the student knows and does not know in mathematics
- To determine areas in need of remediation
- To understand how much a student has learned as a result of instruction
- To measure student progress over time
- To evaluate the effectiveness of instructional programs in mathematics

which link assessment with classroom instruction. This chapter includes extensive information about the use curriculum-based assessment of mathematics. Other reasons for assessing mathematics are to evaluate student progress and monitor program effectiveness, for which both formal and informal appraisal techniques are useful.

The following case study, based on a vignette by Gable and Coben (1990), illustrates why teachers use informal, curriculum-based assessment in their classrooms to assess the performance of students who are experiencing severe problems learning specific math skills.

Although most students in Mr. Kaye's class were experiencing some difficulty learning subtraction with regrouping, Horace was failing miserably. In response to the problem, Mr. Kaye gathered a sample of math papers Horace had completed in class and prepared an informal diagnostic test with 20 subtraction problems. After giving Horace the diagnostic test over a 2-day period, Mr. Kaye analyzed the results by categorizing the errors on a chart. The chart revealed that Horace made five mistakes on the diagnostic test, four of which involved regrouping and one of which was a random error. Mr. Kaye also noticed that all of the regrouping errors involved problems with zeros in the minuend. After confirming this error pattern by examining the other work samples, he conducted a diagnostic interview with Horace. On the basis of these curriculum-based assessment procedures, Mr. Kaye concluded that Horace knew the basic addition and subtraction facts and could handle most three- and four-digit subtractions, except those with zeros in the minuend. When faced with zeros, Horace tended to lose track of the process and make mistakes. Mr. Kaye's solution was to simplify the column labels and then use modeling with specific feedback to teach Horace the simplified regrouping process.

☑ Comprehension Checklist

Many students with special needs require diagnostic assessment and intensive remedial instruction in mathematics, which is the study of numerical patterns, groupings, and correlations. Assessing mathematics achievement involves measuring numerous concepts and skills using both formal, norm-referenced testing and informal, curriculum-based assessment. We assess the math achievement of students with special needs to screen, identify and place students, plan instruction and intervention for them, develop IEPs, evaluate student progress, and monitor program effectiveness.

Formal Assessment in Mathematics

As part of the process of developing instructional objectives and intervention programs in mathematics, the special educator needs an accurate measure of current levels of performance. Only after identifying strengths, weaknesses, and gaps in development can the teacher create appropriate objectives and remedial activities. To obtain this diagnostic information, special educators may select from several formal math achievement tests, which include the multiple-skill tools (reviewed earlier in Chapter 14, Overview of Assessing Academic Achievement) as well as the single-skill instruments reviewed in this chapter.

The mathematics subtests included in most multiple-skill tests, while not covering as much detail as single-skill tests, provide reliable measures of mathematics achievement that is often more than adequate for many diagnostic and instructional uses. When diagnosticians and teachers need even more detailed information about math achievement, however, they frequently use one of the single-skill mathematics tests. Foremost among these is the *KeyMath Revised: A Diagnostic Inventory of Essential Mathematics*.

KeyMath Revised: A Diagnostic Inventory of Essential Mathematics

The *KeyMath Revised: A Diagnostic Inventory of Essential Mathematics* (Connolly, 1998) is an individually administered, norm-referenced diagnostic test of math skills and concepts from kindergarten to grade 9. The *KeyMath-R* is an updated version of the *KeyMath Diagnostic Arithmetic Test* (Connolly, 1988; Connolly et al., 1976), which was originally developed for students with mild mental retardation but later refined and expanded for all students who need comprehensive diagnostic assessment and remedial instruction in mathematics. The authors designed the *KeyMath-R* for special education teachers, educational diagnosticians, and math specialists to use in identifying specific strengths and weaknesses and for planning instructional programs. A summary of the *KeyMath-R* appears in Table 16–1. Two parallel forms allow students to be retested without duplication. The test contains 13 subtests in three strands:

Strand One: Basic Concepts

numeration
rational numbers
geometry

Table 16–1   *KeyMath-Revised: A Diagnostic Inventory of Essential Mathematics (KeyMath-R)*

Type of Test:	Norm referenced and individually administered
Purpose:	To diagnose mathematics achievement
Content Areas:	Basic concepts, operations, and applications
Administration Time:	Approximately 1 hour
Age Levels:	Kindergarten–grade 9
Suitable for:	Students with mild and moderate disabilities, including educable mental retardation, learning disabilities, behavior disorders, sensory impairments (with appropriate adaptations), and physical disabilities
Scores:	Standard scores, grade and age equivalents, percentiles, stanines, and NCEs for the total test and the three content areas
In Short:	The *KeyMath-R* is useful for measuring performance levels and developing instructional objectives. It has excellent content, valuable supplemental features, and adequate technical characteristics.

Strand Two: Operations

addition
subtraction
multiplication
division
mental computation

Strand Three: Applications

measurement
time and money
estimation
interpreting data
problem solving

Materials for the *KeyMath-R*   The well-designed *KeyMath-R* materials include easel kits for both Form A and Form B, test records for both forms, a manual, and a sample report to parents. Supplementary teaching materials and an available computer software scoring and interpretation program enhance the test's usefulness. The software automatically converts scores and connects them to the IEP and the *KeyMath Teach and Practice (TAP)* instructional intervention program. Software options include a score summary profile, a domain performance summary, a narrative report, item objectives, and *TAP* resources. The *KeyMath Revised* is an excellent example of a diagnostic test that includes many valuable instructional features, a summary of which appears in Focus 16–2. These features make it easy for teachers to connect assessment data derived from the *KeyMath Revised* with instructional intervention programs in the classroom.

Administration and Scoring of the *KeyMath-R*   The manual provides extensive information about administering, scoring, and interpreting the *KeyMath-R*. The test, which takes approximately 1 hour to administer, produces a variety of scores, including standard scores ($M = 100$, $SD = 15$), grade and age equivalents, percentile ranks, stanines, and NCEs for the total test and the three strands. In addition, the test provides scaled scores ($M = 10$, $SD = 3$), percentile ranks, stanines, and NCEs for

FOCUS 16–2

Instructional Features of the *KeyMath Revised*

- Contains numerous test items for comprehensively measuring mathematics achievement
- Helps determine scope and sequence in mathematics instruction
- Provides a detailed measure of performance levels in mathematics
- Serves as an instructional guide
- Includes a software program that provides score conversions, a narrative report, and recommendations for intervention
- Provides supplemental materials including remedial activities, worksheets, drills, and games

each of the 13 subtests. Spring and fall norms enable precise assessment of student performance levels at the beginning and end of the school year. Furthermore, a score profile form, one of the strongest scoring features of the test, graphically summarizes results and facilitates visual interpretation of test data. By graphically illustrating strengths and weaknesses, the profile makes it easy to analyze area and subtest performance. A companion software program, *KeyMath Assist,* available for Apple and IBM computers, expedites score conversion and provides a four- to five-page narrative report with student performance data and recommendations for programming. A sample scoring summary form from the *KeyMath-R* appears in Figure 16–1.

Technical Characteristics of the *KeyMath-R* Standardized with a group of more than 3,000 students, the 1997 normative update of the *KeyMath Revised* followed a well-designed test development plan using a representative national sample. The *KeyMath-R* exhibits adequate split-half and alternate-form reliability; however, like many similar tests, some subtest reliabilities fall below acceptable levels. Although the *KeyMath-R* displays excellent content validity, it exhibits limited concurrent and construct validity. Despite this limitation, Larsen and Williams (1994) indicated that the *KeyMath* has a rich history of development, use, and study. In their critical review, they rated the instrument as complete and thorough. Overall, the *KeyMath Revised* displays adequate technical qualities with many excellent measurement features.

Summary of the *KeyMath-R* Because it contains excellent content along with attractive supplemental features, the *KeyMath-R* serves as an effective diagnostic tool for evaluating skills in mathematics. Larsen and Williams (1994) described the instrument as a great asset to educators who need to determine scope and sequence in mathematics instruction. The test organization makes the information especially accessible to teachers. Valuable as a measure of performance levels in mathematics as well as an instructional guide, teachers can use the *KeyMath Revised* together with the *KeyMath Teach and Practice (TAP)* (Connolly, 1985) materials. The *TAP* consists of remedial activities in basic concepts and includes worksheet activities, drills, and games.

Diagnostic Mathematics Inventory/Mathematics System

Unlike the norm-referenced *KeyMath-R,* the *Diagnostic Mathematics Inventory/Mathematics System (DMI/MS)* (Gessell, 1983) is a criterion-referenced assessment tool and curriculum guide. Designed for students from kindergarten through the eighth grade, the *DMI/MS* contains a grade-level–based and an ungraded, objectives-based system. The author designed both systems with the same content and purposes: to identify math performance levels, to determine areas in need of remediation, to develop intervention activities, and to measure student progress over time. A summary of the *DMI/MS* appears in Table 16–2.

The inventory keys each test question to an objective and to practice exercises, making it easy to translate assessment results into programming activities. Other useful features include reference guides to commercial instructional materials and major mathematics textbooks. The *DMI/MS* measures math skills in these areas:

- Whole numbers.
- Fractions and decimals.
- Measurement and geometry.
- Problem solving and special topics.

Figure 16–1 Sample Scoring Summary from the *KeyMath-R*

KeyMath
R E V I S E D

a diagnostic
inventory of
essential
mathematics

AUSTIN J.
CONNOLLY

INDIVIDUAL TEST RECORD

Student's Name _Carrie M._ Sex: M (F)

		YEAR	MONTH	DAY
School _Cedar Hills_ Grade _4_	Test date	87	109	*23*
Mathematics Teacher _Mrs. Guthrie_	Birth date	77	9	14
Examiner _Tom Brown_ Date _10/2/87_	Chronological age	10	1	18

DATA FROM OTHER TESTS

Test	Date	Results
CTBS	5/4/84	Slightly below average
CTBS	4/27/86	About 1.5 yrs below grade
PPVT-R	9/13/87	Average for age

SCORE SUMMARY

Derived-score tables are in Appendix E of the *Manual*. For standard scores and scaled scores, indicate your selection of grade or age and fall or spring norms by circling the number of the appropriate table:

Standard Scores and Scaled Scores
Fall norms (August–January)
Spring norms (February–July)

Grade (Table 1) Table 3
Age Table 2 Table 4

See Table 9 for percentile ranks, stanines, and normal curve equivalents. Obtain grade equivalents and age equivalents from Tables 10 and 11, respectively.

BASIC CONCEPTS

Subtest	Raw Score	Scaled Score	%ile Rank
Numeration	(13)	7	16
Rational Numbers	(2)	10	50
Geometry	(8)	5	5

BASIC CONCEPTS AREA

	Standard Score	%ile Rank
Raw Score (23) →	80	9

Grade / Age Equivalent _2.5_   1.

OPERATIONS

Subtest	Raw Score	Scaled Score	%ile Rank
Addition	(9)	5	5
Subtraction	(8)	9	25
Multiplication	(4)	7	16
Division	(5)	10	50
Mental Computation	(6)	12	75

OPERATIONS AREA

	Standard Score	%ile Rank
Raw Score (32) →	91	27

Grade / Age Equivalent _3.7_   2.

APPLICATIONS

Subtest	Raw Score	Scaled Score	%ile Rank
Measurement	(10)	7	16
Time and Money	(14)	12	75
Estimation	(7)	11	63
Interpreting Data	(10)	13	84
Problem Solving	(10)	15	95

APPLICATIONS AREA

	Standard Score	%ile Rank
Raw Score (51) →	110	75

Grade / Age Equivalent _5.3_   3.

TOTAL TEST

(23) + (32) + (51) = (106)
  1.   2.   3.   Total Test Raw Score

Standard Score	%ile Rank	NCE (optional)	Stanine (optional)	Grade Equivalent (optional)	Age Equivalent
97	42	5	5	4.0	

(From Connolly, A. J. (1998). *KeyMath Revised: A Diagnostic Inventory of Essential Mathematics.* Circle Pines, MN: American Guidance Service. Reprinted with permission of American Guidance Service, Inc.

Table 16–2 *Diagnostic Mathematics Inventory/Mathematics System (DMI/MS)*

Type of Test:	A criterion-referenced, individually administered assessment system and curriculum guide
Purpose:	To diagnose mathematics achievement
Content Areas:	Whole numbers, fractions and decimals, measurement and geometry, problem solving, and special topics
Administration Time:	Approximately 1 hour
Age Levels:	Kindergarten–eighth grade
Suitable for:	Students with mild disabilities, including learning disabilities and behavior disorders
Scores:	Objectives master report, common error report, individual diagnostic report, class grouping report, and estimated norms report
In Short:	The *DMI/MS* provides a system for matching each test item to a math objective and for practicing exercises. This system helps teachers and diagnosticians link assessment results with intervention activities.

Materials for the *DMI/MS* *DMI/MS* materials include a manual, a student response booklet, and several report forms. Evaluators may complete a diagnostic report, a report of frequent errors, a group report summarizing all students in a class, and a report of estimated norm scores.

Administration and Scoring of the *DMI/MS* The manual provides explicit directions for administering each subtest and for scoring student performance. Test results include a diagnostic report, estimated norm scores, a group report, and a report of frequent errors. The *DMI/MS* also provides a system for identifying appropriate objectives for individuals and groups of students. The inventory includes 82 instructional objectives keyed to the test items.

Technical Characteristics of the *DMI/MS* Although norms exist for the *DMI/MS*, evaluators should use them cautiously because the manual provides limited information concerning the process used to obtain the sample group scores. Unfortunately, the manual reports no reliability or validity data for the test.

Summary of the *DMI/MS* The *DMI/MS* is a criterion-referenced diagnostic test of mathematics that measures student mastery of 82 objectives in 29 categories. It is useful for teachers and diagnosticians in planning programs, and the objectives are suitable for inclusion on IEPs.

Other Diagnostic Tests of Mathematics

In addition to the tests just reviewed, teachers and evaluators may select from among other diagnostic tests of mathematics. The brief reviews of representative tests that follow provide an overview of the range and variety of commercially available instruments for measuring the mathematics skills of students with special needs.

Enright Diagnostic Inventory of Basic Arithmetic Skills   The *Enright Diagnostic Inventory of Basic Arithmetic Skills* (Enright, 1983) is an informal, criterion-referenced inventory for groups and individual students from grade 4 through adult. The purpose of the *Enright* is to determine the exact math skill at which to begin instruction and to provide a clear explanation of computation errors. The *Enright* subtests include measures of computation of whole numbers, fractions, and decimals. Four types of tests appear in the *Enright*: tests of basic facts in addition, subtraction, multiplication, and division; wide-range instructional placement tests; skill placement tests; and error analysis skill tests.

Sequential Assessment of Mathematics Inventories   The *Sequential Assessment of Mathematics Inventories (SAMI)* (Reisman, 1985) is an informal classroom survey test that includes a kit of manipulative materials for use in testing. Designed for students from kindergarten through grade 8, the *SAMI* covers 300 math objectives in eight different strands. The *SAMI* provides three different test activities: pencil-on-paper, oral interview, and concrete representation. The *SAMI* enables teachers to obtain an in-depth evaluation of math achievement and provides a profile of student performance in math concepts and skills.

Stanford Diagnostic Mathematics Test-Fourth Edition   The *Stanford Diagnostic Mathematics Test-Fourth Edition* (Beatty et al., 1995) is a norm-referenced test for groups from first through twelfth grade. The purpose of the *Stanford Diagnostic Test-Fourth Edition* is to identify the math achievement levels of groups of students. The test is divided into six levels, each of which includes multiple-choice and free-response items. Two forms of the test are available.

Test of Early Mathematics Ability-2   The *Test of Early Mathematics Ability-2 (TEMA-2)* (Ginsberg & Baroody, 1990) is a norm-referenced, individually administered measure of emerging math concepts. Designed for children from age 3 through age 8, the *TEMA-2* measures concepts of relative magnitude, reading and writing numerals, counting skills, number facts, calculation, calculational algorithms, and base-ten concepts. The purpose of the *TEMA-2* is to determine specific strengths and weaknesses, measure progress, evaluate programs, and guide instruction and remediation. The *TEMA-2* takes 20 to 30 minutes to administer, and its materials include assessment probes and instructional activities.

Test of Mathematical Abilities-2   The *Test of Mathematical Abilities-2 (TOMA-2)* (Brown et al., 1994) is a norm-referenced, individually administered test for students from grade 3 through grade 12. Designed to measure math performance in the major skill areas in math as well as attitude, vocabulary, and general application of mathematics concepts in real life, *TOMA-2* subtests include measures of vocabulary, computation, general information, story problems, and attitude toward math. The *TOMA-2* takes approximately $1\frac{1}{2}$ hours to administer.

☑ Comprehension Checklist

Formal math achievement tests include the subtests on the multiple-skill instruments reviewed in Chapter 14 and the tests just described. When teachers and diagnosticians want more detailed assessment data, they use one of the single-skill mathematics tests. Foremost among these is the *KeyMath Revised: A Diagnostic Inventory of Essential Mathematics.* This well-designed instrument has a long history of development and use. In addition, it features a complete series of teaching and practice materials that teachers can use in conjunction with the test.

Curriculum-Based Assessment in Mathematics

In addition to formal tests such as the *KeyMath-R* and the *DMI/MS,* special education teachers also use curriculum-based assessment techniques to evaluate the mathematics performance of their students. Because it provides a direct link between assessment and instruction, teachers find that curriculum-based assessment is ideal for developing instructional objectives and learning activities. Teachers also use informal measures along with more formal tests, especially in making identification and placement decisions. One of the informal techniques, error pattern analysis, is especially suitable for developing remedial intervention for students who are struggling in math.

Error Pattern Analysis of Mathematics Skills

Error pattern analysis fits mathematics well because students perform most math assignments with pencil and paper. This produces a written record, making it easy to systematically evaluate mistakes and to determine the reasons for the errors. This process of analysis yields information that the teacher needs to plan remedial intervention programs. Various models for analyzing math errors exist. Ashlock (1998) for example, identified four common math errors:

- Wrong operation: The pupil attempts to respond by performing an operation other than the one that is required to solve the problem.
- Obvious computational error: The pupil applies the correct operation, but the response is based on error in recalling basic number facts.
- Defective algorithm: The pupil attempts to apply the correct operation but makes errors other than number fact errors in carrying through the necessary steps.
- Random response: The response shows no discernible relationship to the given problem (pp. 4–5).

Ashlock indicated that defective algorithm techniques account for the largest number of errors among all students. Among the lowest achieving students, however, random responses were the most commonly occurring error.

Ashlock also presented an expanded classification system with eight common error types:

- Basic fact error.
- Defective algorithm.
- Grouping error.
- Inappropriate inversion.
- Incorrect operation.
- Incomplete algorithm.
- Identity error.
- Zero error.

Although various experts employ slightly different systems for categorizing math errors, the process of placing common mistakes into logical groupings serves as the essential element of error pattern analysis in mathematics.

Gable and Coben (1990) described the following common error patterns in mathematics:

1. Incorrect operations

Students making this error complete problems by using the wrong operation, such as subtracting rather than adding.

Problems		*Explanation*
52	87	The student used the wrong operation.
+43	+37	
09	50	

2. Computation mistakes

Students making this mistake use the correct operation but fail to recall a basic math fact.

Problems		*Explanation*
8	9	The student failed to recall a basic math fact.
×6	×7	
45	56	

3. Incorrect algorithm

Students making this error follow the correct operation but use an incorrect or incomplete process in solving the problem.

Problems	*Explanation*
397	The student incorrectly regrouped the hundreds
−58	column.
239	

4. Random responses

Some students make random errors that fail to follow a specific pattern. Often such errors are due to sloppiness or inattention to the task. Teachers detect this chronic problem when mistakes occur on problems previously completed correctly.

Steps in Conducting Error Pattern Analysis   Error pattern analysis works best when teachers use it in a systematic manner. Gable and Coben (1990) recommend a four-stage error pattern analysis implementation procedure, a summary of which appears in Focus 16–3, followed by a detailed explanation of each step in the process.

In the first stage, the teacher gathers representative samples of a student's work. The samples should reflect the curriculum content, include the math problems that the student is having difficulty with, and incorporate enough items to establish a clear pattern. Consistent data are obtained from repeated testing with at least 3–5 items from each subskill area. For example, in the vignette at the beginning of this chapter, Mr. Kaye gathered sample math papers and prepared an informal diagnostic test with 20 subtraction problems that were given over a 2-day period. In this example, the samples were accurately collected with sufficient items to establish a clear pattern.

FOCUS 16–3

A Four-Stage Error Pattern Analysis Procedure

• Gather representative samples of a student's work
• Analyze the error patterns
• Conduct a diagnostic interview
• Record the results and develop an intervention strategy

In stage two the teacher conducts the actual analysis by assessing the errors in the sample papers. This process goes beyond marking each problem as correct or incorrect because the teacher analyzes the incorrect problems to identify the pattern of errors. The teacher then records each error in the appropriate category on a chart and counts the number of errors in each category. The chart provides a permanent record of the analysis. A sample mathematics error analysis chart, adapted from a form developed by Gable and Coben (1990), appears in Figure 16–2. The categories on the sample chart represent frequently occurring math errors, but teachers may add other categories as necessary.

In stage three the teacher conducts a diagnostic interview with the student. **Diagnostic interviews** are a single conference or a series of conferences with the student to help determine the reasons for the errors. Just prior to the interview, students should complete a few math problems that are of the type they are having difficulty with. During the interview the teacher has the student explain the steps used to solve each problem. Having the student talk through each problem gives the teacher insight into the way the student solves problems and the student's attitude toward mathematics. The interview should take place without time constraints or pressure, and the teacher should use nonjudgmental probing questions to gather as much information as possible.

Interviews are often the most valuable part of error analysis. The purpose of the interview is to give students an opportunity to share their thoughts and feelings about the math problems they were asked to complete. The interview gives the teacher vital information about the causes for mistakes and what might help reduce errors. Interviews also help teachers understand student perceptions of math and the cognitive processes that students use to solve math problems. For this to occur, the teacher must avoid conducting the interview like an oral examination, which means the teacher must avoid criticizing, correcting, and sharing opinions. Having students explain how they solve difficult math problems helps them develop awareness of their errors. It also alerts the teacher to students who lack the awareness or motivation necessary for improving their math skills (Smith et al., 1993).

In stage four, the teacher records the error pattern analysis results and develops appropriate intervention strategies. Teachers may use charts such as the Error Analysis Chart in Figure 16–2 to accomplish this. Keeping charts or other appropriate written records enables the teacher to document intervention attempts and to show progress over time.

Figure 16–2   Error Analysis Chart

Student _____   Teacher _____

Date _____   Number of Math Problems Analyzed _____

Description of Math Problems Analyzed _____

_____

Type of Error	Number of Errors	Remediation Strategies
Wrong operation		
Obvious computational error		
Defective algorithm		
Random response		
Other (specify)		
Other (specify)		

Notes _____

_____

_____

Practical Guidelines for Conducting Error Pattern Analysis   The following practical guidelines provide suggestions for conducting error pattern analysis and for ensuring accurate and useful results (Gable & Hendrickson, 1990; Ashlock, 1998).

- When learning how to conduct error pattern analysis, start with one student and set a comfortable time period of about 2 weeks for completing the process.
- Error analysis is best with students who are experiencing severe difficulty learning essential math skills. It is usually not necessary to conduct error analysis with students who are making satisfactory progress in math.
- Analyze and chart student performance as soon as possible after collecting appropriate work samples.
- Diagnosis using error analysis is quite personal and requires student cooperation, especially during the interview. The teacher must be accepting of all student responses, including wrong answers. The student needs to know that all answers are acceptable.

- Separate data collection from teaching. Diagnostic evaluation and teaching are different procedures. Diagnosis involves collecting data for making intervention decisions. Teaching involves giving instruction, training, and guidance. In most situations, teachers should avoid teaching during diagnosis. Put another way, this means that teachers should refrain from labeling responses as right or wrong, instructing students, and correcting mistakes during the error analysis process.
- Conduct multiple diagnoses by setting aside short periods of time for assessment during instruction. The idea is to give students time to reflect and the teacher time to observe behavior by asking them questions such as, "Can you try it another way?" or "Can you think of another way to solve that problem?"
- Watch for patterns to emerge from diagnostic and instructional activities. Rather than focusing on a single bit of diagnostic information for making intervention decisions, the goal of the analysis is to identify consistent patterns from multiple samples of a student's work. This type of analysis is really a problem-solving activity with the goal of finding a consistent pattern of errors that can be remediated as the student learns correct or more precise procedures.

Performance Measurement

Performance measurement is a widely used and practical means for assessing math skills. Teachers use performance measurement procedures with a variety of student work, including class math papers, homework assignments, and teacher-constructed tests. Salvia and Hughes (1990) identified percent correct and performance rate scoring as the most common and useful forms of performance measurement. Percent correct scoring is used with untimed math work. The percent correct score is obtained by calculating the percentage of correctly completed problems divided by the total number of problems multiplied by 100. For example, a math paper with 15 correct answers out of 20 problems would receive a percent correct score of 75% (15 ÷ 20 = .75 × 100 = 75%). With percent correct scoring, the teacher should establish a student mastery level such as 80% or 90% or use a grading scale such as A (94–100), B (85–93), C (75–84), D (65–74), and F (64 and below).

Performance Rate Scoring

Performance rate scoring is the use of timed probes or tests to measure the number of correct responses in a specified period. Teachers have found that this approach is effective in producing long-term gains in math performance, especially in basic addition, subtraction, multiplication, and division. Performance rate is an ideal way to assess simple computations, multiplication facts, and other math skills that students should complete quickly and accurately. The teacher assesses student performance rates by giving timed math assignments and calculating the number of correct responses per minute. For instance, if a student correctly completes 40 math problems in a 5-minute period, the performance rate is 8 problems per minute. Teachers must establish criteria for acceptable performance rates, depending on the type of math assignment. With some assignments, such as simple addition or basic multiplication facts, teachers should expect high rates of performance and accuracy. With other assignments, such as long division or simple word problems, teachers should expect much lower rates of performance. For students who are struggling in math, teachers can use games and team competitions to introduce performance rate activities. For example, teachers can give appropriate rewards to students who finish their assigned math problems within a specified period of time. Alternatively, teachers can place students on teams and arrange for team competitions. The teams that finish within the specified time period receive extra points or rewards.

Other Curriculum-Based Assessment Procedures

Curriculum-based assessment of mathematics encompasses a wide range of methods, procedures, and techniques. In addition to the methods just described in detail, other ways in which teachers can obtain informal, curriculum-based assessment data designed to inform the teaching and learning process include the following:

- Teacher-made math tests
- Clinical observation with anecdotal recording
- Diagnostic checklists
- Interviews
- Conferences
- Student notebooks
- Student exhibitions
- Portfolios
- Student self-assessment
- Student reflections

☑ Comprehension Checklist

Special education teachers may select from among several curriculum-based assessment techniques for evaluating the mathematics performance of their students. Because it links assessment directly with instruction, teachers find that curriculum-based assessment is ideal for developing instructional objectives, preparing learning activities, and remediating deficits. Specific techniques include error pattern analysis, diagnostic interviews, and performance measurement using percent correct and performance rate scoring procedures.

Summary

When students require in-depth, diagnostic evaluation in mathematics, special educators may select from among several multiple-skill and single-skill diagnostic tests as well as a variety of curriculum-based evaluation procedures (see Table 16–3 on page 500). Because the various techniques differ in design and purpose, the special educator should select an appropriate procedure on the basis of individual student needs and the purpose of the assessment. Although laws and professional standards mandate use of individually administered, norm-referenced tests for making placement decisions, most teachers prefer less formal procedures for making classroom-based instructional decisions. Regardless of the specific assessment approach, resulting data should help the teacher to place students appropriately, identify specific math problems, and design appropriate remediation activities.

Chapter Review and Application

Multiple Choice

Directions: Read each item carefully. In the blank beside each item, write the letter of the best response. Each question contains only one best answer. Check your answers with the answer key at the end of the book.

____ 1. In general, the number of available diagnostic mathematics tests is _____
    the number of available diagnostic reading tests.
    a. less than
    b. about the same as
    c. more than

____ 2. Measurement, problem solving, money, and time are examples of _____.
    a. content
    b. operations
    c. applications

____ 3. Numeration, fractions, algebra, and geometry are examples of _____.
    a. content
    b. operations
    c. applications

____ 4. The diagnostic math test that includes a measure of attitudes toward
    math is the _____.
    a. *KeyMath Revised*
    b. *Test of Mathematical Abilities-2*
    c. *Enright Diagnostic Inventory of Basic Arithmetic Skills*
    d. *Stanford Diagnostic Mathematics Test*

____ 5. The diagnostic math test that provides supplemental materials including
    remedial activities, worksheets, drills, and games is the _____.
    a. *KeyMath Revised*
    b. *Test of Mathematical Abilities-2*
    c. *Enright Diagnostic Inventory of Basic Arithmetic Skills*
    d. *Stanford Diagnostic Mathematics Test*

____ 6. Which of the following math tests is criterion referenced?
    a. *KeyMath Revised*
    b. *Test of Mathematical Abilities-2*
    c. *Enright Diagnostic Inventory of Basic Arithmetic Skills*
    d. *Stanford Diagnostic Mathematics Test*

____ 7. Which of the following math tests is group administered?
    a. *KeyMath Revised*
    b. *Test of Mathematical Abilities-2*
    c. *Enright Diagnostic Inventory of Basic Arithmetic Skills*
    d. *Stanford Diagnostic Mathematics Test*

____ 8. This type of curriculum-based assessment in mathematics produces a
    written record, making it easy to systematically evaluate mistakes and to
    determine the reasons for the errors.
    a. Error pattern analysis
    b. Performance measurement
    c. Performance rate scoring

___ **9.** This type of curriculum-based assessment in mathematics is ideal for assessing simple computations, multiplication facts, and other math skills that students should complete quickly and accurately.
   a. Error pattern analysis
   b. Performance measurement
   c. Performance rate scoring

___ **10.** The curriculum-based math assessment procedure that includes a diagnostic interview is _____.
   a. error pattern analysis
   b. performance measurement
   c. performance rate scoring

Short Answers

Directions: Review your understanding of the material in this chapter by answering the following short answer items. Compare your responses to the sample answers at the end of the book. Your responses should contain information that is similar to but not exactly the same as the information in the sample answers.

1. Select a specific math skill such as fractions, counting, computation, measurement, money, or time. What are two curriculum-based assessment procedures that you could use to evaluate student performance in the skill you selected? Name and briefly describe how you would use each assessment procedure.
2. Which norm-referenced, individually admininstered math test would you use to assess the math achievement of a fourth-grade student suspected of having a math disability? Give three reasons for selecting this particular test.
3. Why do we use standardized, norm-referenced tests to assess the math skills of students with disabilities? What are three widely used norm-referenced math tests? Why do we use curriculum-based assessment? What are three widely used curriculum-based math assessments?
4. Conduct the analyzing stage of error pattern analysis with the following sample problems. What math error is the student making? What is an appropriate intervention strategy?

1. 8	2. 9	3. 4	4. 3	5. 9	6. 5	7. 9	8. 4	9. 6	10. 3
×6	×7	×7	×9	×3	×4	×2	×6	×8	×8
45	56	28	26	26	20	18	24	45	24

References

Ashlock, R. B. (1998). *Error Patterns in Computation* (7th ed.). Upper Saddle River, NJ: Merrill/Prentice Hall.

Beatty, L. S., Madden, R., Gardner, E. F., & Karlsen, B. (1995). *Stanford Diagnostic Mathematics Test* (4th ed.). San Antonio, TX: Psychological Corporation.

Brown, V. L., Cronin, M. E., & McEntire, E. (1994). *Test of Mathematical Abilities* (2d ed.). Austin, TX: PRO-ED.

Connolly, A. J. (1985). *KeyMath Teach and Practice (TAP)*. Circle Pines, MN: American Guidance Service.

————. (1988). *KeyMath Revised: A Diagnostic Inventory of Essential Mathematics*. Circle Pines, MN: American Guidance Service.

————. (1998). *KeyMath Revised: A Diagnostic Inventory of Essential Mathematics* (normative update). Circle Pines, MN: American Guidance Service.

Connolly, A., Nachtman, W., & Pritchett, E. (1976). *KeyMath Diagnostic Arithmetic Test.* Circle Pines, MN: American Guidance Service.

Enright, B. E. (1983). *Enright Diagnostic Inventory of Basic Arithmetic Skills.* North Billerica, MA: Curriculum Associates.

Gable, R. A., & Coben. (1990). Errors in arithmetic. In R. A. Gable & J. M. Hendrickson (Eds.), *Assessing Students With Special Needs: A Sourcebook for Analyzing and Correcting Errors in Academics.* New York: Longman, 30–45.

Gable, R. A., & Hendrickson, J. M. (1990). Making error analysis work. In R. A. Gable & J. M. Hendrickson (Eds.), *Assessing Students With Special Needs: A Sourcebook for Analyzing and Correcting Errors in Academics.* New York: Longman, 146–53.

Gessell, J. K. (1983). *Diagnostic Mathematics Inventory/Mathematics System.* Monterey, CA: CTB/McGraw-Hill.

Ginsburg, H. P., & Baroody, A. J. (1990). *Test of Early Mathematics Ability-2.* Austin, TX: PRO-ED.

Harcourt Brace Educational Measurement. (1995). *Stanford Diagnostic Mathematics Test* (4th ed.). San Antonio, TX: Author.

Larsen, J. A., & Williams, J. D. (1994). *Review of the KeyMath Revised.* In D. Keyser & R. C. Sweetland (Eds.), *Test Critiques* (vol. X). Austin, TX: PRO-ED.

Reisman, F. K. (1985). *Sequential Assessment of Mathematics Inventories.* San Antonio, TX: Psychological Corporation.

Salvia, J., & Hughes, C. (1990). *Curriculum-Based Assessment: Testing What Is Taught.* New York: Macmillan.

Smith, T., Finn, D., & Dowdy, C. (1993). *Teaching Students With Mild Disabilities.* Fort Worth, TX: Harcourt Brace Jovanovich.

Table 16–3   Review of Mathematics Achievement Tests

Name of Test	Type of Test	Suitable for Individuals Who Are	Brief Description of Test	Purpose of Administering Test
*Diagnostic Mathematics Inventory/ Mathematics System (DMI/MS) (Gessell, 1983)	Criterion-referenced, individually administered assessment system & curriculum guide	K–grade 8	Measures whole numbers, fractions, & decimals, measurement & geometry, problem solving, & special topics	To diagnose mathematics achievement and to develop instructional objectives using a system for matching each test item to a math objective and to practice exercises
Enright Diagnostic Inventory of Basic Arithmetic Skills (Enright, 1983)	Criterion referenced, individually or group administered	Grades 4–adult	Measures computation of whole numbers, fractions, and decimals using four types of tests: tests of basic facts in addition, subtraction, multiplication, and division; wide-range instructional placement tests, skill placement tests, and error analysis skill tests	To determine the exact math skill at which to begin instruction and to provide a clear explanation of computation errors
*KeyMath-Revised: A Diagnostic Inventory of Essential Mathematics (KeyMath-R) (Connolly, 1998)	Norm-referenced, individually administered diagnostic math test	Kindergarten– grade 9	Measures basic concepts, operations, & applications; includes excellent content & valuable supplemental features	To diagnose mathematics achievement, identify strengths & weaknesses, & develop instructional objectives
Sequential Assessment of Mathematics Inventories (SAMI) (Reisman, 1985)	Criterion-referenced, individually administered classroom survey test	K–grade 8	Covers 300 math objectives in eight different strands using three different test activities: pencil-on-paper, oral interview, and concrete representation using manipulative materials	To obtain an in-depth evaluation of math achievement and to provide a profile of student performance in math concepts and skills
Stanford Diagnostic Mathematics Test (4th ed.) (Beatty et al., 1995)	Norm-referenced, group administered screening test	Grades 1–12	Provides six levels with multiple-choice and free-response items for each level	To identify the math achievement levels of groups of students

*Tests marked with asterisks are featured in tables in this chapter.

Table 16–3 *(continued)*

Name of Test	Type of Test	Suitable for Individuals Who Are	Brief Description of Test	Purpose of Administering Test
Test of Early Mathematics Ability-2 (TEMA-2) (Ginsberg & Baroody, 1990)	Norm referenced, individually administered	3–9 years	Measures concepts of relative magnitude, reading & writing numerals, counting skills, number facts, calculation, calculational algorithms, & base-ten concepts	To determine specific strengths & weaknesses, measure progress, evaluate programs, & guide instruction & remediation
Test of Mathematical Abilities-2 (TOMA-2) (Brown, et al., 1994)	Norm referenced, individually administered	Grades 3–12	Measures vocabulary, computation, general information, & story problems	To measure performance in the major skill areas as well as attitude, vocabulary, & general application of mathematics concepts in real life

Assessment of
Written Language

Overview

In this chapter we explore the knowledge base for assessing written language, beginning with the definition of written language and the skills measured by written language tests. Following this introduction, we examine the most widely used, individually administered tests of written expression and spelling. As you learn each test, you will consider the educational uses of the instrument, the administration and scoring procedures, and the technical qualities. Later in the chapter, we investigate curriculum-based assessment procedures for evaluating written language. These include an error analysis procedure for evaluating spelling skills and a written expression profile for assessing writing ability. You will discover how teachers use these informal assessment tools to guide the teaching and learning process and to ensure that they are including relevant written expression tasks in the curriculum.

Objectives

After reading this chapter, you will be prepared to do the following:

- Understand the assessment of written language.
- Understand the subskills measured by tests of written language.
- Consider why we assess the written language of students with special needs.
- Use single-skill tests of written language.
- Develop curriculum-based procedures for assessing spelling.
- Conduct error pattern analysis of spelling.
- Develop curriculum-based procedures for assessing written expression.
- Assess written expression using the written language profile.

Assessing Written Language

The following narrative includes many of the questions teachers have about assessing written language. It also illustrates why there is a growing interest in curriculum-based assessment of written language among teachers of students with special needs.

Ms. Sirkis, a special education teacher of students with behavior disorders, has never formally assessed written language before, but she has heard a lot about written language assessment recently and is wondering how she can do a better job of assessing the written language of her students. First, she asks herself, what exactly is written language assessment, and what are the different kinds of written language assessment? Next, she asks, why assess written language? Can assessment of written language make a difference in learning and teaching? What can it do for her and her students that other assessment methods don't?

After doing some homework on assessing written language, Ms. Sirkis decides she'd like to try a formal, standardized test of written language, the Test of Language Development-3 (TOLD-3), *along with a curriculum-based evaluation procedure. She uses the results from the* TOLD-3 *to develop her own curriculum-based assessment system tailored to the writing levels of her students. Her newly developed system includes a written language profile scoring form based on similar scoring protocols she found in her research. As she begins to implement her curriculum-based assessment system, she still doesn't know exactly how well it will work, but she decides to begin the process and then fine-tune the system as she goes along.*

Definition of Written Language

Written language is the expression of ideas and feelings in written form. Written language subskills in the school curriculum include written expression, spelling, and handwriting. Of these skills, written expression is the most difficult to assess because of the subjectivity involved in measuring the intricacies of writing.

Because written expression is one of the most complex forms of communication in society, many students with special needs have difficulty with writing. Students without proficiency in written language lack a critical skill for academic success in school and for vocational success in the community. However, unlike the wealth of educationally useful procedures available to assess reading and mathematics, relatively few instructionally sound instruments exist for evaluating written language ability.

Teachers usually rely on curriculum-based assessment to evaluate written language. For this reason, this chapter focuses on the various types of curriculum-based assessment most applicable to instructional settings, and also reviews formal assessment instruments for evaluation of written language.

Why Do We Assess the Written Language of Students With Special Needs?

The following anecdote, written by a teacher of students with learning disabilities, illustrates the way many students with special needs feel about writing. For many students even a writing assignment that requires "just a few words" is an overwhelming task.

Student: "How much do we have to write?"
Young: "One well developed paragraph . . . about 100 to 150 words."

FOCUS 17–1

**Why Do We Assess the Written Language
Skills of Students With Special Needs?**

- To identify current levels of performance in writing and spelling
- To determine specific student strengths and weaknesses in writing and
  spelling
- To identify what the student knows and does not know
- To understand the writing strategies a student knows and uses
- To identify priorities for writing skill development
- To plan a student's intervention program
- To help determine instructional approaches
- To monitor the instructional program
- To determine progress in meeting IEP goals

Student: "I CAN'T WRITE THAT MUCH!!!!"
Young: "Well, write for about twenty minutes."
Student: "TWENTY MINUTES!!!!!"
Young: "Well, then . . . just try a few words." (Young, 1993, p. 3)

Because so many students with special needs experience difficulty in learning
how to write well, it is imperative that teachers know how to assess their written expression skills. The primary reason for assessing written expression is to identify
present levels of writing and spelling performance as the basis for designing intervention programs. Assessment provides the teacher with information about specific
strengths and weaknesses as well as what each student knows and does not know
about writing and spelling. Assessment also helps teachers understand the writing
strategies the student knows and uses. This knowledge leads directly to the establish-
ment of priorities for intervention in writing and spelling. Planning an instructional
program in written expression also includes deciding which particular instructional
methods will be the most responsive to the often unique needs of individual students
and groups of students. Finally, assessment of written expression helps teachers monitor the instructional program and determine student progress in meeting IEP goals.
See Focus 17–1 for additional information concerning assessment of language skills
of students with special needs.

Formal Assessment Instruments
for Evaluation of Written Language

To obtain diagnostic information about student performance in written language,
special educators may select from among several formal, standardized tests. These
tests include the multiple-skill tools reviewed in Chapter 14 and the single-skill instruments reviewed in the following section.

Test of Written Language-3

The norm-referenced *Test of Written Language-3 (TOWL-3)* (Hammill & Larsen, 1996) evaluates the written expression skills for students from ages 7 though 17. Designed to pinpoint a student's current level of performance in written expression and to identify types of writing errors, the test helps teachers develop instructional objectives and plan appropriate intervention activities. The *TOWL-3* uses essay analysis (spontaneous) and other evaluation techniques to measure both spontaneous and contrived written expression skills. A summary of the *TOWL-3* appears in Table 17–1. The *TOWL-3* includes the following subtests:

Spontaneous Formats

1. Contextual conventions: Measures capitalization, punctuation, and spelling
2. Contextual language: Measures vocabulary, syntax, and grammar
3. Story construction: Measures plot, character development, and general composition

Contrived Formats

4. Vocabulary: Measures word usage
5. Spelling: Measures ability to form letters into words
6. Style: Measures punctuation and capitalization
7. Logical sentences: Measures ability to write conceptually sound sentences
8. Sentence combining: Measures syntax

Materials for the *TOWL-3*   The *TOWL-3* kit contains an examiner's manual, 25 student response booklets (Form A), 25 student response booklets (Form B), and 50 Profile/Story Scoring Forms. An optional computer scoring system is also available.

Administration and Scoring of the *TOWL-3*   Evaluators may give the *TOWL-3* to individuals or groups, and it takes about 90 minutes to administer. Students complete the spontaneous expression subtests by writing essays based on stimulus pictures.

Table 17–1   *Test of Written Language-3 (TOWL-3)*

Type of Test:	Norm referenced and individually administered
Purpose:	To diagnose written expression
Content Areas:	Spontaneous and contrived expression
Administration Time:	30–45 minutes
Age Levels:	Grades 2–12
Suitable for:	Students with mild disabilities, including learning disabilities and behavior disorders
Scores:	Percentile ranks and standard scores for the total test and the two subtests
In Short:	The *TOWL-3* is a helpful tool for evaluating the written language skills of individuals and groups. The test is useful for classification, placement, and classroom instruction.

For the contrived subtests, the student responds to dictated stimulus words and sentences, corrects illogical sentences, and combines simple sentences into complex ones. Scores derived from the test include percentiles and standard scores for overall, contrived, and spontaneous writing as well as for each subtest.

Technical Characteristics of the *TOWL-3* The *TOWL-3*, which was standardized on a sample of more than 2,000 students living in 26 states, displays adequate reliability and validity for use as a diagnostic tool. The authors provide data to support the internal consistency, test-retest, and interscorer reliability of the *TOWL-3*. The reliability coefficients average in the .80s at most ages. The manual also includes descriptions of several validity studies conducted with the *TOWL-3*.

The *TOWL-3* was designed to detect and eliminate as many sources of cultural, gender, and racial bias as possible. Steps taken to reduce bias included inclusion of targeted demographic groups (i.e., gender, race, social class, and disabled groups), reliability and validity for targeted groups, analysis of item bias, and avoiding time limits, which are thought to be biased against many groups.

Summary of the *TOWL-3* The *TOWL-3*, a norm-referenced measure of written language, is the most widely used tool for assessing written language. The test meets the nationally recognized standards for assessing the presence of deficits in written language.

Test of Written Spelling-Third Edition

The *Test of Written Spelling-Third Edition (TWS-3)* (Larsen & Hammill, 1994) is a norm-referenced measure of spelling proficiency of students from the first through the twelfth grade. Designed to pinpoint a student's current level of performance in spelling and to identify types of spelling errors made by the student, the test helps the teacher develop instructional objectives and plan appropriate intervention activities. The *TWS-3* consists of two subtests: predictable words that follow phonetic rules and unpredictable words that fail to follow regular patterns. A summary of the *TWS-3* appears in Table 17–2.

Materials for the *TWS-3* The test materials consist of a brief manual and a simple scoring sheet. The materials are contained in a small cardboard carton.

Administration and Scoring of the *TWS-3* It takes 15 to 25 minutes to administer the *TWS-3* to individuals or groups of students. The concise administration procedures consist of dictating words arranged in order of increasing difficulty. Both subtests contain 50 words. Scores derived from the test include percentile ranks and standard scores for the total test and for the two subtests. In addition, the scorer graphs the results on a profile to illustrate strengths and weaknesses between the two subtests.

Technical Characteristics of the *TWS-3* The *TWS-3*, which was standardized on a sample of more than 3,800 students living in 15 states, displays sufficient reliability and validity to qualify for use as an instructional and placement tool. Both internal consistency and test-retest reliabilities average in the .90s, and coefficients at this high level provide strong evidence of test score consistency. The manual also reports research data on the content, criterion-related, and construct validities of the *TWS-3*.

Table 17–2   *Test of Written Spelling-3 (TWS-3)*

Type of Test:	Norm referenced and individually or group administered
Purpose:	To diagnose written spelling proficiency
Content Areas:	Predictable and unpredictable words
Administration Time:	15–25 minutes
Age Levels:	Grades 1–12
Suitable for:	Students with mild disabilities, including learning disabilities and behavior disorders
Scores:	Percentile ranks and standard scores for the total test and the subtests
In Short:	Designed to pinpoint performance in spelling and to identify types of spelling errors, the *TWS-3* helps teachers develop instructional objectives and plan appropriate intervention activities.

Summary of the *TWS-3*   The *TWS-3* is a norm-referenced spelling test that provides useful assessment information about overall spelling proficiency and shows whether teachers should emphasize predictable or unpredictable words in spelling instruction.

Written Expression Scale

The *Written Expression Scale (WES)* measures the written language of children and young adults from 5 to 21 years of age. The *WES* is one of three scales that make up the *Oral and Written Language Scales (OWLS)* (Carrow-Woolfolk, 1995). The other two scales, which were reviewed in Chapter 10, are the *Listening Comprehension Scale (LCS)* and the *Oral Expression Scale (OES)*. The *WES* measures three writing skills: use of conventions, including letter formation, spelling, capitalization, and punctuation; use of linguistic forms, including modifiers, phrases, and sentence structure; and ability to communicate meaningfully, including appropriate content, coherence, unity, word choice, and details. A summary of the *WES* appears in Table 17–3.

Materials for the *Written Expression Scale*   The *Written Expression Scale* is available in a kit that includes a manual, a package of 25 record forms, a package of 25 student response booklets, and an administration card. A computer software scoring program, the *Written Expression Assist for DOS, Macintosh, and Windows,* is available separately. The software provides a score profile, a score narrative, and a descriptive analysis.

Administration and Scoring of the *Written Expression Scale*   It takes approximately 40 minutes to administer the *WES* to individuals or small groups. The evaluator asks the student to complete various writing tasks that are similar to writing activities found in a classroom. Some items have pictures or print, and others are presented orally. Students take the test by writing their responses directly in a response booklet.

Table 17–3   *Written Expression Scale (WES)*

Type of Test:	Norm referenced, administered individually or in small groups
Purpose:	To diagnose written language skills
Content Areas:	Use of conventions, linguistic forms, and ability to communicate meaningfully
Administration Time:	Approximately 40 minutes
Age Levels:	5–21 years
Suitable for:	Students with mild disabilities, including learning disabilities and behavior disorders
Scores:	Age- or grade-based standard scores, percentiles, NCEs, stanines, and age or grade equivalents
In Short:	The *Written Expression Scale* measures the writing skills of children and young adults from 5–21 years of age. The *WES* features a comprehensive sample of written language skills covering a wide age range.

The test manual provides detailed scoring rules along with samples of actual responses. The scoring booklet includes abbreviated scoring rules for quick reference during item-by-item scoring. Evaluators can report *WES* results as age- or grade-based standard scores, percentiles, NCEs, stanines, and age or grade equivalents. The test also provides score comparison procedures for analyzing differences among scores and a score profile that gives a visual representation of performance.

Technical Characteristics of the *Written Expression Scale*   The *WES* was co-normed with the *Listening Comprehension and Oral Expression Scales* using a national standardization sample of 1,795 children and youth. The sample was stratified using the 1991 Current Population Survey data for the demographic variables of gender, race, ethnicity, region, and mother's level of education. The manual reports high internal consistency and test-retest reliability coefficients for the scales. Several validity investigations were conducted using the *WES*, including nine concurrent validity studies and eight clinical studies with 850 subjects.

Summary of the *Written Expression Scale*   Because it provides a detailed sampling of written language and covers a wide age span, the *WES* is valuable in clinical and school settings. The instrument is useful to clinicians, psychologists, and teachers who need accurate test scores and detailed diagnostic information about the written expression skills of students.

Test of Written Expression

The *Test of Written Expression (TOWE)* (McGhee et al., 1995) is a norm-referenced tool for assessing the writing achievement of students from age 6 through 14. The instrument

Table 17–4 *Test of Written Expression*

Type of Test:	Norm referenced, administered individually or in small groups
Purpose:	To diagnose writing achievement
Content Areas:	Ideation, vocabulary, grammar, capitalization, punctuation, and spelling
Administration Time:	Approximately 60 minutes
Age Levels:	6–14 years
Suitable for:	Students with mild disabilities, including learning disabilities and behavior disorders
Scores:	Overall writing standard score, overall writing percentile rank, item analysis, and evaluation of an original writing sample
In Short:	The *Test of Written Expression* measures writing achievement using two methods of assessment: administering 76 items that measure important writing skills or giving a starter storyline to the student, who completes the story to make an original writing sample.

provides two separate assessment methods for measuring a comprehensive set of writing skills, including ideation, vocabulary, grammar, capitalization, punctuation, and spelling. A summary of the *TOWE* appears in Table 17–4.

Materials for the *Test of Written Expression* *TOWE* materials include an examiner's manual, a set of 25 profile/record forms, and a set of 25 student booklets. The materials are available as a complete kit or separately.

Administration and Scoring of the *Test of Written Expression* The *TOWE* can be given to individuals or to groups using two assessment methods. The first method involves administering 76 individual items that measure different writing skills. With this method, diagnosticians can obtain an overall writing score and conduct an item analysis to identify specific strengths and weaknesses. The second method uses a starter storyline that the student completes to make a complete story. This provides an original writing sample for evaluating performance in specific skill areas and for obtaining an overall score based on vocabulary, spelling, capitalization, punctuation, and grammar.

Technical Characteristics of the *Test of Written Expression* The test was standardized with a normative sample of 1,226 students from 21 states. The manual provides evidence of the consistency of *TOWE* scores based on internal consistency, test-retest, and interscorer reliability studies. The manual reports three types of validity investigations: content validity, criterion-related validity, and construct validity. Criterion-related validity was established by correlating *TOWE* scores with writing scores from other tests, including the *Test of Written Language* and the *Diagnostic Achievement Battery*.

Construct validity was investigated by comparing *TOWE* scores with scores from aptitude and achievement tests. Although more study is needed, these investigations provide initial evidence that this instrument is useful as a tool for measuring writing achievement.

Summary of the *Test of Written Expression* The *Test of Written Expression* evaluates the writing achievement of students from age 6 through 14 using two assessment procedures. One procedure involves administering 76 items that measure written expression ability, and the other involves having the student write a complete story from a story starter. This completed story provides a writing sample that can be used independently to obtain a norm-referenced assessment or as a component in a student's portfolio.

Test of Early Written Language, Second Edition

The norm-referenced *Test of Early Written Language, Second Edition, (TEWL-2)* (Hresko et. al., 1996) evaluates the emerging written language skills of youngsters from age 3 through 11. The *TEWL-2* measures skills that relate directly to the learning activities of young schoolchildren, including basic and contextual writing. A summary of the *TEWL-2* appears in Table 17–5.

Materials for the *Test of Early Written Language, Second Edition* The *TEWL-2* test kit includes an examiner's manual, 10 student workbooks each for Form A and Form B, and 10 profile/record booklets each for Form A and Form B.

Administration and Scoring of the *Test of Early Written Language, Second Edition* The basic writing subtest of the *TEWL-2* measures spelling, capitalization, punctuation, sentence construction, and metacognitive knowledge. The contextual writing subtest measures story format, cohesion, thematic maturity, ideation, and story structure. *TEWL-2* scores include standard score quotients, NCEs, percentiles, and age equivalents.

Table 17–5 *Test of Early Written Language, Second Edition (TEWL-2)*

Type of Test:	Norm referenced and administered individually
Purpose:	To identify emerging written language skills
Content Areas:	Basic writing and contextual writing
Administration Time:	45 minutes
Age Levels:	3–11 years
Suitable for:	Students with mild disabilities, including learning disabilities and behavior disorders
Scores:	Standard scores, NCEs, percentiles, and age equivalents
In Short:	The *TEWL-2*, a useful tool for measuring the emerging writing skills of young children, profiles strengths and weaknesses and provides directions for interpretation and instruction.

Technical Characteristics of the *Test of Early Written Language, Second Edition*   The *TEWL-2* was standardized on a population of more than 1,400 children from 33 states. The consistency of the *TEWL-2* scores was examined with studies of the internal consistency and test-retest reliability. The *TEWL-2* manual also reports content, criterion-related, and construct validity research to support the validity of the instrument. This research is promising, but more studies are needed, especially validity studies with the youngest age groups.

Summary of the *Test of Early Written Language, Second Edition*   Because of the increasing emphasis on educational intervention with young children, a need exists for tests like the *TEWL-2*. Although it could benefit from further development and research in response to technical limitations, the *TEWL-2* is a useful tool for assessing the written language of young children. *TEWL-2* results can be used to plan intervention activities for individual children, measure child progress, and evaluate writing skills programs for young children.

☑ Comprehension Checklist

Tests of written language provide teachers, clinicians, and psychologists with standardized measures useful for identifying, diagnosing, and measuring the progress of students with special needs. Some of these tests are survey instruments that measure a range of skills for identifying overall achievement. For example, the *Test of Written Expression* measures ideation, vocabulary, grammar, capitalization, punctuation, and spelling. Other tests focus on specific skills. Examples include the *Test of Written Spelling-3,* which pinpoints spelling performance and identifies specific types of spelling errors, and the *Test of Early Written Language, Second Edition,* which is a 42-item scale that measures emerging writing skills of young children.

Curriculum-Based Assessment of Written Language

Formal assessment is a product-oriented type of testing that centers around numerical outcomes, including scores and standardized results. In contrast, curriculum-based assessment of written language is less structured and more flexible. It focuses on process-oriented, criterion-referenced results that relate directly to daily instruction. Curriculum-based assessment includes observations, informal inventories, and teacher-constructed tests. In addition, there are specific informal assessment procedures for evaluating spelling and written expression.

Observations

Teacher observations of student behavior, also called *clinical observations,* help to identify the strategies students use to complete written language tasks as well as determine the attention span and frustration level of students. Although informal and subjective, the observations of experienced teachers often yield vital assessment information for creating remediation programs and intervention activities. Focus 17–2 discusses the link between instruction and assessment.

FOCUS 17–2

Linking Instruction With Assessment

Teachers have a variety of available options for linking instruction in written language to assessment of written language. The following list includes many ideas for gathering assessment information that is connected directly with classroom instruction. The list also includes strategies for giving feedback to students and parents in ways that occur as a regular part of classroom instruction.

- Using curriculum-based assessment procedures
- Using probes
- Giving teacher-made tests
- Conducting error analysis
- Developing checklists
- Distributing questionnaires
- Conducting interviews
- Holding conferences
- Reviewing work samples
- Grading writing journals and notebooks
- Evaluating writing portfolios
- Giving oral feedback
- Giving written feedback
- Holding discussions with students and parents

Informal Inventories and Tests

Many informal inventories and tests are available, including teacher-constructed measures, commercial inventories, and instruments developed by local school systems and state education agencies. Teacher-made inventories and tests include classroom spelling quizzes, designed to identify student mastery of instructional content, and teacher-created checklists of written expression skills. The widely used *Brigance Diagnostic Inventories* are commercially available inventories that offer several useful subtests for evaluating written language. Available subtests include spelling, grammar and mechanics, and reference skills for the elementary grades, and language arts and communication skills at the secondary level. Informal diagnostic tests like the *Brigance Diagnostic Inventories* serve as both assessment and curriculum guides.

Curriculum-Based Assessment of Spelling

Most of the time when teachers score spelling tests, they simply mark the incorrect words and assign a grade based on a percent correct score. This common grading practice is appropriate in many instructional situations; however, it fails to provide the kind of diagnostic information that teachers need with students who have severe spelling problems. Moreover, it can lead to inaccurate conclusions about the reasons for errors. When teachers need more detailed assessment information, they use more complex curriculum-based assessment procedures.

Comprehensive curriculum-based assessment of spelling involves identifying the overall level of spelling achievement, determining specific strengths and weaknesses, and evaluating spelling error patterns. To achieve this level of assessment, Ariel (1992) recommended the following informal procedure for testing of spelling ability. Teachers can use this informal procedure with individual students or an entire class.

1. Select a list of 30 to 50 words based on any graded list at the grade level of the child or the class.
2. Administer the spelling test.
3. Score the test and tabulate the results. If used with a class, note the lowest 20%.
4. Have the pupils define the words they misspelled. Omit unfamiliar words because they are not in the children's vocabulary.
5. Have the pupils spell any remaining words orally. Keep a record of the spelling, noting the syllabification, phonic use, and speech or hearing difficulties.
6. Compare the original spelling to note differences in oral and written responses.
7. Ask the children to study words missed (for about 10 minutes), and observe their methods of study.
8. Analyze errors and incorporate information from the data obtained from other sources.
9. Draw conclusions about the nature of the spelling problem. Plan educational strategies to overcome the difficulties.
10. Discuss the analysis and teaching plan with the pupil. Provide for pupils to see progress. (p. 448)

Analyzing Spelling Errors   Diagnostic analysis of spelling errors provides the details necessary to develop accurate remediation activities. Steps in the error analysis process include collecting a sample of spelling errors, conducting a diagnostic interview with the student, classifying the errors, determining a corrective strategy, implementing the strategy, and monitoring student progress (Hendrickson & Gable, 1990).

Teachers may record the results of error analysis using a form like the sample spelling error analysis chart in Figure 17–1. This chart, developed from a list of typical student spelling errors by Ariel (1992), places the most common error types in categories and displays the results from analysis of the writing sample that appears in Figure 17–2.

The *Spellmaster Assessment and Teaching System*

The *Spellmaster Assessment and Teaching System* (Greenbaum, 1987) is an example of a commercial error pattern analysis spelling test. The *Spellmaster,* a criterion-referenced test for analyzing spelling errors and developing sequenced instructional remediation, includes eight tests of phonetically regular words, eight irregular words tests, eight homonym tests, and eight entry-level tests. Field-tested with more than 2,500 students, the *Spellmaster* is appropriate for use with students in special education as well as students with limited English proficiency. The *Spellmaster* materials include a manual, a package of student answer sheets, and pads of scoring forms for each diagnostic level.

Figure 17–1   Spelling Error Analysis Chart

Student _____   Teacher _____   Date _____

Description of the Spelling Sample _____

Description of Math Problems Analyzed _____

Total Words _____   Misspelled Words _____   Percent of Correctly Spelled Words _____

Error Category	Error Type	# of Errors	Remediation Plan
Omission errors	Omission of a pronounced letter (e.g., "say" for "stay")	//	
	Omission of a silent letter (e.g., "ofen" for "often")		
	Omission of double letters (e.g., "super" for "supper")		
Substitution errors	Consonant sound confusion (e.g., *t* for *d*, *f* for *v*, *sh* for *ch*, *s* for *z*)	///	
	Vowel sound confusion	⊮⊮ ⊮⊮ ⊪⊪⊪	Focus on vowel sound/sight match in the most common 3-, 4-, 5-letter words from the Hillerich's list of 100 most frequently used words
	Phonetic substitution for a word (e.g., "obay" for "obey")		
	Word substitution ("gals" for "girls")		
Addition/insertion errors	Addition of unnecessary sounds and letters	⫙⫙	
	Addition by doubling ("super-vision" for "supervision")		
	Unnecessary addition of *ed*		
	Addition of unnecessary suffixes		
Confusion of digraphs	Such as "wead" for "weed"		
Phonetic spelling of nonphonetic words	Such as "sum" for "some"		
Confusion between homonyms	Words with similar pronunciation (e.g., "except" for "accept")		
Sequencing errors	One letter out of sequence (e.g., "barn" for "bran")	/	
Sound letter reversals	Such as "form" for "from"		

Notes _____

_____

Figure 17-2 Student Writing Sample

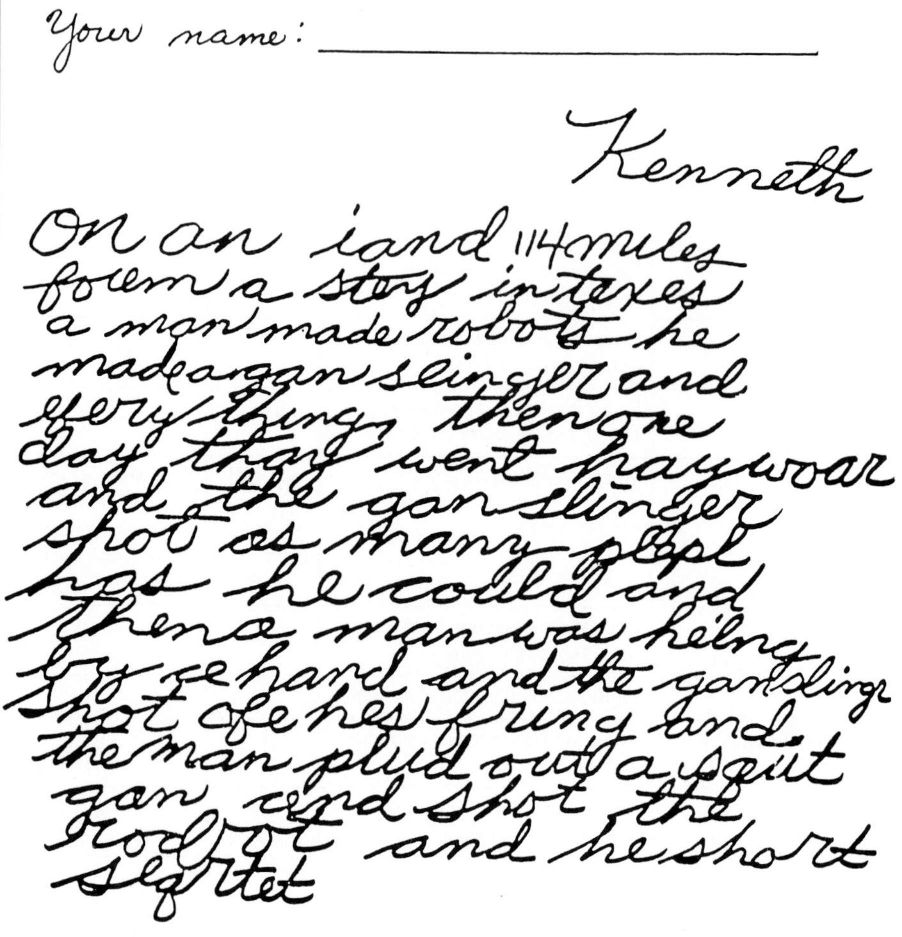
Your name: Kenneth

On an iand 114 miles
foem a stoy in texes
a man made robots he
madeagan sleinger and
evry thing then one
day thay went haywoar
and the gan slinger
shot as many peopl
has he could and
then a man was helng
by he hand and the ganslingr
shot ofe hes fring and
the man plud out a sqit
gan and shot the
rodbt and he short
sqrtet

On an island 114 miles from a city in Texas a man made robots. He made a gun slinger and everything. Then one day they went haywire and the gun slinger shot as many people as he could and then a man was hanging by a hand and the gun slinger shot off his finger and the man pulled out a squirt gun and shot the robot and he short circuited.

Total words: 70 Misspelled: 22 Correctly spelled: 68 %

Grade: 6 IQ: 97 Age: 13 years 1 month

Curriculum-Based Assessment of Written Expression

Informal assessment of written expression skills involves measurement of several elements. Raiser (1996) defined these elements as follows:

Fluency	The quantity of written output as measured by the number of words written in a specific time period.
Average Thought Unit	A measure of writing maturity and complexity based on syntax.
Vocabulary Diversity	The originality, maturity, and variety of words used in writing.
Structure	The mechanical aspects of writing, including capitalization, punctuation, and language usage.
Organization	The coherence of a composition as evidenced by the quality of the narrative, the essay, and the story.

A profile developed by Raiser (1996) for assessing these written language components appears in Figure 17–3. Instructions for using the written language profile appear in Figure 17–4. Teachers can use this curriculum-based assessment tool to guide teaching and learning. The profile provides a way to carefully analyze written language abilities so that teachers can focus instructional time teaching students what they need to know. A list of the 100 most common words, which is used in completing the written language profile, appears in Figure 17–5.

☑ Comprehension Checklist

The curriculum-based strategies that provide assessment information about written language include observations, informal inventories, and teacher-constructed tests. Teachers routinely evaluate written language using informal procedures such as grading class writing assignments, giving weekly spelling tests, and completing informal checklists of written language skills. When teachers need even more detailed assessment information, they often rely on error analysis procedures. Error analysis, using representative samples of student work, can be highly useful in diagnosing spelling deficits. Likewise, teachers rely on various forms of analysis to evaluate written composition samples. These include measuring fluency, calculating average thought units, evaluating vocabulary diversity, rating organization, and identifying structural errors. The next chapter, which deals with portfolio assessment, also provides useful information regarding curriculum-based evaluation of written language. In fact, most of the procedures for portfolio assessment can be applied directly to the assessment of written language.

Summary

Assessment of written language should guide the teaching and learning process. Several types of assessment instruments and procedures are available to achieve this goal (see Table 17–6, p. 526). When special educators need formal norm-referenced assessment information, they may select from among several multiple-skill and single-skill tests that measure writing, spelling, and handwriting skills. These include screening tests as well as comprehensive diagnostic instruments. The norm-referenced tools yield vital assessment

Figure 17–3 Written Language Profile

Name _____   Teacher _____

Age _____   Grade _____   Date _____

To obtain the best scores, analyze three samples over a 2–3 week time period; three 5–10 minute samples work well. Use the same time for each writing session, and repeat the analysis midyear and at year end to chart growth.

Composition	Score	Notes and Target Skills
1. Fluency (word count) Sum of the words per minute from each sample ÷ by the number of samples = fluency		
2. Average Thought Unit Total words − garbles ÷ T-units = average thought unit		
3. Vocabulary Diversity Number of uncommon words ÷ by the total number of words = vocabulary diversity		
4. Organization: Narrative 1 − 5 rating scale (1 = lowest rating, 5 = highest rating)		
5. Organization: Story 1 − 5 rating scale (1 = lowest rating, 5 = highest rating)		
6. Organization: Essay 1 − 5 rating scale (1 = lowest rating, 5 = highest rating)		
7. Structure: Capitalization Count the total number of capitalization errors and note error patterns.		
8. Structure: Punctuation Count the number of punctuation errors and note error patterns.		
9. Structure: Language Usage Count the number of language usage errors and note error patterns.		

Comments _____

_____

_____

Figure 17-4   Instructions for the Written Language Profile

The Written Language Profile is an informal assessment of student abilities intended to guide instructional planning. Through careful analysis of written language abilities, teachers can spend instructional time teaching students exactly what they need to know. The profile will be most effective in classrooms where writing is taking place on a regular basis, preferably daily because effective writing requires frequent practice.

Collecting Samples

Collect three samples over a period of 2–3 weeks to get an accurate measure. Samples should be 75–100 words long; three 5- to 10-minute timed samples work well. Young writers and less experienced writers need the longer time.

Profile Analysis Procedures

1. MEASURE FLUENCY

If you use periodic timed writings, you can measure fluency, which is the number of words written over time. With daily practice in 5–10-minute timed writings, you can expect the number of words to increase. It's easier to compute words per minute if you use the same time each day.

Have students count the words written each day, and write this number at the top of their papers before they turn them in. Then they can chart their own increases on their graphs (e.g., "Words I Wrote in 10 Minutes").

Procedure for Measuring Fluency

a. Count the total number of words (TW). Ignore punctuation and count all words that make sense. Exclude garbles that are incomplete words, conversational asides, false starts, redundancies, or words that do not make sense in context. Subtract garbles from total words (TW).
b. Ignore misspelled words. Try very hard to use context to decipher invented spellings before counting strange-looking words as garbles. With practice, you will become better at decoding unusual spellings.
c. Count names and numbers as one word (e.g., John Paul is one word; 114 is one word). Count compound words written separately as two words (e.g., *every thing* = two words).
d. Teach your students to routinely count the number of words they write and to put the number at the top of the front page of their papers.
e. Divide the TW by the number of minutes written to obtain the number of words per minute (word count). For example, if a student writes 100 words in 10 minutes, then the words per minute is 10: 100 (TW) ÷ 10 (minutes of writing) = 10 words per minute.
f. If you use more than one writing sample, add the number of words per minute from each sample and divide by the number of samples to obtain the average words per minute.

2. CALCULATE AVERAGE THOUGHT UNITS

Average thought units measure writing maturity and complexity based on the syntax of the piece. Syntax is the way words are put together in phrases, clauses, or sentences to make complete thoughts. The formula is:

$$\text{Total Words} \div \text{T-units} = \text{Average Thought Units}$$

Figure 17–4 *(continued)*

Procedure for Calculating Average Thought Units

a. Count the total number of words written using the procedure outlined in procedure for fluency.

b. Count the number of T-units present. A T-unit is the shortest grammatically correct segment that makes a complete thought. When counting T-units, ignore punctuation (many of your students won't use it anyway) and ignore spelling. Do not count garbles, which are incomplete sentences, conversational asides, false starts, redundancies, and words that don't make sense. Try to decipher spelling before counting strangely spelled words as garbles. When in doubt because of handwriting errors, give credit. Ignore "ands" that connect complete thoughts but include "ands" in the Total Word count. For example, the following sentence contains 14 total words and three T-units: "The dog is big/ and the cat is small/ and the rat is smaller/."

c. Divide the Total Words by the number of T-units present. The example contains 14 words and 3 T-units. Therefore, the Average Thought Unit is 4.6. Calculate this as follows: 14 (Total Words) ÷ 3 (T-units) = 4.6 (Average Thought Units)

Interpreting the Average Thought Unit Score

Longer T-units indicate more complex writing. As sentences become more complex, T-units grow very slowly. Expect less than one unit of growth each year. T-unit averages of fewer than 9 words indicate immature writing.

Use the following T-unit averages as benchmarks: 4th graders—8.6 words; 8th graders—11.5 words; 12th graders—14.4 words; 6th and 7th graders with learning disabilities—8.6 words. You may also develop your own benchmarks by analyzing a collection of writing samples from your students.

Teach your students to count T-units. They will learn to recognize complete thoughts and sentence fragments quicker this way than they will with a worksheet. It's also good practice with averaging and decimals; therefore, let them use calculators.

3. MEASURE VOCABULARY DIVERSITY

Vocabulary diversity is the variety of words used in written expression as measured by the percentage of diverse or uncommon words in a composition. Writing should become more original, mature, and diverse as students develop their written expression skills. The formula is:

Number of uncommon words (UW) ÷ Total Words = Vocabulary Diversity

Procedure for Calculating Vocabulary Diversity

a. Count all uncommon words. These are words not on the 100 Most Common Words list (Hillerich, 1978) that appears in Figure 17-5. Count uncommon words used more than once each time they are used.

b. Count the total words in the writing sample.

c. Divide the number of uncommon words by the total words to obtain the vocabulary diversity (percentage of uncommon words).

Interpreting the Vocabulary Diversity Score

The 100 Most Common Words make up 60% of words that students use in writing in grades 2–6. Uncommon words make up 40% of words used. A score above 40% indicates higher writing development. Students can learn to do this analysis.

Figure 17–4   *(continued)*

4. RATE THE ORGANIZATION: NARRATIVE

A narrative is the type of composition that tells an event or a story. Rate the narrative quality of the sample by answering the following questions: Is the piece clearly focused? Is it logically sequenced? Does it have a definite beginning, middle, and end? Does it make sense? Use rating scale scoring with a range of 1 to 5 to obtain a narrative score. A rating of 1 indicates a poor narrative. A rating of 5 indicates a superior narrative.

5. RATE THE ORGANIZATION: STORY

A story is an account of a happening or group of happenings. Rate the quality of the story by answering the following questions: Are the characters well developed? Is the setting well developed? Does the story include a problem to solve? Does the story present a problem resolution? Use rating scale scoring with a range of 1 to 5 to obtain a story score. A rating of 1 indicates a poor story; a rating of 5 indicates a superior story.

6. RATE THE ORGANIZATION: ESSAY

An essay is a composition on a specific subject. Rate the quality of the essay by answering the following questions: Do the paragraphs contain lead/topic sentences? Does the essay provide supporting details? Does the essay include a conclusion? Use rating scale scoring with a range of 1 to 5 to obtain an essay score. A rating of 1 indicates a poor essay; a rating of 5 indicates a superior essay.

7. MEASURE THE STRUCTURE: CAPITALIZATION

Identify capitalization errors including sentence beginnings, proper names, important words in titles, and abbreviations. Score capitalization by counting the number of capitalization errors, and look for patterns of errors.

8. MEASURE THE STRUCTURE: PUNCTUATION

Identify punctuation errors including periods, question marks, exclamation points, commas, semicolons, and quotations (e.g., "I can go," said Tommy). Score punctuation by counting the number of punctuation errors, and look for patterns of errors.

9. MEASURE THE LANGUAGE USAGE

Identify language usage errors including subject and verb agreement, object agreement, verb tense consistency throughout the piece, appropriate pronoun usage, and other errors. Score language usage by counting the number of usage errors, and look for patterns of errors.

Figure 17–5   100 Most Common Words

> The 100 most common words are found on most basic sight word lists; they are the words children and adults need most often in their writing. If your students know how to spell these 100 words, they will know 60% of all the words they need to know how to spell when writing about their own self-selected topics.
>
> When students learn to spell these words, they will then need to worry only about the other 40% they need to spell in their writing. Students should keep this list, the Dolch sight word list, and their own personal list in their writing process folios for reference.
>
> The words *I, and,* and *the* account for 11.8% most commonly used words. Add the words *a* and *to* and you have 18.2% of the words. Add *was, in, it, of, my,* and *you* for 26.1%. The following list of 100 words make up 60% of all the words used by the children in Hillerich's study (1978). These words came from the free writing (unassigned writing) of regular education students in grades 2–6.
>
> **100 MOST COMMON WORDS IN ABC ORDER**
>
> | | | | |
> |---|---|---|---|
> | a | for | mother | them |
> | about | from | my | then |
> | after | get | no | there |
> | all | go | not | they |
> | am | got | now | things |
> | an | had | of | think |
> | and | have | on | this |
> | are | he | one | time |
> | around | her | or | to |
> | as | him | our | too |
> | at | his | out | two |
> | back | home | over | up |
> | be | house | people | us |
> | because | I | put | very |
> | but | if | not | was |
> | by | in | now | we |
> | came | into | said | well |
> | can | is | saw | went |
> | could | it | school | were |
> | day | just | see | what |
> | did | know | she | when |
> | didn't | like | so | who |
> | do | little | some | will |
> | don't | man | that | with |
> | down | me | the | would |

information for making identification, staffing, and placement decisions and for developing and evaluating intervention programs. In instructional settings, teachers often rely on less formal, curriculum-based measures of composition and spelling, including error pattern analysis procedures, teacher observations, inventories, tests, and checklists. Some of these criterion-referenced assessments, including error analysis, rely on student work samples. Assessment using actual student work directly links assessment with instruction. This linkage is especially helpful when teachers need to develop specialized remediation programs for students with severe written language deficits.

Chapter Review and Application

Multiple Choice

Directions: Read each item carefully. In the blank beside each item, write the letter of the best response. Each question contains only one best answer. Check your answers with the answer key at the end of the book.

_____ 1. Which test measures use of conventions, linguistic forms, and ability to communicate meaningfully?
   a. *Written Expression Scale*
   b. *Test of Written Expression*
   c. *Test of Written Language-3*
   d. *Test of Written Spelling*

_____ 2. Which test measures spontaneous and contrived expression?
   a. *Written Expression Scale*
   b. *Test of Written Expression*
   c. *Test of Written Language-3*
   d. *Test of Written Spelling*

_____ 3. Which test measures ideation, vocabulary, grammar, capitalization, punctuation, and spelling?
   a. *Written Expression Scale*
   b. *Test of Written Expression*
   c. *Test of Written Language-3*
   d. *Test of Written Spelling*

_____ 4. When teachers informally measure the quantity of written output, they are assessing _____.
   a. organization
   b. vocabulary diversity
   c. structure
   d. average thought unit
   e. fluency

_____ 5. When teachers measure writing maturity and complexity based on syntax, thoughts, and sentences, they are assessing _____.
   a. organization
   b. vocabulary diversity
   c. structure
   d. average thought unit
   e. fluency

_____ **6.** When teachers measure the originality, maturity, and variety of words used in writing, they are assessing _____.
    a. organization
    b. vocabulary diversity
    c. structure
    d. average thought unit
    e. fluency

_____ **7.** When teachers measure the mechanical aspects of writing, including capitalization, punctuation, and language usage, they are assessing _____.
    a. organization
    b. vocabulary diversity
    c. structure
    d. average thought unit
    e. fluency

_____ **8.** When teachers measure the coherence of a composition as evidenced by the quality of the narrative, the essay, and the story, they are assessing _____.
    a. organization
    b. vocabulary diversity
    c. structure
    d. average thought unit
    e. fluency

_____ **9.** The process of measuring vocabulary diversity involves counting the _____.
    a. garbles divided by T-units
    b. number of uncommon words
    c. words per minute
    d. capitalization and punctuation

_____ **10.** The process of measuring fluency involves counting the _____.
    a. garbles divided by T-units
    b. number of uncommon words
    c. words per minute
    d. capitalization and punctuation

Short Answers

Directions: Review your understanding of the material in this chapter by answering the following short answer items. Compare your responses with the sample answers at the end of the book. Your responses should contain information that is similar to but not exactly the same as the information in the sample answers.

1. Explain how curriculum-based assessment tools (such as the *Written Language Profile* and the *Spelling Error Analysis Chart* that appear in the chapter) connect assessment of written language with instruction in written language.
2. Read the following writing sample that Alisha, a fourth-grade student, wrote in 15 minutes. Use the *Written Language Profile* in the chapter to analyze her writing.

My Grandmother

My grandmother is a strong black lady who marched with Dr. Martin Luther King back in the 60's. She was at that time pregnant with my father and have two young daughter at home. My grandmother spent time in jail for this march, but she never gave up her right to speech. My grandmother raises five children and worked an 8 hour job. She never let them go hunger or dirty and she was alway there to make sure they was on their best behavior. My grandmother is still alive and well. But she can not do the things she like to do for very long without getting try. Doing her time traveling with my grandfather in the navy my grandmother would travel with her children every where. I love you my grandmother very much.

3. Identify three norm-referenced, individually administered tests of written language appropriate for comprehensive diagnostic assessment of the written language skills of an elementary student with special needs. Which of these three instruments would you use? Why?

4. What are the advantages and the disadvantages of assessing the written language of students with special needs using standardized, norm-referenced tests? Using curriculum-based assessment?

References

Ariel, A. (1992). *Education of Children and Adolescents With Learning Disabilities.* New York: Merrill/Macmillan.

Carrow-Woolfolk, E. (1995). *Oral and Written Language Scales.* Circle Pines, MN: American Guidance Service.

Greenbaum, C. R. (1987). *Spellmaster Assessment and Teaching System.* Austin, TX: PRO-ED.

Hammill, D. D., & Larsen, S. C. (1996). *Test of Written Language-3.* Austin, TX: PRO-ED.

Hillerich, R. L. (1978). *A Writing Vocabulary of Elementary Children.* (Eric Document Reproduction Service No. ED 161 084.)

Hendrickson, M. J., & Gable, R. (1990). Errors in spelling. In R. A. Gable & J. M. Hendrickson (Eds.), *Assessing Students With Special Needs: A Sourcebook for Analyzing and Correcting Errors in Academics.* New York: Longman, 78–88.

Hresko, W., Herron, S. R., & Peak, P. K. (1996). *Test of Early Written Language* (2d ed.). Austin, TX: PRO-ED.

Larsen, S. C., & Hammill, D. D. (1994). *Test of Written Spelling-3 (TWS-3).* Austin, TX: PRO-ED.

McGhee, R., Bryant, B., Larsen, S., & Rivera, D. (1995). *Test of Written Expression (TOWE).* Austin, TX: PRO-ED.

Raiser, L. (1996). *Written Language Profile.* Unpublished manuscript, University of North Florida, Jacksonville.

Young, G. M. (1993). Images. In K. Gill (Ed.), *Process and Portfolios in Writing Instruction.* Urbana, IL: National Council of Teachers of English, 3–9.

Table 17–6 Review of Written Language Tests

Name of Test	Type of Test	Suitable for Individuals Who Are	Brief Description of Test	Purpose of Administering Test
*Spellmaster Assessment and Teaching System (Greenbaum, 1987)	Criterion referenced, individually administered	In special education, as well as students with limited English proficiency	Includes eight tests of phonetically regular words, eight irregular words tests, eight homonym tests, and eight entry-level tests	To analyze spelling errors and to develop sequenced instructional remediation
*Test of Early Written Language, Second Edition (TEWL-2) (Hresko et al., 1996)	Norm referenced, individually administered	3–11 years	Measures basic writing and contextual writing	To identify the emerging written language skills of young children
*Test of Written Expression (TOWE) (McGhee et al., 1995)	Norm referenced, administered individually or in small groups	6–14 years	Measures ideation, vocabulary, grammar, capitalization, punctuation, and spelling using a 76-item test, or a starter storyline given to the student, who completes the story to make an original writing sample	To diagnose writing achievement
*Test of Written Language-3 (TOWL-3) (Hammill & Larsen, 1996)	Norm referenced, administered individually or in groups	7–17 years	Measures spontaneous and contrived expression	To evaluate the performance of students with writing deficits
*Test of Written Spelling-3 (TWS-3) (Larsen & Hammill, 1994)	Norm referenced, individually or group administered	Grades 1–12	Measures predictable and unpredictable words	To pinpoint performance in spelling and to identify types of spelling errors to help teachers develop instructional objectives and plan appropriate intervention activities
*Written Expression Scale (WES): one of three scales that make up the Oral and Written Language Scales (OWLS) (Carrow-Woolfolk, 1995)	Norm referenced, administered individually or in small groups	5–21 years	Measures conventions, linguistic forms, and ability to communicate meaningfully	To obtain a comprehensive sample of written language skills covering a wide age range

*Tests marked with asterisks are featured in tables in this chapter.

CHAPTER 18

Portfolio Assessment

Overview

In this chapter we investigate the processes for using student portfolios as assessment tools. Our study begins with a description of portfolios, which includes an explanation of the portfolio concept, an examination of the growing interest in portfolio assessment, a review of the advantages and disadvantages of portfolio assessment, and a discussion of portfolios for students with disabilities. Next we examine procedures for planning, building, and using portfolios in ways that ensure reliable appraisal of student performance. Later in the chapter we examine specific portfolio assessment processes, including scoring systems and reporting procedures. Finally we consider portfolio conferences that provide opportunities for review, reflective discussion, and student self-assessment.

Objectives

After reading this chapter, you will be prepared to do the following:

- Implement the portfolio concept.
- Administer portfolio assessment.
- Use process and product portfolios.
- Understand advantages and disadvantages of portfolio assessment.
- Develop portfolios for students with special needs.
- Develop portfolio contents and materials.
- Create a portfolio management system.
- Consider the key reliability considerations of portfolio assessment.
- Understand the connection between portfolio and performance assessment.
- Use holistic and analytical scoring rubrics.
- Use external and internal scoring protocols.
- Integrate student self-assessment in portfolio evaluation.
- Hold individual portfolio conferences.
- Direct peer and small-group portfolio conferences.

Growing Interest in Portfolio Assessment

The following narrative shows the many questions teachers have about portfolios and also illustrates why there is a growing interest in portfolios by teachers of students with special needs.

Mrs. Geneva is a special education teacher who teaches students with learning disabilities. She has never used portfolios before, but, because she has heard so much about portfolios of late, she is wondering whether portfolio assessment could be used in her class. But first, she asks herself: What exactly are portfolios and what kind of assessment are they most like? Are there different kinds of portfolios? Next, she asks: Why use portfolios? Is the use of portfolios in education a trendy phase that will quickly pass, or can portfolios really make a difference in learning and teaching? What can portfolio assessment do for her that other assessment methods don't? What about her students—what can portfolios do for them?

Mrs. Geneva does some research, consults some educators, and decides to try portfolios because of their purported advantages such as increased sense of student "ownership" of work and physical documentation of improvement over the course of a year. She gets some helpful information from these resources on implementing portfolios in a general education classroom. She doesn't know, though, how to tailor the portfolio for her students with learning disabilities. None of the articles she read mentioned this, and none of her colleagues have ever dealt with portfolios for students with special needs. She wonders: Will her students' portfolios be different from those of "typical" students? How will portfolios meet instructional needs? What specifically can they do for children with special needs that other assessment methods don't? Will her students be able to handle the paperwork and self-reflective activities involved in creating a portfolio? Who does she talk with to find out? She decides to visit with the district's itinerant counselor and consult a special education teacher in another school who she has heard uses "celebration" portfolios with success.

Portfolios in the Classroom

A portfolio literally is a flat, portable case for carrying documents, drawings, and similar materials. Artists, architects, photographers, and investors all use such carrying cases as holders for their valuable materials. The portfolio concept, as applied to education, is based on this idea. Artist's portfolios, for example, consist of carefully selected collections that show their finest paintings, photographs, or other works. Likewise, student portfolios should consist of carefully selected schoolwork representing the students' best work. Portfolios are not static compilations but dynamic collections that artists update periodically. Like an artist's portfolio, the contents of a student's portfolio are not fixed. Students may eliminate older samples of work when they update their collection with more recent accomplishments.

Defining Portfolios and Assessment

A **student portfolio** is a systematic collection of student work and related material that depicts a student's activities, accomplishments, and achievements in one or more school subjects. The collection should include evidence of student reflection and self-evaluation, guidelines for selecting the portfolio contents, and criteria for judging the quality of the work. The goal is to help students assemble portfolios that illustrate their talents, represent their writing capabilities, and tell their stories of school achievement (Stiggins, 1997). **Portfolio assessment** is an ongoing process that captures the many activities and accomplishments associated with reflective teaching and learning that occur in portfolio-based instruction. By evaluating progress using a collection of authentic samples of student work, portfolio assessment provides an ongoing record of student performance and mastery of specific competencies (Vavrus, 1990).

Emphasis on Performance

Rather than emphasizing test scores to measure student progress, portfolio assessment focuses on evaluation of samples of a student's best work. Clearly, measuring student learning with portfolios is much different from traditional grading, in which teachers assign grades based on test scores and other assignments such as homework. Teachers then use the test scores and other grades to calculate a report card grade. Although this is an efficient method of evaluation, it may fail to provide details about student performance. In contrast, when teachers use portfolios, they are more concerned with maintaining the details and less concerned with efficiency. Although most portfolios focus assessment on the process of learning and the quality of the final portfolio product rather than on test scores, tests are a valid measure of student performance that can be included in portfolios. Even though some portfolios avoid tests altogether, others routinely incorporate tests as a valuable assessment element (Stiggins, 1997).

Alternative, Authentic, and Performance Assessment

Because there are several types of **alternative assessments,** one can easily become confused about the similarities and differences among them. One reason for the confusion is that educators use a variety of names to describe alternative assessment, including *authentic assessment, curriculum-based assessment, classroom-based assessment, informal assessment, portfolio assessment,* and *performance assessment.* The fact is that, although differences exist among these assessments, there are more similarities than differences.

Portfolio assessment, which relies on evaluation of genuine student work samples, is one type of authentic, alternative assessment. Authentic assessment involves using informal, criterion-referenced appraisal procedures that take place as a regular part of instruction and that relate to real-life situations. A basic authentic assessment principle is that students should demonstrate skills rather than respond to test questions about what they know. In addition, authentic assessment procedures should enable students to participate in the assessment process. Compared with objective, norm-referenced testing, authentic assessment tends to be decentralized and portfolio based. This allows for more open-ended, unstructured evaluation procedures that are an integral part of instruction rather than a separate activity divorced from the learning process.

Authentic assessment is important because it allows us to obtain realistic and practical information about student performance. Teachers are especially enthusiastic about authentic assessment because it emphasizes measuring progress based on what students know and can do in the classroom rather than how well they answer questions on a test. Authentic assessment also provides a more realistic context for assessment by linking evaluation with classroom instruction. Finally, authentic assessment communicates to the student and others that we care about evaluating performance using realistic, practical measures.

A strong connection also exists between portfolios and performance assessment. Performance assessment is authentic, curriculum-based assessment that emphasizes teacher observation and clinical judgment. For example, a teacher's observation of interaction in an inclusive classroom might be used to make professional judgments about a student's social skills. Teachers might keep a record of their observations of social skills by completing a checklist, filling out a rating scale, or preparing a written description. An example of performance assessment at the secondary level might be an on-the-job evaluation of a student using a criterion checklist. A job coach might complete this assessment by judging the quality of the student's work in relation to the written performance criteria. As you can see from these examples, performance assessment is like portfolio assessment in that it provides detailed information while avoiding use of traditional measures such as teacher-made tests (Stiggins, 1997).

Another important consideration is that alternative assessment procedures, such as portfolio evaluation and performance assessment, are not brand new. Teachers have always collected samples of students' work, used checklists of behavior to observe students, and judged student performance with rating scales. Furthermore, we have solid evidence and vast experience to support the effectiveness of alternative assessments (Deno, 1985; Salvia & Yssledyke, 1995; Tindal & Marston, 1990; Worthen, 1993). Unfortunately, some uses of alternative assessment fail to meet the standards of high quality and good reliability associated with more formal, norm-referenced testing. For this reason, we must do our best to follow the standards for conducting high-quality assessment, which means carefully developing assessment instruments such as checklists, rating scales, and evaluation forms, and making sure that we keep accurate records of the results (Stiggins, 1997).

Focus on Writing and Reading

Most student portfolios focus on writing and reading activities, although more and more teachers are introducing portfolios in science, math, and other subjects as well. Having students collect writing samples is an established way to begin portfolio-based instruction. Assessment may include measurement of how much writing a student accomplishes and the stages through which written documents progress from the rough draft to the final product.

Likewise, having students develop reading portfolios is another excellent way to initiate portfolio-based instruction and assessment. Reading portfolios can consist of a list of readings, which document how much a student has read and identify a student's particular interests. Such reading portfolios are more than a simple listing and should include elements such as annotations by students, book reports, vocabulary lists, and invented endings. Reading portfolios can also be much more complex. They may include peer feedback, teacher impressions, and self-reflections that allow students to discuss and react to reading materials. These portfolio elements can help students organize what they understand and feel and demonstrate what they have learned through their readings. Having students prepare reading portfolios can also motivate and encourage them to pursue additional reading.

Process and Product Portfolios

Process and product portfolios represent the two major types of portfolios. A **process portfolio** documents the stages of learning and provides a progressive record of student growth. A **product portfolio** demonstrates mastery of a learning task or a set of learning objectives and contains only the best work. Cole et al. (1995) described process evaluation as the major and more dynamic type of portfolio. Teachers use process portfolios to help students identify learning goals, document progress over time, and demonstrate learning mastery.

Process portfolios may include a variety of materials such as unfinished work, journals, reflections, notes, independent work, conference reports, teacher evaluations, peer evaluations, self-evaluations, and even test results. However, rather than a random collection of work samples, the process portfolio should contain carefully selected materials that illustrate particular learning.

In general, teachers prefer to use process portfolios because they are ideal for documenting the stages that students go through as they learn and progress. Information about using process portfolios with diverse learners appears in Focus 18–1. In the initial stages, the teacher and the students identify the materials that will go into the portfolio, and the teacher helps the students specify their learning goals. After this initial step, the portfolio begins to take shape. At this point students include interim evidence in their portfolios that demonstrates progress toward reaching their learning goals. For example, a process portfolio in the interim stages might contain an outline for a paper, a rough draft of the paper, and an edited second draft of the same manuscript with teacher comments and student reflections. Completed process portfolios also contain the final output as evidence of mastery (Cole et al., 1995).

FOCUS 18–1

Portfolio Assessment and Diversity

Because process portfolios provide the teacher detailed diagnostic information, they are especially responsive to the needs of diverse learners who have learning deficits. For example, when students with limited English proficiency prepare writing portfolios that include rough drafts, teachers can identify specific areas in need of remediation. If a student makes mistakes using articles or helping verbs, the teacher can quickly identify the error pattern and start remediation. Likewise, students who use nonstandard English can be easily identified using portfolio assessment, and remediation programs can be started.

Product Portfolios

Managing and producing a process portfolio takes time, and the notebook or storage container can be bulky. For this reason, teachers sometimes have students prepare a more concise portfolio called a *product portfolio*. Product portfolios, which are used less often in the classroom, are shorter, more accessible documents. The materials in the portfolio should be final products illustrating success at the mastery level. Teachers and students may include summary statements that reflect the level of student learning. In some situations, teachers may have students transform their process portfolios into product portfolios. The most practical time for this transformation is at the completion of a program or the end of a school year. The school then keeps a copy of the product portfolio for future reference (Cole et al., 1995).

Celebration Portfolios

Although process and product portfolios represent two major types, there are many creative ways to develop portfolios. For example, Stiggins (1997) recommends **"celebration" portfolios,** which students can use as mementos of their favorite learning experiences and activities. Students are free to create these portfolios without teacher-prescribed requirements. The teacher asks students to select materials in response to the question "What are your favorite class materials and activities, and why are these your favorites?"

This type of imaginative portfolio helps students learn to identify special work and develop understanding of the meaning of quality. Because students develop their own standards, the celebration portfolio helps them learn to make choices and reflect on their own strengths and interests. For this reason, the celebration portfolio is particularly useful with children with special needs who may have poor self-esteem or fear of failure. Sharing their celebration portfolios with their families and others gives them a way to communicate school successes.

A "Big Books" Portfolio Project

In the following narrative account of a "Big Books" portfolio project, Katherine Curtis, a special education teacher in Orange Park, Florida, discusses her concept of the benefits of portfolios. Her "Big Books" activity contained elements of both process and product portfolios. The process elements were the sloppy, neat, and final copies of the story. The final products were the "Big Books" that the students prepared and presented to students in other classes.

This year I designed a "Big Book" portfolio activity for my fifth- and sixth-grade students with disabilities. This particular portfolio project required them to use a variety of academic skills to create their Big Books. They developed written expression skills as they created their stories, which they accomplished by picking a topic and then writing sloppy copies, rough drafts (which I edited), and neat copies. They learned creative art skills by designing a picture for the cover of their big books. Presentation skills were also part of the project. My students practiced reading their books in class, and this prepared them for the final step of reading their story to children in a kindergarten or first-grade class.

This portfolio activity also helped improve student self-esteem and confidence. I was pleased to observe my students gain self-assurance as a result of their hard work and determination. The portfolio helped meet many of my students' affective IEP goals. The activity was so successful that I plan to continue using it. The project showed me the many benefits of portfolio-based instruction.

Samples of student work from the "Big Books" project appear in Figure 18–1. The samples include a "sloppy copy," a rough draft (with the teacher's comments), and a neat copy of the "Big Book" story called "The Dog I Never Had" written by Amber, a student in the class.

Language Arts Assessment Portfolio (LAAP)

The *Language Arts Assessment Portfolio (LAAP)* (Karlsen, 1992) is a commercially available classroom assessment system that makes extensive use of portfolio evaluation procedures. The *LAAP* measures student achievement and progress in reading, writing, listening, and speaking. Three separate *LAAP* kits are available: Level I is for grade 1, Level II is for grades 2–3, and Level III is for grades 4–6. Materials in each kit include a teacher's guide, a set of 30 blackline masters, a set of 30 evaluation booklets, a set of 30 self-evaluation booklets, and portfolio folders. Teachers can use the *LAAP* to individualize assessment and instruction using teacher evaluation, student self-evaluation, and a collection of student work. This provides an authentic and meaningful assess-

Figure 18–1 Amber's Sloppy Copy, Rough Draft, and Neat Copy from her Big Book Story "The Dog I Never Had"

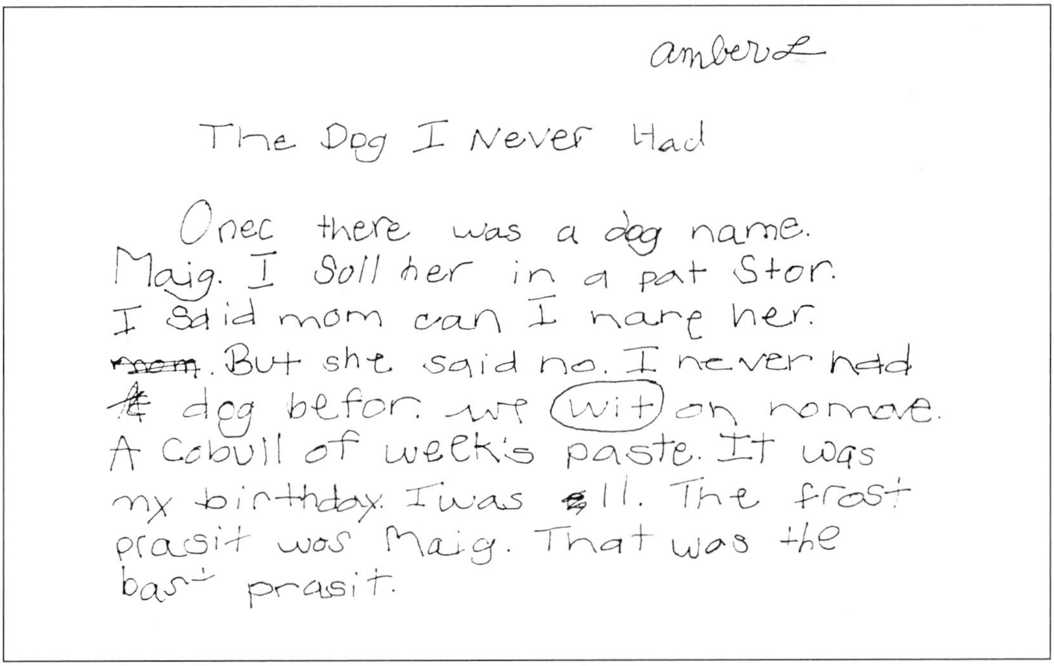
amberL

The Dog I Never Had

Onec there was a dog name.
Maig. I Soll her in a pat Stor.
I said mom can I hare her.
~~mom~~. But she said no. I never had
~~a~~ dog befor. we (wit) on nomae.
A Cobull of week's paste. It was
my birthday. I was ~~8~~ 11. The frost
prasit was Maig. That was the
bast prasit.

Figure 18–1   *(continued)*

Amber
9-16-93

The Dog I Never Had

Maggie Once there was a dog name.
~~Maig~~. I ~~fett~~ *saw* her in a *pet* ~~pak~~ Store.
I said "Mom, can I have her?"
But she said no. I never had a dog
before. We ~~wiitt~~ *went* ~~houme~~ *home*. A ~~coubuh~~ *couple*
of weeks ~~fister~~ *passed*. ~~If~~ *It* was my *first*
birthday. I was 11. The ~~feist~~
present
~~brasit~~ was ~~Maig~~ *Maggie*. That was the
best   *present.*
~~bast~~ ~~prasit.~~

Amber

The Dog I Never Had

Once there was a dog named
Maggie. I saw her in a pet store. I
said, "Mom, can I have her?" But she
said no. I never had a dog before. We
went home. A couple of weeks passed.
It was my birthday. I was 11. The
first present was Maggie. That was
the best present.

ment because it relies on students' language arts materials, including the books they read, the stories they write, and the oral presentations they make. An optional *LAAP* training video shows how to use the system and includes scenes of *LAAP* in classroom use and author interviews.

☑ Comprehension Checklist

Widespread use of portfolios by teachers, schools, school systems, and entire states has made portfolio evaluation an increasingly important assessment topic. Portfolio assessment, which relies on samples of real student work rather than test scores, is the type of curriculum-based, authentic assessment that emphasizes systematic collection of work to demonstrate achievement and reflective learning. Students usually present their work in an organized, well-planned notebook or another appropriate container. The concept, based on artists' and architects' portfolios, uses samples of a student's best work to show mastery learning; however, many teachers also have students develop creative and individualized portfolios, such as celebration portfolios. Although most portfolios focus on written expression and related language arts activities, portfolios are also useful in other disciplines such as math and science.

Why Do We Use Portfolio Assessment With Students Who Have Special Needs?

Like all evaluation procedures, portfolio assessment has both advantages and disadvantages. Although the benefits of portfolio assessment typically outweigh the drawbacks, an understanding of the limitations helps us avoid potential pitfalls. Some teachers readily adapt to portfolio-based instruction because it fits easily into their teaching style. Regardless of individual teaching styles, the widespread interest in portfolios is due, in large part, to disillusionment with traditional teaching and testing practices. At the same time, many educators are enthusiastic about opportunities for reflective teaching and learning that allow students to actively participate in the learning process.

Because portfolios facilitate this type of reflective teaching and learning, more and more teachers are using portfolios as instructional and assessment tools. Although portfolio assessment is not entirely new, it has recently come into more widespread use as educators reexamine standards for student performance. Several factors account for the growing interest in portfolio assessment. One factor is the expanding use of whole language instruction. Like portfolio-based instruction, whole language instruction focuses on the language arts, especially written expression. A second factor contributing to the growing interest in portfolios is the movement toward assessment reform, which, as part of overall school restructuring, emphasizes performance evaluation using criterion-referenced measures rather than formal, standardized tests. Finally, dissatisfaction with standardized testing has led many teachers to embrace portfolio assessment because it provides a more realistic and relevant alternative to traditional testing. Although most teachers are familiar with portfolios in general, they should carefully consider the advantages and disadvantages of portfolio assessment before implementing the system in their own classrooms.

Advantages of Portfolio Assessment

Portfolio-based assessment provides several distinct advantages. These include the following:

- Promoting student self-evaluation, reflection, and critical thinking.
- Measuring performance based on genuine samples of student work.
- Providing flexibility in measuring how students accomplish their learning goals.
- Enabling teachers and students to share the responsibility for setting learning goals and for evaluating progress toward meeting those goals.
- Giving students the opportunity to have extensive input into the learning process.
- Facilitating cooperative learning activities, including peer evaluation and tutoring, cooperative learning groups, and peer conferencing.
- Providing a process for structuring learning in stages.
- Providing opportunities for students and teachers to discuss learning goals and the progress toward those goals in structured and unstructured conferences.
- Enabling measurement of multiple dimensions of student progress by including different types of data and materials.

Disadvantages of Portfolio Assessment

Like all assessment procedures, portfolio assessment has certain disadvantages, which include the following:

- Requiring extra time to plan an assessment system and conduct the assessments.
- Gathering all of the necessary data and work samples can make portfolios bulky and difficult to manage.
- Developing a systematic and deliberate management system is difficult, but this step is necessary in order to make portfolios more than a random collection of student work.
- Scoring portfolios involves the extensive use of subjective evaluation procedures such as rating scales and professional judgment, and this limits reliability.
- Scheduling individual portfolio conferences is difficult and the length of each conference may interfere with other instructional activities.

Portfolios for Students With Special Needs

Although the basic portfolio format and content are the same for all students, the portfolios of students with special needs may have some distinctive characteristics. Because the contents of portfolios are flexible, portfolios are particularly useful in special education. First, their flexibility gives students with special needs opportunities to demonstrate achievement in a variety of creative ways. This flexibility is especially helpful for students who perform poorly on tests and traditional class assignments. Instead of taking tests, for example, students can often demonstrate progress through drawings, audiotapes, videotapes, checklists of skills, or behavior charts. Second, portfolios make it easy to individualize learning activities, which lets teachers tailor assignments to the special learning needs of each student. Next, portfolios enhance motivation by allowing students to focus their efforts on the areas of greatest interest to them. Fourth, portfolios promote mastery learning because students can be given the time and the practice necessary to become proficient at particular skills before they must move on to new skills; therefore, portfolios enable teachers to arrange the learning environment so that students begin at their level of achievement and progress at their own pace rather than at some externally imposed level and pace. Finally, students with special needs often have serious deficits in reading and written expression. Portfolios provide an ideal way for them to build their reading and writing skills and to develop the self-confidence necessary to try new written language activities. (See Focus 18–2.)

The following account by special education teacher Susan Oliver describes how she successfully incorporated portfolios into her special education class.

Because portfolios are such a valuable instructional tool and a hot topic right now, I decided to begin using them in my primary class for students with severe and multiple disabilities. Although I had attended an excellent workshop on portfolios and I had talked with teachers who were using portfolios in regular classes, I knew that my students needed flexibility in selecting items for their portfolios. For example, instead of written essays and book reports, my students included lists of new signs or new vocabulary words that they had learned and lists of favorite stories and songs listened to in class. Many of my students also included their best drawings or art projects, lists of favorite class activities, letters from parents, and checklists of recently learned skills. Perhaps the most individual item was in Timmy's portfolio. Timmy, who is autistic, decided to include two of his favorite pieces of wire sculpture. One of his favorite activities is to collect pieces of wire that he shapes into objects of interest. For his portfolio, he decided to include two of the wire sculptures that he had shaped into the Chevrolet "bowtie" symbols that he sees on automobiles.

As I reflect on my portfolio experience, I think that the most motivating part of the project for the students was when they shared their work with other adults in the school and with their parents. For me as the teacher, the portfolios were most useful as tools for communicating with parents; as a way to introduce students in a positive light to new teachers, therapists, paraprofessionals, and volunteers; as vehicles for documenting mastery of skills; and as tools for measuring progress in practical and interesting ways. For these reasons, I plan to continue using portfolios, and I would not hesitate to recommend them to other teachers of students with severe, profound, and multiple disabilities.

FOCUS 18–2

Why Are Portfolios Useful With Students Who Have Special Needs?

- The flexibility of portfolios encourages students to demonstrate progress in creative ways.
- Portfolios encourage individualization in response to the special learning needs of each student.
- Portfolio assessment enhances student motivation.
- Portfolios promote mastery learning.
- Portfolio assessment is an ideal way to evaluate the skills of students with special needs.

At the same time, I didn't realize how much effort and time it would take to set up and manage all of this. In the end, however, my efforts were worthwhile because my students really enjoyed and learned from the experience.

☑ Comprehension Checklist

Although portfolios offer several distinct advantages, the major benefit is promoting student self-evaluation and reflective teaching and learning. The major drawback concerns the extra time required to plan and conduct portfolio instruction and assessment. For students with special needs, portfolios offer some attractive characteristics including flexibility, enhanced student motivation, and opportunities for students to develop proficiency by mastering targeted skills.

The Portfolio Assessment Process

The process of assessing student portfolios involves three major steps. First, the teacher and the student need to clearly identify the portfolio contents, which are samples of student work, reflections, teacher observations, and conference records. Second, the teacher should develop evaluation procedures for keeping track of the portfolio contents and for grading the portfolio. The evaluation procedures include the planning and record-keeping necessary to build portfolios that accurately measure student progress and achievement. Most portfolios include student self-management as part of the overall evaluation system. Third, the teacher needs a plan for holding portfolio conferences, which are formal and informal meetings in which students review their work and discuss their progress. Because they encourage reflective teaching and learning, these conferences are an essential part of the portfolio assessment process.

Selecting Portfolio Contents

Selecting what should go into the portfolio is one of the first decisions in the process. Student portfolios may include a variety of elements that depend on many considerations such as the grade level, the subject, the learning objectives, and the student's IEP. Although the specific contents of a particular portfolio can vary, most portfolios contain several basic contents, and the best portfolios include a combination of student- and teacher-selected items.

Student ideas are important in the selection process because they portray learning from the student's point of view. The teacher, however, may require additional items to measure student progress and respond to particular instructional goals. Along with including student ideas, portfolios should relate to instructional goals. For students with disabilities, the collection of materials in the portfolio should relate to IEP objectives as well as goals for the grade level, the program, the school, and the district. Additionally, portfolios can be an excellent vehicle for showing multiple dimensions of student progress and learning. For example, process portfolios convey the steps by which work is accomplished along with the accomplished work itself. This provides details about the student's academic proficiencies and shows student growth and achievement. To achieve this, portfolios should include different types of data and materials (Wesson & King, 1996).

Portfolio Holders

Students should have the opportunity to provide input in selecting and designing their portfolio holder. Appropriate holders keep materials of different sizes, help organize these materials, and give a sense of responsibility and ownership. Paper file holders or briefcases with flaps, pockets, and attached bands or strings may be appropriate, but some teachers prefer cardboard or plastic file boxes. Because these holders are expensive, some teachers use cardboard boxes, flat-bottom shopping bags, or similar containers that students can decorate with many different kinds of materials, including cutouts, paints, markers, vinyl, logos, and construction paper. Portfolio holders should be durable, creative, low cost, functional, neat, and stylish (Miller, 1995). See Focus 18–3.

Sample Contents

A list of typical portfolio contents (Wesson & King, 1996) for elementary students with disabilities appears in Table 18–1. This list gives ideas about possible items that can go into portfolios. It is not an exhaustive list, and portfolios need not include all of these items. Some portfolios have specific contents; others have a wider range of content across several subjects in the curriculum.

FOCUS 18–3

Technology Tip

Portfolio holders need not be limited to file folders, notebooks, or boxes. They can also include electronic containers. Teachers and students have a wide array of available electronic design options for preparing, storing, and presenting portfolio materials. Possibilities range from basic word processing documents to totally electronic portfolios which are entire portfolios that students prepare on computers and then store on disk or CD-ROM. Students may use word processing, multimedia presentation, and graphic design software to prepare their electronic portfolios. Students may present their portfolios on disk, CD-ROM, or web pages posted on the Internet.

For meeting the needs of students with disabilities, teachers should consider a number of useful accessibility options, including specialized hardware such as adapted keyboards, touch screens, and speech recognition for students with physical impairments and synthesized speech output for students with visual impairments. Useful software adaptations are also available for keyboard, display, and mouse functions. Students with written expression deficits may also benefit from learning how to use basic spell checking and grammar checking programs to correct their written documents.

Table 18–1   Portfolio Contents

Item	Example
Writing samples	Copies of writing samples, which may include rough drafts, revisions, and completed papers
Reading samples	A list of books read during the grading period that may include titles, authors, dates completed, and student appreciation ratings of the books
Reading response journal	Excerpts from a student journal or reflections log
Conference records	Completed conference record forms
Handwriting samples	A sample of a student's best handwriting
Audiotapes	A tape of the student reading orally. The student may reread the same piece periodically to measure progress.
Photographs	Photos of student projects that show mastery of the material
Videotapes	Students working cooperatively on a language arts project such as a skit that shows understanding of a story
Parent reflections	Parent notes or observations that show student progress
Teacher reflections	Notes that the teacher makes during observations that document instructional decisions
Drawings, paintings, or self-portraits	Artwork that the student prepares as part of an assignment
Student reflections	A self-evaluation in narrative or rating scale form that the student completes after finishing a major assignment
Checklist of skills	Skills the student needs to master, such as phonics rules, or writing conventions such as capitalization and punctuation
Charts and graphs	A self-evaluation chart of student behavior that shows improvement over time

Johns and Vanleirsburg (1991) conducted a study of the contents that teachers prefer in student portfolios. In the investigation, 43 teachers who had used portfolios were asked to indicate the items they would include in a literacy portfolio. A summary of the results appears in Table 18–2, which lists the contents by rank according to the percentage of teachers who rated the item as something they would definitely or possibly include in their portfolios.

In some situations, the portfolio contents are prescribed by state or school district standards. For example, Vermont's Portfolio Project (Abruscato, 1993) developed guidelines for writing portfolios that require six samples of student work, including the student's response to a formal writing assignment called the *uniform writing assessment*. Several states and many school districts have developed similar portfolio requirements. The Vermont guidelines require the following items:

- A table of contents.
- A "best piece."
- A letter.

Table 18–2   Teacher Ratings of Portfolio Comments

Portfolio Item	Percent of Teachers Indicating Inclusion
Writing samples related to literacy experiences	97
Listing of materials read	88
Samples of student work on important reading skills or strategies	84
Student self-evaluation	82
Checklists of relevant reading behaviors	79
Teacher observations and insights	77
Collaboratively produced progress notes	66
Classroom tests	58
Audiotapes	45
Standardized tests	35
Photographs of reading activities	28

- A poem, short story, play, or personal narrative.
- A personal response to a cultural, media, or sports exhibit or event or to a book, current issue, math problem, or scientific phenomenon.
- One prose piece from any curriculum area other than English or language arts (for fourth graders) and three prose pieces from any curriculum area other than English or language arts (for eighth graders).
- The piece produced in response to the uniform writing assessment as well as related outlines, drafts, and so on (Abruscato, 1993, p. 475).

Portfolio Evaluation Procedures

Teachers quickly form impressions of performance when they observe students as they work on their portfolios, hold conferences with students, and review portfolios. As a result, teachers almost always know the effort that students put into their portfolios and the progress they are making. Teachers form these impressions regardless of whether they grade a portfolio; however, when teachers grade portfolios, they must support their evaluation with evidence that goes beyond their subjective impressions. The contents of the portfolio itself are the primary document that provides this evidence. Portfolio contents should include a series of materials that teachers can use to evaluate what students have learned and how well they learned it. Well-designed portfolios provide more evidence of achievement than poorly designed portfolios, and the best ones tell a story that clearly demonstrates student progress over time. Although portfolios are creative documents that might include a variety of measures, most incorporate the following essential measures: a tracking and evaluation system, criteria for evaluating the entire portfolio and its contents, evidence of student self-assessment, and evidence of portfolio conferences. One of the initial steps in this evaluation process is developing the management system.

Developing a Management System

Because portfolios may be arranged in many different ways, they may include a variety of materials. This variety requires successful portfolios to have an organizational focus and a management system. For example, reading items in a language portfolio could be placed in one section, while written expression materials appear in another section. Alternatively, portfolios may reflect thematic units or specific curriculum goals. Materials may appear in chronological order to show progress over time, or they may appear together with the same theme in response to specific goals. Regardless of the arrangement, teachers should develop a management system that enables them to keep records of the elements in the portfolio. One of the first steps is developing a tracking and evaluation procedure for monitoring overall student progress. An ideal way to accomplish this is with a portfolio contents checklist. Sample checklists appear in Figures 18–2 and 18–3. The portfolio management checklist in Figure 18–2 is designed for teachers. The student portfolio checklist in Figure 18–3 is for student use.

Figure 18–2   Portfolio Management Checklist

Teacher _Deirdre McDowell_   Date _Second 9 Weeks_

Class _5th & 6th Grade_

Student Names: John, Tamara, Keisha, Kim, Jose, Melody, Jan, Flo, Johann

Contents:
- Writing sample rough draft
- Writing sample revisions
- Writing sample final paper
- List of books read
- Reading response journal
- Conference record forms

Marking Key

\+   Complete

+/–   Needs improvement

–   Not complete

Notes

Figure 18–3 Student Portfolio Checklist

Student _Keisha_   Teacher _Ms. McDowell_

Class _Fifth Grade_

Portfolio Item	Activity Log				
Writing sample—rough draft	9/22				
Writing sample—revisions	9/25	9/26			
Writing sample—final paper					
List of books read	9/16	9/24 –added			
Reading response journal					
Conference record forms					
Picture for My Big Book			9/28		

Notes _____

_____

_____

Scoring Portfolios

Although portfolio assessment should include an overall management system, the evaluation process involves more than keeping a checklist. The specific scoring procedures depend on the type of portfolio and the reason for the assessment. It is possible for students to develop their own individualized portfolios, but this requires the teacher to develop separate scoring criteria for each one. Although valuable in some learning situations, this is usually difficult to implement in instructional settings with groups of students (Wolcott, 1993).

Most teachers set requirements for the number of items and the specific materials that go into the portfolios. This standardization provides criteria for accurately and effectively assessing portfolios and helps to develop a reliable scoring system that produces consistent results across students. Some educators oppose standardization of portfolios for scoring and grading purposes because they believe it limits the value of portfolios as individual learning tools; however, most educators support standardization of at least some aspects of the portfolio to facilitate evaluation (Wolcott, 1993). A compromise is to let students choose items for the portfolio with the teacher giving some criteria. For example, the teacher tells students they must complete all assignments but include in their portfolios only 5 in-class writings (of 10 that were assigned), two essays (of three written), and two collaborative writings (of four). This way the teacher gets a "standard" to grade, and students have some autonomy.

Rubrics

Thorndike (1997) points out that scoring student performance usually takes one of two forms: fixed response or variable response. Fixed response scoring involves matching answers to one or more correct responses, such as marking the questions on a multiple-choice test as either correct or incorrect. Variable response scoring is more complicated. With variable response scoring no one correct answer or set of answers exists. Instead, scoring relies on sets of criteria often referred to as **rubrics,** which are scoring criteria that describe an array of possible responses and specify the qualities or characteristics that occur at different levels of performance. Most portfolio assessment systems rely on rubrics such as the sample holistic and analytical portfolio scoring systems that appear later in this chapter. Likewise, teachers use rubrics whenever they create variable response, curriculum-based scoring systems for grading student performance. The increasingly popular statewide assessment systems for measuring student performance in written expression, mathematics, and other academic skills are based on rubrics.

According to Thorndike (1997), the best rubrics for scoring provide clear criteria for evaluating student proficiency and performance that are keyed to educational objectives in the student's curriculum. Rubrics include various types of checklists, rating scales, and observation systems that teachers use to assess student products and performances. The best rubrics provide samples of student responses that illustrate student performance at below average, average, and above average levels. When scorers receive adequate training in using explicit scoring criteria, rubrics produce consistent and effective assessment data. On the other hand, incomplete scoring criteria used by poorly trained scorers usually produce unreliable results with inadequate validity.

Reliability Considerations

Because portfolio assessment is a type of informal criterion-referenced measurement, scoring is subjective. In order to make the process as reliable as possible, teachers should develop rubrics that identify criteria and serve as standards, and then judge each portfolio in reference to these criteria and standards. The standards may be informal criteria presented in a teacher-made checklist or more formal competencies developed by a school system or a state department of education. Because these standards are subjective, teachers must exercise professional judgment when rating student performance. As with any system that involves professional judgment, reliability is always a central concern.

Developing and maintaining a reliable system can be a challenging task. For example, in the first year of Vermont's statewide portfolio assessment system, different teachers scored the same student portfolios quite differently. When experts studied the problem, they found that scoring differences reflected low reliability in the grading system rather than differences in the quality of student work. Recognizing the importance of this reliability problem, Vermont changed the rubrics to improve reliability. These changes included providing additional training for the teachers who served as scorers, eliminating the most-difficult-to-score items from the student portfolios, and modifying the scoring protocols by reducing the number of scoring dimensions. Vermont's struggle to improve reliability illustrates why many teachers and schools use multiple-choice tests (which are easier to make reliable) to measure student achievement even though they do not capture critical details of important competencies (Murnane & Levy, 1996). This example also illustrates why portfolio assessment has limited use in the entitlement process of identifying children who qualify for special education services due to a disability.

In response to these reliability concerns, Vavrus (1990) suggested that the key to successful scoring is setting standards that relate to students' learning goals. This can be difficult for teachers who are implementing portfolios for the first time. To overcome startup problems, teachers should develop a scoring form listing the criteria they will use to grade the portfolio. A sample scoring form, based on a form developed by Farr and Tone (1994), appears in Figure 18–4. Beginning teachers may also wish to consult with more experienced teachers to obtain information about how they set standards to ensure reliability.

Figure 18–4 Portfolio Scoring Summary

Student _____ Teacher _____

Date _____ Grade _____ School _____

Rating : 1 – Below Average   2 – Average   3 – Above Average   4 – Excellent

Assessment	This Review	Since the Last Review	Comments
Amount of writing (completes writing tasks, writes on a variety of topics, revises ideas)			
Quality of writing (neatness, organization, vocabulary, mechanics)			
Attitude toward writing (motivation, effort, determination)			

Another way to improve reliability is to develop an evaluation scale that lists a progression of performance standards with representative examples of work at each level of performance. The teacher can determine what students should demonstrate at each level and then describe what constitutes inadequate, satisfactory, and exemplary work. This is most easily accomplished after teachers have successfully used portfolios in classes and have the opportunity to collect samples of student work that can be used as examples. This process of describing characteristics at each level makes it possible to locate where a student's work toward a particular goal falls in terms of the set of standards (Vavrus, 1990).

Holistic and Analytical Scoring Protocols

Most teachers ensure accurate assessment by developing one scoring protocol for evaluating all student portfolios. The scoring protocol can be holistic or analytical. **Holistic scoring** involves evaluating the portfolio in its entirety and giving a single overall score. **Analytical scoring** involves evaluating each piece separately and combining the individual scores to obtain an overall score. The question of whether teachers should use holistic or analytic scoring depends on several factors, including the purpose of the portfolio, the intended use of the final product, and the setting in which the students are developing their portfolios. Most teachers find that holistic scoring is preferable for evaluating large groups of portfolios. In contrast, analytical scoring tends to be better in small-group situations in which teachers and students have the time to focus on the process as well as the final product (Wolcott, 1993).

As with all evaluation procedures, strengths and weaknesses exist for each type of portfolio scoring (Spandel & Stiggins , 1990). The benefits of holistic assessment include the following:

- For many teachers holistic scoring "feels right" because they can judge how well the parts work together.
- Holistic scoring is faster and less expensive than analytical scoring.
- Holistic scoring measures the quality and the coherence of the entire work. This avoids problems that arise when evaluating the material as isolated pieces.
- Holistic scoring may be easier for beginners to understand and learn than analytical scoring.

The possible drawbacks to holistic scoring include the following:

- Holistic scoring provides general information that lacks the specifics necessary to diagnose and pinpoint strengths and weaknesses.
- Holistic scoring has the potential for bias if a rater scores a portfolio in response to ideas, handwriting, or opinions rather than the work as a whole.
- Because holistic assessment yields an overall score, the ratings may not reflect relative strengths and particular deficits.

In contrast, analytical scoring may provide teachers with the following benefits:

- The relative strengths and weaknesses of particular materials can be determined with analytical scoring, which is especially important with students who have disabilities.

- Analytical scoring has the potential for providing the type of appraisal that teachers need as a basis for developing remediation programs. Again, teachers of students with special needs often require this type of assessment information.
- Analytical scoring may also help students identify particular deficits that need improvement.

Possible problems with analytical scoring include the following:

- The extra time and expense associated with scoring each individual piece in a portfolio.
- The difficulty in defining specific criteria for each individual work in a collection.
- The possible frustration that new raters may experience because of the complexity associated with analytical scoring.

An example of a holistic scoring form appears in Figure 18–5, followed by an example of an analytical form in Figure 18–6. These sample forms, based on scoring sheets developed by Wolcott (1993), are most appropriate for use at the middle school and secondary level. Teachers at the elementary level should modify the individual items to make them more suitable with younger students. These sample forms can also be modified in other ways to meet individual scoring needs.

Internal and External Scoring

Another scoring consideration involves internal and external scoring. **Internal scoring** relies on scorers who have direct contact with the portfolio authors; this includes

Figure 18–5 Holistic Portfolio Scoring Form

Student ___Eloysa___   Date ___1/17/98___

Scorer ___Ms. Chen___   Overall Score _Very Good – B_

Rating Pinpoints	Excellent	Very Good	Good	Fair	Below Average	Poor
Quality of Content		✔				
Organization			✔			
Style and Grammar				✔		
Self-Evaluation		✔				
Originality	✔					

Comments

Eloysa –

I enjoyed your writing. It is lively and creative. However, you still

need to work on grammar. Overall, your portfolio shows progress.

Figure 18–6   Analytical Portfolio Scoring Form

Scorer ___Ms. Chen___   Student ___Eloysa___   Date ___1/17/98___

Pinpoint	Informal Essay	Formal Essay	Best Essay	Spontaneous Writing Sample #1	Spontaneous Writing Sample #2	Total Score
Clarity (Purpose & Thesis)	4	4	4	3	3	18
Organization	2	2	2	2	2	10
Quality of Content	4	4	4	3	4	19
Vocabulary	3	3	3	2	2	13
Sentence Style	2	3	3	1	1	10
Sentence Structure	2	2	3	1	1	9
Punctuation & Spelling	2	2	3	1	1	9
Originality	4	4	4	4	4	20
Self-Assessment Skills (reflections)	3	3	3	3	3	15
Overall Score	36 26	36 27	36 29	36 20	36 21	180 123

Rating Scale

Excellent   = 4

Very Good   = 3

Good   = 2

Fair   = 1

Poor   = 0

Highest Possible Score = 180

Notes   Nice work, Eloysa. Your strengths as a writer remain with your originality and ability to communicate clearly. Next quarter, let's concentrate on improving your writing style and structure (punctuation, spelling, sentence style, and sentence structure) — especially spontaneous writing.

teachers who score the portfolios of their own students. External scoring relies on scorers who have had no contact with the portfolio authors. In many situations teachers are responsible for grading their own students' portfolios without any input from external sources. Because teachers know their students so well, they may lack the objectivity of external scorers, and in some situations they might even be too critical of their own students. Further, when the teacher is the only scorer, no opportunity exists for checking interrater reliability. A practical solution is to agree to a "portfolio swap" with a teacher in another classroom. If the second teacher's opinion differs greatly from your own, you may want to revisit the student's portfolio and reconsider the grade. If the other teacher's evaluation is similar to yours, this will confirm the reliability of your assessment. Because reliability tends to increase with more than one scorer, external raters can help improve the consistency of portfolio grading. At the same time, however, using external scorers can increase scoring costs and scoring time (Wolcott, 1993).

Student Self-Assessment

Student self-assessment, an element that distinguishes portfolio assessment from traditional evaluation, is not one specific procedure; it includes various types of reflections and self-evaluations. Self-assessment involves having students review their entire portfolio, reflect on a series of revisions, compare two work samples to show growth in a specific topic, or self-evaluate a single work sample. An example of a self-reflection written by a student with special needs appears in Focus 18–4. Self-assessment options range from informal written statements, such as student comments in the margins, to more formal self-evaluations in which students respond to specific questions. For example, when reviewing a writing sample, students might consider the following questions:

What do I like best about this writing sample?
What was most important to me when I wrote this?
If I wrote this over again, what would I change?
Is this like my other writing? Why/Why not?
Has my writing changed since I wrote this? How?
Is this my best writing? Why/Why not?

Helping students develop their self-evaluation skills is an essential part of portfolio assessment. However, because students are not automatically reflective, teaching them self-assessment can be difficult. Of course, giving students experience with collecting their work and writing reactions to it will help. For this reason, it is important to give students enough time on a regular basis to reflect. This is accomplished when students have time to get out their portfolios, review what is in them, read everything, and, most important, think and write about what they have accomplished. In other words, portfolios should be part of regular instruction, not a separate activity. Even when teachers encourage reflection, most students need additional assistance. One

FOCUS 18–4

Example of a Self-Reflection Written by a Student With Special Needs

"This piece is important because it is the first time I ever had characters talk to each other. You know with quotation marks. The other extremely important thing about this paper is that I actually wanted to do a revision. Two revisions. And I like the final copy. I've never done a revision on purpose before" (Hill & Ruptic, 1994, p. 44–45).

way to do this is to circulate while students are working on their portfolios. Ask questions that encourage and promote reflection:

- "That's a great comment about how your writing has changed! When did you notice this change?"
- "What could you write about your drawing? That's good! Will you write that comment beneath your drawing?"
- "I didn't know that you liked to read comic books. Are you going to report them in your list of books read? What is it about them that make them fun?"

Another way to help students learn self-assessment is by having them select two pieces, one that they like and one that they do not like. Students should read their selections and write comments such as why they liked or disliked each piece or what they noticed about themselves as writers. Other ideas include having students maintain reflective reading and writing logs. Examples of these appear in Figures 18–7 and 18–8. Portfolio conferences also provide students with opportunities for

Figure 18–7   My Writing Log

Name _____ Demetrius _____

Grade _____ 5 _____

Rating Guide   Best   ✓ ✓ ✓ ✓
                  Very Good   ✓ ✓ ✓
                  Good   ✓ ✓
                  Poor   ✓

Date	Title	Rating Overall	Review
2/22	Thank you letter	✓✓	This was okay.
3/2	Book report – President Kennedy	✓✓✓	This report was good.
3/13	Book report – Martin Luther King	✓✓✓✓	I liked this most.
3/14	Portfolio conference record	✓	I don't like this. I don't like the goals.

Figure 18–8   Reading Log

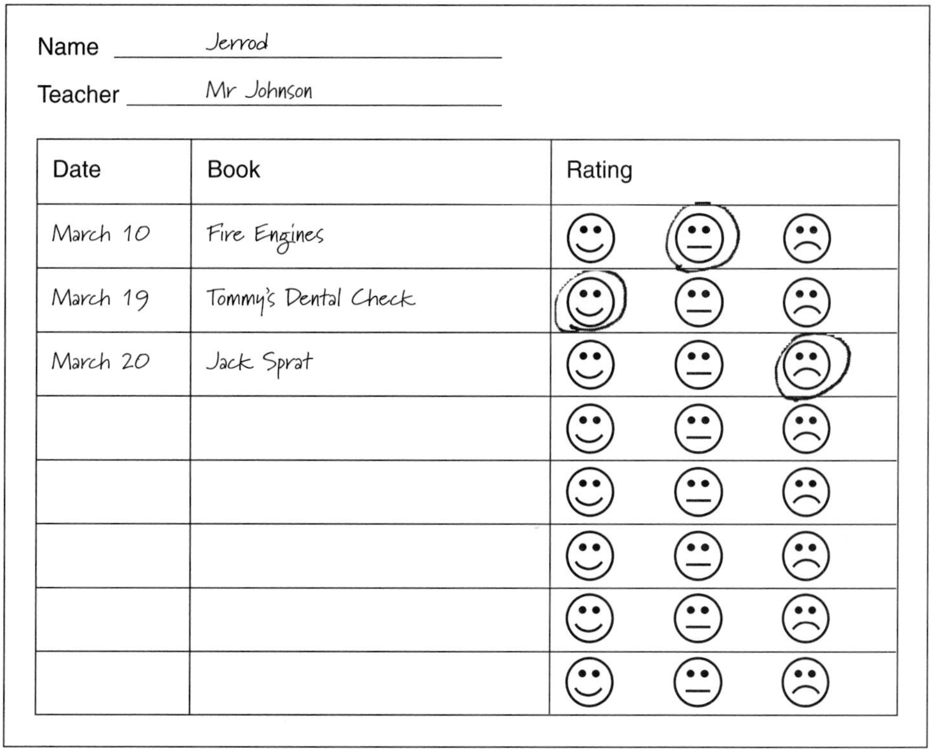

Name _____ Jerrod _____

Teacher _____ Mr Johnson _____

Date	Book	Rating		
March 10	Fire Engines	☺	(😐)	☹
March 19	Tommy's Dental Check	(☺)	😐	☹
March 20	Jack Sprat	☺	😐	(☹)
		☺	😐	☹
		☺	😐	☹
		☺	😐	☹
		☺	😐	☹
		☺	😐	☹

self-evaluation. Through conferences with their teacher, students may discuss their learning goals, evaluate their progress, and receive immediate feedback. More specific information about conferences appears in the next section of this chapter.

☑ Comprehension Checklist

Portfolios may include a variety of different materials depending on their intended use. In most situations, the school or the teacher requires certain basic materials in all student portfolios; teachers and students may include unique and creative elements as well. Moreover, some portfolios allow for students to include optional materials that reflect their particular learning goals and interests.

Successful portfolio assessment requires careful planning and record keeping. Most teachers use portfolio content checklists as an essential element in a management and tracking system. The checklists help the teacher monitor the progress of individual students and the entire class. More specific evaluation involves use of either holistic or analytical scoring protocols. With holistic scoring the scorer rates the entire portfolio using overall scoring; with analytical scoring the scorer rates each portfolio item separately.

Helping students develop self-evaluation skills is also an important part of portfolio assessment. Teachers should give students enough time on a regular basis to engage in reflective learning activities. This means that students should have structured time to think and write about what is in their portfolio.

Portfolio Conferences

Portfolio conferences, a key element in the portfolio assessment process, consist of meetings in which students review learning goals and discuss progress. Most conferences occur between individual students and their teacher. Conferences are important because they give students opportunities to consider their interests and to assess their abilities. According to Farr and Tone (1994), conferences provide opportunities for reflective discussion and review and help teachers assess student progress.

The portfolio conference process involves several steps. When teachers first introduce portfolios, they need to describe and discuss conferences with their students before scheduling any meetings. Initial conferences occur soon after the students begin to compile their portfolios. Prior to conferencing, students should write down their learning goals and evaluate their progress toward achieving those goals; students should bring this written information to the conference. Often the best way to accomplish this is to have students fill out a conference record form before the meeting (Farr & Tone, 1994).

Two sample conference record forms follow. The first form (Figure 18–9) is divided into a student report section and a teacher comments section. In the report section, students list their learning goals and evaluate their progress toward meeting those goals. Students complete this section prior to meeting with the teacher. During the conference, the teacher and student use this form as the basis for discussion. At the end of the conference, teachers provide written feedback by filling out the comments section. The second sample form (Figure 18–10), based on a form developed by Farr and Tone (1994), is less formal. It simply provides a way for the teacher and the student to write down notes during the conference. Because this is completed during the conference, students need not prepare this form in advance. After the conference, students place the record form in their portfolio. This record form documents the conference and provides valuable evaluation information.

Figure 18–9 illustrates a typical form that teachers might use with middle school or high school students. Teachers can modify this basic form for use in other situations. For example, with students who are very young or unable to write, the teacher may conduct the conference as a personal interview by asking them a series of questions and making notes about their responses.

Scheduling Conference Time

Finding the time to schedule and hold conferences can be one of the most difficult challenges in portfolio implementation. Most individual portfolio conferences take about 15 minutes to conduct, and Farr and Tone (1994) recommend that teachers hold four portfolio conferences with each student during a typical academic year. For teachers with many students, 15 minutes of conferencing with each student four times a year takes a significant amount of time.

Figure 18–9   Portfolio Conference Report

Name _____Demi_____   Date _____   Grading Period _____

Student Report

My learning goals To get done with my big book dinosore story and read more books. I
want to ead my dinasour story to the other class.

_____

Progress in meeting my goals Okay. my dinasour picture is done. I need to get done
with my story

_____

My new goals I want to learn to write on the computer

_____

_____

Teacher Comments

Notes on student's goals and progress Your overall progress is good, and you have a very
good story idea. You need to update your student checklist and begin work on your reading
response journal. Make sure to put this conference record form in your portfolio.

For this reason, finding the time to hold conferences is a concern of all teachers. Finding conference time is especially difficult for teachers who rely primarily on direct instruction. Because of this, teachers arrange time for conferencing by incorporating student-centered learning activities, such as whole language instruction, as part of the daily routine. For example, teachers can conference with students while the rest of the class engages in student-centered assignments. including cooperative learning groups, sustained silent reading, portfolio work sessions, or individual class assignments that students complete independently. The goal is to make conferences a normal part of ongoing class activities rather than a separate activity that interferes with instruction. When this is not possible, teachers may be able to obtain assistance from a teaching assistant, teacher aide, or parent volunteer to help with the class while the teacher meets with students (Farr & Tone, 1994).

Despite these potential solutions, the time problem is a legitimate concern in most instructional situations; consequently, teachers need to balance the benefits of conferences against the time it takes to hold them. In some situations, finding the time is so difficult that teachers employ alternatives to individual conferences.

Figure 18–10   Conference Notes

Name ___Fabrice___   Date of Conference ___March 23___

Teacher's Notes	Student's Notes

Fabrice,
  I think your portfolio is very, very good. I really enjoyed your summer camp story, and I hope you get to go to camp again this summer. I think when your Mom reads your story about how much you want to go, it might help!
 	
                K. Eggen
	I just wrote my story about summer camp and how much I want to go. It would be a lot of fun and I hope my Mom lets me. I like this story the best because I really want to go.

Peer and Small-Group Conferences

Alternatives to individual student teacher conferences include peer conferences and small-group conferences (Farr & Tone, 1994). Peer conferences are meetings between two students to discuss portfolio goals, activities, and progress. Peer conferences are valuable in many instructional situations, especially with older students. In order for the conferences to be effective, the teacher should establish clear guidelines including time limits and activities. Peer conferences work best later in the school year after students have completed individual conferences with their teacher. Teachers can introduce peer conferencing by modeling an appropriate conference to the entire class.

Small-group conferences consist of meetings with three to five students. They may be organized around reading or writing groups or some other appropriate grouping. Small-group conferences give students opportunities to discuss their portfolios with peers. Although not as effective as individual conferences, small groups are especially useful if the teacher finds it difficult to find time for individual conferences. As with all conferences, students should keep a brief written record describing their participation in each peer conference (Farr & Tone, 1994). A sample peer conference record form appears in Figure 18–11.

Figure 18–11   Peer Conference Review Form

Portfolio Owner _____

Portfolio Reviewer _____

Date of the Review _____

1.   What do you think is really good about this portfolio? Why?

2.   What do you think is the best piece in the portfolio? Why?

3.   What is **one** thing the writer can do to make this portfolio better?

☑ Comprehension Checklist

Conferences are meetings with students to review learning goals and discuss progress. Teachers usually document conferences with some type of form that also provides valuable evaluation information. Because finding time to schedule and hold conferences is often difficult, teachers must balance the benefits of conferences against the time it takes to hold them. In some situations, teachers save time by employing alternatives to individual conferences, such as peer and small-group conferences.

Summary

Chapter 2 included a biographical sketch of special education teacher Brenna Bateh. This account described, in general terms, how Ms. Bateh incorporated assessment into her instruction. This biographical sketch described how she was experimenting with a language arts portfolio activity to help her secondary students with disabilities develop more reflective learning strategies. In the following narrative we see how she has incorporated process and product portfolios, holistic and analytical scoring, student self-management, and portfolio conferences into one of her classes.

One of the high school special education classes that I teach regularly is basic English grammar. In order to pass the first nine-week term, my students must learn to write simple and compound sentences. I have always taught this class using a traditional approach with lectures, worksheets, homework assignments, and class tests. Many students successfully learned to write sentences using these methods, but many students also failed. For this reason, I decided to try a portfolio approach to see if this method would help more students acquire sentence-writing skills and become more reflective learners.

Because of my experience with portfolios, I knew that developing effective assessment procedures was a key to success. Therefore, I wrote a couple of assessment forms, including a self-management checklist for my students, an analytical scoring form for detailed grading, and a holistic form for overall grading. (Copies of these assessments appear in Figures 18–12, 18–13, and 18–14.) I showed my students how to use the self-management checklist to keep up with their portfolio assignments. I then used the analytical form as my primary grading tool. I arranged for two external graders to score the final sentences written by my students. These graders used the holistic scoring form. The external graders were two of my faculty colleagues who volunteered to help. At the beginning of the term, I shared the forms with my students and showed them how we were going to use each form to evaluate their portfolios.

After using portfolios to teach sentence structure, my class experienced a higher level of understanding and higher grades at the end of the term. Using portfolios helped me and the students to monitor levels of comprehension. By monitoring, I could intervene when a student

Figure 18–12   Student Self-Management Checklist

Simple and Compound Sentences		
	Portfolio Item	Completion Date
Worksheets	Identifying the subject in simple sentences	
	Identifying the verb in simple sentences	
	Memorizing the seven coordinating conjunctions	
	Identifying the coordinating conjunction in compound sentences	
	Identifying the comma in compound sentences	
Sentences	5 simple sentences (practice #1)	
	10 simple sentences (practice #2)	
	10 simple sentences (final)	
	5 compound sentences (practice #1)	
	10 compound sentences (practice #2)	
	10 compound sentences (final)	
Assessments	Reflection #1	
	Reflection #2	
	Portfolio Conference Record #1	
	Portfolio Conference Record #2	

Figure 18–13 Analytical Scoring Form

Simple and Compound Sentences						
Name _____ Scorer _____ Date _____						
Pinpoint	Worksheets	Practice Sentences	Final Sentences	Reflections	Conferences	Total Score
Subjects						12
Verbs						12
Idea						12
Conjunction						12
Style & punctuation						12
All work completed						20
Self-assessment skills						16
Conference skills						8
Overall scores	24	24	24	8	8	88

Figure 18–14 Holistic Scoring Form

Simple and Compound Sentences					
Student _____ Scorer _____ Date _____ Overall Score _____					
Rating Pinpoint	Excellent	Very Good	Average	Weak	Poor
Quality of Content (Subject, verb, conjunction, idea)					
Punctuation					
Style, Neatness, Creativity					

needed special assistance. The use of external graders helped students gain confidence in their ability to express their thoughts to others.

More and more teachers like Ms. Bateh are implementing portfolio-based instruction and assessment. In addition, many programs, schools, and entire school systems are relying on portfolios as assessment tools to measure student performance and achievement. Although not entirely new, portfolio assessment has recently come into more widespread use as educators question the effectiveness of traditional testing and reexamine standards for student performance. Portfolio assessment is a type of curriculum-based, authentic evaluation that relies on samples of genuine student work to measure student progress. Student portfolios usually focus on written expression and related language arts activities, including reading. Most contain a similar set of basic contents, but teachers and students may include unique and creative elements as well.

Successful portfolio assessment requires careful planning and record keeping. Most teachers develop a contents checklist that they use as a management tool for monitoring the progress of individual students and the entire class. Teachers also use holistic and analytical scoring protocols. Holistic scoring is generally preferred with large groups of portfolios, whereas analytical scoring is usually better in small-group situations that focus on the process as well as the final product. Portfolio conferences, for the purpose of discussing learning goals and measuring progress, are also part of the assessment process. They provide opportunities for reflective discussion and review, and this self-evaluation helps students focus their thoughts and carefully consider their portfolio. The overall benefit of portfolio assessment is that it promotes reflective teaching and learning and makes assessment authentic and meaningful. Furthermore, portfolios provide special insights about the successes of students with disabilities.

Chapter Review and Application

Multiple Choice

Directions: Read each item carefully. In the blank beside each item, write the letter of the best response. Each question contains only one best answer. Check your answers with the answer key at the end of the book.

_____ **1.** A variety of informal, criterion-referenced appraisal procedures that take place as a regular part of instruction.
   a. Portfolio assessment
   b. Authentic assessment
   c. Performance assessment

_____ **2.** A type of authentic, curriculum-based assessment that is an ongoing process of evaluating progress using a collection of samples of genuine student work that students put together in a notebook or some other container or holder.
   a. Portfolio assessment
   b. Authentic assessment
   c. Performance assessment

_____ **3.** A type of authentic, curriculum-based assessment that emphasizes teacher observation and clinical judgment.
   a. Portfolio assessment
   b. Authentic assessment
   c. Performance assessment

_____ **4.** Most portfolios focus on
   a. artistic expression.
   b. reading but not writing skills.
   c. the basic skills of reading, writing, and arithmetic.
   d. reading and writing skills.

_____ **5.** In a study of the contents that teachers prefer most in portfolios, the number one choice was _____.
   a. teacher observation
   b. student self-evaluation
   c. checklists of reading behaviors
   d. writing samples

_____ **6.** When teachers score the portfolios of their students, they are serving as _____ scorers.
   a. internal
   b. external

_____ **7.** When a teacher agrees to a "portfolio swap" with another teacher, the teachers are serving as _____ scorers.
   a. internal
   b. external

_____ **8.** Farr and Tone (1994) suggest that most individual portfolio conferences take about _____ minutes to conduct.
   a. 5
   b. 10
   c. 15
   d. 20

_____ **9.** _____ conferences are meetings between two students.
   a. Individual
   b. Small-group
   c. Peer

_____ **10.** _____ conferences consist of meetings with three to five students.
   a. Individual
   b. Small-group
   c. Peer

Match Type of Portfolio With Description

Directions: Match the type of portfolio with its description. Select from the following types of portfolios: process, product, and celebration. You may use terms more than once. Check your answers with the answer key at the end of the book.

_____ **1.** This portfolio demonstrates mastery and contains only the best work.
_____ **2.** Most teachers use this major and more dynamic type of portfolio.
_____ **3.** This portfolio documents the stages students go through in reflective teaching and learning activities.
_____ **4.** Students are free to create this portfolio without teacher-prescribed requirements.

Match Scoring Protocol With Description of Scoring

Directions: Write the correct name of the scoring protocol (either analytical or holistic) in the blank beside each description. Use the terms more than once. Check your answers using the answer key at the end of the book.

_____ **1.** This type of scoring evaluates the portfolio in its entirety and produces a single overall score.

_____ **2.** This type of scoring evaluates each item separately and combines the individual scores to obtain an overall score.

_____ **3.** This type of scoring provides a way to judge how well individual portfolio items work together.

_____ **4.** This is the fastest and least expensive type of scoring.

_____ **5.** This type of scoring provides a way to evaluate relative strengths and weaknesses of particular portfolio items.

_____ **6.** This type of scoring can serve as the basis for developing remediation programs.

Provide Practical Examples

Directions: Give a specific, practical example of student work that fits each of the following portfolio categories. Check your examples with the examples in the answer key at the end of the book.

1. Writing samples _____
2. Reading samples _____
3. Conference records _____
4. Parent reflections _____
5. Audiotapes _____
6. Teacher reflections _____
7. Student reflections _____

Short Answers

Directions: Review your understanding of the material in this chapter by answering the following short answer items. Compare your responses to the sample answers at the end of the book. Your responses should contain information that is similar to but not exactly the same as the information in the sample answers.

1. What criteria (i.e., pinpoints) would you include in a holistic scoring form for assessing a reading portfolio that included reading samples and a reading response journal?

2. What criteria (i.e., pinpoints) would you include in an analytical scoring system to assess a reading portfolio that included reading samples and a reading response journal?

References

Abruscato, J. (1993). Early results and tentative implications from the Vermont Portfolio Project. *Phi Delta Kappan* 74, 474–77.

Cole, D. J., Ryan, C. W., & Kick, F. (1995). *Portfolios Across the Curriculum and Beyond.* Thousand Oaks, CA: Corwin Press.

Deno, S. L. (1985). Curriculum-based measurement. *Exceptional Children* 52, 219–32.

Farr, R., & Tone, B. (1994). *Portfolio and Performance Assessment: Helping Students Evaluate Their Progress as Readers and Writers.* Fort Worth, TX: Harcourt Brace.

Hill, B. C., & Ruptic, C. (1994). *Practical Aspects of Authentic Assessment: Putting the Pieces Together.* Norwood, MA: Christopher-Gordon Publishers.

Johns, J. L., & Vanleirsburg, P. (1991). How professionals view portfolio assessment. In C. B. Smith (Ed.), *Alternative Assessment of Performance in the Language Arts: What Are We*

Doing Now? Where Are We Going? Bloomington, IN: Eric Clearinghouse on Reading and Communication Skills, 242–48.

Karlsen, B. (1992). *Language Arts Assessment Portfolio.* Circle Pines, MN: American Guidance Service.

Miller, W. H. (1995). *Alternative Assessment Techniques for Reading and Writing.* West Nyack, NY: The Center for Applied Research in Education.

Murnane, R. J., & Levy, F. L. (1996). *Teaching the New Basic Skills.* New York: The Free Press.

Salvia, J., & Yssledyke, J. E. (1995). *Assessment* (6th ed.). Boston: Houghton Mifflin.

Spandel, V., & Stiggins, R. J. (1990). *Creating Writers: Linking Assessment and Writing Instruction.* New York: Longman.

Stiggins, R. J. (1997). *Student-Centered Classroom Assessment* (2d ed.). Upper Saddle River, NJ: Merrill/Prentice Hall.

Thorndike, R. M. (1997). *Measurement and Evaluation in Psychology and Education* (6th ed.). Upper Saddle River, NJ: Merrill/Prentice Hall.

Tindal, G. A., & Marston, D. B. (1990). *Classroom-Based Assessment: Evaluating Instructional Outcomes.* Upper Saddle River, NJ: Merrill/Prentice Hall.

Vavrus, L. (1990). Put portfolios to the test. *Instructor.* August, 48–53.

Wesson, C. L., and King, R. P. (1996). Portfolio assessment and special education students. *Teaching Exceptional Children* 28, 44–48.

Wolcott, W. (1993). Addressing theoretical and practical issues of using portfolio assessment on a large scale in high school settings. In T. Vernetson (Ed.). *Florida Educational Research Bulletin on Alternative/Portfolio Assessment.* Sanibel, FL: Florida Educational Research Council, 123–32.

Worthen, B. R. (1993). Critical issues that will determine the future of alternative assessment. *Phi Delta Kappan* 74, 444–54.

CHAPTER 19

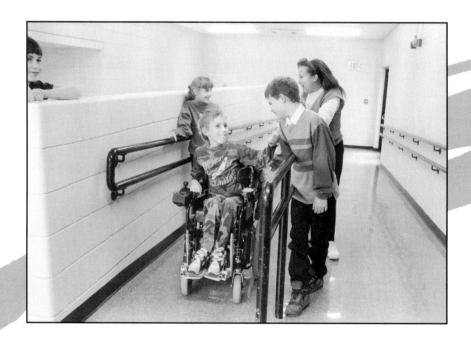

Assessment in
Inclusive Settings

Overview

In this chapter you explore the procedures for assessing students with disabilities in inclusive settings. Your study of this increasingly important topic begins with questions teachers have about inclusive assessment. Next you investigate the definition of inclusion as it relates to assessment of students with special needs. Your study of inclusive assessment includes a review of promising new approaches, and you also learn about test design modifications and test accommodations for students with disabilities. Finally you explore the alternative grading criteria that teachers use in response to unique student abilities, interests, behavior, and educational goals.

Objectives

After reading this chapter, you will be prepared to do the following:

- Understand the definition of inclusion.
- Modify assessment practices for students with disabilities in inclusive settings.
- Understand why we provide assessment accommodations for students with disabilities.
- Provide appropriate test modifications.
- Respond to the critics of such accommodations.
- Use team assessment.
- Assess teamwork in cooperative learning.
- Modify teacher-made tests.
- Use alternative grading criteria.

Questions Teachers Have About Inclusive Assessment

The following narrative illustrates some of the questions teachers have about assessment in inclusive settings.

Maria Aspera, a special education teacher recently assigned to an inclusion class, has never assessed children with special needs in a general education setting. As a result, she has many questions. For instance, what assessments are best in inclusion classrooms? Are there special tests for inclusion settings? How much does traditional classroom testing need to be modified for students with disabilities? And how useful is curriculum-based assessment, especially portfolio assessment, in evaluating students with special needs in inclusion classes?

Maria decides to find answers to these questions by doing some research. She finds a lot of information on inclusion in general and on methods for successful inclusion, but she finds very little information on assessment in inclusive settings. She discovers that she needs to learn more about accommodations and modifications in testing and that assessment in inclusive settings requires teamwork and ongoing communication between the general and special education coteachers. She locates some helpful suggestions regarding the most frequently occurring testing and grading problems of students in regular classes and learns that not all students with disabilities require extensive modifications in assessment. To her relief, Maria realizes that most modifications for students with special needs involve minor alterations of procedures rather than major adjustments. As she begins her new teaching assignment, she decides that her goal is to provide appropriate assessment in ways that are as similar as possible to the testing and grading used with the general education students in the class.

Growth of Inclusive Education

Keeping pace with changes in assessment practices and services for students with disabilities is challenging. Many innovations have occurred, one of the most significant of which has been the growing number of schools and entire districts that educate students with disabilities in general classrooms. As a result, assessment practices are also changing, although not as quickly as some educators would prefer.

Definition of Inclusion

The Individuals with Disabilities Act Amendments of 1997 (IDEA 97) defines *inclusion* as the participation of children and youth with disabilities in the general education classroom and the general curriculum with appropriate aids and services. Gearheart et al. (1996) define inclusion as educating children to the maximum extent appropriate in the regular school and classroom they would otherwise attend with appropriate support services. The related concept of *full inclusion* refers to attaining the greatest integration possible for all students with disabilities, including pupils with severe and multiple disabilities. More specifically, *full inclusion* refers to full membership in the general classroom with the full supports necessary to make inclusion successful (Sailor et al., 1993). The term *full supports* describes the importance of providing necessary support services in general education classrooms to ensure a quality educational program. Inclusion also encompasses placement in a variety of educational settings. In addition to the general education classroom, inclusion extends to community-based instruction and educational activities such as school clubs and athletics that occur outside the classroom.

Inclusion gives students with disabilities the opportunity to participate in typical school activities with their peers who are not disabled. The advantages of inclusion for students with disabilities include improved academic performance and social development. This conclusion is based on assessment data from the last 15 years that indicate that excluding students with disabilities from general education may result in lower achievement and social skill development (Baker et al., 1995).

Experts expect that inclusion will result in public school classrooms composed of much more diverse groups of students (Putnam et al., 1995). As a result, teachers need to develop new instructional methodologies and assessment procedures that respond to the greater diversity of student needs. In other words, the concept of the general education classroom is changing; therefore, the notions of teaching, learning, and assessment must change as well.

Although assessment in inclusive settings requires changes, many current evaluation practices work equally well in inclusive and noninclusive educational settings. For example, many curriculum-based assessment procedures, such as teacher-made testing, grading of homework assignments, and grading of classwork, already occur in the same way in most classrooms. In fact, teachers should use established assessment procedures whenever possible as long as they meet the increasingly diverse needs of the students. Fortunately, teachers may use established assessment procedures in many inclusive settings.

Assessment Issues in General Education

Key issues in general education, identified in focus group discussions among special and general education teachers, include concerns about standards and assessment in inclusive settings (Trump et al., 1996). When asked about inclusion, many general education teachers feel that required modifications for students with special needs lead to a watered-down curriculum. In contrast, special education teachers often express concerns about the emphasis in general education on testing as a means of accountability. This causes pressure on general educators to make sure that their students perform well on tests. Because students with special needs tend to perform poorly on tests, general educators may be hesitant to accept inclusion due to fears about a negative impact on the testing performance of the total class. These are the types of issues that educators are dealing with as they develop strategies for assessing students with disabilities in inclusive settings. Although many of the basic procedures for successful inclusion have been established, not all issues surrounding inclusion have been resolved. Unresolved issues include inclusion of students with severe disabilities, coteaching, support services, and assessment. Educators who are teaching students with special needs in inclusive settings are still in the process of developing the best possible solutions to these issues and concerns.

Why Do We Modify Assessment for Students With Disabilities in Inclusive Settings?

The following narrative, based on a vignette by Salend (1995), shows why we modify assessment for students with disabilities in inclusive settings. The scenario illustrates some of the most commonly used assessment modifications and also shows how assessment modifications help students with disabilities succeed in inclusive classrooms.

Ms. McBride, a general education teacher in a newly formed inclusion class, was disappointed by the student performance on her teacher-made tests. In class discussions and activities, her students appeared to understand the material. On the tests, however, many students received grades of Cs, Ds, and Fs. The scores of several students with disabilities were especially low. Confused and frustrated, Ms. McBride asked her students why they were having difficulty. They responded with the following comments: "I didn't understand some of the questions." "I skipped some questions because there were too many on the page." "The directions were confusing." "I lost my place on the answer sheet." "I didn't have enough room for my answers." "I thought the true-false questions were tricky."

After discussing the problem of low test grades with the special education coteacher, Ms. McBride decided to try out some test design modifications suggested by the special educator. Together the teachers implemented several accommodations, including providing an improved test format, writing more explicit directions, changing response modes, varying the types of items, and improving test readability. Although some students continued to score poorly, the teachers noted a marked improvement in the performance of many students. The teachers and the students were pleased with the results because the testing modifications allowed the students with disabilities to demonstrate what they had learned, and the improved tests benefited all of the students in the class.

This account illustrates the effectiveness of modifying assessment by making design modifications to teacher-made tests. Because performance on teacher-made tests is a key element in evaluating achievement and assigning semester grades, classroom tests given to all students, including students with disabilities, must be well designed and sensitive to unique learning needs.

New Approaches to Assessment in Inclusive Settings

Modifying assessment by redesigning teacher-made tests is just one example of the new approaches to assessment that teachers are using in inclusive settings. Other approaches include team assessment, assessing teamwork in cooperative learning, and portfolio assessment. New assessment procedures are necessary to meet the needs of the increasing numbers of students with disabilities who receive all or part of their education in general classes. In addition to the following information, information about inclusive assessment also appears in Chapter 6, especially in the section on accommodations in test administration that are useful in inclusive settings.

Team Assessment

One of the most useful assessment approaches in inclusive classrooms is team assessment, which is a process that involves all teachers in the evaluation process, not just special education teachers. Team assessment helps general education teachers, in particular, who have many concerns about testing and grading students with disabilities. Some concerns result from a lack of training and experience in appropriate techniques for modifying evaluation procedures with mainstreamed students. Other concerns arise from the resistance of a few teachers to altering their traditional testing and grading practices. However, successful inclusion depends in part on the willingness of teachers to modify their measurement procedures in response to the needs of individual students.

Team assessment is necessary because the inclusion classroom is different from the traditional classroom. The goals, teachers, curriculum, and assessment procedures are all different (Tiegerman-Farber & Radziewicz, 1998). Because the inclusion classroom changes assessment, general and special education teachers as well as the other members of the assessment team must work together in implementing new assessment procedures. Fortunately, most teachers are willing to collaborate as coteachers in developing and implementing new assessment techniques that benefit all students while accommodating the needs of students with disabilities.

One of the team assessment elements that teachers should consider is how well the members of the assessment team work together. Teachers can use the team analysis checklist in Figure 19–1 to assess team collaboration and effectiveness. The 25 items in the checklist cover the most important aspects of team success, including team goals, structure, interpersonal relations, resolution of conflicts, information exchange, consensus, assignment of responsibility, and team assessment. The checklist is best used as an informal tool for evaluating overall effectiveness and identifying specific problems that the team needs to address.

Team assessment requires a substantial amount of time, professional commitment, and interpersonal communication (Coufal, 1993). Active participation of all team members in gathering and interpreting assessment data is a key element. Team assessment represents a change in the decision-making approach that results in a more complete assessment of student needs based on discussion among team members with diverse expertise. In team assessment, all team members should help interpret assessment data. The benefit of team assessment is more complete evaluation of student needs within the most appropriate educational environment.

Cooperative Learning Assessment

Cooperative learning is an instructional strategy that works well in inclusive settings. Experts (Cohen, 1994; Pomplan, 1996; Webb, 1995) indicate that students with disabilities who participate in cooperative groups, including cooperative assessment groups, are more likely to make successful transitions into general education classes. Some students with disabilities, however, need social and group skills training to ensure successful participation. Research studies by Pomplan (1997) and Carlson et al. (1988) provide further evidence to support the use of cooperative learning in inclusive classrooms. These studies suggest that nonroutine, open-ended tasks maximize the participation of students with disabilities in heterogeneous cooperative groups.

Appropriate assessment is one of the key components in cooperative learning. Further, assessing teamwork in cooperative learning is as important as assessing individual student work. The following cooperative learning assessment procedures, developed by Johnson et al. (1998), include ways to assess teamwork and individual work. Teachers can easily adapt these procedures for use in inclusive classrooms.

Figure 19–1   Team Analysis Checklist (TAC)

Item	Yes	No
Team Purpose		
1. I understand the purpose of the team.		
2. I believe it is possible to accomplish the team purpose.		
Team Structure		
3. I know the expertise of each team member.		
4. I know the major tasks associated with the team objectives.		
5. I know who serves as team leader.		
6. I accept the leadership of the team leader.		
Interpersonal Relations		
7. I am accepted as a valuable contributor by my fellow team members.		
8. I perceive most of the other members as valuable team contributors.		
9. All team members can fully express their views.		
10. Fair consideration is given to the views of all team members.		
11. No individual dominates the rest of the team.		
Resolution of Conflicts		
12. The team solves conflict together.		
13. The team strongly discourages personal attacks.		
14. I accept team decisions even if they conflict with my own view.		
Records, Reporting, and Responsibility		
15. The activities and decisions of the team are recorded.		
16. The team members share recording and reporting duties.		
Information Exchange		
17. I have regular opportunities to contribute my professional knowledge to the team.		
18. Other team members have regular opportunities to contribute their professional knowledge to the team.		
19. The team frequently seeks information from outside sources.		

Figure 19–1 *(continued)*

Item	Yes	No
Gaining Consensus		
20. The members have opportunities for input in making team decisions.		
21. The members reach consensus prior to making team decisions		
Assigning Responsibility		
22. After the team makes a decision, members accept responsibility for specific follow-up and implementation activities.		
23. Follow-up and implementation responsibilities are shared equally among team members.		
Team Assessment		
24. The programs developed by the team are regularly assessed by the team.		
25. All team members have opportunities to participate in program change and program evaluation activities.		

When teachers use cooperative learning, they are responsible for ensuring that appropriate assessment takes place. The steps in assessing cooperative learning are similar to those in assessing any lesson:

- Specify the objectives.
- Develop the assignment.
- Determine grading criteria.
- Explain the assignment and share the grading criteria with students.
- Monitor the efforts of the cooperative groups.
- Intervene and provide support as necessary.
- Evaluate the results.

Teachers may use several assessment strategies to evaluate results, including the following:

- Observing group performance as it occurs.
- Interviewing individual students and groups of students.
- Evaluating individual and group performance on classwork and homework.
- Grading teacher-made tests given to individuals or groups.

Although these strategies are familiar to most teachers, Johnson et al. (1998) have also designed specialized approaches to assessment in cooperative learning situations. Specialized assessment approaches include peer editing, peer assessment of class presentations, self-assessment, peer assessment, group assessment, and group celebration. An explanation of each approach follows.

Peer Editing   **Peer editing** involves having the other members of the cooperative group grade the compositions of individual students. In peer editing, all group members certify that each member's paper meets the criteria set by the teacher. Group members work together in developing their papers, and each group member receives two grades. One grade is an individual grade based on the quality of the manuscript. The other grade is a group grade that reflects the sum quality of the group's papers.

One way to structure peer editing uses the following steps. First, the teacher assigns students to cooperative learning pairs with at least one good writer in each pair. Second, the teacher gives the students individual writing assignments. Third, the teacher has the students describe what they are planning to write to each other. Fourth, students work individually on their papers, but they also share material with each other and help their partners. The teacher monitors the work of the pairs and assists as necessary to help students develop their writing skills and their cooperative skills. Finally, when the assignments are complete, the teacher helps the students do the following:

- Discuss how well they worked together by describing specific actions they engaged in to help each other.
- Plan what behaviors they are going to emphasize in future cooperative writing assignments.
- Thank each other for the help they received.

Students with special needs may require additional instruction, support, coaching, and encouragement to develop peer editing skills. The special education teacher can often provide this support directly. Teachers may also arrange for teaching assistants, peer tutors, or volunteer tutors to provide extra support while students learn how to work with others on cooperative writing assignments.

Peer Assessment of Class Presentations   Any presentation given by a student can be evaluated by peers as well as the teacher. One way to encourage group interdependence and to foster peer assessment is to structure class presentations so that all members must learn the material being presented. This is accomplished by assigning students to cooperative groups of four, giving each group a topic, and requiring the group to develop a presentation that each group member can give in its entirety. The presentation criteria should include a specific time frame and active participation by the audience. The groups should have sufficient time to prepare and rehearse so that all group members can give the presentation. The teacher then divides the class into four sections (one in each corner of the classroom). One member of each group goes to each section and gives the presentation to the audience in their section. Assessment involves having the audience rate the presentation using a rating form. The rating form should include items for assessing the quality of the information, the interest generated by the presentation, the ease of understanding, the organization, creativity, originality, and audience participation. The students give one copy of the completed rating form to the presenter and one copy to the teacher. The teacher also observes parts of all the presentations. Finally, the groups meet to evaluate the effectiveness of the presentations, to celebrate their successes, and to discuss ways to improve their presentation skills in the future.

Self-Assessment and Peer Assessment   Arranging for students to assess themselves and each other should be an element in most cooperative learning lessons. Students with special needs in inclusive settings may need considerable guidance to develop self-assessment and peer assessment skills. Students who lack these skills need opportunities to develop them over time. This can be accomplished in many ways, including modeling, role playing, coaching, and direct instruction. The goal is for students to discuss and reflect on their learning and that of others.

Teachers can use cooperative learning assessment checklists such as those in Figures 19–2 and 19–3 to help students develop self-assessment and peer assessment competencies. The checklist in Figure 19–2 is for student self assessment. Teachers should help students learn how to rate their own collaboration skills with the self-assessment checklist. The checklist in Figure 19–3 is for peer assessment. Teachers should give students instruction in using the peer assessment checklist in Figure 19–3 to rate the participation of their peers in their cooperative group. Students can use the completed checklists to compare their self-ratings with the ratings from their peers. The checklists provide data that teachers and students can use to ensure they are making positive contributions to the learning of all group members. Teachers can also use the results in grading individual students and cooperative learning groups, or teachers may develop their own assessment checklists to fit particular cooperative learning assignments. For example, teachers of young students should develop simplified checklists and rating scales.

Figure 19–2   Cooperative Learning Assessment Checklist Self-Assessment Form

Your Name _____	Rate yourself using the following scale: 4 - Excellent, 3 - Very Good, 2 - Good, 1 - Poor	
Assessment Item	Rating	Comments
1. I was on time.		
2. I was prepared.		
3. I contributed to the learning of others in my group.		
4. I listened to the other members of the group.		
5. I worked together with others in my group.		
6. The other members would like to work with me again.		
Notes		

_____

_____

_____

Figure 19–3   Cooperative Learning Assessment Checklist Peer Assessment Form

Person Being Rated _____   Rater _____

Rate yourself using the following scale:
4 - Excellent, 3 - Very Good, 2 - Good, 1 - Poor

Assessment Item	Rating	Comments
1. The group member was on time.		
2. The group member was prepared.		
3. The group member contributed to the learning of others.		
4. The group member listened to others.		
5. The group member worked together with others.		
6. I would like to work with this group member again.		

Notes

_____

_____

_____

Group Assessment   Because individual assessment is more common in the classroom than group assessment, the typical cooperative learning group has students learn in a group but individually demonstrate what they have learned. In real life, most organizations focus on the success of the organization as a whole. The emphasis is on the success of departments in the organization and teams in departments rather than the success of individual employees. For this reason, cooperative learning assignments in school should require group reports, exhibits, performances, and presentations in which the students work together and are graded as a group.

Group Celebration   Group celebrations should occur at the end of cooperative learning lessons after completion of assessment and grading. Celebrations may be simple, such as having students congratulate each other, or they can be more elaborate, such as a group cheer, a dance, a song, or an event. Group celebrations give students the opportunity to salute their success and reflect on how well they collaborated to achieve their learning goals. One way to celebrate success is to arrange an activity in which students share how well they are achieving their academic goals and what they learned through collaboration. Recognizing the learning efforts of group members and their contributions to the learning of others is an important element in rewarding and reinforcing group interdependence.

Assigning Grades in Cooperative Learning   The way teachers assign grades in cooperative learning depends on the amount of interdependence they wish to develop among students. Teachers have a number of options for assigning grades. Examples of some of the available options follow.

- Individual grading with extra points based on all members reaching criterion: This grading procedure encourages group members to study together so that everyone learns the material. Students are graded individually but also receive extra points if all group members achieve a preestablished criterion level. An example of this procedure follows.

Group Member	Individual Points	Extra Points*	Total Points
Jaros	95	3	98
Marinko	92	3	95
Taka	90	3	93

*Criteria for Extra Points: If all group members receive at least 90 individual points, all group members receive 3 extra points.

- Individual grading with extra points based on the lowest score: In this grading system the group members prepare with each other to take the exam. The group members receive extra points based on the lowest individual score in the group. An example follows.

Group Member	Individual Points	Extra Points*	Total Points
Jaros	99	4	103
Marinko	87	4	91
Taka	80	4	84

*Criteria for Extra Points: 90–100 = 5 points, 80–89 = 4 points, 70–79 = 3 points

- Individual grading with extra points based on the group average: After group members help each other study for the test, students take the exam individually and receive individual scores. The scores of all group members are then averaged, and the average is added to each student's score. An example follows.

Group Member	Individual Score	Average Score	Total Score
Jaros	88	82	170
Marinko	82	82	164
Taka	77	82	159

- Random selection of one group member's work to grade: The students in the group complete the assignment individually and then help each other to make sure all the papers are correct. Because the group certifies all papers as correct, it matters little which paper is randomly selected by the teacher for grading. All group members receive the same grade.

- Assigning the lowest member's grade to all members of the group: The group members help each other study for the exam. Then students take the exam individually, but all group members receive the lowest grade in the group. This grading procedure helps group members encourage, support, and assist the low-achieving members of the group. This sometimes results in significant increases in the performance of low-achieving students. Teachers can avoid the problem of penalizing advanced and high-achieving students by using group grades like this only for extra credit or rewards. Thus, a low grade from a group exam can potentially increase but never reduce a student's individual grade.
- Averaging individual grades with a collaboration score: The group members work together to learn the assigned material and then take individual exams. The grades of the group are then averaged. The teacher also observes the group to determine the level of collaboration (e.g., leadership, shared decision making, listening). The group then receives a collaboration grade that is added to their average grade to arrive at a total score.
- Individual grading with celebration rewards: The members of the group help each other study for the exam, but they take the test individually and receive individual grades. The group is rewarded with free time, extra time in the yard, snacks, stickers, or other appropriate reinforcers if they all achieve a predetermined level of success.

The procedures for assessing the performance of students in cooperative learning groups described here were developed by Johnson et al. (1998) for assigning grades. Teachers should select a particular procedure from these available options, depending on the nature of the assigned task and the amount of interdependence they wish to foster in the group.

Peer Tutoring Assessment

Another evaluation strategy that is useful in inclusive settings is peer tutoring assessment. Peer tutoring is an instructional strategy in which a student tutor teaches another student in a tutor-tutee relationship designed to promote academic learning and social skill development. Successful peer tutoring involves planning, tutor training, teacher support, and assessment. Some teachers assess the progress of tutees by having tutors complete daily progress sheets. Teachers can also monitor progress by observing tutor-tutee pairs, conducting interviews, and having tutors and tutees complete simple questionnaires.

Adaptations During Testing

Although teachers are continuing to develop adaptations for testing students in inclusive settings, a number of appropriate and effective techniques already exist. A list of some of the most effective modifications during testing appears in Focus 19–1. This list, developed by Wood (1998), includes general suggestions for giving test and specific adaptations for students with particular learning problems.

Fortunately, not all students with disabilities require assessment adaptations. Furthermore, appropriate modifications for students who require them usually involve minor alterations of procedures rather than major adjustments. The goal is to

FOCUS 19-1

General Suggestions for Giving Tests

1. Students with language or memory deficits often have difficulty with recall of specific information or understanding questions posed in multiple-choice, true-false, or even fill-in-the-blank format. These students often can convey what knowledge they have in a format involving longer answers. For example, "tell me what you know about the pilgrims' homes, jobs, foods, or daily life" or "explain what happens to air when heated."

2. Include a prompt (visual or mnemonic) to remind students of an activity.

3. Include an open-ended question; for example, "What did you learn in this chapter?" "Tell me what you know about magnets."

4. Allow students to take a test with three colors of pens to indicate support used (black = took test without any assistance; red = took test with notes; blue = took test with book and notes).

5. Hand out colored stickers to students to place by test sections they are choosing not to answer. The stickers may be earned.

6. Children take a learning style test (using a computer) and are told of their style preference. Before a test the students gather in common groups based on style strength (visual, auditory, kinesthetic) for study purposes.

   Kinesthetic: Twister, darts, flash cards
   Visual: Chalkboard, magazines, flash cards
   Auditory: Tape recordings, quizzing orally

7. At the end of each class, write down four or five questions about material just covered. This way you will have a study guide, and you will be sure you have covered the material appearing on the test.

Adaptations During Test Administration

Problem	Adaptations
Poor comprehension	1. Give test directions both orally and in written form. Make sure all students clearly understand.
	2. Avoid long talks before tests.
	3. Allow students to tape-record responses to essay questions or entire tests.
	4. Allow students to take the test in an alternate site, usually the resource classroom.
	5. Correct for content only, not for spelling or grammar.
	6. Provide an example of the expected correct response.
	7. Remind students to check tests for unanswered questions.
	8. When the test deals with problem-solving skills, allow use of multiplication tables or calculators during math tests.

FOCUS 19–1 *(continued)*

	9. Read tests aloud for students who have difficulty reading.
	10. Give a written outline for essay questions.
	11. Tape-record instructions and questions for a test.
	12. Use objective rather than essay tests.
Poor auditory perception	1. For oral spelling tests, go slowly, enunciating each syllable and sound distinctly.
	2. Avoid oral tests.
	3. Seat students in a quiet place for testing.
	4. Allow students to take tests in an alternate site, such as the resource classroom.
	5. Place a TESTING sign on the classroom door to discourage interruptions.
Poor visual perception	1. Give directions orally as well as in written form.
	2. Check students discreetly to see whether they are on track.
	3. Give exam orally or tape-record it.
	4. Allow students to take the entire test orally in class or in the resource room.
	5. Seat students away from distractions (such as windows and doors). Use a carrel or put desk facing wall.
	6. Avoid having other students turn in papers during the test.
	7. Meet visitors at the door and talk in the hallway.
	8. Hang a DO NOT DISTURB—TESTING sign on the door.
	9. Use an alternate test site if student requests it.
Student works poorly with time constraints	1. Allow enough time for students to complete the test. Mainstreamed students may require longer periods of time.
	2. Provide breaks during lengthy tests.
	3. Allow split-halves testing. Give half the test on one day and the remaining half on the second day.
	4. Allow students to take the test in the resource room if necessary.
	5. Allow students to complete only the odd- or even-numbered questions. Circle the appropriate questions for students who may not understand the concept of odd and even.
	6. Use untimed tests.
	7. Give oral or tape-recorded tests. Students with slow writing skills can answer orally to the teacher or on tape.

FOCUS 19–1 *(continued)*

Anxiety/ Embarrassment	1. Avoid adding pressure to the test setting by admonishing students to "hurry and get finished" or "do your best; this counts for half of your six-weeks' grade."
	2. Avoid threatening to use a test to punish students for poor behavior.
	3. Give a practice test.
	4. Give a retest if needed.
	5. Don't threaten dire consequences for failure.
	6. Grade on percentage of items completed.
	7. Have students take the regular test with the class and the adapted test in the resource room.
	8. Make modified test closely resemble regular test to avoid embarrassing self-conscious students.
	9. Avoid calling attention to mainstreamed students as you help them.
	10. Confer with students privately to work out accommodations for testing.

Wood, J. W. (1998). *Adapting instruction to accommodate students in inclusive settings* (3d ed.). Upper Saddle River, NJ: Merrill/Prentice Hall, 484–87. Reprinted with permission of Merril/ Prentice Halll Publishing Company.

provide appropriate evaluation using techniques that are as similar as possible to the testing and grading used with all students in the class.

Modifying Teacher-Made Tests

In general education settings, student success is often measured by performance on teacher-made tests. The problem is that these tests frequently fail to give students with learning and behavior disabilities the opportunity to demonstrate what they have learned. This occurs because students with disabilities may have deficits in attention, memory, organization, reading, or writing that hinder performance on teacher-made tests. For these reasons, teachers need to incorporate test design accommodations that minimize the effect of attention and memory problems. Test design accommodations include modifications in format, directions, response modes, test items, test setting, and test timing (Mercer & Mercer, 1998; Salend, 1995).

Test Format Modifications

Students with disabilities sometimes master the academic content necessary for successful performance on a test but perform poorly on the test due to problems with the test format. Long, poorly designed, cluttered, or distracting tests can negatively affect student performance. Teachers can reduce format problems by giving tests that have these features:

- Are clean and printed darkly on a solid, clear background.
- Are typed (not handwritten) in a familiar style.
- Have proper spacing and sequencing of items.
- Avoid separate answer sheets requiring students to transfer responses.
- Present questions in a structured, stable, predictable sequence (this helps students make the transition from item to item).
- Provide adequate space for responding to each item.
- Have a reading level that is not too high for the students.

In addition to these test format considerations, some students may need specialized equipment. Students who are visually impaired, for example, may need large-print or braille versions of tests. Students with hearing impairments may need the services of an interpreter. Likewise, students with reading disabilities may need audiocassettes of tests and markers to focus attention and maintain their place.

Test Directions

In some situations, students with special needs may receive poor marks on a test due to difficulty in following the test directions rather than lack of knowledge of the test content. Teachers can minimize this problem by using cues that help students understand and follow test directions. Cues include color coding, font variations, underlining, bolding, symbols, and enlarging the print. Cues can highlight key parts of items and emphasize changes in specific items. For example, a model showing changes in item type or test directions can be placed in a box. Symbols such as arrows or "go" signs can delineate continuations, and "stop" signs can indicate the end of a section. Teachers, paraprofessionals, or class volunteers can also provide cues. For example, some students need a proctor to read test directions and questions.

Response Modes

Teachers may need to modify the response modes of test items for students with written or verbal communication difficulties. For example, when the mechanics of written language are not important in grading answers, students can record responses on an audiocassette, or they can take an oral exam. Students can also dictate answers to a scribe, review their answers, and then direct the scribe to revise grammar, punctuation, and word choices in the responses. Word processors, pointers, communication boards, typewriters, and other adaptive devices also can assist students. Finally, some students may need aids such as calculators, word lists, or arithmetic tables.

Test Items

Teachers should consider the needs of their students with disabilities when selecting the types of items to include on tests. With multiple-choice items, for example, teachers can improve student performance by doing these things:

- Presenting response choices in a vertical format.
- Avoiding double negatives.

- Keeping the response choices as brief as possible.
- Avoiding potentially confusing choices such as *all of the above* or *none of the above.*
- Limiting the number of choices to no more than four items.

Students who have difficulty recording their answers should have the option of circling their response selection.

With matching items, teachers should keep several design features in mind, including the following:

- Limiting sections to no more than 10 item pairs.
- Providing an equal number of choices in both columns with one correct response for each pair.
- Presenting longer items in the left-hand column.
- Organizing matching items so they all appear on the same page.
- Placing an answer space next to each item instead of having students draw lines.

Other test formats include true-false, fill in the blank, short answer, and essay. Appropriate modifications for these items include the following:

- Requiring only a brief response or an outline on short-answer or essay questions.
- Defining unfamiliar or abstract vocabulary.
- Providing a group of possible answers for fill-in-the-blank questions.
- Avoiding the use of *never, not, sometimes,* and *always* in true-false questions.
- Providing subsections that break up essay questions into manageable sections.

Modifying the Test Setting and Timing

Some students may need to take tests in an alternative setting such as alone in a quiet room, in a study carrel, in a small group, or in a special education class. Sometimes students also benefit from extended time to complete a test by giving breaks during testing or by testing over several sessions instead of one long session.

Students with disabilities can benefit from and have a right to testing modifications such as these that enable them to successfully demonstrate their knowledge and skills in general education classes. Reasonable modifications are essential so that capable students with special needs are tested fairly in ways that give them the opportunity to earn good grades.

Alternative Grading

Many students with disabilities who receive their education in general classes require and can benefit from alternative grading criteria. In some cases, **alternative grading** procedures are written into a student's IEP. In other situations, alternative grading is provided to students as needed without specifying a particular procedure in the IEP. Regardless of whether alternative grading appears in a student's IEP, the general education teacher and the special education teacher should work together as a team in the grading process. This means that the type of grading system used and the grading responsibilities of the teachers should be agreed upon prior to instruction.

Results from a comprehensive study of class grading (Bursuck et al., 1996) indicated that most teachers support the use of alternative grading with students who have special learning needs. The most common alternative grading procedures

FOCUS 19–2

Alternative Grading

- Pass/fail grading
- Multiple grading
- Grading for effort
- Portfolio-based grading
- Competency-based grading
- Point systems
- Contract grading
- Qualitative grading
- IEP grading

identified in this study were pass/fail grades, multiple grades, grading for effort, and portfolio-based grading. An explanation of how to use these and other alternative procedures follows (Mercer & Mercer, 1998; Salend, 1998; Wood, 1998). A list of alternative grading procedures appears in Focus 19–2.

Pass/Fail Grading

Pass/fail grading involves establishing minimum criteria for receiving a passing grade. Students who successfully meet the criteria receive a grade of "pass," and those who fail to demonstrate the required skills and knowledge receive a grade of "fail."

Multiple Grading

Multiple grading enables teachers to assign grades in more than one area. For example, students can earn two grades: one for effort and one for performance. Multiple grading also provides a way to grade students based on ability.

Grading for Effort

Some teachers use grading for effort with students whose ability is so low that they are unable to meet even minimum performance standards.

Portfolio Grading

Portfolio grading is another promising technique for evaluating students with special needs in inclusive settings (Mercer & Mercer, 1998). Teachers assign portfolio grades based on evaluation of the authentic samples of student work that appear in a portfolio. Rather than emphasizing grades such as test scores, the portfolio approach relies more on holistic grades. This encourages reflective teaching, learning, and assessment. As a result, students have many opportunities to evaluate their performance, to receive feedback during portfolio conferences, and to think about their learning experiences and progress. Portfolio grading has the potential for expanding measurement into new and challenging areas. More detailed information about portfolio grading and assessment appears in Chapter 18, which is an entire chapter on this exciting and useful approach to evaluating student performance.

Competency-Based Grading

With competency-based grading, students demonstrate attainment of required skills. Teachers should establish criteria for successful attainment of competencies prior to instruction so that students know what is expected. Students then receive grades based on their progress in reaching specified criterion levels for each competency or skill. Teachers often list the required competencies on a checklist, which helps monitor student progress. Teachers assign grades according to the number of successfully mastered skills.

Point Systems

Point systems assign points for successfully completing learning activities, tests, and assignments. A sample point system may consist of the following:

10 points for each of 10 homework assignments completed
20 points for each of 5 class quizzes
50 points for completing the class project or paper
10 points for daily participation in class

Students can earn all the points or partial points for a particular assignment depending on their level of performance. At the end of the grading period, students receive grades corresponding to the total number of points earned. Students with the highest number of points earn a grade of "A"; students with lower point totals earn lower grades.

Contract Grading

Contract grading involves having the teacher and the student sign a contract that describes the work that the student will complete within a specified time period. Students may contract for grades of "A," "B," or "C" depending on the amount or quality of work they complete. For example, students who contract for an "A" may be expected to write an extra paper during the grading period or complete specific enrichment activities such as documenting books, articles, or chapters read on a particular topic. The contract is written and signed prior to instruction. The teacher and the student then monitor progress in fulfilling the contract, and the teacher assigns a final grade at the end of the grading period.

Qualitative Grading

Qualitative grading relies on narrative statements—not numbers like point totals, or letter grades from A to F—that the teacher writes to describe the quality of a student's performance. The narrative statements can describe student performance, effort, attitude, behavior, interest, and learning style. For example, team teachers in an inclusion class may decide to evaluate the performance of a student with a severe disability using narrative paragraphs rather quantitative grades. Examples of completed student work can be used to support the qualitative statements.

IEP Grading

IEP grading is based on student attainment of IEP goals. The teacher measures progress and assigns grades using the evaluation criteria for each IEP objective. IEP grading is individualized for each student.

As you can see from this description of alternative grading procedures, teachers can select an appropriate grading procedure from an array of available options. Sometimes teachers combine two or more grading procedures. The particular alternative grading system that the teacher develops will depend on the needs of the individual student with consideration given to student ability, motivation, interest, behavior, and educational goals.

Questions Teachers Ask About Alternative Grades and Test Accommodations

Because so many alternative grading and testing procedures exist and new practices appear frequently, teachers have many questions about how to best modify grades and provide appropriate testing accommodations. Among the many questions that teachers ask are these:

- How can I make sure that grading modifications and testing accommodations maintain the integrity of the test, the course, and the curriculum?
- Do alternative grading and testing give students with disabilities an advantage over other students?
- How can I find the time and locate necessary resources to implement testing accommodations?
- Should students with disabilities be graded using the same grading system as their peers without disabilities?
- Should grades reflect student competence?
- Should grades reflect student growth, progress, and effort?

Responding to these questions is challenging, and teachers have a variety of opinions about the best answers. For this reason, decisions about needed adaptations should be made by IEP teams rather than individual teachers. Further, experts (Salend, 1998; Yell & Shriner, 1996) point out that the IEP is the legal document that defines an appropriate educational plan, and, as a result, student IEPs should outline the decisions of the team regarding needed modifications in grading and testing. Students with disabilities also have a legal right, under IDEA 97, to take large-scale and statewide assessments. However, because these types of assessments can create problems for students with disabilities, educators must consider procedures for reducing the possible negative effects. Again, it is the responsibility of the IEP team to address the problems and issues, and, when students need accommodations or exemptions from these assessments, IEPs should include appropriate plans for providing these services.

On a more practical level, most teachers rely on a variety of support services in providing students with needed accommodations. Although many programs have well-established support services, teachers often find that they must also develop their own support systems. For example, teachers may use paraprofessionals, resource teachers, parent volunteers, or community volunteers to assist students with accommodations such as giving oral tests, tape-recording instructions, transcribing tape-recorded test responses, and monitoring students who take tests in alternative settings.

Although few teachers question students' rights to reasonable and appropriate modifications and accommodations, most agree that alternative testing and grading should only be used when necessary. Further, students should be weaned from modifications whenever possible. This helps to ensure maximum success in the general education setting for students with special needs.

Summary

Inclusion of students with disabilities in general education means that regular classrooms are composed of a much more diverse group of students than in the past. As a result, teachers in inclusive settings must provide significant testing modifications to meet individual student needs. Although most teachers are familiar with inclusion in general, they have many questions about inclusive assessment. Furthermore, the wide variety of alternative testing procedures makes inclusive assessment complex and challenging. On the other hand, this variety also provides a range of options from which to select the best test procedure for each student.

Clearly teachers must continue efforts to improve assessment procedures for students with disabilities in inclusive classrooms. In order to achieve this goal, teachers must be familiar with appropriate procedures for assessment in inclusive settings. Teachers equipped with this knowledge can make sure that students with special needs receive fair and accurate assessment regardless of the setting in which they receive their education.

Chapter Review and Application

Multiple Choice

Directions: Read each item carefully. In the blank beside each item, write the letter of the best response. Each question contains only one best answer. Check your answers with the answer key at the end of the book.

_____ **1.** This cooperative learning activity uses cooperative learning pairs.
    a. Peer editing
    b. Peer assessment of class presentations
    c. Self-assessment
    d. Group celebration

_____ **2.** Teachers who wish to achieve the highest possible increase in the performance of low-achieving students should _____.
    a. assign individual grades with extra points based on all members reaching criterion
    b. randomly select one group member's paper to grade

      c. grade individually but give group celebration rewards

      d. assign the lowest member's grade to all members of the cooperative learning group

_____ 3. With this cooperative learning grading procedure, all group members receive the same grade, and it matters little which group member's paper the teacher selects to grade.

      a. Assign individual grades with extra points based on all members reaching criterion

      b. Randomly select one group member's paper to grade

      c. Grade individually but give group celebration rewards

      d. Assign the lowest member's grade to all members of the cooperative learning group

_____ 4. With this cooperative learning grading procedure, the students receive an individual grade.

      a. Assign individual grades with extra points based on all members reaching criterion.

      b. Randomly select one group member's paper to grade.

      c. Grade individually with group celebration rewards.

      d. Assign the lowest member's grade to all members of the cooperative learning group.

_____ 5. Student performance can be negatively affected by long, cluttered, distracting tests. Such tests require modifications in _____.

      a. test format

      b. test directions

      c. response modes

      d. test items

_____ 6. When teachers modify classroom tests by arranging for students to record responses on an audiocassette tape, take an oral exam, or dictate answers to a scribe, they are modifying the _____.

      a. test format

      b. test directions

      c. response modes

      d. test items

_____ 7. This alternative grading procedure involves assigning grades in more than one area.

      a. Competency-based grading

      b. Contract grading

      c. Qualitative grading

      d. Multiple grading

_____ 8. This alternative grading procedure involves specifying the amount of work students are willing to complete in a period of time for a particular grade.

      a. Competency-based grading

      b. Contract grading

      c. Qualitative grading

      d. Multiple grading

____ **9.** This alternative grading procedure uses narrative statements that a teacher writes to describe the quality of a student's performance.
   a. Competency-based grading
   b. Contract grading
   c. Qualitative grading
   d. Multiple grading

Short Answers

Directions: Review your understanding of the material in this chapter by answering the following short answer items. Compare your responses to the sample answers at the end of the book. Your responses should contain information that is similar to but not exactly the same as the information in the sample answers.

1. You recently agreed to coteach in an inclusion class with a fifth-grade teacher. What assessment questions and concerns do you think the teacher may have? What will you do to help answer the questions and ease the concerns?
2. Which alternative grading criteria do you think you would be most likely to use? Name three specific alternatives, and explain why you would use each of them.
3. In response to poorly designed teacher-made tests, students with disabilities often make comments like these: "I didn't understand some of the questions," "I skipped some questions because there were too many on the page," "The directions were confusing," "I lost my place on the answer sheet," "I didn't have enough room for my answers," and "I thought the true-false questions were tricky." As a teacher, what can you do to modify your classroom tests to minimize these concerns?
4. Which guideline for test taking in Focus 19–1 seems the most practical to you? Describe why the guideline is practical, and give an additional test-taking tip that was not mentioned in the guidelines.
5. You have been asked to make some brief remarks at an upcoming faculty meeting about the benefits of assessment modifications for students with disabilities in inclusive settings. What are the three or four ideas you would share with your colleagues about inclusive assessment in the elementary school? Why did you select these particular topics?

References

Baker, E., Wang, M., & Walberg, H. (1995). The effects of inclusion on learning. *Educational Leadership* 52 (4), 33–35.

Bursuck, W., Polloway, E. A., Plante, L., Epstein, M. H., Jayanthi, M., & McConeghy, J. (1996). Report card grading and adaptations: A national survey of classroom practices. *Exceptional Children* 62, 301–18.

Carlson, H., Ellison, D., & Dietrich, J. (1988). *Servicing Low Achieving Pupils and Pupils With Learning Disabilities: A Comparison of Two Approaches.* Duluth, MN: University of Minnesota, Duluth, and Duluth Public Schools (ERIC Document Reproduction Service no. ED 283 341).

Cohen, E. G. (1994). Restructuring the classroom: Conditions for productive small groups. *Review of Educational Research* 64 (1), 1–35.

Coufal, K. (1993). Collaborative consultation for speech/language pathologists. *Topics in Language Disorders* 14 (1), 1–4.

Gearheart, B. R., Weishahn, M. L., & Gearheart, C. J. (1996). *The Exceptional Student in the Regular Classroom* (6th ed.). Upper Saddle River, NJ: Merrill/Prentice Hall.

Johnson, D. W., Johnson, R. T., & Holubec, E. H. (1998). Supplemental text for foundations of cooperative learning; Chapter seven: Assessment and evaluation. Jacksonville, FL: Workshop handout.

Mercer, C. D., & Mercer, A. R. (1998). *Teaching Students With Learning Problems* (5th ed.). Upper Saddle River, NJ: Merrill/Prentice Hall.

Pomplan, M. (1996). Cooperative groups: Alternative assessment for students with disabilities? *Journal of Special Education* 30, 1–17.

———. (1997). When students with disabilities participate in cooperative groups. *Exceptional Children* 64, 49–59.

Putnam, J. W., Spiegel, A. N., & Bruininks, R. H. (1995). Future directions in education and inclusion of students with disabilities: A delphi investigation. *Exceptional Children* 61, 553–77.

Sailor, W., Gee, K., and Karasoff, P. (1993). Full inclusion and school restructuring. In M. E. Snell (Ed.), *Instruction of Students With Severe Disabilities* (4th ed). New York: Merrill/Macmillan, 1–23.

Salend, S. J. (1995). Modifying tests for diverse learners. *Intervention in School and Clinic* 31, 84–90.

———. (1998). *Effective Mainstreaming: Creating Inclusive Classrooms* (3d ed.). Upper Saddle River, NJ: Merrill/Prentice Hall.

Tiegerman-Farber, E., & Radziewicz, C. (1998). *Collaborative Decision Making: The Pathway to Inclusion.* Upper Saddle River, NJ: Merrill/Prentice Hall.

Trump, G., Allen, G., & Hange, J. (1996). *Teacher Perceptions of and Strategies for Inclusion: A Regional Summary of Focus Group Interview Findings.* Charleston, WV: Appalachia Educational Laboratory.

Webb, N. M. (1995). Group collaboration in assessment: Multiple objectives, processes and outcomes. *Educational Evaluation and Policy Analysis* 17, 239–61.

Wood, J. W. (1998). *Adapting instruction to accommodate students in inclusive settings* (3d ed.). Upper Saddle River, NJ: Merrill/Prentice Hall.

Yell, M. L., & Shriner, J. G. (1996). Inclusive education: Legal and policy implications. *Preventing School Failure* 40 (3), 101–8.

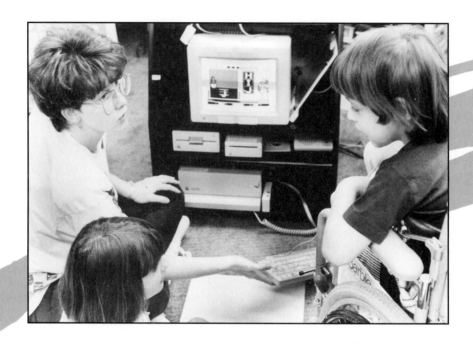

C H A P T E R   2 0

Technology Issues and Future Perspectives

Overview

This final chapter provides an overview of technology issues and future perspectives in assessing students with special needs. In this chapter you investigate how teachers are using computer technology to better assess students with special needs. Your review of technology includes a study of computer-based test development, scoring and reporting, administration, and interpretation. You also consider technology issues such as accessibility of computer-based assessment for students with special needs, and you also have the opportunity to examine future trends in assessment. In your study of future trends, you learn about the continued expansion of the testing movement and consider current issues regarding fairness in testing and minimum competency testing. Your study of technology issues and future trends will help you gain a sense of the challenges facing special educators and the significant changes that will take place in assessment in the future.

Objectives

After reading this chapter, you will be prepared to do the following:

- Use computer-based test development, scoring, reporting, administration, and interpretation programs.
- Understand the technology issues related to assessing students with special needs.
- Describe the continued expansion of testing in school and society.
- Discuss the issue of fairness in testing.
- Define minimum competency testing.
- Discuss the concerns of teachers regarding minimum competency testing.

Technology Issues

The rapid spread of technology, especially computer technology, influences all aspects of assessing students with special needs. Test development, scoring, reporting, administration, and interpretation are all changing as the cost of computers and related technology decreases and the capabilities increase. Technology will certainly become even more important in the future. For example, teachers will likely use computers for all kinds of instructional tasks, including assessment. In addition to the desktop computers now in widespread use, teachers will also rely on networked computers, notebook computers, handheld computers, Internet access, and other technology in an effort to provide the best possible assessment services for students with special needs.

Widespread implementation of computers and related technology will enable teachers to assess students with disabilities in new and exciting ways. As computers evolve, a major outcome will be testing that reduces barriers for students with special needs. Many technology solutions are being explored, such as large adjustable keyboards, touch screens with raised-line images, and speech recognition programs. As computer-based assessment develops, students will be able to hear audio explanations, highlight specific areas of the screen, listen to verbal descriptions of graphic material, and view on-screen sign language explanations of test materials. Research is ongoing to discover the best ways to use computers in assessment, and much of this research focuses on test development (Chung & Baker, 1997; Hurst et al., 1997; Mislevy & Chang, 1998).

Test Development

Developers of commercial, standardized instruments have used a number of sophisticated computer programs in the test development process for quite some time. Teachers are now beginning to use test development software as well, which helps teachers improve their tests and their test-writing skills while making it easier for teachers to modify tests for students with special needs. The increasing variety of test development and item analysis software programs available for teachers includes test-generation programs.

Test-Generation Programs   Test-generation programs enable teachers to type in questions, scoring criteria, test format information, and other test specifications using relatively simple, menu-driven computer software programs. Teachers can revise, review, modify, update, and print out the resulting test. They can also mix together multiple-choice, short-answer, true-false, and other types of questions by selecting them manually or having the computer randomly select them. Programs for creating pencil-on-paper and computer-based tests are available from a variety of sources. For example, Assessment Systems Corporation (www.assess.com) offers several development programs including Examiner, Question Mark, and FastTEST. Examiner (Assessment Systems Corporation, n.d.) is a Windows-based item-banking and test administration program for creating paper-on-pencil or computer-based tests. Question Mark (Assessment Systems Corporation, n.d.) is a program for creating computerized tests that can be administered from a local PC or over a network. Question Mark supports a number of question format types and allows incorporation of multimedia into questions. FastTEST (Assessment Systems Corporation, ND) makes it easy to enter test questions into item banks and then quickly create tests for printing. An optional module allows administration on a PC. Teacher's Helper Plus (Visions Technology in Education, n.d.) is a teacher/student utility availabe in Windows and Macintosh formats. Teacher's Helper Plus enables teachers to make worksheets, thematic units, and tests in multiple choice, matching, fill-in, true/false, and picture formats.

Although test-generation programs such as these have many attractive features, they also display certain limitations, which include test security concerns when using computer-based test administration, the lack of access to the computer hardware and software necessary to use these programs, and flexibility limitations imposed by computer-based test-generation programs that make it difficult to adapt tests for learners with special needs.

Another test-generation option that teachers are using is on-line e-mail communication to discuss and exchange teacher-made tests. More and more schools are installing networks so that teachers within the school can share all types of information with each other, including tests. Teachers who have Internet access can use e-mail to share teacher-made tests with colleagues from other schools and school districts.

IEP Development   Many school systems provide teachers with computer programs to assist in developing IEPs and measuring student progress in achieving IEP goals. Teachers and IEP teams use these programs to formulate short- and long-term objectives and to accomplish other IEP development tasks, such as completing the cover page. Teachers can create objectives or select them from a data bank and modify them as necessary to fit individual students. For example, teachers can use programs such as IEP Master (B.A.S.I.C., ND) (www.iepmaster.com) to quickly and easily generate individualized IEPs for students with disabilities. The steps in creating computer-based IEPs using programs such as IEP Master begin with entering each student into an IEP data bank. Next the teacher selects the content area, such as math or motor skills. An objective for the area is then identified along with appropriate tasks. The IEP is completed by selecting the level of mastery, adding grading period codes, and specifying other required services. Although computer-based IEPs hold much promise for the future, certain limitations may reduce the usefulness of such programs. For example, teachers who use programs such as these may need extensive and expensive technical support. Technical support needs include assistance with the hardware and software problems that frequently arise, especially with new systems and programs. Teachers also need training so that they can learn to use the new IEP software efficiently.

Computer-Based Assessment of Behavior   Much potential exists for developing innovative computer-based behavioral assessment procedures. Computers can assist teachers in conducting interviews, completing checklists, filling out rating scales, carrying out direct observations of student behavior, and helping students monitor their own behavior. Experts in behavioral assessment are also exploring additional uses of computer technology to assist in designing, implementing, and monitoring behavioral assessment and treatment programs.

Test Scoring and Reporting

Test services have been using computers for years to score tests, interpret results, and produce reports. They employ the ubiquitous bubble-in scoring forms. After computers read the forms, they score them and print out various reports. School systems continue to use testing services, especially for scoring the group achievement tests administered at the end of the school year. Testing services provide scores, test reports, and analysis of results for individual students, classes, schools, and school systems.

Until recently, computer-based test processing was provided only by large, commercial testing services. Recent developments in personal computers have brought computer scoring and reporting capabilities to the local school systems and individual teachers. For example, computer scoring and reporting software is available for most of the individually administered standardized tests that special education teachers use in the classroom, such as the *Peabody Individual Achievement Test-Revised* (Markwardt, 1998) and the *KeyMath Diagnostic Test of Arithmetic-Revised* (Connolly, 1998). A sample computer-generated diagnostic report from the *KeyMath-R* appears in Chapter 6. Teachers and diagnosticians use software like this to help them score, interpret, and disseminate assessment data.

Records Management and Grade Reporting   Computerized records-management and grade-reporting programs enable teachers to keep student records in a manner comparable to the traditional student record booklet. Teachers maintain attendance, test scores, grades on papers, homework assignments, and other information in this way. Records-management software also averages test score grades and produces weighted averages. Teachers can track the progress of individual students and measure group performance using these programs.

Many teachers use grading software programs such as Grade Point by Paper Trail Software (www.tcd.net/~papertrl/) and Grade Quick by Jackson Software (www.jacksoncorp.com) to simplify the many grading tasks that take time away from teaching. Teachers can use grading software to create progress reports, average grades, prepare report cards, prepare for conferences, develop parent reports, plan for remedial instruction, track assignments, and create checklists. Teachers can also use grading software as a motivating tool by giving students daily access to their grades. An electronic system for providing this access is described in Focus 20–1.

In addition to using software to assist with grading, teachers are also using other types of electronic records-management software to help them with performance, portfolio, and authentic assessment. One of the most widely used software programs in this category is the Learner Profile, a description of the use of which appears in Focus 20–2.

Scoring Essay Tests   Increased emphasis on writing skills coupled with computer delivery has combined to produce promising new software for scoring essay tests. Available prototype software uses rubrics like those discussed in Chapter 18. Pilot tests (Educational Testing Service, 1998) provide possible indications that computerized scoring of essays has the potential to become as reliable as teacher scoring. If this occurs in the future, then some essays will be scored by the teacher and computer together. Differences in scores can be resolved by the teacher or by a second teacher.

FOCUS 20–1

Using Grading Software as a Motivating Tool

One innovative use of electronic grading software involves using obsolete computers to provide students with real-time access to their grades. Amaro (1997) described how to give students hands-on, daily access to their grades by using a surplus computer equipped with a simple gradebook program. Giving immediate access to grades helps eliminate surprises for students who think they have good grades but don't, and it makes it possible for students to set exact goals for raising their grades. As a result, students with low grades will be motivated to work harder to boost their averages; students with high grades will be encouraged to continue to work hard to maintain their grades. Teachers who use this system should maintain an original copy of the grades on a secure computer and use floppy disks to update the student-accessible computer. Care must also be taken to ensure privacy so that students cannot view the grades of their peers. This approach to grading makes averages real to students with special needs because they often fail to understand how averages work and may see grading as a process under the control of the teacher.

Although automated scoring of multiple-choice questions is commonplace, computerized scoring of essay tests represents a significant jump in technology, and much needs to be done before teachers can use such technology. At present, available rubrics measure factors that correlate with high and low scores assigned to essays by experienced teachers. These factors include length of essay, word choice, word variety, and structure. Longer essays that incorporate sentence structure variety and sophisticated vocabulary, for example, receive high scores because these qualities are valued by teachers. Although much remains to be developed, natural language processing programs for scoring essays may develop further so that teachers can use them to help in scoring large numbers of essays in a relatively short time. However, this type of computer scoring will not likely replace teacher scoring. Content knowledge, creativity, and originality of ideas are all qualities that are still unmeasurable by computer.

Computerized Test Administration

Computerized testing involves the actual administration of tests using computers. Like other forms of computer-based assessment, large testing services have been using computerized test administration for some time. New technology is beginning to bring computer testing capabilities to personal computers. One of the most useful aspects of computer-based administration is adaptive testing.

Computer Adaptive Testing   **Computer adaptive testing** (CAT) is a recent advance in computer administration that enables interaction between the test and the test taker. CAT matches a test's difficulty with a test taker's ability. By interacting with test takers, adaptive tests provide an optimal number of test items for each test taker.

FOCUS 20–2

Electronic Tracking of Student Progress

More and more teachers are using electronic progress-tracking software to help them with performance, portfolio, and authentic assessment (Ungar, 1998). For example, the Learner Profile (Sunburst Communications, n.d.) (http://www.sunburst.com) is an electronic management software program that includes collections of performance indicators for a variety of curricular areas. Teachers can also add rubrics or learning indicators to accommodate specific district, school, or classroom objectives. The Learner Profile is available for desktop, laptop, and handheld computers in both Windows and Macintosh formats. This means that teachers with laptops or handheld computers can use the software to collect data unobtrusively while interacting with their students. Once teachers gather the data, they can generate reports for report cards, parent-teacher conferences, and portfolios. Collections of performance indicators are available for academic, vocational, physical education, special needs, early learning, and extracurricular activities. The special education collection, for example, is designed especially for young students or older students with severe disabilities. Topics include object performance, visual development, following directions, identification/matching, imitation, and language structure. The special education set includes over 100 categories containing over 1000 observables. Observations are made by an individual student, a group of students, or the whole class. Student progress on observations is described by choosing one of the following descriptors: "developing," "mastered," or "integrating." Other collections include a set of general observables that focuses on collaborative skills, life-long learning, class participation, work habits, and problem solving. Software for student self-assessment is also available. The self-assessment software allows students to actively participate in the assessment process by providing a simple, easy way for students to reflect on and make thoughtful judgments about their work. Because electronic tracking software is so new, it has several drawbacks, including limited availability of programs from which to choose and a lack of laptop and handheld computers for teachers to use in the classroom. Improved versions of tracking software along with greater availability of portable computers may make this technology more useful in the future. Overall, these programs hold promise for giving teachers greater control over and better organization of student and group information.

CAT produces a different set of test items for each test taker based on the test taker's responses. For example, when a test taker correctly answers an item, the test responds by providing a more difficult item. In contrast, when a test taker answers incorrectly, the test adapts by giving an easier item. Adaptive tests use fewer items than conventional tests, and this makes them faster, easier to take, and more accurate. As more adaptive test-development programs become available for personal computers, teachers will be able to develop adaptive tests for students with special needs.

Multimedia Assessment   In the near future, advanced multimedia computer technology will allow for assessment using video, audio, and sophisticated graphics. With multimedia assessment, test takers actually interact with test information. This use of technology goes beyond paper versions of tests by offering capabilities for measuring complex learning. For example, performance assessment using computer simulation will allow student assessment such as virtual driving tests and computer-simulated surgical procedures. Networked computers will be used to assess teamwork. Likewise, on-line Internet programs will assess problem-solving skills associated with search behavior and search performance. Experts (Chung & Baker, 1997) are already using on-line multimedia technology to develop constructed response tasks such as concept mapping. Constructed response tasks measure student learning processes and conceptualization skills. A typical constructed response task involves having students create a concept map on an environmental science subject like the food chain. Students use an on-line computer to develop their concept maps, which are based on students' existing knowledge of the subject. Students submit their initial concept map via the Internet and receive feedback about which concepts need work. At this point students are given access to Web pages on environmental science so they can search for information, modify their concept maps, and request feedback. Students create their maps using on-line computer access to a set of concepts and links. Students can add, delete, or move concepts or links at will. The concept maps can include text, graphics, sound, pictures, or video. For example, a student may wish to show understanding of the food chain by including a graphic depicting eel grass and a video clip of a shark eating a fish. This illustration shows how multimedia technology can be used with constructed-response tasks such as concept maps to enable assessment of student learning processes in ways that go beyond the capabilities of conventional paper testing

Computer-Based Test Interpretation

Teachers and diagnosticians may select from among a number of available software programs that interpret test results and generate narrative reports for individual students. Report-writing software is available for achievement tests, intelligence tests, behavior rating scales, language tests, and other types of widely used instruments. Most report-writing programs produce a description of the assessment instrument, the student's specific test results, interpretive information, and recommendations based on the student's particular scores and item responses. Most experts recommend using computer-generated reports as the foundation for preparing professional evaluations. This use of reports provides report writers with significant assistance in the time-consuming and difficult process of developing diagnostic evaluations.

Guidelines for Computer-Based Testing and Interpretation

Although most teachers are enthusiastic about the possibilities of using computers and related technology to make assessment more efficient and responsive to the needs of students, many teachers have questions about the possible misuses of computer testing. Teachers are concerned about the validity of computer-based testing, about the accessibility of computers for students with disabilities, and about the possible misuse of automated test interpretation.

Validity of Computer-Based Testing   When a test is available in both pencil-on-paper and computer-based administration formats, the test scores from both administration formats should yield equivalent or parallel results. This is accomplished by conducting validity research that compares both sets of scores to establish equivalency. Because computer-based assessment alters the mode of administration and thus changes the test, conventional tests cannot simply be transferred to the computer. For example, most paragraphs that measure reading comprehension fit on one page in a conventional response booklet, but on the computer the paragraph fills up more than one computer screen. Therefore, with computer-based assessment, the test taker must scan back and forth on the screen to read a paragraph and answer the comprehension questions. This makes a computer-based test different from the same test in pencil-on-paper format. Furthermore, reading a paragraph from a computer screen is unlike reading the same paragraph from a test booklet. For these reasons, developers of computer-based tests must establish the equivalence of the conventional and computer forms to ensure the validity of the resulting scores.

Ensuring Accessibility of Computer Administration   Computer-based testing raises new issues of equity and access for students with disabilities (Educational Testing Service Net, 1998). For example, traditional assessment provides accessibility for test takers with disabilities by offering a variety of accommodations such as braille, audiocassettes, extended time, sign language interpreters, and human readers. These access strategies may or may not be directly transferrable to computer-based assessment. Computers and technology have introduced new access challenges that are being addressed by assistive technologies or adaptive computing, and many of these adaptations can be adopted for computer-based testing.

Computerized testing may even improve accessibility for some students. For example, students with certain physical disabilities who have difficulty writing responses in a test booklet can successfully respond to the same questions using a computer with an adapted keyboard or another appropriate alternative input device. On the other hand, providing adaptive input devices alone may not address the range of issues faced by students with disabilities who need to take computer-based tests. To avoid the problem of unfair administration, test takers with special needs must receive proper training along with appropriate adaptations prior to administration of a computer-based test. This means that test givers need to be aware of the accessibility issues associated with computer-based testing, and test developers must concentrate efforts on creating tests that reduce or eliminate barriers.

Judging the Appropriateness of Computer-Based Test Interpretations   By far the greatest concern among professionals is the possibility for misuse of automated test interpretation. To avoid potential pitfalls, professionals who use computer-based interpretative reports must adjust or modify automated reports to account for individual student needs. Potential problems with automated interpretation include the following:

- Inexperienced professionals who treat computerized reports as objective without considering possible limitations and problems.

- Developers of computer-based interpretation programs who fail to provide information about the limitations of such reports.
- Developers who fail to provide information validating the use of their computer-based report programs.

☑ Comprehension Checklist

Special educators are finding more and more uses for computer-based technology in assessment. Clearly computer-based assessment will continue to become easier to use, less expensive, and more powerful. Although questions remain about limitations, difficulty of use, expense, and accessibility, computer-based assessment is rapidly gaining acceptance because of the potential for saving valuable time, increasing accuracy, motivating students, and easing the burden of record keeping. As the technology is widely adopted, teachers will create new and innovative assessment approaches that will help identify performance levels, develop IEPs, and measure progress.

Future Perspectives

Perhaps the most significant future trend is continued expansion of the testing movement. Soon after World War II, psychologists, educators, and other professionals began developing tests for virtually everything. This rapid pace of test development has continued since then. Key factors contributing to an increase in testing include increasing demand for fairness in testing and for teacher and school accountability. As a result, testing has become a way of life in the United States, and the future of assessment is clearly one of continued expansion.

The effect of this expansion is particularly dramatic in special education. As a result, special educators, working in concert with professionals from related disciplines, need to monitor advances in testing to make sure that new assessments translate into solutions for students with disabilities. The following section describes growth in testing and discusses how future developments might impact, positively or negatively, the education of students with special needs.

Continued Expansion of the Testing Movement

Although testing affects the lives of all Americans, the effect is especially evident in the schools. Prior to the late 1970s, for example, most school systems had few eligibility testing requirements for placing students into special education. Since then new laws with rigid standards require all school systems to employ extensive eligibility testing as part of the placement process. These eligibility testing standards have focused attention on developing better norm-referenced instruments, especially standardized achievement and intelligence tests. More importantly, the new standards have helped to ensure appropriate identification and education of students with disabilities.

Expansion of Norm-Referenced Testing The continued growth and refinement of norm-referenced testing produce many benefits, but negative effects occur as well.

Special educators are all too familiar with students in special education who have been tested over and over. Some students have cumulative records containing so many test reports and related information that multiple file folders are needed to hold the large volume of material. Although attorneys require all this information in complicated legal cases to protect the child, the family, and the teacher, a point of diminishing returns occurs when additional testing is not worth the time and expense because it fails to provide any significant new information. Also, such "overtesting" may foster negative attitudes about assessment for all those involved.

Teachers have many other questions about the continued expansion of testing, such as "What new tests need to be developed?" "How much testing will be computer based?" "How can developers design new tests so that they help students with special needs to the maximum extent possible?" and "What is the role of curriculum-based assessment?"

Expansion of Curriculum-Based Assessment   Along with the growth of norm-referenced testing, the testing movement has also expanded to include new and promising approaches in curriculum-based assessment (CBA). Teachers are especially interested in CBA approaches because these procedures help them develop better IEPs, improve accountability, and link assessment with instruction. Teachers are finding that CBA techniques like error pattern analysis and portfolio assessment are especially helpful in inclusive settings. See Chapters 15, 16, 17, and 18 for specific information about these and other CBA techniques.

Like all forms of assessment, CBA has drawbacks. Some curriculum-based procedures, for example, tend to focus on isolated tasks and skills that may be important in a particular setting but are difficult to generalize in other situations. Furthermore, CBA suffers from the reliability and validity problems associated with all forms of criterion-referenced testing. This can lead to bias by producing inconsistent, ineffective data. Teachers need to be aware of these drawbacks so that they can avoid using CBA in unfair ways. Despite these weaknesses, continued expansion of CBA clearly holds much promise for the future.

Fairness in Testing

One of the containing concerns associated with the testing movement is fairness in testing. **Fairness in testing** refers to equity of tests for all students regardless of race, ethnicity, language, gender, or cultural background. A major fairness-in-testing problem is the disproportionate number of students from minority groups who receive low scores on standardized tests and other assessment instruments. Discrimination in assessment may also occur in other forms. One form involves inaccurate referrals for placement into special education as a result a student's minority status, gender, or age. For example, teachers may underrefer students from minority groups for programs serving those who are gifted. In contrast, teachers may also underrefer students from majority groups for programs serving students with mild mental retardation.

Discrimination can also occur when evaluators administer and score tests. Common administration and scoring errors include failure to establish rapport prior to assessment and mishandling the administration of a test or interview (e.g., rushing or upsetting a student) because of preconceived ideas based on a student's background, appearance, or language. Other questions about fairness in testing result from technical inadequacies of tests such as normative groups that fail to include students from diverse backgrounds.

Critics continue to raise questions about fairness in testing, and there are certainly many difficult and controversial issues related to nondiscriminatory assessment. Some critics argue that because developers create tests within the context of their culture, elements of bias are bound to appear. Although it may be impossible to develop tests that are entirely culture free, test developers and users must continue efforts to reduce partiality to a minimum and to take prejudice into account in the use of test results.

The success of students from historically underrepresented groups on tests is another fairness-in-testing issue (Thorndike, 1997). Some students from minority groups, such as recent immigrants from Southeast Asia, are highly motivated to perform well on individual tasks such as tests of academic achievement. In contrast, some Native American students focus more on group success and group tasks and less on individual performance associated with tasks such as taking individually administered tests. The challenge is to refine the overall approach to assessment to account for differences such as these. This refinement might lead to more adaptive testing based on students' abilities, interests, and experiences. For example, the test scores of majority students may require an interpretation different from the test scores of some minority students. The challenge is to agree on what types of interpretations are appropriate for students from diverse backgrounds. The goal is to incorporate those adjustments that provide the most accurate and the fairest test score interpretations and assessment decisions.

Forms of Bias   In a discussion of fairness as it relates to the technical qualities of tests, Rust and Golombok (1989) described three forms of bias: item bias, internal bias, and external bias. **Item bias** refers to unfairness that exists within individual items on a test, an example of which is a question about temperature based on the Celsius scale in a nation that uses the Fahrenheit scale. Item bias is the easiest form of bias to correct. Test developers usually rely on various forms of error pattern analysis to identify questions that are unfair to groups of individuals. After identifying unfair items, the developers either modify or eliminate the biased questions in the test.

Internal bias refers to differences in average scores among two or more groups due to the qualities of a test rather than actual differences among the groups. Internal bias has received the most attention from both experts in testing and policymakers. As a result, developers of standardized tests routinely include evidence to show that their tests avoid internal bias. For example, when developers prepare a new test, they compare scores from the new test with those from an existing test that is free from internal bias. This comparison includes scores from specific groups of students, such as students from minority groups and students with disabilities. If scores from the new test are consistent with those from the existing test across the various groups, the new test avoids internal bias. On the other hand, if scores from the new test fail to match scores from the existing test, internal bias may exist. Any bias problems must be corrected prior to publication.

The third type of bias, **external bias,** occurs when decision makers use test results in an unfair manner. External bias can occur when school systems place students unfairly on the basis of test scores. For example, this happens when the placement procedure creates a staffing pattern in which minority students are overrepresented in classes for children who are mentally retarded and underrepresented in classes for children who are gifted. In an attempt to avoid this type of bias, the law requires schools, agencies, and institutions to follow established guidelines that incorporate strict rules designed to eliminate external bias and ensure fairness.

Because it is so important that tests be fair and that students, parents, and teachers believe that tests are fair, efforts must continue to eliminate the effect of discrimination in assessment. Fortunately, test developers and policymakers are continuing to improve assessment so that it is as fair as possible for all students.

Minimum Competency Testing

Minimum competency testing is an aspect of assessment that affects all areas of society, including education. In addition to the widespread use of minimum competency tests in education, business, industry, and government all rely on these tests to determine whether individuals have entry-level knowledge and skills. Teachers, for example, are familiar with minimum competency tests on a personal level because most states require teachers to pass them as part of the teacher licensing and certifying process. In addition to general considerations, minimum competency tests have particular implications for students with disabilities. Educators use **minimum competency tests** to determine whether students demonstrate the minimal skill level necessary for completion of specific grades and school subjects, and ultimately for graduation from school. Most minimum competency tests are criterion-referenced tests and checklists of skills rather than norm-referenced tests. They typically rely on a pass-fail scoring system in which passing is based on a preestablished cutoff level (often 80% correct). State legislation requiring administration of minimum competency tests to students is largely responsible for the development of these instruments. Virtually all states require minimum competency testing for students, and some have separate minimum competency tests for students with disabilities. In addition, many local school districts have developed minimum competency tests for use in specific programs, including programs in exceptional student education.

Benefits of Minimum Competency Testing Benefits of minimum competency tests include the following:

- Establishing standards for basic knowledge, skills, and performance levels.
- Furnishing a tool for measuring competence at the basic level.
- Establishing criteria for identifying students who fail to demonstrate minimum proficiency.
- Measuring important knowledge and skills for educational decisions related to graduation, promotion, retention, and instructional intervention.

Disadvantages of Minimum Competency Testing Many issues and problems also surround the minimum competency testing movement (Perkins, 1982; Thorndike,

1997). One of the greatest concerns is higher failure rates among minority students. Other disadvantages include the following:

- Students who fail may be stigmatized.
- Students who fail may be unfairly labeled.
- The tests place the burden of failure on the student.
- The tests may lead to neglect of the needs of gifted, talented, and average students by stressing minimum standards.
- Teachers often feel pressured to teach to the tests.

Unfortunately, many minimum competency tests focus on lower-order facts and information necessary to pass the tests rather than higher-level thinking and problem-solving skills. In addition, as a result of the pressure to obtain good test scores, teachers may spend instructional time in test preparation rather than in teaching what students need to learn next. For these reasons, minimum competency tests seem to focus more on ensuring that students below a certain level do not graduate rather than on educating students and raising educational standards.

Further criticism of the movement suggests that teachers sometimes fall into the trap of focusing the curriculum on minimum competencies instead of including minimum competencies as one aspect in the total curriculum. In response to this problem, experts recommend redesigning procedures for measuring minimum skills so that they complement teaching practices and include observations and performance samples of students along with test scores.

Accountability

Accountability refers to documenting what students are learning and how well they are progressing in their learning. In education, evidence of accountability is usually obtained from results of state and district large-group testing programs that produce scores from norm- and criterion-referenced tests, including minimum competency tests. According to Elliott et al. (1998), the importance of this issue can be seen in concerns about educational accountability that regularly appear in newspapers, magazines, radio programs, and political speeches. Educators also have questions about assessment and accountability. In particular, teachers are concerned with the implications of accountability for students, parents, and school personnel. They are even more concerned about pressure to "teach the test" so that the students in their school and school district produce "good" test scores.

Test scores are important because decision makers typically use results from state and district assessment programs as the basis for educational accountability. For example, when test scores rise in a particular school or district, decision makers conclude that the educational program is doing well. Likewise, falling test scores indicate problems in the educational program. The result is decisions about curriculum, allocation of resources, and policy development that emanate from these assessments.

Until recently, the scores of students with disabilities were not at issue because most of them were excluded from participation in state and district assessment programs (Erickson et al., 1996; Vanderwood et al., 1998). However, regulations in the newest version of the Individuals with Disabilities Education Act require the participation of students with disabilities in general state and district assessment programs. Appropriate accommodations must be provided as necessary. Regulations also permit alternate assessment for a small percentage of students with disabilities who are unable to participate in the regular testing program.

These new regulations enable the participation of students with disabilities in state and district assessments in one of three ways (Elliott et al., 1998). When possible, students take the tests without accommodation. Other students take the tests with accommodations. Finally, some students take an alternate or different assessment. The IEP team is responsible for making the decision about student needs for accommodation or alternate testing. In order to make appropriate decisions, the team members must know the tests that are being given and the accommodations that meet each student's needs. Fortunately, each state has developed assessment accommodation policies that provide guidelines for making appropriate decisions (Thurlow et al., 1997).

These new requirements for participation in district and state testing programs are another example of the dramatic changes taking place in how schools assess and educate students with disabilities. Educators are in the process of finding solutions to the many questions about assessment programs, accommodations, and alternate testing. The goal is to make the educational system accountable for the learning progress of all students, including those with disabilities.

☑ Comprehension Checklist

Although it is clear that the testing movement will continue to expand, the direction of this expansion is more difficult to predict. Future innovations will certainly include widespread application of computer-based assessment and other technological advances. In addition, the issues of fairness in testing and accountability will remain critical concerns. Finally, questions about the efficacy of minimum competency testing must also be resolved.

Summary

Assessment in special education will continue to evolve in response to changes in society and technology. Changes will include the revision of existing tests and evaluation procedures as well as the introduction of new tests and measurement techniques. For the most part, these changes will result in improvements in assessment that will help teachers solve current problems in special education. New directions in assessment, such as increased use of computers and related technology, will help special educators find solutions to contemporary issues, including fairness in testing and minimum competency testing. Because evolution will be a key feature of assessment in the future, special educators must be sensitive to new ideas that arise out of their experiences and must be open to learning innovative measurement techniques.

Although educators may disagree about the usefulness of particular assessment procedures, they generally agree that assessment is important, and they understand the need for evaluation. Because assessment must occur, the goal is to ensure that testing has a clear purpose. Much support exists when educators clearly define the reasons for assessment and show ways in which the results will help students. However, achieving this goal requires further improvement of assessment practices by refining existing tools and introducing fresh approaches. The challenge is to use assessment in new ways that help children grow, develop, and achieve as much as possible.

For the special education teacher, assessment—the process of using tests and other measurement instruments to make educational decisions—is an indispensable tool in providing a full range of appropriate educational services to students with special needs. For this reason, special education teachers must have a working knowledge of assessment concepts and procedures. As special educators consider their future role, they need to continue to develop their assessment skills. The future of assessment in special education is bright.

Chapter Review and Application

Multiple Choice

Directions: Read each item carefully. In the blank beside each item, write the letter of the best response. Each question contains only one best answer. Check your answers with the answer key at the end of the book.

_____ 1. Computer software that enables teachers to _____ is available.
   a. create standardized test instruments
   b. develop national norms
   c. develop IEPs

_____ 2. Commercial test services use computers to _____.
   a. help students self-monitor test-taking skills
   b. interpret results
   c. carry out observations of student behavior

_____ 3. Records-management software helps teachers _____.
   a. maintain attendance
   b. analyze standardized test scores
   c. develop a behavior management system

_____ 4. Computerized essay scoring measures factors that include _____.
   a. word choice
   b. overall achievement
   c. intelligence

_____ 5. Computer adaptive testing _____.
   a. provides maximum accessibility for students with physical impairments
   b. matches a test's difficulty with a test taker's ability
   c. matches a test's results with a test taker's adaptability

_____ 6. Video, audio, and sophisticated graphics are used in _____.
   a. computer adaptive testing
   b. computer-based records management
   c. multimedia assessment

_____ **7.** Report-writing software uses information based on _____.
      a. students' raw scores from testing
      b. concept maps and links
      c. text, graphics, and video

_____ **8.** The greatest concern among professionals regarding computer-based testing is _____.
      a. misuse of automated test interpretation
      b. equivalency of computer-based and conventional tests
      c. accessibility of computer-based tests for students with disabilities

_____ **9.** A negative effect of the expansion of norm-referenced testing has been _____.
      a. more focused attention on norm-referenced testing
      b. new laws with specific standards
      c. repeated testing of some students with disabilities

_____ **10.** Minimizing external test bias involves changing _____.
      a. individual test items
      b. the use of test results by decision makers
      c. individual tests

Short Answers

Directions: Review your understanding of the material in this chapter by answering the following short answer items. Compare your responses to the sample answers at the end of the book. Your responses should contain information that is similar to but not exactly the same as the information in the sample answers.

1. Describe ten ways a teacher of students with special needs can use computer-based records management.

2. Design and create a hypothetical multimedia computer test in a specific skill area that includes video, audio, graphics, and other elements.

3. Item bias is one type of bias that affects fairness in testing. Give an example of item bias that can occur in teacher-made classroom tests. How could a teacher identify the item bias in the test? How could a teacher prevent or correct the item bias?

4. Computer-based testing encompasses development, scoring, reporting, administration, and interpretation. Which of these aspects of computer-based assessment would you be most likely to use as a teacher of students with special needs? How would you use it? Which aspect would you be least likely to use? Why?

5. Use the information in the future perspectives section of this chapter as the basis for considering ways in which assessment of students with special needs might change in the next decade. In particular, identify three specific areas that you think will change the most and describe the impact of the change, either negatively or positively, on the education of students with special needs.

References

Amaro, R. (1997). Hooked on real-time grades: Daily access to their scores on my IBM clones keeps kids motivated. *Electronic Learning* 16 (4), 62.

Assessment Systems Corporation. (n.d.). *Examiner.* St. Paul, MN: Author.

———. (n.d.). *Question Mark.* St. Paul, MN: Author.

———. (n.d.). *FastTEST.* St. Paul, MN: Author.

B.A.S.I.C. (n.d.) *IEP Master.* Plano, TX: Author.

Chung, G., & Baker, E. (1997). *Year 1 Technology Studies: Implications for Technology in Assessment.* Los Angeles: National Center for Research on Evaluation, Standards, and Student Testing, University of California.

Connolly, A. (1998). *KeyMath Diagnostic Test of Arithmetic* (rev. ed.). Circle Pines, MN: American Guidance Service.

Educational Testing Service. (1998). Coming to your test soon: Computerized scoring of essays. Princeton, NJ: *ETS Developments* 43 (3), 6, Author.

Educational Testing Service Net. (1998). Equity and access in assessment. Princeton, NJ: Author. (www.ets.org/research/equity.html)

Elliott, J., Ysseldyke, J., Thurlow, M., & Erickson, R. (1998). What about assessment and accountability? Practical implications for educators. *Teaching Exceptional Children* 31, 20–27.

Erickson, T., Thurlow, M., & Ysseldyke, J. (1996). Neglected numerators, drifting denominators, and fractured fractions: Determining participation rates for students with disabilities in statewide assessment programs (Synthesis Report 23). Minneapolis, MN: University of Minnesota, National Center on Educational Outcomes. (ERIC Document Reproduction Service no. ED 404 801)

Hurst, K., Casillas, A., & Stevens, R. H. (1997). *Exploring the Dynamics of Complex Problem-Solving With Artificial Neural Network-Based Assessment Systems.* Los Angeles: National Center for Research on Evaluation, Standards, and Student Testing, University of California.

Markwardt, F. C. (1998). *Peabody Individual Achievement Test* (rev. ed.). Circle Pines, MN: American Guidance Service.

Mislevy, R. J., & Chang, H. (1998). *Does Adaptive Testing Violate Local Independence?* Los Angeles: National Center for Research on Evaluation, Standards, and Student Testing, University of California.

Perkins, M. R. (1982). Minimum competency testing: What? Why? Why not? *Educational Measurement: Issues and Practices* 1, 5–9.

Rust, J., & Golombok, S. (1989). *Modern Psychometrics: The Science of Psychological Assessment.* London: Routledge.

Sunburst Communications. (n.d.) *Learner Profile.* Pleasantville, NY: Author.

Thorndike, R. M. (1997). *Measurement and Evaluation in Psychology and Education* (6th ed.). Upper Saddle River, NJ: Merrill/Prentice Hall.

Thurlow, M., Seyforth, A., Scott, D., & Ysseldyke, J. (1997). State assessment policies on participation and accommodations for students with disabilities: 1997 update (Synthesis Report 29). Minneapolis, MN: University of Minnesota, National Center on Educational Outcomes.

Ungar, S. (1998). Learner profile: Track your student's progress. *Pen Computing Magazine* 5 (23), 90.

Vanderwood, M., McGrew, K., & Ysseldyke, J. (1998). Why we can't say much about the status of students with disabilities in education reform. *Exceptional Children* 64, 359–70.

Visions Technology in Education (n.d.). Teacher's Helper Plus. Eugene, OR: Author. http:/www.visteched.com.

Answers to Chapter Review and Application

Chapter 1

Multiple Choice

1.	a	8.	c
2.	c	9.	b
3.	d	10.	c
4.	c	11.	b
5.	b	12.	a
6.	d	13.	c
7.	a		

Match Terminology

1. Measurement
2. Test
3. Assessment
4. Test
5. Measurement
6. Assessment
7. Test

Match Historical Figures

1.	Seguin	4.	Binet
2.	Doll	5.	Dunn
3.	Gesell	6.	Skinner

List Assessment Influences

1. Ethical obligations
2. Federal laws
3. Multiple tests
4. Multiple levels of assessment
5. Professional standards
6. Contributions from other disciplines

Short Answers

1. The three historical landmarks that have had the most significant influence on current assessment practices in special education are intelligence testing, individual achievement testing, and curriculum-based assessment. Intelligence testing is significant because the concept dramatically changed assessment when it was introduced. Intelligence testing remains significant today because it is an integral part of testing students with special needs.

All students with special needs are given individually administered intelligence tests as part of the identification and placement process, and intelligence test scores are a key consideration in diagnosing specific types of disabilities such as learning disabilities. Individual achievement testing is another significant landmark because it is a contribution to assessment that was developed by special educators for special educators. When tests such as the *KeyMath* and other similar measures were introduced, they provided diagnosticians and special education teachers with formal, standardized tools for assessing the learning needs of individual students and for developing specific teaching and intervention activities. Unlike group achievement tests, which report results in the form of test scores and general levels of performance, these individually administered tests provide specific data and information for diagnosing remediation needs and for prescribing specific intervention activities. Finally, curriculum-based assessment is significant because it links assessment and instruction in ways that enable teachers to evaluate student performance in direct relation to what has been taught in the curriculum.

2. Three of the changes in assessment incorporated into the IDEA amendments of 1997 are (1) new requirements for participation of children and youth with disabilities in state and district assessment (testing) programs, (2) updated requirements for developing and reviewing Individualized Education Programs (IEPs), especially increased emphasis on participation in general education with appropriate support services, and (3) more flexibility in conducting reevaluations. Of these changes, the one that will have the most impact on assessment and on special education in general is the increased emphasis on participation of students with disabilities in general education. This change means that more students with disabilities will participate fully in general education. As a result, teachers will need to modify existing assessment procedures and develop

new procedures designed for students with special needs who receive most of their education in the general classroom.

3 Ethics and professional standards are important in assessing students with special needs for several reasons. The most important reason is to protect the rights of the student and the family, especially the right to receive accurate and fair assessment. Other reasons include providing guidelines that specify appropriate practices for professionals who test children with special needs. For example, children and their families have a right to privacy in testing and in reporting test results. The right to privacy is a basic standard that must be preserved. Teachers have a responsibility to understand what is meant by the right to privacy, and they must ensure privacy in the way they use tests and test results. Maintaining privacy in testing helps to protect children with special needs and their families from many of the potential negative effects of testing.

Chapter 2

Multiple Choice

1.	c	7.	c
2.	d	8.	b
3.	b	9.	a
4.	b	10.	a
5.	d		
6.	a		

Match Levels of Assessment

1. Measuring progress
2. Screening
3. Instructional intervention
4. Classification and placement

Short Answers

1. Provide responses with information similar to those in Figure 2–13.

Chapter 3

Multiple Choice

1.	c	6.	d
2.	a	7.	b
3.	b	8.	d
4.	a	9.	d
5.	d		

Short Answers

1. Validity, the effectiveness of an assessment instrument, is the most important technical characteristic of tests. Validity is concerned with whether a test measures what it was designed to measure. The basic question of validity is "Does the test do what it is supposed to do?"

2. To confirm that a particular test had high validity, my primary question would be "Does the content of the test cover the domain, or learning area, of the test?" In answering this question, I would review the test items and the test manual for evidence of content validity. I would also ask the question "Does the test provide evidence of both criterion-related and construct validity?"

3 The major effect of constructing such a test without input from the other teachers would be to diminish the content validity of the test. The content validity would be questionable because the test probably fails to include items reflective of particular skills and competencies taught by the other teachers. The teacher could improve the validity of the test by arranging for the other teachers to review and revise the test.

Figure 2–13

Assessment Procedures		
Measurement	Process	Outcome
90% of the time for 30 consecutive days	Classroom behavior chart	Achieved on 12/10
90% of the time for 30 consecutive days	Teacher and staff observation	
90% of the time for 30 consecutive bus rides	Bus driver observation and report	

4. Reliability is the accuracy or consistency of test scores. Reliability is important in testing because reliable tests produce consistent scores that are accurate across various conditions and situations. They also enable measurement of true differences in performance with a minimum of error or unexplained variability in a score or a group of scores.

5. Test A is more reliable than Test B. Furthermore, Test A has acceptable reliability because all three coefficients meet or exceed .90. In contrast, .85 is the highest coefficient for test B.

6. Items A and C represent criterion-referenced interpretations, and B and D represent norm-referenced interpretations.

7. National norms are valuable for comparing the performance of individual children and groups of children to the performance of similar children from the norm sample group. Teachers may develop informal classroom norms by collecting results from class tests for a period of time and using this collection of data as the basis for comparisons. Although these classroom norms cannot be used to place or label children or to compare children in the class to children outside of the class, they are helpful in evaluating the performance of the class and of individual groups of children in the class.

8. Yes, a norm-referenced test can be interpreted in both a criterion-referenced manner and a norm-referenced manner. Using a norm-referenced test in a criterion-referenced manner involves interpreting the results without association to the norm group. Instead, student performance is compared with the student's earlier scores from the same test.

9. This fluctuation in scores, from a low of 81 to a high of 89, is not significant because it is normal for scores from the same test to vary somewhat each time the test is given. This variation is called the *standard error of measurement*.

Chapter 4

Multiple Choice

1.	a	5.	c
2.	c	6.	d
3.	b	7.	a
4.	c	8.	b

Short Answers

1. Raw scores, the simple numerical result of testing, are usually meaningless by themselves. Raw scores must be transformed into criterion-referenced or norm-referenced scores to give them meaning. Transformed scores include criterion-referenced scores such as simple numerical reports, percent correct scores, and letter-grade scores; they also include norm–referenced scores such as age and grade scores, percentiles, standard scores, stanines, and NCEs. These transformed scores summarize performance in a variety of useful ways.

2. The argument for using this grade score is based on the apparent ease with which grade scores can be understood and interpreted and on the widespread use of grade scores. There are many arguments against using grade scores to describe and interpret performance. One reason for avoiding grade scores is the strong possibility for inaccurate interpretation of grade scores, especially extremely high or low scores. A second problem with grade scores concerns unequal and unpredictable grade-score units. Some grade scores are also estimated, which can lead to problems. Finally, grade scores may not indicate skill development.

3. The first interpretation is accurate because Shemika's score was obtained by comparing her performance to the average performance of seventh graders in the norm sample group (i.e., the seventh grade test). Stated another way, Shemika scored third grade when her performance was compared with the seventh-grade norms. Even though she received a score of third grade, this does not mean that she is reading on the third-grade level. Her actual reading behavior is probably very different from the reading behavior of average third graders. This example illustrates a major problem with grade-level scoring in that it often leads to inaccurate interpretation.

4. a. Grade-equivalent scores produce unpredictable and unequal units because the changes in behavior of children are significantly different at different grade levels. For example, the difference between the reading behavior of 2nd and 3rd graders is much greater than the difference between the reading behavior of 11th and

12th graders. This leads to unequal and unpredictable grade-score units.

b. Percentile scores yield equal units near the mean of 50 but unequal units at the extremes. In other words, scores near 50 are more equally distributed than extremes scores.

c. Standard scores are calculated in a manner that produces approximately equal units between the scores, including scores at the extremes. This characteristic of approximately equal units makes standard scores more precise than other norm-referenced scores.

5. The NCE score of 35 represents the highest performance because it is less than one standard deviation below the mean (28.94). The standard score of 65 represents the lowest performance because it is more than two standard deviations below the mean (70).

6. Norm-referenced scores provide a way to compare the performance of individual children and groups of children to the performance of similar children in the norm group. This is the main advantage of norm-referenced scoring.

7. Criterion-referenced tests have the advantage of allowing teachers to measure and interpret assessment results in relation to a functional level or criterion of performance. The criterion can be content related or related to student progress over time.

8. I would include the following topics in the workshop: standards for scoring, types of test scores, how to use criterion-referenced scores in the classroom, how to interpret and give meaning to norm-referenced scores, and the principles of using scores. I would emphasize the use of criterion-referenced scores and the interpretation of norm-referenced scores.

9. I prefer to use the following criterion-referenced scores: simple numerical reports, percent correct scores, and graphical reports. Of these three scores, graphical reports are best for illustrating performance and showing progress over time. My preferred norm-referenced score is the percentile. Percentiles are relatively easy to understand, they are widely used, and they are more accurate than age and grade scores.

10. I would interpret this score as a below-average score and further explain that the student

scored better than 25 percent of similar students in the norm group but worse than 75 percent of similar students.

11. The advantage of this placement process is that it is objective and relatively easy to implement. The many limitations of this practice include using a test score as the sole criterion for making an educational decision. This is poor practice and violates the standards for scoring. Another problem with this practice is that it involves averaging grade scores, which leads to inaccurate interpretation of student performance. Furthermore, this practice ignores other important factors in making the placement decision such as the child's age, social maturity, and previous placement.

Chapter 5

Multiple Choice

1. d		**5.** c	
2. a		**6.** b	
3. c		**7.** c	
4. a		**8.** b	

Short Answers and Practical Application Activities

1. I would locate available tests in a particular teaching area using the Eric Test Locator (http://www.ericae/testcol.htm/) and current assessment textbooks (available in university libraries). After locating the available tests, I would review catalogues from the test publishers, and I would look over the tests themselves by examining specimen sets available in testing centers. To obtain even more information on the suitability of each instrument, I would read the test reviews in *Mental Measurements Yearbook*, *Test Critiques*, or professional journals.

2. I would expect to find comprehensive reviews of standardized tests in *Mental Measurements Yearbook* and *Test Critiques*. These test review collections provide critical reviews written by experts in the field. Test manuals provide descriptions of the test, instructions for giving and scoring the test, information about interpreting the results, and technical information about how the test was developed and standardized.

3. The catalogs provided by the American Guidance Service (AGS) and PRO-ED, for example, both contain informative and attractively designed advertisements for various types of tests, including tests of academic achievement, language tests, and intelligence tests. The AGS test descriptions tend to be more detailed than the PRO-ED descriptions. Although the descriptions are "infomercials" for the tests, they provide helpful information, including current prices and ordering information.

4. I located a review of a developmental scale in *Mental Measurements Yearbook*. The reviewers emphasized the following strengths of the test: useful content, ease of administration, and ease of scoring. The main weakness pointed out by both reviewers related to technical qualities such as weak reliability, poor validity, and inadequate norms. The reviewers generally agreed on the merits and demerits of the instrument.

Chapter 6

Multiple Choice

1. c
2. a
3. b
4. d
5. c
6. c
7. c
8. c
9. b

Short Answers

1. Although it may appear that assessment, especially the paperwork associated with it, takes time away from teaching, in reality good teaching includes assessment. In fact, assessment provides essential information for making the best possible educational decisions. Assessment helps teachers to document teaching and learning and to provide appropriate educational services for children with special needs. Other benefits of assessment include providing concrete evidence of learning, identifying present levels of performance, assisting with the development of instructional objectives, and measuring progress. Perhaps even more important, assessment helps teachers to identify reasons for lack of progress and to revise unsuccessful instructional intervention programs.

2. The two steps in the process of preparing for assessment that seem the most important to me are gathering information from others and reviewing the assessment tool. Gathering information from others seems especially important because parents and other school personnel, for example, often provide vital information about a child that cannot be obtained through any other method. For example, parents may report circumstances at home that explain changes in student behavior and performance in school. Likewise, parents and other teachers may have insight about student reinforcement preferences, learning styles, and behavior patterns that are extremely important in the assessment process.

   Reviewing the assessment tool is another critical step in the process of preparing for assessment. No excuses exist for errors that occur because of inadequate preparation. Prior to giving any test or using another type of assessment procedure, the evaluator should review and practice administration and scoring. This ensures that when the evaluator gives the test to a child, the results will be as reliable and valid as possible.

3. I would consider the following test accommodations for a child with a learning disability: more testing time, including longer breaks between sections and extra time for specific sections of the test. In addition to accommodations such as these, I think it is important for children with learning disabilities to become informed about standardized tests. This includes understanding standardized tests, handling different types of test questions, and learning what their standardized test scores mean. Perhaps the best way to help students understand standardized tests is by arranging for students to take practice tests with the same accommodations that they would use during actual testing. The main accommodation I would consider for a child who is deaf is providing a sign language interpreter.

4. Even the best test does not ask all the right questions. For this reason, gathering and recording anecdotal assessment information is very important. For example, in situations involving students who exhibit verbal and physical aggression, notes, comments, and other

details about their behavior are essential in assessing the problem, developing a behavior management plan, and measuring changes in the behavior.

5. In a brief written report from a screening test, I would include basic identifying information about the student and a summary of the test score results. I would limit my report in this way because screening tests yield such a small amount of assessment data for making decisions. In a comprehensive diagnostic report, I would include detailed identifying information, extensive background information, a summary table of test score results, and a full discussion and interpretation of the results, along with appropriate recommendations. The type of recommendations would depend on the reasons for testing and the needs of the student. I would include all of this information because comprehensive testing yields a large amount of assessment information for making decisions.

6. The sample case-study report on Bill does a good job of following the report-writing guidelines. The report is well organized with clear findings and common themes across subtests. Relevant material from the *Peabody Individual Achievement Test-Revised* is included in the report along with relevant information from other sources, such as Bill's IQ. The report communicates clearly and displays excellent grammar and style. The report is cautious when discussing problematic findings. Rather than using percentile scores to describe performance, the report relies primarily on stanines. Because the *PIAT-R* is a screening test, the report makes appropriate recommendations for further evaluation. Overall, the report is accurate and thorough with excellent interpretive information and helpful recommendations for further evaluation.

7. The computer-generated report that appears in Table 6–2 is remarkably accurate and thorough and contains a wealth of useful information. The strengths of the report include the large amount of information it provides and the ease with which it generates this information. Producing the report is easy. The evaluator simply inputs the raw scores along with some other identifying information about the

child. The result is a complete diagnostic report that includes a summary of scores, an interpretation of the meaning of those scores, and detailed recommendations for intervention. However, the computer-generated report also displays several weaknesses. Information about the child's behavior and attitude during testing is not included. In contrast, the report does include a lengthy description of the *KeyMath* that reads more like an advertisement for the test than a diagnostic report. Finally, the report may contain too much analysis of the test scores, especially the subtest scores, which should be interpreted with extreme caution. The limitations of subtest scoring should be described in the report.

Chapter 7

Multiple Choice

1.	b	9.	d
2.	a	10.	a
3.	b	11.	b
4.	c	12.	b
5.	a	13.	c
6.	b	14.	a
7.	d	15.	a
8.	a	16.	b

Match Type of Behavior

1. Verbal language
2. Performance
3. Verbal language
4. Performance
5. Verbal language
6. Performance
7. Performance
8. Verbal language

Match Type of Intelligence Test

1. Group
2. Individually administered, general
3. Specialized
4. Infant, toddler, or preschool
5. Individually administered, general
6. Group
7. Specialized
8. Infant, toddler, or preschool
9. Individually administered, general

True-False

1. T	4. T
2. F	5. F
3. T	6. F

Short Answers

1. Three major issues in intelligence testing with students who have special needs are the limited ability of intelligence tests to predict non-academic and vocational success, the inaccuracy of IQ scores at the extremes, and cultural bias against minority groups. Bias against minority groups causes the greatest concern because of the disagreement surrounding this issue which has resulted in a long-running debate over the correct use of intelligence tests with students from deprived and culturally different backgrounds. This includes the increasing numbers of students with limited English language proficiency as well as students with disabilities.

2. Four reasons for using intelligence tests in special education are to obtain an estimate of learning ability, to identify students with disabilities, to classify students according to their specific disability, and to periodically re-evaluate the learning ability of students.

3. Group intelligence tests are useful for screening the intelligence of groups of children, they are quick to administer, and they are inexpensive. Group intelligence tests have several disadvantages. First, the multiple-choice format limits the range and variety of questions on these tests. Second, most group tests are not suitable for students who have reading problems. For students with poor reading skills, a low score may reflect reading problems rather than low intelligence. Likewise, students with visual-perception problems who have difficulty filling in computer-scored answer sheets and who often skip items may receive low scores on group tests due to visual-processing deficits and poor test-taking skills rather than intellectual deficiencies.

4. The *Cognitive Abilities Test (CogAT)* and the *Test of Cognitive Skills, Second Edition (TCS/2)* are two of the available group intelligence tests. The *CogAT* assesses the reasoning and problem-solving abilities of students from the 1st through the 12th grade. Consisting of subtests that measure verbal, quantitative, and non-verbal (spatial) abilities, the *CogAT* takes approximately 90 minutes to complete. The test produces verbal, quantitative, nonverbal, and composite scores. The *TCS/2* contains four subtests: sequences, analogies, memory, and verbal reasoning. The *TCS/2* measures the learning ability of students from grades 2 through 12 and takes approximately 50 minutes to administer. *TCS/2* scores may be used with scores from the *Comprehensive Tests of Basic Skills (CTBS)* or the *California Achievement Test* to predict achievement in later grade levels.

5. Because the two parts of the *WJ-R* are co-normed, this battery and others like it are ideally suited for identifying students with significant discrepancies between learning ability and academic achievement. Such comparisons are a necessary step in the process of classifying and placing students with specific learning disabilities.

6. I would use the *WISC-III* because it is the foremost and the most widely used, individually administered, general test of learning ability. The *WISC-III* is co-normed with the *WIAT*, which enables comparison of student learning ability and academic achievement.

7. I would use the *Comprehensive Test of Nonverbal Intelligence (CTONI)*, which measures six types of nonverbal reasoning abilities. Because the *CTONI* requires no oral responses, reading, writing, or object manipulation, it is especially appropriate for use with children who are nonverbal.

8. I would use the *Wechsler Preschool and Primary Scale of Intelligence-Revised (WPPSI-R)*. Designed for young children from 3 years to 7 years 3 months of age, the *WPPSI-R* has superior technical qualities that make it the test of choice among psychologists. Because of its popularity among practitioners and researchers, the *WPPSI-R* is considered the classic preschool intelligence test.

9. I would use the *Bayley Scales of Infant Development, Second Edition (BSID-II)*. The *BSID-II* is the most carefully designed and widely administered infant developmental scale. Designed for infants from 1 month to 30 months, it includes a mental scale, a motor scale, and a be-

havior rating scale. Useful as a tool for early identification of infants with disabilities, the *BSID-II* features separate mental and motor tests to facilitate diagnosis of individual needs.

Chapter 8

Multiple Choice

1. c	**6.** c
2. c	**7.** d
3. b	**8.** b
4. d	**9.** b
5. a	**10.** a

Match Principles of Developmental Assessment

1. d	**3.** c
2. b	**4.** a

Match Descriptions of Developmental Assessment

1. Developmental diagnosis
2. Screening
3. Specialized
4. Readiness

Match Developmental Tests

1. Screening
2. Readiness
3. Specialized
4. Screening
5. Diagnostic
6. Readiness
7. Diagnostic

True-False

1. F	**4.** T
2. T	**5.** F
3. F	**6.** F

Short Answers

1. The five uses are
   a. Screening young children for potential developmental and learning problems.
   b. Assisting in the diagnosing of disabilities of young children with developmental and learning problems.
   c. Assessing the readiness skills of young children with special needs.
   d. Obtaining data for writing IEPs and developing intervention programs.
   e. Measuring the developmental progress of young children with special needs.

   Special education teachers would be most likely to use developmental assessment to help write IEPs, to develop intervention programs, to measure progress, and to assess readiness skills.

2. I would use the *DIAL-3* rather than the *Denver II* for the following reasons. The *DIAL-3* is designed for use in educational settings and has more educationally relevant content. In contrast, the *Denver II* was initially developed for use in hospital settings. The *DIAL-3* uses a more appropriate scoring system than the *Denver II*. Possible *DIAL-3* scores include potential problem, OK, and potential advanced. These are more accurate screening scores than the *Denver II* scores of advanced, normal, caution, or untestable. Finally, the *DIAL-3* has superior technical characteristics.

3. The *LAP-D Standardized Assessment* and the *Battelle Developmental Inventory (BDI)* are the two appropriate tools for use in the initial identification and placement process. Both of these tests are norm referenced. Norm-referenced tests compare the performance of an individual child to the performance of similar children in the norm sample group. The *Brigance Early* is a criterion-referenced test and should not be used for identification and placement.

4. A case history is important because it is one of the best sources of information about infants and toddlers with special needs and their families. Because it is more difficult to test very young children than older children and because the test scores of young children are less stable than those of older children, evaluators rely heavily on information from sources such as case histories. A complete case history includes biographical information, medical history, developmental history, educational history, and social history.

5. The *Birth to Three Assessment and Intervention System* consists of a screening test, a criterion-referenced developmental checklist, and an intervention manual. These components make up a complete system for classroom and home-based diagnostic assessment and intervention

with infants and toddlers who have special needs. *Birth to Three* subtests include measures of language comprehension and expression, cognitive development, social and personal development, and motor development. The *Birth to Three* materials emphasize parental involvement and training and home instruction as the key intervention program features. *Birth to Three* is best suited for infants and toddlers who have mild and moderate developmental disabilities.

Chapter 9

Multiple Choice

1.	a	**7.**	a
2.	d	**8.**	d
3.	d	**9.**	a
4.	b	**10.**	b
5.	a	**11.**	c
6.	c		

Match Definitions With Key Terms

1.	j	**7.**	a
2.	i	**8.**	d
3.	k	**9.**	c
4.	h	**10.**	b
5.	g	**11.**	f
6.	e		

Short Answers

1. Screening for vision and hearing impairment—Screening procedures may include reviewing a child's cumulative record or observing a child directly. Teachers who observe unusual visual or auditory behaviors that may indicate a vision or hearing problem should refer the child to a specialist.

   Exercising caution with students who have physical or sensory impairments—Children with visual impairments may not be able to see the details in the complex drawings on visual-processing tests. For this reason, care should be taken to make sure a child can see the drawings before giving a visual-processing test.

   Assessing older students carefully—When testing older students, check the age range of the perceptual or motor test to make sure it was designed for use with them.

   Determining the need for training—Children with limited experience and exposure to

perceptual and motor tasks may need practice with the types of behaviors on the test. Examples of tasks include building with 1-inch cubes, throwing and catching bean bags, and walking a balance beam.

   Observing behavior carefully—Teachers should confirm the results of testing through daily observation of the child in the classroom. If this fails to confirm the results of testing, the test results should be carefully reviewed for accuracy.

2. I would use the *Test of Auditory-Perceptual Skills, Revised,* because it measures a wide range of auditory-processing behaviors, it can be given in about 25 minutes, and it also includes a hyperactive rating scale that might help determine the effects of the child's behavior on the test results.

3. I would select the *Developmental Test of Visual Perception: Second Edition* because it includes eight separate subtests that measure a wide variety of visual-processing behaviors. The other tests listed in the question are screening tests that measure a limited range of behaviors.

4. I would use the *Observable Characteristics of Modality Strength* chart to assess the modality strengths of a small group of children. This method would provide me with assessment information derived from observation of the actual behavior of the children in class rather than their behavior as measured indirectly by a test.

5. I would use the *Peabody Developmental Motor Scales* because these scales provide a set of 282 activity cards matched with the items on the test. These activity cards would help in developing appropriate intervention activities.

Chapter 10

Multiple Choice

1.	d	**6.**	a
2.	b	**7.**	d
3.	a	**8.**	c
4.	d	**9.**	a
5.	c	**10.**	d

Short Answers

1. The three procedures that I would be most likely to use in my classroom are (1) observing the child's language in natural settings such as

the classroom, the home, or with peers; (2) completing criterion-referenced checklists of specific language behaviors; and (3) interviewing the parent. I would use these procedures because they seem the most practical and the most efficient. In fact, most teachers frequently use observations, interviews, and checklists to assess a variety of behaviors, including language behaviors. These informal assessments help teachers develop IEPs, design intervention programs, and measure student progress.

2. The informal measures for assessing morphology and syntax described in the chapter include spontaneous language sampling, assessing mean length of utterance, and developmental sentence analysis. These measures display several distinct advantages over formal testing. First of all, they place fewer controls on the student than structured language tests. This enables students to exhibit phrases and sentences in spontaneous speech not observed during formal language testing. Informal measures also provide an opportunity to observe language during interactions with others in natural settings. Finally, the informal measures enable evaluation of the words and sentences a student knows well enough to use in everyday language. These techniques seem best with younger children and, of them, developmental sentence analysis seems best overall because it provides opportunities to assess more aspects of language than the other procedures.

3. The *PPVT-III* is a well-designed, easy-to-use tool for obtaining an estimate of an important component of oral language: receptive language vocabulary. Several reasons exist for its widespread use. In addition to displaying excellent technical characteristics, the outstanding design of the *PPVT-III* makes it easy to administer, score, and interpret. This makes the instrument useful to a wide range of professionals including special educators, school and clinical psychologists, educational diagnosticians, counselors, and speech and language pathologists who use the *PPVT-III* with children and adults at all levels of ability. An available Spanish version of the *Peabody Picture Vocabulary Test* is another valuable feature that makes the instrument so popular.

I would probably not use the *PPVT-III* in my classroom. Instead, I would prefer to use curriculum-based assessment procedures that link assessment more closely with instruction.

4. Assessing CLD students who may have language disorders is the most critical issue because students should not be tested for language disorders until they have adjusted to the new culture. This makes it difficult to accurately identify language problems while a student is acquiring a new language. Other critical issues include the questionable validity of some assessment procedures used with CLD students, including information from outside sources, especially when the outside information is more than 6 months old. Finally, providing enough qualified evaluators and trained teachers for the increasing numbers of CLD students is an important issue.

Chapter 11

Multiple Choice

1. c		6. a	
2. b		7. c	
3. a		8. b	
4. d		9. c	
5. d		10. b	

Short Answers

1. Instruments and procedures for assessing behavior are distinct in several ways. First, student behavior encompasses a broad range of nonacademic behaviors, including social-emotional development such as self-concept and attitudes, and affective behavior such as emotions. Unlike assessment in most other domains, school, family, neighborhood, and community influences are considered in the assessment process. Further, assessment of behavior involves measuring complex interaction patterns and acceptable limits for behavior. Making decisions about interactions and limits is more subjective than grading academic work such as math worksheets and spelling tests. For these reasons, the assessment of behavior differs in form and content from the assessment of cognitive indicators. This is why most behavior assessment relies on rating scales, checklists, inventories, interviews, and observations rather than tests.

2. Behavior rating scales are written questionnaires containing lists of behaviors that raters complete by assigning a rating (usually based on a scale of 1 to 5) to each item on the checklist. Raters are usually teachers, parents, or other primary care givers who are familiar with a student's typical conduct. Most scales are general screening instruments that take only 20 minutes or so to complete and provide an overview of behavior rather than in-depth diagnostic information. For these reasons, behavior rating scales are not often used for instructional purposes such as developing intervention programs. Instead, these instruments are best used in screening and initial identification.

3. Ecological assessment involves evaluating the behavior problems of children within the ecological context in which the behavior occurs, which is the family, the school, the neighborhood, the community, and the culture. Ecological assessment helps teachers expand their insight into the behavior problems of students by revealing information about the interaction between a child's behavior problems and the ecosystem in which the child develops. By identifying the ecological variables, teachers can assess the intensity of their effects on each child's conduct and academic performance. This assessment process helps teachers select appropriate intervention strategies and curriculum activities.

Ecological assessment methods focus on the environmental elements that affect and are affected by the child. The minimum elements in ecological assessment include evaluation of student–teacher interaction, student– curriculum match, peer interactions, school and classroom climate, and variables outside the school setting that affect school behavior. Assessment data regarding these elements are obtained from direct observation supplemented by interviews with teachers. Other elements that may be considered include space and facilities, teaching and learning settings, social environments, responsibility for management, classroom safety and order, staff collaboration, student academic progress, emotional climate, cultural differences, and parent and teacher communication.

Chapter 12

Multiple Choice

1.	d	7.	d
2.	c	8.	c
3.	b	9.	c
4.	a	10.	a
5.	b	11.	b
6.	c		

True-False

1.	F	4.	T
2.	F	5.	F
3.	T		

Short Answers

1. Adaptive behavior is the ability to adjust to personal and social demands in the environment, especially to changes in the environment. The adaptive behavior scales measure behaviors related to personal self-sufficiency, independence in the community, and personal-social responsibility. Although individual scales have various age ranges, most scales measure the adaptive behavior of children and adults beginning around age 4 or 5 and going through retirement.

2. An informant is a person who provides the information required to rate the items on a scale, usually a teacher, parent, grandparent, teacher aide, or another primary care giver. Although most informants give accurate answers, some give biased or distorted answers. Reasons for inaccurate responses include student behavior that varies in different settings, unreliable informant information, differences in informant interpretation of student behavior, differences in familiarity with a student, and biased informants. When evaluators have serious doubts about the validity of a set of responses, they must gather additional information by interviewing another informant. Interviewing more than one informant enables an evaluator to compare responses for consistency. Evaluators should attempt to conduct more than one interview whenever possible. For example, teachers can provide information from observations of student behavior in an educational setting. Parents, on the other

hand, can supply information about at-home behaviors such as sleeping, leisure activities, and eating.

3. The *Vineland Adaptive Behavior Scales* are individually administered and norm referenced. Designed to assess personal and social skills, the *Vineland* measures communication, daily living skills, socialization, and motor skills. Subtests for measuring both adaptive and maladaptive behavior are included in the scales. The interview edition of the *Vineland* has an age range of birth to 18 years of age, and the classroom edition has an age range of 2–12 years. The *Vineland* is used in special education to identify and place students with disabilities and to obtain evaluation data for developing intervention programs.

Chapter 13

Multiple Choice

1.	b	**6.**	d
2.	a	**7.**	c
3.	c	**8.**	d
4.	a	**9.**	d
5.	a	**10.**	b

Short Answers

1. Career assessment encompasses evaluation of a broad range of practical life skills that are part of living and working as an adult. Career skills include social behaviors, functional academics, and daily living activities necessary for success on the job and in the community. Special educators usually begin to assess and teach career-related competencies in the elementary grades. Unlike the broad range of career skills, vocational assessment has a more specific connotation. It refers to the particular skills necessary for success in specific jobs, professions, or trades. Because vocational skills are limited to particular job skills, special and vocational educators usually begin to assess and teach vocational skills when students reach high school.

2. Transition services are coordinated activities that help students with disabilities successfully move from school to postschool activities. Transition services are important because students with disabilities need coordinated assistance to ensure success in postschool activities. For this reason, transition planning needs to begin as early as possible but no later than age 14, and it should continue until the student makes a successful transition from education to the adult world of living and working in the community.

Functional assessment is emphasized in transition planning and services because it measures student performance in real-life, natural settings and identifies proficiency in performing practical, applied skills. For high school students, this means assessing performance at home, at school, on the job, and in the community. Functional assessment not only recognizes the importance of academics and specific job competencies but also includes daily living, personal-social development, and community-based skills as equally important learning domains.

Functional assessment is also a key component in assessing student needs for transition services and in developing Individual Transition Plans (ITPs). The ITP process requires special educators to collaborate with other professionals from agencies and institutions (e.g., vocational rehabilitation) to identify suitable postschool services and to develop linkages so that students can access those services.

3. Written tests are useful for assessing many different career and vocational skills. Written tests are relatively inexpensive and easy to administer and can be given and scored in short time periods. The major drawback of written tests, inherent in all pencil-on-paper testing, is that the test results may differ from actual student performance in real work situations.

One of the written tests I would consider using is the *Reading Free Vocational Interest Inventory-Revised,* a picture test of vocational interests. I would use the inventory to help in vocational planning and placement and as a guide for developing instructional objectives and activities. The *Brigance Diagnostic Inventory of Essential Skills* is another written test I would consider using. Because the *Brigance* was specifically designed for teachers to use in the classroom with students who have special needs, it would be useful as a criterion-referenced assessment tool and as a curriculum guide. Finally, I would consider using the *Employability Assessment Instrument* to measure job readiness skills, develop instructional objectives and activities, and monitor student progress in developing employability skills.

4. Situational assessment is the use of systematic observation to evaluate work- and career-related performance on the job or in real or simulated environments such as vocational training settings, simulated workstations, job tryouts in the community, and other community-based environments. On-the-job assessment is a specific type of situational evaluation for measuring vocational behavior in actual work settings.

   In recent years, special educators have adapted traditional situational assessment to measure student vocational and career-related skills in many different work- and community-based settings. Situational assessment is ideal for use in community-based instructional programs that occur "on location" at the workplace or in other community sites such as the shopping mall, bus stop, grocery store, post office, drugstore, public library, and park.

   The most significant advantage of situational assessment is the ability to assess students in real-life settings rather than in artificial testing situations. This produces genuine, authentic assessment results that can be linked directly with the curriculum. The main drawbacks are problems in transferring and generalizing results from one situation to another and problems in controlling the reliability and validity of the assessment data. If not carefully controlled, reliability and validity problems can limit the usefulness of data from situational and on-the-job assessment.

5. Julie's progress chart (Figure 13–3) includes data illustrating how quickly she learned to operate a paper cutter. The chart clearly documents her progress in learning this task. The chart is useful for communicating progress with many people, including Julie, her parents, and other faculty and staff.

Chapter 14

Multiple Choice

1.	d	6.	a
2.	c	7.	a
3.	a	8.	c
4.	c	9.	c
5.	a	10.	b

Short Answers

1. The group tests of academic achievement are really screening tests that give an overview of achievement rather than specific diagnostic information. Almost all group tests rely on a multiple-choice format and are usually brief and often machine scored. When developers write test questions for group tests, they limit the items to content that fits on machine-scored, multiple-choice response sheets. For these reasons, the group tests have limited usefulness with children who have special needs. However, despite their limitations in special education, the group tests are widely used in education.

   Individual tests, on the other hand, sample a greater range of behaviors, and evaluators score them by hand rather than by machine.

Figure 13–3

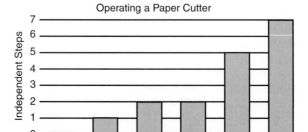

Julie's Progress Chart

Operating a Paper Cutter

Unlike the group tests, the individually administered diagnostic tests provide in-depth information that translates into instructional objectives. For example, the *Wechsler Individual Achievement Test (WIAT)* is designed for assessing and reevaluating students, answering academic questions about students, and planning instructional intervention programs for them. The *WIAT,* and tests like it, can also examine the amount of discrepancy between achievement and ability, which is especially important in diagnosing learning disabilities. For these reasons, the individually administered, multiple-skill achievement tests are best with children who have special needs.

2. A review of the test items in the *PIAT-R* and the *WRAT-3* reveals that the *PIAT-R* has many more test items that sample a much wider range of academic skills and behaviors than the *WRAT-3.* For example, the *PIAT-R* includes subtests for measuring reading comprehension and written expression skills. The *WRAT-3* fails to measure either one of these important academic skills. Similarities exist in the types of items both tests use to measure reading recognition, mathematics, and spelling skills, but, again, the *PIAT-R* has more items and a wider range of items than the *WRAT-3.* For these reasons, the *PIAT-R* is appropriate for use in many more situations than the *WRAT-3.* In fact, the *WRAT-3* should be used only as a gross screening measure for deciding whether a child has potential problems in academic achievement. In contrast, the *PIAT-R* is a highly useful, well-developed screening test of academic achievement, helps identify children who may have significant deficits in academic achievement, and gives teachers ideas about where to begin and how to design instructional intervention programs.

3. The *WIAT* and the *K-TEA* have similar subtests in the following areas:

WIAT Subtests	K-TEA Subtests
Basic reading	Reading decoding
Reading comprehension	Reading comprehension
Mathematical reasoning	Mathematical computation
Numerical operations	Mathematical applications
Spelling	Spelling

The difference between the two tests is that the *WIAT* also provides subtests for measuring listening comprehension, oral expression, and written expression.

4. Mr. Smith should consider using one of the following multiple-skills tests: the *WIAT,* the *K-TEA,* the *Brigance Diagnostic Inventories,* or the *PIAT-R.* The particular instrument that he should use depends on the purpose of testing. If he is interested in an overview of achievement, then the *PIAT-R* would be a good choice. If he is more interested in developing specific objectives and intervention activities, then the criterion-referenced *Brigance Inventories* would be best. The norm-referenced *WIAT* and the *K-TEA* would be excellent choices if he is interested in standardized diagnostic data for making staffing, placement, and instructional intervention decisions.

5. Each type of testing is best in certain situations. The formal, standardized tests are especially useful for identifying, classifying, and placing students with special needs; evaluating overall academic progress or lack of progress; measuring progress over long periods of time; identifying specific strengths, weaknesses, and gaps in skill development; and making comparisons among children. The informal, curriculum-based achievement tests are more flexible and more directly connected with classroom instruction. For these reasons, curriculum-based assessment is especially helpful for evaluating progress in learning specific skills that may be unique to an individual student, class, program, or school; measuring daily and short-term progress; and evaluating the value of particular educational interventions in response to the learning problems of children with special needs.

Both types of testing are necessary and actually complement each other. Planning and implementing the best possible educational programs for children with special needs requires both formal and informal assessment.

Chapter 15

Multiple Choice

1. b		**3.** c	
2. c		**4.** d	

5. c   **8.** c
6. a   **9.** a
7. c   **10.** b

Short Answers

1. The three approaches for assessing reading achievement discussed in the chapter are norm-referenced testing, informal reading inventories, and curriculum-based assessment. Norm-referenced testing provides standardized scores that enable comparing a student's performance with the performance of others. This makes norm-referenced testing useful for diagnosing reading disabilities and classifying and placing students. In addition, the norm-referenced, single-skill, diagnostic reading tests produce detailed information for identifying specific reading problems, writing instructional objectives, developing IEPs, and creating intervention activities.

   Informal reading inventories are most useful for planning reading intervention programs. Because the informal inventories contain graded word lists for testing word recognition ability and graded reading passages for evaluating oral reading, silent reading, and comprehension, they provide teachers with valuable assessment information that is linked with classroom instruction in reading.

   In addition to using informal reading inventories in reading instruction, special education teachers and diagnosticians also use many curriculum-based assessment strategies to measure reading performance and to develop instructional objectives and activities. With curriculum-based assessment, teachers use student work such as class papers, homework, and class tests to evaluate reading skill and development. Curriculum-based assessment also allows teachers to conduct evaluation as part of the ongoing teaching and learning activities in the classroom. This links assessment directly with the curriculum.

2. When teachers use CBA, they rely on student classwork such as class papers, homework, oral reading, and class tests to evaluate reading skill and development. This allows teachers to conduct evaluation as part of ongoing teaching and learning activities. This links assessment with instruction by enabling teachers to evaluate student performance in direct relation to the cur-

riculum. Thus, teachers can make educational decisions on the basis of actual reading behavior. For these reasons, teachers have a special interest in this type of assessment.

   Making the connection between classroom reading instruction and assessment is important in developing IEPs, monitoring student progress, and evaluating the reading program. In addition, curriculum-based assessment of reading informs the teaching and learning process by making it more reflective and responsive to student learning needs.

3. The specific curriculum-based techniques described in the classroom include clinical observation, diagnostic checklists, miscue analysis, and cloze procedures. Of these techniques, I would definitely use clinical observation because it is such a natural part of the teaching and learning process. The other technique that fits my teaching style is the use of checklists, such as those of oral reading and silent reading, for measuring skill development and performance.

4. I think Ms. Marisol should use the *Woodcock Reading Mastery Tests-Revised* to obtain the in-depth, diagnostic assessment. The *WRMT-R* is a good choice because it is the foremost diagnostic reading test, and the complete battery contains four reading achievement subtests plus three readiness subtests. This comprehensive group of subtests makes the *WRMT-R* ideal for making staffing decisions, creating instructional objectives, and developing remedial intervention activities. The *WRMT-R* also includes many diagnostic features such as an error analysis procedure for identifying specific strengths and weaknesses and five interpretive profiles. In addition, the *WRMT-R* measures reading vocabulary in science-mathematics, social studies, and humanities. These features illustrate the diagnostic power of this well-designed, single-skill diagnostic test.

Chapter 16

Multiple Choice

1. a		**6.** c
2. c		**7.** d
3. a		**8.** a
4. b		**9.** c
5. a		**10.** a

Short Answers

1. Two curriculum-based assessment procedures for evaluating student proficiency in computation are error pattern analysis and performance rate scoring. I would use a four-stage error pattern analysis procedure. The first stage involves gathering representative samples of a student's computation work. The second stage consists of analyzing the error patterns in those samples. The third stage is a diagnostic interview with the student. The final stage includes recording the results and developing an instructional intervention strategy. Because students must be able to perform computations quickly and accurately, performance rate scoring is ideal for assessing computations. It uses timed probes or tests to measure the number of correct responses in a specified period. For example, if a student correctly completes 40 addition problems in a 5-minute period, the performance rate is 8 problems per minute.

2. I would use the *KeyMath-Revised: Diagnostic Inventory of Essential Mathematics* to assess the math achievement of a fourth grade student suspected of having a math disability. I would use the *KeyMath-Revised* because it is specifically designed for students who need comprehensive diagnostic assessment and remedial instruction in mathematics. Furthermore, it helps to identify specific strengths and weaknesses and to plan instructional programs. Finally, the *KeyMath- Revised* provides extensive supplementary teaching materials and a computer software scoring and interpretation program, which are features that enhance the test's usefulness.

3. Because norm-referenced tests enable comparison of the math performance of individual students with the performance of others, we use them to identify, classify, and place students. Widely used norm-referenced math tests include the *KeyMath-Revised*, the *Test of Early Mathematical Ability-2*, and the *Test of Mathematical Abilities-2*. Norm-referenced math tests are also useful in the classroom, but most teachers prefer curriculum-based assessment because it provides a direct link between assessment and the classroom curriculum. Some of the most commonly used curriculum-based math assessment procedures are error pattern analysis, performance measurement, and performance rate scoring.

4. The student missed five of the ten problems. All five errors are computation errors in which the student failed to recall the basic math facts of multiplying by eight and by nine. Intervention should focus on having the student review and practice the multiplication tables of eight and nine.

Chapter 17

Multiple Choice

1. a		**6.** b
2. c		**7.** c
3. b		**8.** a
4. e		**9.** b
5. d		**10.** c

Short Answers

1. The *Written Language Profile* and the *Spelling Error Analysis Chart* directly connect assessment of written language with instruction in written language in several ways. Because they are curriculum-based assessment (CBA) instruments, the profile and the chart are designed for teachers to use in the classroom as a regular part of instruction. This design helps link these assessment tools with classroom instruction. Another way the profile and the chart connect with instruction is that they both rely on samples of authentic student work. The profile and the chart also produce detailed assessment data for pinpointing remediation activities based on the specific errors made by the student. In other words, curriculum-based assessment tools like these produce data that directly inform the teaching and learning process. This links assessment and instruction by producing information that helps teachers focus instructional time on what students need to know.

2. The completed written language profile from Alisha's writing sample appears in Figure 17–6.

3. The *Written Expression Scale*, the *Test of Language Development-3* and the *Test of Written Expression* are three norm-referenced, individually administered tests of written language appropriate for comprehensive, diagnostic assessment of the written language skills of elementary students with special needs. I prefer the *Written Expression Scale* because it is one test in a complete language battery: the *Oral*

Figure 17–6 Completed Written Language Profile From Alisha's Writing Sample

Name _Alisha_   Teacher _John Venn_

Age _11_   Grade _4_   Date _4/2_

Composition	Score	Target Skills
1. Fluency (word count) Sum of the Words per Minute from each sample ÷ by the number of samples = fluency	9 wpm	Increase overall fluency
2. Average Thought Unit Total words − garbles ÷ T-units = average thought unit	8.5	None
3. Vocabulary Diversity Number of uncommon words ÷ by the total number of words = vocabulary diversity	32%	Increase overall diversity
4. Organization: Narrative 1 − 5 rating scale (1 = lowest rating, 5 = highest rating)	3	Focus the paragraph on one theme.
5. Organization: Story 1 − 5 rating scale (1 = lowest rating, 5 = highest rating)	3	Develop the grandmother as a character.
6. Organization: Essay 1 − 5 rating scale (1 = lowest rating, 5 = highest rating)	3	Write a topic sentence that connects the paragraph.
7. Structure: Capitalization Count the total number of capitalization errors and note error patterns.	0	You're doing well with this!
8. Structure: Punctuation Count the number of punctuation errors and note error patterns.	2	Be sure to put commas before coordinating conjunctions.
9. Structure: Language Usage Count the number of language usage errors and note error patterns.	5	You need to work on subject-verb agreement and verb tense.

Notes _____

_____

_____

and Written Language Scales (OWLS). The *OWLS* battery also includes a *Listening Comprehension Scale* and an *Oral Expression Scale.* Although the tests can be given separately, the complete *OWLS* enables assessment of written language, listening skills, and oral expression. The *OWLS* provides more assessment data for making instructional intervention decisions than the other two instruments.

4. The primary advantage of standardized, norm-referenced assessment of written language is that it enables comparison of the performance of individual children with that of peers in the norm sample group. This ability to compare performance is essential in situations involving classification and placement decisions. Because norm-referenced tests have a standardized set of administration and scoring procedures, they are also helpful for making classroom-based instructional intervention decisions when the teacher needs comparative assessment data that are independent of the specific curriculum in the classroom.

   The major advantage of curriculum-based assessment (CBA) of language is that the data produced are linked to classroom instruction. This linkage makes CBA a much more natural part of the teaching and learning process. However, CBA is an informal, criterion-referenced type of assessment that does not enable comparisons among students. This is the most significant disadvantage.

Chapter 18

Multiple Choice

1. b	6. a
2. a	7. b
3. c	8. c
4. d	9. c
5. d	10. b

Match Type of Portfolio With Descriptions

1. Product	3. Process
2. Process	4. Celebration

Match Scoring Protocol With Description of Scoring

1. Holistic	2. Analytical

3. Holistic	5. Analytical
4. Holistic	6. Analytical

Provide Practical Examples

1. Writing samples: rough drafts, revisions, completed papers
2. Reading samples: lists of books read, book appreciation ratings
3. Conference records: completed conference record forms
4. Parent reflections: parent notes that describe progress
5. Audiotapes: a tape of oral reading
6. Teacher reflections: teacher observation notes
7. Student reflections: a self-evaluation in narrative form

Short Answers

1. In your response, include pinpoints similar to the following: portfolio quality (content), portfolio organization, style and grammar, self-evaluation, and amount and variety of reading.
2. In your response, include some pinpoints that are similar to the following: list of reading samples, appreciation ratings with narrative comments, reading response journal, conference record forms, reflective book reports, audiotape of student reading a favorite passage, videotape of a skit, and artwork showing understanding of a favorite reading.

Chapter 19

Multiple Choice

1. a	6. c
2. d	7. d
3. b	8. b
4. c	9. c
5. a	

Short Answers

1. It is understandable that some general education teachers have concerns about testing and grading students with disabilities. One hopes that most of their concerns stem from a lack of training and experience rather than resistance to modifying traditional evaluation procedures to meet the individual needs of students with disabilities. If this is the case, then the concerns can be resolved through appropriate training

and experience. It is also fortunate that most teachers are willing to work together as a team to try new techniques that will benefit all students, including those with special learning needs.

Questions teachers have about inclusive assessment include the following: What assessments are best in inclusion classrooms? Are there special tests for inclusion settings? How much does traditional classroom testing need to be modified for students with disabilities? How useful is curriculum-based assessment, especially portfolio assessment, in evaluating students with special needs in inclusion classes?

I would share with the teacher that some students require few if any assessment modifications, and for those students who do need specialized testing and grading, the needed modifications are usually straightforward and easy to implement. In those cases where extensive modifications are needed, helpful support services are available.

2. The three alternatives that I would be most likely to consider using are portfolio, competency-based, and IEP grading procedures. I would use portfolio-based grading because it allows teachers to assign grades based on evaluation of authentic samples of student work. I also prefer portfolio grading because it encourages reflective teaching, learning, and assessment. This gives students opportunities to evaluate their performance, receive feedback during portfolio conferences, and think about their learning experiences and progress.

Competency-based grading also has features that make it useful as an alternative grading procedure. With competency-based grading, teachers grade students based on their progress in reaching specified criterion levels for each skill. Teachers often use competency checklists to monitor progress. The checklist of skills helps teachers assign grades according to the number of successfully mastered skills.

I would use IEP grading with students who need extensive testing and grading modifications. This would include students with severe and multiple disabilities who have limited ability and require extensive modification in curriculum and assessment. Because IEP grading is based on student attainment of IEP goals,

teachers measure IEP progress and assign grades using the evaluation criteria for each IEP objective. This enables the teachers to individualize grading for the student.

3. The problem that these students are commenting about is that teacher-made tests frequently fail to give students with learning and behavior disabilities the opportunity to demonstrate what they have learned. For example, students with disabilities sometimes master the academic content necessary for successful performance on a test but perform poorly on the test due to problems with the test format. Long, poorly designed, messy, or distracting tests negatively affect student performance. This occurs because students with disabilities may have deficits in attention, memory, organization, reading, or writing that hinder performance on teacher-made tests, especially poorly designed ones. Teachers can reduce format problems and other testing design problems by incorporating test design modifications that minimize the effect of attention and memory problems. Test design accommodations include modifications in format, directions, response modes, test items, test setting, and test timing. Furthermore, students with disabilities can benefit from and have a right to these testing modifications. Reasonable modifications are essential so that capable students with special needs are tested fairly in ways that give them the opportunity to earn good grades.

4. Many students with special needs expect to fail tests and have few, if any, test-taking skills. As a result, these students need to learn practical, concrete test-taking skills. Giving practice tests is one of the best ways to help students learn test-taking skills. The practice tests should be brief and designed so that students can experience success. Practice tests give students much-needed hands-on experience. This is much more valuable than abstract academic lessons about test-taking rules such as scheduling time, discovering clue words, reading carefully, and reviewing.

One idea for helping students improve their test-taking skills that wasn't mentioned in the guidelines is using diagnostic interviews with students. Teachers can use diagnostic interviews to help students learn new test-taking skills and reduce test-taking errors. The questions teachers ask in diagnostic interviews should be based on review of a student's prior test performance.

5. The topics that I would share with my colleagues would include the questions teachers have about inclusive assessment, why we provide assessment modifications for students with special needs in inclusive settings, and alternative grading criteria. I would also define inclusion and explain the need to use a team approach. These topics would give an appropriate overview of inclusive assessment. More detailed information could be shared in a handout on inclusive assessment.

Chapter 20

Multiple Choice

1. c		**6.** c	
2. b		**7.** a	
3. a		**8.** a	
4. a		**9.** c	
5. b		**10.** b	

Short Answers

1. Teachers of students with special needs can use computer-based records management for a wide variety of assessment and record-keeping tasks. These include the following:
   - Keeping attendance data such as absences, tardies, and withdrawals
   - Recording daily grades and producing weekly grade reports
   - Maintaining parental contact records such as notes and phone calls
   - Storing students' personal information including addresses, phone numbers, ages, and medications
   - Tracking homework assignments
   - Keeping daily checklists of individual student progress in achieving goals
   - Keeping track of daily lunch orders
   - Storing bus transportation information
   - Recording, averaging, and reporting test scores and grades
   - Storing student schedule information such as days and times for speech therapy or occupational therapy

2. A multimedia computer test in applied mathematics that uses money skills would be very beneficial for assessing students with special needs. The test would involve giving students $300 to buy school clothes. They would spend the $300 using an on-line computer to shop in three electronic stores on the Internet. Students would view visual, audio, and graphic descriptions of clothing to compare prices and features. After shopping for the best clothing at the best prices, students would select items for purchase and place them in an electronic shopping cart. Before making their final selections, students could remove clothing from the cart and replace it with other items of better style or price. Students would then prepare a final list of clothes purchased with the $300 and write a brief description of why they chose these particular items.

3. One example of item bias in a teacher-made test is placing a problem-solving item that involves a particular type of borrowing in a math test when the students have not been taught that borrowing concept. The teacher could use item analysis to identify the item bias. Item analysis reveals how many students missed the borrowing item. If all, most, or a even a majority of the students missed the item, it would indicate possible bias. This could be corrected by removing the borrowing item from the test item or teaching borrowing prior to giving the test.

4. The aspect of computer-based assessment that I would be most likely to use as a teacher of students with special needs is test scoring and reporting. Available computer-based scoring and reporting software includes records management and grade-reporting programs. In particular, grading software and learner profile software would be especially useful for simplifying the many grading tasks that take time away from teaching. Grading software can be used to create progress reports, average grades, prepare report cards, prepare for conferences, develop parent reports, plan for remedial instruction, track missing assignments, and create checklists.

   The type of computer-based testing that I would be least likely to use is computerized test administration because classroom applications of this technology are not yet widely available. However, the potential benefits of this type of computer technology are significant, and I expect that, in the future, many teachers will use computer adaptive testing and multimedia assessment with students who have special needs.

5. Of the areas of change described in the future perspectives section of the chapter, the three that I think will undergo the most change are curriculum-based assessment, fairness in testing, and minimum competency testing. Of these three, curriculum-based assessment (CBA) will have the most beneficial impact as more teachers use this type of assessment. As a result, teachers will continue to refine CBA to make it more responsive to the needs of students with disabilities. Many of the fairness-in-testing issues will also be resolved as test developers and decision makers continue to make progress in reducing test bias. In contrast, I believe that nega-tive effects from minimum competency testing will continue because decision makers believe they can use minimum competency tests to raise educational standards. This means that students must pass criterion-referenced, minimum competency tests to complete specific grades and school subjects and, ultimately, to graduate from school. Although all students should meet certain standards, the validity of using criterion-referenced, minimum competency tests to accomplish this goal is questionable. In many cases, the negative result is that teachers feel pressure to teach tests and to focus the curriculum on minimum competencies.

Glossary of Assessment Terms

Abnormal distribution   A pattern in which scores cluster at either the high or the low end rather than the middle or the average of a distribution. See also *skewed distribution*.

Accommodations in testing   Modifications and adjustments in test administration that give students with special needs a fair opportunity to demonstrate their knowledge and skills.

Accountability   Documenting what students are learning and how well they are progressing in their learning.

Achievement tests   Most frequently used in educational settings, achievement tests measure learning in academic subjects such as reading, spelling, written expression, mathematics, and general information.

Acquiescence   The tendency to respond positively to all items on self-report inventories and other types of questionnaires.

Adaptive behavior   The ability to adapt to the environment, especially by developing independent personal and social behavior; acquiring functional, practical competence in communication, daily living, and social interaction; and adjusting to changes in the environment.

Affective domain   Opinions, attitudes, and behaviors derived from emotions and feelings rather than from thought.

Age score   A score that represents typical or average performance for individuals of a particular chronological age.

Alternate-form reliability   An estimate of accuracy that involves comparing scores from two forms of the same test.

Alternative assessment   A group of informal assessment techniques that emphasize open-ended, criterion-referenced evaluation that occurs as an integral part of instruction rather than a separate testing activity (see also *portfolio assessment* and *authentic assessment*).

Alternative grading   Procedures such as pass/fail grading, assigning multiple grades, grading for effort, portfolio grading, and IEP grading that teachers use in the classroom to meet the individual needs of students with special needs (see also *IEP grading*).

Analytical scoring   Evaluating each part of a portfolio or other student work separately and combining the individual scores to obtain an overall score (see also *holistic scoring*).

Anecdotal assessment information   Refers to procedures that evaluators follow when they include written notes and comments about students on scoring sheets and in written assessment reports.

Anecdotal recording   Systematic observation of behavior in which the observer writes down the behaviors and interactions that occur during a specific time interval.

Assessment   The process of using tests and other measures of student performance and behavior to make educational decisions. Assessment consists of an assortment of techniques for evaluating, estimating, appraising, and making conclusions about the behavior, performance, and learning of students.

Assessment environment   The setting, circumstances, and conditions surrounding an evaluation.

Assessment proficiency checklist   An informal tool that provides a practical, applied way to measure an evaluator's skill in administering and scoring an assessment instrument.

Auditory-motor processing   Refers to the process of coordinating sensory information from the ears with fine and gross motor body movements.

Authentic assessment   An assessment approach that links evaluation and instruction by measuring student performance in direct relation to what has been taught in the curriculum (also see *alternative assessment, curriculum-based assessment,* and *portfolio assessment*).

Average thought unit   A measure of writing maturity and complexity based on syntax.

Behavior rating scales   Written questionnaires containing lists of behaviors that raters complete by assigning a rating (usually based on a scale of one to five) to each item on the checklist. Raters are usually teachers, parents, or other primary care givers who are familiar with a student's typical actions and conduct.

Behavioral observation   A procedure for directly observing behavior that involves recording student actions using specific techniques to ensure accurate measurement.

Bell-shaped curve   The bell-shaped curve or bell curve is another name for a normal distribution because the shape of a normal distribution, when graphed, looks somewhat like a bell (see also *normal distribution*).

Career assessment   Evaluating the broad range of practical life skills that are part of living and working as an adult, including the social behaviors, functional academics, and daily living activities necessary for success on the job and in the community.

Celebration portfolios   Portfolios that students use as mementos of their favorite learning experiences and activities.

Child-study team   A team of professionals who coordinate the screening activities associated with the referral process that leads to identifying students with disabilities. A team usually includes a school administrator, a counselor, regular teachers, and special education teachers.

Classifying and placing students   The process of determining the nature and severity of a student's learning or behavior problem and deciding whether the student qualifies for special education services. The process requires use of an interdisciplinary assessment team of professionals who work together to obtain a complete diagnosis of a student's specific problem and needed services.

Clinical observation   A curriculum-based assessment technique that relies on direct observation of student behavior and systematic recording of observation findings. The technique is useful for obtaining diagnostic data concerning a student's actual performance in the classroom and other educational settings; practitioners often use checklists of behavior to record their observations and maintain a record of results.

Cloze procedures   A group of curriculum-based assessment techniques that consists of informal tests of word-prediction abilities for measuring comprehension skills and the way students use cues to identify words. The most common cloze procedure, visual cloze, involves selecting a brief passage (about 250 words), altering it by deleting every fifth word of the text, and having a student read the altered passage aloud while filling in the blanks.

Community independence   Refers to autonomy in the community, which, for young children, includes playing at school, at home, and in the yard with minimal supervision, and for teenagers and adults includes self-reliance in the community as related to work, recreation, and leisure activities.

Computer adaptive testing   A type of computer-based test administration that enables interaction between the test and the test taker.

Construct validity   A measure of effectiveness that refers to how well a test assesses a theoretical construct or attribute. Examples of constructs include traits such as intelligence, mathematical reasoning ability, receptive language vocabulary, and gross motor skill. Establishing construct validity entails a lengthy process of putting together scientific research data about the relationship between test performance and the theoretical construct measured by the test.

Content validity   A measure of effectiveness that refers to how well a test covers a domain or learning area. The process of establishing content validity involves developing test specifications, writing test items, conducting field tests, reviewing and revising the test, and compiling the final test.

Cooperative learning assessment   Specialized assessment approaches that include peer editing, peer evaluation of class presentations, peer assessment, and group assessment.

Criterion-referenced score   A score that describes performance in relation to a functional level rather than the performance of others.

Criterion-referenced testing   Testing that is closely related to instruction and that measures student knowledge on relatively small and discrete units.

Criterion-related validity   A measure of effectiveness that involves analysis of the relationship between a test and other independent criteria. The two types of criterion-related validity are as follows: predictive validity, which entails measuring the effectiveness of a test in predicting future performance, and concurrent validity, which consists of correlating a test with a comparable test or other measure of proven validity.

Critical moment   The optimal time during which a child is physically, psychologically, and emotionally ready to learn a particular skill. Other terms for this phenomena include the *critical period* and the *teachable moment*. Developmental assessment helps professionals identify critical moments by determining mastered, emerging, and unlearned skills.

Critical period   See *critical moment.*

Culturally and linguistically diverse   Children from minority cultures who know and use two languages.

Culture fair   The fairness or equity of tests to all students regardless of cultural background. Culture-fair tests attempt to provide equal opportunity for success by students of different cultures and life experiences. As a result, developers of culture-fair tests must limit test content to material that is common to all cultures or is unfamiliar to students from a variety of different cultural backgrounds (see also *fairness in testing* and *nonbiased testing*).

Curriculum-based assessment   An assessment approach that measures educational success based on student progress in the local school curriculum rather than in relation to scores on standardized, norm-referenced tests. Curriculum-based assessment involves using class tests, homework assignments, classwork, and teacher impressions (based on direct observation) to make assessment decisions (also see *authentic assessment*).

Deciles   A type of percentile that expresses percentile scores in 10 equal units or tenths (see also *percentile score*).

Developmental age   A type of age score designed to compare individual performance to the average performance of children of the same chronological age.

Developmental assessment   A specialized type of assessment for measuring the performance of young children, especially infants, toddlers, and preschoolers from birth to around 6 years of age. Developmental assessment provides, on the basis of the predictable patterns that children follow as they grow and develop, a means to determine whether a child is following the normal sequence of skill acquisition at expected age levels.

Developmental learning areas   The traditional developmental learning areas include fine motor, gross motor, communication and language, social, cognitive, and self-help skills.

Developmental milestones   Critical skills in early childhood development such as walking, saying one or two words, and toilet training.

Developmental scales   Specialized tests of the performance of young children that consist of scales or checklists of behavior arranged in chronological order.

Developmental screening   A special type of assessment for identifying the general performance levels of young children from birth to approximately 6 years of age. Screening alerts parents and professionals to children who may have a developmental delay or learning problem. In addition, teachers often rely on developmental screening to determine overall levels of functioning and to develop initial programming goals with new students.

Developmental sentence analysis   An assessment procedure for collecting and analyzing a speech sample to measure the ability to spontaneously formulate and produce words and sentences. Developmental sentence analysis involves examination of eight grammatical categories that represent syntactic ability.

Deviation IQ   A standard score that provides an index of general mental ability based on the deviation between a student's score and the average score for students in a norm group of the same age.

Diagnostic interviews   One or a series of conferences with a student to determine the reasons for errors in academic work. During an interview a teacher has the student explain in a step-by-step manner the process used to solve each problem.

Diagnostic-prescriptive model   A system of assessment that involves conducting an initial evaluation to identify present levels of performance (diagnosis), using the results to determine appropriate intervention objectives (prescription), and conducting periodic reevaluations to measure progress and revise the objectives.

Direct observation   The process of assessing performance by listening to or watching a student over a period of time in a structured, systematic manner. Examples of direct observation include keeping progress graphs on students, counting incidents of misbehavior to establish a baseline for evaluating subsequent treatment, and using audio- or videotapes to measure change in behavior over time.

Distribution   A procedure for grouping a large set of scores into a meaningful arrangement that visually summarizes and illustrates the relationship among the scores. The process involves organizing scores in rank order from highest to lowest, grouping them in intervals, and graphing them.

Duration recording   A method for accurately measuring sustained behaviors by recording the total time that a target behavior occurs during a specified time period.

Ecological assessment   An assessment technique that considers both student and environmental characteristics (such as the classroom setting, the community, and the family situation) in the evaluation process. In ecological assessment, the evaluator analyzes student behavior within the context of the environment, setting, or situation in which the behavior occurs.

Employability skills   The generic skills important to qualify for entry-level jobs in the workplace regardless of the particular occupation or profession.

Error pattern analysis   A curriculum-based assessment procedure that involves systematically measuring student mistakes and using the results to plan a remedial program. The procedure is also called *error analysis* and *miscue analysis* (see also *miscue analysis*).

Event recording   A behavioral assessment procedure that involves counting the number of occurrences of a target behavior during a specified period of time.

Expressive language   Sending messages and translating thoughts, ideas, and signals into vocal expression or motor expression (the latter includes writing and sign language or other nonvocal forms of communication).

External bias   The use of test results in an unfair manner.

External scoring   Relies on scorers who have had no contact with the students (see also *internal scoring*).

Fairness in testing   Refers to equity of tests for all students regardless of race, ethnicity, language, gender, or cultural background (see also *culture-fair testing* and *nonbiased testing*).

Faking   A common validity problem with self-report inventories caused by respondents who attempt to distort the test results in a positive direction.

Fine motor   Addresses movement and response speed controlled by the small muscles of the body, including hand and finger dexterity, drawing, and manipulating small objects.

Fluency   The quantity of output as measured by the total output in a specified time period, such as the number of words written in 20 minutes.

Functional assessment   Measuring and evaluating student performance in real-life, natural settings (e.g., at home, in school, on the job, and in the community) for the purpose of identifying proficiency in performing practical, applied skills.

Functional skills   Practical life skills associated with independence in daily living activities, employment, and participation in the community.

Gaps in development   Major skill deficits that impede the development of higher-level skills. For example, problems with the basic locomotion skill of walking may block the development of higher-level locomotion skills such as running, jumping, skipping, and hopping (see also *splinter skills*).

Grade score   A score that describes student performance according to scholastic grade levels. Other terms for grade score include *grade equivalent score, grade-referenced score,* and *grade placement score.*

Graphical report   A reporting procedure that produces a profile or visual representation of performance. The procedure is especially useful for illustrating progress over time and for analyzing strengths and weaknesses across skills.

Gross motor   Refers to movement controlled by the large muscles of the body, including those that regulate walking, throwing, catching, and balance.

Group intelligence tests   Tests designed to be given to more than one student at a time and often given to large groups as a screening measure for initial identification of those who may need comprehensive assessment of their intellectual ability.

Group Tests   Given to groups of students rather than individuals, groups tests are usually brief screening instruments that give an overview of performance rather than specific diagnostic information.

Holistic scoring   Evaluating portfolios and other student materials in their entirety and giving a single overall score (see also *analytical scoring*).

IEP grading   A procedure for measuring individual student progress and assigning grades using the evaluation criteria in a student's IEP (see also *alternative grading*).

Inclusion   Participation of students with disabilities in the general education classroom and in the general curriculum, with appropriate aids and support services.

Individual education plan (IEP)   A written document developed jointly by parents, professionals, and, if appropriate, the student that guides the development and implementation of an appropriate education for the students.

Individual family service plan   A written document prepared by professionals and the family with an infant or toddler who has disabilities that guides the development and the implementation of an appropriate family service plan.

Individually administered intelligence tests   Tests that an evaluator administers to one student at a time to obtain comprehensive data about intellectual ability. Individual tests exist for all age groups, and most individual tests contain subtests that sample various behaviors, including verbal language, motor performance, and visual reasoning.

Informal reading inventories   Commercial and teacher-made instruments for diagnosing reading difficulties, planning instructional intervention, and measuring student progress.

Informant   A teacher, parent, grandparent, teacher aide, or other primary care giver who provides the information required to rate the items on a scale such as an adaptive behavior scale.

Inner language   The use of language in thinking, planning, and cognition.

Instructional intervention   The process of developing instructional objectives, establishing intervention priorities, instructing students, and evaluating the effectiveness of the instruction.

Intelligence   A trait or construct associated with cognitive or intellectual capacity that is related to the potential or ability to learn. Intelligence is an abstract quality associated with all types of intellectual processes, including abstract thinking, mental reasoning, using sound judgment, and making rational decisions.

Internal bias   Differences in average scores among two or more groups due to the qualities of a test rather than actual differences between the groups.

Internal scoring   Relies on scorers who have direct contact with the students; this includes teachers who score the work of their own students (see also *external scoring*).

Interrater reliability   Often referred to as *interobserver reliability,* this type of reliability is obtained by comparing the observations of two observers who independently watch or listen to a student in a classroom and in other settings.

Item bias   Unfairness that exists within individual items on a test.

Kinesthetic   The learning modality that relies on a combination of feeling, balance, and motion.

Language   The use of organized voice sounds and written symbols to communicate thoughts and feelings. Language occurs at both receptive and expressive levels of communication.

Learning modalities   The primary or preferred sensory modes for learning new or difficult information, including visual, auditory, and kinesthetic modalities.

Least restrictive environment (LRE)   A term that refers to the extent to which students with disabilities participate in regular education. LRE involves educating students who have disabilities with their nondisabled peers. Under LRE, special classes, special schools, or other removal from regular education should occur only when, as a result of the nature or severity of the disability, educating a student in regular classes with the use of supplementary aids and services cannot be achieved satisfactorily.

Letter grade   Represents a classic means of describing student performance and is usually derived from a percent correct score and assigned according to a grading scale.

Limited English proficiency   Refers to bilingual students who display inadequate skills in understanding and speaking the English language.

Mainstreaming   Educating students with disabilities in regular classes and providing opportunities for students with disabilities to interact with their nondisabled peers in other educational settings.

Mean   The average number in a distribution and the most commonly used measure of central tendency. In most instances, the term *average* refers to the mean rather than to the other specific measures of central tendency. The formula for calculating the mean involves summing all the scores and dividing by the number of scores.

Mean length of utterance (MLU)   An assessment procedure for evaluating the ability to form words, phrases, and sentences. MLU assessment is ideal for measuring the language level of young children. The MLU procedure involves tape recording and later analyzing a spontaneous speech sample containing a minimum of 50 consecutive utterances.

Measurement   The process of determining ability or performance level by using objective information such as numbers, scores, and other quantitative data. Types of measurement include testing, observing behavior, conducting interviews, completing rating scales, filling out checklists, and performing clinical evaluations.

Measures of central tendency   Statistics, including the mean, median, and mode, that describe the typical or representative scores in a group of scores.

Measures of variability   Statistics, including the standard deviation and the standard error of measurement, that summarize the spread or dispersion of test scores.

Measuring student progress   An assessment process that involves measuring and evaluating student progress on daily lessons, over time, and globally.

Mental age (MA)   A score that estimates mental ability in relation to the average performance of the individuals in the norm group at each successive chronological age.

Minimum competency tests   Tests that help to determine whether students demonstrate the minimal skill level necessary for completion of specific grades and school subjects and, ultimately, for graduation from school.

Miscue analysis   A procedure for systematically measuring and evaluating student reading errors for the purpose of planning remedial reading programs (see also *error pattern analysis*).

Momentary time sampling   A behavioral assessment procedure that involves obtaining a sample of the percentage of time in which a target behavior occurs by recording the occurrence or nonoccurrence of the behavior at the end of specified time periods (e.g., at the end of 5 minutes or at the end of every minute).

Morphology   The study of the smallest meaningful units of language, called *morphemes*. For example, the word *boy* has one morpheme, but the plural form of the word *(boys)* has two morphemes because *-s* is a separate language unit.

Motor proficiency   Refers to movement output, especially the efficiency of movements controlled by the muscles of the body. The two major types of motor activity are fine and gross motor movement.

Multiple Intelligences   Different dimensions of intelligence, including unique cognitive behaviors and cognitive learning styles such as emotional intelligence and interpersonal intelligence.

Multiple-skill achievement tests   Tests that provide an overview of performance in more than one subject area. For example, a multiple-skill test of academic achievement might include subtests for assessing reading, mathematics, and spelling.

Negative response bias   The tendency to respond negatively to questions on self-report inventories and other types of questionnaires.

Nonbiased testing   Testing that minimizes inequalities due to racial, cultural, ethnic, gender, or language background (see also *culture-fair testing* and *fairness in testing*).

Normal curve equivalent (NCE)   A statistically transformed standard score that fits a normal curve of equal units. NCEs have a mean equal to 50 and a standard deviation equal to 21.06. NCE values within 21.06 points of 50 (50 ± 21.06, or 28.94 to

71.06) represent average scores. Scores of 28.94 and lower fall more than 1 standard deviation (SD) from the mean of 50 and indicate below average performance. Scores of 71.06 and higher are more than 1 SD from the mean and represent above average values.

Normal distribution   A pattern in which scores cluster around the average of a distribution with an even formation of scores above and below the average. Because the shape when graphed looks somewhat like a bell, another name for the normal distribution is the *bell-shaped curve,* or *bell curve.*

Norm-referenced score   A score that enables interpretation of student performance in relation to the performance of others by comparing the score of an individual to the scores of those in a norm group.

Norm-referenced testing   Testing that compares an individual score to the scores of those in a comparison group. The comparison group, called the *norm group* or *normative sample,* consists of a carefully selected group of students who take the test in a precise manner.

On-the-job assessment   A specific type of situational evaluation for measuring vocational behavior in actual work settings.

Partial interval recording   A behavioral assessment procedure that involves dividing a period of time into brief intervals (e.g., a 1-minute time period into 10-second intervals or a 10-minute period into 1-minute intervals) and observing whether a target behavior occurs at any time during the interval.

Peer editing   Having other members of the cooperative group review the work of individual students.

Percent correct score   A criterion-referenced score that describes performance as the percentage of correct answers on a test.

Percentile score   A score that shows relative standing by ranking a student in comparison to those in a corresponding norm group. A percentile is any 1 of 99 scores divided into a distribution of 100 equal ranks ranging from 1 to 99. The 50th percentile signifies the average ranking or average performance.

Perception   The process of comprehending or giving meaning to information received by the senses. Assessment of perception involves measuring the way in which students process information from the senses, especially visual and auditory information.

Perceptual-motor performance   The process of integrating information received by the senses with corresponding movements of the body, including visual-motor, auditory-motor, and tactile-motor movements.

Performance behaviors   Behaviors sampled by intelligence tests that rely primarily on fine motor proficiency and perceptual ability rather than language ability.

Performance measurement   A curriculum-based assessment approach for assessing math and other types of academic achievement. The most common and useful forms of performance measurement are percent correct and performance rate scoring of class worksheets, homework assignments, and class tests. Percent correct is the percentage of correct responses on a worksheet, assignment, or test. Performance rate refers to the number of correct responses in a specified time period.

Performance Rate Scoring   The use of timed probes or tests to measure the number of responses in a specified period.

Performance scale   A subtest of the *Wechsler Intelligence Scale for Children-Third Edition (WISC-III)* that consists of items requiring responses based on visual reasoning ability and fine motor proficiency.

Personal self-sufficiency   With young children, personal-self-sufficiency refers to the ability to perform self-help skills such as dressing, eating, hygiene, and toileting. With older children, personal self-sufficiency encompasses a wide range and variety of daily living skills such as selecting and caring for appropriate clothing, eating independently in cafeterias and restaurants, and performing other daily activities.

Personal-social responsibility   A term that encompasses behaviors such as trustworthiness, commitment, appropriate socialization, proper interpersonal interaction, and self-direction. For young children, personal-social responsibility refers to behaviors such as complying with parents, getting along with siblings, and playing constructively. For older children, personal-social responsibility includes behaviors such as taking care of personal items, making friends at school, and completing homework.

Phonology   The study of the smallest units of sound in language, called *phonemes.* American English includes 44 speech sounds or phonemes. Phonemes have no meaning by themselves but contribute to word meaning. For example, the word *boy* includes three phonemes: *b, o,* and *y.*

Portfolio assessment   An ongoing process of evaluating the activities and accomplishments associated with reflective teaching and learning that occur in portfolio-based instruction (see also *alternative assessment, authentic assessment,* and *curriculum-based assessment).*

Portfolio conferences   A key element in portfolio assessment that consists of meetings in which students review learning goals and discuss progress.

Practical measurement concepts   Concepts that focus on the applied, functional features and the practical aspects of assessment instruments.

Pragmatics   The use of language in context, especially during social interaction. The essence of pragmatics is the process of sharing intents that occur in a wide variety of contexts, including those involving two people, small groups, and large groups. For example, the verbal sharing of intents includes intimate communication such as whispering as well as formal communication such as introductions at a reception.

Preparing for assessment   The process of reviewing cumulative records, gathering information from others, studying the assessment tool, and organizing an assessment session.

Prevocational skills   The personal, social, and applied academic skills that are necessary for success on any job.

Principles of developmental assessment   Guidelines that professionals follow when they use the developmental approach to assess the behavior and performance of young children with special needs.

Principles of using test scores   Practical suggestions for using test scores accurately and effectively with appropriate caution to avoid errors.

Process portfolios   Portfolios that document the stages of learning and provide a progressive record of student growth.

Product portfolios   Portfolios that demonstrate mastery of learning tasks or sets of learning objectives, and contain only the best work.

Prompting during assessment   Using verbal cues, modeling, and physical prompts while administering a test or conducting another type of assessment procedure.

Quartile   A type of percentile score that expresses percentiles in four equal units or fourths.

Quotient score   Includes two distinctly different kinds of scores. One type is an age score that expresses performance based on the ratio of functioning age to chronological age. Some older intelligence tests use this score, which is called a *ratio intelligence quotient* (ratio IQ). Similar age-based quotient scores exist for other types of tests. The other kind of quotient score is a standard score that expresses performance on the basis of the relationship between an individual score and the average score in a norm sample group. When used with intelligence tests, it is called a *deviation intelligence quotient* (deviation IQ). Similar deviation quotient scores exist for other types of tests.

Random responses   A validity problem associated with self-report inventories and other assessment tools in which respondents answer questions inconsistently.

Ratio IQ   An age score derived from an intelligence test that expresses mental ability on the basis of the ratio of a student's mental age to chronological age. The formula for calculating a ratio IQ is mental age divided by chronological age multiplied by 100.

Raw score   The simple numerical result of testing, typically the number of items answered correctly. In most situations, evaluators avoid using raw scores to report test results. Instead, they convert raw scores into various types of transformed scores.

Readiness tests   A special category of developmental scales designed to measure a child's knowledge of the basic skills necessary for success in the beginning years of school. Most readiness tests measure the behavior of children between the ages of 4 and 7 years.

Receptive language   The process of understanding and giving meaning to the communication (most often verbal language) of others.

Regular Education Initiative (REI)   A proposal advocating that general education accept primary responsibility for educating students with disabilities, which involves complete integration of students with disabilities into regular classes and removal of labels on students with disabilities. REI calls for significant changes in assessment, including the participation of all teachers in evaluating students with special needs.

Reliability An essential technical quality of assessment instruments that refers to the accuracy and consistency of test scores and other measures of the skills, abilities, and behaviors of students. Methods for estimating reliability include test-retest, alternate-form, split-half, and interrater reliability.

Rubrics Scoring criteria that describe an array of possible responses and specify the qualities and characteristics that occur at different levels of performance.

Screening instruments Brief, easy-to-administer tests, rating scales, checklists, and direct observation techniques that provide an overview or sketch of behavior rather than a detailed analysis.

Screening process The process of determining general levels of performance or behavior through the use of concise, abbreviated tests and evaluation procedures.

Self-concept Refers to students' feelings about themselves in various life situations.

Self-injurious behavior (SIB) Responses that result in physical damage to the student exhibiting the behavior. Although self-injurious behavior takes many forms, common examples include head banging, hand biting, hair pulling, scratching, and eye poking.

Semantics Understanding and expressing word meanings and word relationships. Word meanings and relationships include vocabulary, synonyms, antonyms, word categories, ambiguities, and absurdities. For example, word relationships include the associations that exist between words such as *8:45* and a *quarter to nine,* and *house* and *home.*

Simple numerical report Criterion-referenced scores that express performance as the number of right and wrong answers on a test, such as 45 of 50 correct responses (i.e., 45/50).

Single-skill achievement tests Tests that are especially useful for gathering in-depth diagnostic information about student performance in a single content area.

Situational assessment The use of systematic observation techniques to evaluate work- and career-related performance on the job or in real or simulated environments such as vocational training settings, simulated workstations, job tryouts in the community, and other community-based settings.

Skewed distribution A distribution that occurs when scores cluster at either the high or the low end rather than in the middle of a distribution. A positive skew occurs when scores cluster around the low end of a distribution; a negative skew results from scores that bunch up at the high end of a distribution.

Sociogram An assessment technique for measuring social acceptance and peer popularity by having students rate each of their classmates in a nonobtrusive manner for the purpose of analyzing the group structure in a classroom and identifying the popularity of individual students.

Splinter skills   Behaviors developed in isolation from related skills, such as learning to write the letters of the alphabet without understanding the meaning of the letters (see also *gaps in development*).

Split-half reliability   A measure of accuracy based on the correlation between two halves of the same test that is obtained by giving a test once, splitting the test items in half, and comparing the two halves to each other.

Spontaneous language   The candid, unrehearsed verbal expression of students that occurs naturally in real-life situations.

Standard deviation   An estimate of the variability of scores based on the average distance of individual scores from the mean of the distribution. Groups of scores with higher variability yield larger standard deviations than those with lower variability.

Standard error of measurement   An estimate of the variability of individual test scores that testing specialists employ as a measure of the accuracy or reliability of a test.

Standard score   A general term for a variety of scores that express performance by comparing the deviation of an individual score from the average score for students in a norm group of the same chronological age or scholastic grade level. The most widely used standard scores have means of 100 and standard deviations of 15.

Standardization   Refers to structuring test materials, administration procedures, scoring methods, and techniques for interpreting results. Standardization makes it possible to give a test in the same way to a group of students or to the same student more than once. This helps to ensure accuracy and consistency in measuring progress, determining levels of performance, and comparing performance to others.

Standards for scoring   Guidelines for scoring tests and reporting test scores that include recommendations for fairly reporting test results and suggestions for avoiding pitfalls and problems in scoring.

Stanine   A standard score with a mean of 5 and a standard deviation of 2 that is based on a scale of 1 to 9. Average stanines occur around the mean of 5. Stanines above 1 SD from the mean (5 + 2 = 7) fall in the above-average range, and stanines below 1 SD (5 − 2 = 3) fall in the below-average range.

Statistics   Numbers, including test scores, that summarize large groups of data by putting them into manageable form.

Stereotypy   Behaviors characterized by idiosyncratic, highly consistent, repetitive, rhythmic movements of the body or body parts. Also referred to as *stereotypic* or *self-stimulatory behavior*, examples of stereotypy include head weaving, rocking, arm and finger flapping, posturing, and mouthing hands or objects.

Student behavior   A broad term that encompasses a range of nonacademic behaviors including social-emotional development.

Student portfolio   A systematic collection of student work and related materials that depicts a student's activities, accomplishments, and achievements in one or more school subjects.

Student self-assessment   A variety of procedures in which students engage in various types of reflections and self-evaluations.

Syntax   The way morphemes or words go together to form phrases and meaningful sentences. For example, the sentence "I am going to the store" is syntactically correct, but the sentence "I going store" is incorrect.

Task analysis   An instructional technique and a curriculum-based assessment procedure that involves breaking down a difficult task into small steps.

Teachable moment   See *critical moment.*

Team approach   A method that provides a way for professionals to combine efforts with parents to obtain the best possible assessment data for meeting the needs of the child and the family. The team approach relies on the expertise of professionals from various disciplines as well as the family.

Test   A test contains a standard set of questions for the purpose of producing a score, a set of scores, or some other numerical result. Tests are usually given once in a prescribed manner and in a structured setting.

Test norms   Sets of scores developed from the scores of subjects in the norm group, which includes carefully selected students who take the test in a precise manner. Many types of norms exist, including national, state, and local norms.

Test-retest reliability   A process for evaluating accuracy that involves giving a test twice to a carefully selected group and comparing the resulting scores to obtain an estimate of test consistency.

Test scores   The numerical result of testing that summarizes test results using numbers and provides an effective and efficient way to describe student performance in an objective manner.

Transition services   A coordinated set of activities designed to facilitate movement from school to postschool activities, including postsecondary education, vocational training, integrated employment (including supported employment), continuing and adult education, adult services, independent living, and community participation.

t-score   A standard score with a mean of 50 and a standard deviation of 10. A t-score of 50 denotes average performance, whereas a t-score of 40 (1 SD below the mean) suggests below-average performance, and a t-score of 60 (1 SD above the mean) connotes above-average performance.

Validity   A term that refers to the effectiveness of assessment instruments and is considered the most important technical characteristic of a test. The basic question of validity concerns "How well does the test measure what it was designed to measure?" or "Does the test do what it is supposed to do?"

Verbal language behaviors   Behaviors sampled by tests that require students to give verbal responses to oral questions from an evaluator such as answering factual and comprehension questions, defining vocabulary words, identifying similarities, and solving arithmetic problems.

Woodcock, R., 453, 454, 478
Woodcock, R.J., 163, 435, 440
Woodcock, R.M., 317
Woodcock, R.W., 30, 91, 163,
165, 250, 271, 283, 312,
314, 342, 354, 370, 376,
435, 442
Woods, M.L., 461, 477
Worthen, B.R., 532
Wylie, R.C., 338

Yell, M.L., 584
Young, G.M., 505
Yssledyke, J.E., 148, 532, 603,
604

Zeislaft, B., 224, 238
Zelman, J., 209
Zigmond, N., 467
Zola, M., 465

SUBJECT INDEX

Abnormal distribution, 56–57
Accommodations in testing,
126–128, 584
Accountability, 603–604
Achievement quotient (AQ),
93
Achievement tests, 415–416
curriculum-based, 416–417
formal, standardized,
416–417
group tests, 417–418
individually administered, 9,
149, 155–168, 418–436
mathematics, 484–490
multiple-skill, 418–435
reading, 440–461
single-skill, 414
types, 414
use in special education,
414–417
written language, 505–512
Acquiescence, 340
Adaptive behavior, 8, 357
controversial aspects,
359–360
indirect measurement,
358–359
purpose of assessment,
360–361
role of informant, 359
scales, 362–371
Affective domain, 320
Age scores, 92–96

Alternate-form reliability, 67
Alternative assessment,
531–532
American Association on
Mental Deficiency, 8
American Association on
Mental Retardation, 6, 8
American Association for the
Study of the
Feebleminded, 8
American Council on
Education, 111
American Guidance Service,
111
American Psychological
Association, 14–15
Analytical scoring, 548–549
Anecdotal assessment, 130,
132, 331–332
Arena assessment, 197
Assessment, 2, 3, 4–11, 122
anecdotal information, 130,
132, 331–332
culturally diverse students, 7,
29, 154, 196, 303–305,
323, 600–602
curriculum-based, 10–11,
43–44
ethical issues, 12–15
functional, 306, 381–382
inclusive settings, 567
information required,
109–110
and instruction, 513
large groups, 5, 7
legal considerations, 29, 31
modality-based, 5, 7, 254–257
preparing for, 123–124
proficiency checklist, 130,
131
prompting during, 128–129
students needs during,
125–128
tool selection, 113–116
Assessment analysis checklist,
113–114
Assessment decisions, 108–116
Assessment environment, 124
Assessment Instrument Review
Form, 113–115
Assessment instruments. *See*
tests
Assessment process, 22–46
classifying and placing students, 28–32

Individual Education Plan
(IEP), 32–40, 126–127
instructional intervention,
40–42
measuring student progress,
42–46
screening students, 22–28
Assessment proficiency check-
list, 130, 131
Assessment reports, 132–140
Assistive technology, 306
Attention Deficit/Hyperactivity
Disorder, 343–345
Auditory-motor processing,
245
Authentic assessment, 531–532

Behavior
maladaptive, 130
performance, 149
self-injurious, 330
stereotypy, 330
Behavioral observation,
329–337, 397
recording, 331–336
Behavior assessment, 9,
319–322
attention-deficit hyperactivity
disorder, 343
attitudes and interests, 342
computer based, 593
culturally diverse students,
323
observation, 329–337
principles, 321
rating scales, 322–329
self-concept, 338–341
Bell curve, 55, 179
Bias in testing, 10, 154–155,
340, 600–602
Boehm Resources Guide for
Basic Concept Teaching,
294
Buros Institute of Mental
Measurement, 111

Career assessment, 380
functional assessment, 381–382
transition services, 381
See also Vocational assessment
Career development stages,
380–381
Carnegie Foundation for the
Advancement of Teaching,
111